EAGLES OVER THE SEA
1935–1942

Eagles over the Sea 1935–1942

A History of Luftwaffe Maritime Operations

Lawrence Paterson

This book is dedicated to Fast Eddie Clarke.
One of a kind.

Copyright © Lawrence Paterson 2019
First published in Great Britain in 2019 by
Seaforth Publishing,
A division of Pen & Sword Books Ltd,
47 Church Street,
Barnsley S70 2AS
www.seaforthpublishing.com

British Library Cataloguing in Publication Data
A catalogue record for this book is available from the British Library

ISBN 978 1 5267 4002 1 (HARDBACK)
ISBN 978 1 5267 4003 8 (EPUB)
ISBN 978 1 5267 4004 5 (KINDLE)

All rights reserved. No part of this publication may be reproduced or transmitted in any form or by any means, electronic or mechanical, including photocopying, recording, or any information storage and retrieval system, without prior permission in writing of both the copyright owner and the above publisher.

The right of Lawrence Paterson to be identified as the author of this work has been asserted by him in accordance with the Copyright, Designs and Patents Act 1988.

Pen & Sword Books Limited incorporates the imprints of Atlas, Archaeology, Aviation, Discovery, Family History, Fiction, History, Maritime, Military, Military Classics, Politics, Select, Transport, True Crime, Air World, Frontline Publishing, Leo Cooper, Remember When, Seaforth Publishing, The Praetorian Press, Wharncliffe Local History, Wharncliffe Transport, Wharncliffe True Crime and White Owl

Typeset and designed by JCS Publishing Services Ltd

Printed and bound in Great Britain by TJ International Ltd, Padstow

Contents

Acknowledgements	vii
Glossary	ix

1 **The War to End All Wars**
   The Birth of German Naval Aviation — 1

2 **Renaissance**
   The Rebirth of Germany's Military — 13

3 **Early Lessons**
   The Spanish Civil War — 44

4 **War** — 81

5 **Turning North and West**
   The Invasion of Norway and Western Europe — 144

6 **The End of the Beginning**
   The Atlantic Battleground — 245

7 **Blue Water, Grey Steel**
   The Mediterranean and Eastern Fronts — 289

8 **Torpedoes Los!**
   The Arctic and Malta Convoys and the Crimean Battle — 340

   Appendix
   Main Aircraft of the Luftwaffe Maritime Forces 1935–1942 — 426

Notes	439
Bibliography	454
Index	458

Acknowledgements

THIS BOOK BEGAN LIFE as a single volume to tell the story of Luftwaffe maritime operations. However, the more I delved into the story the more I realised just how expansive was the topic I was trying to cover. This is not just the story of the Kriegsmarine's attempt at creating a Fleet Air Arm, but also the metamorphosis of those units and other more orthodox bomber formations that gravitated towards specialising in maritime strikes using either torpedo, mine or bomb. Likewise, the story cannot begin at 1939 and the outbreak of war. Nor can it really be told from 1935 and the unveiling of both the Luftwaffe and Kriegsmarine to the world, but a brief look as far back as the First World War is necessary to give a sense of where the entire impetus for German naval aviation began. Thus, one book became two. This volume splits the story in late 1942, and will pick up where I left off in the second volume to follow.

There are many people I would like to thank for help and support during the researching and writing. First, my wife Anna Paterson, who has enough work to do in her jobs as a professional proof reader and editor without me hassling her for advice. My kids James and Megan are always very supportive of whatever hare-brained scheme I come up with next, as is my mother, Audrey 'Mumbles' Paterson and Don 'Mr Mumbles'. That kind of familial support can never be overstated.

I am also indebted to all at Seaforth Publishing, with their constant hard work and willingness to let me get on with whatever comes up. I have dealt with Rob Gardiner and Julian Mannering since the days when they were Chatham Publishing, and have the highest regard for everything that they do and the great books they manage to create out of pages of jumbled manuscript.

This is my first foray into the world of the Luftwaffe, and it was quite an eye-opener. As always, the more you learn the more you realise you don't know. As well as pages and pages of original documents available through the National Archives of the UK and USA and the Bundesarchiv in

Germany, there is also a phenomenal amount of knowledge freely shared by people on the internet, for which I am very grateful. It is easy to sneer at internet sources, as for every gem there is the equivalent lump of coal (if not more than one), but it can be a very valuable resource for connecting with people who have made the study of certain subjects one of their life's great passions. As with printed books, there is never any replacement for your own independent verification, but it can be a fantastic starting point, if not more. There are myriad forums discussing the Luftwaffe and its role in the Second World War, dealing with everything from strategic operations to the minutiae of uniforms and decorations. Though I am often just a bystander in many of these 'conversations', they have been both informative and enlightening and push your deeper research in directions that may not have seemed so obvious before. I will list some of the most informative in the Bibliography, though the list will be by no means complete.

Likewise, thank you to the many authors who have written fascinating books about the Luftwaffe, without whom I would not have known where to begin.

Glossary

ASW	Anti-submarine warfare.
B.d.U.	*Befehlshaber der U-Boote*, Commander-in-Chief, submarines.
B-Dienst	*Beobachtungsdienst des feindlichen Funkerverkehrs*, Kriegsmarine radio monitoring and cryptographic intelligence service.
Bordflieger	Shipboard air units, or, alternatively, the pilot of such an aircraft.
OKH	*Oberkommando des Heeres*, Army High Command.
OKL	*Oberkommando der Luftwaffe*, Air Force High Command. Properly established during February 1944, previously designated the *Oberbefehlshaber der Luftwaffe* (*Ob.d.L.*: C-in-C Luftwaffe).
OKM	*Oberkommando der Kriegsmarine*, Naval High Command.
OKW	*Oberkommando der Wehrmacht*, Armed Forces High Command.
Fliegerdivison	Early-war subdivision of a *Fliegerkorps*. Kept in use for certain specialised formation.
Fliegerführer	Theatre air commander, e.g. *Fliegerführer Atlantik*.
Fliegerkorps	Largest operational level subdivision of *Luftflotte*. Numbered consecutively with Roman Numerals, e.g. IX.*Fliegerkorps*.
F.d.Luft	*Führer der Seeluftstreitkräfte*, Commander of maritime combat aviation.
F.d.U	*Führer der U-boote*, early-war designation for Commander submarines.

Geschwader	Luftwaffe equivalent to an RAF Group or a USAAF Wing.
Gruppe	Luftwaffe equivalent to an RAF Wing or a USAAF Group (plural *Gruppen*)
Kampfgruppe	Independent bomber formation of *Gruppe* size.
Kette	Flight of three aircraft.
Kommandeur	Commander of a unit, particularly in Luftwaffe use for *Gruppe* commander.
Kommodore	In the Luftwaffe a *Geschwader* commander, not an actual rank.
Küstenflieger	Luftwaffe equivalent to the Fleet Air Arm.
Luftwaffe	German Air Force from 1935 onwards. The term 'operational Luftwaffe' is used here to separate orthodox Luftwaffe units from the *Küstenflieger* and other naval flying units.
Luftflotte	Luftwaffe Air Fleet equivalent to an American numbered Air Force. Numbered consecutively with Arabic numerals, e.g. *Luftflotte* 4.
Luftmine	Air-dropped mine.
Kriegsmarine	German Navy between 1935 and 1945.
Marinegruppen-kommando	Regional command of Kriegsmarine security forces such as minesweeping, submarine hunters, patrol boats and so on, e.g. *Marinegruppen-kommando West*. Abbreviated to '*MGK*'.
Oberbefehlshaber der Luftwaffe	Commander-in-Chief, Luftwaffe, the military post held by Hermann Göring.
Reichsmarine	Pre-war German Navy, renamed Kriegsmarine in 1935.
RLM	*Reichsluftfahrtministerium*, Reich Air Ministry; civilian office headed by Hermann Göring.
Staffel	Roughly the Luftwaffe equivalent to an Allied Squadron (plural *Staffeln*)
Staffelkapitän	Squadron Commander, abbreviated to '*Staka*'.

GLOSSARY

Equivalent Rank Table

Luftwaffe	Kriegsmarine	Royal Air Force/ US Army Air Force
Generalfeldmarschall (*GFM*)	Grossadmiral	Marshal of the Air Force/General of the Army
Generaloberst (*Genobst*)	Generaladmiral	Air Chief Marshal/ General
General der Flieger (*Gen.der Flg*)	Admiral	Air Marshal/ Lieutenant General
Generalleutnant (*Genlt*)	Konteradmiral	Air Vice-Marshal/ Major General
Generalmajor (*Genmaj.*)	Vizeadmiral	Air Commodore/ Brigadier General
Oberst (*Obst.*)	Kapitän zur See	Group Captain/ Colonel
Oberstleutnant (*Obstlt.*)	Fregattenkapitän	Wing Commander/ Lieutenant Colonel
Major (*Maj.*)	Korvettenkapitän (*K.K.*)	Squadron Leader/ Major
Hauptmann (*Hptm.*)	Kapitänleutnant (*Kaptlt.*)	Flight Lieutenant/ Captain
Oberleutnant (*Oblt.*)	Oberleutnant zur See (*Oblt.z.S*)	Flying Officer/First Lieutenant
Leutnant (*Lt.*)	Leutnant zur See (*Lt.z.S.*)	Pilot Officer/Second Lieutenant
Stabsfeldwebel (*Stabsfw.*)	Stabsoberfeldwebel	Warrant Officer/ Master Sergeant
Oberfeldwebel (*Obfw.*)	Stabsfeldwebel	Flight Sergeant/ Technical Sergeant
Feldwebel (*Fw.*)	Feldwebel	Sergeant/Staff Sergeant
Fähnrich (*Fhr.*)	Fänrich zur See	Officer Cadet/Flight Cadet

Unterfeldwebel (Ufw.)	*Obermaat*	Corporal/Sergeant
Unteroffizier (Uffz.)	*Maat*	Corporal/Corporal
Hauptgefreiter (Hptgfre.)	*Matrosenhauptgefreiter*	Senior Aircraftman/Private First Class
Obergefreiter (Ogfre.)	*Matrosenobergefreiter*	Leading Aircraftman/Private First Class
Gefreiter (Gfr.)	*Matrosengefreiter*	Aircraftman 1st Class/Private First Class
Flieger (Flg.)	*Matrose*	Aircraftman 2nd Class/Private

Luftwaffe Operational Organisation

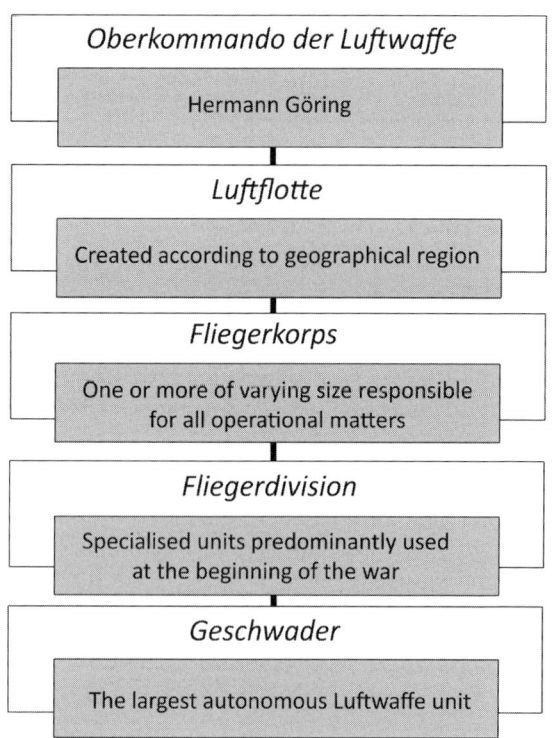

GLOSSARY

Tactical Level Luftwaffe Organisational Notes

Though local circumstances could dictate modification to existing unit structure, the general form of a Luftwaffe *Geschwader* was as follows:

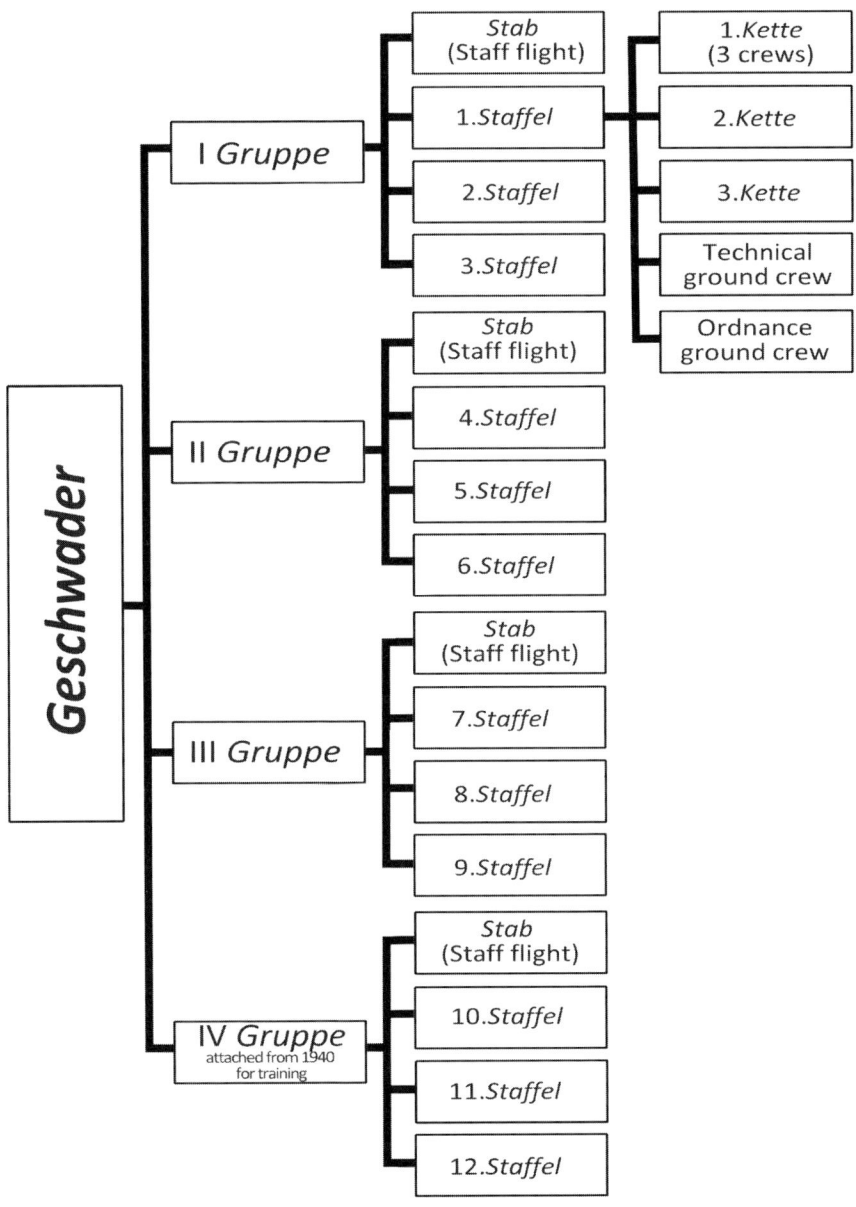

Geschwader: The largest homogeneous Luftwaffe flying unit roughly the equivalent of an RAF Group or a USAAF Wing. Comprising three '*Gruppen*', the *Geschwader* was named according to its purpose and its individual identity suffixed by Arabic numerals, such as KG 26. Amongst the most common identification prefixes within this work are:
Fighters: JG (*Jagdgeschwader*), day fighter single-engine aircraft such as the Bf 109.
Heavy Fighters: ZG (*Zerstörergeschwader*), day fighter twin-engine aircraft such as the Bf 110.
Bombers: KG (*Kampfgeschwader*), heavy or medium bombers such as the He 111.
Dive-bombers: StG (*Sturzkampfgeschwader*), typically Ju 87 Stukas during the early years of the war.
Advanced Training: LG (*Lehrgeschwader*), often each *Gruppe* of a different aircraft type.
The *Geschwader* was commanded by a *Geschwaderkommodore*, typically of rank between *Oberstleutnant* or *Major*. He would have a small staff and a *Stabschwarm* (staff flight) of perhaps four aircraft, including one belonging to the *Geschwaderkommodore*.

Gruppe: The basic autonomous Luftwaffe flying unit, roughly equivalent to an RAF Wing or a USAAF Group. Typically comprising a *Stabschwarm* (staff flight) and three *Staffeln* commanded by a *Gruppenkommandeur*, who could be a *Major* or *Hauptmann*. He would have a small staff including administration, operations, medical and technical officers. Each *Gruppe* was identified with a roman numeral (e.g. II.*Gruppe* of 26th Bomber *Geschwader* would be II./KG 26). The exception to this rule were those *Gruppen* acting in autonomous specialised maritime of reconnaissance roles, such as the *Küstenfliegergruppen* (coastal maritime aircraft) *Aufklärungsgruppen (F)* (The 'F' designates '*Fernaufklärungsgruppen*', meaning 'long-range reconnaissance'), *Bordfliegergruppen* (aircraft carried aboard surface ships), *Seeaufklärungsgruppen* (maritime reconnaissance) and *Trägergruppen* (carrier aircraft), which were designated using Arabic numerals.

Staffel: Roughly the equivalent to an Allied Squadron, comprising from nine to twelve aircraft and commanded by a *Staffelkapitän* (abbreviated to '*Staka*') generally of a rank between *Hauptmann* and *Leutnant* as the most junior example. The *Staffeln* were numbered consecutively within the *Geschwader* with Arabic numerals (e.g. third *Staffel* of 26th Bomber *Geschwader* would be 3./KG 26) therefore it would always be possible to identify the first three *Staffeln* as belonging to I *Gruppe*, *Staffeln* 4-6 to II *Gruppe*, and so on. Each *Staffel* generally comprised three *Ketten* of three aircraft each, and associated ground crew.

Luftwaffe aircraft identification codes

Luftwaffe aircraft markings are a multifaceted and intricate subject that involves symbols and colour codes each denoting a unit or position within the command structure. The system evolved continuously until 24 October 1939, when a compact four-character code was introduced. This is simply an introduction to the adopted four-character numbering system used to identify all aircraft, except for *Jagdgeschwader*, which had a separate complex system and are outside the scope of this study. The code is divided, with an alpha-numeric pair of characters to the left of the *Balkankreuz* (straight-sided cross) that adorned Luftwaffe aircraft, and two letters to the right. The two letters to the left indicated the parent *Geschwader* (or *Gruppe*) to which the aircraft belonged. To the right of the *Balkankreuz* the numeral, usually colour-coded, was the individual aircraft number, and the letter indicated the *Staffel*.

Four-digit *Staffel* letters: *Geschwader* Stab.: A

    (I *Gruppe*) Stab.: B   1.*Staffel*: H   2.*Staffel*: K   3.*Staffel*: L
    (II *Gruppe*) Stab.: C   4. *Staffel*: M   5.*Staffel*: N   6.*Staffel*: P
    (III *Gruppe*) Stab.: D   7. *Staffel*: R   8.*Staffel*: S   9.*Staffel*: T
    (IV *Gruppe*) Stab.: E   10.*Staffel*: U   11.*Staffel*: V   12.*Staffel*: W

You will find frequent mentions of such four-digit codes within the text to identify various aircraft, written thus: M2+SL. In this particular case the letters denote aircraft 'S' of 3.*Staffel* ('L') belonging to *Küstenfliegergruppe* 106 (M2). Below is relevant unit two-digit coding (used from October 1939) for the units mentioned within this book:

1./BFl.Gr. 196: T3
5./BFl.Grp.196: 6W
KG 26: 1H
KG 30: 4D
KG 40: F8
KG 54: B3
KG 77: 3Z

KG 100: 6N
KGr. 126: 1T (also used by aircraft of III./KG 26 between January 1942 and February 1943)
Kü.Fl.Gr. 106: M2
Kü.Fl.Gr. 306: K6 (shared with Kü.Fl.Gr. 406, to which it was attached)
Kü.Fl.Gr. 406: K6
Kü.Fl.Gr. 506 and KGr. 506: S4 (originally M7)
Kü.Fl.Gr. 606 and KGr. 606: 7T (originally 8L)
Kü.Fl.Gr. 706: 6I
Kü.Fl.Gr. 806 and KGr.806: M7
Kü.Fl.Gr. 906: 8L
Küstenfliegerstaffel Krim: 6M
LG1: L1
Minensuchgruppe der Luftwaffe: 3K ('*Mausi*' aircraft)
SAGr. 125: 7R
SAGr. 126: D1
2.*Seenotstaffel*: N7
3.*Seenotstaffel*: M6
5.*Seenotstaffel*: P7
6.*Seenotstaffel*: K3
7.*Seenotstaffel*: J9
8.*Seenotstaffel*: M1
10.*Seenotstaffel*: 5W
Trägergruppe 186: J9
Transozeanstaffel and KG.z.b.V 108: P5

1

The War to End All Wars
The Birth of German Naval Aviation

The story of German military aviation stretches back to the end of the nineteenth century, when a small balloon section was established during November 1883, initially incorporated into a railway troop but becoming autonomous after four years. Experimental large rigid airship designs developed by former Army Officer Count Ferdinand von Zeppelin eventually steered an almost reluctant military towards airships, while in 1908 the German General Staff concluded that the aeroplane must also become part of the future military arsenal. Within two years a flying school was formed in Döberitz and the first military aircraft acquired by the German Army entered service, forming the nucleus of the *Fliegertruppen des deutschen Kaiserreiches* (Imperial German Flying Corps), which in October 1916 would become the *Deutsche Luftstreitkräfte* (German Air Combat Forces).

Successful Army experiments with balloon reconnaissance also led the German Navy to reopen investigations into their viability after initial trials had been cancelled in 1890. Their primary role was to be scouting for enemy units and minefields, roles traditionally carried out by destroyers and high-speed small craft. However, communications failures between a torpedo boat and the crew of its towed balloon during trials near Kiel led to the cancellation of all attempts at developing aerial reconnaissance. The decision resonated with *Admiral* Alfred von Tirpitz, Secretary of State of the Imperial German Naval Office, who had previously dismissed the idea out of hand as contrary to his faith in surface ships fulfilling this purpose.

But for the enthusiasm for naval aviation of Prince Heinrich of Prussia, younger brother to the Kaiser, Wilhelm II, the matter may have rested there. Heinrich, promoted to the rank of *Großadmiral* on 4 September 1909 after thirty-eight years of naval service, was arguably more popular than his older brother, particularly abroad, where his diplomatic skills far surpassed those of Wilhelm. Heinrich, in his role as Inspector General of the Imperial Navy, attended the Döberitz flying school and graduated as Germany's first naval pilot determined to develop a seaplane force. He remained instrumental in the development of naval aviation, unmoved by Tirpitz's general disapproval of the diversion of resources that included a 200,000-Mark investment by the *Reichsmarineamt* which he considered better used by the surface fleet. Meanwhile, after British naval authorities enquired about the purchase of German-made Zeppelins, Germany was finally spurred into the building of their first naval airship, *L1*, which was ready for testing in October 1912. Following successful trials, the Navy Airship Detachment (*Marine Luftschiffabteilung*) was formed on 8 May 1913 under the command of *Korvettenkapitän* Friedrich Metzing.

However, the entire German airship project soon suffered two heavy blows. Metzing and fifteen of his crew were killed when *L1* crashed in high winds during fleet manoeuvres in September 1913, and the second airship commissioned, *L2*, exploded at altitude, killing all on board. Nonetheless, the new commander of the Airship Detachment, *Kaptlt.* Peter Strasser, was able to steer his fledgling unit through the minefield of critics determined to see the airship programme aborted, and *L3* took to the skies in May 1914.

Parallel to Strasser's airship unit was the Naval Flying Detachment (*Marine Fliegerabteilung*) which had been established in 1911 following Heinrich's graduation as a pilot. Early trials were made using civilian aircraft on loan, as initial expectations of interest from German aircraft manufacturers proved misplaced. Seaplanes were far more expensive and specialised to construct than land-based aircraft, and naval specifications demanded that all naval aircraft be amphibious. This, combined with the fact that the majority of manufacturers were located considerable distances from Germany's coastline, conspired to keep the fledgling service arm impoverished. It was not until May 1912 that the first pair of German-built Albatros B1 two-seat reconnaissance aircraft were received by the Naval Air Service.

Nevertheless, the detachment gradually grew in size and the pace of seaplane development increased. An experimental centre for naval aviation was established in West Prussia near Putzig, forty-four kilometres north of Danzig. Boasting a concrete slipway, an 800m airstrip and all necessary buildings and workshops for a functioning airfield, the first aircraft, a Fritzsche Rumpler, arrived to be equipped with floats during the autumn of 1911. On 3 May the following year an Albatros D 2 took off from the solid runway and successfully alighted on

Testing of an early German torpedo bomber during the First World War.

water, as it had been decreed that all German naval aeroplanes were to be of amphibian configuration. This, however, was a difficult requirement to meet owing to the weight of a dual float-and-wheel assembly and the marginal engine power then available. By discarding the wheels fitted to the central Coulmann float of the Albatros WD 3 (70hp Mercedes), *Oblt.z.S.* Walter Langfeld was able to make the first water take-off on 5 July 1912. When the wheels were fitted again, a system was used that enabled them to be raised clear of the water. To reduce water resistance further and allow acceleration to flying speed, the wingtip floats could also be raised by means of a large handwheel on the port side of the engine nacelle. However, official dissatisfaction with the slow progress of the marine aeroplane led to the first German Seaplane Competition, held at Heiligendamm in August-September 1912. Various manufacturers submitted what were basically landplanes fitted with floats, and although only two (Aviatik and Albatros) met the stated requirements, the official view was that the problems of amphibious operations had been solved.

On 1 June 1913 the 1.*Marine Flieger Abteilung* was formed in Kiel-Holtenau with a complement of 100 officers and men. To evaluate current

The seaplane tender *Stuttgart*, operational from May 1918 as an 'aircraft carrier' capable of supporting three machines.

foreign marine aircraft techniques, several machines were bought from other countries, including an Avro 503 seaplane from Britain. Following acceptance tests, Langfeld flew the Avro to Heligoland in September 1913 for the autumn fleet manoeuvres, carrying a passenger; the first flight by a seaplane from the German mainland to Heligoland. Four seaplanes were deployed in the manoeuvres, three of which were considered unsuitable for operational use, but the Avro produced excellent results. Meanwhile, the production of a single-engine biplane with floats, the Friedrichshafen FF 29, began at Flugzeugbau Friedrichshafen, and the FF 29 entered service with the Imperial German Navy in November 1914, by which time the nation had been at war for four months.[1] That same month *Oblt.z.S.* Friedrich von Arnauld de la Perrière, brother of the soon-to-be famous U-boat commander Lothar, was placed in command of the first German naval air unit deployed on foreign soil after he established *Seeflugstation* Zeebrugge on the harbour mole. A former passenger terminal was converted to form the core of the seaplane base, with hangars, ammunition storage and personnel quarters added or requisitioned. A railway spur linked the base with Lisseweg, where German forces had established a major aircraft repair facility.

The *Marine Flieger Abteilung* began the war with a strength of only twelve seaplanes; six in Heligoland, four in Kiel (to where the detachment had moved its headquarters) and two in Putzig; between them mustering thirty officer and three NCO pilots, with few trained observers. Naval air observers (land or sea) did not have to hold commissioned rank, as was required in the Army Air Service. Although underequipped and predominantly relegated to reconnaissance, with limited attacks on enemy shipping, the naval aircraft detachments gradually grew in strength, as did Strasser's airship numbers as they proved their worth both in reconnaissance and as part of the aerial bombardment of Great Britain, authorised by the Kaiser in January 1915. Indeed, Strasser was a known advocate of area bombing, writing to his mother after the commencement of Zeppelin raids on British cities:

> We who strike the enemy where his heart beats have been slandered as baby killers and murderers of women. What we do is repugnant to us too, but necessary. Very necessary. A soldier cannot function without the factory worker, the farmers, and all the other providers behind them. Nowadays there is no such animal as a non-combatant; modern warfare is total warfare.

Germany fielded seventy-eight naval airships during the First World War which flew a combined total of 1,148 reconnaissance missions and hundreds of bombing raids, delivering 360,000kg of bombs, the majority against British harbours, ports, towns and cities. Strasser had been named *Führer der Luftschiffe* (*F.d.Luft*) and continued to fly combat missions until he was killed on 5 August 1918 during a raid on Boston, Lincolnshire, when his airship, *L70*, was shot down near the Norfolk coast by a British D.H.4. aircraft, all twenty-three men aboard being killed.

Nordholz, near Cuxhaven on the North German coast, was the main naval airship base and *F.d.Luft* headquarters, with subsidiary bases on the North Sea coast and within the Baltic. Small numbers were also employed within the Adriatic and Black Seas, and *L59* attempted a supply journey from Bulgaria to East Africa, turning back at Khartoum when the planned rendezvous area with German troops was overrun by British forces.

Naval aircraft were concentrated in 1.*Marine Flieger Abteilung* at Kiel-Holtenau, 2.*Marine Flieger Abteilung* at Wilhelmshaven and the *Marine-Freiwilligen Fliegerkorps* in Berlin-Johannisthal. During September 1915 the former two units were renamed *Seeflieger Abteilungen*, reporting directly to *Befehlshaber der Marine Luftfahrt Abteilungen* (*BdL*, Commander Naval Air Units), *Konteradmiral* Otto Philip. Large numbers of seaplanes were ordered, the Hansa Brandenburg KDW being introduced in 1916 as a single-seat seaplane fighting scout alongside forty

Rumpler 6 Bis, and 114 Albatros W 4s were built beginning in 1917. Additionally, naval units had begun to field land-based aircraft, initially to protect U-boat bases and other naval installations on the Western Front, and on 21 December *Oblt.z..S.* Egon von Skrbensky arrived at Mariakerke (Ghent) with 113 officers and men to create the *1.Marine Landflieger Abteilung* (Naval Land Aircraft Unit). Since the Navy had no facilities of its own for training single-seat pilots, when Fokker E monoplanes were introduced into naval landplane units naval pilots were sent to the single-seater school attached to *Kampfeinsitzerstaffell* (*Kest I*) on Sonthofen aerodrome near Mannheim, the first pilot to undertake this conversion course, *Flugmaat* Boedicker, being attached to *2.Marine-Feldflieger-Abteilung* at Neumunster.

The basic unit of the Imperial German Naval Air Force was the *Seeflugstation* (Seaplane Station) or *Landflugstation* (Landplane Station). By mid-September 1916 there were some forty single-seat land fighters operating with the *Marine Flieger Abteilungen*, most of them Fokker E monoplanes. While a number of these were concentrated in Nieuwmunster for defending conquered Belgian territory, at least half of the fighter strength was deployed defending airship bases from

1930s postcard of a Dornier 'Wal' operated by the Lufthansa airline.

Allied air attack. As the service grew during the war, a number of semi-autonomous *Staffeln* (flights) were created; the *Marinefeldjagdstaffel* (Naval Fighter Squadron) commanded by *Lt.z.S.* Sachsenberg, operating with success in the area of the Fourth German Army occupied by the German Marine Corps. As air-to-air fighting activity increased, the *Staffel* was joined by other naval landplane fighter units until, towards the end of 1918, the five *Marinefeldjagdstaffeln* were formed into the *Marinefeldjagdgeschwader* under Sachsenberg's command, with a strength of over fifty fighters. This was achieved despite aircraft production and allocation being held firmly under Army control, rendering naval fliers the junior partners in aviation matters. However, the success of the naval aviators was undeniable. During 1917-1918 they sank in the North Sea four merchant vessels, four patrol boats, three submarines, twelve other ships and a Russian destroyer. They had also managed to gain aerial superiority over the North Sea, shooting down 270 Allied aircraft for a loss of 170 of their own.[2]

Two other major developments in German naval aviation took place in 1917. Firstly, the order to create three *Küstenflieger Abteilungen* in September for the patrol of coastal waters and assistance in coastal artillery spotting against enemy warships, and, secondly, the establishment that same month of the 1.*Torpedostaffel*, flying Hansa Brandenburg GWs, Friedrichshafen FF 41As and Gotha WD 11s in Germany's first torpedo plane squadron.

Bombing had also been pursued by the German Navy. The land-based *Riesenflugzeug* (literally 'Giant Aircraft'; a large bomber possessing at least three engines) was evaluated as a possible addition to the naval airship for bombing and long-range scouting purposes. However, experience with the Staaken VGO 1/RML 1 (*Reichs Marine Landflugzeug 1*) was plagued by difficulties. Engine troubles and structural failures of undercarriage assemblies had eventually been overcome, and the aircraft participated in some bombing operations on the Eastern Front, until, during a fully-loaded night take-off late in August 1916, a double engine failure resulted in a crash into a Russian forest. The machine was completely rebuilt and modified to take an additional two engines. At this time a transparent Cellon covering intended to render aircraft partially invisible and reduce searchlight illumination was under consideration, and the fuselage and tail unit were covered with this material. On the first test flight, at Staaken aerodrome near Berlin on 10 March 1917, engine failure resulted in the aircraft yawing wildly, and this was compounded by a control system malfunction. The pilots were unable to prevent the machine from crashing into the corner of one of the airship sheds.

Shipboard aviation had also begun in earnest almost immediately after the outbreak of war, largely due to Heinrich's command of the Baltic Sea Fleet. The British freighter SS *Craigronald* had been seized as a prize while moored in Danzig at the outbreak of war and renamed *Glyndwr*, and the 2,425-ton ship was immediately impressed into service as an aircraft mother ship. Although no hangars were built on board, four seaplanes could be carried on the fore and aft decks. A heavy cargo crane was used to load and unload the aircraft, and the vessel was initially used as a training ship in the Bay of Danzig for the fledgling naval aircraft service. Two German cargo ships were also converted into bona fide seaplane tenders within the Baltic Sea; the SMH *Answald* and SMH *Santa Elena*, commissioned into the High Seas Fleet as *Flugzeugschiff* I and II respectively. Both received hangars fore and aft which could hold three and four aircraft each. Anti-aircraft guns were added, though the initial conversion proved unsatisfactory and they did not see action until 1915, following further modification. However, once in service they contributed greatly to the power of the German Baltic Fleet, keeping Russian naval forces on the defensive. The ex-British freighter SS *Oswestry*, which had been taken as prize in August 1914 and renamed *Oswald*, was also converted in 1918 to the role of aircraft tender and attached to IV Torpedo Boat Flotilla, carrying four FF 29s.

Additionally, the cruiser SMS *Friedrich Carl* had been provided with two aircraft in 1914, but was sunk by mines shortly thereafter and the aircraft were operationally unused. On 15 January 1915 an FF 29 became the first aeroplane to be launched from a submarine, the *U12*. The unarmed scout aircraft was lashed to the U-boat's forward deck and piloted by the Zeebrugge naval airbase commander *Oblt.z.S.* von Arnauld de la Perrière. The U-boat's bow was submerged after releasing the aircraft's ties, and de la Perrière successfully took flight. However, Imperial Navy observers were unimpressed, and the decision was made not to use U-boats as aircraft carriers thereafter.[3] Elsewhere, the battlecruiser *Derfflinger*, light cruiser *Medusa* and several *Sperrbrecher* made effective use of embarked aircraft, as did the armed merchant cruiser SMS *Wolf*.

When SMS *Wolf* left Kiel on 30 November 1916 on a 15-month voyage, during which she traversed three oceans as a commerce raider. She carried a Friedrichshafen FF 33E seaplane on board for scouting

An HD 42 (later He 42) two-seater biplane, relegated to training duties for maritime pilots throughout the Second World War.

purposes. Named *Wölfchen*, the seaplane played an important part in *Wolf*'s marauding activities and carried out over fifty flights in this role. During the voyage *Wölfchen* was operated without the display of any national insignia other than the German War Ensign, which was flown from the innermost starboard rear interplane strut as occasion demanded. Crewed by *Lt.z..S.* Stein and *Oberflugmeister* Fabeck, the seaplane contributed to the *Wolf* sinking or capturing twenty-eight Allied vessels and returning home laden with booty from her victims.

Within the North Sea, German naval command finally came to understand the value of shipborne aircraft and ordered the construction of seaplane tenders capable of matching the speed of the Grand Fleet, something that mercantile conversion could not achieve. Two cruisers were ordered to be adapted, the SMS *Roon* and *Stuttgart*, and work began on *Stuttgart* on 21 January 1918 at the Imperial Dockyard in Wilhelmshaven. On 16 May she was commissioned as an 'aircraft carrier'. Two large hangars had been installed aft of the funnels, with space for two seaplanes; a third was carried atop of the hangars. *Stuttgart* provided air cover for minesweeping operations within the North Sea but was never used in the offensive mode employed by Prince Heinrich within the Baltic.

Though *Stuttgart* had finally provided an aircraft tender that could keep pace with the High Seas Fleet, her small payload of only three aircraft was unsatisfactory, and plans were drawn up on Heinrich's insistence for the construction of a flight-deck-equipped 'true' aircraft carrier. The answer was found in the incomplete hull of 12,585-ton Italian turbine-powered steamer *Ausonia*, which had been under construction in Hamburg's Blohm & Voss shipyard at the outbreak of war. Conversion plans were drawn up by *Lt.z.S.dR* Jürgen Reimpell of 1.*Seeflieger Abteilung*, his final design proposals being completed by 1918. The ship was to carry two 82m hangar decks for wheeled aircraft and a third 128m hangar deck for seaplanes, all mounted above the existing structural deck. The flight deck itself was 128.5m long and 18.7m wide, and the ship was designed to carry either thirteen fixed-wing or nineteen folding-wing seaplanes, along with a maximum of ten wheeled aircraft. *Ausonia* could carry up to ten fighter aircraft and a combination of fifteen to twenty bombers and torpedo-floatplanes, but she was never completed. With the emphasis placed on U-boat construction, the final building drive of the Imperial Navy was never to reach fruition, as the war ended in November 1918, with Bolshevik revolution within the Kaiser's Navy.

Of 2,138 naval aircraft fielded between 1914 and 1918, 1,166 were lost. The years of war yielded many 'aces' within the *Marine Flieger Abteilungen*, including three winners of the coveted *Pour le Mérite*: Theo Osterkamp with thirty-two victories, Gotthard Sachsenberg with thirty-one and Friedrich Christiansen with thirteen.[4] However, the armistice did not see the end of their fighting as Sachsenberg was approached in January 1919 by *General* von der Goltz while demobilising the *Marinegeschwader* with a request to form a volunteer air unit that could serve in support of the 'Iron Division', composed of *Freikorps* troops and the remnants of the German 8th Army in the Baltics. Within weeks, Sachsenberg had recruited many former colleagues and formed *Kampfgeschwader Sachsenberg*, officially designated *Fliegerabteilung Ost*. Sachsenberg's unit was despatched by German Defence Secretary Gustav Noske to join the fighting against Russian Bolshevik forces encroaching on German interests within the Baltic states. The Inter-Allied Commission of Control had insisted in the armistice agreement that German troops remain in the Baltic countries to prevent the region from being reoccupied by the Red Army, though the true motivation of the Iron Division was deeply rooted in the desire to install pro-German leadership within the region and possibly instigate the fall of the Bolshevik government of Russia, returning the monarchy to power. Sachsenberg's approximately 700 personnel were based at Riga, Latvia, and gave aerial support to *Freikorps* units fighting 'Reds' on the Baltic borders of Germany, Lithuania, Latvia, Estonia and Finland. Sachsenberg managed to amass a considerable number of aircraft before the Versailles Treaty of 28 June 1919 banned German military aircraft production. They established local air superiority and were mainly used thereafter for reconnaissance and ground-attack missions in support of *Freikorps* operations. However, after fierce fighting against Estonian troops and Latvian nationalists who had turned against the Germans following several reported massacres, the Iron Brigade was forced to retreat. Increasing international pressure from countries concerned about German expansion in the Baltic region finally prompted Reich President Friedrich Ebert to issue an order to end all official military operations. Volunteer units began to withdraw from the Baltic states during September 1919, and by December *Kampfgeschwader Sachsenberg* had returned to the East Prussian town of Seerappen and disbanded, its aircraft being recycled.[5]

Pre-war cigarette card showing a man of the SA taking part in glider training as an 'auxiliary policeman'.

Under the terms of the Versailles Treaty, German air forces were banned, although the German Navy had been allowed to retain a small number of aircraft for mine clearance work:

ARTICLE 198.

The armed forces of Germany must not include any military or naval air forces.

Germany may, during a period not extending beyond October 1, 1919, maintain a maximum number of one hundred seaplanes or flying boats, which shall be exclusively employed in searching for submarine mines, shall be furnished with the necessary equipment for this purpose, and shall in no case carry arms, munitions or bombs of any nature whatever.

In addition to the engines installed in the seaplanes or flying boats above mentioned, one spare engine may be provided for each engine of each of these craft.

No dirigible shall be kept.

ARTICLE 199.

Within two months from the coming into force of the present Treaty the personnel of air forces on the rolls of the German land and sea forces shall be demobilised. Up to October 1, 1919, however, Germany may keep and maintain a total number of one thousand men, including officers, for the whole of the cadres and personnel, flying and non-flying, of all formations and establishments.[6]

Based at Nordeney and Holtenau, the aircraft provided great assistance for the hard-pressed minesweeping ships. By October 1919, 11,487 fixed and 12,386 drifting mines had either been swept or destroyed. Within two months all of the minesweeping aircraft were then scheduled to have been handed over to Allied authorities for disposal, but *Kaptlt.* Walther Faber, a former combat pilot with the *Marine Flieger Abteilung* and later Adjutant and Training Advisor to the Naval Air Service Chief of Staff (*Adjutant und Referent Chef des Stabes Marineluftfahrt*) from August 1917, managed to retain six operational machines within the Baltic well into the 1930s, despite the naval air service having been officially dissolved during 1920.

2

Renaissance

The Rebirth of Germany's Military

*K*APITÄNLEUTNANT FABER REMAINED CONVINCED of the validity of maintaining a naval air service despite a general disinterest by the naval staff, who considered capital ships to be the pre-eminent weapon and aircraft merely a reconnaissance tool. Faber was made a head of department within the *Reichsmarineamt* Air Transport Section, while also acting as a member of the Air Peace Commission established by the *Reichswehr* to liaise with the Inter Allied Aeronautical Control Commission tasked with overseeing the disarmament of all German aerial forces and root out any transgressions of the Treaty terms. Nevertheless, he firmly held the six aircraft that he had managed to spirit away beyond the reach of Allied observers, and by 1921 had fifteen trained pilots included within the Reichsmarine ranks; a paltry number, though important for the maintenance of any hope of resurrecting a naval air arm.

At this juncture the seaplane ace and one-time commander of Zeebrugge's naval air station *Leutnant* Friedrich Christiansen, credited with thirteen victories, encouraged covert development of a maritime aircraft by a man whose name would soon to be synonymous with Luftwaffe air power, Ernst Heinkel. Born in Grunbach, Baden-Württemberg, Germany, Heinkel had long harboured a fascination with flight as the future of transportation, and after constructing his own aircraft in 1911 went on to work at Albatros, playing a major role in the design of the Albatros B II reconnaissance and trainer aircraft. After leaving Albatros he worked as chief designer and technical director of the Hansa-Brandenburg company, creating land- and seaplanes from 1914 onwards. It was through this work that he first co-operated closely with Christiansen, who approached Heinkel as one of the Navy's finest 'aces' for the development of faster and more manoeuvrable seaplanes than those already in service.

By 1921 Heinkel had been appointed head designer of the recently re-established Caspar-Werke, owned by former naval plot Karl Caspar, and Christiansen approached him to encourage the design of a small floatplane capable of being launched by submarine. In the Pacific, the Japanese-American arms race had begun, and both parties were interested in advanced German aeronautical designs, which also provided a means to circumvent Versailles restrictions, as the actual construction of these licensed designs could take place outside German territory. The Japanese naval attaché in Berlin, Araki Jirō, had already ordered illegal aircraft designs from Heinkel during 1921 (the HD 25 and HD 26 biplanes), while Christiansen successfully negotiated the construction of a seaplane named the 'Caspar U 1' for the US Navy (USN). This cantilever biplane was capable of being stored within a submarine-borne cylindrical container, reassembled in just over a minute on the surface and launched by catapult. Two U 1 prototypes were bought by the USN in 1922 for successful trials, in turn prompting the German Navy to purchase a single U 1 for its own tests. This was the first naval aircraft ordered since the imposition of the Versailles Treaty, and an important indication that perhaps naval aviation still garnered some interest within the upper echelons of the *Reichsmarine*. A second, improved design, the HS 1, was made for construction by the Swedish Navy, though arguments with Caspar over design rights led Heinkel to depart the company and establish his own design bureau, followed by a construction company, Heinkel-Flugzeugwerke, in a rented ex-naval hangar at Warnemünde. Heinkel concentrated on design work, his prototypes hidden in sand dunes near his construction hangar and out of sight of inspectors, while larger-quantity production took place at the Svenska AB Aero Works in Sweden. During 1924 Heinkel received orders for catapult aircraft, shipborne fighters and floatplanes from the Imperial Japanese Navy. After Heinkel once again warned the Japanese authorities of the ban on aircraft construction in Germany, the Japanese assured him that, as erstwhile enemies from the First World War and members of the Allied inspection commission, they would warn him of any pending inspections, allowing incriminating material to be secreted away. The *Reichsmarine* was already negotiating secretly with their Japanese counterparts to exchange technological information, which was also proving immensely beneficial to the reconstruction of the German U-boat service.[1]

Meanwhile, Faber had also begun the first small naval pilot training course in Stralsund during 1922 as part of the II *Abteilung der Schiffsstammdivision Ostsee*, a second intake being trained during the following year. In January 1923 French and Belgian troops occupied the industrial Ruhr region after the Weimar Republic announced its inability to meet expensive reparations payments demanded by the Versailles Treaty. Turmoil and the complete collapse of the German economy immediately followed, fuelling rage within Germany at the foreign 'invaders' and moving large tracts of the population to the political right wing. Faced with such aggression, the military also girded themselves for potential future conflict. As well as having accumulated nearly 100 million Marks in 'black funds' by the illegal sales of ships due to be scrapped under the terms of the Versailles Treaty, they took a portion of a secret 'Ruhr Fund' established by the German Cabinet without parliamentary knowledge to bolster the military beyond treaty limits. The Navy's share amounted to 12 million gold Marks and, along with other small boosts to research and development, the *Reichsmarine* invested in Faber's tiny maritime aviation unit, ordering the purchase of ten Heinkel HS 1 floatplanes from the Swedish Navy. Faber had even been granted a small staff of four men, and his office had been given its own designation of 'AII1' by the head of the Reichsmarine, *Admiral* Hans Zenker, responsible for all naval aeronautical issues. Faber's AII1 office remained responsible for providing an air defence consultant for each major naval station and maintaining an up-to-date archive of reference material on all matters related to naval aviation; attempting to keep aerial matters in the minds of the *Reichsmarine* officers still otherwise rooted in fleet strategic thinking.

In the interim, the illegal monetary fund provided direct support for aircraft manufacturers Heinkel, Junkers, Dornier and Rohrbach (the latter two having established major aircraft plants in foreign countries), and for the purchase of the Caspar Works in 1926, which continued to develop commercial aircraft bearing an uncanny resemblance to fighter, bomber and reconnaissance types in use by other air forces. Among the designs thus developed was the prototype of the huge Do X 'flying ship', created by the Swiss subsidiary of Dornier; a twelve-engine giant larger even than the famous Boeing Clippers of Pan American, and planned to meet the requirement for a patrol seaplane capable of landing and refuelling at sea. Only an unacceptably low service ceiling made it necessary to abandon this design. The Dornier company had already produced a smaller, twin-engine flying boat which entered production designated the Do J *Wal* (Whale). The *Wal* was a highly successful design, used frequently by explorers and on the marine mail routes, crewed by

A Heinkel He 59; the Luftwaffe's first multipurpose torpedo bomber.

three and capable of carrying up to ten passengers. It was powered by two piston engines mounted in tandem in a 'push-pull' configuration in a central nacelle on a parasol wing. The aircraft's maiden flight took place on 6 November 1922 in Italy to circumvent treaty restrictions. Most of its production was also carried out in Italy until 1931, when the *Wal* began to be produced in Germany. The militarised version, designated Do 15, carried a crew of between two and four in an open cockpit in the forward part of the hull and had a bow-mounted moveable machine-gun, augmented by one or two others amidships. The aircraft was soon on order for the naval air forces of Spain, Argentina, Chile and the Netherlands.

The illegal monetary boost also established the 'civilian' firm Severa (*Seeflugzeug-Versuchsabteilung*, or Seaplane Research Unit) for the development of naval aircraft types and pilot training at Norderney and Kiel-Holtenau. Founded in conjunction with the newly established government-sponsored national airline Deutsche Lufthansa A.G at an annual cost of 1.25 million Marks, Severa provided refresher courses for battle-experienced observer and pilot officers of the last war and trained new officer recruits as observers in a private naval aviation school created at Warnemünde. The 'Communication Experimental Command' located in the same facility also developed highly successful radio equipment for future military aircraft. Under the cover afforded by the newly established German Commercial Flying School (*Deutsche Verkehrsfliegerschule*, or *DVS*) for 'civilian' aircrew, the Warnemünde centre began training observers as well assuming responsibility for all boats and ships for use by naval aviation units. Between 1925 and 1926 Severa spearheaded development of seaplanes and their armament, slowly accumulating airfields and seaplane bases from which to expand its training regime, most notably the 'Seaplane Testing Station for the United German Aviation Companies' at Travemünde, headed by *Kaptlt.* Hermann Moll (retired). Officially, Severa was concerned with commercial flights and the transport of target drones for use by anti-aircraft artillery units still permitted in the peacetime German military. However, these target flights simultaneously enabled the training of observers in reconnaissance techniques for use with the fleet. An average of only six pilots and observers were trained annually, though this still represented a genuine revival of the naval air arm. Naval flying schools were finally established at Warnemünde in October 1928 for the training of both pilots and observers, each course lasting for two years and hosting twenty-seven students in each intake. Aircraft testing was carried out at Rechlin and Travemünde.

An interesting distinction within the early German Air Force as opposed to others was that the observer was the commander of the aircraft, generally outranking the pilot. Therefore, their training was both varied and comprehensive as they were able to assume the duties of any other crewmen. They were trained pilots to 'C' standard, denoting 150 flying hours as pilot, before beginning observer training which included navigation by day and night, blind-flying techniques, gunnery and bomb-aiming. This high pre-war standard produced decidedly skilled aircraft commanders, but was relaxed after the outbreak of war in 1939, when the rule of the observer being senior officer was dropped and training was reduced incrementally over the years that followed as losses mounted on all fronts and the demand for replacements grew.

In 1929 Heinkel developed the HD 42 biplane for use with the covert military-training *DVS*. Its fuselage was a welded steel-tube truss and the engine cowling used lightweight metal, but the rest of the fuselage was fabric-covered. Equipped with floats, the HD 42 was sold to the Swedish Navy, which provided positive operational feedback. The aircraft was subsequently redesignated He 42 and secretly provided to the small naval air units disguised as the *DVS*.

In the wider sphere of Germany's air forces as a whole, facilities for the covert training of pilots and observers had been established outside Germany's borders. By 1926, with the strong support of *Gen* Hans von Seeckt, Chief of the General Staff, an agreement had been reached with Russia for training to take place at Lipetsk near Moscow, and in smaller centres within the expansive landscape of the Ukraine. Fifty Fokker D XIII aircraft were subsequently shipped by steamer from Stettin to Leningrad and then overland to the flying school. Within Germany's borders, the number of private flying schools had blossomed, as had Deutsche Lufthansa A.G. pilot training centres, and by the end of the 1920s the German Air Sports Association (*Deutscher Luftsportverband*, or *DLV*) numbered over 50,000 members spread throughout various clubs. During 1930 the Nazi Party's SA (*Sturmabteilung*, colloquially known as 'brownshirts', the paramilitary arm of the Nazi Party) established a flying branch, and the SS followed suit during the following year; both were Nazi Party-sponsored organisations and counted as auxiliary 'police' units when convenient for international observers. During 1932 the National Socialist Flying Corps was also established as a semi-civilian counterpart, though it was not regarded as a Party organisation despite its title, and in September 1933 the '*Flieger* SA' and SS were absorbed into the *DLV* as a whole. Gliding, unrestricted by the Versailles Treaty, was also strongly promoted, with *Hptm.* Kurt Student of the Air Technical Branch organising courses in glider instruction, allowing fundamental aeronautics to be taught to prospective military pilots. Future fighter pilot Winfried Schmidt followed this path:

> In 1933 I had the opportunity to fly with gliders, which pleased me a lot. The next year I joined a private aviation club, soon included in the *Luftsportverband* (*LSV*), created at that period to become the basis for the new (and still secret) Luftwaffe. In this club I was quickly promoted to flying powered aircraft. Still as civilians, we flew the Klemm 25. This aircraft was so light and slow that we were not authorised to start if the weather was too windy![2]

The airline Deutsche Lufthansa A.G. was an important part of Germany's aerial revival. Founded in Berlin on 6 January 1926, the company was the result of a merger between the small Deutscher Aero Lloyd airline (formed in 1923 by co-operation between shipping companies Norddeutscher Lloyd and Hamburg America Line) and

Adolf Hitler and Hermann Göring pictured at the first inspection of the newly created '*Richthofen Geschwader*'.

Junkers Luftverkehr, the in-house airline of the Junkers aircraft company, both of which were virtually crippled with heavy debts and required the support of government funding. The merger was planned to reduce that required level of monetary assistance, and coincided with the lifting of restrictions on commercial air operations previously imposed by the original terms of the Treaty of Versailles. The Paris Air Agreement of 1926 relaxed restrictions on German aviation, cancelling technological limits on the quality of German commercial aircraft and allowing the construction of airships once more. In return, the Weimar government agreed to halt the subsidising of civilian aero-clubs. However, sturdy limitations remained on the training of military personnel:

> The German Government shall take suitable steps to ensure . . . That members of the *Reichswehr* or Navy may not, either individually or collectively, receive any instruction or engage in any activities in connection with aviation in any form.

That, as an exceptional measure, members of the *Reichswehr* and of the Navy may, at their own request, be authorised to fly or to learn to fly as private persons, but only in connection with amateur aviation and at their own expense. The German authorities shall grant them no special subsidies or special leave for the purpose.

It is to be understood that these exceptional authorisations shall . . . exclude all training in flying of a military character or for a military purpose.

Such authorisations may be granted up to a maximum of thirty-six. This maximum may only be reached in six years as from January 1, 1926, with the proviso that not more than six authorisations may be granted in any one year . . . Members of the *Reichswehr* and of the Navy who hold a pilot's licence issued before 1 April 1926 may continue to act as pilots if they do not exceed the maximum number of thirty-six. These thirty-six pilots, who may not be replaced and whose names shall appear on a special list, are not included in the number of pilots referred to in the above paragraphs.

Nevertheless, as an exceptional measure, fifty police officers may be given aeronautical training and hold a pilot's certificate. It is agreed that these pilot's certificates will not be issued to the police officers to enable them to engage in aviation, but solely to enable them to acquire the technical knowledge required for the efficient supervision of commercial aviation.[3]

Though the ban on military aviation remained in place, a large measure of Germany's air sovereignty had been restored, and many members of the military were covertly transferred to legitimate commercial flying schools. Lufthansa's saleable route network expanded rapidly, soon to include the world's first night passenger flights (necessitating long-range and 'blind-flying' training that would serve future bomber crews well), all under the auspices of the former managing director of Junkers Luftverkehr, the half-Jewish veteran observer of the Imperial Air Force, Erhard Milch.

During the 1920s and 1930s the *Reichsmarine* deliberately avoided joint aerial exercises or discussions on strategy and tactics with the German Army. Memories lingered of Army control over aircraft production during the First World War that had rendered naval squadrons unable to meet demands for modern machines, as did fears of the absorption of naval aviators into the Army.

The Heinkel He 60, a successful two-seater reconnaissance aircraft initially designed for shipboard use.

However, by this time Faber was no longer involved as the head of AII1. He was transferred briefly to the post of navigation officer aboard the cruiser *Medusa* on 10 April 1923, until moved in June to the post of *Referent Inspektion Torpedo-und Minenwesen*, Kiel. There, his expertise was put to good use as he assisted in the development of air-launched torpedoes and mines. He was replaced at AII1 by *Kaptlt.* Hans Ritter (a former naval pilot), who was in turn superseded by *Kapitän zur See* Rudolf Lahs on 1 April 1928; the latter was a former torpedo-boat officer of no aviation experience. The office had increased dramatically in size and lay under the umbrella of the 'Naval Transport Division' commanded by *Kapitän zur See* Walter Lohmann, chief of the Naval Maritime Transport Department (*Seetransportabteilung der Marine*) and the man who had been tasked with both the accumulation of the naval 'Black Fund' and its distribution.

The AII1 office was expanded and renamed with Lahs' assumption of command, now designated *Gruppe BSx* and sprouting a number of sub-offices, many headed by men who would later become major luminaries within the Luftwaffe:

   Military and Tactical: *K.K.* Hans Ferdinand Geisler (transferred to the Luftwaffe in 1933)

Training: *Oblt.z.S.* Wolfgang von Gronau (replaced by *Kaptlt.* Ulrich Kessler, the latter transferred to the Luftwaffe in 1933)

Technical: *K.K.* Joachim Coeler (transferred to the Luftwaffe in 1933, replaced by *K.K.* Hans Siburg who also transferred to the Luftwaffe in 1933)

Intelligence: *Lt.z.S.* Werner Bartz (replaced by *K.K.* Beelitz, a former Zeppelin officer).

During 1928 Lohmann was forced to resign from his post after it became publicly known that he had also poured money into various non-military ventures to bolster the dwindling secret fund. His ventures ranged from the Berliner Bacon Company (attempting to wrest the lucrative British bacon market from Danish firms) to a firm attempting to raise sunken ships by encasing them in ice. However, it was involvement with the Phoebus Film Company, which collapsed financially in August 1927, that compromised him. Lohmann's stake in the company was revealed by investigative journalist Kurd Wenkel, though, somewhat paradoxically, it was not Lohmann's backing of rearmament that scandalised the journalist, but rather the fact he had been influencing the film company to make increasingly nationalistic features supporting the burgeoning right-wing political parties.[4] However, the cessation of Lohmann's activities forced only a brief delay in the establishment of new business fronts behind which the military could continue its secret work. New Commander-in-Chief of the *Reichsmarine*, *Admiral* Erich Raeder himself pressed Chancellor Hermann Müller and the Reich Defence Minister, Wilhelm Groener, for authority to continue and was given the green light.

During the summer of 1929, clandestine naval air training was reorganised on Groener's orders, the Defence Minister being intensely involved in secretly rearming the Weimar Republic. He informed Fleet Command on 1 September that:

> The Coastal Air Section which had been guided by the Navy was dissolved in the latter part of April for considerations of internal foreign policy. The Navy has been able to make a contract with a private air company, the *Luftdienst G.m.b.H.*, whereby the Navy will hire aeroplanes at a fixed hourly rate. The company has rented the (naval air) installations at Holtenau and Norderney . . . .The *Luftdienst G.m.b.H.* personnel are available only for duties which can be considered permissible in terms of the Paris Agreement of 1926 (target flight, towing of targets). For all other duties,

Erich Raeder, Commander-in-Chief of the Kriegsmarine until 1942 and champion of an independent naval air arm, though he perhaps never truly appreciated its potential.

that is especially for gunnery observation and for the direction of naval guns, naval personnel are to be assigned to the aeroplanes as observers.[5]

Only eight aircraft were to be available at any given time, although the new directive guaranteed that 3,000 flying hours were to be available at a price to the Navy of 4.53 Reichsmarks per hour; additional hours available at 70 Reichsmarks. The hours were divided between three separate stations: Baltic, 950 hours; North Sea, 1,550 hours and Naval Command, 500 hours. While at face value the limitations appeared undesirable to the naval air service, they yielded more flying hours than had ever been available previously, and helped established a small but well-trained cadre around which to continue developing the service branch. By the summer of 1930, despite complaints from the British and French embassies at the apparent German abrogation of previous agreements, the *Reichsmarine* was able to select and train a small number of air cadets annually.

On 20 September 1929, *Kapitän zur See* Konrad Zander, a career naval officer and former torpedo-boat commander from the First World War, took command of *Gruppe BSx*, which was subsequently renamed

Gruppe LS. His official title was Director of the Air-Protection-Group, Naval Command (*Chef der Abteilung Luftverteidigung der Marineleitung*), and as such he brought his considerable energies to bear on refining the training regime already established for the small naval aviation wing. He lengthened the training period for new pilots from six months to a year, and that of observers from a single year to two. Zander concentrated on refining the training itself to achieve greater efficiency per Reichsmark spent, and succeeded in no small measure. He also created training courses for flight engineers, radio operators and ground crew personnel, further underlining the Navy's desire for a genuinely autonomous service, separate from the growing strength of the developing air force. In January 1931 the first formalised regulations for the co-operation of fleet and naval air units were issued; the aircraft were referred to as 'motor tenders' to disguise their true nature.

Zander was relocated to the post of Inspector of Torpedo and Mine Affairs in October 1932, though he would later figure prominently in the continuing development of the naval air service. Former U-boat commander *Fregattenkapitän* Rudolf 'Ralph' Wenninger took his place, and by the time of Zander's exit a multipurpose aircraft for the dropping of bombs, mines and torpedoes, the Heinkel He 59, had been developed alongside the He 60 reconnaissance/fighter floatplane.

A large, twin-engine biplane with a crew of four, the He 59 was constructed under the cover of being a maritime rescue aircraft, but in fact it was a versatile reconnaissance bomber capable of operating from

The Dornier Do 18, an improvement on the previous *Wal* that was used to provide long-range reconnaissance during the early years of the war.

both land and water. The aircraft possessed high endurance, an ample bomb load and powerful armament, and demonstrated dependable seaworthiness. The initial prototype, the He 59A, flew in September 1931 with a wheel undercarriage, but subsequent versions were all fitted with floats, beginning with the He 59B-1, of which sixteen were built, one being taken to Lipetsk in Russia for testing in January 1932. The subsequently improved He 59B-2 was the first model placed into major production. The first sixteen were built by Walter Bachmann's aircraft production firm based in Ribnitz, which specialised in seaplanes. A glazed nose that had been provided for the bombardier was replaced by a smaller glazed bomb-aimer's position, and all-metal construction was employed.

The He 60 single-engine, two-seat biplane reconnaissance aircraft was intended for launch by shipboard catapult, and the original prototype flew in 1933. However, the 660hp BMW VI engine was found to be underpowered for the heavy airframe, resulting in sluggish handling. A second prototype equipped with a 750hp version of the same engine offered no significant improvement, so the final production model, the He 60C, reverted to the original powerplant. Aircraft were delivered for training purposes during 1933, and the next year the type began to equip front-line units, including on-board aircraft of *Bordfliegerstaffel* 1./BoFl. Gr.196. The He 60 was of similar mixed construction to the He 59. Both types were designed in 1930 by the talented engineer Reinhold Mewes, who had accompanied Heinkel on his departure from the Caspar Works.[6]

The *Reichsmarine* had also begun testing dive-bomber designs, and Kiel's Deutsche Werke had constructed a prototype shipboard catapult, the K1, under Ernst Heinkel's direction. Heinkel had already developed a catapult for the Japanese Navy which had been successfully installed aboard the battleship *Nagato*, and his new construction was fitted aboard a small scow for testing purposes (designated *Schleuderprahm* 11). It propelled an He 60 successfully into the air during trials in Travemünde. An improved catapult model, K2, was the first to see active use. Heinkel himself had overseen the catapult's successful operation on 22 July 1929, when an He 12 mailplane was launched from the liner SS *Bremen* on its record-setting maiden transatlantic run, a 110-kilometre flight to New York Captain Joachim von Studnitz and wireless operator Willi Kirchhoff. Lufthansa subsequently installed a K2 aboard their catapult ship *Westfalen* within the North Sea, where it was used in conjunction with a Dornier *Wal* flying boat.

While this progress was gratifying, the Achilles Heel of German maritime aircraft operations would later prove to be the torpedo to be carried into action. In 1934 the *Reichsmarine* were latecomers in developing a 45cm aerial torpedo after purchasing the patents of the Horten Naval Torpedo from Norway, short-sightedly reasoning that there was little naval application for a torpedo of that diameter, as opposed to the 53cm version found aboard surface ships and U-boats. Manufactured by the German firm 'Eisengießerei und Maschinen-Fabrik von L. Schwartzkopff', the LT ('*Luft Torpedo*') F5 entered service with the maritime flying units, carried by the He 59.[7] The 650kg weapon had limited drop-parameters, requiring the carrying aircraft to not exceed 75 knots (140km/h) airspeed and be at a height of between 15 and 20m from sea level. A minimum water depth of more than 23m was required for the torpedo's initial drop, which negated all effectiveness in shallow coastal waters such as found on Great Britain's North Sea coast. With a range of 2,000m and maximum speed of 33 knots, the torpedo carried a 200kg Hexanite explosive warhead. However, the marked lack of co-operation between the Kriegsmarine and Luftwaffe frustrated the testing of the design, and it was spectacularly unsuccessful, as the Luftwaffe would soon discover in action in Spain. It is difficult to say whether the Torpedo Experimental Institute (TVA) and the Kriegsmarine's own Torpedo Department simply lacked the initiative to concentrate on developing the torpedo, or whether they were preoccupied by the G7 steam and electric models for U-boat use which, ironically enough, also suffered from major design flaws that rendered them almost completely unreliable. For its part, the Luftwaffe still failed to see the true value of the aerial torpedo, believing that the same results were achievable using less-costly bombs equipped with different fuse combinations. Their reasoning was also, no doubt, fuelled by the thought that such an approach would also lessen the need for specialised torpedo training on the behest of the *Reichsmarine*, which they jealously believed could diminish their hold on maritime air operations. However, with its shortcomings not yet evident, plans were instituted to amass a stockpile of 600 LT F5 torpedoes by 1939. In the event, war began with a stock of fewer than 100 and only five to ten new models being produced each month.

Nonetheless, Zander's groundwork had set the Naval Air Service on firm footing for the moment when Hitler assumed power in 1933 and made German rearmament a matter of the highest priority. The majority of militarily advanced countries included air power within both the navy and army; each arm of service responsible for its specialised training requirements. Perhaps the most notable examples of these were the Japanese, American and French armies and navies. Great Britain, on the other hand, had established an independent air service in 1918; the Royal Air Force, created by an amalgamation of the British Army's Royal Flying Corps and the Royal Naval Air Service. Other commonwealth countries such as Canada, Australia and New Zealand subsequently followed suit, as did Egypt, Brazil and Finland. Göring's desire for a similarly independent service posed significant problems for Raeder's navy.

> It has been consistently held by all the larger navies that naval components, whether surface ships, submarines or air forces, must be controlled by a single commander-in-chief, and for this reason naval air forces must be an integral part of the navy. In Germany, Air Force General Göring and his circle had made the repeated assertion: 'Everything that flies belongs to us!' Such a concentration could have advantages in engine development, general flight training, and industrial expansion, but the proponents of the Göring thesis apparently could not realise that the employment of aeroplanes and air forces in land warfare is totally different from their employment in naval warfare. On land, the attack and defence will be predicated on the principles of *land* warfare, and hence the pilot must be a master of the methods and tactics of land warfare. Naval warfare requires men, machines, and tactics especially fitted to the techniques of *sea* combat, only here the requirements are more difficult to fill, since the element of water is so utterly different from the element of earth. The resulting tactics and methods are so different that only flyers trained in the tactics of naval warfare and trained in the ways and idioms of the sea can be really useful in naval operations.[8]

Furthermore, Raeder noted that one of the primary advantages offered by naval-trained pilots and crew was the facility offered by long-range reconnaissance; far beyond the visual reach of surface craft and U-boats.

> A single observer's report often changes the whole position of his commander-in-chief. A prime essential in such a reconnaissance report, therefore, is its accuracy . . . Such reports are the result of extensive training and long experience . . . Accordingly, up to 1933 our naval flyers had been trained with these things especially in mind and had become familiar with naval doctrine by living constantly within the Navy.[9]

On 8 January 1933 the new *Reichswehr* Minister, von Blomberg, had amalgamated both the Army and Naval flying staffs into the *Reichswehr* under the cover name '*Luftschutzamt*'. However, at the end of the month Hitler was appointed to the post of Chancellor, and in turn also selected a man to assume the newly created post of Reich Minister for Air; officially tasked with the maintenance and expansion of German civilian aeronautics, but in reality primarily concerned with the continued development of the air force as an independent branch of military service. Hermann Göring, a former fighter pilot and holder of the *Pour le Merit*é, was the man appointed to take charge, and he threw himself into the role with vigour. Göring had distinguished himself as both a pilot and the last leader of *Jagdgeschwader* 1, the unit made famous by its original commander, Baron Manfred von Richthofen. In 1922, after meeting Hitler for the first time, he joined the Nazi Party, and by 1933 he had already commanded the SA to considerable effect, been named Interior Minister of Prussia and President of the Reichstag. The Göring of the

The two-man crew of an He 60 preparing to board their aircraft.

mid-1930s was not the same person who, as a child, had railed against the discipline of his boarding school until removed from it, as a teenager had scaled peaks in the Alps, and as an adult had been credited with shooting down twenty-two enemy aircraft during the First World War. Arrogant, highly intelligent and ruthless, Göring was shot in the leg in the failed 1923 'Beer Hall Putsch', in which the Nazis had first attempted to seize power, and subsequently became a morphine addict following surgery, remaining so for the rest of his life. His post-First World War weight gain escalated, and by the time that the Nazis had achieved power he was corpulent and frequently ridiculed for his vanity, outlandish costumes and narcissism. However, his political acumen was considerable, and initial popularity with the Führer assisted his consolidation of both political and, with command of the new Luftwaffe, military power. The vainglorious Göring would soon become the bane of the German Navy as he worked tirelessly to bring everything that flew within Germany under his control, his personal animosity towards the aristocratic head of the *Reichsmarine*, Erich Raeder, compounding an already bitter struggle for ownership of Germany's aerial forces.

Raeder was almost the polar opposite of Göring. Born in Schleswig Holstein to an authoritarian headmaster and his wife, daughter of a royal court musician, the young Raeder was taught to value thrift, cleanliness, discipline and the fear of God above all else. Entering the Imperial Navy at the age of 18, he rose rapidly in rank due to his diligence and application, including two years on the staff of Prince Heinrich of Prussia. Although he was deemed aloof and even 'cold' by those closest to him professionally, his undoubted aptitude for naval leadership led him to serve as Chief of Staff to Admiral Franz von Hipper, a proponent of the creation of a 'balance fleet' centred on battleships that would serve as a deterrent to the risk of war with Britain. This theory never left Raeder, who rose to command the *Reichsmarine* in October 1928 and steered its rebuilding programme in that direction. Punctilious, diligent and a devout Christian, Raeder was singularly unequipped to deal with the nature of political manoeuvring that would dominate the Third Reich in both civilian and military matters, and his opposition to Göring over matters of a naval air arm was doomed to failure from the outset.

> Of all the men close to Hitler, however, Göring was the one with whom I had my most violent battles . . . While he might have been a brave and capable flier in World War One, he lacked all the requisites for command

of one of the armed services. He possessed a colossal vanity which, while amusing to some, and pardonable if it had been associated with other more significant qualities, was dangerous because it was combined with limitless ambition.[10]

Though the newly created *Reichsluftfahrtministerium* (*RLM*, Reich Air Ministry) comprised barely more than Göring's personal staff, Blomberg relinquished control of the combined Army and Navy flying staffs and ordered the incorporation of the *Luftschutzamt* into new Ministry. This could arguably be considered the birth of the Luftwaffe, as all aerial components now rested under the control of Hermann Göring. He, and those senior officers who assisted in the establishment of the Luftwaffe (all of them former Army pilots or staff), maintained that the art of flying remained of primary importance to prospective pilots and crew; specialist training, such as that required for nautical operations, was a secondary consideration. This distinction would have wider ramifications on the entire future of what had seemed a promising German naval air service. At the creation of this new independent branch of service, the newly appointed staff included an office designated *Abteilung* 1 and headed by *Oberst* Eberhard Bohnstedt, with *Fregattenkapitän* Rudolf Wenninger as his Chief of Staff. The office was further subdivided into two subsections: L1 (Army) and L2 (Navy), prescient observers being able to discern future Luftwaffe control over all air activity. A conference held during December between the Naval Staff and the Air Ministry failed to reach accord on the boundaries of control over naval air units, as each side issued opposing directives entrenching their own positions. Coincidentally, on the other side of the hill, the Royal Navy found itself in a similar position until 1939, when the Fleet Air Arm (established by the RAF in 1924 to encompass aircraft carried aboard ship) was returned to Royal Navy control. The RAF's Coastal Command, responsible for maritime patrols, suffered from severe disregard until as late as 1943, being neglected in favour of purely land-based and aerial doctrine.

On 22 January 1934 the Naval Staff issued a proposal that the Luftwaffe be composed of three parts: Operational Air Force, Army Air Units and Naval Air Units. Of these only the first would remain under the singular authority of the Reich Air Ministry, while the latter two would be commanded by officers of the respective service, with material and men provided by Göring's ministry. For the naval aviation unit, an officer designated *Führer der Marineluftstreitkräfte* (*F.d.Luft*, Commander of

Naval Air Forces) would be appointed by Göring and transferred to the command of the Fleet. The proposal was ignored and answered with a counter-initiative.

While the controversy of control continued, Göring, with former Lufthansa executive Erhard Milch appointed his deputy, speedily continued to consolidate the power of the fledgling air force, and the Luftwaffe came into being as an independent air force on 15 May 1934, albeit still under the camouflage required by its contravention of the Versailles Treaty. With the Minister frequently absorbed by his political appointments, it often fell to Milch to organise the distribution of increased though still covert aircraft production, and he vehemently opposed the allocation of any bomber or fighter units to the navy. Interestingly, from the 1934-35 production schedule of a planned 4,021 aircraft, the majority were trainers, obviously with the rapid expansion of the air force in mind, closely followed by land-based aircraft.

Elementary Trainers — 1,760
Operational Type (Land) — 1,714
Miscellaneous (including experimental bomber types) — 309
Operational Types (Coastal) — 149
Communications — 89.[11]

Pre-war Heinkel He 59 overflying one of Germany's capital ships during exercises in the North Sea. (James Payne)

Reinhard Hardegen photographed here later in his career as a highly successful U-boat commander, still wearing the Luftwaffe Observer's badge following pre-war service in both 1./Kü.Fl.Gr.106 and 5./Bo.Fl. Gr.196.

Nevertheless, by December 1933 Raeder was able to muster two squadrons as part of his naval strength: *Seefliegerstaffel* Holtenau (cover-name '*Luftdienst e.V.*') and *Seefliegerstaffel* List (cover name '*Deutsche Verkehrsfliegerschule GmbH, Zweigstelle* List'). Furthermore, the navy controlled the training schools *Seefliegerschule* (pilot school) Warnemünde I and II (cover name '*Deutsche Verkehrsfliegerschule GmbH*, Warnemünde'), *Beobachterschule* (observer school), Warnemünde and the *Bomberschule See* (maritime bomber school) in Bug near Rügen, as well as the testing facility *Seeflugzeugerprobungsstelle* (S.E.S) in Travemünde. Interestingly, one of the early officer cadets (*Offizieranwärter*) of the Crew 33 that received training at Warnemünde was Reinhard Hardegen, who qualified first as an observer and later a pilot, serving in the naval air arm until 1939 and his transfer to the U-boat service.[12]

On 1 April 1934, Göring established six regional Luftwaffe commands; *Luftkreis* I – VI. Outwardly, they were to control civilian aviation throughout Germany disguised as *Gehobenes Luftamt*, but in reality they allowed the founding of a co-ordinated Luftwaffe command structure. In Kiel, *Luftkreise* VI was founded, its geographic location making this office responsible for co-operation with the navy. At the head of the regional

Luftkreiskommando VI was the returning *Konteradmiral* Konrad Zander (designated *Inspekteur der Marineflieger*), transferred to the Luftwaffe and promoted *Generalmajor* in March 1935. Under his remit were all flying units, ground organisation and air defence of the German coastal areas, as well as taking charge of all ships and boats that had been used by the German Commercial Flying School (*DVS*) at Warnemünde, which now operated under the office of *Luftzeuggruppe VI (See)*. Zander was immediately subordinate to Göring as Luftwaffe Commander-in-Chief in every respect. However, regarding training, equipment, maintenance of both personnel and materiel, and shipboard and carrier aircraft units, Zander was referred to the corresponding departments within the Kriegsmarine chain of command. His Chief of Staff was named as *Fregattenkapitän* Otto Stark. On 1 July the new post of *Führer der Marineluftstreitkräfte* (*F.d.Luft*, redesignated *Führer der Seeluftstreitkräfte* on 27 August 1940) was commissioned in Kiel. Its purpose was to facilitate proper liaison between air force and navy as officer in command of the flying units. Initially a post subordinate to Zander, and thus two steps from Göring, in wartime the *F.d.Luft* was tactically subordinate to the Kriegsmarine's Fleet Command (*Flottenkommando*) and was occupied at the outset by *Oberst* Hans-Ferdinand Geisler, a veteran of the First World War naval squadrons before transfer from the *Reichsmarine* to the Luftwaffe in 1933.

Meanwhile, on 11 January 1935, naval command placed before Göring the following proposal for the effective training of officer observers (who also served as the on-board commanders of the aircraft) drawn from the navy for service in the naval air forces:

Three years' normal officer's training;

Three years' experience at sea as *Leutnant* and watch officer aboard small vessels;

Three years' command with naval air units as an observer.

After the final three years, 20 per cent of these men could volunteer for service with the Luftwaffe, while the remaining 80 per cent would return to the navy, all naval aviation units' senior officers to be drawn from the ranks of the men who opted for Luftwaffe service. Göring received the proposal without comment, as the unveiling of the new Wehrmacht would soon take place and he had already outmanoeuvred his naval counterpart.

Raeder later submitted an amended proposal regarding the training of observers for naval aviation units, asking that 100 per cent of observers in such units be naval personnel. This was to be the objective by 1940, though in the intervening period a shortfall of fully trained men would be assuaged by naval officer cadets beginning observer training immediately following their final officers' examinations. The *Reichsmarine* would make good the loss of personnel by their transfer to the Luftwaffe by recruiting an additional 140 officer cadets every year.

However, this proposal also failed to meet with Luftwaffe approval, and a counter-proposal was similarly refused by Raeder. Regardless, the Luftwaffe expanded its training syllabus to include aspects of naval warfare essential for any meaningful contribution to naval aviation. In a co-operative spirit, the *Reichsmarine* founded a small staff of instructors to provide specialised training to existing combat units in naval tactics, ship recognition and the basic principles of naval strategy. The aerial exercises over German coastal waters that followed were conducted primarily by *Lehrgeschwader Greifswald* (Greifswald Training Wing) and a *Staffel* of III./KG 157; the former commanded by *Major* Hans Jeschonnek, who would later become Chief of Luftwaffe Operations Staff in 1938. The Heinkel crews of *Oberst* Dr Otto Sommer's III./KG 157, based in Delmenhorst, were the first operational Luftwaffe crews to receive training in flying over sea areas, their He 111B and H bombers being the first to be equipped with extra flotation gear within the wings to provide buoyancy in the event of an emergency ditching. However, while this development may have appeared favourable to the *Reichsmarine*, in effect it served to highlight to Göring the capability of his Luftwaffe in dealing with naval aviation, relegating a separate naval air arm yet further into the backwater of military priority.

During 1934 the rate of Luftwaffe rearmament had increased under Milch's effective administrative leadership, in what became known as the 'Rhineland Programme', which called for a total of 4,021 aircraft to be manufactured in Germany between the beginning of January 1934 and the end of September the following year. This formidable projected total included eighty-one He 60s and twenty-one Dornier Do 15 long-range reconnaissance aircraft, fourteen He 51W and twelve He 38 fighters, and twenty-one He 59 multipurpose aircraft for naval aviation. Four improved Dornier Do 18 flying boats were also planned to be built. An improved design based on the original *Wal*, the Do 18 retained the high wing, metal hull and push-pull engines in tandem. The power was boosted by the use of Junkers Jumo 250 engines, and general aerodynamics and handling were improved. However, by the outbreak of war the Do 18 was found to be virtually obsolete. Underpowered and vulnerable to enemy fire, it

Hans-Ferdinand Geisler, pictured here later in the war at the rank of *General der Flieger*.

was still used in some quantity owing to the lack of a suitable long-range reconnaissance replacement aircraft for the *Küstenflieger*.

Almost predictably, the programme failed to keep pace with plans, not least of all due to engine production lagging behind the manufacture of airframes, though by March 1935 three new units were able to be formed from delivered aircraft: *Küstenaufklarüngsstaffel* (Coastal Reconnaissance Squadron) 1./126 at List, *Küstenaufklarüngsstaffel* 2./116 at Nordeney and *Küstenjagdstaffel* (Coastal Fighter Squadron) 2./136 at Kiel-Holtenau.[13] During October a revised production schedule, *Lieferplan Nr.1*, was enacted, which would produce a total of 462 naval and 200 naval training aircraft.

Finally, in March 1935, Hitler revealed to the world Germany's rearmament and the existence of an independent Luftwaffe. Ex-*Reichsmarine* officer *Oberstlt.* Ulrich Kessler, commander of the *Fliegerwaffenschule*, Warnemünde, witnessed the immediate prelude to the announcement.

> [Kessler] had been travelling with British Air Vice-Marshal Sir John Salmond, who had been visiting Germany as a representative of Imperial

Airways to study the German Lufthansa Air Line and particularly training in blind landing (the Lufthansa had been training many English pilots in blind flying) . . . One day Sir John and the British Air Attache, then Col Don, paid an official visit to Göring, with [Kessler] acting as interpreter. Sir John and Göring discussed the restrictions of the Versailles Treaty, with Göring complaining especially about the ban on military aviation. Sir John pointed out that in this respect Germany had been granted equality in theory in December 1932, to which Göring replied with some heat that Germany had not needed that other nations grant her moral equality, that what she had been waiting for fifteen years was real equality. 'Now.' he added, 'he had been building up a little Air Force of his own.' [Kessler] hesitated to translate this latter statement, but Göring insisted. 'A little one?' was Sir John's reply, to which Göring said, 'Well, I would call it little.' Göring thereupon promptly notified Hitler that he had let the cat out of the bag, and public announcement followed the same day.[14]

Göring was named Luftwaffe Commander-in-Chief (*Oberbefehlshaber der Luftwaffe*), subordinate to the head of the Armed Forces. Those units previously disguised as flying clubs or police formations — the latter generally comprised of SA paramilitaries — were handed over officially to the strength of the Luftwaffe. Beneath the expansive Luftwaffe umbrella were flak units and, eventually, parachute, infantry and even armoured formations.[15] The naval aircraft units also passed into this all-pervasive realm, including all naval officers and men who had so far received air force training. (Although exact figures are unknown, it is thought to have been approximately eighty officers, including at least twenty-seven from Crew 33 and thirty-six from Crew 34.) They were released by Raeder for Luftwaffe service as pilots and observers, and included within the Luftwaffe's personnel, organisation and supply branches in the vain hope that their attachment could engender a greater understanding of naval interests in aerial matters. To that end, Raeder personally wrote to each senior naval flier who was being transferred, urging them to always remember the naval perspective in their future endeavours. Retired and reserve naval officers were also recalled for posting to administrative offices within the Luftwaffe ground staff, and during 1935 forty officers ranging in rank from *Leutnant zur See* to *Konteradmiral* were transferred to the Luftwaffe.

Meanwhile, the *Reichsmarine* was renamed the Kriegsmarine by Hitler and embarked upon its own expansion plan; building vessels allocated to increasing the size of Raeder's surface fleet and U-boat strength, though the latter initially remained a poor relation to the former. The original plans of Raeder's drive for a new, balanced fleet included the construction of two aircraft carriers, recorded on 11 November 1935 in the overall construction proposal.[16] These would be Germany's first dedicated aircraft carriers since the initial interest in converting *Ausonia* at the end of the last war. Building such a ship from the keel up was a hitherto unexplored area of Geramn naval development, and 36-year-old Naval Chief Architect Dr Wilhelm Hadeler was obliged to begin his planning virtually from scratch. He chose as his original models the British *Courageous*-class carriers and the Japanese *Akagi* which would later take part in the raid on Pearl Harbor. Two German engineers were part of a delegation that toured HMS *Furious* during Britain's 'Navy Week' in 1935, photographing her sister-ship *Glorious* during the same event. Of more use was an official Japanese tour of *Akagi* granted to a small group of naval architects at Sasebo Navy Yard during the same year, blueprints of both *Akagi* and *Soryu* being handed over before the Germans departed.

Hitler authorised the construction plans of the two carriers, given the budgetary and construction designations 'A' and 'B' and to be included in the fiscal years 1936 and 1938 respectively. The intended commissioning year was to be 1939; 'A' was scheduled to be commissioned on 1 April 1939, and 'B' on 1 October. A further two carriers were also added as a later product of the 'Plan Z' naval rearmament scheme authorised in early 1939, but this never gained traction before the outbreak of war and swiftly altered priorities.

The Deutsche Werke Kiel AG was awarded the contract for carrier 'A' on 16 November 1935, though construction was delayed because the shipyard was already working to capacity, with the battleship *Gneisenau*, the heavy cruiser *Blücher*, four destroyers and four U-boats filling the slipways that teemed with workers. The carrier's keel was finally laid on 28 December 1936 in Slipway 1, from which *Gneisenau* had been launched twenty days previously. Carrier 'B' had been awarded to Krupp's Germania shipyard. The machinery contract was issued on 11 February 1935, and construction of the ship itself following on 16 November. However, construction of this vessel was delayed even further, and the keel was not laid until the second half of 1938, after the heavy cruiser *Prinz Eugen* had been launched. Building of 'B' then proceeded at a deliberately slow pace to capitalise on potential experience gained during the building of 'A', the hull of which was launched on 8 December 1938.

Meanwhile, with the assumption of Luftwaffe control over naval aviation, Raeder was compelled to request the continued establishment of naval air squadrons, and was promised twenty-five, totalling 300 aircraft, during 1935. The original proposal included three mixed groups of coastal aircraft (each with a squadron of short- and long-range reconnaissance and general-purpose aircraft), two ships' aircraft groups with two squadrons, three mixed groups of carrier-borne aircraft (each with a squadron of fighter, general-purpose and dive-bomber aircraft), and three coastal fighter squadrons. Apart from the fighter and carrier-borne units, the rest were to consist entirely of He 60 short-range reconnaissance, Do 18 long-range reconnaissance and He 59 multipurpose aircraft. At the right time, the He 60 was scheduled to be replaced as ships' reconnaissance aircraft by the He 114, and later the Arado Ar 196; the Do 18 by the Ha 138 that was in development (later known as the BV 138) as a long-distance flying boat, and the He 59 by the improved He 115 as a general-purpose aircraft. Although early trials of the Heinkel He 115 V1 had been a spectacular failure, Heinkel chief test pilot Friedrich Ritz stating baldly that 'The bird was cursed with absolutely terrible flight characteristics', continued development resulted in a fine aircraft that was popular with naval aviators. The air bases at List, Hörnum, Nordeney, Wilhelmshaven, Kiel, Grossenbrode, Bug auf Rugen, Warnemünde, Swinemünde, Nest and Pillau were all used during the build-up phase; carrier aircraft were based at Bremerhaven and Holtenau.

This plan would enable the Luftwaffe to form *Gruppen*, each containing constituent parts of a *Jagdstaffel* (a fighter squadron of approximately twelve aircraft), *Fernaufklärungsstaffel* (long-range reconnaissance squadron) and a *Mehrzweckstaffel* (multipurpose squadron), under the control of the *Gruppenstab* (Group Staff Unit). Three such *Gruppen* would in turn form a *Geschwader* (*See*) (naval combat wing). By October 1936 it was planned to have two autonomous naval *Geschwader*, though the target production required was never fully attained.

Nonetheless, even this proposed strength was soon deemed inappropriately small for the needs of the Kriegsmarine, particularly in view of potential war against Great Britain and France. Fast aircraft would be required for reconnaissance duties both to the east and west, and Raeder and his staff firmly believed that the Luftwaffe's thinking remained rooted in continental warfare, and that it was therefore unable, or unwilling, to fulfil naval requirements. As he saw it, a strong independent naval air arm was the only solution, and during April the following year Raeder requested an increase to sixty-two squadrons

Pre-war photograph from *Seeflieger* magazine showing an He 59 in Kiel harbour while a flight of He 60s pass overhead.

totalling approximately 800 aircraft, many of which were specified as high-performance types with wheel undercarriages for attacks against naval targets and enemy naval bases.

> Only fast aircraft can be used for long-range reconnaissance in the Channel; flying boats cannot stand up to fighter defence on account of their low speed and lack of manoeuvrability. They are open to enemy attack for about two-thirds of their journey. Requirements are the same both as regards the patrol of the east coast of England and that of the Gulf of Finland (Leningrad).
>
> For offensive operations against naval targets, against English or French bases and mercantile ports, including those on the west coast of England and the Irish coast, bomber formations of Luftwaffe *Luflotte* 2 are by all accounts to be provided. It is doubtful, however, whether bomber formations of the operational Air Force, which are used for large-scale massed attacks on special concentrations at the front, <u>could be released at any given time for such special tasks</u>. It is imperative that the Navy should be in a position to deal, at least in part, with such tasks.[17]

Raeder asked for six long-range bomber squadrons to be attached to the naval air service for the purposes of minelaying, with the incumbent specialist training required. In total he wanted:

Twenty-five general-purpose squadrons (He 115)
Nine flying boat squadrons (Do 18)
Three long-range reconnaissance aircraft squadrons (wheeled)
Six long-range bomber squadrons (wheeled)
Seven ship-borne squadrons (small floatplanes)
Twelve carrier squadrons (fighters, dive-bombers, torpedo bombers).

The new request met with Göring's agreement in principle to realise such a plan by 1942, within the framework of existing prearranged Luftwaffe expansion. The issue of operational control of the naval air arm had yet to be finalised, the Luftwaffe being content to solidify the chain of command 'later' in a memorandum despatched to Raeder by *Generalmajor* Albert Kesselring, Luftwaffe Chief of Staff. In the interim the Luftwaffe established a command specifically for naval operations, *Luftwaffenkommando See*, and placed it under Kriegsmarine tactical command. Raeder felt this also insufficient, though his assertion that the Kriegsmarine should have a say in developing the aptitude of naval fliers was, in turn, unacceptable to Göring. An impasse had already been reached which would never truly disappear during the years that followed.

Heinkel He 59B ashore on a seaplane base hardstanding for replenishment.

Close co-operation between the three branches of the Wehrmacht had already been formalised in published military doctrine by the end of 1935. One of the most influential officers of Göring's small staff was *Generalleutnant* Walther Wever, an outstanding former army staff officer who had been transferred to the Reich Air Ministry on 1 September 1933 as Office Chief, and was soon elevated to Chief of the Air Command Office; in effect a *de facto* Chief of Luftwaffe General Staff.[18] It was he who oversaw the creation of Regulation 16: The Conduct of Aerial War' (*Die Luftkriegführung*), which was eventually issued in 1935. Regulation 16 encouraged wide flexibility in the use of Luftwaffe assets, listing strategic bombing, air superiority and the direct support of Army and Navy operations as principles upon which the air forces should be employed.

> Air Force/Naval Co-operation.
>
> Should there be no maritime co-operation possible, the air force will be able to use its strongest forces available in air operations.
>
> The primary targets of the air force in this environment are the enemy fleet and air units. This will degrade his ability to execute naval operations.
>
> The air force can also support the navy by carrying out operations against enemy ports as well as against his import and export.
>
> These attacks may not always be carried out in co-ordination with naval operations, but have to be in co-operation with naval objectives.
>
> Only a part of the air force will be used to carry out naval operations, and then secure means of communication have to be established between navy and supporting section of the air force.
>
> The operations of the army, navy and air force have to be co-ordinated in such a manner that maximum overall effectiveness is achieved.

However, an important distinction between Luftwaffe and Kriegsmarine co-operation as opposed to that with the Army lay in the fact that at no point did Regulation 16 advocate aerial units being placed directly under Kriegsmarine control. This is in contrast to Army co-operation, in which it was stated that:

Direct co-operation with and direct support of the Army are missions primarily of those units of the Luftwaffe which are allocated to and assigned under Army control for reconnaissance and air-defence purposes. The types of forces in question include reconnaissance, anti-aircraft artillery, aircraft reporting and, if the current situation on the ground requires and the overall situation permits, fighter forces.

On 1 October 1936 the Luftwaffe reorganised its composite units and *Luftkreiskommando* VI stood at the following strength with newly-created *Küstenfliegergruppen* (coastal aircraft groups) created by the renaming of *Seefliegerstaffeln*. Each of the new *Gruppen* comprised three *Staffeln*; the first a short-range tactical reconnaissance squadron, the second long-range reconnaissance and the third multipurpose. The vast majority were commanded by former naval officers (denoted by an *):

Befehlshaber im Luftkreis : *General der Flieger* Konrad Zander*
(also *Inspekteur der Marineflieger* until 1 April 1937)
Chief of Staff: *Oberst* Hermann Bruch*

Führer der Marineluftstreitkräfte: *Oberst* Hans-Ferdinand Geisler* (Kiel)
Küstenfliegergruppe 106: *Oberstleutnant* Ulrich Kessler* (List/Sylt)[19]
  Küstenaufklärungsstaffel 1./Kü.Fl.Gr.106: *Hptm.* Wolfgang Bühring*, Heinkel He 60
  Küstenaufklärungsstaffel 2./Kü.Fl.Gr.106: *Major* Axel von Blessingh*, Dornier Do 18 (and depot ship *Hans Rolshoven*, later transferred to the *Seenotdienst*)
  Küstenaufklärungsstaffel 3./Kü.Fl.Gr.106 *Major* Hans-Arnim Czech*, Heinkel He 59 (Had returned from temporary duty on mission to the Japanese Navy to train as an aircraft carrier pilot aboard the *Akagi* and to study the Japanese aircraft industry).

  Küstenaufklärungsstaffel 1./206: *Hptm.* Hermann Busch*, Heinkel He 60 (Nordeney)
  Küstenaufklärungsstaffel 2./206: *Hptm.* Joachim Hahn*, Dornier Do 18 (Kiel-Holtenau relocated to Nordeney, 1 July 1937)
  Küstenaufklärungsstaffel 3./206: *Hptm.* Hans Hefele*, Heinkel He 59 (Kiel-Holtenau, relocated to Nordeney, 1 February 1937)
(All units of *Küstenfliegergruppe* 206 were subordinated to external staffs; no command unit was ever created)

Küstenaufklärungsstaffel 1./306: *Major* Friedrich Schily, Heinkel He 60 (Nordeney)
(Likewise, raised without a command unit)

Küstenjagdgruppe 136: *Major* Georg-Hermann Edert* (Jever)
All squadrons equipped with He 51 floatplanes for coastal fighter protection.
    Küstenjagdstaffel 1./136: *Oblt.* Hans Hans Busolt (Kiel-Holtenau) (former Army officer)
    Küstenjagdstaffel 2./136: *Hptm.* Werner Restemeyer (Jever)
    Küstenjagdstaffel 3./136: *Oblt.* Hannes Trübenbach (Kiel-Holtenau, relocated to Sarz 1 November 1936)

Also, the *Bordfliegerstaffel* 1./BFl.Gr.196 had been created; a catch-all squadron from which shipborne aircraft and crews were drawn, the remainder being stationed ashore and taking part in coastal reconnaissance and, later, anti-aircraft missions.
Bordfliegerstaffel 1./BFl.Gr.196: *Hptm* Heinrich Winner*, Heinkel He 42 and He 60 (Nordeney, relocated to Wilhelmshaven, 1 January 1937)

Logistically, Zander controlled the following supply units:
    Luftzeuggruppe VI *(See)* Kiel (responsible for ships and boats used in support of naval aviation), established 1 April 1934;
    Luftzeugamt (See) Travemünde, established 1 October 1936;
    Luftpark (See) Holtenau, established 1 October 1934;
    Luftpark (See) Nordeney, established 1 October 1934;
    Luftpark (See) Swinemünde, established 1 January 1936;
    Luftpark (See) Tönning, established 1 April 1936;
    Luftpark (See) Ribnitz, established 1 February 1938;
    Luftwaffen-Munitionsanstalt Diekhof, established 1 June 1934;
    Luftwaffen Munitionsanstalt Hesedorf, established 1 May 1937.

The aircraft with which the naval air force was equipped had all been under development during the years of Versailles restrictions, and plans for the expansion of the Luftwaffe's maritime component were now well under way, albeit not without hindrance from the Reich Air Ministry. However, even at this early stage the Luftwaffe was about to taste action for the first time, and among those units to be blooded were seaplanes of a hastily assembled squadron. The *Aufklärungsstaffel See/88* (AS/88) was attached to the Condor Legion and despatched to wage war in Spain.

3

Early Lessons

The Spanish Civil War

On 18 July 1936 armed revolution erupted in Spain. After years of political and social turmoil, a left-wing coalition government narrowly elected during February became the object of a military coup mounted by the right-wing bulk of the army, led by General Francisco Franco. The subsequent revolt polarised the nation into Republican and Nationalist camps and led to all-out civil war. Franco, who had been virtually banished from Spain to command the military on the Canary Islands, immediately assumed command of the Nationalist Spanish Army of Africa, based in Morocco, and appealed for assistance from sympathetic fascist Italy and Germany in transporting his troops to the Iberian Peninsula. The Republican Navy controlled the maritime approaches to southern Spain. Mussolini offered some Italian aircraft to assist in the transporting of Franco's men, while Hitler quickly authorised German aid, although Spain had never featured prominently in his immediate plans for German expansion. On 27 July *Flugkapitän* Henke departed Berlin in his Junkers Ju 52 and collected twenty-two Moroccan troops for transport from Tetuan to Jerez de la Frontera. Further Ju 52 transport aircraft soon followed, and began airlifting Franco's 30,000 soldiers to Seville, from where the fighting began in earnest.

Ideologically opposed to any prospect of a communist-controlled Spain, Hitler had authorised this covert military intervention, beginning Operation *Feuerzauber*, which would eventually result in the formation of the Condor Legion, originally commanded by the bear-like *Generalmajor* Hugo Sperrle. By the end of August twenty Ju 52s were still involved in the transporting of Nationalist troops and equipment in what was one of the first military airlifts in history, ultimately carrying 13,523 men and 300 tons of supplies into action. Commanded by *Oblt.* Rudolf Freiherr von Moreau, the Luftwaffe aircraft had been painted in civilian markings until two were ordered modified as bombers by Moreau. On 13 August these two aircraft attacked the Republican battleship *Jaime I* in the Bay of Malaga, damaging it with two SC250 bombs and killing forty-seven sailors. The ability of this transport aircraft to switch roles so adeptly illustrated the success of the clandestine build-up of the Luftwaffe through apparent civilian means.

Sonderstab W (Special Staff W) in Berlin recruited volunteers to fight in the Condor Legion under the orders of Luftwaffe *General* Helmuth Wilberg.[1] Although it was under Luftwaffe command, the Kriegsmarine assisted by contributing a small group of officers to maintain a shipping detachment responsible for the covert transport of men, weapons and equipment carried out through the private 'commercial' company Hisma. This umbrella organisation, the '*Hispano-Marroqui de Transportes, Sociedad Limitada*' to give its full title, was founded on Wilberg's orders on 31 July 1936 and registered in Tetuan; overseeing the German transport operations that included the Junkers Ju 52 air bridge. The first eighty-five German volunteers arrived on a Panamanian-registered German steamer, *Usaramo*, on 1 August 1936, in civilian clothes and under the command of *Major* Alexander von Scheele.[2] They had been officially 'discharged' from Luftwaffe service for the duration of their Spanish deployment, serving to barely camouflage their military status. Within the ship's holds were equipment for the maintenance of the Ju 52s, six Heinkel He 51s, twenty 20mm anti-aircraft guns, bombs, ammunition and other military hardware and equipment; all as requested by Franco.

The Luftwaffe contingent of the Condor Legion, which later came to include armoured personnel (codenamed '*Gruppe* Imker') and a naval contingent (codenamed '*Gruppe* Nordsee'), received the designation '88', though it was too large for a *Geschwader* and too small for a *Fliegerkorps*. Its cover name within Spain was 'Negrilla', literally meaning 'bold'. The component units of this Luftwaffe force all carried the '88' suffix, among them a seaplane unit designated *Aufklärungsgruppe See* 88 (Reconnaissance Group Sea 88, or, AS/88). On 14 October 1936 the Nord Deutscher Lloyd liner *Eisenach* docked in Seville. On board were six passengers, 329 tons of military equipment and two disassembled Heinkel He 60 single-engine floatplanes. The aircraft were taken to the Spanish naval base at Puntales, Cadiz, which had been captured by Nationalist forces soon after fresh troops arrived from Morocco. There reassembly began, under the supervision of four of the ship's passengers: observers *Hptm*. Dr Karl-Heinz Wolff and *Leutnant* Hans Siegmund Storp and two Luftwaffe mechanics. Both aircraft were immediately put into service in Nationalist colours with no discernible German insignia on machines or men, the aircraft being colourfully named 'Sea Beast' and 'Terror of the Seas' by their crews. The following month two twin-engine Heinkel He 59s also arrived by ship, accompanied by pilots *Obfw.* Johann Gaessler and *Uffz.* Bernhardt Wines and observers *Oblt.* Werner Klümper and Dieter Leicht. Two more He 60s were landed by steamer during December.

Former Kriegsmarine officer *Hptm.* Wolff had been given command of the small untried unit, and the first pair of aircraft began maritime patrols from Puntales during October. These comprised reconnaissance for the benefit of the Nationalist navy, and bombing attacks on the Republican air base at El Rompedizo. On 16 October a Republican Breguet 19 biplane was shot down into the sea by an He 60, the first aerial victory for Wolff's command.

The Condor Legion received its official formation orders at the end of November 1936, and Wolff's small unit gained its AS/88 designation. By the year's end it had five operational He 60s and a single He 59, aircraft No.521 having been written-off in a forced alighting at sea. During December AS/88 transferred to the Moroccan port of Melilla, based in the Base de Hidroaviones de El Atalayón (Mar Chica). The

Werner Klümper, photographed here in 1943 after rising to command the torpedo bombers of KG 26.

badly concealed relocation of the German aircraft to Morocco raised considerable tension with Great Britain and France, who mobilised troops near the Moroccan border despite repeated denials from Berlin that German military units were present in the Spanish North African territory. German Press outlets subsequently went on the offensive; 'France Wants War in Morocco' the headlines screamed, accusing the French government of inventing a German presence as a pretext for occupying Morocco.

Meanwhile, AS/88 began regular patrolling, 30 January 1937 marking an important milestone in its Spanish deployment. On that day the crew of an He 59 reconnaissance aircraft sighted the Spanish mailship SS *Delfin* sailing between Almeria and Málaga. The 1,253-ton steamer, on its first voyage after being returned to active service following a period spent as a prison ship in Málaga, carried a cargo of flour bound for Republican troops. Escorted by two He 60s, *Oblt*. Werner Klümper took off from Melilla in an He 59 and, after locating the reported steamer in fine clear weather, attempted an F5 torpedo attack. Although the approach was perfect, his initial attempt failed, as the temperamental weapon did not detach from its cradle. With no indication of any fault on the aircraft's weapon release panel, Klümper made a second run, which likewise suffered another hang-up. Finally, during the course of a third attack, his flight engineer managed to free the torpedo by unscrewing the aircraft's floorboards and prising opening the securing lock using a screwdriver when signalled by Klümper. However, once free, the released torpedo splashed into the water and ran a clearly visible circular trajectory, missing the steamer completely.

The *Delfin*'s captain had immediately headed for the coastal shallows when Klümper began his attack, and after grounding the steamer he ordered his ship abandoned, instructing the crew to row their lifeboats ashore. Above them, Klümper and his escort departed the scene, the He 59 landing at Melilla. Klümper then returned in a second He 59, armed this time with four 250lb bombs, all confidence in the potential of the F5 torpedo now gone. Hours later, Klümper found *Delfin* once more and attacked, but this time missed with his bomb run. In the interim, the Spanish crew had returned, only to abandoned ship immediately a second time at the seaplanes' approach, refusing point-blank to re-board after making landfall once the Germans had departed again.

Republican plans to tow the stranded *Delfin* from shore were thwarted by damage to the only available escort ship *Xauen*, suffered during

An He 60 of AS/88 escorting Nationalist flying boats.

air attacks on Málaga and the steamer was subsequently sighted and torpedoed by the Italian submarine *Ciro Menotti*, commanded by Lt Cdr Vittorio Moccagatta. The Italian claimed to have 'sighted a ship sailing along the coast, with lights off, at the Torrox lighthouse', and hit it with two torpedoes, sinking *Delfin* in shallow water. However, the battered ship remained salvageable until Klümper returned on 2 February and finally hit it with delay-fused bombs. One burst through the decking and entered the engine room, where it exploded. Four scrambled Republican fighters then forced the AS/88 aircraft to break away and return to Melilla. Although not a particular success story, this was the first German combat aerial torpedo attack and — eventually — successful anti-shipping mission since the end of the First World War, albeit in conjunction with the Italian Navy, which also claimed the sinking. Klümper was later presented with a certificate signed by Göring that credited him with the destruction of SS *Delfin*.

Between his attacks on the beached steamer, Klümper achieved another distinction when he intercepted the 2,733-ton steamer SS *Nuria Ramos*, bound for Barcelona from Oran with a cargo of coal and 200 foreign volunteers to the Republican cause. On 31 January, accompanied by an He 60 piloted by *Leutnant* Dieter Meicht, Klümper fired warning shots across the steamer's bow, threatening to launch a torpedo until the *Nuria Ramos* diverted to Melilla, where it was surrendered to Nationalist forces.[3]

During February 1937 *Hptm.* Wolff departed Spain to return to his original unit, II./KG 157 in Germany, his place as commander of AS/88 being taken by *Hptm.* Günther Klünder. Like Wolff, the 29-year-old Klünder had also originally enlisted in the Kriegsmarine before transfer to the Luftwaffe in April 1935 for observer training. Before volunteering for the Condor Legion, Klünder was an officer observer in 1.(Mz)/Kü.Fl. Gr. 106 based on the island of Sylt, only recently promoted *Hauptmann*.[4] Under his command, AS/88 took part in the capture of Málaga, suffering their first combat casualty on 5 February, when He 59 No.523 was brought down at sea by Republican fighters and severely damaged. The observer, *Lt.* Dieter Leicht, was severely wounded, and died after he and his crew were recovered by the Nationalist cruiser *Canarias*, which sank the aircraft's remains with cannon fire. Ten days later, AS/88 transferred from Melilla to a temporary base in Málaga, from where it continued operations following the arrival of fresh aircraft from Germany to boost unit strength. A Republican bombing raid on the seaplane station on 9 April failed to destroy any aircraft, although *Gfr.* Siegfried Paendieck was killed. By April the unit had transferred to the base at Cadiz, and the Spanish *Revista de Historia Naval* credits them as taking part in the intense bombing of Valencia during May. It records that the 3,717-ton *Kardin* (ex-*Cabo Creux*), sailing under the British flag, was sunk by AS/88 bombs in Valencia Harbour on 28 May 1937, with seven men killed and eight injured. This merchant ship was later refloated, only to be sunk once again by bombing in February 1939 and again refloated and returned to service under its original name. Klünder's squadron was later moved once more to Pollensa on the Balaeric island of Mallorca. In the interim, AS/88 also scored another first aerial victory when an He 59 shot down one of the seven active Republican Dornier *Wal* flying boats near Cartegena on 28 June.

In Malaga, AS/88 was bolstered by the arrival of a Junkers Ju 52/3m fitted with floats, for use as a liaison and transport aircraft, and by the beginning of August seven operational He 59s were in operational service. From Mallorca, AS/88 took part in the blockade of Republican ports along the Mediterranean coast, under the tactical direction of Nationalist Air Force Mallorca commander LtCol Ramon Franco. Aggressive patrolling resulted in several skirmishes with Republican warships and aircraft, and a second torpedo dropped on 9 June against the Republican destroyer *Antequera* missed by a 'narrow margin'.[5] During July Klünder returned to Germany, to be replaced by *Hptm.* Hans Hefele, who would serve as AS/88 senior officer until January 1938.

Hefele had enlisted in the *Reichsmarine* in March 1924, and began flight training during 1931. Transferred to the Luftwaffe in October 1933, he had served at the *Erprobungsstelle* Travemünde before being promoted *Major* and appointed *Staffelkapitän* 3.(M)/Kü.Fl.Gr. 206 and, concurrently, as Commandant of the naval air station at Borkum.[6] Under Hefel's direction AS/88 continued its patrolling, the target list expanded by Nationalist authorities to include targets in all Spanish harbours, except British ships at anchor and blockade runners flying Greek, Panamanian, Danish or Norwegian flags. Hefele himself was shot down on 30 July when his He 59 was hit by anti-aircraft fire from Republican destroyers escorting the Greek merchant ship SS *Laris*, which was hit on the stern and damaged by bombs. The small Soviet-built motor torpedo-boat (MTB) *Lancha 41*, which also formed part of the Republican escort, was also hit and sunk. Hefele and his crew were rescued by Nationalist cruiser *Canarias*, which took their damaged seaplane in tow back to Pollensa for repair.

The activities of AS/88 expanded to include attacks against railway transport hubs and fuel storage depots, as well as anti-shipping patrols. Among the missions flown, Hefele also managed to make several reconnaissance missions near the British naval base at Gibraltar, building up a significantly detailed picture of the situation in harbour and on the ground which was later passed on to Berlin. The number of ships hit and damaged by AS/88 machine-gun fire and bombing gradually mounted, though an attack on the British steamer *Cervantes* on 9 October started a brief diplomatic incident after one He 59 narrowly missed with bombs, and a second with a torpedo. Following subsequent British protests, the military commander of Palma de Mallorca, Admiral Francisco Basterreche, candidly admitted in an 'off-the-record' conversation with the British consul Alan Hillgarth, a British intelligence officer, that the attacking aircraft had been piloted by Germans. When the French vessel *Oued-Mellah* was subsequently attacked and sunk by He 59s near Barcelona on 24 October, the incident elicited a similar diplomatic protest, though Nationalist Admiral Francisco Moreno disavowed any knowledge of the attack. On the following day the 73-ton French auxiliary ship *Chasseur 91* was attacked by two He 59s while refuelling Air France aircraft in the harbour at Fornells, Menorca. Machine-gunned and bombed, the ship broke in two and sank, but with no casualties.

Matters came to a head on 30 October, when a single AS/88 He 59 strafed and bombed the 2,349-ton SS *Jean Weems* fifteen miles off the Spanish coast. The British merchant ship was carrying a declared cargo

Martin Harlinghausen (left) and *Oblt.* Franz Wieting photographed for the English language edition of *Signal* magazine in North Africa during 1941 as Staff of X.*Fliegerkorps.* Wieting was awarded the Knight's Cross on 19 June 1940 while part of 6./KG 30 for success against merchant and military shipping in the North Sea. He was killed in a plane crash on 29 June 1941.

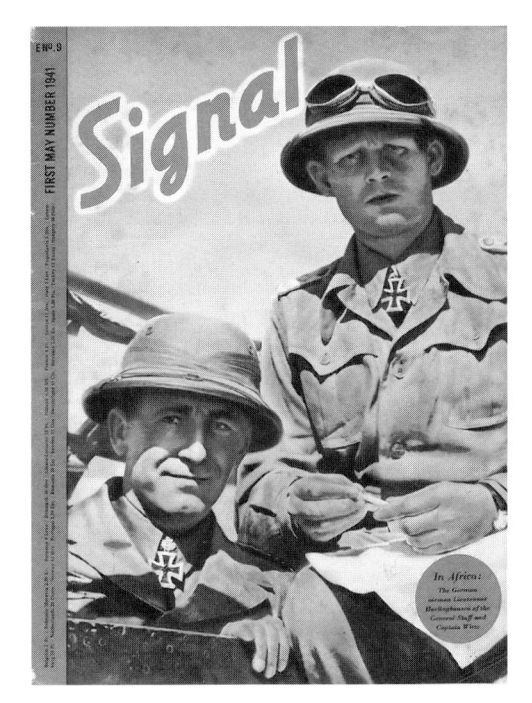

of wheat, leather and condensed milk from Marseilles to Barcelona under Republican government charter. The German pilot reported sighting a cargo of what appeared to be cotton, as well as eight trucks painted grey-green. Following warning shots across the bows, the ship stopped and the crew took to their lifeboats. The abandoned steamer was subsequently hit by four 50kg bombs and broke in two, sinking within ten minutes. Among the twenty-six survivors were two observers of the Non-Intervention Committee formed in 1936 following ratification of the Non-Intervention Agreement to prevent personnel and matériel reaching the warring parties of the Spanish Civil War.[7] The resultant backlash from both the British press and government resulted in a Nationalist apology and an offer of compensation.

Condor Legion operations as a whole had already raised the ire and condemnation of the wider world, not least of all following the April 1937 bombing of Guernica, in which no AS/88 aircraft took part. However, as far as Germany was concerned the combat experience of war in a foreign 'testing ground' was invaluable. The men of AS/88 were regularly rotated back to Germany and replaced by fresh arrivals eager for experience. During 1937 AS/88 gradually began handing its He 60 fighters over to Spanish aviation units, the squadron focus concentrated on He 59 bombing and torpedo operations. In January 1938 Hefele was rotated and replaced by *Hptm.* Martin Harlinghausen, who would lead AS/88 throughout 1938. Like his predecessors, Harlinghausen had originally enlisted in the *Reichsmarine*, and transferred to the Luftwaffe in October 1933 with the rank of *Oblt.z.S.* Following General Staff Training he was made *Staffelkapitän* of 3./Kü.Fl.Gr. 506, situated in Dievenow, outside Swinemünde. One of his first missions after his arrival in Spain was to attack the CAMPSA fuel tanks in Valencia on the night of 19 January, which he subsequently successfully carried out, leaving the depot in flames. Harlinghausen had brought a new attack technique with him, experimenting with it for the first time over Valencia. As the He 59's low cruising speed rendered it vulnerable to ground fire during an attack run, he ordered his pilot, *Lt.* Zenker, to cut the throttle to idle during the approach to target, rendering the attacking aircraft virtually silent as it dropped its payload. With bombs released, Zenker swiftly pushed the biplane into full throttle and climbed away unscathed from the confused ground fire. Although the ponderous aircraft remained vulnerable during its low-level escape, its chances of avoiding anti-aircraft fire were greatly enhanced.

Harlinghausen's AS/88 continued attacks on both land and maritime targets throughout 1938. However, daylight attacks on shipping were becoming less frequent, as they were left more and more to land-based dive-bombers. Instead, AS/88 found itself more often attacking port installations by day and supply trains with bombs and cannon fire by night. On 15 March He 59 No.529 was shot down by anti-aircraft fire from guns mounted on a train it was attacking near Vinaroz. Hit in the starboard engine and fuselage, the aircraft made an emergency landing in an olive grove and was destroyed by its crew before they were captured by Republican troops. The five men aboard numbered four Germans: *Obfdw.* Rudolf Rücker, *Obfw.* Alfred Tonollo (pilot), *Obfw.* Hermann Strohmaier (observer) and *Obfw.* Bruno Stötzer. In company with them was Portuguese volunteer Jose Caetano Rocha Sepulveda Velloso. The prisoners were later exchanged for Republican PoWs and returned to their respective nations.

Six days later, *Oblt.* Hajo Jürgens and his crew (*Uffz.* Kurt Keitzel, *Uffz.* Kurt Werner and *Lt.* Karl Zunker) were all lost when their aircraft was shot down in flames by a Republican Dewoitine D.510 nightfighter of 1st Escuadrila Grupo 71 near Cambrils. Three of the crew burned to death within the twisted remains of their aircraft after it had crashed, and a fourth died in hospital forty minutes after being recovered by Republican troops.

During the Spanish Civil War only three AS/88 aircraft were literally 'shot down'. Five others damaged and forced down by enemy ground fire or aircraft were later written off, and another nine were written off through bad landings, running out of fuel or inclement weather. One was caught in the blast of its own bombs. All casualties were He 59s, though the aircraft's ruggedness was demonstrated by Harlinghausen himself when his aircraft was hit by ground fire over Barcelona but managed to return with half its wing fabric missing, the fuselage twisted out of shape and the lower wing broken in several places. As well as the loss of seventeen aircraft, AS/88 also suffered seventeen men killed.

Logistics had also proved to be a major and almost insurmountable hurdle for AS/88. The He 59 in particular was a complex machine that required constant maintenance and attention. Unfortunately, most spare parts were still in Kiel within Kriegsmarine warehouses, whereas the aircraft had already passed to Luftwaffe control. Bureaucratic wrangling between the two Services conspired to keep AS/88 from effectively maintaining its optimal number of machines at combat readiness. Moreover, the necessary servicing required after completing 300 flying hours had to be undertaken in Germany, and as ground-attack missions increased the hours flown by AS/88 this milestone was reached more rapidly than anticipated. The sole solution was for aircraft requiring the major overhaul to fly to Cadiz, where they were disassembled, shipped back to Germany, reassembled and flown to the repair depot; a process that could take as long as three months from beginning to end.

The performance of AS/88 has variously been described in other texts as either disappointing or an unqualified success. The truth lay perhaps somewhere between these extremes. Eleven torpedoes were launched in combat, of which only two succeeded in sinking ships. The Danish refrigerator ship SS *Edith* was attacked with bombs on 12 August 1937 by four AS/88 He 59s as it travelled from Marseilles to Valencia with a cargo of frozen meat. A single torpedo was also launched, but missed. Not so the bombs; *Edith* was hit and set ablaze, the crew of twenty plus a French officer representing the Non-Intervention Committee all abandoning ship. The derelict vessel was left adrift until hit by a torpedo from *Lt.z.S.* Hans Reefe's He 59 during the following day and sunk in deep water thirty miles off Barcelona.[8]

An He 60, two Arado Ar 95s and a Dornier *Wal* flying boat of the Condor Legion.

The following year, on 21 June, the 4,798-ton British steamer SS *Thorpeness*, carrying 7,000 tons of wheat from Marseilles to Valencia, was attacked at 2150hrs by He 59 No.530, captained by Harlinghausen himself. The ship lay darkened at anchor near the mole of Valencia Harbour, and was seen by Harlinghausen by the light of a weak crescent moon. Aware of the problematic launch parameters of the F5 torpedo, Harlinghausen ordered the aircraft throttled back to 120km/h and released the torpedo from a height of only 5m above sea level. The weapon ran true and impacted amidships, *Thorpeness* slowly heeling over and sinking. The ship had already been bombed by Italian aircraft during the previous January, suffering fatalities and multiple wounded. This time almost the entire crew reached shore unscathed, apart from a single Chinese member, who was subsequently posted as missing. Contemporary reports repeated in newspapers worldwide claimed that the attacking aircraft returned to machine-gun the sinking ship, though Harlinghausen made no mention of this, and claimed that his approach and attack had remained unobserved, leading Franco to inform the British authorities that *Thorpeness* had struck a mine. However, the attack by a lone raider had been observed by at least one crew member and immediately reported, the ship's captain being quoted as saying that it was a 'deliberate and premeditated attack to sink a British ship anchored at sea', though he was unable to identify the aircraft.[9]

The sinking of the *Thorpeness*, followed by the bombing and sinking of the 3,054-ton British SS *Sunion* by AS/88 aircraft the following day, prompted fresh complaints in the British Parliament about the obvious foreign involvement in attacks on British shipping, despite Spanish Nationalists' adamant assertion that *Thorpeness* had been sunk by a mine.

> British Ships Sunk. Protests To Rome And Berlin?
>
> Mr Lloyd George made one of his now infrequent interventions at question time in the Commons today, when the bombing of the *Thorpeness* and the *Sunion* was raised by the Conservative Mr Sandys. The Prime Minister replied that the government were seeking an early explanation from the Burgos Government. The veteran ex-Premier asked whether a protest was to be sent to those to whom these bombing engines belonged, or whether Mr Chamberlain was confining the protests to the Franco Government whereas these engines belonged to the Italian and German Governments. Mr Lloyd George asked whether Mr Chamberlain was going to protest to the government who supplied those machines and pilots. The Prime Minister said that these machines must be considered exactly in the same categories as other arms and equipment — supplies from foreign countries to either side in Spain.[10]

Despite international protests, AS/88 served throughout the civil war, continuing both anti-shipping raids and targeting land objectives, including an attack on a Tarragona railway yard in October 1938 that badly damaged a passenger train with shrapnel, killing thirty civilians. Two newly developed Heinkel He 115s began operations with AS/88 during March 1939. The aircraft had been designed as a replacement for the antiquated He 59, Ernst Heinkel winning the contract against competition from the Blohm & Voss Ha 140.[11] Supervising the performance of the two new aircraft in Spain was *Fliegerstabsingenieur* Dr Gerhard Geike of the *Erprobungsstelle See*, Travemünde. Provided with the honorary Spanish rank of *Teniente Colonel* (Lieutenant Colonel), Geike was on hand to study the potentially corrosive effect of the Mediterranean Sea water on the aluminium aircraft skin. Both aircraft departed Germany in civil markings, crewed by Luftwaffe men who flew via Italy to the AS/88 base at Mallorca. Painted with Spanish markings, they made several reconnaissance flights, encountering no opposition. Although the aircraft performed well, their subsequent return to Germany during May flowing the end of hostilities showed that the airframe and floats had suffered high levels of salt corrosion that had begun to cause severe structural damage.

During January Harlinghausen had returned to Germany, and his place as AS/88 commander was taken by *Hptm.* Helmer Smidt, who was still in charge when hostilities officially ended on 1 April 1939 with the Republican capitulation following the fall of Madrid. There remains some ambiguity over the exact number of ships destroyed by AS/88, though the most reliable lists record forty-two vessels sunk, nineteen damaged (including the Republican destroyer *Almirante Valdés*) and one steamer captured. Certainly this cannot be described as an inconsequential part of the overall role played by Germany's aerial presence during the Spanish Civil War. Indeed, of the total number of ships sunk or captured by Nationalist forces during the conflict, approximately one-third were accounted for by the seaplanes of AS/88 during the course of 850 operational sorties.

Alongside the German pilots and crews, at least eighteen Spanish Nationalist personnel also served as part of AS/88, the small Spanish contingent being commanded by pilot Captain Carlos Pombo Somoza. At the end of hostilities the Condor Legion returned to their homeland, AS/88 leaving three He 59s for the Nationalist Air Force, while the remaining seven serviceable machines were also repatriated to Germany. A victory parade of the Condor Legion and Italian legionnaires was held before General Franco at Madrid's Barajas Airport on 12 May, and the two *Staffel* commanders (and observers), *Majors* Martin Harlinghausen and Karl-Heinz Wolff, as well as observers *Hptm.* Franz Brey, *Oblt.* Hans-Siegmund Storp and *Uffz.* Ernst Arno Kleyenstüber, were all awarded the Spanish 'Individual Military Medal'; the country's third-highest military decoration. Brey's award was in recognition of his aircraft having sunk nine enemy vessels, making him the highest single-scoring aircraft commander of AS/88.[12]

A second victory parade was held in Berlin during June before the German dictator and his assembled generals. Thousands of Condor Legion veterans were presented with the Spanish Cross (*Spanienkreuz*) that had been initiated during April 1939 and awarded in varying classes, and Harlinghausen was presented with the Wehrmacht's Spanish Cross in Gold with Swords and Diamonds (*Spanienkreuz in Gold mit Schwertern und Brillanten*), awarded to only twenty-eight men in recognition of repeated acts above and beyond the call of duty during the Spanish Civil War.

Most importantly, first-hand combat experience had been gained by the naval pilots and tactics had begun to evolve, including the dangerous technique adapted from Harlinghausen's silent approach of completely switching off the aircraft's engines and gliding into the attack undetected before restarting them. However, while the Wehrmacht as a whole, and particularly the Luftwaffe, had taken the opportunity to rotate officers and men through the war zone in an effort to gain experience which could be passed on in training regimes within Germany, what of the

A *Bordflieger* Heinkel He 60; this machine was officially listed as belonging to the cruiser *Leipzig*, photographed here aboard the *Admiral Scheer* in Spanish waters during the Spanish Civil War.

tactical development of these tried and tested revolutionary new ideas? Unfortunately for the naval air service, the primary Luftwaffe lesson had been the advantages of close-support aircraft for ground forces. Little strategic bombing had been carried out by the Luftwaffe, which perhaps contributed to the stubborn refusal to develop a truly effective bomber force for use in future war. Likewise, the Luftwaffe reported AS/88's achievements as meagre at best. The disappointing performance of the F5 torpedo seems to have resulted in a virtual abandonment of further development, rather than providing potential impetus for a search for solutions. The Heinkel He 59 had performed well despite being virtually obsolete, a testament to the effectiveness of the mixed Luftwaffe-Kriegsmarine crews and their inventiveness at overcoming logistical and supply hurdles in an operational theatre. The negative result of such adaptation, however, was that the He 59 was therefore considered adequate for the likely future role of maritime aviation; reconnaissance.

This apparent indifference to the possibility of naval air power as an effective offensive weapon can be laid not just at the door of the Luftwaffe, but also at that of Erich Raeder, who remained rooted in the naval tradition of large fleet actions that saw no role for aircraft beyond scouting missions. While the USA and Japan in particular saw the potential of aircraft at sea, as did Great Britain, though arguably to a lesser degree, the possibilities demonstrated by the destruction of so many enemy ships during the Spanish conflict appears to have been completely lost on both the Luftwaffe and Kriegsmarine. Back in Germany, the struggle for control of the neglected naval air arm continued within the offices of military bureaucrats in Berlin. Though many men who had been on the ground with AS/88, and Harlinghausen himself in particular, could see the potential of a well-trained and equipped naval air force, the lessons of the Spanish Civil War failed to help their cause. Germany headed towards war with an incomplete naval air arm, and an incoherent combat doctrine regarding maritime aerial operations.

However, there were others within the Luftwaffe who were also well aware of the necessity of strong maritime air units. During the summer of 1938, as the situation between Germany and Czechoslovakia deteriorated, *General der Flieger* Helmut Felmy, commander of *Luftwaffengruppenkommando* 2 (redesignated *Luftflotte* 2 in February 1939), sent a detailed memorandum to Göring outlining the unpreparedness of waging potential war with Great Britain. He readily acknowledged that both the Royal and Merchant Navies would be primary targets, though the Luftwaffe possessed virtually no experience and little training at waging an aerial campaign over water. Therefore he strongly urged the establishment of a dedicated Luftwaffe maritime strike force of heavy bombers for anti-shipping attacks and preparations for a major minelaying campaign that could strangle Britain's ports.

The uneasy and unsettled compromise agreements that had been reached by Raeder and Göring over naval aviation reignited during February 1937, after Raeder requested a private conference with the Minister of War, *General* Werner von Blomberg, to settle the matter once and for all. Upon Göring learning of this attempt to circumvent his authority, he requested a verbatim transcript of the meeting, which Raeder immediately refused. Instead, the two service chiefs scheduled their own face-to-face meeting, which took place on 11 March 1937. In preparation, the Naval Staff prepared a lengthy dossier for presentation to Göring, detailing the argument in favour of an air arm under naval control, but to no response, as the impasse between the two chiefs remained as fixed as ever. Subsequent conferences on the subject also failed to reach a solution, and the controversy dragged on. Meanwhile,

General Franco and *Generalmajor* Wolfram Freiherr von Richthofen review men of the Condor Legion at Madrid's Barajas Airport on 12 May 1939 before their return to Germany.

Göring had been named by Hitler as the head of the government's 'Four-Year Plan' of rearmament and the German drive toward self-sufficiency. In this role the head of the Luftwaffe now exercised greater power over the allocation of weaponry to each service branch, complicating the issue as far as Raeder was concerned, and allowing Göring to deny further naval requests for aircraft, claiming that economic concerns could not match both naval and air force requirements. During a meeting held by the Luftwaffe General Staff at Göring's Karinhall on 26 October to discuss the means by which to wage war on Great Britain and its maritime strength, Hans Jeschonnek forcefully persuaded Göring to authorise the manufacture of as many four-engined He 177 bombers as possible, despite the design being far from complete and laden with problems. Nonetheless, there was an overconfident expectation that the manufacture of such aircraft would allow Luftwaffe units to tackle the issue of maritime interdiction and, following a further meeting held on 24 November 1938, the Luftwaffe finally and flatly denied Raeder's sixty-two squadron demand.

> In view of the productive capacity of the German aircraft industry, the long-term [expansion] policy of the Luftwaffe can only be carried out if construction is entirely concentrated on two types of aircraft for the future air forces, namely, Ju 88 and He 177.
>
> A simultaneous expansion of the Naval Air Force from twenty-five to sixty-two *Staffeln* is impossible and appears unnecessary, since the Luftwaffe is prepared to take over all offensive tasks and part of the reconnaissance duties with its thirteen bomber *Geschwader* detailed for air/sea warfare . . .[13]

As an answer to Kriegsmarine demands, the Luftwaffe had instead pledged to devote thirteen bomber *Geschwader* for special training in offensive operations against targets at sea, using bombs, torpedoes and minelaying. In total, in the event of war in the west, the *RLM* envisioned thirty *Geschwader* for operations against the British mainland, thirteen for operations in the 'economic war' and against targets at sea, and fifteen for operations against France. Naval Staff requested that at least some of the bomber units be placed under Kriegsmarine tactical command, but Göring's express orders forbade such a measure, the bomber units being placed instead under Felmy's tactical command in *Luftwaffengruppenkommando 2*. Göring had successfully outmanoeuvred

Raeder, and possessed an almost unassailable upper hand in all future negotiations between the two services. Meanwhile, however, the result of Raeder's meeting with Blomberg was formalised on 31 March, when the latter issued a directive that stated:

In the whole theatre of war the primary task is combat:

a. of the Army against the enemy's ground forces

b. of the Navy against the enemy at sea

c. of the Air Force against the enemy air force.

The only exception to this rule is the combat of the Army and Navy in defence against an enemy air force attacking troops, ships or fortifications. For this defence, the Army and Navy will use their own equipment and those units of the Air Force which have been permanently assigned to them . . . All other exceptions fall within the jurisdiction of the Armed Forces Command and will be ordered by this command.

The division of the theatre of war into a theatre of the Army (operational zone), a theatre of the Navy (coastal defence district), and a theatre of the Air Force (Reich air defence district), as has been directed, must not lead to a strict isolation of the branches from one another.[14]

With this directive, the War Ministry authorised the Kriegsmarine to handle responsibility for all defensive matters in Germany's coastal areas, within each 'Coastal Defence District', the commanding admiral being responsible for all defensive matters against attack from the air as well as from the sea. Bolstered by this clear stance from the Minster of War, Raeder scheduled another conference with Göring for 11 May 1937, at which the naval chief once again requested an answer to the written proposals that had been handed to him during their previous meeting, noting in a circulated memorandum that no agreement in principle on the navy's position had been reached between the two services. In yet another face-to-face meeting, Raeder noted that it was 'absolutely essential' that Göring accept the provisions of his original presentation.[15] Nonetheless, the meeting was yet again inconclusive. Worse still, from Raeder's point of view, the Luftwaffe now voiced the urgent request that all fighter and reconnaissance squadrons in coastal areas be handed over to its control, in defiance of Blomberg's decision.

This unsatisfactory and vague situation continued for the months that followed. At no point did the *RLM* emphatically refuse Kriegsmarine requests, and tacit agreement was made regarding joint training and research, though all to the betterment of the Luftwaffe rather than offering genuine support for a naval air arm. Göring continued to exercise dominance over military production and allocation, and the War Ministry provided no further clarity regarding the situation before the office was abolished in 1938, following Blomberg's ignominious fall from power in a personal scandal surrounding his second wife, which in large part had been engineered by Hermann Göring himself. In its stead, Hitler became Wehrmacht supreme commander, creating the office of *OKW* as he did so. With Hitler now his immediate military superior, the politically adept Göring consolidated both his personal power and that of the Luftwaffe, while Raeder's position within Berlin's convoluted hierarchy weakened over the same period.

None of this was apparent outside the bureaucratic halls of Berlin when, on 8 December 1938, the hull of the *Graf Zeppelin* was finally launched amid the grandeur of a spectacular ceremony attended by Hitler and military leaders of all three services. With the first dedicated aircraft carrier now in existence, though far from finished, Raeder's drive for a maritime air service appeared to have been rekindled once more. At the height of the event Göring mounted the dais festooned with flower garlands and delivered a brief laudatory speech, after which Helene von Brandenstein-Zeppelin, daughter of the ship's namesake, christened the carrier before it slid stern-first into the water.

The ship was impressively built, its well-armoured hull being divided into nineteen watertight compartments. The control 'island' lay to starboard of the heavily armoured flight deck, its weight counteracted by the below-deck hangar. The flight deck itself was protected by Wotan Weich steel armoured plate up to 45mm thick, with a 60mm-thick armoured deck located beneath to protect the inner workings of the ship against aerial attack. Around the waterline, an armoured belt provided defence against torpedoes and reached a maximum of 100mm thickness in the midships area.

Four Brown, Boveri & Co turbines, each providing 50,000hp, made *Graf Zeppelin* the most powerful ship built thus far in Europe, theoretically capable of a top speed of 34.5 knots. Perhaps the

The launching of the *Graf Zeppelin* on 8 December 1938.

most contentious part of the design had been the installation of sixteen 150mm L/55 C/28 guns in twin casemates. Originally, the Kriegsmarine had requested eight 203mm guns, the equivalent main armament carried by a heavy cruiser, illustrating the fact that they had not as yet grasped the aircraft carrier's true role. Raeder and his officers continued to see this impressive ship as a supporting craft, capable of engaging enemy warships in a traditional surface action, as opposed to an entirely new entity in the field of naval battle. Twelve twin-mounted 105mm L/65 G/33 and twenty-two 37mm L/83 C/33 twin-mounted and seven 20mm L/115 C/30 single anti-aircraft guns rounded out the fearsome weaponry.

Furthermore, rather than develop aircraft specifically for carrier use, the Germans chose instead to modify existing aircraft designs, with a single exception. As designed, the ship would carry forty-two aircraft: twelve adapted Junkers Ju 87 dive-bombers, twenty Fieseler Fi 167 torpedo bombers and ten adapted Messerschmitt Bf 109s, operated by a total of fifty-one officers and 255 NCOs and enlisted men as flying and ground crew.

Hermann Göring speaks at the launch of the *Graf Zeppelin*, flanked by Raeder at far left and Hitler at far right.

The *Technische Amt RLM* (Technical Office of the State Ministry of Aviation) requested Messerschmitt draw up plans for a carrierborne version of the Bf 109E fighter, to be designated Bf 109T (for '*Träger*', or, 'carrier'). As will be seen later, the construction of *Graf Zeppelin* was a stop-start affair that serves almost as an illustration of the fate of the entire naval air arm. By December 1940, when the first major work stoppage occurred on *Graf Zeppelin*, the decision was made to complete only seven of the carrier's Bf 109T-1s, the remainder to be completed as land-based aircraft (T-2) and subsequently posted to Norway. As work was about to be resumed in 1942, the surviving T-2s were reconfigured as carrier aircraft, seven being handed over to the Kriegsmarine during May. By December forty-eight T-1s were on strength, the majority stationed in Pillau in expectation of deployment aboard *Graf Zeppelin*. However, when completion of the carrier was finally cancelled, they returned to Luftwaffe service in April 1942.

The Fieseler Fi 167 was a different case. It was ordered by the Reichs Air Ministry in early 1937, which specified the need for an all-metal biplane capable of both torpedo- and dive-bombing, specifically for use aboard the aircraft carriers. Both Fieseler and Arado were given the opportunity to tender for the order, which required the aircraft to have a maximum speed of 300km/h and an operational range of 1,000 kilometres. Arado offered the Ar 195, a derivative of the Ar 95 fitted with an arrester hook and catapult-launching gear. Three prototypes were constructed, but none achieved the specified performance.

The Fieseler design, on the other hand, exceeded expectations in every respect, including an unusually low stalling speed that could allow the aircraft to make an almost vertical landing aboard a moving ship. An interesting naval adaptation to the design was the ability to jettison the fixed undercarriage in case of an emergency alighting on water, while the lower wing assemblies contained air bags that could keep the aircraft afloat for sufficient time to enable the crew to abandon it. After only two prototypes had been tested, production of twelve aircraft began. Although the Fi 167 showed great promise, as the construction rate of the carrier itself progressively slowed, so too did Fi 167 production. Upon the halt of *Graf Zeppelin* building work in 1940, the aircraft was deemed surplus to requirements and the semi-completed airframes were finished and transferred to *Erprobungsstaffel* 167, a testing unit that was used in German-held Dutch waters, engaged in research into naval aircraft camouflage. Others were sold to Croatia, where their excellent take-off and landing capabilities made them useful Army supply aircraft during 1944 and 1945. Upon the brief resumption of *Graf Zeppelin* construction in 1942, the Fi 167 was not reinstated, as the Ju 87D-4 was intended to be used as a torpedo bomber. Prototypes were built which could carry a 750–905kg aerial torpedo on a PVC 1006 B rack, allowing use of the *Lufttorpedo* LT 850, the German version of the Japanese Type 91 aerial torpedo. A reorganised aircraft complement for *Graf Zeppelin* numbered thirty Ju 87s and twelve Bf 109s.

An adapted Junkers Ju 87B, the Ju 87C, was to form the backbone of the *Graf Zeppelin*'s offensive power, the 'Stuka' dive-bomber already having proved its capabilities by leaving its mark in Spain. Five prototype Ju 87Cs were built, four of which had folding wings and an arrester hook, for testing and extensive service trials, including catapult launches and simulated deck landings. Unlike other carrier designs, all the aircraft would be launched by catapult, rather than making a conventional take-off using the length of the flight deck. To this end, two 23.5cm-wide, 23.5m-long compressed-air fast-start catapult tracks were installed near the bow, from which it was theoretically possible to launch eight aircraft within three-and-a-half minutes.

Of the 170 Ju 87C-1s that were finally ordered, only a small number were completed before work on *Graf Zeppelin* was suspended in May 1940, and the order was cancelled in its entirety. Existing airframes were completed as conventional Ju 87B-2s.

However, the stop-start events surrounding *Graf Zeppelin* and its aircraft were still some time in the future when Göring issued Organisation Order No. 6072./37 on 29 July 1937, for the formation of the first *Trägerfliegerverband* (aircraft carrier unit). *Geschwader* 186 was to be established in Bremerhaven, comprising *Geschwader* staff, three Fi 167 multipurpose *Staffeln*, one Ju 87 *Staffel* and a single Bf 109 fighter *Staffel*. Each *Staffel* was to comprise eight operational aircraft and four reserve, the carrier to control a total of five *Staffeln*; four on board and one ashore for training and replacement purposes.

Trägergruppe I./186 was activated at Bug on the island of Rügen, but was disbanded on 22 October after delays in construction of the carriers became evident, the unit being considered too costly to maintain without a specific purpose. Instead, on 1 November, a single fighter squadron (*Trägerjagdstaffel*) of Bf 109s was created, designated 6./186, and placed under the command of *Hptm.* Heinrich Seeliger. A Stuka *Staffel*, 4./186, was soon added, equipped with Ju 87Bs under the command of *Hptm.* Erich Blattner, and six months later, in July 1939, a second Bf 109 *Staffel*, 5./186, was formed under *Oblt.* Gerhard Kadow. Only weeks before the outbreak of hostilities the three *Staffeln* were organised into *Trägergruppe* II./186 under the command of *Major* Walter Hagen, and *Graf Zeppelin* was expected to be ready for trials by the summer of 1940. Their first employment on an operational level was in conjunction with the existing *Küstenfliegergruppen*, when they were ordered to prepare for the German annexation of Memel in 'Operation Order 1./38', grouped under the command of *Führer der Marineluftstreitkräfte Generalmajor* Geisler on 14 December 1938 and standing in readiness in an operation codenamed 'Transport Exercise Stettin'. In the event they were unnecessary, Memel being relinquished without conflict by Lithuania under pressure from the Western powers as they continued their policy of appeasement to Hitler's territorial ambitions.

In the meantime, during early 1938, the Luftwaffe General Staff announced a structural reorganisation in which the Naval Air Command would be abolished, necessitating the relinquishing of independent control of the Naval Air Arm by the Kriegsmarine. Predictably, this resulted in fierce naval opposition to the planned reshuffle, and a

A second victory parade of the Condor Legion, including the men of AS/88, took place in Berlin in June 1939.

compromise was reached during February when the Luftwaffe was reorganised into three main *Luftwaffengruppenkommandos* (*Lw.Gr.Kdo.s*) and two smaller *Luftwaffenkommandos* (*Lw.Kdos.*), with the naval sector radically diminished in size and priority:

Luftwaffengruppenkommando 1 (*Ost*) in Berlin (formed from the amalgamation of *Luftkreiskommandos* II and III), under the command of *General* Kesselring;

Luftwaffengruppenkommando 2 (*West*) in Braunschweig (formed from the amalgamation of *Luftkreiskommandos* IV and VII), under the command of *General* Felmy;

Luftwaffengruppenkommando 3 (*Süd*) in Munich (ex-*Luftkreiskommando* V), under the command of *General* Sperrle;

Luftwaffenkommando Ostpreussen in Königsberg formed from *Luftkreiskommando* I), under the command of *Generalleutnant* Keller;

Luftwaffenkommando See in Kiel (formed from *Luftkreiskommando* VI), under the command of *General* Zander.

Testing the catapult-launching gear on a Bf 109T planned to equip the *Graf Zeppelin* aircraft carrier.

One year further on, the rapidly expanding Luftwaffe was again reorganised, the three *Luftwaffengruppenkommandos* renamed *Luftflotten* (Air Fleets) and comprising balanced components incorporating bomber, fighter, ground-attack and reconnaissance units, as well as ground-based signals, logistics and anti-aircraft components that enabled each to be self-contained and capable of completely independent operation.
Luftflotte 1: (Berlin) under the command of *General* Kesselring
Luftflotte 2: (Braunschweig) under the command of *General* Felmy
Luftflotte 3: (Munich) under the command of *General* Sperrle.[16]
Luftwaffenkommando Ostpruessen remained initially independent, until transferred to *Luftflotte* 1 in March 1939, its regional headquarters remaining in Königsberg. However, as part of the restructuring, the post of *Luftwaffenkommando See* was abolished on 1 February 1939, after the simmering tensions between the Luftwaffe and Kriegsmarine finally came to a head early in 1939, when yet another Kriegsmarine-Luftwaffe conference took place to decide finally the delineation of responsibility and control. On 27 January Raeder and Göring met, the results formalised in a joint statement issued on 3 February.

The major points promised close co-ordination between the two services, with information exchanged and frequent consultation on operational matters where interests overlapped. However, operations against the entire British Isles and 'sea areas not open to naval operations' were to remain in Luftwaffe hands, and though aircraft could be placed at the disposal of the Kriegsmarine, they remained under Luftwaffe command. Tactical participation of naval air units in naval engagements would only take place when specifically requested by the Kriegsmarine, or when 'generally agreed upon', and for planned participation in future engagements only those units trained by the Kriegsmarine could be considered for use. Minelaying theoretically required naval agreement but would be exclusively handled by the Luftwaffe, while the co-ordination of German coastal reconnaissance would remain the domain of the Kriegsmarine, echoing Blomberg's previous decree. Perhaps most importantly, control of all naval air logistics and training establishments would pass to the Luftwaffe from 1 April 1939, under the command of Luftwaffe Administrative Commands (*Luftgaus*) I (Königsberg), III (Berlin) and XI (Hannover), while the Naval Air Equipment branch (*Luftzeug*) would be retained but subsumed by *Luftgau* XI. Göring was determined that all flying units concerned with naval warfare remain under Luftwaffe control, as did all boats and ships that had served in connection with naval aviation. To this end, *Luftzeuggruppe See* was created under the command of *Oberst*. Hermann Moll, responsible for all aspects of operating 590 vessels spread between seven regional groups at the beginning of 1939. Zander's *Luftwaffenkommando See* had also been abolished also by 1 April, and its duties thereafter were exercised by a new Luftwaffe representative assigned to the Naval Staff, 'Luftwaffe General attached to Naval Command' (*General der Luftwaffe beim Oberbefehlshaber der Marine*, or *Gen.d.Lw.b.Ob.d.M.*). This new office would be under *RLM* command during peacetime, but placed under the tactical command of *OKM* in time of war.

> During peacetime he is in administrative command of all Naval Air forces. At the same time he is Inspector General of all Naval Air units [now limited to *Küstenfliegerstaffeln, Bordfliegergruppe*, and *Trägerverbände*, the official post designated '*Inspekteur der Luftwaffeninspektion der Seeflieger*']. In this capacity he acts under the Chief, Training, Reich Air Ministry. To give a maximum of consideration to the training requirements requested by the Commander-in-Chief, Navy, the General of the Air Force will be directed to work in close co-operation with the Commander-in-Chief, Navy, and to give due heed to the requests by the Commander-in-Chief, Navy. Directives concerning the training of Naval Air Forces issued by the Chief, Training Air Force, will be submitted to the Commander-in-Chief, Navy, for agreement before submittal to Commander-in-Chief, Air Force, for signature.[17]

Furthermore, details regarding naval air units were finally decided. The Naval Staff had required the fulfilment of three primary roles: long-range reconnaissance in distant maritime environments by high-endurance flying boats; the operation of specialised naval weaponry such as mines and torpedoes both on the enemy coast and the open sea by aircraft of high load-carrying capacity and having heavy defensive weaponry and high speed and endurance; and armed reconnaissance by fast and well-armed fighter aircraft. In response, by the autumn of 1941 Göring pledged to provide nine long-distance reconnaissance squadrons (F-*Staffeln* – 108 aircraft), eighteen multipurpose squadrons (M-*Staffeln* – 216 aircraft), twelve carrier squadrons (T-*Staffeln* – 152 aircraft for both *Graf Zeppelin* and the second carrier, due to be commissioned in spring 1942), and two shipboard squadrons (*Bord-Staffeln* – 42 aircraft) for Kriegsmarine use. Göring promised to begin renegotiating aircraft types to be made available 'upon the return of *General* Udet from his holidays'.[18]

The types of aircraft to fulfil each role between the years 1938 and 1941 were already mapped out in a communication despatched by *Generalstab* 1. *Abteilung* in Berlin on 31 January 1939, combining seaplanes and land-based wheeled aircraft:

	1938	1939	1940	1941
F-*Staffeln*	4 x Do 18	6 x Do 18	3 x Do 18	3 x Do 18
	2 x He 59		3 x Ha 138	3 x Ha 138
			1 x Ju 88	3 x Ju 88
Mz-*Staffeln*	5 x He 60	6 x He 115	9 x He 115	9 x He 115
	4 x He 59	3 x He 59	6 x Bf 110	9 x Bf 110
		3 x Do 17		
Träger-*Staffeln*	1 x Ju 87	4 x Ju 87	2 x Fi 167	6 x Fi 167
	1 x Bf 109	2 x Bf 109	2 x Ju 87	4 x Ju 87
			2 x Bf 109	2 x Bf 109
Bord-*Staffeln*	2 x He 60	2 x Ar 196	2 x Ar 196	2 x Ar 196

Almost immediately, the Luftwaffe began forming a wheeled aircraft group of Dornier Do 17Ms and refitting an 'Mz' group with Heinkel He IIIJ bombers; the latter scheduled to re-equip with Bf 110 twin-engine fighters and the former with Junkers Ju 88s during the autumn of 1940, both types not yet being in abundance.

The previously agreed thirteen bomber *Geschwader* of the operational Luftwaffe (the term used by the Kriegsmarine to denote standard Luftwaffe units) allocated for naval warfare remained in place, though they were not specifically referred to within the signed protocol. Raeder asked that from 1942 the assigned Ju 88s be upgraded to Heinkel He 177s, and that the twin-engine Bf 110 'Destroyers' be replaced by Me 210s then in development and showing great promise. Göring gave his personal assurance that a further increase in naval aircraft strength could be negotiated with the Kriegsmarine after 1941, though this vague assurance is unlikely to have carried much weight with Raeder and his officers.[19]

Under the terms of this agreement the Luftwaffe had successfully appropriated responsibility for aerial reconnaissance of British naval bases and coastal areas. They also assumed control of air warfare against enemy naval forces which were considered beyond the range of the Kriegsmarine surface fleet, leaving only the interdiction of vessels outside British coastal areas to the Kriegsmarine. Although this was undoubtedly a major compromise on Raeder's part, and deeply unsatisfactory from the naval standpoint, the Kriegsmarine commander's position had weakened to such a degree against Göring's that he was left with little choice than to agree, in the hope of influencing the development of greater naval aviation units in the future. In this matter, however, he was mistaken, as Göring had effectively taken his first steps in dismantling the naval air arm and subsuming all aerial forces to his control. Even if it was engaging the enemy, the Kriegsmarine would be required to juggle dual command of any Luftwaffe aerial forces involved, a difficult and protracted method of directing any potential combat. The agreement also had a negative impact upon planned U-boat operations, as Karl Dönitz related years later in his autobiography:

> Aircraft would be detailed for duty with the navy only when required for reconnaissance purposes or to take part in a tactical air battle in the event of a fleet engagement . . . It meant that continuous joint training in combined operations between U-boats and aircraft would not be possible . . . These combined exercises were of the greatest possible value to the pilots taking part. The aircrews always displayed a high degree of devotion to duty; time and again, when the state of the exercise demanded it, they flew over the open sea until their fuel was down almost to the last drop.[20]

The multipurpose Fieseler Fi 167 designed to be used aboard the *Graf Zeppelin* for carrying bombs or a torpedo. A promising aircraft, it was soon seen to be surplus to requirements and production was discontinued.

The result of this curtailment of such continuous training, as opposed to sporadic exercises, and the subsequent flawed navigational abilities of maritime aircrew, would only become truly apparent once war had been declared.

At the very least, Raeder was fortunate in the man allocated by Göring to the Kriegsmarine as 'Luftwaffe General attached to Naval Command'. *Generalmajor* Hans Ritter was an experienced former First World War naval fighter pilot who had transferred to the Luftwaffe in 1935 with the rank of *Fregattenkapitän*. He had already served in the *Reichsmarine*'s developing air arm and commanded Luftwaffe flying schools and personnel replacement battalions before he was appointed to the post of *Gen.d.Lw.b.Ob.d.M*. His fundamental duties were to prepare the Maritime Air Forces for operational use and to supervise their serviceability, supply and training in co-operation with the Luftwaffe Quartermaster General. However, despite his obvious affinity for the Kriegsmarine, Ritter was neither particularly required by the Naval Staff, nor included in their tactical planning. Most operational matters were dealt with directly between the respective staffs, rarely including Ritter within the chain of command. The existence of the *Gen.d.Lw.b.Ob.d.M* position was intended more to placate

Kriegsmarine concerns with the removal of Zander's more effective *Luftwaffenkommando See*. Luftwaffe records stipulated the exact size of Ritter's small office. He was to have a Chief of Staff, two typists, three *Uffz.* drivers, a single heavy staff car and two light staff cars. The Chief of Staff position was filled by *Oberst i.G.* Ernst-August Roth, another former First World War naval pilot. Between 1924 and 1935 he had held a series of positions within the developing naval air arm, including chief pilot and acting head of *Erprobungsstelle Travemünde* during 1928, before promotion to *Kapitänleutnant* and subsequent transfer to the Luftwaffe during 1934. He had commanded *Küstenfliegergruppe* 106 with the rank of *Oberstleutnant* from October 1937 before reaching the rank of *Oberst* and transferring to Ritter's staff.

The post of *Führer der Marineluftstreitkräfte* remained in existence below Ritter in the chain of command, though more often than not liaising directly with Kriegsmarine staff and bypassing the newly created higher office. On 1 April *Generalmajor* Joachim Coeler was appointed *F.d.Luft*, replacing Geisler, who was promoted to *Generalleutnant* and placed briefly into the Luftwaffe manpower pool pending reassignment. Coeler had risen to the rank of *Oblt.z.S.* as a naval pilot during the First World War. He was an enthusiastic proponent of the maritime air force, and a former Technical Officer within *Gruppe* BsX. During the 1920s he had served as a naval flying instructor, followed by various *Reichsmarine* staff positions before transfer to the fledgling Luftwaffe in October 1933.

Within the Luftwaffe Staff, the position of Naval Liaison Officer to the Commander-in-Chief Luftwaffe (*Marine-Verbindungsoffizier beim RLM/Oberbefehlshaber der Luftwaffe*) had been held by *Kapitän zur See* Hellmuth Heye until April 1939, and from August *Fregattenkapitän* Wilhelm Mössel was appointed to the position to oversee Kriegsmarine interests within Luftwaffe High Command, a post he held until the war's end.

Generalleutnant Geisler was only briefly without an official position, soon being placed at the disposal of *Luftlotte* 2 for 'special duties'. He was tasked with examining the conduct of potential naval air warfare against Belgium and Great Britain. Specifically, his small staff were to investigate the organisation of *Luftflotte* 2 reconnaissance of sea areas in conjunction with naval air units, co-ordination between tactical reconnaissance and combat units, and co-operation between Kriegsmarine surface units and bomber formations. He was furthermore asked to theorise the likely direction of such operations should hostilities begin. His findings were less than inspiring, as he reasoned that the primary task of *Luftflotte* 2 would be the destruction of the British fleet, and neither the capabilities of the available aircraft (Heinkel He 111s) nor the training of their crews were adequate to undertake this objective. Instead, the greatest hope lay in bombing British aircraft factories with small bomber formations while attempting to establish a blockade of the British Isles.

Among those flying units directly subordinate to *Generalmajor* Ritter was the *Seenotdienst*; the air-sea rescue service formed by ex-First World War naval pilot *Obstlt.* Konrad Goltz. The first dedicated air-sea rescue ship had been launched on 11 March 1934, and entered service with the *DVS* as it acted as camouflage for the developing Luftwaffe. This small 196-ton vessel, the *Kirschan* (*Flugsicherungsschiff* A), was soon followed by two larger ships; the 375-ton *Günther Plüschow* (*Flugsicherungsschiff* B) and the 880-ton *Bernhard von Tschirschky* (*Flugsicherungsschiff* C) in 1935, and then the 985-ton *Hans Rolshoven* (*Flugsicherungsschiff* D) during 1937. The Luftwaffe also took control of the 350-ton naval salvage ship *Phoenix* and the 890-ton Luftwaffe salvage vessel *Greif*. All vessels had a similar configuration, with a flat working deck aft capable of accommodating a seaplane or, aboard the larger ships, a flying boat, which could be taken aboard by means of the aircraft crane. The small *Kirschan* had two loading trees, only capable of handling smaller floatplanes, towards the ship's bow. By the outbreak of war the *Seenotsdienst* mustered a dedicated force of six larger ships, with supporting smaller vessels, and twelve He 59s. A total of ten *Seenotstaffeln*, comprising the aircraft contingent of the *Seenotdienst*, would be established during the Second World War, the first during April 1939, based between Norderney and List and, by the outbreak of war, a second *Seenotstaffel* in the east at Pillau-Neutief. Their aircraft were painted white with Red Cross insignia and civilian markings, though they retained the national Swastika on the tail. By German reckoning they were protected by Article 18 of the 1929 Geneva Convention, entitled *Convention for the Amelioration of the Condition of the Wounded and Sick in Armies in the Field*:

> Article 18. Aircraft used as means of medical transport shall enjoy the protection of the Convention during the period in which they are reserved exclusively for the evacuation of wounded and sick and the transport of medical personnel and material.
>
> They shall be painted white and shall bear, clearly marked, the distinctive emblem prescribed in Article 19 [as a compliment to Switzerland, the

heraldic emblem of the red cross on a white ground, formed by reversing the Federal colours] side by side with their national colours, on their lower and upper surfaces.

In the absence of special and express permission, flying over the firing line, and over the zone situated in front of clearing or dressing stations, and generally over all enemy territory or territory occupied by the enemy, is prohibited.

Medical aircraft shall obey every summons to land.

In the event of a landing thus imposed, or of an involuntary landing in enemy territory and territory occupied by the enemy, the wounded and sick, as well as the medical personnel and material, including the aircraft, shall enjoy the privileges of the present Convention.

The pilot, mechanics and wireless telegraph operators captured shall be sent back, on condition that they shall be employed until the close of hostilities in the medical service only.

However, events in 1940 would later serve to nullify this claimed protection, as the aircraft were viewed as belligerent due to their activities in connection with Allied coastal convoys.

The *Seenotsdienst* was initially divided into two theatres of operation:
Seenotzentrale (Sea Rescue Command) *Nord*
(Wilhelmshaven – subordinate to *Marinegruppenbefehlshaber West* and *F.d.Luft* West)
    Seenotbezirk (Rescue District) Nordeney.
       1 *Kette* (three aircraft) 1.*Seenotstaffel* (He 59)
       Hans Rolshoven
    Seenotbezirk List.
       2 *Kette*, 1.*Seenotstaffel* (He 59)
       Bernhard von Tschirschky
Seenotzentrale Ost
(Wilhelmshaven – subordinate to *Marinegruppenbefehlshaber Ost* and *F.d.Luft* Ost)
    Seenotbezirk Holtenau
       Phonix
       Greif

Seenotbezirk Bug
  Günther Plüschow
Seenotbezirk Nest
  Krischan
Seenotbezirk Pillau
  2.*Seenotsstaffel* (He 59)

While the He 59 served with distinction as a rescue aircraft, being roomy and stable on reasonably rough seas, during the autumn of 1939 proposals to substitute a wheeled aircraft, probably a Bf 110 or Junkers Ju 88, for the He 115B and C were already being placed before the Naval Staff, as the Heinkel floatplane was deemed unlikely to stand up to the demands of modern warfare in terms of durability and manoeuvrability in combat. However, although initial approval was tentatively granted following trials of conventional wheeled aircraft in *Küstenflieger* units, Kriegsmarine command harboured reservations about the idea of removing a tried and tested floatplane from service. Indeed, trials of the aircraft indicated that changing to the use of land aircraft over the sea was largely unadvisable on account of the psychological strain on the crews.

> The high speed to be expected of wheeled aircraft must not be rated as an exclusive gain. Since such tasks as shadowing, bad weather flying, smoke laying and escort duties were more easily carried out at medium speed.[21]

Indeed, before the outbreak of hostilities in 1939, young Stuka pilot Helmut Mahlke, then of Wilhelmshaven's shipboard *Staffel* 1./B.Fl.Gr.196 and later a Stuka pilot of 4./186, remembered discussing the rationale behind naval forces not using wheeled aircraft.

> As naval flyers, and shipboard ones at that, we were already familiar with the dangers of low-level flying, even in peacetime. And if hostilities did break out, we were only too well aware that every type of seaplane currently in service would be just as vulnerable to enemy fire – if not more so – than any dive-bomber. Although this was a situation beyond our control, my views on the subject had almost got me into hot water when *General* Geisler, the *Führer der Marineluftstreitkräfte*, paid an official visit to our *Staffel*. Seated next to him at lunch, I rather foolishly asked the general why our maritime units couldn't be equipped with land-based aircraft, which were altogether faster, more manoeuvrable, more powerful and more heavily armed – and thus stood a far better chance of surviving in combat

EARLY LESSONS

Heinkel He 115V-3, *Werknummer* 1555, civilian number D-ABZV. This was the first He 115 to sport the fully glazed nose that remained unchanged in later design models. (James Payne)

The same Heinkel as in the previous image, only this time in military colours. The *Balkenkreuz* outboard of the large painted numbers indicates a factory-operated aircraft. This particular aircraft first flew March 1938 and was involved in weapons testing at Travemünde from 14 August 1939, and was later used as a test bed for prototype A-series BMW 132 engines, under new serial number TI+HB. (James Payne)

– than our present lame-duck seaplanes. But the general was having none of it. He flatly rejected any such idea, giving as his reason the seaplane's ability to put down on water in the event of an emergency, something he regarded as an indispensable safety measure in maritime operations. I expressed my doubts about this, saying that if they came down in the water a crew usually ended up in a dinghy anyway, irrespective of whether they had been flying a seaplane or a landplane. I explained that only shipboard *Staffeln* such as ourselves were wholly dependent on seaplanes. And I was certain in my own mind that if we were to become involved in a naval engagement on the high seas our chances of getting back on board our ship would be slim. It was far more likely that we would have to attempt an emergency landing on open water, and even for us the floats would then be of questionable value as they were unable to stand up to anything rougher than sea strength three. My poor opinion of the safety value of floats on an aircraft clearly did not go down at all well. That very same evening every naval air unit was in receipt of a teleprint from the *F.d.Luft*, which, if I remember rightly, read something along the lines of: 'With immediate effect, I forbid any discussion whatsoever among the commissioned ranks regarding the deployment of land aircraft over the sea. Geisler.'[22]

Demands were therefore made to the Luftwaffe to replace the He 115 with another floatplane, but the already strained armaments industry was unequal to the task. During August 1939 the Luftwaffe requested that Raeder relinquish any Bf 110 and Ju 88 aircraft thus far accumulated during trials and instead accept the continued use of the He 115, future deployment of BV 138 seaplanes and the introduction of the newly developed Dornier Do 217, which adequately fulfilled requirements for a multi-role, long-range, twin-engine, all-metal aircraft capable of maritime operations as a secondary consideration. Dornier had begun development of the Do 217 as an improved version of the Do 17 (the famous 'flying pencil', so named because of its narrow fuselage), with greater structural integrity allowing heavier armament and a larger bomb load. Initially, the Luftwaffe had pressed for Dornier to produce a floatplane version, the Do 217G, known colloquially as a 'sea Stuka' in the misguided belief that the effectiveness of the Ju 87 could be replicated in a larger aircraft. Although the idea received support from both the Luftwaffe and Kriegsmarine, the high alighting speed that would be required was enough to shelve the project. Furthermore, the ineffectiveness of horizontal bombing of ship targets had already

A Kriegsmarine *Leutnant* aircraft observer, indicated by his Luftwaffe observer's badge, seconded to the Luftwaffe for a four-year term.

been noted during the aircraft's development. At the *Erprobungsstelle Travemünde* military aviation test centre at Greifswald, training and operational naval air units practised level-bombing the ship *Zähringen* with concrete bombs. The results were a 2 per cent hit rate, whereas Ju 87 dive-bombers repeated the assault with a 40 per cent hit rate. The superior accuracy of dive-bombing was clearly demonstrated, and the Do 217 was subsequently delayed by insistence on an ability to dive-bomb, something of an obsession with Luftwaffe designers at the behest of Ernst Udet, a devout disciple of the art. Eventually, the maritime Do 217 version was shelved in favour of the He 115 and Ju 88 during 1938, as its specifications failed to match the requested criteria. However, despite the project's cancellation, Dornier continued development unofficially and at the end of August 1938 after the floatplane variant and dive-bombing capability were both dropped. A land-based bomber with torpedo capability was developed instead, which would later see action with the operational Luftwaffe.

Meanwhile, as the expected *Graf Zeppelin* completion date was rapidly approaching, on 6 February 1939 the Reich Air Ministry ordered the complete unit structure for use aboard the carrier to be assembled by November, the two existing *Staffeln* to provide seed components to assist in the creation of the new *Staffeln*. The final planned organisation comprised:

Stab *Trägergeschwader* 186
Trägerstukastaffel 1./186
Trägerstukastaffel 2./186
Trägerstukastaffel 3./186
Trägerstukastaffel 4./186 (already formed)
Trägerjagdstaffel 5./186
Trägerjagdstaffel 6./186 (already formed)

Support units for all carrier *Staffeln* were quickly formed, garrisoned in Bremerhaven while awaiting posting to *Graf Zeppelin*. Owing to a lack of available torpedoes, the Fi 167 *Staffeln* were originally omitted, a situation planned to be rectified by November 1940 with a reduction in both Stuka and fighter units, but ultimately never to be.

Work on completing *Graf Zeppelin* continued at its planned pace until the end of 1939, with completion expected for the end of the following year. By September 1939 the ship was 85 per cent complete, with machinery installed, boilers prepared and 150mm guns already fitted (though their control system was still lacking). However, fresh demands placed on German shipyards for increased U-boat construction forced further severe delays, the aircraft carrier always considered the least important construction priority, behind major surface units and U-boats.

Europe was sliding inexorably towards war, despite the Führer's promises to his service heads that such a conflict would be years in the future. The overburdened German armaments industry struggled to keep pace with the varying demands of all three services as the storm finally broke over Poland on 1 September 1939 and the Wehrmacht began their invasion, codenamed '*Fall Weiss*'. Within two days Germany found itself at war with both Great Britain and France; a conflict that neither the Kriegsmarine nor the Luftwaffe were adequately prepared for.

4
War

WHEN WAR WAS DECLARED with Great Britain and France on 3 September 1939, the Heinkel He 115 was beginning to enter service. However, owing to the imperfections of the LT F5 torpedo, the new floatplane was unable to carry the weapon as it was incapable of flying slowly enough to launch it successfully without stalling. During October 1939, trials conducted by the TVA in altering the torpedo's aerial rudder to allow use by the He 115 resulted in an unacceptable 50 per cent failure rate. Nevertheless, the He 115 began operational missions, relegated to reconnaissance and bombing roles. By 2 September the *Kriegsgliederung der Luftwaffe* reported the *See-Luftstreitkräfte* standing at a strength of thirty-one He 59s (thirty of them operationally ready), eighty-one He 60s (sixty-six operationally ready), sixty-three Do 18s (fifty-four operationally ready) and eight He 115s spread among its squadrons; the carrier group 4./Tr.Gr. 186 numbering twelve Ju 87s, and 5. and 6./Tr.Gr. 186 twenty-four Bf 109s between the two *Staffeln*.

Two distinct operational commands were established to allow smoother control over operations in the North Sea or the Baltic Sea. These were *Führer der See-Luftstreitkräfte West* and *Führer der See-Luftstreitkräfte Ost* respectively; each tactically subordinate to the relevant *Marinegruppenkommando* (*MGK*) that had been established to co-ordinate surface forces within the same regions. At the formation of the two posts *Generalmajor* Hermann Bruch, former Chief of Staff to Zander at *Luftwaffenkommando See*, commanded the western branch, while *Generalmajor* Joachim Coeler headed that in the east, both men having been former naval officers before transfer to the Luftwaffe. However, their positions changed almost immediately war was declared, when the two officers swapped posts. The allocation of available *Staffeln* to each regional command was made by the Kriegsmarine; Ritter was responsible for all related administration and logistical support pertaining to the deployment in his role as *Gen.d.Lw.b.Ob.d.M.*

F.d.Luft West
Küstenfliegergruppe 106, *Obstlt.* Hermann Jorden, Norderney
- Stab/Kü.Fl.Gr. 106: no aircraft
- 1./Kü.Fl.Gr. 106: He 60, He 115 (*Hptm.* von Schrötter)
- 2./Kü.Fl.Gr. 106: Do 18 (*Oblt.* Bischoff)
- 3./Kü.Fl.Gr. 106: He 59 (*Hptm.* Stein) (based at Rantum)

Küstenfliegergruppe 406 *Maj.* Heinrich Minner, List
- Stab/Kü.Fl.Gr. 406: no aircraft
- 1./Kü.Fl.Gr. 406: He 115 (*Hptm.* Lienhart Wiesand)
- 2./Kü.Fl.Gr. 406: Do 18 (*Maj.* Bartels)
- 3./Kü.Fl.Gr. 406: He 59 (*Hptm.* Bergemann)

Bordfliegergruppe 196, Wilhelmshaven
- 1./B.Fl.Gr. 196: He 60/Ar 196 (*Maj.* Lessing)

F.d.Luft Ost
Küstenfliegergruppe 306, *Obstlt.* Heinz von Holleben, Dievenow
- Stab/Kü.Fl.Gr. 306: 1 x He 60, 1 x He 59 (moved to *F.d.Luft West* command on 4 September, based at Hörnum)
- 1./Kü.Fl.Gr. 306: He 60 (*Hptm.* Heyn) (moved to *F.d.Luft West* command on 4 September, based at Hörnum)
- 2./Kü.Fl.Gr. 306: Do 18 (*Hptm.* Hartwig)

Küstenfliegergruppe 506, *Obstlt.* Wolfgang von Wild, Pillau
- Stab/Kü.Fl.Gr. 506: 1 x Ju 52, 3 x He 59
- 1./Kü.Fl.Gr. 506: He 60 and He 114 (*Hptm.* Hermann Busch)
- 2./Kü.Fl.Gr. 506: Do 18 (*Hptm.* Herbert Hartwig) (moved to *F.d.Luft West* command on 4 September and placed under staff of Kü.Fl.Gr. 306)
- 3./Kü.Fl.Gr. 506: He 59 (*Hptm.* Ludwig Fehling) (moved to *F.d.Luft West* command on 12 September)

Küstenfliegergruppe 606, Kamp (Formerly 2./Kü.Fl.Gr. 706)[1]
- 2./Kü.Fl.Gr. 606: Do 18 (Hptm. Hans Bruno von Laue – temporarily replacing Hptm. Rudolf Wodarg on attachment to Staff/Luftwaffenkommando East Prussia) (moved to *F.d.Luft West* and placed under the staff of Kü.Fl.Gr. 306)

Küstenfliegergruppe 706, *Obstlt.* Hermann Edert, Kamp
- Stab/Kü.Fl.Gr. 706: 1 x Ju 52
- 1./Kü.Fl.Gr. 706: He 60 and He 114 (*Maj.* Kaiser) (based at Nest)[2]
- 3./Kü.Fl.Gr. 706: He 59 (*Hptm.* Gerd Stein) (moved to *F.d.Luft West* and placed under the staff of Kü.Fl.Gr. 106)

Bordfliegergruppe 196, Holtenau
  5/B.Fl.Gr. 196: He 60 (*Hptm.* Wibel)
II./*Trägergeschwader* 186 (established in Kiel-Holtenau), *Maj.* Walter Hagen
  Stab II/Tr.Gr. 186:
  4./Tr.Gr. 186: Ju 87B (based at Stolp)
  5/Tr.Gr. 186: Bf 109B (based at Brüsterort)
  6/Tr.Gr. 186: Bf 109B (based at Brüsterort)

Outside of direct Kriegsmarine tactical control, *Luftflotte* 2 had been allocated the task of investigating aerial naval operations, and Felmy ordered the creation of a specific command for maritime operations using high-performance land-based aircraft, the 10.*Fliegerdivision*, established in Hamburg on 5 September 1939, commanded by *Generalleutnant* Hans Ferdinand Geisler and based initially at Blankenese. Geisler took aboard as his Chief of Staff the gifted and experienced *Maj.* Martin Harlinghausen of AS/88 fame. Within less than a month Geisler's command was renamed X.*Fliegerkorps*. Stationed in North Germany, the main force incorporated Heinkel He 111H bombers of *Generalmajor* Robert Fuchs' KG 26 and, from November, the new Junkers Ju 88 bombers of KG 30 under the command of *Geschwader Kommodore*

The size of the He 115 can be fully appreciated in this overhead shot of a crew preparing for take-off.

Generalmajor Hans Siburg (replaced by *Obstlt.* Walter Loebel in January 1940). Until 1941, most of KG 26's observers were either members of the Kriegsmarine or *Seeluftstreitkräften*, and the crews as a whole had already been introduced to a new training regime incorporating the techniques required for nautical warfare; ship identification and marine navigation, as well as weather patterns and their relative sea state. They began their first small-scale joint manoeuvres with Kriegsmarine units in waters south of Norway.

During September, *Hptm.* Edgar Petersen began to lobby for the adoption of a relatively new aircraft to enable long-distance maritime reconnaissance. The former Army flight instructor and *Staffelkapitän* of 1./KG 51 had been moved to the staff of Geisler's fledgling 10. *Fliegerdivision* as a navigation specialist, and began pushing for the use of the Focke-Wulf Fw 200. He had initially favoured the Junkers Ju 90, but was swayed by the fact that only two prototype aircraft existed and there was, as yet, no established production line for more. The Fw 200, on the other hand, had already proved its endurance during peacetime.

The prototype Fw 200 V1 (initially civil registered as D-AERE and named *Saarland*, then re-registered D-ACON and named *Brandenburg* in the summer of 1938 in preparation for its record flight to New York that August) had first flown at Neulander Field in Bremen, the Focke-Wulf factory airfield, on 27 July 1937. At the controls was Kurt Waldemar Tank, a former First World War cavalry officer who had become a leading aeronautical engineer and test pilot. Tank was working for the prestigious Albatros Flugzeugwerke when the company was merged with Focke-Wulf in 1931, and during 1936 began design work on the Fw 200 Condor long-range commercial transport to specifications agreed with Lufthansa. British and American airlines were developing and using large four-engine flying boats for transatlantic journeys from Europe to South America, though their weight and bulk prevented them from carrying large payloads. Instead, Tank developed a sleek, lighter landplane; an all-metal, low-wing monoplane crewed by four and capable of carrying twenty-six passengers. The aircraft was designed to operate at a maximum ceiling of 3,000m, allowable without the use of oxygen and a pressurised cabin.

To prove the aircraft's potential, at 7.30am on 10 August 1938 D-ACON lifted off from Flugplatz Berlin-Staaken to begin a Great Circle course across the North Atlantic, and landed at Floyd Bennett Field, Brooklyn, New York, at 1.50pm local time the following day. The

Heinkel He 115 weapons test flight over Travemünde. (James Payne)

flight, which had carried no passengers, had covered 6,371.3 kilometres in just a fraction under twenty-five hours, and marked the first non-stop flight between the two points by a heavier-than-air aircraft. The crew comprised Lufthansa pilot *Kapitän* Alfred Henke, Luftwaffe *Hptm.* Rudolf Freiherr von Moreau (co-pilot), Paul Dierberg (flight engineer) and Walter Kober (radio operator).[3] Two days later the aircraft made a return crossing, shaving five hours off owing to more favourable winds.

The Condor had proved itself as a long-distance aircraft, and made a series of demonstration flights, including Berlin to Hanoi, French Indo-China, during November, during which it set a new speed record, though the aircraft was eventually wrecked after ditching near Manila on 6 December 1938 due to fuel starvation, either through crew error or mechanical malfunction. There were no casualties, and though the Condor was recovered it was deemed beyond repair.

Nonetheless, a military variant of the Condor, the Fw 200 V10, had been requested by the Imperial Japanese Navy, and at the outbreak of war four such aircraft were near completion in Bremen. They were purloined by Petersen and combined with six existing civilian models for the formation of his new unit on 1 October 1939: the *Fernaufklärungsstaffel* (long-distance reconnaissance squadron), initially under the direct command of *Ob.d.L.*, though non-operational until 1940. During the pre-war development of the Luftwaffe the late Walther Wever had been a strong advocate of strategic bombing by long-range aircraft, leading to the Dornier Do 19 and Junkers Ju 89 prototypes. However, following his death the concept of strategic bombing had been abandoned by men who favoured tactical aircraft, particularly the dive-bomber. This frustrated German bomber design thereafter; even development of the heavy He 177 was delayed through an irrational desire to incorporate a dive-bombing capability. The Fw 200 was a compromise between the two camps, but although its later reputation among the Allies as the 'Wolf of the Atlantic' was born from some reality, the aircraft was never entirely suitable for its intended role, and one wonders what could have been achieved if Wever's original vision had been allowed to flourish. Among the deficiencies of the Fw 200 were lack of a proper bombsight and relatively poor forward vision, particularly compared with the Heinkel He 111H and its extensively glazed cockpit. This forced Condor crews to attack at low level, approaching targets at a height of around 50m before releasing bombs only 240m or so from the target. Crews came to know this manoeuvre as the 'Swedish turnip tactic', allowing the highest chance of a damaging hit or near miss, but also rendering the relatively fragile airframe vulnerable to small-calibre anti-aircraft weapons that were soon issued to merchant ships. Furthermore, the barometric altimeters in use at that time were notoriously unreliable at low altitude, requiring instead good spatial judgement and timing on behalf of both pilot and observer for a successful attack.

On the front line in the days leading up to war the *Seeluftstreitkräfte* was engaged in reconnaissance of the North and Baltic Seas. As the Wehrmacht began its invasion of Poland on the morning of 1 September the floatplanes were immediately in combat, its first casualties being suffered less than twenty-four hours after fighting began, in an accident when He 60 M7+NH of 1./Kü.Fl.Gr. 506 crashed while taking off for a reconnaissance of the Bay of Danzig. Pilot *Uffz*. Hans August Damrau misjudged his take-off run and the aircraft's floats struck the harbour mole in Pillau-Neutief. The Heinkel crashed into the sea and caught fire after impact, killing Damrau and observer *Lt.d.R*. Hoffmann. In the West, Do 18 M2+JK 'I' of 2./Kü.Fl.Gr. 106 crashed in darkness and bad weather on 3 September. The wreckage was later recovered by the *Seenotdienst* ship *Günther Plüschow*, which had been despatched to investigate a large oil patch believed to be from the missing aircraft, and the bodies of observer *Oblt.d.R.* Georg Müssig and pilot *Uffz.* Friedrich Römermann were found six days later.

Newly trained observer *Lt.z.S.* Paul Just later recalled the beginning of hostilities in his post-war autobiography:

> I am ordered from the school to the front: *Küstenaufklarüngsstaffel* 1./306 on the North Sea island Norderney. But the English remain inactive like the French. We landed our float biplane on a lake in Pomerania and prepared for combat missions. With the single-engine Heinkel He 60 we are to bombard the last Polish units in small bunker positions on the Hela peninsula . . . We wear leather aviator overalls, with hood and glasses. The observer has binoculars, and in the on-board compartment are the nautical chart, compass and navigation triangle, in front of his knees the radio. With Morse signals he can relay reconnaissance information to the command post.[4]

The initial tasks allocated to the naval fliers during the first days of war with Poland revolved around attacks on the Hela Peninsula and its heavy gun emplacements, and in bombing the garrison at Gydnia. Just and his He 60-equipped *Staffel* joined in the attack, a task for which the He 60 was not designed:

> But here we are supposed to be a bomber. The explosive bombs with detonators in place weigh five kilos each. To prime them, I have to remove a safety pin. Bomb mountings are not available in the He 60, so I put the bombs under the seat. If they roll around, I have to hold them with my feet.[5]

More appropriately, the dive-bombers and fighters of the *Graf Zeppelin*'s *Trägergeschwader* 186 had also been taken on to the strength of *F.d.Luft* Ost, and were in combat from the outbreak of hostilities. Indeed, the first Luftwaffe loss attributed to enemy action was a Junkers Ju 87B-1 of 4./Tr.Gr.186 that had been thrown into action against Polish targets. Equipped with heavy SC500 bombs, the Stukas were provided with air cover by Bf 109 fighters of *Trägergeschwader* 186, both squadrons operationally subordinated to *Jagdgeschwader* 1, commanded by *Obstlt.* Carl Schumacher.

During the last days of peace the carrier squadrons of *Trägergeschwader* 186 had moved from Kiel-Holtenau to the east: the fighter squadrons

5./186 and 6./186 on 22 August and 24 August respectively to Brüsterort, the Stuka *Staffel* 4./186 to Stolp-West in Pomerania. *Major* Walter Hagen, the commander of *Trägergeschwader* 186, was a highly experienced pilot, having served with the *Seeflieger* during the previous world war and spent years in the interim as a pilot and test pilot for the German airline industry. Joining the Luftwaffe in 1935, he had continued his role as test pilot before being appointed commander of the *Graf Zeppelin*'s aircraft group. Stuka pilot Helmit Mahlke later wrote of him:

> A modest individual, he was a superb pilot who had played a pivotal role in the earliest days of naval aviation. He was also an incomparable leader of men who treated those under his command with respect, consideration and absolute fairness. We could not have wished for a better commanding officer.[6]

A mixture of naval and Luftwaffe personnel had flowed into Hagen's command during the weeks leading to war. They were hurriedly formed into operational units at Kiel-Holtenau, with a few He 50s available for training alongside the newly available modified Stuka Ju 87Bs finishing production. The squadron was treated as an extension of the *Graf Zeppelin* complement, and by 1 September only one Stuka *Staffel* was fully equipped and operational, having been posted to Stolp for what the men believed were impending exercises.

Hauptmann Erich Blattner's 4./Tr.Gr. 186 was in fact the strongest single unit within *Generalmajor* Hermann Bruch's *F.d.Luft Ost* command, which had established its headquarters at the *Seefliegerhorst* Dievenow (Pomerania), on the north-east corner of the island of Wolin. Blattner, a former Lufthansa pilot, led his squadron into action, initially against Polish naval bases, beginning with a one-and-a-half-hour attack on Gdynia Harbour beginning at 0215hrs on 2 September. The next morning *Uffz.* Wilhelm Czuprina and his gunner/radio operator *Funkmaat* Erich Meinhardt were killed when their Stuka was hit and brought down by flak during an attack against the Hela Peninsula. During this bombing raid the Stukas severely damaged the 2,250-ton modern minelayer *Gryf*, hits on her bow setting her ablaze, as well as 1,540-ton destroyer *Wicher*, which was hit amidships, the tender *Smok*, and a patrol boat.

The Polish minelayer *Gryf* had already been attacked by Stukas of the Luftwaffe's *Lehrgeschwader* 1 (LG1, formerly *Lehrgeschwader Greifswald*) on the first day of hostilities, while travelling in company

The *Seenotdienst* vessel *Hans Rolshoven* (*Flugsicherungsschiff* D), used for the recovery of downed aircraft.

with six minesweepers from Gydnia to lay mines at the entrance of the Bay of Danzig. With the *Gryf* damaged by several near misses and with twenty-two men killed, including the commander, Captain Wiktor Kwiatkowski, the 290 mines were jettisoned, and the ship was taken to the Hela Peninsula to serve as a flak platform. There German destroyers briefly shelled them, *Gryf* being hit twice before a return hit on *Z1 Leberecht Maass* forced the Germans to retreat. Moved to the floating dock for repair, she was then hit repeatedly by the carrier squadron's Stukas, and left burning and partly submerged. The *coup de grâce* did not come until 4 September, when the *Staffelkapitän* of 3./Kü.Fl.Gr. 706, *Hptm.* Gerd Stein, led his He 59 aircraft in an attack that afternoon and finished the ship off with more hits, the hulk continuing to burn for two days. The He 59 seaplanes of both Kü.Fl.Gr. 506 and Kü.Fl.Gr. 706 were added to the offensive against the Hela Peninsula by this stage of the battle, though *Obstlt.* Wolfgang von Wild, commander of Kü.Fl.Gr. 506, harboured grave doubts about the aircraft's suitability for what would be a conventional night bombing role against artillery positions.[7] In his War Diary, the entry from 5 September clearly records his opinion:

> *Kdr.* Kü.Fl.Gr. 506 repeatedly informed *F.d.Luft* several times by telephone of his doubts concerning the military expediency of planned

attacks by bomber squadrons on 6 September 1939. A successful attack cannot be counted on as the small target can only be properly targeted from low level. The attacking crews will meet very heavy flak (ten heavy anti-aircraft batteries and between thirty and forty anti-aircraft machine guns). The battery has so far been bombarded with 50 tons of bombs, of which 20 tons were SC500s, without any success whatsoever. Considering the defence, the operation seems unwarranted and a waste of ammunition, especially since the *Gruppe*'s request to attack the Westerplatte was originally rejected in order to save ammunition.[8]

Nonetheless, the attacks went ahead between 0400hrs and 0420hrs on 6 September, and *Lt.z..S.* Claus Münscher's He 59 M7+XL of 3./ Kü.Fl.Gr. 506, was brought down by flak from a height of 500m, all four crewmen being killed. The aircraft hit the sea, and a Polish patrol boat despatched to the site collected a pilot's glove, collar, and pieces of the wing for identification.

> Attack carried out according to orders. Heavy defensive fire. Aircraft 'X' shot down. Success of attack equal to zero. Request *F.d.Luft*: Should the ordered additional attacks be carried out?
>
> Response from *F.d.Luft*: No further attacks.[9]

Too late for Münscher and his crew, on 6 September, *SKL* prepared the following order to Group Baltic, to be issued four days later:

> Multipurpose aeroplanes are no longer to operate against heavily protected objectives on land. The use of multipurpose aeroplanes for long-range reconnaissance operations in the North Sea is more urgent: thus, the aeroplanes are to be spared during operations in the Baltic Sea which are still necessary for the time being.

The Stukas of *Trägergeschwader* 186 had been despatched to sink Polish gunboats which fired on German positions around Rewa, before spending an extended period in support of ground operations, two aircraft making forced landings after being hit by ground fire, and another being shot down in flames during the battle for the marshlands at Oxhöfter-Kämpe on 14 September; *Oblt.* Hans Rummel and *Oberfunkmaat* Fritz Blunk were both killed. Stuka crewmen reported enemy machine-gun fire from

Recovering a damaged Heinkel He 60 crash-landed due to engine failure in September 1940.

the quarantine station east of Amalienfelde (marked by a large red cross on white ground), returning fire in what they considered a violation of international convention.

After the British declaration of war on 3 September, several units were removed from the Baltic battlefield and transferred west, creating a confused tangle of administrative hierarchy as individual *Staffeln* were placed under different *Gruppe* commands. On 12 September, 3./ Kü.Fl.Gr. 506 was the latest assigned to *F.d.Luft West* and ordered to transfer to the North Sea. Following the expected defeat of Gdynia Blattner's Stuka squadron, redesignated two days previously from 4./ Tr.Gr. 186 to 3.(St)/Tr.Gr. 186, was also to be placed at the disposal of *Marinegruppenkommando West* (*MGK West*), leading *SKL* to issue notice to Ritter that 'for reasons of tactical command Naval Staff no longer needs a Commander, Naval Air, Baltic, for the Baltic Sea due to the reduction of staff and senior personnel'.

Following the subjugation of all Polish naval bases and the clearing-up of defensive minefields that had clogged Danzig Bay, Commanding Admiral, Baltic, considered the minimum allocation of aerial forces suitable for his requirements to be one long-range reconnaissance squadron, one Stuka squadron and three multipurpose squadrons for the effective maintenance of reconnaissance and combat operations for control of the Baltic Sea. However, on 20 September the Luftwaffe's Chief of General Staff, *Generaloberst* Hans Jeschonnek, expressed 'the urgent desire' for Blattner's Stukas to be removed from naval control and transferred to *Luftflotte* 1. The Naval Liaison Officer attached to Luftwaffe General Staff, *Fregattenkapitän* Mössel, received the following reply to Jeschonnek from *SKL*:

a. Naval Staff considers that there is still a limited number of tasks for the Stuka squadron in the Baltic Sea area at present, not only as support for the fight on Hela, but also for possible employment in the fight against submarines etc.

b. Some time ago Naval Staff issued an order that this squadron is to be assigned to Group West for tasks in the North Sea as soon as there are no more tasks in the Baltic Sea.

c. The Naval Staff believes that if this squadron were assigned to *Luftflotte* 1 in the course of the general transfer of air forces from the east to the west, the Stukas would not immediately be able to operate against land targets there. On the other hand, the Naval Staff sees possibilities for using this squadron in the North Sea theatre against sea targets. As a matter of fact, possibilities for such operations have already presented themselves.

d. However, if it appears in the further progress of the war against Great Britain that, owing to limited range of the Stukas or to lack of opportunities for attack, the squadron is in the wrong place, Naval Staff will at once make it available.

e. Naval Staff therefore asks to have 3.(St)/Tr.Gr. 186 left with the Navy at present.

Within five days the Kriegsmarine had their answer, as Göring himself ordered the Stukas immediately placed under the command of *Luftflotte* 2. Raeder and his staff were predictably and justifiably outraged at yet another incursion into what small amount of control the Kriegsmarine still exercised over aerial units:

> The withdrawal of this squadron is opposed to the demand of Naval Staff, who will feel the loss of the squadron for breaking resistance on Hela Peninsula as well as for operations against naval targets in the North Sea all the more, as by order of Armed Forces High Command the naval air units are tactically assigned to Commander in Chief, Navy, and the order of Commander in Chief, Air Force, is, therefore, contradictory to the basic instruction issued in agreement with the Führer.[10]

Nonetheless, the decision was taken, and the highly effective Stuka unit was shortly removed to purely Luftwaffe control. Blattner's squadron transferred briefly to Danzig, from where it continued to batter the Hela Peninsula, before moving to Radom, south of Warsaw, for two days, where it was temporarily subordinated to *Stukageschwader* 77. By 28 September

Heinkel He 59 C-2, DA+RYX, of the *Seenotdienst* showing its Red Cross and civilian colours.

Blattner and his men and machines had returned to Kiel-Holtenau. As the inter-service wrangling continued in the higher command echelons, the men of 3.(St)/Tr.Gr. 186 were pragmatic when informed of their impending reassignment.

> Our personnel had come exclusively from the ranks of the Navy before being transferred to the Luftwaffe. But because it was not known at this juncture just how long it would be before our aircraft carrier, the *Graf Zeppelin*, entered service – which, in the event, she never did – the Luftwaffe was demanding that, in the interim, our *Gruppe* should be placed under the control of its own *Luftflotte* 2. The Navy's opposition to this demand – made mainly as a matter of prestige, I suspect – was put to the *OKW*, which came down firmly on the side of the Luftwaffe. Naturally, we knew nothing of these goings-on at our lowly level. We were simply surprised and delighted when, at the beginning of November 1939, we received orders to transfer to Wertheim, near Würzburg, for service under *Luftflotte* 2. On 8 November 1939 we landed at Wertheim, thereby taking our place as a tactical unit on the Luftwaffe's operational order of battle alongside all its other *Stukagruppen*. The move was very welcome from a flying point of view, but it did pose a number of problems for our ground staff, which would continue to plague the *Gruppe* for a long time to come. Still nominally a carrier-based unit, we had been furnished with very little transport of our own. The *Gruppe* itself had been allocated a single Ju 52 transport aircraft, while the HQ and each *Staffel* was provided with one 3-ton lorry, one small car and one motorcycle for use while lying in harbour. Obviously, this was totally inadequate for a normal Stuka unit's day-to-day operations, let alone for a rapid transfer from one airfield to another.[11]

While the aircraft of *Trägergruppe* 186 were soon removed from *F.d.Luft Ost*, the remaining squadrons continued their activities over Poland and the Baltic Sea. On 16 September *SKL* suggested that boarding commandos be formed from personnel of both 1./Kü.Fl.Gr. 306 and 1./Kü.Fl.Gr. 706 to augment the naval forces already tasked with the interdiction of merchant ships carrying contraband to Great Britain. Each small commando unit would comprise a naval officer observer supported by a Luftwaffe radioman and one or two soldiers drawn from the ground staff. They were to be carried into action aboard an He 59, which was capacious enough to accommodate the extra men, two float-equipped Ju

An armed prize crew boards an He 59 for the enforcement of the Baltic blockade.

52s able to carry larger parties of men if required also being added to the complement. The officers received basic training in the intricacies of Prize Law and were soon operational within the Baltic Sea. The interdiction missions were mounted by pairs of aircraft, one maintaining a protective circle above while the other landed near the target vessel, which had been requested to stop by gunfire, a thrown message from the Heinkel, or flashed Morse signals. Once alongside, the officer was able to inspect the ship's manifest. Any vessel suspected of carrying contraband was directed to Swinemünde, where it would be more thoroughly inspected and possibly interned as a legitimate Prize of War. Following their brief training in the art of boarding merchant ships, on 24 September *SKL* recorded that: 'Naval air forces are permitted to carry out war against merchant shipping in compliance with prize regulations'.

It was soon found that prevailing winds often prevented safe landings, and that the most effective method of inspection involved signalling the suspect vessel while remaining aloft, directing the ship toward a German port or one of the *Vorpostenboote* waiting in predetermined locations.

Once again, Paul Just was at the forefront of this new *Küstenflieger* inititave, this time as observer and aircraft commander aboard a Kü.Fl. Gr. 306 Heinkel.

> The He 59 is a good aircraft, but the two 600hp BMW engines can only give a maximum speed of 240km/h, the highest cruising speed only 205 km/h. The He 59 was intended for four men: Pilot and navigator up front, the radioman who doubled as an air gunner behind, and another gunner, the flight engineer, astern in the lower hull . . . Eight to ten aircraft are constantly on the move, and every day sixty to eighty merchant ships are inspected by the *Vorpostenboote*. It puts a great strain on the crews, with no possibility of collecting military glory . . .
>
> My pilot, *Bootsmann* Brötsch, sits behind and above me. If I want to enter the control dome for a turn at the stick, I knock on his leg. He trims the machine, we understand each other with a look, and he drops out of his seat in the hull, I pull myself up. Of course, the change is prohibited, but the He 59 sails so well through the air, that probably nothing can happen; until the day it happens. When I'm up in the pilot's seat, I unexpectedly see a crooked horizon. The machine is suddenly leaning almost 45 degrees to port. Brötsch is back in his seat in a flash. The machine straightens up, but the drone of the port motor is missing; the propeller has stopped. Theoretically, one engine should be sufficient to keep the He 59 airborne. Brötsch gives the starboard engine full power. The flight engineer, who also takes constant care of the aircraft when on the ground, feverishly searches for the cause of the failure. We can only hope that he is successful, because the aircraft has started to lose height.
>
> Brötsch doesn't need to say anything: we will be down soon. Worried, I look at the sea state, which is quiet, but with a few foam heads. Two steamers are all that are in sight, and as we go further down they disappear behind the horizon. We turn to face against the wind and wave direction. With the slow-running starboard engine we hold ourselves on course above the sea. But the He 59 lurches powerfully and it looks for a moment like the ends of the floats could hit the water and submerge. The fierce vibrations of the floating aircraft puts a great strain on us . . .
>
> We radio a distress signal, because if the motor stops we will not be able to get it going again on our own. [The engineer shouts] 'Everything is okay, I can't find anything. Brötsch, give it another try!' The starter makes the [port] engine pop and puff, the propeller turning in fits and starts before suddenly the engine runs again. We are amazed, and the pilot is happy.[12]

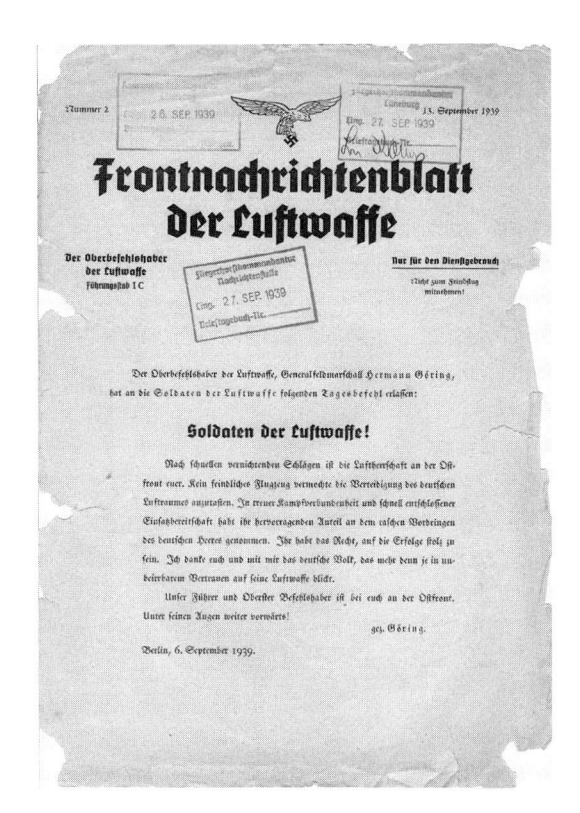

(*Left*) Advertisement from the pages of the propaganda magazine *Signal* for the new 'Schnellbomber', the Junkers Ju 88, soon to become probably the most versatile Luftwaffe aircraft.

(*Right*) The *'Frontnachrichtenblatt der Luftwaffe'* issued by the Luftwaffe's intelligence branch and including information on enemy aircraft types as well as general related news and propaganda. Issue Number 2 released less than a fortnight since hostilities with Poland began ends with the exhortation: 'Our Führer and Supreme Commander is with you on the Eastern Front. Before his eyes, forward!'

In the west, co-operation between *Admiral* Alfred Saalwachter (*MGK West*) and both Joachim Coeler's *F.d.Luft West*, Felmy's *Luftflotte* 2 and Geisler's 10.*Fliegerdivision* was initially very positive. Despite the fact that the Luftwaffe and Kriegsmarine had failed to co-ordinate the most basic tenets of cohesive maritime war (each used different map grids, there was no established mutual communications net, no common code or cypher system, and inadequate telecommunications between operational headquarters and command stations), an element of goodwill had been fostered, not least of all due to Coeler's obvious enthusiasm for his aircraft to begin maritime operations. Overcoming the difficulties imposed by the joint control of naval air units, local organisational measures were taken between the various headquarters: Saalwachter based in Wilhelmshaven, Coeler in Jever thirteen miles to the west, Felmy in Brunswick, and Geisler's office located in Hamburg, which boasted a highly developed signals net. The Luftwaffe and Naval offices immediately exchanged grid-square charts, enabling a composite overlay to be created to ease operational co-ordination. Communications systems were rapidly improved upon, and a Luftwaffe liaison officer was quickly assigned to Saalwachter's staff. Felmy requested that a U-boat be assigned the task of sending direction-finder signals to aid aircraft navigation, but this was refused by *B.d.U.* on the grounds of meagre

The graceful lines of the Focke Wulf Fw 200 'Condor' betray its civilian airliner heritage. While high hopes were attached to the aircraft for maritime operations, it eventually proved less than ideal for the task despite relative combat success.

U-boat strength available for the war against British trade, a converted trawler *Vorpostenboot* being allocated instead for the same purpose.

Over the North Sea, aircraft controlled by *F.d.Luft West* mounted continuous reconnaissance missions to form a picture of shipping movements and the distribution of the Royal Navy's Home Fleet. Aircraft also monitored the entrance to the Skagerrak for any indications of enemy minelaying, as well as any British naval forces despatched to reinforce Poland. First blood was drawn by one such reconnaissance flight within two days of the start of war with Great Britain. During the morning of 5 September eight He 115s of 1./Ku.Fl.Gr. 106 took off from Norderney to fly their parallel search patterns. At approximately 0600hrs the crew of *Lt.z.S.* Bruno Bättger's M2+FH sighted Avro Anson Mk.I K6183, VX-B, of 206 Sqn, RAF, south of the Dogger Bank, and attacked. The Anson was also engaged on maritime reconnaissance, as part of the new Coastal Command, having taken off from its home airfield at Bircham Newton to hunt for U-boats. Pilot Officer Laurence Hugh Edwards, a New Zealander who had trained with the RNZAF, engaged the He 115, and a fifteen-minute battle followed. The Anson's dorsal gunner, 22-year-old LAC John Quilter, was killed by gunfire. Edwards was unable to bring his forward machine gun to bear, and the Anson was soon on fire as it went down into the sea. Two other occupants, 23-year-old Sgt Alexander Oliver Heslop (of 9 Squadron, RAF) and 18-year-old AC1 Geoffrey Sheffield, were both killed, but Edwards manage to swim free of the wreckage despite suffering burns to his face and other minor wounds. The victorious He 115 alighted and rescued Edwards, who became the first RAF officer to be captured during the Second World War.[13] Bättger's triumph was to be short-lived, however, as his aircraft was shot down on 8 November by a 206 Sqn Anson. Bättger was posted as missing in action, but the bodies of pilot *Uffz.* Friedrich Grabbe and wireless operator *Fkmt.* Schettler were later recovered.

However, Coeler's *F.d.Luft West* staff also suffered casualties during the first week of war. On 5 September a Junkers Ju 52 transport carrying six passengers was misidentified by flak gunners aboard the 'pocket battleship' *Admiral Scheer* and shot down. All aboard were killed, including *Hptm.* Günther Klünder, former commander of AS/88, who had been seconded to the staff of *Führer der Seeluftstreitkräfte*.

Only three He 60s were lost during the period between the opening of hostilities with Poland and the end of the year, all during September

1939. As well as the fatal crash in Pillau on 3 September, a second He 60 from 1./Kü.Fl.Gr. 506 crashed in the harbour on 11 September, shortly before alighting, after the pilot was momentarily blinded by sunlight. However, both he and the observer escaped unscathed. On 22 September an He 60 made an emergency landing off Kaaseberga near Kivik, Sweden, owing to engine problems during a reconnaissance sweep of the Bay of Danzig. Drifting toward Swedish territorial waters, the aircraft was subsequently taken in tow by the Swedish destroyer *Vidar* and landed at Ystad. Both the pilot, *Oblt.* Gerhard Grosse, and observer *Lt.z.S.* Helmut von Rabenau were initially interned but repatriated on 8 June 1940. The aircraft was not returned to Germany until 4 November of that year.

On 26 September the second He 59 destroyed during the month was lost when M2+SL of 3./Kü.Fl.Gr. 106, one of nine patrolling the North Sea, was forced down by failure of the port engine. Observer *Oblt.z..S.* Deecke could see that the aircraft was steadily losing height and stood no chance of making landfall, and so ordered pilot *Fw.* Worms to put the Heinkel down, a strong breeze running the sea to a moderate and potentially dangerous swell. Unfortunately, as soon as the aircraft touched down, the starboard float struts broke on the choppy water and the wing cut under the sea surface. The aircraft was completely written off, its wreckage being recovered by the salvage ship *Hans Rolshoven* and the crew rescued and landed at Borkum.[14]

Three of the few unsatisfactory He 114s in service were also lost during September. On 6 September T3+NH was destroyed while being lifted aboard the supply ship *Westerwald*, which was idling near Greenland in support of the 'pocket battleship' *Deutschland*. The aircraft smashed against the ship's hull and was dropped back into the water, its engine later being salvaged. Five days later, observer *Lt.z..S.* Ralph Kapitzky and his pilot, *Uffz.* Nowack of 1./Kü.Fl.Gr. 506, were both slightly injured while alighting at their home base at Putzig following action against Polish troops at Grossendorf. During the attack on infantry positions, rifle and machine-gun fire had damaged the aircraft's control system, causing Nowack to lose control during the landing run.[15] Theirs was one of ten He 114s operated by the *Staffel*. A second was lost a week later when it crashed while alighting owing to an unexpectedly strong tailwind, though there were no casualties.

Six of the long-range reconnaissance Dornier Do 18s were also lost during September. Four days after the fatal crash of Do 18 M2+JK in

Baltrum, an aircraft of 2./Kü.Fl.Gr. 606 capsized during a night alighting at 2304hrs at Hörnum, after being diverted from Witternsee because of fog. Of its crew, observer *Oblt.z.S.* Helmut Rabach was posted as missing, his body never being recovered, flight engineer *Uffz.* Karl Evers was killed, pilot *Uffz.* Ernst Hinrichs was badly injured, and wireless operator *Hptgfr.* Herbert Rusch slightly injured. The aircraft, 8L+WK, was virtually destroyed and later written-off, and Hinrichs died of his injuries in hospital two days later. The *Staffel* 2./Kü.Fl.Gr. 106 lost two aircraft within a day of each other, the first following an emergency alighting with engine trouble in the North Sea. *Kapitänleutnent* Karl Daublebsky von Eichhain rescued the crew, adrift in their lifeboat, with his coastal Type II U-boat *U13*. He also attempted to take the aircraft in tow, but repeated attempts failed in a worsening sea state. During the following morning the seaplane tender and *Seenotdienst* ship *Günther Plüschow* reached their position and also attempted to take the crippled Dornier in tow, but the waterlogged aircraft subsequently flooded and was finally sunk by gunfire at 1230hrs on 13 September.

That same day, near the sand dunes of Ameland, Do 18 M2+LK of the same *Staffel* washed ashore after being damaged by Dutch Fokker D.XXI fighters of 1st JaVA. Unlike the other Low Countries, The Netherlands actively defended their territorial air and sea space, and the Dutch fighters had been scrambled after a naval reconnaissance Fokker T.VIII-W floatplane was attacked six miles outside territorial waters off Schiermonnikoog Island by a German He 115 floatplane of *Küstenfliegergruppe* 406. The German crew had not recognised the approaching aircraft as Dutch, maintaining that, as it came out of the sun towards them, the national insignia of tricolour roundels looked either British or French. The Heinkel crew opened fire and brought the aircraft down, whereupon the T.VIII-W capsized. Recognising their error too late, the Heinkel crew descended alongside the upturned Fokker to assist the crew, some of whom were slightly injured. However, the He 115 was also slightly damaged by a short steep sea, and further assistance arrived in the form of the Do 18 flying boat commanded by *Lt.z.S.* Horst Rust. This too suffered minor damage upon alighting, but the Heinkel was eventually able to take off and transport the injured Dutch crew to hospital on Norderney. Meanwhile, alerted to the drama unfolding at sea by observers ashore, a patrol of three Fokker D.XXIs took off from Eelde, intending either to force the German aircraft to remain stationary and await naval interception, or attack should they attempt to flee. By the time they arrived at the scene the Heinkel had already left, but they sighted the stationary Dornier and fired initial warning shots ahead of the floatplane to prevent take-off. Pilot *Fw.* Otto Radons initially set course for the flying boat to head towards the Dutch coast, but then attempted to lift off and escape. A second strafing attack hit the Dornier, puncturing its hull, which began to leak in the heavy swell. Abandoned, the aircraft drifted ashore and was virtually destroyed by the surf, while Rust and his crew, who had taken to their lifeboat and paddled to the coastline, were captured and interned at Fort Spijkerboor, being taken to Great Britain as prisoners of war in May 1940.

Although the Luftwaffe immediately apologised for the incident, Dutch authorities also admitted some measure of culpability, and in an attempt to minimise such an event recurring, the Dutch Air Force substituted an orange triangle for their tricolour roundels, and their established red, white and blue rudder markings being changed for orange overall. This, however, did not prevent the misidentification of a Dutch DC-3 on 26 September, which was attacked by an He 115 of 1./Kü.Fl.Gr. 406, damaging the airliner and killing Swedish passenger Gustav Robert Lamm.

The forces available to *F.d.Luft West* were steadily increased as the war in Poland progressed in Germany's favour. Gydnia fell on 14 September, Polish forces withdrawing to the Oksywie Heights, which in turn fell within five days. The Hela Peninsula was isolated and finally battered into submission by 2 October, and four days later the final Polish military units surrendered following the battle of Kock, marking the end of the German's Polish campaign.

While '*Fall Weiss*' neared completion in the east, the units of *F.d.Luft West* shared with *Luftflotte* 2 responsibility for the reporting of shipping movements and naval activity within the North Sea. The picture that was forming at MGK West instigated an intensification of operations against merchant shipping sailing in defiance of the declared blockade of Great Britain, in which both Kriegsmarine surface forces and naval aircraft could co-operate. The Luftwaffe crews of *Luftflotte* 2 still lacked the required naval training to guide German destroyers effectively towards suspicious merchant vessels, so the onus fell to *F.d.Luft West*, with its contingent of Kriegsmarine observers.

On 26 September 2./Kü.Fl.Gr. 306, 2./Kü.Fl.Gr. 406 and 2./Kü.Fl. Gr. 506 were scheduled to mount eighteen separate reconnaissance flights over the North Sea in what had become a familiar routine. However, on

Junkers Ju 87 Stukas entering their dive. These aircraft frequently mounted raids against maritime targets and proved effective in their allocated role as dive-bombers. However, only the Ju 87s of *Trägerstukastaffel* 4./186, planned for the *Graf Zeppelin* carrier, were officially attached to the Luftwaffe's maritime strike forces, and then only for the attack on Poland.

this occasion they located strong elements of the Royal Navy Home Fleet that had thus far eluded them. Three main groups were reported and, to maintain contact, aircraft of 1./Kü.Fl.Gr. 406 and 2./Kü.Fl.Gr. 506 (transferred from the east and placed under the direction of Karl Stockmann's Stab/Kü.Fl.Gr. 406) were also despatched to strengthen the reconnaissance sweep. The first group (Home Fleet) was observed heading east, and comprised two battleships, one aircraft carrier and four cruisers. The second (Humber Force), was sailing west, and consisted of two battlecruisers, (mistakenly) one aircraft carrier and five destroyers, and the final group, 'heading for the west at high speed', comprised two cruisers and six destroyers. Rather than spread the aircraft too thinly, contact was maintained on the two heavy groups only, and all W/T transmissions from the shadowing aircraft were immediately forwarded by *F.d.Luft West* to 10.*Fliegerdivision* so that they could prepare a bombing attack. Furthermore, Coeler ordered two multipurpose torpedo-carrying *Staffeln* to prepare an attack to follow-up the bombers, though the time taken to prepare the aircraft delayed take-off until 1330hrs.

At 0830 on 25 September the Home Fleet, comprising the battleships HMS *Nelson* and *Rodney* (of the 2nd Battle Squadron), the aircraft carrier HMS *Ark Royal* (with the Blackburn Skuas of 800 Sqn, the Blackburn Skuas and Rocs of 803 Sqn, and the Fairey Swordfish of 810, 818, 820 and 821 Sqns embarked), and the destroyers HMS *Bedouin*, *Punjabi*, *Tartar* and *Fury*, had sailed from Scapa Flow, steering a westerly course to provide cover for the cruisers and destroyers of the Humber Force returning to British waters, escorting the submarine HMS *Spearfish* which had been damaged by German depth charges. The destroyers HMS *Fame* and *Foresight* were already at sea, and soon joined the main force, followed later by the destroyers HMS *Somali*, *Eskimo*, *Mashona* and *Matabele*.

At 1100hrs GMT three of the distant shadowing Dornier flying boats were sighted by Swordfish reconnaissance aircraft from *Ark Royal*, and nine Skuas were flown off in groups of three at hourly intervals to intercept. The first flight had trouble locating the shadowing aircraft, finally sighting 2./Kü.Fl.Gr. 306 Do 18 K6+XK and engaging in a protracted air combat, hitting the Dornier thirty-six times before it escaped using its superior speed. A second Do 18 of the same *Staffel* survived forty minutes in combat against Skuas of 803 Sqn, suffering fifty-five hits before managing to escape and later making an emergency landing. It was later recovered successfully. However, *Leutnant zur See* Wilhelm Frhr. von Reitzenstein's Dornier Do 18, M7+YK of 2./Kü.Fl.Gr. 506, was attacked by a flight from 803 Sqn at approximately 1203hrs GMT. Reitzenstein was sighted flying close to the surface of the water, and Lt B.S. McEwan RN and his air gunner, Acting Petty Officer Airman B.M. Seymour, disabled the Dornier's engine, forcing it to make an emergency descent. All four crewmen took to their liferaft and were captured by HMS *Somali*, their crippled aircraft being sunk with gunfire. The shooting-down of Reitzenstein's Dornier was the first confirmed German aircraft lost in aerial combat.¹⁶ A second Do 18 of 3./Kü.Fl.Gr. 106 was also lost, but to engine malfunction rather than enemy action. It made an emergency descent near Juist, whereupon the starboard float struts broke apart and the wings hit the water. Although it was later recovered by the *Seenotdienst* ship *Hans Rolshoven*, the Dornier was written-off. Nonetheless, the *Küstenflieger* aircrafts' dogged perseverance in maintaining contact allowed a co-ordinated bombing attack to be made on the Home Fleet.

> In the morning our air reconnaissance contacted heavy enemy forces north and west of the Great Fisher Bank. Despite strong enemy fighter defence and anti-aircraft gunfire, the shadowing aeroplanes succeeded in guiding four dive-bombing Ju 88s and one squadron of He 111s of 10 *Fliegerdivision* to the attack by sending out direction-finder signals.

The ships' positions had been successfully reported and at 1345hrs, when the British Home Fleet was approximately 120nm west of Stavanger, HMS *Rodney*'s Type 79Y radar reported aircraft approaching. Nine He

The large size of the multipurpose Heinkel He 59 is evident in this photo of a machine from *Küstenfliegergruppe* 906 taken in Norway.

111H bombers of the only operational '*Löwen Geschwader*' *Staffel*, 4./ KG 26, from their forward airfield at Westerland, and four Ju 88A-1 bombers of 1./KG 30 from Jever airfield, were closing on their target at an altitude of 2,000m, attacking in the face of heavy anti-aircraft fire of all calibres but no fighter cover. All of the defending British aircraft had landed and been struck down to defuel, as dictated by Royal Navy policy at the time, which relied on anti-aircraft fire for fleet protection. Despite the strong defensive fire, no attacking bombers were hit, although it at least prevented German success.

All four Ju 88s targeted the *Ark Royal*, that flown by *Uffz*. Carl Francke, a former aeronautical engineer, being one of the last to make his dive-bombing attack with *Ark Royal* manoeuvring below him. A single SC 500 bomb exploded off the port bow, sending a huge column

A Dornier Do 18, the long-distance reconnaissance of the early war *Küstenflieger*, photographed here ashore at Aalborg, Denmark in 1940 with engine and open nose position protected by tarpaulins. In the background is the *Flugsicherungsschiff* BS 11 *Phönix*. (Bundesarchiv)

of water higher than the flight deck and causing the ship to whip and list alarmingly. Aboard the Ju 88 the water column was sighted along with a visible flash, though none of the crew could confirm whether it was an actual hit or simply the flash of gunfire obscured by smoke and water. One of the two bombs dropped was an established miss, but the second Francke reported as a 'possible hit on bows; effect not observed'. Over-optimistically, *MGK West* counted the hit as definite, and by the time Francke had landed the wish had solidified into fact.

> Result: One 500kg bomb hit by a Ju 88 on an aircraft carrier; two 250kg bomb hits by He 111 on one battleship. One miss by a Ju 88 on a cruiser. Results of hits by a Ju 88 on another battleship and a second aircraft carrier(?) were not observed owing to interception of the aeroplane. The fate of the hit aircraft carrier, which was not sighted again by further air reconnaissance, is unknown. If not sunk, at least heavy damage is presumed by the effect of the 500kg bomb. Own losses: Attacking formation; none. Reconnaissance formation; two Do 18s.

No British ships had actually been damaged, though HMS *Hood* had suffered a glancing blow from a bomb dropped by *Lt.* Walter Storp's Ju 88 that bounced off the armoured hull plating, a large patch of grey paint being removed to show the red primer beneath. A second wave of bombers from KG 26 and KG 30 was cancelled, as arming the aircraft had taken too long, while *F.d.Luft West* was soon informed that his own He 59 torpedo bombers, which were almost ready to take off, would be unable to operate against the enemy owing to the extreme range. Nonetheless, the Germans believed that they had been triumphant. Further reconnaissance missions located heavy ships but failed to find any trace of HMS *Ark Royal*, though she docked in Scapa Flow two days later. In fact, the Kriegsmarine were not inclined to believe that the carrier had been sunk. They instead correctly reasoned that, as a result of incorrect location fixing, the aircraft had in fact sighted the Humber Force, which they no longer believed included an aircraft carrier. Nonetheless, the co-operation of the Luftwaffe and Kriegsmarine in this operation had proceeded smoothly and without significant issues. *SKL* recorded their summary of the event:

> The success of the aerial attack by the operational Luftwaffe without any losses, entailing a distance of over 300 miles, is most satisfactory. It must be

> rated all the higher since it was the first operation of the war by the British Fleet in the North Sea, which has shown it in a very impressive manner the dangers of an approach to the German coast and, beyond that, the striking power of the Luftwaffe which threatens it. Any attempt by surface forces to penetrate into the Heligoland Bight or through the Kattegat and Baltic Sea entrances into the Baltic Sea must appear completely hopeless to the British Fleet after today's experience – if it should be included at all in its operational plans.
>
> The disposition of the bomber formations of the operational Air Force – providing for only four dive-bombing Ju 88 aeroplanes on Westerland at present, out of the small number so far available – rendered a more extensive use of the particularly suitable dive-bomber formations impossible. This must be regretted all the more as, after today's experience, the British are not likely to repeat the operation, and the use of stronger Stuka formations would probably have had an annihilating effect. The co-operation of the reconnaissance formations of the Naval Air Force with the attacking formation of the operational Air Force, which is still rather inexperienced in flying over the sea, is particularly satisfactory: they stubbornly maintained contact with the enemy with remarkable persistence and despite the strongest fighter defence. Our Radio Monitoring Service worked well. In addition to the observation of heavy enemy forces in the North Sea yesterday, it was possible to gain important information as to course and speed of certain enemy groups by the decoding of enemy radiograms to enemy aeroplanes. The enemy anti-aircraft defence was of medium strength. The enemy fighters proved inadequate as to speed and daring.[17]

German propaganda seized on the thin evidence of success and triumphantly reported the sinking of the *Ark Royal*, the *Völkischer Beobachter* and the Luftwaffe magazine *Der Adler* both publishing graphic artists' impressions of the carrier wreathed in smoke and flames. Francke received a telegram of congratulations from Göring, and was promoted and awarded the Iron Cross First and Second Class, though at no point did he claim to have actually sunk the ship.[18]

However, while the Kriegsmarine appeared content with the result of the combined operation, the resulting analysis by Luftwaffe staff had far-reaching consequences, as it contributed to an overinflated view of the effectiveness of Luftwaffe forces acting in isolation in action against enemy naval units. A report forwarded to Göring on 30 September by his Operations Staff Officer summarised that:

> a. It can be assumed according to available data that the aircraft carrier was probably sunk. (The aircraft carrier not visible on the second comprehensive reconnaissance.)
>
> b. According to the observations of the Ju 88 which attacked the carrier, it seemed that the strongly-cased 500kg SD delayed-action bomb caused an explosion inside the carrier among the oil reserves. (Apparent fires, smoke clouds.)
>
> c. Even small Luftwaffe forces (thirteen aircraft) are in a position to inflict considerable damage on heavy naval forces.
>
> d. In the rough sea (state four to five) the ships' anti-aircraft guns were unable to break up the attack.[19]

Göring published an order on 29 September that all long-range reconnaissance over the North Sea was henceforth to be handled by *Luftflotte* 2, and frequent mistakes in Luftwaffe navigation resulted in an increased number of erroneous sighting reports which, though generally considered unreliable by *MGK West*, still required investigation by naval air units. The resultant waste of resources in duplicated and fruitless missions served to upset the uneasy calm that had been reached over operational jurisdiction between Luftwaffe and Kriegsmarine tactical control.

On 3 October *SKL* enquired to Luftwaffe General Staff, Operations Division, about the possibility of the operational Luftwaffe conducting war against merchant shipping in accordance with prize regulations, and any plans for the conduct of war against merchant shipping during the 'siege of Britain'. The answer, noted in the *SKL* War Diary, was both disappointing and predictable:

> 1. War against merchant shipping in accordance with prize regulations cannot be carried out by the units of the Luftwaffe.
>
> 2. Luftwaffe General Staff regards the main objective of the fight against Great Britain up to about spring 1940 to be against British Air Force

armament factories. Suitable aircraft in sufficient numbers for effective participation in the blockade of Britain by sea west of Ireland will not be available until the end of 1940 or the beginning of 1941. Up to that time the blockade in the North Sea area by the Luftwaffe remains a task of secondary importance. It is planned effectively to support the blockade by combined attacks on the main enemy ports of entry and naval bases.

Meanwhile, elements of the *Küstenflieger* were also engaged in support of German destroyers attempting to intercept contraband merchant shipping in the Kattegat and Skagerrak bound for Great Britain, though this resulted in few seizures of cargo ships. In the Baltic the Naval Air Units continued to maintain their own blockade by stopping and searching steamers. Thirty-one had been intercepted by 9 October, and six taken as prizes to Swinemünde. Beginning on the evening of 27 September, aerial reconnaissance reported many ships hugging the coasts of Sweden, Denmark and Norway, sheltered by those nations' neutrality. Only four steamers were successfully seized as prizes out of a total of forty-four stopped and searched, the majority travelling in ballast. However, the German concentration of aircraft, U-boats, S-boats and armed trawlers in the Skaggerak approaches had all but paralysed Danish export trade to Great Britain, and gave rise to Royal Navy Admiralty orders for a special reconnaissance patrol of Lockheed Hudsons to search the entrance to the Skagerrak to confirm reports of continuous German aerial patrolling, and 'attack if circumstances prove favourable'. However, bad weather intervened during the following day, and most of the planned missions were cancelled. Grimsby fishing trawlers reported frequently sighted German flying boats; never more than two flying together, flying very low over the fishing fleet at between 200 to 500ft, though thus far no trawlers had been attacked.

On the evening of 7 October the battleship *Gneisenau* and light cruiser *Köln* sailed from the Jade into the North Sea, accompanied by the destroyers *Wilhelm Heidkamp*, *Friedrich Ihn*, *Diether von Roeder*, *Karl Galster*, *Theodor Riedel*, *Max Schulz*, *Bernd von Arnim* and *Friedrich Eckoldt*. They were to bolster the war against merchant shipping while also attempting to lure British heavy surface forces from their bases into bomber range, in the mistaken belief that the major German units might be attempting to break into the Atlantic Ocean. After one day at sea, one of the ship's two Arado Ar 196A-1s, T3+CH of 1./B.Fl.Gr. 196, was lightly damaged by its own catapult air pressure while being prepared for

A Do 18 in flight; aircraft 'E' of its *Küstenfliegergruppe*'s 3rd *Staffel*.

launch 30nm west of Utsire, after the ship was approached by a British reconnaissance aircraft.

While the *Gneisenau* group headed north, the *Küstenflieger* continued to traverse the North Sea, looking for the Home Fleet. HMS *Selkirk* and *Niger* were machine-gunned and attacked with bombs by Do 18s on 7 October while sweeping for mines off Swarte bank, 45 miles ENE of Cromer, though the strafing caused only light damage. The following day, *Lt.z..S.* Hans Wilhelm H. Hornkohl's Do 18D3, M7+UK of 2./Kü.Fl. Gr. 506, was attacked by three Hudson Mk.Is of RAF Coastal Command 224 Sqn engaged on the delayed 'special reconnaissance' of the Skaggerak approaches and shot down 60 miles north-east of Aberdeen. The pilot, *Fw.* Willy Erich Nahs, managed to ditch the aircraft successfully, and after the circling Hudsons watched all four crew climb into their dinghy, they sank the aircraft with gunfire. The Danish freighter SS *Teddy* rescued the four Germans, who were landed in Sweden and interned after attempts by the destroyers HMS *Jervis* and *Jupiter* to intercept and take the German airmen prisoner failed. They were soon repatriated to Germany, arriving home on 25 October.

During the day following the loss of Hornkohl's aircraft, *B-Dienst* established that heavy British forces had put out into the North Sea, detecting the 1st British Battleship Squadron, 2nd Cruiser Squadron and destroyers of the 6th and 7th Destroyer Flotillas. They had not,

A Junkers Ju 88 of KG 30 'Adler', clearly showing the Eagle insignia adopted by the unit that became maritime specialists.

as yet, been found by aerial reconnaissance, and a greater-than-normal number of aircraft was despatched to the hunt, both *Küstenflieger* and aircraft of Geisler's X.*Fliegerkorps*; the new nomenclature having been bestowed upon 10.*Fliegerdivision* on 2 October with a view to its imminent expansion. At 0800hrs the first of three sightings were reported by aircraft of 2./Kü.Fl.Gr. 606, aircraft 'J' signalling the sighting of three enemy battleships and two destroyers in quadrant 4611, swiftly followed by aircraft 'F' reporting three cruisers and two destroyers in quadrant 3419, and aircraft 'E' three heavy cruisers and two destroyers in quadrant 3151, all located between the Shetland Islands and Norway. The latter two groups (designated 'C' and 'B' respectively and separated by 50nm), were listed as headed on a 90° course, while the direction of travel of the first reported group (designated 'A' and 80nm from 'Group B'), was not included in the sighting report. Immediately, *F.d.Luft* designated the battleships of 'Group A' as the priority target.

At 0820hrs X.*Fliegerkorps* were informed by telephone of the three sighted enemy groups and, determined to demonstrate the capabilities of his forces, Geisler despatched a total of 127 He 111s and twenty-one Ju 88s of KG 26, KG 30 and LG 1 to intercept in staggered attacks throughout the course of the day. While KG 30 had previously been the sole operator of Ju 88s, *Lehrgeschwader* 1, which had been formed as a demonstration unit, and therefore had each *Gruppen* equipped with different aircraft types, had started to take on the Junkers fast bomber. Eventually, nearly all of LG 1 would be converted to the Ju 88, IV./LG 1 remaining the only *Gruppe* of the *Geschwader* to continue operating Ju 87s instead, and frequently served as part of the Luftwaffe's maritime interdiction forces.

The staff of *Küstenfliegergruppe* 406 were ordered to co-ordinate an attack on 'Group C' by He 59s of 3./Kü.Fl.Gr. 706 at 0840hrs, and within hours five torpedo-armed aircraft were airborne, accompanied by three others carrying smoke floats. However, the results obtained by this large aerial commitment were negligible. Weaknesses in nautical navigation among the conventional Luftwaffe crews had rendered sighting reports wildly inaccurate, the problem compounded by poor weather conditions which resulted in the previously smooth interplay of sighting, shadowing and attack, demonstrated previously against the *Ark Royal*, quickly becoming a shambles. The three separate groups later transpired to be just one that had been reported in various locations owing to imprecise navigation. The Royal Navy's 2nd Cruiser Squadron, HMS *Southampton*, *Glasgow* and *Edinburgh* and five 'J'-class destroyers, collectively known by the Admiralty as the 'Humber Force', had been sent to sweep northward off the Norwegian coast to prevent any planned German breakout of capital ships into the Atlantic indicated by *Gneisenau*'s sailing.

No concerted Luftwaffe attack was mounted, though small groups attempted to bomb sporadically, and erroneous reports of success were received by wireless in Germany. Of two 500kg bombs, 121 250kg and fifty-one 50kg bombs dropped during sixty-one separate attacks, seven hits were claimed; five 250kg bomb hits on cruisers, one amidships, causing flame and smoke and an explosion three minutes after impact, and two 50kg bomb hits despite heavy enemy flak. The Royal Navy recorded that HMS *Jaguar*, returning to Rosyth for fuel, had suffered an attack by two aircraft which had dropped six bombs, and an attempted dive-bombing attack by a Ju 88 which was deflected by anti-aircraft fire. The 2nd Cruiser Squadron came under attack at various intervals between 1120hrs and 1645hrs, though no ship was hit and only bomb splinters were found aboard HMS *Southampton*. At 1518hrs the two destroyers HMS *Jervis* and *Jupiter* were bombed by four aircraft which missed, but *Jupiter*'s engines broke down and forced *Jervis* to take her in tow for Scapa. In return, one Ju 88 was lost over the sea, though the crew were rescued, and three He 111s were lost, two crews being recovered.

On the part of the *Küstenflieger*, *Hptm.* Gerd Stein, *Staffelkapitän* of 3./Kü.Fl.Gr. 706, recorded in his KTB at take-off:

> I realise right now that if the enemy maintains his course, he will be out of my range. In the hope that the enemy will either be held up by the effect of the expected bombing raids made by the long-range division, or forced to alter course, I still head for the expected interception point.[20]

Thus the *Küstenflieger* attempted its first torpedo operation of the war, sending out eight He 59s of 3./Kü.Fl.Gr. 706 equipped with the less-than-ideal F5. However, despite hours of searching they failed to contact the enemy, and lost He 59 8L+UL, which attempted an emergency alighting and crashed in heavy seas north-west of Sylt, the crew being drowned. A second He 59 was damaged by the same weather when, low on fuel, it was also forced to put down on the sea. The rest of the *Staffel* returned to their base after over eight hours in the air. Another aircraft, a Do 18 of 2./Kü.Fl.Gr. 606, was also forced to make an emergency descent at sea near Lister, Norway, the crew and aircraft later being interned in Kristiansand until freed by the German invasion in April 1940.

In total, *F.d.Luft* later calculated that, at midday during the unfolding battle, twenty-three Do 18s were airborne in either picket lines or search patterns, plus the eight He 59s of 3./Kü.Fl.Gr. 706, as well as 132 aircraft of X.*Fliegerkorps*. Nonetheless, despite the obvious failure in location and co-ordinated attack, the Kriegsmarine placed great store in the very fact that Luftwaffe aircraft were theoretically capable of dominating sea space far from German waters.

> Apart from the immediate results of the bombing attacks, great strategic and operational importance is to be attached to the appearance of German operational air forces in the area of the northern part of the North Sea at such a long distance from their home bases. The fact that the enemy has become aware of the complete control of the entire North Sea area by the German Air Force will not be without a decisive effect on his considerations regarding operations in German coastal waters. In this way, he has been clearly shown for the first time the long range of German bomber forces and the danger to his bases and ports on the east and west coasts.[21]

A Heinkel He 111 observed from the navigator's position aboard another. The heavily glazed cockpit afforded the Heinkel crew excellent visibility, though it was vulnerable to enemy fire.

Eager for more tangible success, photographic-reconnaissance Heinkels of KG 26 detected a concentration of Royal Navy capital ships in the Firth of Forth on the morning of 16 October, and successfully evaded Spitfires attempting to intercept them. Their radioed reports of the sighting, including the belief that HMS *Hood* was within the estuary, brought twelve Junkers Ju 88A-1s of *Hptm.* Helmuth Pohle's KG 30 to readiness on the island of Sylt. The Ju 88s departed in four separate waves of three aircraft each; Pohle leading the way, followed by the second group led by his executive officer, *Oblt.* Hans Siegmund Storp, a veteran of service in AS/88 during the Spanish Civil War and brother to *Oblt.* Walter Storp, former commander of the testing unit *Erprobungsstaffel Ju 88* and now also in KG 30. They had been informed by Luftwaffe intelligence that there were no Spitfire squadrons based in Scotland, and were content to rely on their aircrafts' speed to outrun any defences.

After making landfall as planned, the Ju 88s dive-bombed various capital ships within the estuary between 1434hrs and 1654hr. They had been ordered to sink the *Hood* but hamstrung by operational instructions that had been issued by Hitler, forbidding attacks on ships in dry dock, or

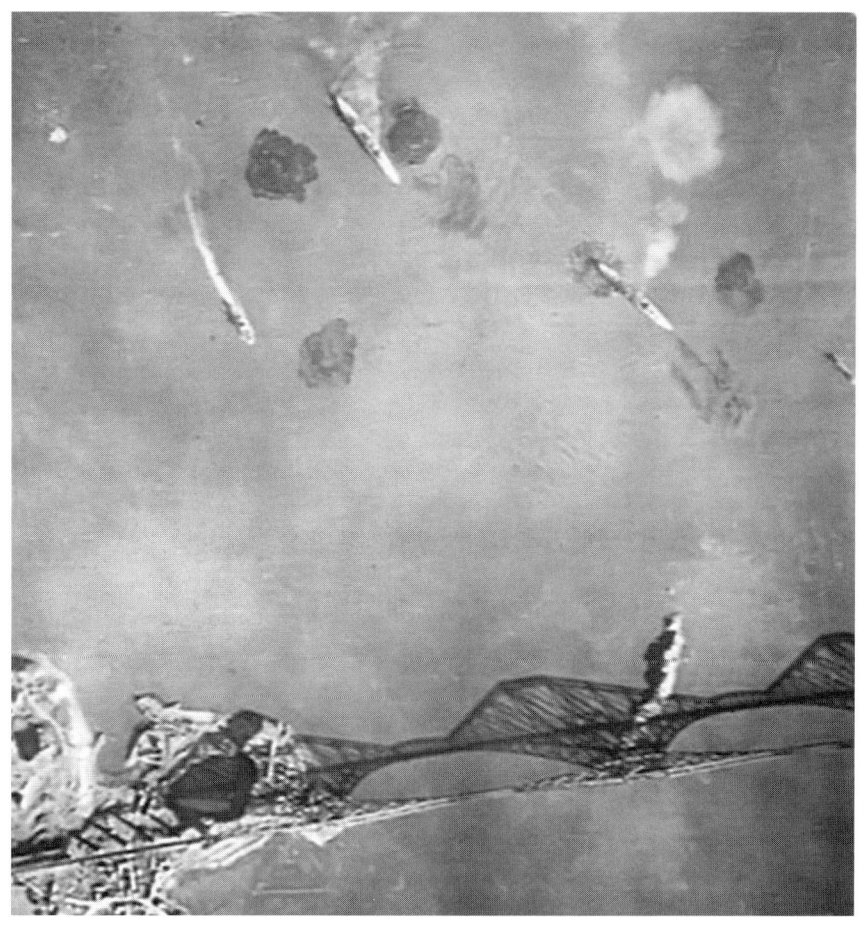

German aerial reconnaissance photograph of Royal Navy shipping in the Firth of Forth, 16 October 1939, that presaged an attack by KG 30.

on any land targets on Britain, to minimise the risk of civilian casualties. The ship believed to have been HMS *Hood* was in fact *Repulse*, which had clearly been placed into dry dock and was therefore off limits. There remained, however, several cruisers and the carrier HMS *Furious* as Pohle led the first attack against HMS *Southampton*. His steep 80-degree dive angle tore the canopy roof from his aircraft, taking with it the defensive rear machine gun, but he released bombs successfully at 550m and pulled out of the dive to the estuary's north bank, where he planned to orbit and observe subsequent attacks. Storp's second wave followed, his aircraft

Walter Storp, former naval officer in the *Reichsmarine* before transfer to the Luftwaffe at the rank of *Oberleutnant* in 1935. Storp's KG 30 Ju 88 hit HMS *Hood* in September 1939, but the bomb bounced off. Storp survived the war at the rank of *Generalmajor*, credited with 435 combat missions.

again targeting HMS *Southampton*. A single bomb hit the bow, slicing through three decks before bursting out of the hull above the waterline and exploding, blowing the admiral's barge and a pinnace moored alongside into the air. The raid was observed by passengers on a train stopped at the southern arch of the Forth Bridge, at first believed to be the Germans' target, as Storp's and two other Ju 88s of his second wave flew parallel to observers on the bridge while coming out of their dives.

By this time, the unexpected arrival of Spitfires from Edinburgh's 603 Sqn scattered the attacking bombers as they gave chase. Storp's Junkers was hit by machine-gun fire, stopping his port engine and killing rear gunner *Ogfr.* Kramer. Further strikes disabled the elevators, after which the Junkers crashed into the sea near the coast at Port Seton; the first German aircraft brought down over Britain in the Second World War. Storp was thrown clear by the impact, and he and his two surviving crew, *Fw.* Hans Georg Heilscher and Hugo Rohnke, were picked up by the fishing boat *Dayspring* and taken ashore as prisoners. Storp gave the fishing boat's captain, John Dickson Snr, his gold ring as a token of gratitude for their rescue. Glasgow's 602 Sqn also arrived, ignoring an unidentified twin-engine aircraft sighted three miles from the scene of the action to intercept three distant aircraft, which turned out to be a trio of naval Skuas on a training flight from Donibristle. Retracing their path, they approached the previously unidentified aircraft, which was now identified as a Junkers. It was commanded by Pohl, who continued to circle while observing the attack. Bullets hit the port wing as Pohl hurriedly sought cloud cover but was outpaced by the pursuing Spitfires. As they attempted to climb away, the Ju 88's cockpit was struck again by machine-gun fire, killing pilot *Fw.* Werner Weise and rear gunner seventeen-year-old *Gefr.* August Schleicher, and wounding the radio operator, nineteen-year-old *Uffz.* Kurt Seydel. Fuel tanks were soon ruptured and the starboard engine damaged, and Pohl was forced to ditch near a trawler that he fervently hoped would be the Luftwaffe *Seenotdienst* boat *Fl.B213*, based in Hörnum and positioned for the purpose of rescuing crews shot down during the raid. However, the trawler was British, and Pohl and his radio operator were pulled aboard, where the latter died of his wounds. Pohl had received wounds to his face and was later transferred to a military hospital in Edinburgh Castle before incarceration in Grizedale Hall. Although Weise's body was never recovered, Schleicher's was found, and both he and Seydel were later

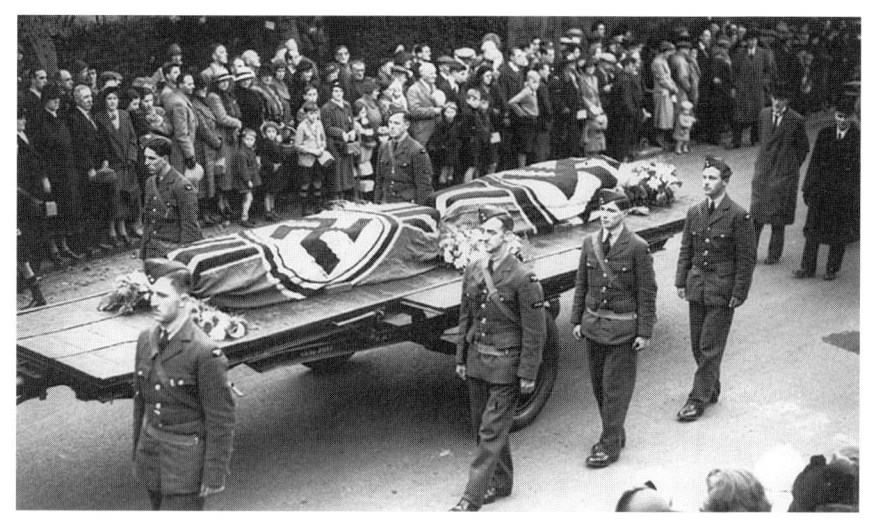

The Edinburgh funeral procession of seventeen-year-old *Gefr.* August Schleicher and nineteen-year-old *Uffz.* Kurt Seydel killed over the Firth of Forth, 16 October 1939.

given military funerals as RAF pipers played *Over the Sea to Skye* as a lament. Nearly 10,000 people lined Edinburgh's streets for the funeral procession of the two German airmen, 603 Sqn's chaplain, the Reverend James Rossie Brown, delivering a moving eulogy and later personally writing to their families in Germany to assure them that their sons had been buried with full military honours. A pair of wreathes were placed on the airmen's graves at Portobello Cemetery, reading: 'To two brave airmen from the mother of an airman', and 'With the deep sympathy of Scottish mothers'. The dehumanising effect of war had not yet touched this part of Scotland.

As Pohle was being shot down, the fourth wave of Ju 88s attacked HMS *Mohawk* in an inbound Scandinavian convoy escort, bombs from *Lt.* Horst von Riesen's Junkers bursting close alongside and sending lethal flying splinters scything through crewmen. Machine-gun fire from the bombers' gunners added to the casualties, and the ship's first lieutenant and thirteen men were killed. The captain, Cder Richard Frank Jolly, was mortally wounded in the stomach but stayed at his post until HMS *Mohawk* reached its berth in Rosyth, where he suddenly collapsed, dying five hours later.[22]

In total, HMS *Southampton*, *Edinburgh* and *Mohawk* had all been damaged, and sixteen Royal Navy men were killed and forty-four injured for the loss of two Luftwaffe aircraft, albeit crewed by the *Staffel*'s senior officers. One of the Junkers of the third wave to attack was chased at low level over the centre of Edinburgh by Spitfires, but escaped, although stray bullets from the engagement hit a building under refurbishment and wounded a painter in the stomach.

The following day four KG 30 Ju 88s on an armed reconnaissance mission (German terminology for 'shipping harassment') over Scapa Flow, led by the newly promoted *Gruppenkommandeur* I./KG,30, *Major* Fritz Doench, attacked the unseaworthy and partly stripped obsolete battleship HMS *Iron Duke*, lying in the Flow as guardship only days after the sinking of HMS *Royal Oak* by Günther Prien's *U47*. Two 500kg bombs hit the dilapidated ship, which was severely damaged and forced to beach in Ore Bay with a heavy list to port and one rating killed. A single Junkers piloted by *Oblt.* Walter Flaemig was brought down in flames by anti-aircraft fire from Rysa Little, crashing at the mouth of Pegal Burn on the Isle of Hoy. Only wireless operator *Uffz.* Fritz Ambrosius survived. He released the upper escape hatch and was dragged away by the slipstream, still clutching the release handle. Although he was able to open his parachute as the aircraft plunged to the rocks below, he sustained serious injuries because his parachute had caught fire and he landed heavily. He spent a month in hospital after his capture. A second wave of KG 26 Heinkels also attacked the beached ship as workmen of the salvage firm Metal Industries Ltd were engaged in pumping out the vessel and patching the hull, but the bomb run was inaccurate and they failed to hit anywhere near the target.

While the losses suffered by X.*Fliegerkorps* were considered relatively acceptable, there was growing Luftwaffe concern over the comparatively heavy casualty rate suffered by squadrons operating the Do 18, at that time the only available long-range reconnaissance aircraft. Ten had been lost since the beginning of the war, and construction of a more robust replacement aircraft was once again prioritised, the Dornier being considered extremely vulnerable to enemy air attack. To underline the point, on 17 October 8L+DK of 2./Kü.Fl.Gr. 606 had been shot down by Gloster Gladiators of 607 Sqn. Tasked with shadowing enemy shipping following an early-morning search mission for a missing Ju 88 of I./KG 30, *Oblt.z.S.* Siegfried Saloga reported a 'light cruiser' some 125nm east of Sunderland, which they later misidentified as the Polish destroyer *Grom*, whereas it was actually HMS *Juno*. A second Dornier was ordered to join Saloga, and at 1240hrs three Gladiators of 607 Sqn were sent off from Acklington to see off both Do 18s. At approximately 1330hrs they engaged Saloga's aircraft. The flying boat was damaged, and retired quickly towards the east, eventually having to ditch 35nm east of Berwick less than a quarter of an hour later, stalling as it flared for alighting and crashing into the sea. Flight mechanic *Uffz*. Kurt Seydel was killed, while Saloga, pilot *Uffz*. Paul Grabbert and radio operator *Oberfunkmaat* Hillmar Grimm abandoned the aircraft in their liferaft, which proved to have been pierced by gunfire. The swimming Germans were later pulled from the sea by the crew of HMS *Juno*.

In the meantime, Saloga's earlier contact report triggered the despatch of six He 115s of 1./Kü.Fl.Gr. 406 from List at 0957hrs on an armed reconnaissance of the area Flamborough Head-Aberdeen, along with an additional three equipped with bombs. At 1020hrs they were followed by thirteen He 111s of KG 26, which took off from Westerland and headed for the area under the scrutiny of the He 115s. At 1507hrs two He 115s of the *Bombenkette* found and attacked HMS *Juno* six sea miles north of Berwick, dropping four SC250 bombs without result. The Heinkel floatplanes were later attacked by the Gladiators of 607 Sqn, but the combat was inconclusive. The KG 26 bombers failed to located *Juno* and returned to their airfield.

Increased numbers of He 115s were arriving at *Küstenflieger* squadrons, though they were still incapable of carrying torpedoes into action owing to the F5's deficiencies. Furthermore, their potential vulnerability to determined enemy defence was soon made glaringly apparent during a badly fumbled operation mounted in co-operation with X.*Fliegerkorps* on 21 October. Convoy FN24 from Methil to Orfordness was reported steaming north of Flamborough Head, and *MGK West* requested and was immediately granted permission to co-ordinate an air attack. Ten He 115s of 1./Kü.Fl.Gr. 406 were armed with bombs and prepared for the raid, and the initial attack wave was increased to include three Ju 88s of 1./KG 30. As the two aircraft types had vastly different capabilities, take-offs were staggered to allow the Heinkels to arrive on target first, followed shortly by the faster Junkers bombers. However, the plan misfired badly, as the Ju 88s outpaced the slower floatplanes and arrived well in advance, delivering their bombing attacks and retreating at equally high speed. By the time the *Küstenflieger* were within sight of the target, at 1545hrs, RAF Spitfires of 72 Sqn and eleven Hurricanes of 46 Sqn were on protective patrol, alerted by the previous attack.

The Heinkels flew into heavy defensive fire, and their loose formation was soon broken up by the British fighters, each of the floatplanes attempting emergency manoeuvres against the more agile fighters. Within minutes four had been shot down. *Oberleutnant zur See* Heinz Schlicht and his two crewmates, *Lt.* Fritz Meyer and *Uffz.* Bernhard Wessels, were brought down into the sea, their aircraft crashing five miles off Spurn Head, Yorkshire and killing all on board. The crew's bodies were carried by the tide until they were washed ashore at Mundesley and Happisburgh, Norfolk, and they were buried on 2 November. A second Heinkel, commanded by *Oblt.z.S.* Albert Peinemann, crashed while attempting to ditch after being severely damaged by the attacking fighters. Pilot *Uffz.* Günther Pahnke and Peinemann were both slightly injured, but radio operator *Uffz.* Hermann Einhaus was unscathed, and all were rescued by a British merchant ship. The following day their abandoned Heinkel was examined by the crew of a Do 18, who landed alongside before sinking it with gunfire. A third crew, led by *Oblt.z.S.* Günther Reymann, was also taken prisoner after an emergency alighting by pilot *Fw.* Rolf Findeisen, who was badly injured and admitted to hospital after being put ashore on British soil.

The fourth Heinkel brought down was piloted by *Uffz.* Helmuth Becker, who was killed in combat with Spitfire K9959, piloted by Australian Flt Lit Desmond Sheen of 72 Sqn.

> Just nineteen days after his 22nd birthday . . . Des later described that battle as 'Really good fun; as exciting a five minutes as anything you could wish for'.
>
> 'A' Flight was scrambled at 2.15pm, and 'B' Flight's Blue section was put on readiness. Green section, led by Des in Spitfire K9959, was scrambled at 2.30pm. He and Flying Officer Thomas 'Jimmy' Elsdon were ordered to proceed to Spurn Head, and soon sighted a loose formation of 12-14 aircraft, which they identified as Heinkel He 115 three-seater floatplanes.
>
> Des and Elsdon intercepted the formation about 15 miles south-east of Spurn Head. As the Spitfires neared, the three enemy subsections 'split up and employed individual evasive tactics of steep turns, diving, climbing and throttling back'.
>
> Des 'fired all I had at one of them', attacking from 'dead astern', at about a hundred yards' distance. Then: 'as I closed on my He 115, its rear gunner attempted to put me off my aim by blazing away with his weapon, but I soon silenced him. The next burst may have killed the pilot, for the Heinkel started to fly very erratically, and with this I turned away to look for another target.'[23]

The Heinkel broke away and later ditched near the Danish ship *Dagmar Clausen, Oblt.z.S.* Gottfried Lenz having been wounded by the Spitfire's bullets, and *Uffz.* Peter Großgart was rescued by the neutral steamer and returned to Germany two days later.

The disaster of 21 October was referred to by Raeder in conference with Hitler two days later, as Raeder attempted once more to urge greater naval control of such aerial operations or, at the very least, enhanced co-operation between Kriegsmarine and Luftwaffe forces.

> The attack by He 115s in the coastal waters off southern England resulted in the loss of four aircraft; this area therefore appears unsuitable for attacks. The C-in-C Navy declares that conclusions have already been drawn from this experience, namely that the anti-aircraft defences are apparently very strong along the southern part of the coast of England. The C-in-C Navy asks that no measures be taken as rumoured — for

instance, that combined operations over the sea are being considered —
for it is absolutely necessary to train and operate naval aircraft in closest
co-operation with naval forces. The Führer declares that there is no
question of such measures.[24]

However, the entire event played further into the hands of the Luftwaffe elements that wanted to wrest control of maritime operations from the Kriegsmarine. On 15 November Göring ordered the reduction of the *Küstenflieger* to just nine long-range reconnaissance and nine multipurpose *Staffeln*. He strongly requested that Raeder withhold the slow seaplanes from enemy coastal operations, noting that the Luftwaffe was supposed to be the authority of activity over open sea if no fleet operations were taking place.

The grievous losses did little for the moral of *Küstenfliegergruppe* 406, the *Kommodore Obstlt.* Karl Stockmann complaining bitterly about the effectiveness of his seaplanes and requesting, unsuccessfully, that at least one *Staffel* be converted to Fw 200 bombers. Instead, his staff unit was diverted to responsibility for the formation of a new long-distance reconnaissance unit, the *Transozeanstaffel* under the command of *Major* Friedrich von Buddenbrock, previously of the *F.d.Luft Ost* staff. During August 1939 Hermann Göring, as Minister for Air, had ordered that all Lufthansa seaplanes be placed at the disposal of Luftwaffe command. Although he recommended the continuation of transatlantic passenger flights until the eve of war, the few available transocean Lufthansa aircraft operating in conjunction with catapult ships in the Atlantic were ordered back to Germany via Spain shortly after hostilities began, the catapult ships being directed to dock in neutral Las Palmas. By 15 September 1939 the Luftwaffe had authorised the formation of the *Transozeanstaffel*, and the first pair of former Lufthansa Do 26 flying boats, *Seeadler* and *Seefalke*, alighted at Friedrichshafen for transfer onwards to Travemünde in September. Four other Do 26s either in trials or under construction were soon added to the specialised *Staffel*, which was completed by the addition of three large Lufthansa Blohm & Voss Ha 139 floatplanes named *Nordmeer*, *Nordwind* and *Nordstern*, and two smaller Dornier Do 24s. The catapult ship *Friesenland* was used for the operation of the Ha 139s, docked in Travemünde and made ready for exercises in January 1940. While the *Staffel* was still in its gestation, its personnel were subject to posting to units already in combat, aircraft commander/observer *Hptm.* Rücker being ordered by *F.d.Luft* to transfer to KG 26 on 10 January, leaving only a single observer officer on strength until the arrival of Kriegsmarine *Oblt.z.S.* Heinz Witt, though Witt was qualified as an observer and not as an aircraft commander. Buddenbrock subsequently complained to *Generalmajor* Hans Ritter as *Gen.d.Lw.Ob.d.M.*, asking how the *Transozeanstaffel* was to reach operational readiness with such a shortage of observer commanders.

In reality, none of the *Transozeanstaffel* aircraft would be combat ready for several months, as they were being adapted from civilian to military use with the assistance of engineers from Dornier and Blohm & Voss. This entailed the fitting of machine guns, bomb-carrying gear and accompanying ballast to the erstwhile civilian aircraft, which was not without its difficulties. Not until February 1940 did *MGK West* request their immediate despatch to the covert German naval base inside Soviet Russia, Basis Nord, for the purpose of North Atlantic reconnaissance. The small Kriegsmarine outpost had been established at the small fishing port of Zapadnaya Litza, 120km west of Murmansk in the Motovsky Gulf. However, the aircraft were deemed unready, as trials were ongoing to establish the operational radii available to the various aircraft using the less fuel-economical water take-offs necessitated by the rather primitive facilities at the Soviet port. The results were disappointing. Naval command estimated that the 'range for Ha 139 aeroplanes is 2,500km, for Do 26 aeroplanes 3,000km, i.e. just barely enough for the flight from North Base to Germany'. The *MGK* request was subsequently refused, and Buddenbrock's *Staffel* would not see action until April 1940, during the invasion of Norway.

Meanwhile, in October 1939, the dislocation of naval air units caused by transfer of individual *Staffeln* from east to west as Poland approached collapse prompted a wholesale reorganisation of the *Küstenfliegergruppen*, most individual *Staffeln* being renumbered while *Küstenfliegergruppe* 306 was disbanded and two entirely new *Gruppen* formed. While **Küstenfliegergruppe 106** remained unchanged, the following exhaustive reorganisation took place:

Kü.Fl.Gr. 306 was disbanded.
Stab/Kü.Fl.Gr. 306 became Stab/Kü.Fl.Gr. 406;
1./Kü.Fl.Gr. 306 became 3./Kü.Fl.Gr. 806;
2./Kü.Fl.Gr. 306 became the core of 3./Kü.Fl.Gr. 406, with some men and equipment distributed elsewhere as reinforcements.
Kü.Fl.Gr. 406 was reorganised:

Stab became Stab/Kü.Fl.Gr. 506, replaced by former Stab/Kü.Fl.Gr. 306;
1./Kü.Fl.Gr. 406 became 1./Kü.Fl.Gr. 506, replaced by former 2./Kü.Fl.Gr. 506;
3./Kü.Fl.Gr. 406 became 3./Kü.Fl.Gr. 506, replaced by 2./Kü.Fl.Gr. 306.

Kü.Fl.Gr. 506 was reorganised:
Stab/Kü.Fl.Gr. 506 became Stab/Kü.Fl.Gr. 806, replaced by former Stab/Kü.Fl.Gr. 406;
1./Kü.Fl.Gr. 506 became 1./Kü.Fl.Gr. 806, replaced by former 1./Kü.Fl.Gr. 406;
2./Kü.Fl.Gr. 506 became 1./Kü.Fl.Gr. 406, replaced by new *Staffel*, 2./Kü.Fl.Gr. 506;
3./Kü.Fl.Gr. 506 was disbanded, replaced by renumbered 3./Kü.Fl.Gr. 406.

Kü.Fl.Gr. 606, consisting solely of 2./Kü.Fl.Gr. 606, was disbanded when 2./Kü.Fl.Gr. 606 was redesignated 2./Kü.Fl.Gr. 906. However, the decision was taken on 1 November to re-form the *Küstenfliegergruppe* with three *Staffeln* raised from scratch: 1./Kü.Fl.Gr. 606, 2./Kü.Fl.Gr. 606 and 3./Kü.Fl.Gr. 606, plus Stab/Kü.Fl.Gr. 606. However, although this unit was originally destined for purely maritime operations and equipped with seaplanes, a fresh caveat was placed upon Kü.Fl.Gr. 606, requiring that it be re-equipped with Dornier Do 17 bombers with land undercarriages. Under the command of *Obstlt.* Hermann Edert, the new squadrons would be considered a land-based *Kampfgruppe*; a standard bomber formation. A single bomber of 1./Kü.Fl.Gr. 606, 7T+CH, was kept in readiness at all times for maritime operations, the remainder eventually alternating between land and sea missions, though the latter became less prevalent with each passing week once the *Küstenfliegergruppe* was operational.

Kü.Fl.Gr. 706 was disbanded:
Stab/Kü.Fl.Gr. 706 became Stab/Kü.Fl.Gr. 906;
1./Kü.Fl.Gr. 706 became 1./Kü.Fl.Gr. 906;
3./Kü.Fl.Gr. 706 became 3./Kü.Fl.Gr. 906. Not until 1 January 1940 did Kü.Fl.Gr. 706 begin to re-form, 1./Kü.Fl.Gr. 706 being created in Kiel-Holtenau, equipped with He 59s rather than their previous He 60s. In July 1940 Stab/Kü.Fl.Gr. 706 was formed in occupied Stavanger, and 2./Kü.Fl.Gr. 706 following three years later in Tromsø.

Kü.Fl.Gr. 806 was created in Dievenow:

Stab/Kü.Fl.Gr. 806 from former Stab/Kü.Fl.Gr. 506;
1./Kü.Fl.Gr. 806 from former 1./Kü.Fl.Gr. 306;
2./Kü.Fl.Gr. 806 from former 3./Kü.Fl.Gr. 506;
3./Kü.Fl.Gr. 806 built from scratch.
Kü.Fl.Gr. 906 was created in Kamp:
Stab/Kü.Fl.Gr. 906 (in Kamp) from former Stab/Kü.Fl.Gr. 706 (He 60);
1./Kü.Fl.Gr. 906 (in Nest) from former 1./Kü.Fl.Gr. 706 (He 60/He 114);
2./Kü.Fl.Gr. 906 (in Pillau) from former 2./Kü.Fl.Gr. 606 (Do 18);
3./Kü.Fl.Gr. 906 (in Norderney) from former 3./Kü.Fl.Gr. 706 (He 59).

There was no respite from operations while this organisational upheaval was taking place, and the aircraft continued to fly. On 22 October six German destroyers carried out a sortie against merchant shipping in the Skagerrak as part of a general Kriegsmarine initiative to consolidate control of the North Sea approaches to the Baltic. Multiple reconnaissance flights mounted by the naval air arm revealed numerous steam trawlers in the Dogger Bank and Hoofden areas, thought likely to be British or working in conjunction with Allied intelligence-gathering. Channel lights continued to burn brightly along the British coast, as they did in Dutch waters, in addition to the remains of one of the unfortunate He 115s shot down during the botched attack on Convoy FN24 and Seydel's Do 18 drifting twenty miles east of Hartlepool. The destroyers seized two neutrals west of Lindesnes, one Swede and one Finn, carrying contraband to England, while fourteen other neutrals were stopped and released.

However, the reconnaissance demands were stretching the naval air arm to exhaustion. At the end of October *MGK West* flatly informed *SKL* that there were insufficient aircraft available to cover the tasks allocated effectively. Each large-scale operation that was mounted resulted in exhaustion of the available crews, rendering them ineffective on the following days. Only the Do 18 was suitable for long-range missions, the numbers having been reduced by the ten lost during the previous month and the receipt of only three replacement aircraft. The He 115 was increasingly coming into use as a medium-range multipurpose aircraft, but its limitations too had been starkly illustrated by the disastrous raid on Convoy FN24. *Admiral* Saalwachter, in conjunction with *F.d.Luft West*, estimated that a total of 378 naval aircraft would be required to provide the essential operational number of 126 in readiness at any given time. The total available to them at the end of October was listed at eighty-five machines.

The resultant staff conference between the two services served only to see the Reich Air Ministry recommend that three of the twelve multipurpose squadrons either at readiness or forming be transferred to Geisler's X.*Fliegerkorps*. Raeder, of course, rejected the proposal, reminding Göring in a letter of the original agreement of naval air strength reached during the previous spring. Nonetheless, the letter did not better his cause, and naval air strength continued to dwindle through attritional loss and gradual diversion towards standard Luftwaffe use.

Consequently, during the first week of November Raeder's staff issued a fresh directive to *MGK Ost* and *West* (with a copy sent to *Generalmajor* Ritter), in which they outlined the employment of naval air formations during what they termed the 'struggle against Britain'. Bearing in mind the aircraft types available, they ordered concentration on open sea reconnaissance, confining combat missions to anti-submarine actions and opportunistic attacks on small enemy surface vessels. Torpedoes were only to be used in favourable weather conditions that offered 'good tactical possibilities'. Minelaying, too, was only to be undertaken in optimal weather conditions, and only then in close co-operation with X.*Fliegerkorps*.

The German *Luftmine* (LM) mine series, developed by the Kriegsmarine, eventually consisted of five different series of sea mines, designated LMA, LMB, LMC, LMD and LMF. All were influence mines designed primarily for dropping from aircraft by means of large parachutes. Both the LMA and LMB were ground mines, while the remaining three were moored. The LMA mine was developed between 1929 and 1934, though due to its relatively low charge weight (300kg of hexanite) it was not extensively used and manufacture discontinued early in the war. The LMB mine was developed during the same period and was of similar construction, carrying 705kg of hexanite explosive and therefore of slightly larger dimensions.

The LMC mine was an experimental model, development of which started in 1933. A moored mine designed to be laid from aircraft such as the He 59, development was discontinued when it became apparent that the He 59 would not remain in combat operations. The work thus far completed on the LMC was instead transferred to the LMD, which could be laid by any mulitpurpose aircraft. The LMD was intended to have the same general dimensions as the LMB mine, but, once again, development was stopped in 1937 and transferred to the LMF, a cylindrical moored influence mine with a warhead carrying 290kg of hexanite, designed for aircraft use but first deployed by S-boats in 1943. During 1940 the Luftwaffe also began developing aerial mines separate from the Kriegsmarine, ending in the creation of the *Bombenmine* (BM) series.

The minelaying instructions to X.*Fliegerkorps* marked one of the few occasions on which there had been unity in Kriegsmarine and Luftwaffe thinking. At the outbreak of war the *SKL* had wanted to delay the instigation of aerial minelaying until sufficient aircraft and stocks of LMA and LMB mines were available to mount a concerted minelaying offensive that would cause major problems for British countermeasures. However, a review of mine production and availability led naval planners to opt instead for the immediate commencement of aerial minelaying to augment the thick barrages already sown off the English coast in dangerous inshore missions carried out by destroyers, S-boats and U-boats. Despite opposition from the Luftwaffe, who favoured accumulating a larger stockpile before starting minelaying, and thus striking one major blow rather than many smaller ones, the *Küstenflieger* launched their inaugural minelaying missions in November. Instructions were issued that included the use of He 59 aircraft to lay LMA mines between the moles of British harbour entrances.

On 20 November He 59s of 3./Kü.Fl.Gr. 906 laid mines in the Thames Estuary and near Harwich as the start of operations codenamed *Rühe* (Silence). Of the nine aircraft despatched, five turned back because of navigational difficulties, as each mine needing to be dropped precisely where planned. During the nights of 22 and 23 November there was further minelaying, by aircraft of Kü.Fl.Gr. 106 and 906, which dropped them in the Thames River and estuary as well as at Harwich, in the Humber, in the Downs and, in an effort to disrupt supply of the British Expeditionary Force in France, in the approaches to Dunkirk Harbour. Between 20 November and 7 December five missions were flown on which forty-six LMA and twenty-two LMB mines were dropped.

The results were almost immediate. At approximately 2100hrs on 21 November HMS *Gipsy* was sunk while departing Harwich for a North Sea patrol, in company with four other destroyers. A single seaplane had been sighted flying low offshore, but as there was a Short Sunderland seaplane base nearby, no guns were fired. The intruder was finally identified as an He 59 by searchlights from Landguard Fort, but they were ordered to be doused to allow the quick exit of the five destroyers from harbour. Fighters were belatedly scrambled from nearby RAF

Martlesham Heath, but failed to intercept the minelayer, which had dropped two LMAs, and at 2123hrs HMS *Gipsy* detonated one of them, breaking in half and sinking in shallow water, killing twenty-eight men. The destroyer's captain, Lt-Cdr Nigel J. Crossley, died of severe wounds six days later. The steamer SS *Hookwood* was also sunk in the Thames Estuary, near the Tongue light vessel, while travelling from Blyth to Dover on 23 November. Two crewmen were killed.

In fact the magnetic mine offensive had begun to fail as early as 22 November, when an He 115 of 3./Kü.Fl.Gr. 106 was fired upon by an anti-aircraft machine-gun team near Shoeburyness. Evidently startled by the sudden barrage, the Heinkel's crew dropped their LMA mine and hastily departed. The parachute mine landed in the mudflats of the estuary, its descent being observed and the mine pinpointed. The Royal Navy summoned specialists Lt Cdrs John Ouvry and Roger Lewis from HMS *Vernon*, and alongside British Army explosive experts they waded out to the exposed mine that night, and by the following day had defused it. The weapon's secrets were subsequently revealed after close examination ashore, and countermeasures soon put into place which would nullify the advantage given by the magnetic mine. Nonetheless, the fact that British engineers were feverishly working on an answer to the magnetic mine only spurred Raeder to demand yet more vehemently that the Luftwaffe also begin minelaying in earnest before the opportunity passed.

On the night of 5 December several aircraft were lost on minelaying missions. By this stage He 115s of 3./Kü.Fl.Gr. 506 had also joined the operations, and aircraft S4+BL crashed on take-off from Nordeney after the flaps were retracted at insufficient altitude, the aircraft flipping over, destroying its LMA payload and killing the radio operator and observer. Only the pilot, *Uffz*. Rose, was rescued. A second He 115, S4 +EL, was also lost from the *Staffel* while flying across the Wash to Sheringham, when it collided with the Chain Home radio location mast at West Beckham. The stricken Heinkel narrowly missed the Sheringham gasholder and finally crashed on to the beach a short distance from Sheringham lifeboat station at 0315hrs, killing all three crewmen. Two more He 59s were completely written off during that night's operations. The port engine of M2+VL of 3./Kü.Fl.Gr. 106 caught fire shortly after take-off from Borkum and the aircraft crashed, losing its LMB mine at sea, killing three of the crew and leaving gunner *Uffz*. Wolf badly injured, and M2+OL of the same *Staffel* crashed on

Borkum's North Beach and was later found in 4m of water with all four crewmen dead.

A third He 59 made an emergency landing near Schiermonnikoog and was later towed by *Vorpostenboote V801* and *V805* back to Borkum, and another of 3./Kü.Fl.Gr. 906 was damaged by a strongly running swell after making an emergency landing near Ameland. The aircraft was recovered, but suffered further damage to the starboard float during retrieval by the *Seenotschiff Hans Rolshoven*. Preliminary Kriegsmarine investigations established that, other than the collision over Great Britain, the remaining losses and damage were predominantly caused by the inclement weather conditions and the resultant icing, and perhaps also by the overloading of the aircraft necessitated by the mission task. Ice within the seaplane bases had become a major issue, and by 17 December the increasingly severe winter caused all further operations to be cancelled.

Nine days previously, a conference between the Naval Staff and *F.d.Luft West*, *Generalmajor* Coeler, had taken place to review progress of the aerial minelaying. Coeler stated that the He 59 had proved itself 'exceptionally suitable' for such operations, able to carry two LMA or one LMB mine as far as the Downs, River Thames, Dunkirk, Calais and the Humber. The smaller He 115 had also performed well, being capable of carrying a single LMA or LMB mine as far as Southampton. However, in his view the minelaying operations had placed a disproportionately heavy strain on both personnel and material. The necessity of laying mines accurately, the long approach flights, exacting navigation requirements, bad weather conditions, seven to eight hours blind flying at night and frequent heavy overloading of aircraft all demanded the highest crew efficiency.

> The regrettable losses which have occurred lately are mostly due to heavy overloading of the aeroplanes, the difficulties encountered in night take-offs and to weather conditions (icing). British anti-aircraft defence at night has so far only been slight. *F.d.Luft West* believes that use of fighters over the Thames area would be of little use. Balloon barrages, on the other hand, which the British are apparently planning to put up, would be quite a hindrance.[25]

Since accurate navigation was essential for successful minelaying operations, Coeler planned to begin training specialist navigators for the various target areas. In turn, the Naval Staff encouraged Coeler to use 'all available means' to lay mines in English waters as quickly as possible, since it was to be expected that British anti-aircraft and anti-mine defence would only grow stronger. A projected output of 120 newly produced aerial mines was expected for December, although portions of this number were to be held in reserve for Luftwaffe operations in the Firth of Forth and the Clyde, which the Kriegsmarine hoped would take place towards the end of December. For his part, Göring had also pledged to place the training of crews of the operational air force who had been chosen for minelaying operations under Coeler's direct control.

Ironically, it was Coeler's determined drive to undertake aerial minelaying that further reduced the standing of the *Seeluftstreitkräfte* in the eyes of the operational Luftwaffe. With minelaying seaplanes grounded by bad weather, only land-based aircraft were capable of continuing the fight. Subsequently, in January 1940, Göring ordered Coeler to 'take all necessary steps' to develop aerial minelaying by the operational Luftwaffe. The Luftwaffe had long harboured misgivings about naval air units conducting minelaying, seeing it as their sole prerogative. Correspondingly, alongside the production of LMA and LMB mines, aircraft specifically adapted for minelaying were also to be built: the first *Gruppe* of He 111H-4s was to be operational by March, followed shortly thereafter by a second, and there were future plans for the use of Do 217s, Ju 88s, Fw 200s and He 177s.

On 17 January, following renewed and protracted negotiations with the Luftwaffe, General Staff *SKL* recorded a lengthy War Diary entry entitled 'Promotion and further development of aerial mining'.

> In this special province the *F.d.Luft West* is placed directly under the Commander-in-Chief, Luftwaffe, to make suggestions with regard to the further development of the apparatus as well as the training of the specialised personnel, and in so doing work in direct conjunction with the offices concerned belonging to the Luftwaffe General Staff. Within the scope of this special assignment, *F.d.Luft West* has under his command;
>
> 1, 7. *Staffel*, KG 26
>
> 2. one *Staffel* of I. *Gruppe*, KG 30
>
> 3 (later, after formation) 1. *Staffel*, KG 40.

(At present as experimental and training formations, at the same time to clear up undecided questions with regard to aerial mine warfare.)

A course for aerial minelaying personnel is being arranged at the Luftwaffe Ordnance School (Naval Air) at Dievenow. Three minelaying bomber wings are to be formed later. The Naval Staff welcomes the concentration of training of the aerial minelaying units under *F.d.Luft West*, whose <u>main</u> tasks — maritime reconnaissance, occasional bombing of naval targets, aerial mine warfare against short-range targets, and operations against merchant shipping — must remain unaffected by the assumption of the new duty and be ensured by suitable arrangements.

The Air Force General attached to Commander in Chief, Navy, considers that <u>no</u> weakening of the naval air formations in favour of the aerial minelaying formations is to be expected. Effects on personnel are at present slight, so that <u>no</u> detrimental effects of any consequence to the personnel situation are to be feared.

Marinegruppenkommando West, too, welcomes the fact that *F.d.Luft West* has been entrusted with the formation and training of the minelaying squadrons because of his experience, and considers this command the best guarantee that these formations will operate in close conjunction with *MGK West* and will participate in other naval operations. Three commands will have to co-operate in the future conduct of air operations against Great Britain:

<u>F.d.Luft West</u>: maritime reconnaissance and occasional bombing of naval targets, attacks on merchant shipping, aerial mine warfare against short-range targets;

<u>X.Fliegerkorps</u>: bombing of naval forces at sea and in port, also harbour installations, attacks on merchant shipping;

<u>Minelaying Air Corps</u>: Aerial mine warfare along the entire coast of Great Britain and in her harbours.

Marinegruppenkommando West in so doing draws special attention to the fact that mine warfare by air and surface forces is the same, and that minelaying operations by naval forces must be kept up continuously and carefully synchronised. They consider the appointment of a General, Luftwaffe, to *MGK West* as the representative of the Commander-in-Chief, Luftwaffe, a serviceable solution to the question of close co-operation; he will direct the operations of the X.*Fliegerkorps* and Aerial Minelaying Corps on behalf of the Commander-in-Chief, Luftwaffe after adjusting them to the requirements of naval warfare by issuing operational instructions.

Reorganisation of the Staff of the Commander, Naval Air, has already commenced, with a view to such an organisation. The Commander, Naval Air's former Chief of Staff, *Oberst.* [Hans-Arnim] Czech, takes over the minelaying formations, *Oberstleutnant* [Hans] Geisse will take over the duties of the latter. The Naval Staff considers that it is quite a feasible proposition to carry out the organisation as suggested by *MGK West*. With regard to operations by aerial minelaying formations, *MGK West* takes the view — in fundamental agreement with Naval Staff — that mine warfare carried out by air forces off the more distant coasts of England, especially on the west and south-west coasts, should not be commenced until it can be done suddenly, simultaneously and on a large scale, since by this means, the greatest — and in conjunction with the other means of naval warfare perhaps even decisive — effect, can be attained.

In the Group's opinion, aerial minelaying operations should be limited to the area formerly considered, perhaps extended to the east coast from Dover to Newcastle, until the aeroplanes and aerial mines necessary for the large-scale operation are ready.

It is not yet possible to give a final verdict on the question of whether it was correct to use the aerial mine for the first time as early as November 1939, i.e. at a moment before a sufficiently large number of mines and mine-carrying aeroplanes were available. The fact remains that the aerial mine was used on the south-east coast of England and that its existence thereby became known to the enemy. Patrol flights and defensive patrols, attacks on our airfields, preparation of fighter formations, and erection of numerous balloon barrages on the east coast clearly show that the enemy is conscious of the danger threatening him and has resolved on large-scale countermeasures.

Naval Staff, in agreement with *MGK West*, considers that, since the dropping of mines from aeroplanes on the east coast has been begun and detected by the enemy, we should now continue this with all the means at our disposal, following up our former objective in the conduct of offensive mine warfare in the North Sea, namely that of making the east coast of England and its ports impassable until any merchant traffic is completely suspended.

Conditions on the west coast of England are different. Although the enemy must also be expecting the dropping of mines from aeroplanes in this area, he will probably — in the endeavour to protect the east coast ports which are particularly endangered and at the same time to protect the interior from air raids — first build up his main line of defence on the east coast with fighters, searchlights, anti-aircraft batteries and balloon barrages. He will not set to work on the effective defence of the west coast until the east has been protected, possibly not even until the western ports are actually threatened with attacks by aerial mines.

Under these circumstances it seems best to leave the aerial mining of the west coast and its important ports and bays until a moment when the stock of mines and the number of suitable mine-carrying aeroplanes will enable the execution of a large-scale minelaying offensive or continuous minelaying operations on the enemy west coast.

By the beginning of February the Luftwaffe's minelaying specialty unit had been expanded, and Coeler was ordered to create 9.*Fliegerdivision*, *Oberst* Czech being appointed his Chief of Staff and Operations Officer. Operationally subordinated to the *Oberbefehlshaber der Luftwaffe* (*Ob.d.L.*), and administratively to *Luftflotte* 2, the new unit was charged with responsibility for all future aerial minelaying, and comprised all of KG 4, *Gruppe* III./KG 26, *Staffel* 7./KG 26, I./KG 30 and *Gruppe* I./KG 40. Before long, 3./Kü.Fl.Gr. 106 was requested to be transferred to Coeler's new command. Raeder refused, citing operational necessity, but in the end only managed to retain temporary control of *Küstenfliegergruppe* 106.

Meanwhile, the onset of winter and a steady drain of casualties forced Coeler to suspend minelaying activities by the *Küstenflieger*, and the last mission of 1939 was completed on 17 December. During the following weeks Göring used his privileged position within Hitler's inner circle to persuade his Führer to appoint the operational Luftwaffe as the

Gruppenkommandeur I/KG 30, *Major* Fritz Doench (right) and two of his pilots photographed in March 1940.

sole aerial minelaying agency. Despite Raeder informing Hitler of the Kriegsmarine's viewpoint on the matter, and imminent minelaying plans on 23 February — issuing orders to *MGK West* that day to resume minelaying by the formations with *Küstenflieger* units 'as it sees fit' on the assumption of the Führer's agreement — Hitler ordered all naval aircraft minelaying to cease in a memorandum to *SKL* just three days later, the task henceforth being removed from the Kriegsmarine's sphere of activity. Göring's machinations had borne fruit, although Hitler was once more swayed to change his mind by Raeder in conference during early March, following British press announcements that they had developed a successful countermeasure to the magnetic mine. With the support of Jodl as *OKW* Chief of Staff, Raeder pointed out that mine production was steadily increasing, allowing immediate commencement of a fresh aerial minelaying offensive. He was adamant that swift action was necessary before such countermeasures could be widely introduced.

Naval enquiries to the Luftwaffe Chief of Staff showed that, as of 15 March, ten He 111H-4 aircraft were ready for minelaying use, this number expected to increase to twenty-five within ten days and thirty-one by the beginning of April, thus equipping an entire *Gruppe*. A total of fourteen Ju 88s of the 'Storp' *Staffel* (1./KG 30) would be brought up to *Gruppe* strength during the first half of April, rendering two complete *Gruppen* in readiness as mine-carriers. By 1 May the 9.*Fliegerdivision* would have three mine-carrier groups (two groups of He 111H-4 and one group of Ju 88s). In the meantime, three *Staffeln* were available for immediate mining operations: *Hptm.* Gerd Stein's He 111-equipped 7./KG 26 (Stein was the former commander of 3./Kü.Fl.Gr. 906), *Oblt.* Walter Storp's Ju 88s of 8./KG 4 (Storp having transferred from KG 30 and begun training his *Staffel* for minelaying at the beginning of March), and the He 115s of 3./Kü.Fl.Gr. 506. Despite disagreements between

Generalmajor Joachim Coeler, *F.d.Luft West* and commander of 9.*Fliegerdivision*.

OKM and the Reich Air Ministry regarding the efficacy of the magnetic mines themselves, by mid-March there was a stock of 268 LMA and 286 LMB mines, each total expected to increase by a further 350 by the end of April.

Between 2 April and the German attack on the Low Countries and France on 10 May 1940, six minelaying missions were mounted off south-eastern England and the French Channel ports in conjunction with (and under the control of) Coeler's 9.*Fliegerdivision*. In total, 188 mines were laid, though they accounted for a meagre seven ships sunk, totalling 14,564 tons. Ultimately, Felmy's original vision of a concerted lethal campaign using huge numbers of mines had been undermined by Raeder's determination to use available stocks as quickly as possible and, while the *Küstenflieger* had been originally tasked with continuing minelaying in advance of the ground assault in the west, on 12 March the task was once again made the sole domain of Coeler's forces by order of Göring himself.

Away from the problems of jurisdiction over aerial minelaying, in conference with *F.d.Luft West*, *SKL* had also pressed for the commencement of aerial torpedo missions to provide operational experience for crews, particularly during bright, clear nights. Coeler requested that the relevant instructions be issued, and on 9 November 1939 *SKL* delivered a directive that all naval air force units be permitted full use of weapons against darkened ships sighted west of longtitude 3°E, proposing night patrols by torpedo-carrying aircraft on particularly bright nights. The aircraft of X. *Fliegerkorps*, on the other hand, were only permitted (from January 1940) to attack darkened vessels within 30 miles of the British coast, owing to what the Kriegsmarine perceived as their inferior maritime navigational training and potential confusion of targets.

Despite the loosening of *Küstenflieger* constraints on torpedo use, there were few successes with this temperamental weapon, the first being on 18 December, when an He 59 of 3./Kü.Fl.Gr. 706 torpedoed and sank the 185-ton steam trawler *Active* off Rattray Head. The vessel's cook, George Watt, was killed in the sinking, which marked the first successful use of an aerial torpedo in the Second World War. Twice during early November He 59s had scrambled to intercept enemy destroyers; the first time failing to make contact, and on the second launching a single torpedo which completely missed its target. During the morning attack, approximately 70 miles east of Lowestoft, the He 59 released a torpedo at the Polish destroyer *Blyskawika* from a range of 1,000 yards off its port

The wreck of the Heinkel He 111 1H+JA of Stab./KG 26 shot down near Humbie, Scotland, on 28 October 1939; the first German aircraft to be brought down on mainland Britain since the war had begun. *Leutnant* Adolf Hiehoff (observer) and *Uffz*. Kurt Lehmkuhl (pilot) were captured, the latter wounded in the back by two bullets from pursuing Spitfires. Both *Uffz*. Gottlieb Kowalke (flight engineer) and *Gefr*. Bruno Reimann (wireless operator) were killed.

bow. The torpedo track was visible to lookouts, and was avoided by course alteration as anti-aircraft guns opened fire, driving the slow-moving seaplanes away. Following this failure and the obvious shortcomings of the F5 weapon, Hitler ordered production stopped as of 28 November, until improvements could be made. A stock of seventy-six F5 torpedoes remained, while modifications were tested to improve performance and also allow their use by the faster He 115s.

During November, *Küstenflieger* losses mounted steadily through enemy action, accidents, mechanical failure and at least one incident of friendly fire, in which a Bf 110 damaged a Do 18 of 2./Kü.Fl.Gr. 906 returning from patrol and misidentified as British. Although there were no casualties the Dornier was compelled to make a forced alighting, later being recovered by the ship *Hans Rolshoven* and repaired. On 29

November *SKL* recorded in its War Diary a 'black day for the Naval Air Force', with five of the seventeen Do 18 reconnaissance aircraft shadowing light naval forces and a convoy in the Shetland-Bergen passage lost. All five belonged to *Küstenfliegergruppe* 406. Two were shot down by British aircraft, both crews being rescued and interned in Norway, and a third was also interned after coming down with engine failure near Mandel, Norway. The fourth was forced to alight near the Faeroes after losing a propeller in stormy weather; all four men were rescued by the Danish coastguard vessel *Islands Falk* and interned. The final Dornier crashed into the sand dunes at Hörnum in darkness, killing all on board. Two Do 18s of 2./Kü.Fl.Gr. 106 were also badly damaged that same day after colliding in the darkness.

On Christmas Eve Raeder approved the despatch of a teletype to Luftwaffe command regarding the operational readiness of the Naval Air Arm. Within its text he urged the upgrading of the *Küstenfliegergruppen*, and stressed the potential unsuitability of the obsolete Heinkel He 111J undergoing trials for maritime operations. One had been written-off at Kamp after failure of the starboard engine immediately following take-off on 27 November, a second at Dievenow on 14 December, and a third had crashed on 5 January.

> 1. The freezing of the naval air bases on the North Sea coast makes sea reconnaissance over the main theatre of war impossible. Land-based groups (Kü.Fl.Gr. 806 with He 111J aeroplanes) cannot be used as substitutes, since these aeroplanes are so antiquated they cannot be made serviceable in less than three months. The Air Force General attached to the Commander-in-Chief, Navy, reported that use of the He 111J aeroplanes for operations over the North Sea cannot be endorsed owing to technical deficiencies.
>
> 2. Immediate replacement of the He 111J aeroplanes of Kü.Fl.Gr. 806 with He 111H or P aeroplanes, later on with Ju 88s, is imperative, since otherwise the tasks set by the Führer cannot be carried out. This request is not based on the limited ice period, but mainly on the need to increase the fighting power and speed of our naval reconnaissance aeroplanes.
>
> The He 115 and Do 18 are in every respect inferior to all British types of aeroplanes which have so far been encountered over the sea (Blenheims, Wellingtons).[26]

The Dornier Do 26 flying boat 'Seeadler' during its pre-war service with Lufthansa; one of the civilian aircraft impressed into the Luftwaffe to form the *Transozeanstaffel*, commanded by *Major* Friedrich von Buddenbrock. Flying overhead is a Dornier Do 18.

As if to underline his second point, Do 18 8L+CK of 2./Kü.Fl.Gr. 906 was shot down on 27 December by a patrolling Hudson of 220 Sqn, making an emergency descent on to the sea. *Hptgfr.* Josef Reitz was killed by the Hudson's gunfire. Aircraft commander *Lt.z.S.* Dietrich Steinhart, *Hptfw.* Schmidt and *Uffz.* Czech were all rescued by the Swedish steamer *Boden* and landed in Gothenburg, where they were interned until January 1940. Theirs was the final loss suffered by the naval air units in 1939.

At sea, aircraft of the *Bordflieger Staffel* had also suffered casualties. Three Arados had been damaged aboard *Gneisenau*; one by mishandling while being hoisted aboard after descent, two others by storms encountered on 29 November after sailing in company with sister ship *Scharnhorst*, the light cruiser *Köln* and nine destroyers to patrol the area between Iceland and the Faeroe Islands. The *Gneisenau* group was intended to draw enemy forces away from pursuit of the 'pocket battleship' *Admiral Graf Spee*, which was under increasing Royal Navy pressure while on its successful Atlantic raiding voyage. The group encountered the British auxiliary cruiser HMS *Rawalpindi* which, hopelessly outgunned, bravely turned to fight and was sunk in forty minutes. However, both German battleships suffered the effect of heavy seas and high winds while returning to Germany, all three Arados carried aboard *Scharnhorst* being considerably damaged.

The object of the Royal Navy's attention far to the south, the *Admiral Graf Spee*, had been on a commerce-raiding mission since the outbreak of war, having departed Germany on 21 August. Under strict instructions to avoid combat with enemy naval units, *Kapitän zur See* Hans Langsdorff had used his single Arado Ar 196A-1 seaplane to advantage, finding targets and also successfully avoiding enemy warships by the use of highly effective aerial reconnaissance. Commanded by *Oblt.z.S.* Detlef Spiering and flown by *Flugzeugführer Uffz.* Heinrich Bongards, the aircraft suffered a cracked engine block following a reconnaissance flight on 6 October and was inoperative for several days while the five on-board support personnel fitted a spare engine.

The difficulties of operating a catapult aircraft at sea were many, enemy interference being the least of the aircrew's concerns. If, once aloft, on-board navigation in the vast expanses of the ocean was imprecise, any planned return rendezvous of ship and aircraft could be foiled, leaving the aircraft stranded. Even once contact had been re-established, all but the calmest sea rendered floatplane alightings difficult. *Oberleutnant* Helmut Mahlke was observer aboard the He 60 floatplane of 1./BFl.Gr. 196 carried aboard the 'pocket battleship' *Admiral Scheer* during its 1938 voyage into the Mediterranean, his pilot being *Lt.* Köder.

> In order to put down safely we usually had to ask the *Scheer* for the 'duck-pond.' This she would produce by performing a sharp 30-degree turn to port; the turbulence of her wake would smother the heavy swell to create a relatively calm patch of water within her turning circle. And if the duck-pond wasn't sufficient, we had to resort to the landing mat. As its name suggests, the landing mat was just that: a small rectangular

mat of reinforced canvas that would be paid out from a swinging boom on the port side of the ship forward, and streamed on the surface of the water close alongside. For a pilot, landing on the mat was the ultimate test. It was so narrow that he could not afford to be more than a metre off the centreline if the aircraft was to be recovered intact. A few more centimetres to the right and the starboard wingtip would be smashed against the side of the ship. A few more centimetres to the left and the port float would miss the landing mat and the machine might be lost altogether.[27]

Reconnaissance missions by Spiering and Bongards from *Admiral Graf Spee* resumed on 22 October, though the Arado's propeller was damaged soon afterwards while the aircraft was being hoisted back aboard ship. Once repaired, on 9 November, following a further reconnaissance flight, a crack was once again discovered in the engine block at exactly the same place as previously. As there was no second spare engine, the crack was bordered with a steel band and cemented together to enable the aircraft to fly once more, albeit with less than optimal performance. Spiering led the aircraft on further flights before radio failure on 2 December rendered communication with the ship impossible and necessitated an emergency landing at a prearranged rendezvous point. During this touchdown the Arado's port float was damaged, gradually filling with water and threatening to capsize the battered aircraft before Langsdorff's ship arrived to retrieve it. After further repairs, more reconnaissance flights were made until, on 11 December, a succession of hard alightings split the engine block completely, beyond the scope of on-board repair. The aircraft was ordered to be dismantled.

Two days later, on 13 December, the Royal Navy hunting party of HMS *Exeter*, *Ajax* and *Achilles* found *Graf Spee* off the River Plate, Commodore Harwood immediately attacking. Despite heavy damage to the British ships, *Graf Spee* was hit by seventy shells and suffered thirty-six men killed and sixty more injured, including Langsdorff, who was wounded by shell splinters while on the bridge. Pilot *Uffz.* Bongards and mechanic *Ogfr.* Hans-Eduard Sümmerer were both killed during the exchange of fire, and the partly dismantled aircraft was set on fire and completely burnt out.

Within four days the much-storied scuttling of *Admiral Graf Spee* took place in the River Plate estuary, and the remaining members of *Bordfliegerkommando* 1./BFl.Gr. 196 from the heavy cruiser were interned in Argentina. Of those, three successfully returned to Germany by June 1940, including *Oblt.z.S.* Spiering. Following his return, Spiering was transferred to the Luftwaffe, promoted *Hauptmann* on 1 March 1942, and transferred to KG 26, the Luftwaffe's torpedo group. Appointed *Staffelkapitän* to 7./KG 26, he was listed as missing in action after his Ju 88A-4, 1H+AR, was lost during an attack on Allied ships near Syracuse on 27 July 1943.

5

Turning North and West

The Invasion of Norway and Western Europe

THE NORTHERN EUROPEAN WINTER of 1939/1940 was the coldest on record for over one hundred years, caused by arctic air currents from the Siberian interior that lasted from mid-December 1939 through to March 1940. Northern Germany was particularly affected, with record-setting conditions that clogged harbours with thick ice and frequently rendered seaplane bases inoperative. Emphasis was instead placed on the *Küstenflieger*'s few available wheeled aircraft and those of the operational Luftwaffe.

> Air reconnaissance and proposed reconnaissance of lights [minelaying] along the enemy south-east coast had to be abandoned because of the weather. Since air reconnaissance by the Naval Air Force is frequently prejudiced or rendered impossible by ice, X.*Fliegerkorps* has already taken over as much of the air reconnaissance over the North Sea as possible. The previous tacit agreement on this was expressly confirmed by the Commander-in-Chief, Air Force, in the following tele print:
>
> Until further notice X.*Fliegerkorps* will, in direct agreement with Naval Group Command West, take over as many reconnaissance assignments over the North Sea as possible, if Commander-in-Chief, Navy's reconnaissance forces are not adequate. X.*Fliegerkorps* will make the decisions regarding Operations.[1]

The conversion of *Küstenfliegergruppe* 806 to the Heinkel He 111J continued to be fraught with difficulties, as the type was plagued with problems, particularly regarding its inefficient powerplant. Four were lost or severely damaged due to engine failure between 27 January and 8 April 1940, and another two collided after landing, while taxiing to their dispersal areas. By the beginning of February the conversion period had been completed and twelve aircraft were declared operational at Sagan-Küpper, and another twenty at Kiel-Holtenau, five machines being held in reserve at Nordhausen. However, towards the end of the previous year the obvious shortcomings of the obsolete Heinkel had prompted both 1./Kü.Fl.Gr. 806 and 3./Kü.Fl.Gr. 806 to continue using He 59s, He 60s and He 114s when possible, alongside the landplane bombers, to enable both operational missions and training to continue amidst repetitive breakdowns and malfunctions. With 2./Kü.Fl.Gr. 806 temporarily attached to the staff of *Küstenfliegergruppe* 906 for Heinkel He 111 conversion (and its place taken by 1./Kü.Fl.Gr. 906), those crews still operational continued to mount patrols over the Skagerrak and North Sea, hunting for enemy submarines and intercepting merchant ships with a Prize Crew carried aboard the He 59s. On the last day of December 1939 the strength of *Küstenfliegergruppe* 806 was reported by *F.d.Luft Ost* as:

- 1./Kü.Fl.Gr. 806: five crews operationally ready; two He 111s and one W 34 in service; ten He 111s and one W 34 out of service.
- 3./Kü.Fl.Gr. 806: eight crews operational, including two trained in blind flying; four He 60s, two He 114s, six He 111s and one W 34 in service; one He 114, four He 111s and one W 34 out of service.
- (Attached) 1./Kü.Fl.Gr. 906: nine operational crews; three He 60s, three He 114s, five He 59s and two W 34 in service; one He 60, one He 114 and four He 59s out of service.

The small Junkers W 34 was a single-engine passenger and transport aircraft developed during the 1920s, and thereafter used as a training aircraft or pushed into active service as a stop-gap measure, armed with ventral and dorsal machine guns and capable of carrying six 50kg bombs. It was used in both training and combat roles by the *Küstenfliegergruppe*, though as early as December 1939 it was decided that no responsible command could assign the type to maritime operations. Nevertheless, it remained a useful training aircraft, although not without peril, as on 30 January, when the W 34L TY+HL of 3./Kü.Fl.Gr. 806, involved in blind-flying exercises at Holtenau, crashed from a height of only 20m after the engine had been insufficiently warmed-up before take-off. Pilot *Obfw.* Murswiek and *Uffz.* Helmut Niklas were killed, and another pilot in training, *Uffz.* Emil Podstufka, and wireless operator *Ogfr.* Karl-Rudolf Holz were both severely injured and later succumbed to their wounds.

In the meantime, the conversion of *Küstenfliegergruppe* 606 to the Dornier Do 17 proceeded more smoothly, though presumed pilot error caused the loss of *Uffz.* Georg Lindauer's aircraft only 400m from the beach at Deep after it crashed into the sea during exercises, killing the entire crew. Flying practice also caused the loss of *Scharnhorst*'s 1./ BFl.Gr. 196 Ar 196A-2 T3+NH, flown by pilot *Uffz.* Hans Ritter and commanded by observer *Lt.z.S.* Heinz-Paul Steudel. Ritter crashed while performing a low-altitude turn in the Schillig Roads off Wilhelmshaven, and the aircraft immediately submerged, killing both men. Their bodies were recovered by a vessel of the Wilhelmshaven *Hafenschutzflottille* and later returned to *Scharnhorst*.

> The *Staffel* provided a final escort for the two dead before they were transferred to their home towns. Three officers and one NCO attended the funerals.[2]

The Arado wreck was subsequently located by *Hafenschutzflottille* vessels using mine-detection equipment, recovered by crane and taken ashore by the tug *Hermes* for its valuable metals to be salvaged. The destroyed Arado had originally joined *Scharnhorst* on 13 February 1940, as one of two Ar 196s, T3+HH and T3+NH, accompanied by a total of three crews attached the battleship's complement who came aboard the next day. *Staffelkapitän Hptm.* Gerrit Wiegmink transferred to the battleship as senior flight officer, while the three crew commanders/observers were naval officers: *Oblt.z.S.* Jürgen Quaet-Faslem, *Oblt.z.S.* Peter Schrewe and *Lt.z.S.* Steudel. Quaet-Faslem had joined the *Reichsmarine* in the late 1920s, serving in the naval air arm since his days as a *Fähnrich*. In 1942 he would transfer to the U-boat service and later command U_{595}, which was sunk on its maiden patrol on 14 November 1942. Captured by the United States Navy, Quaet-Faslem was described as 'among the less pleasant of the U-boat captains so far encountered. He was bitter, taciturn, and barely civil, and the hatred in his eyes was apparent to all who talked to him.'[3] Peter Schrewe had also enlisted in the *Reichsmarine*, though in April 1934 as an officer cadet. He too transferred to U-boats in 1942, being in command of U_{537} when it was sunk with all hands in the Java Sea on 10 November 1944. All three pilots, *Obfw.* Kroll, *Uffz.* Hans Ritter and *Uffz.* Ludwig, were Luftwaffe personnel, as were the seven technical support crew.

Following the death of Steudel and Ritter, replacement aircraft T3+KH was brought aboard *Scharnhorst* on 11 March, crewmen *Lt.z.S.* Ernst-Joachim von Kuhlberg and *Oblt.* Gerhard Schreck following within a fortnight.

A rather fanciful German war artist's impression of Dornier Do 17 bombers over British shipping near Dover. *Küstenfliegergruppe* 606 re-equipped with these wheeled bombers in late 1939, considered a land-based '*Kampfgruppe*' thereafter.

As new Ar 196A-2s were taken on strength with the *Bordfliegerstaffel* during March 1940, its last He 42, Sd+CC, and last three Ar 196A-1s were taken out of service, while the Staff took control of small W 34 BB+MR from *F.d.Luft* purely for transportation purposes. The shore-based aircraft of the *Bordfliegerstaffel* flew periodic reconnaissance and ASW missions from Wilhelmshaven, as well as intercepting encroaching RAF Blenheims as they probed German defences along the North Sea coast, where the bombers of Geisler's X.*Fliegerkorps* continued to mount harassing attacks on merchant shipping.

Increasing numbers of fast Ju 88s had been declared operational with KG 30, a second operational *Gruppe* having been formed around a cadre taken from the Ju 88 training unit (*Lehrgruppe* 88) and declared operational early in December 1939, and III./KG 30 following during January in the same fashion. A newly established *Geschwaderstab* under the command of *Obstlt*. Walter Loebel (previously the commander of I./KG 26), brought KG 30 to its full complement and parity with

Heinkel-equipped KG 26. Henceforth, Geisler ordered the Heinkels of the '*Löwen*' *Geschwader* KG 26 to concentrate their efforts primarily on merchant shipping, leaving the Ju 88s of the '*Adler*' *Geschwader* to attack the Royal Navy. During February a new unit designated *Kampfgruppe* 126 (KGr.126) was established from III./KG 26, under the command of former *Küstenflieger Hptm.* Gerd Stein; charged with minelaying while simultaneously conducting operational tests of the Heinkel He 111 bomber in the role of torpedo carrier.[4]

Although weather conditions frequently curtailed flying, sporadic operations were still mounted, resulting in steady casualties both among merchant shipping targets and the maritime bombers themselves. As the Royal Navy's Home Fleet had now temporarily abandoned Scapa Flow for the distant anchorage of Loch Ewe, Luftwaffe maritime strike forces switched their attention to shipping off the Scottish coast.

On 9 January armed reconnaissance was carried out between the Thames and Kinnaird Head, and over the course of the day aircraft successfully attacked unescorted merchant shipping. The 689-ton steamer SS *Gowrie* was sunk four miles east of Stonehaven, all crewmen being rescued, followed by the 1,985-ton SS *Oakgrove* twelve miles SE by E of the Cromer Knoll Light Vessel, sending 2,900 tons of iron ore to the bottom and killing its Master, William Duke Falconer.[5] The 1,103-ton coastal freighter SS *Upminster* was also severely damaged further south, off Cromer, sinking the next day. Master Alfred Hunter, Able Seaman James Stubbs and Able Seaman William Robertson Young were all killed. Survivors described how the two Luftwaffe aircraft 'swooped down and attacked us first with machine guns and then with bombs'.[6] The British cargo ships SS *Northwood* and SS *Reculver*, the trawler *Chrysolite* and the Danish steamers SS *Ivan Kondrup* and *Feddy* were also damaged by further attacks along the east-coast shipping lanes. Misty weather prevented RAF fighter defences from establishing contact with the German bombers, though *Fw.* F. Pfeiffer's Ju 88 of 2./KG 30 came down near Sylt after being hit by anti-aircraft fire.

In Berlin, Raeder's staff were enthusiastic about the attacks against merchant shipping off the British coast, reasoning that they were 'highly suited for the intimidation of enemy and neutral ships alike', particularly when mounted in conjunction with ongoing minelaying. Throughout January X.*Fliegerkorps* continued its operations along the east coast, and harvested a grim tally of ships sunk or damaged, both in convoy and sailing independently. Attacks against Scapa Flow were less successful in the face of heavy anti-aircraft defences, and hampered in at least one case the icing of a Ju 88's bombsight during an attempted dive-bombing attack. However, the enthusiasm among Kriegsmarine officers was noticeably lacking among their Luftwaffe counterparts, who considered the assault on mainland Britain to be their highest priority.

> The Naval Staff attaches great significance to these most gratifying successes on the part of the Air Force and considers operations by X.*Fliegerkorps* in support of naval warfare as often as possible of great importance. Since the Luftwaffe itself seems to attach little value to the results obtained, the Luftwaffe General Staff is being informed of the Naval Staff's opinion.[7]

The Luftwaffe had ample reason to share the Kriegsmarine's gratification at the results of the anti-shipping missions mounted in the North Sea. On the other side of the hill, RAF Fighter Command was feeling overstretched and unable to keep pace with the demands placed upon it for protection of merchant shipping along Britain's east coast. Air Chief Marshal Sir Hugh Dowding considered that the primary responsibility of Fighter Command was the protection of aircraft factories and London against the threat of massed bomber attacks. He believed that the protection of mercantile traffic at sea lay within Coastal Command's sphere of responsibility, although he had willingly included four planned fighter squadrons allocated to Trade Defence, yet they were not scheduled to begin formation until the financial year beginning April 1940.

Dowding in no way denied the use of his fighters to protect the vulnerable shipping, but he agreed with a joint political memorandum issued by Lord Stanhope and Sir Kingsley Wood during June 1939 that, in the event of war and enemy air attacks on east coast merchant shipping, Fighter Command would be unable to provide effective protection unless the ships were routed close inshore, and even then they considered it unlikely that sufficient warning could be given to launch a successful fighter interception. The existing Radio Direction Finding (RDF) system did not, as yet, detect low-flying bombers, and the likelihood of it providing effective assistance to fighters operating more than five miles offshore was slim. Likewise, aerial defence of the remote anchorage at Scapa Flow remained problematic to Fighter Command, stretching its meagre resources to the absolute limit.

An He 115 dropping an aerial mine. (James Payne)

Dowding was forced to move several squadrons nearer the coast and further from the industrial centres thought likely to be the target of the Luftwaffe before long. Four Fighter Command squadrons under formation, 235, 236, 248 and 254 Sqns, were temporarily transferred to Coastal Command in lieu of the planned Trade Defence units; a situation with which neither Dowding nor his counterpart in Coastal Command, Air Marshal Sir Frederick Bowhill, were particularly pleased, as both wished to retain the squadrons permanently, Dowding as a nucleus for the fixed creation of Trade Defence which he believed was likely to be made solely his responsibility in the near future, and Bowhill for long-range maritime reconnaissance. Nonetheless, the squadrons were equipped with Blenheims and transferred to coastal operational airfields during February 1940. Unfortunately for the protection of merchant shipping, apart from 254 Sqn the remainder were generally used for maritime reconnaissance and escorting naval operations, rather than for their planned purpose.

The harassment of British trawlers by X.*Fliegerkorps* in the North Sea continued, though not without Luftwaffe losses at the hands of

TURNING NORTH AND WEST

Dowding's fighters. On 3 February Heinkels of KG 26 attacked shipping off the north-east coast and faced defensive fire from Royal Navy ships as well as interception by RAF fighters. Heinkel 1H+FM of II./KG 26 was detected by the Danby Beacon Chain Home base on the North Yorkshire Moors at 0903hrs, sixty miles out to sea. Three Hurricanes of 43 Sqn, based at Acklington, intercepted after the Heinkel, commanded by observer *Uffz*. Rudolf 'Rudi' Leushake, had already attacked a trawler. Flight Lieutenant Peter Townsend led the Hurricanes into a fierce counterattack, killing Leushake and damaging the starboard engine. A second attack by Fg Off Patrick Folkes caused further damage and mortally wounded mechanic and ventral gunner *Uffz*. Johann Meyer in the stomach. Further attacks hit wireless operator and dorsal gunner *Uffz*. Karl Missy in the leg, which was later amputated, and forced the Heinkel to crash-land on a snow-covered field, coming to rest near the farm cottages at Bannial Flat Farm, Whitby. It was the first enemy aircraft to crash on English soil. Missy and pilot *Fw.* Hermann Wilms were captured, and had to be protected from an angry mob of locals by being held in the nearby farmhouse until removed under guard for hospital treatment. Theirs was the sixth Heinkel of KG 26 lost to enemy aircraft during 1940, and the eleventh since war had begun.

Two merchant ships were sunk that day; one unidentified vessel east of Farne Islands and the Norwegian SS *Tempo* off St Abbs Head, but for the loss of three Heinkels. As well as Leushake's, aircraft, 1H+HL of 3./KG 26 was shot down by Fg Off John Simpson of Acklington's 43 Sqn while attacking shipping south-east of the Farne Islands, *Lt.* Luther von Bruning and his crew all being killed. Simpson last saw the Heinkel trailing smoke as it disappeared into a bank of sea mist before crashing in Druridge Bay.

Feldwebel Franz Schnee's Heinkel, 1H+GK of 2./KG 26, was also shot down by 43 Sqn, Sgts Frank Carey and Ottewill brought it down it off the Northumberland coast as it attacked a small convoy. Flight mechanic *Uffz*. Willi Wolf was killed by the machine-gun fire and both engines were disabled, forcing pilot *Obfw.* Fritz Wiemer to ditch the He 111 approximately fifteen miles off Tynemouth. It sank in a little over a minute, leaving the crew bobbing in their kapok lifejackets until they were rescued by the trawler *Harlech Castle* and landed in Grimsby. Air gunner *Uffz*. Karl-Ernst Thiede was badly wounded as he was taken aboard, and subsequently died of his injuries. Another crew member suffered a broken leg during the crash. Although the Germans had managed to discard personal papers and the like before being picked up, owing to a major oversight by one of the captured Germans a signals table was found in one of the airmen's pockets, giving wireless frequencies, recognition signals and call signs for use by KG 26.[8]

That same day, three Ju 88s from 2./KG 30 took off from Westerland and attacked ships of the 5th Minesweeping Flotilla operating in the Moray Firth. Under air attack during drifting snow flurries fifteen miles north of Kinnaird Head, HMS *Sphinx* was hit by a single bomb that exploded in the forward structure, causing extensive damage and rapid flooding. HMS *Harrier* attempted to take the minesweeper in tow, but failed due to the deteriorating weather conditions, and *Sphinx* finally capsized. The upturned hull drifted ashore two miles north of Lybster. Fifty-four men had been killed in the first loss of a Fleet Minesweeper during the Second World War. In return, the Ju 88 belonging to the *Staffelkapitän* of 2./KG 30, *Hptm*. Heinz-Wilhelm Rosenthal, was brought down by ground fire.

During late January and early February, German aerial reconnaissance reported the frequent presence of numerous unidentified fishing vessels and apparently neutral ships in the area of the Dogger Bank. Unsure of their purpose or identity, *MGK West* planned to send the 1. *Zerstörerflottille* to launch a surprise stop-and-search operation against what were strongly suspected to be enemy trawlers reporting German shipping and aerial movements. Originally scheduled for the night of 26/27 January, the operation, codenamed *Wikinger*, was postponed owing to adverse weather conditions, and did not begin until 22 February, when *Z16 Friedrich Eckoldt*, flying the pennant of flotilla commander *Fregattenkapitän* Fritz von Berger, *Z4 Richard Beitzen*, *Z13 Erich Koellner*, *Z6 Theodor Riedel*, *Z3 Max Schultz* and *Z1 Leberecht Maass* sailed at midday, carrying additional boarding parties for the searching and possible seizure of suspect vessels. Initially, the Luftwaffe had been asked to provide fighter cover for the departing destroyers, though communication problems resulted in no fighters making an appearance. There were, however, other German aircraft on operations.

During the previous day Geisler's X.*Fliegerkorps* had planned further missions against merchant shipping along Britain's east coast, the Heinkels of KG 26 being ordered to attack any targets of opportunity between the Orkney Islands and Thames estuary. Anything outside of this specific operational region was deemed off-limits for this mission. The morning flights originally scheduled were cancelled owing to bad

TURNING NORTH AND WEST

Luftminen being prepared for loading aboard an He 111.

weather, and the first aircraft did not take off until 1745hrs that evening; two *Staffeln* departing Germany; 4./KG 26 to fly against targets between the Thames and Humber estuaries, and 6./KG 26 to concentrate on shipping further north.

The He 111 bombers of 4./KG 26 left from Neumünster Airfield. Among the first to become airborne was 1H+IM, piloted by *Fw.* Jäger, who took a northerly course until he was over the island of Sylt, where he banked left and followed a heading of 241 degrees out over the dark North Sea. Shortly after 1900hrs Jäger's crew detected a wake on the sea below them, with an indistinct shadow preceding it. Although they did not know it, they had reached the six German destroyers travelling in line-ahead formation to the north-west, producing a bright wake as they ran at high speed along the mine-free passage '*Weg* I', a six-mile-wide gap in the defensive '*Westwall*' minefield that protected the German Bight. The aircraft, in turn, was heard and then sighted by lookouts aboard the leading ship, the *Friedrich Eckoldt*, flying at an altitude of only 500-800m and passing overhead without incident, but failing to show any of the agreed recognition signals dictated by protocol. Although it displayed no hostile intent, the aircraft turned and passed over a second time, still unidentified by the Kriegsmarine sailors below.

Jäger and his observer, *Fm.* Schräpler, were convinced that they had contacted a single freighter, the ship itself at no time being clearly sighted and showing no identification signals even after a second pass, but he remained hesitant to attack as the Heinkel had not yet reached its designated target area. The tension was broken when the second and third ships in line, the *Richard Beitzen* and *Erich Koellner*, fired several 20mm warning shots at the aircraft that they now suspected to be a British reconnaissance flight. Aboard the Heinkel, *Fm.* Döring immediately returned fire using his ventral machine gun. Only at the last moment did lookouts aboard the tail-end ship, the *Max Schultz*, report the aircraft as carrying German markings, but the destroyer's brief and urgent radio message on the communal wavelength was ignored. Aboard the *Max Schultz*, *Oblt.z.S.* Günther Hosemann reported definitely having seen the aircraft's markings, and firmly identified it as German in the flash of the warning shots, though others remained sceptical. At 1943hrs the *Max Schultz* detected the aircraft approaching for a third time from astern, emerging from a cloudbank with the moon directly behind it. A brief radio message was sent: '*Flugzeug ist gesichtet worden in der schwarzen Wolke des Mondes*' (aircraft detected in the black cloud in front of the moon) as Jäger began his bomb run at an altitude of 1,500m, convinced by the gunfire that their target was hostile.

Four bombs were dropped. Two impacted the sea immediately behind the *Leberecht Maass*, the third hit the destroyer between the forward superstructure and funnel, and the fourth missed completely. Although there was no visible smoke or flame, the crippled destroyer slowed and veered to starboard, signalling for assistance from its flotilla-mates, but as other destroyers steered to render aid they were ordered back into formation lest they run on to the flanking German minefields. The lead ship, the *Friedrich Eckoldt*, slowly approached the *Leberecht Maass* to investigate the damage visually as rescue equipment and towing gear were made ready. When it was only 500m away, the still-unidentified aircraft returned for a second bombing run thirteen minutes after its first. Two out of another four bombs hit the damaged destroyer, a huge fireball blowing upwards from the second funnel as the ship was enveloped in thick smoke until the gentle breeze dispersed the choking cloud. Aboard the *Friedrich Eckoldt*, horrified observers saw that the *Leberecht Maass* had been broken in two, both bow and stern jutting out of the water as she sank in 40m of water. Above them, the Heinkel crew broke away and headed west, only at that moment sighting the shapes of accompanying ships below them.

The remaining destroyers steamed slowly towards the wreck and its survivors swimming in the frigid North Sea water. The *Erich Koellner* stopped engines in order to drift toward survivors swimming between the two parts of the wreck, with boats swung out to begin the rescue, along with those lowered from the *Friedrich Eckoldt* and *Richard Beitzen*. Suddenly, at 2004hrs, another huge explosion was observed, lookouts aboard the *Richard Beitzen* confusingly reporting a fresh air attack, though there had been no sighting of aircraft. The *Theodor Riedel*, only 1,000m from the explosion, was heading towards the fireball when its hydrophones detected a submarine contact to starboard, causing fresh confusion among the German destroyers. Fearing a British submarine attack, the *Theodor Riedel* ran down the contact and dropped four depth charges, which exploded too close to the ship's hull and jammed the rudder, causing the ship to run in lazy circles until manual control was established. The remaining destroyers continued their rescue operation until a lookout aboard the *Erich Koellner* also reported a submarine sighting. Flotilla commander Berger ordered all rescue operations to be halted immediately, and for the submarine to be hunted to exhaustion, at that point establishing that the *Max Schultz* was no longer answering

The destroyer *Leberecht Maass*, accidentally sunk by a KG 26 Heinkel due to chronic miscommunication between air and naval units at every command level.

radio calls. The *Erich Koellner* had not even cast off one of her own boats, which was being readied to rescue men from the water. It remained tethered to the destroyer, and was dragged under its stern as it increased speed to engage the 'enemy submarine'. The *Erich Koellner*'s captain then attempted to ram a sighted 'submarine', but it appears to have been the drifting bow of the *Leberecht Maass*. Meanwhile, it seems that the hapless *Max Schultz*, which was stubbornly remaining silent, had had the misfortune to hit a mine recently laid in '*Weg* 1' by the British destroyers HMS *Intrepid* and *Ivanhoe* nearly two weeks previously, though none of this was apparent at the time.[9] Confused and hurried messages from the scene were relayed to *MGK West*, and onwards to *SKL*, where the scale of the disaster began to unfold:

> 2018hrs: 'The *Leberecht Maass* sunk in grid square 6954, lower left quadrant.' (This spot lies on 'Route 1' more than ten miles from our own nearest minefields in the declared area.)
>
> 2050hrs: 'The *Max Schultz* also missing. Probably submarine.'
>
> Group West left it to the Commander's discretion to break off the operation and at 2215hrs informed the flotilla that patrol boat *V803* had been sent to search for survivors. Commander, 1.*Zerstörerflottille*, called off the operation and put in to Wilhelmshaven in the early hours of 23 February. Close investigation should reveal the full facts about the loss of the two destroyers. Pending the result of an examination of '*Weg* 1' for enemy mines, it is at present assumed that both destroyers were torpedoed by an enemy submarine.

However, doubts swiftly followed as to the cause of the two destroyers' loss, as *SKL* recorded later that night, after Jäger had landed and reported sinking a ship fifty kilometres from the actual scene:

> KG 26 reported attacks on the British coast and the following incident:
>
> About 2000hrs spotted armed, darkened steamer of 3,000 to 4,000 tons, course 300°, near Terschelllng Bank. Several attacks were made from 1,300 metres. One hit was scored on the forecastle, two hits amidships, ship caught fire and sank. No further observations due to darkness. Light anti-aircraft and machine-gun fire from the ship.

(Margin note: Is this the sinking of the *Leberecht Maass* and *Max Schultz*?) The attack on a steamer near Terschelllng Bank is most regrettable and contravenes the regulations issued to the Luftwaffe for the conduct of war on merchant shipping. Air attacks at sea are permitted only in a strip thirty miles wide along the British coast. Closer investigation has been ordered.

At 2036hrs Berger ordered the remaining four destroyers to retreat after recovering the boats that had been left for survivors while they hunted an imaginary submarine. However, most survivors had died of hypothermia in the freezing water during the 25-minute chase of the phantom submarine. Only sixty of the 330 crew members of the *Leberecht Maass* were rescued, and none of the 308 men from the *Max Schultz*. A single man was also posted as missing from the *Erich Koellner*. The planned sailing of a *Vorpostenboot* to hunt for survivors was curtailed by heavy fog, and no more were found. Later, as if to compound the Wehrmacht's misery, at 0032hrs a returning He 111 banking low over the island of Borkum from the west was misidentified as British and shot down by Kriegsmarine flak gunners at Holtzendorff's battery.

The early variant Heinkel He 111J with which *Küstenfliegergruppe* 806 was equipped and which soon proved obsolete and particularly unsuited for maritime operations.

The '*Wikinger*' disaster was investigated by a commission of mixed Luftwaffe and Kriegsmarine officers, chaired by *Generalmajor* Coeler, who was considered ideal because his office was unconnected with the events, and including *Kapitän zur See* Helmuth Heye (former Kriegsmarine Liaison Officer to Göring between 16 March 1938 and April 1939, and current commander of the heavy cruiser *Admiral Hipper*) and *Obstlt.* Loebel of KG 30. By early March the committee had established the facts and identified a catastrophic breakdown in communications between the Luftwaffe and Kriegsmarine as the root cause of the disaster, including the following timeline of notifications and notification failures that had occurred on the day:

12:18: X.*Fliegerkorps* sent a teletype message to *MGK West* that KG 26 will operate against coastal shipping south of the Humber between 1930hrs and 0000hrs. *MGK West* failed to inform the '*Wikinger*' destroyers of the aerial operation, and failed to inform X.*Fliegerkorps* of the destroyers' movements.

12:35: *MGK West* wasted an opportunity to rectify this when it sent two radio messages to the destroyers in the North Sea; the first with meteorological information, the second with notice of a British bomber that had been shot down nearby, mentioning nothing of KG 26 operations.

Between 13:00 and 15:00: *MGK West* contacts the '*Seeluftstreitkräfte*' to request reconnaissance aircraft for the destroyers' path (impossible due to ice conditions at the seaplane bases), and to the '*Jagdfliegerführer* Deutsche Bucht' for air cover during the afternoon and the next morning, when they were expected to return from the Dogger Bank. Neither of these two headquarters was in contact with X.*Fliegerkorps*, and therefore the bomber crews remained ignorant of German destroyer operations.

16:15: To protect the bombers on their way over the East-Frisian Islands and the coastline, X.*Fliegerkorps* sent a teletype message to *MGK West* to request removal of barrage balloons and ask that naval flak batteries be notified of the bombers' operation (which evidently still failed to safeguard the returning aircraft near Sylt).

17:00: *MGK West* requested X.*Fliegerkorps* to prepare covering bombers for the next morning to assist the expected return of the destroyers if possible. This message aroused the curiosity of X.*Fliegerkorps*' Chief of Staff, *Major* Harlinghausen, who had received no notification of destroyers operating in the North Sea that night.

17:35: *Major* Harlinghausen called *MGK West* to ascertain whether the Kriegsmarine was operating destroyers in the same area as KG 26 bombers. Although the potential for accidents soon became clear, bomber crews were already on the runways and exercising radio silence, and therefore received no notification. The Kriegsmarine likewise made no radio signal concerning the matter to Berger, at sea.

The enquiry rightly concluded that the attacks on the *Leberecht Maass* could only be attributed to Jäger's aircraft. It noted:

> This night attack was the first which this crew had ever undertaken. Experience with this kind of operation, including recognising and determining a target, was also lacking. It was only their second-ever night flight over sea, and as such they suffered from lack of experience in managing navigational data. The crew of the aircraft were not informed of the possibility of encountering German vessels . . . In every case, a continuous and extensive briefing of the higher staffs appears necessary. There are no complaints about the conduct of the aircraft or the destroyers.

While *SKL* accepted the enquiry's findings, *Admiral* Alfred Saalwachter at *MGK West* was extremely defensive, replying to Raeder that it was impossible to brief every vessel under his control of air operations, and noting that the Heinkel had indeed disobeyed standing orders in attacking a ship outside of its operational zone, especially one not firmly identified. Though not without some validity, Saalwachter's complaint appears more likely to be an officious attempt to deflect blame from exceedingly poor staff work. A furious Hitler himself issued his own directive on the matter, in which he demanded 'flawless reciprocal briefing' of command elements on movements on land, sea and air within the same operational area, and also requested the tightening of regulations regarding recognition signals.

While North Sea operations by X.*Fliegerkorps* continued, the Royal Navy had gradually bolstered its anti-aircraft defences of Scapa Flow with an eye to the Home Fleet returning to the strategically positioned anchorage. Satisfied that enough measures had been taken, Admiral

Forbes ordered HMS *Valiant* and *Hood* under escort by six destroyers to re-enter Scapa Flow on 7 March, followed soon thereafter by other heavy units. Luftwaffe reconnaissance flights soon detected the Royal Navy vessels, and *SKL* pressed for attacks to be mounted in order to render the Orkneys militarily untenable once more. German planning for the invasion of Denmark and Norway was already well advanced, and the return of heavy forces to the Orkneys threatened an already thinly stretched naval assault and supply plan that extended along almost the entire length of the Norwegian coast. Raeder and his Staff also correctly surmised that the continuing concentration of major naval forces in Scapa Flow could possibly presage a landing on Norway under the guise of support for Finland's ongoing struggle against the Soviet Union.

An armed reconnaissance flight over Scapa Flow was mounted by three Ju 88s of 2./KG 30, although iced windows prevented firm identification or attempted attack on ships below, and *SKL* even doubted whether the crews' navigation had accurately placed them over Holm Sound. Scrambled Hurricanes of 111 Sqn chased the Junkers and shot down *Oblt*. Frithjof Sichart von Sichartshoff's aircraft forty miles east of the Orkneys, the entire crew being lost and reported in Germany as missing in action.

Despite this failure, *SKL* requested that a major air attack be mounted as soon as weather conditions permitted. They railed against the Luftwaffe having sent only three aircraft, 'since in this case the anti-aircraft fire can concentrate on the small number of attackers', and strongly advised that bombing be mixed with mines laid in the Sound, though the latter request was ignored by the Luftwaffe. The raid was finally mounted on 16 March, after a weather reconnaissance flight confirmed conditions acceptable though still subject to rain and snow showers. Eighteen Ju 88s of KG 30, led by *Kommodore Major* Fritz Doench, were assigned the task of dive-bombing the heavy ships at anchor, while sixteen He 111s of KG 26 bombed ground defences and the islands' airfields. Although five aircraft were forced to abort due to technical problems, the remainder began their attack at 1950hrs.

The bombers approached virtually undetected via a roundabout route that swept wide over the North Sea at low altitude, only ascending once they had made landfall. The Ju 88s split into small groups and dive-bombed through a fortuitous break in the drifting cloud cover. In total the German fliers claimed two definite hits on a battleship, one hit on either a battleship or battlecruiser, another hit each on an identified battle

TURNING NORTH AND WEST

cruiser and heavy cruiser, and two near misses on capital ships, close enough to assume that some measure of damage was inflicted. A total of 140 SD50 fragmentation bombs and two bombloads of incendiaries was dropped by the KG 26 Heinkels on Hatston Aerodrome and the hamlet of Brig o' Waithe on the road between Kirkwall and Stromness, as well as on blockships in Skerry Sound, damaging cottages and cratering the airfield at Hatston with eight holes 800 yards from the hangars. At Brig o' Waithe, 27-year-old road labourer James Isbister was killed, the first British civilian killed by German bombs of the war, and seven others were injured.

> When the bombs started to fall James Isbister was at home with his wife Lily and baby son Neil, who now lives in Kirkwall. Across the road a bomb blew apart the house occupied by Mrs Isabella McLeod. James ran to her aid but collapsed a few feet from his own front door, struck down by a shower of shrapnel. The attack was over in minutes, and although others were injured, including Mrs McLeod, who crawled from the shattered remains of her home, James Isbister was the only fatality.[10]

Heavy fires were left behind by the Heinkels as they retreated out to sea, no attempt having been made to bomb the oil storage tanks at Stromness. No aircraft were lost to enemy action, though *Uffz.* Werner Mattner and his crew crash-landed on the Danish Baltic island of Lalaand near Magelundgaard Farm. Following a serious navigation error, the crew mistook the island for Sylt in the early morning darkness and belly-landed on flat pasture after exhausting their fuel. Escaping from their aircraft and no doubt realising their mistake, they set fire to the cockpit and were quickly arrested. However, their internment by Danish authorities did not last long. Of the other aircraft, several reported being fired upon by German warships, though it was later found to have been gunnery practice carried out by '*Schiff 36*', the auxiliary cruiser *Orion*, soon to depart on its maiden raiding cruise into the Pacific and Indian Oceans.

The results of the attack on the anchored ships, while not insignificant, were well below German assumptions. HMS *Norfolk* suffered a single near miss to starboard and was hit by one bomb on the port side quarterdeck abaft 'Y' turret. It passed through the main and lower decks and exploded in the 'Y' shell room, holing the ship below the waterline and causing extensive flooding. In addition, the 'X' and 'Y' magazines were intentionally flooded as a precaution against ammunition exploding.

Recovering an Arado Ar 196 of the *Bordfliegerstaffel*. The officer observer sits astride the canopy to ensure that the steel lifting hawser is firmly attached. (James Payne)

Three midshipmen and a warrant engineer were killed, and four officers and three ratings wounded. Although the steering gear was damaged, the ship was later able to steam at 10 knots for repairs at the Clyde. HMS *Iron Duke* was also damaged once again by a near miss, but it made little difference to what was essentially a depot hulk.

> The X.*Fliegerkorps* has achieved excellent results in the successful attacks on Scapa. The detailed results cannot be checked for the present. According to available reports there is no doubt of some severe and some moderate damage to battleships or heavy cruisers. The ship hit by two 1,000kg bombs must be claimed as out of action for some time. (The Admiralty admits slight damage to one ship only.) The unexpected inadequacy of fighter and anti-aircraft defence in Scapa during the attack is surprising, since it allowed our formation to carry out their attack without losses. It cannot yet be foreseen whether the British Home Fleet, with the knowledge of the severe threat from the air to this base once more

confirmed, will now avoid Scapa as a permanent anchorage and move again to the ports and bays of the west coast.

In the interest of the conduct of warfare in the North Sea and of bringing German forces out into the Atlantic, every endeavour must be made to render it unpleasant for the British naval forces to stay in the Orkneys base, which represents a very severe flank threat to the Shetlands-Norway area.

Naval Staff regrets that we did not succeed in using the aerial mine on Scapa at the same time as the bombing attack. This might possibly have given rise to further great successes.[11]

However, within days *B-Dienst* reports of Royal Navy capital ships putting to sea from Scapa Flow, coupled with an address to the House of Commons by Chamberlain in which he described the raid as a failure, with only one warship damaged, gave rise to serious doubts at *SKL* about the actual results claimed by the Luftwaffe. Again they pressed Göring for permission to lay mines in Scapa Flow using the *Küstenflieger*, but were rebuffed once more. Instead, Heinkel He 111H-4s of '*Stein*' *Staffel* made ready to undertake minelaying missions against the Orkneys, but were prevented by increasingly bad weather. The Kriegsmarine chafed

The mixed Luftwaffe and Kriegsmarine personnel of the *Bordfliegerstaffel* operating shipboard aircraft. (James Payne)

at their enforced inactivity while Britain came closer to effectively countering the threat of magnetic mines permanently. With U-boat and surface forces tied down by preparations for Operation *Weserübung*, the *Küstenflieger* were considered the only offensive naval units available now that ice had begun to clear from the seaplane bases sufficiently for regularly scheduled operations to resume.

The base at Hörnum occupied by *Küstenfliegergruppe* 406 and 2./Kü.Fl.Gr. 906 became the target of a retaliatory raid by Bomber Command on the night of 19/20 March, though it was not the first attention given to the Sylt Island airfields by the RAF. During December 1939 Bomber Command had experimented with maintaining a standing patrol of Armstrong Whitworth Whitleys over the German seaplane bases during the hours of darkness, with the object of interfering with *Küstenflieger* minelaying. Bombs had been dropped on both Hörnum and Borkum, targeting lights sighted on the water which the British believed were connected with the launching and landing of seaplanes. On 14 December five bombs were dropped on seaplanes near Rantum, and six nights later six bombs were dropped along lights in Westerland Bay, Sylt, special care being taken to avoid hitting land. However, the first full-scale raid against the base itself was ordered by the British government, who chose the remote Hörnum seaplane station on the southern end of Sylt owing to the lack of civilian dwellings in the vicinity. The anchorage used by the seaplanes was hardly ideal. It was windswept and exposed, experienced large tidal variation and frequently rough seas, and the pack ice that had formed in December was only just releasing its grip on the three jetties and single slipway. Nonetheless, its strategic location made it invaluable to the *Küstenflieger*, and the British bombing raid was the largest undertaken thus far, and the first specifically against a German land target. Bomber Command's 4 Group sent eight aircraft from 10 Sqn, seven from 51 Sqn, seven from 77 Sqn and eight from 102 Sqn, while 5 Group despatched twenty Handley Page Hampdens. Three aircraft were forced to turn back with technical trouble and another was unable to locate the target, but the remainder bombed on target. The first aircraft reached Sylt at 2000hrs, beginning the raid that continued at intervals over the following six hours. In total, the British dropped forty 500lb bombs, eighty-four 250lb bombs and 1,260 incendiaries.

A single 51 Sqn Whitley avoided attack by an Ar 196 floatplane belonging to Wilhelmshaven's 1./BFl.Gr. 196, but was subsequently damaged by the heavy German flak and its tail gunner was wounded.

RAF reconnaissance photograph of Hörnum seaplane base, taken in preparation for the Bomber Command raid of the night 19-20 March 1940.

A second Whitley of the same squadron was caught by searchlights immediately after dropping its bomb load, and successfully shot down by the gunners below. In flames, the aircraft staggered onwards, heading north to the Danish island of Rømø, where it turned out to sea and finally, at 2335hrs, crashed and exploded in the tidal area north of Morsum, Sylt, killing all five crewmen. Despite the RAF's efforts, little serious damage was suffered at Hörnum, though the base's infirmary took a direct hit. Numerous parked *Küstenflieger* aircraft sustained some measure of splinter damage, but all were fully repaired within forty-eight hours, the Naval Staff attributing the lack of British success more to 'extremely good fortune' than the effectiveness of flak and fighter defence. The British bombing had been accurate, though the calibre of bombs themselves was poor and insufficient to cause significant damage.

Geisler's X.*Fliegerkorps* maintained its pressure on merchant shipping for the remainder of March, even two aircraft from the specialised pathfinder unit KG 100 flying to attack shipping in the Thames and Scheldte estuaries, but with no reported success. By their reckoning, KG 26 Heinkels had made approximately 200 attacks on enemy ships within the North Sea, accruing a claimed total of forty-six vessels sunk, amounting to 70,000BRT of merchant shipping. Alongside a further seventy-six ships claimed as damaged, the total was considered ample return for the operational Luftwaffe's maritime bomber arm. On 6 April 1940 KG 26 *Kommodore Oberst*. Robert Fuchs was awarded the Knight's Cross for his *Geschwader* leadership, the first such award granted to a member of the Luftwaffe's bomber arm.

During February the Heinkel He 111Js of *Küstenfliegergruppe* 806 began armed reconnaissance missions over the North Sea, concentrating both on the Skagerrak and along the British east coast. Aircraft of 3./Kü.Fl.Gr. 806 transferred to the grass runway of Uetersen Airfield in Schleswig-Holstein, twenty-one kilometres north-west of Hamburg, to provide easier access to its main operational area. During February a flight of seven aircraft on an armed reconnaissance had an inconclusive clash with Blenheims sent to intercept them off the English east coast, but not until 20 March was the first *Küstenflieger* He 111 brought down as a result of enemy action.

On that day *Lt.z..S.* Helmut Ostermann's aircraft, M7+EL, engaged fishing boats sighted off the Dutch coast, which promptly returned fire with anti-aircraft weapons and damaged the Heinkel's engines. Ostermann and gunner *Obfw.* Alfred Hubrich were both wounded, and as the bomber lost height its pilot, *Fw.* Hermann Kasch, had no alternative but to ditch. Distancing the stricken bomber from the fishing vessels, Kasch brought the Heinkel down off the Dutch coast north-west of Waddeneilanden, from where the crew were rescued by Dutch cutter *Vier Gebroeders*. Taken ashore at Ijmuiden, they were briefly interned until repatriated to Germany on 22 March, classified as shipwrecked mariners.

Engine failure following a fire caused the loss of another of the *Gruppe*'s Heinkels on 3 April, when *Fw.* Heinrich Baasch was forced to ditch off Hatter Rev, deep within the Kattegat, during a routine reconnaissance mission. All four crew, led by *Oblt.z..S.* Werner Beck, abandoned the aircraft in a rubber dinghy, initially refusing assistance from Danish fishing boats in the hope that they would come ashore in Germany. However, the prevailing current took their small dinghy to the eastern side of Samsø Island near Lillballe, where they were subsequently arrested by Danish police and interned for what amounted to only six days.

While Geisler's *Fliegerkorps* carried the weight of winter attacks on enemy shipping, work had been completed during March 1940 on technical improvements to the LT F5 torpedo, the upgraded model being designated the LT F5a. These included a major alteration to the rudder, which would finally allow the He 115 to become an operational torpedo carrier, theoretically replacing the outdated He 59. However, the torpedo's performance remained far from ideal, as the He 115 had to fly as slow and low as possible to stand any chance of a successful launch, despite the maximum launch speed having been increased from the original 75 knots to 140 knots, and drop height from 20 to 50m. Hitler's restriction on production was lifted, and by the end of March torpedo stocks had risen to 135 modified F5a torpedoes. The inter-service bickering and lack of co-operation between the Kriegsmarine and Luftwaffe is no better demonstrated than by the lack of technical development of this potentially mainstay weapon. The *Seeluftstreitkräfte* had jealously guarded the results of its original pre-war weapons trials, and the Luftwaffe had provided no assistance in the furnishing of torpedo-launching equipment. Pointless brinkmanship over authority of the naval air arm robbed German maritime aviation of one of its major weapons. The solution was co-operation and compromise, towards which neither service appeared willing to work, and German crews continued to fight with substandard weaponry. Harlinghausen, a veteran of Spanish Civil War torpedo operations and fully aware of the weapon's potential in his role as X.*Fliegerkorps* Chief of Staff, was an advocate of establishing a unified aerial torpedo development office, but this single ambition was not actually achieved until 1942.

While the war with Britain at and over the sea had continued unabated since September 1939, the western front facing France had remained static as the 'Phoney War' dragged into its eighth month. Yet, as early as 27 September 1939, Adolf Hitler had summoned his military chiefs to the Reich Chancellery and ordered plans to be prepared for the invasion of The Netherlands, Belgium and France to be launched during October. Designed as a single massive blow to the west before Great Britain could fully mobilise, Hitler's demand was beyond the capability of the Wehrmacht, which was heavily engaged in Poland. Subsequent operational delays finally forced postponement until 1940 of what had become a planned two-part operation; the initial attack against the

Low Countries and north-eastern France, known as '*Fall Gelb*' and the subsequent exploiting drive into the French mainland, '*Fall Rot*'.

While the difficult process of planning this ambitious campaign was still under way, fears of a likely Allied occupation of Norway began to mount in Berlin. Hitler was worried that such an attack by the Allies would halt the crucial import of raw materials, particularly iron ore from mines in northern Sweden, routed to Germany through Narvik and via seaborne traffic that trailed along the neutral Norwegian coast. Raeder fully endorsed Hitler's point of view, and was convinced that Great Britain would indeed attempt to sever this Scandinavian supply chain, an occupation of Norway also effectively barring Kriegsmarine access to the Atlantic and hindering naval operations within the North Sea. Norway had already begun to display a marked anti-German posture which was heightened by the Soviet Union's war of aggression against Finland, Stalin's and Hitler's representatives having signed the Soviet-German non-aggression pact during August 1939. Raeder firmly believed that

An Arado Ar 196 stowed away with wings folded within its hangar aboard the battleship *Tirpitz*. (James Payne)

political and military pressure from a combination of the Allies and Norway could be applied to Sweden, finally choking mercantile trade to Germany, and possibly even forcing Sweden into the war on the side of the Allied powers. However, *Vizeadmiral* Otto Schniewind, Chief of Staff at *SKL*, and his Chief of the Operations Division, *Vizeadmiral* Kurt Fricke, believed it improbable that Great Britain was planning or even capable of such an operation. Instead they believed a German occupation of Norway to be extremely risky, both strategically and economically. Even if their assessment of Allied capabilities was proved wrong, they reasoned that any British occupation of Norway would probably bring them into opposition with the Soviet Union and result in legitimate German countermeasures that could extend German operational bases to Denmark and Sweden. Furthermore, a German seizure of Norway could remove the country's neutral territorial waters and its protection of iron-ore shipments that were permitted, by agreement, to use such sea space as a transit route in safety.

The point of decision came during February 1940, when the Royal Navy ignored Norwegian neutrality and attacked the German auxiliary *Altmark*, which had moored inside Norwegian territorial waters, and rescued 299 captive British sailors. Hitler correctly believed that the British harboured as much ambivalence toward Norwegian neutrality as he himself did, and subsequently ordered an invasion of Denmark and Norway to take precedence over the invasion of France and the Low Countries. *Generaloberst der Infanterie* Nikolaus von Falkenhorst was charged with creating the plan and given supreme command of the operation, and on 1 March 1940 the *SKL* recorded detailed instructions from Hitler on the method by which Norway was to be taken; the Kriegsmarine and Luftwaffe to 'bear the weight of the first operation'. The invasion, codenamed *Weserübung,* was confirmed; *Wesertag* being set for 9 April 1940.

In this instance, Raeder's assessment of Allied intentions towards Norway was correct. The Allies had formed plans to neutralise Norway and thus German use of its sea lanes under the guise of an expeditionary force sent to aid Finland in their battle against the Soviets. This land force would reach Finland only after disembarkation in Norway and transit through Sweden, once the relevant permissions had been secured. By landing in Narvik, the all-important Swedish Gällivore iron-ore mines were to be occupied, the stated rationale for such a move being the maintenance of Allied lines of communication to the expeditionary force in Finland.

The small Junkers W 34 was used in both training and combat roles by the *Küstenfliegergruppe* during the early weeks of war, before it was relegated to training and transport. This particular aircraft crashed in fog in The Netherlands in 1941. (James Payne)

While planning continued, British troops began to be gathered in Scotland while French transport ships assembled in Brest and Cherbourg. However, Sweden refused the Allied application for transit rights to Finland on 12 March, and Finland's Scandinavian neighbours urged the acceptance of new Soviet armistice terms to end the costly winter war. Bowing to pressure, Finland subsequently sued for peace with the Soviet Union on 13 March, and the pretence upon which the original Allied plan hinged was gone, and its form abandoned. Instead, British and French ships were ordered to begin minelaying along the Norwegian coast, forcing German shipping to sail further offshore and outside the safety of neutral waters, where they could be attacked by the Royal Navy. This was in direct contravention of an agreement signed between Great Britain and Norway on 11 March 1940, by which exports to Germany, even of contraband, were permitted, provided they did not exceed the levels of 1938 trade. Following the successful sowing of minefields, 'Operation R4' would then see the landing of the

18,000 British, French and Polish troops on Norwegian soil (those that had already been earmarked for Finland) in response to the predicted German reaction to the Allied infringement upon Norwegian neutrality. Disguising their offensive actions as the defence of neutral Norway, the Allied convoys were scheduled to begin sailing on 8 April.

Concurrently, the Kriegsmarine was fully committed to the largely amphibious invasion of Norway, and as *Weserübung* forces put to sea in preparation for *Wesertag*, Allied reconnaissance noted the appearance of German ships moving along the Norwegian coast, speculating that they were attempting a breakout into the Atlantic. On 8 April at 0600hrs the British government informed Norway that they were to begin sowing mines within Norwegian territorial waters; four destroyers already having begun mining Vestfjord an hour before the declaration. Troops of the joint Anglo-French 'Plan R4' were readied for landing at Stavanger, Trondheim, Bergen and Narvik, and had already embarked aboard their transport ships in preparation. Although Germany was outwardly outraged, in Berlin there was a certain degree of satisfaction with the Allied announcement. The Western Powers had now flagrantly violated Norwegian neutrality, providing a small measure of public justification for the impending German invasion, which could now be camouflaged as a counter-stroke to the Allies' activities.

Generalleutnant Hans Geisler was placed in command of aerial forces deployed for *Weserübung*, X.*Fliegerkorps* remaining the organisational umbrella beneath which all participating aircraft were placed, including the Heinkel He 115s of 1./ and 2./KüFl.Gr. 506 (eight and ten aircraft respectively), with 1./Kü.Fl.Gr. 106 (ten aircraft) attached (3./Kü.Fl.Gr. 506 remaining in Norderney under command of *Küstenfliegergruppe* 106). At the peak of the fighting in Norway, X.*Fliegerkorps* would muster 710 combat aircraft. Geisler delivered briefings to his subordinate commanders on 6 April, after the first naval troop transports had already sailed from Germany.

The three *Küstenflieger Staffeln* committed to the first wave of *Weserübung* under the command of *Major* Heinrich Minner as *Gruppenkommandeur* Kü.Fl.Gr. 506 were given patrol sectors that covered the North Sea approaches to south-west Norway. Beginning at 0600hrs, 1./Kü.Fl.Gr. 106 was tasked with covering four separate sectors that covered the entrance to the Skagerrak, stretching from Hanstholm in Denmark to Bergen, and 1./ and 2./KüFl.Gr. 506 covering the North Sea as far west as the Orkneys between Bergen and Trondheim. Furthermore, the first *Rotte* of two aircraft from 1./Kü.Fl.Gr. 506, led by *Staffelkapitän Hptm.* Lienhart Martin Wiesand, was instructed to fly immediately to Trondheim upon completion of its patrol and find suitable berthing for the incoming seaplanes. The remainder were directed to Stavanger until Trondheim was reported ready. Minner was mindful of the risk of fuel starvation on such extended patrolling, and included in his written orders of the day the warning that:

> Navigational difficulties in finding and reaching a landing site must be kept in mind!!
>
> If fuel shortage forces any planned flight path to be aborted, the western part of each patrol sector is of greater importance than the northern. Any premature flight cancellation is to be reported by radio.[12]

Minner forbade attacks against sighted submarines and merchant ships, as the large commitment of U-boats and troopships provided ample opportunity for mistaken identity, despite the briefing including clear recognition signals to be displayed by all German vessels during *Weserübung*.

The Luftwaffe's role in the invasion plan was crucial; they were responsible for reconnaissance and potential naval interdiction, as well as for the transportation of Luftwaffe paratroopers charged with the capture of important airfields. Once German boots were on Norwegian soil, the Luftwaffe would also be responsible for the lion's share of the major supply operation required by the invading ground forces.

For their part, the *Küstenflieger* forces not directly involved in the opening of the attack on Norway were primarily charged with reconnaissance and ASW missions over the North Sea and Skagerrak. The logistical difficulties of ground operations along Norway's rugged coastline also called for the formation of a special seaplane transport *Geschwader* for *Weserübung*. Named *Kampfgeschwader zur besonderen Verwendung* 108 ('Combat Group for Special Purposes', or, KG.z.b.V. 108) a single example of the newly operational BV 138A and a small number of Dornier Do 24 flying boats were incorporated into the formation, which consisted mainly of Ju 52(M) floatplanes and He 59s that had been transferred from Norderney's 3./Kü.Fl.Gr. 906 which handed its elderly Heinkels over as it began converting to the He 115.[13] The invasion of Norway also marked the combat debut of Focke-Wulf

Fw 200 Condors of *Hptm*. Edgar Petersen's *Fernaufklärungsstaffel* (long-distance reconnaissance squadron), soon redesignated 1./KG 40 and in action from 10 April onwards, eight Condors also being brought into service as transports with 4./KG.z.b.V. 107 and 2./KG.z.b.V. 108.

Two days before the invasion began, *Küstenfliegergruppe* 406 mounted eighteen separate Do 18 long-range reconnaissance missions to the area between the Pentland Firth and Shetland Islands, to discern whether there had been any Royal Navy response to the invasion fleet setting sail from German waters. The British had become increasingly alarmed at the activity reported by its aerial reconnaissances, not only at sea, but also on land as large columns of heavy traffic were detected moving at night with unshaded headlamps along the autobahn that stretched between Hamburg and Lübeck. Desultory bombing attacks were made on the streams of traffic, with little real success. However, at sea, the opposing naval forces had already begun to blunder into one another in poor weather conditions. In rough seas and thick fog. On 8 April the Polish submarine *Orzel* sank the 5,261-ton German troopship SS *Rio de Janeiro* of 1.*Seetransportstaffel* (carrying 313 Luftwaffe troops and flak weapons bound for Bergen), and noted a large number of uniformed soldiers among the wreckage. Norwegian fishing boats and a destroyer

The unsuccessful Heinkel He 114 floatplane, soon replaced by the far superior Arado Ar 196.

came to the surviving Germans' aid, also noting a startling number of troops, and the Reuters News Agency immediately reported the sinking of a 'German troopship' near Kristiansand. South of Oslo, HMS *Trident* sighted a 'large laden tanker steaming westward outside territorial waters'. It was the naval tanker *Stedingen*, carrying Luftwaffe fuel for future operations after the expected capture of Stavanger Airfield, which was the target of a German parachute landing on *Wesertag*. The tanker's Master, *Kapitän* Schäfer, turned to starboard and ran for Norwegian waters when *Trident* surfaced to fire a warning shot. Two live rounds followed, and the German crew scuttled their ship and abandoned it, Schäfer being taken prisoner as a single torpedo finished off *Stedingen*. *Weserübung* was no longer shielded by secrecy.

Late on eve of the invasion, Ar 196A-2 6W+BN from the *Admiral Hipper*, bound for Trondheim and commanded by *Oblt.z.S.* Werner Tacham and flown by *Lt.z.S.* Johannes Polzin, inadvertently landed in Norwegian territorial waters near Lyngstad, where the aircraft was seized by the Norwegian torpedo boat *Sild* and towed into harbour. Both crewmen were interned, though they were subsequently freed by advancing German forces during May. The captured aircraft was to be flown to Britain for examination after the invasion had begun, but was crashed en route. This was not the sole loss to *Bordfliegerkommando* 196 during *Weserübung*. Two aircraft aboard the heavy cruiser *Blücher* were destroyed when the ship was shelled by the 28cm Norwegian guns of Oscarsborg Fortress as she attempted to pass through Drøbak Sound to attack Oslo during early morning darkness on 9 April. Two hits were instantly scored on the ship's port side, the first hitting the battle station of the anti-aircraft guns' commander, the second exploding near the aircraft hangar, killing all four of the Luftwaffe technical crew and one of the pilots. Both aircraft were set aflame, one sitting ready on the catapult and the other within its hangar. Although the ship returned fire, the damage had been done. The flames spread, causing sympathetic explosions of stored ammunition and equipment that eventually ruptured several bulkheads in the engine rooms and ignited the ship's fuel stores. *Blücher* slowly capsized as the crew and embarked troops for the Oslo assault abandoned ship. The single Arado carried aboard the cruiser *Karlsruhe* was also destroyed, heavily damaged by a torpedo from HMS *Truant* that disabled the ship as she sailed from Kristiansand after successfully landing troops following the surrender of the Norwegian garrison. All of the aircraft's complement were successfully evacuated before the cruiser was scuttled by two torpedoes fired from the accompanying torpedo boat *Greif*.

A Do 18 of 2./Kü.Fl.Gr. 406 was also among the first casualties suffered by the *Küstenflieger*. Twelve RAF Hampden bombers were despatched during the morning on 9 April to attack German forces at Bergen, but were recalled on account of poor weather conditions. That same afternoon the twelve Hampdens, accompanied by twelve Vickers Wellingtons of 9 Sqn, repeated the attempt, and at dusk attacked the cruisers *Königsberg* and *Köln* in Bergen Harbour. Claiming a direct hit and several near misses, the British aircraft turned for home, when Sqn Ldr George Peacock took his Wellington for a second pass over the target area, despite heavy anti-aircraft fire. As he did so, his front gunner, Sgt A.K. Griffiths, opened fire at *Lt.z.S.* Wolfgang Cohrs' Do 18, K6+HL, returning from a North Sea patrol, which was hit and shot down in flames. Cohrs', pilot *Oblt*. Heinrich de Vlieger, *Uffz*. Hanz Liesner and *Fw.* Helmut Suhr all died in the crash.[14]

Although the cruiser *Königsberg* had suffered no damage in Peacock's raid, the following day she was hit and holed by dive-bombing Fleet Air Arm Skuas. Within three hours she had capsized and sunk, her Ar 196A-2, T3+CH, being carried with her to the bottom. The aircraft's crew and technicians were taken ashore, and fought as infantry for ten days before they were transferred back to Wilhelmshaven, pilot *Uffz*. Josef Kampfle being wounded during fighting at the seaplane base in Flatøy.[15]

At 1030hrs on *Wesertag* German reconnaissance aircraft sighted the Royal Navy's Home Fleet west of Bergen, under the command of Admiral Charles Forbes aboard his flagship, HMS *Rodney*. In anticipation of major British fleet movements, Geisler had kept KG 26 and KG 30 aircraft in readiness for potential interception and, after briskly ordering them into action, forty-one He 111s and forty-seven Ju 88s attacked the Royal Navy capital ships over a period of three hours. The battleship HMS *Rodney* was hit by an SC500 bomb, which smashed through the upper deck aft of the funnel but did not explode and exited sideways after bouncing off the armoured deck. HMS *Glasgow* and *Southampton* suffered minor damage from near misses, one man being killed and four injured aboard the former. The *Staffelkapitän* of 3./KG 30, *Hptm*. Arved Crüger, incorrectly claimed a direct hit on either *Southampton* or *Galatea*. The destroyer HMS *Gurkha* was, however, sunk after leaving the protective umbrella of fire of the other ships to obtain a more advantageous firing position. She was last seen by the attacking aircraft lying stationary and wreathed in smoke, with a severe list to port. Sixteen crewmen were killed before she went down, most of the crew being rescued by HMS *Aurora*.

The German seizure of Norwegian airfields was of the highest priority, to allow reinforcing troops and equipment to be flown in and also to provide advanced front-line bases for covering aircraft. This objective was largely achieved during the first day. Likewise, the provision of seaplane bases in captured harbours was also realised, aircraft of 1./Kü.Fl.Gr. 506 flying to Trondheim, although the *Staffelkapitän* of 1./Ku.Fl.Gr. 506, *Hptm*. Wiesand, was killed when his He 115 was hit by Norwegian ground fire and made a forced descent in Trondheim Harbour. The remaining aircraft were soon joined by the 2nd *Staffel*, and immediately began reconnaissance flights covering the North Sea area between Bergen and the Orkney Islands, co-ordinated by Geisler's staff at X.*Fliegerkorps*. However, fuel was critically short, the *SKL* reporting that 'every aspect of the supply question [was] difficult'. Rail transport to Trondheim from the supply head established in captured Oslo was impossible, and the seaplanes faced short-term grounding unless fuel could be provided.

In Stavanger, which had also been swiftly conquered, 1./Kü.Fl.Gr. 106 arrived late on the first day to also begin operations. A single He 115 was shot down while en route over Trondheim, alighting and being abandoned by its crew before sinking in flames. Ships had arrived in harbour carrying sufficient fuel for four hours' flying time for the seaplanes of *Küstenfliegergruppe* 506. The RAF also mounted an attack by two Blenheims on Stavanger Aerodrome and the assembly of seaplanes within the harbour, machine-gunning the aircraft and setting a petrol pump on fire, though causing no severe damage.

It was in Narvik, the most northerly German landing zone, that Allied forces mounted their strongest counterattacks. Although the Wehrmacht had captured the vital ore harbour on the first day, by 13 April all eight supporting Kriegsmarine destroyers and the ammunition ship *Rauenfels* had been sunk by the Royal Navy. Under increasing pressure from Norwegian and Allied forces, *General* Eduard Dietl, commander of the 3.*Gebirgsdivision* and all Narvik forces, was forced to abandon the town and retreat into the hills. Dietl's forces required fresh supplies of heavy weapons and ammunition if they were to stand any chance of success, and the five long-range Dornier Do 26 reconnaissance aircraft of the *Transozeanstaffel* were taken off maritime missions and incorporated into 9./KG.z.b.V 108 to operate as transport for heavy material and reinforcements that could not be dropped by parachute.[16] Wilhelm Küppers, the radio operator on Do 26V-2 P5+BH, recalled:

> During the Norwegian campaign we flew an almost constant round of sorties bringing in anti-tank guns, munitions, mines and mountain troops for Narvik. These flights were combined with reconnaissance along the Norwegian coast. The more perilous moments of any such sortie were the landings on the narrow fjords around Narvik and the subsequent take-offs. We skirted along neutral Swedish airspace to avoid anti-aircraft fire before diving down almost vertically — almost helicopter-like — for the surface of the water with our engines throttled back. The aircraft had to be rapidly unloaded, but it was amazing what could be achieved with the threat of death so close; we expected naval or artillery fire to come crashing down around us at any moment. Two tons of equipment could be off-loaded under such circumstances — with much sweat and cursing — in under twenty minutes. Take-offs were just as 'suicidal', especially in the narrow Beisfjord with its high cliffs. Taxiing out into the middle of the fjord was often done under fire from British ships. Our take-off runs had to be finely judged in order to avoid the cliffs. Engines were run up to full power and we were lucky if we managed to pass more than ten metres over these obstacles. Each successful take-off under such circumstances represented a considerable feat of airmanship for such a large and heavy seaplane weighing up to twenty tons.[17]

Dietl's men also desperately needed combat air support, and four He 115s of 1./Kü.Fl.Gr. 106 flew from Stavanger on 12 April. The aircraft sighted the battleship HMS *Warspite*, but were driven away by heavy flak, and an attempted attack on the destroyer HMS *Ivanhoe* was also unsuccessful. With the harbour still in German hands at that point, the aircraft spent the hours of darkness moored, refuelled and ready for the return flight during the following day. However, as they passed over Vestfjord, He 115 M2+EH was shot down by Royal Navy ships, the aircraft commander, *Lt.z.S.* Joachim Vogler, being taken prisoner and his three crewmen lost.

Interestingly, the *Küstenflieger* also faced the He 115 in combat, as the Norwegian Ministry of Defence had ordered six He 115Ns for the Royal Norwegian Navy Air Service (RNoNAS) on 28 August 1939. Six more had been ordered in December 1939, but delivery was forestalled by *Weserübung*. The six already in service were spread along the coast, from the naval air stations at Sola and Flatøy in the south to the one at Skattøra Naval Air Station outside Tromsø in the north. At the beginning of the German invasion the single Norwegian He 115 at the seaplane base at Hafrsfjord near Stavanger (numbered F60) was captured by the Germans, but in return two Luftwaffe He 115s were seized soon thereafter by Norwegian forces. One machine from 2./Kü.Fl.Gr. 506 was captured by police officers at Brønnøysund, Nordland, on 12 April, and aircraft M2+FH of 1./Kü.Fl.Gr. 106 was taken by an improvised militia unit of Norwegian riflemen at Ørnes in Glomfjord, Nordland, after the aircraft made a forced descent owing to fuel starvation.[18] Numbered F62 and F64 respectively and manned by Norwegian aircrews, and they flew several missions against the German invaders. During June F64 successfully flew to Britain, but F62 was recovered by German forces, unserviceable and abandoned at Skattøra after Norwegian evacuation, and later repaired and returned to Luftwaffe service.

With the Luftwaffe wresting local air superiority form the Allies and posing a direct threat to Allied troop landings, the Admiralty ordered cruiser HMS *Suffolk*, escorted by four destroyers, to proceed towards Skudesnesfjorden and shell Stavanger Airfield. The raid was to be supported by two air strikes; twelve Wellingtons to bomb the airfield before dawn to sow disruption and also illuminate the target area with flames, and a mid-day attack by a dozen Blenheims to suppress potential enemy retaliation. Code-named Operation *Duck*, the initial Wellington raid never took place, as most of the bombers failed to locate the target in bad weather, while the two that did failed to bomb after observing only damaged hangars and no aircraft. Nevertheless, the surface force met as planned with the submarine HMS *Seal*, which had been posted as a navigational beacon to the firing area, and *Suffolk* launched one of its two Supermarine Walrus aircraft to assist in target location.

> We approached the Norwegian coast in the dark . . . The normal catapult officer was sick and the chap who was put in charge of the catapult had never done it before, and I thought he was a blinking idiot anyway. We were the first aircraft off and were revving up on the [catapult] and we gave the signal to launch. The ship rolled so that the catapult pointed down to the sea and he dropped the flag and we were fired off straight into the sea . . . it stove in the bottom of the hull and wiped the two wingtip floats off, but we staggered into the air. The other aircraft had a better launch.

We couldn't establish radio communication with the ship... they could hear us, but we couldn't hear them. Anyway, we were passing through the magnetic bearing of the airfield, it was beautiful clear weather and we could see one aircraft taking off and we were hoping for the best. Then the ship opened fire... they fired armour-piercing shells and were hoping to damage the runways. And I looked through my binoculars and I couldn't see a thing. I could see the airfield but couldn't see a shot falling anywhere.[19]

Two Hudson bombers had also been despatched for spotting purposes, one turning back with mechanical problems and the second being plagued by communications difficulties and unable to make radio contact with the cruiser. The pilot did, however, drop his bomb load of incendiaries on the airfield, destroying a Ju 52 of Stab/KG 30 and providing a small conflagration for targeting purposes. With dawn edging nearer, HMS *Suffolk* opened fire at 0515hrs on 17 April, and over the next forty-nine minutes 217 8in shells were fired towards that airfield at a range of 20,000 yards.

A Junkers Ju 88 of I./KG 30 following a forced landing. The nose insignia displays the plunging eagle of the *Geschwader*, while the umbrella in crosshairs on the starboard engine indicates the aircraft is from I *Gruppe*.

Despite the Hudson crew's best efforts, the shells missed Stavanger-Sola Airfield, overshooting and instead hitting the Sola seaplane base just to the north. The operational readiness of the *Küstenflieger* aircraft thus far moved to Stavanger was relatively slight, owing to a severe shortage of ground staff and the great demands made both on the available personnel and material. While aircraft attacks had thus far caused little extra disruption, *Suffolk*'s shellfire destroyed buildings (including the commander's house), a truck, two fuel stores, four He 115s of 1./Kü.Fl.Gr. 106 and three He 59s that had been taken on to the strength of KGr.z.b.V. 108 as transport aircraft. All light and power installations were also disabled, hampering initial German damage control efforts.

However, the British ships were not to escape without retaliation, and reconnaissance aircraft scoured the area for the attackers, a Do 18 of 2./Kü.Fl.Gr. 106 sighting HMS *Suffolk* as the cruiser was west of Haugesund and driving hard for Britain. Geisler's bombers were swiftly readied and ten He 111s from I./KG 26 spearheaded an attack, eight focussing on *Suffolk* and the remaining pair attempting to bomb the escorting destroyers. The only damage caused was to HMS *Kipling*, from two near-misses that cracked engine mounts and disabled the aft torpedoes. Two torpedo-carrying He 115s of 3./Kü.Fl.Gr. 506 also attempted an attack, but weather conditions prevented them from launching their weapons successfully. Dornier Do 18s maintained contact with the speeding British ships as weather gradually began to clear, until the warships sailed under a virtually cloudless sky, the sun rising to allow excellent visibility to the west in the North Sea.

Fighter cover for the retreating ships had been arranged with Coastal Command, though only two of three planned Blenheims took off, and were soon sent on a wild goose chase against imaginary German destroyers. One of the Blenheims reached Bergen and made a low-level strafing run against He 59D seaplanes of KGr.z.b.V. 108, before being attacked and driven away by a defending Bf 110. Meanwhile, the planned Blenheim noon attack on Stavanger Airfield did take place, destroying a Bf 110C of 1./ZG 76 and a single Ju 52 and killing two Luftwaffe ground crew, though it failed to have any detrimental effect on Luftwaffe retaliation against the ships of Operation *Duck* as KG 30 added its weight to the attack.

> At 1037 HMS *Suffolk* was hit by a heavy bomb from a steep dive bomber on the starboard side of the upper deck just for'ard of 'X' turret. The bomber approached down sun and was expected to make a high-level

TURNING NORTH AND WEST

attack. The ship was brought beam-on to meet this attack, but on reaching an angle of sight of 65 to 70 degrees, at a height of about 10,000 feet, the aircraft dived on the ship, releasing the bomb at an estimated heighted of from 4 to 5 thousand feet. The weight of the bomb is estimated at 500 kilos . . . The bomb passed through the Ward Room, Warrant Officers' Flag, and storerooms on to the Platform Deck, from starboard to port, and exploded in the inflammable store close to the bulkhead of the After-Engine Room. The effect of this explosion penetrated forwarded to the After-Engine Room, and aft, through 'X' Shell Room to 'X' Cordite Handing Room. It is believed that a charge exploded in the Cordite Handing Room which penetrated the Cordite Hoist Trunk and vented into 'X' Gunhouse. The empty cordite cage at the top of the hoist was broken, and the charge in the Right Traversing Rammer caught fire. The roof of the Turret was lifted. 'X' shell handing room and all Oil Fuel Tanks in the vicinity of the explosion were holed. The bulkhead of the After-Engine Room was blown in, the Engine Room seriously damaged and flooded, and the force of the explosion vented up through the Engine Room Exhaust Trunks and up the hatches leading to the War Room Flat. A column of flame was seen to reach the height of the gaff on the main mast, destroying the ensign. Fires started in the Ward Room Flat, the Warrant Officers' Flat, and the Storerooms underneath, and in the entrance to the Officers' Galleys.

The second W/T Office and the After-Gyro Compass Room was wrecked. The Main W/T Office was unable to transmit as a result of the blast. The After 8-inch Magazine had to be flooded. About 1,500 tons of water entered the ship in about 20 minutes. The immediate effect on the ship's fighting efficiency was a reduction of maximum speed to about 18 knots, 'X' and 'Y' turrets out of action and Main and Second W/T Offices out of action. A considerable volume of water had entered the ship aft. Signals had to be passed by V/S to *Kipling* for transmission . . . At 1050 *Kipling* reported a mine ahead. This mine was suspected as having been laid by a Flying Boat which had been observed flying very low across the horizon ahead of the mean course made good. The object passed close on the starboard hand. I cannot say with any certainty whether, it was, in fact, a mine, but lookouts had reported that a low-flying aircraft had been dropping something ahead of the ship.[20]

Sporadic Ju 88 attacks continued. The cruiser's steering motor was temporarily put out of action, the seaplane hangar was strafed, the lower-deck scuttles were blown in, and the hull was punctured by severe

The close confines of a Ju 88 cockpit in action. At right is the pilot, left, the observer/bombardier, at the back is the wireless operator/rear gunner. The photograph was probably taken by the fourth crewman, the flight engineer/lower gunner. The diagonal line on the window near the pilot was for use as an 'artificial horizon' and visual dive indicator.

splinter damage which caused further flooding. Twenty-two He 111s of KG 4 were also thrown into the fray, eleven attacking successfully, although British aircraft had now reached the ships and established some form of air cover, despite also having been fired on by British anti-aircraft gunners through faulty recognition; the Blenheim and Junkers Ju 88 were frequently mistaken for one another. A shadowing Do 18 of 1./Kü.Fl.Gr. 406, commanded by *Lt.z.S.* Max Keil, was shot down by three 801 Sqn Skuas and all four-crew killed before the fighting ended with the final Luftwaffe withdrawal. HMS *Suffolk* finally reached Scapa Flow battered but afloat, and repairs were undertaken that saw the ship later returned to service. Thirty-two sailors were killed during the action or died of wounds, and a further thirty-four injured.

Despite their losses, 1./Kü.Fl.Gr. 106 was called upon to send aircraft to Narvik the following day, 18 April. Three He 115s were despatched, but forced to abort their mission in terrible weather conditions. *Oblt.z.S* Heinz Witt's aircraft, M2+ BH, crashed into Storsadlen Mountain, 112 kilometres south-west of Trondheim, in freezing rain. Witt was killed instantly, while pilot *Fw.* Otto Arnold died the following day beside the wreckage. Radio operator/gunner *Uffz.* Karl Georg set fire to the remains of the aircraft before making his way towards German lines and finally reaching Trondheim. The bodies of his crewmates lay next to the burnt wreckage for three weeks before being found and buried by German soldiers.

Another reconnaissance mission to Narvik, planned for 22 April, also came unstuck. Heinkel He 115B-2 M2+AH, equipped with optional ice runners under the floats, had been flown by a crew from 1./Kü.Fl. Gr. 106 from Sylt to Hommelvik in the Trondheimsfjord. The aircraft was scheduled to be taken on the *Staffel* strength of 1./Kü.Fl.Gr. 506 and begin reconnaissance missions over the North Sea, but *Oblt.z.S.* Rudolf Schrader and his crew, pilot *Lt.z.S.* Siegfried Schulz and *Uffz.* Erich Günther, were instead tasked with their Narvik flight during the following day. As they passed north-east of Namsos, engine trouble resulted in a fire which forced a landing on the frozen surface of Lake Limingen in the northern part of Trondelag, close to the Swedish border. Despite extinguishing the flames they were unable to rectify the fault, and abandoned the aircraft, setting it on fire and attempting to walk to Sweden in the the hope of being repatriated to Germany. Their path was blocked, however, by Norwegian troops, and they were captured and handed over to a French army unit before being transported to a prisoner of war camp in Scotland.

Strong Allied forces had landed around Namsos with the objective of retaking Trondheim, and were constantly bombed by the Luftwaffe, particularly effectively by Ju 87 Stukas of *Stukageschwader* 1, which had been moved to forward airfields at Stavanger and Værnes-Trondheim. The latter was a grass aerodrome, and the spring thaw made the operation of heavy aircraft difficult at best. Local Norwegian residents were paid to work on immediate improvements. By 28 April an 800m wooden runway had been constructed, allowing the Heinkels of KG 26 to use the airstrip, described by *Admiral* Boehm to Raeder as '. . . small, sodden and miserable at this time of the year with low clouds hanging down from the surrounding mountains'.[21] The larger maritime bombers also took their toll, both dive-bombing Junkers Ju 88s and level-bombing Heinkel He 111s. The danger of the high-level bombing attacks was magnified by explosions ashore sending torrents of rock crashing on unwary vessels below the steep fjord sides. The French cruiser *Emile Bertin* of 'Group Z', a fire support group of ten warships, was heavily damaged in a dive-bombing attack on 19 April after *Lt.* Werner Baumbach's Junkers Ju 88 of 5./KG 30 scored a direct hit which passed straight through the unarmoured light cruiser without exploding. With limited air support, the entire position at Namsos soon became untenable, and a withdrawal was hastily planned, codenamed Operation *Klaxon*. An evacuation force of destroyers entered the fjord, in which strong French naval units were already present, Royal Navy heavy cruisers being positioned to seaward in support. Only two of the Royal Navy armed trawlers that had also been present in Namsos had survived the relentless bombing, and they assisted with the transfer of troops from shore to the waiting ships. The small trawlers also added whatever firepower they possessed to air defence, as the *Klaxon* ships were still attacked, despite patches of thick fog periodically obscuring them from German aircraft.

Lieutenant Richard Been Stannard was in command of the anti-submarine trawler HMT *Arab*, which had been despatched to Namsos in late April, and his valiant actions as he assisted in the evacuation were to earn him the Victoria Cross.

> Thursday 2nd May 0200 – proceeded up Fjord, met fleet leaving, transported wounded, *Aston Villa*'s and *Gaul*'s crews, to HMS *Griffin* proceeded down fjord, ordered to proceed to England. Decided I would keep well north as I was on my own and my speed was about 5/6 knots. 0500 – Clear of Namsen Fjord. 1000 – Speed 3 knots.
>
> Attacked by [unidentified] Heinkel 115 who signalled by V/S in plain language 'Go east or be sunk'. (Had sent out W/T message half-an-hour before reporting a friendly or captured cargo ship about eight miles north was being escorted by seaplane, heading S.E.) Could not intercept her owing to lack of speed. A suitable answer was sent in reply. The pilot of this machine seemed a novice or else thought we had no ammunition left, as he circled us, closing towards us each time. He was keeping up a continuous fire with his two guns, but I decided to hold my fire until he was closer. He banked at 800 yards just forward of the beam so opened fire with all Lewis guns and Oerlikon. Could see the H.E. Oerlikon shells bursting on him. The Heinkel 115 came down about two miles astern of us, but I did not attempt to save the crew.[22]

Men of *Küstenfliegergruppe* 906 celebrate the claimed sinking of 30,000 BRT of enemy shipping.

As the *Klaxon* evacuation was under way, the retreating Allied ships were sighted by *Küstenflieger* reconnaissance aircraft and shadowed by aircraft of *Küstenfliegergruppe* 506, which guided Stuka dive-bombers into the attack. The He 115s played an essential role because navigation, particularly radio navigation, was impossible on long flights in the two-seat Ju 87, the most potent anti-shipping dive-bomber that the Germans possessed. Over the course of the evacuation the British destroyer HMS *Afridi* and sloop HMS *Bittern*, as well as the French destroyer *Bison*, were all sunk by the dive-bombers. They did, however, successfully lift 1,850 British and 2,345 French troops, as well as an undetermined number of Norwegian soldiers and thirty German prisoners of war (including the crew of M2+AH) from Namsos and transport them to Britain.

Although Norway was steadily falling to the *Weserübung* forces, attritional losses continued to sap the strength of the *Küstenflieger*. Enemy bombing and strafing of seaplane harbours, aerial combat and occasional accidents caused by the unforgiving Scandinavian weather all accrued a grim tally of losses and damage. The *Transozeanstaffel* had finally been committed to action, and three of its large Do 26 seaplanes were destroyed during the fighting in Norway. The first, V2 (ex-*Seefalke*),

Pilot and observer aboard a Dornier Do 17, a spare magazine for one of the onboard MG 15 defensive machine guns clipped in place behind them.

was shot down on 9 May by three Blackburn Skuas of 803 Naval Air Squadron (NAS), Fleet Air Arm, operating from the aircraft carrier HMS *Ark Royal*. Piloted by Lufthansa veteran *Oblt.z.S.* Siegfried Graf Schack von Wittenau, the Dornier was carrying eighteen *Gebirgsjäger* reinforcements to Narvik when it was engaged by the Skuas, crashing in Efjorden in Ballangen after a running battle that inflicted serious damage on the flying boat. One of the Skuas was forced to land at Tovik after being hit by defensive machine-gun fire. Too far from German-held territory, the Do 26 crew and *Gebirgsjäger* then attempted to run for the Swedish border and face internment, but were apprehended after six days of running skirmishes with pursuing Norwegian troops, Schack von Wittenua being wounded in both legs before capture. On

28 May 1940 both V1 (ex-*Seeadler*) and V3 (ex *Seemöwe*) were strafed by three Hurricanes of 46 Sqn RAF, set ablaze and sunk only minutes after successfully mooring at Sildvik in Rombaksfjord near Narvik,. The flying boats were carrying arms and ammunition to the beleaguered German Narvik forces, and three valuable mountain guns were still aboard and lost when the aircraft sank.

The Luftwaffe continued to supply and reinforce ground forces while also conducting continuous coastal and North Sea reconnaissance missions, attacks on British supply and naval shipping and air support for ground attacks, and providing a strong protective umbrella by using patrolling fighter aircraft and strategically placed anti-aircraft units ashore. Scapa Flow was also bombed in attempts to hinder ongoing Royal Navy involvement in the struggles around Narvik, while the *Küstenflieger* continued to make harassing attacks on British trawlers and coastal merchant shipping, as well as carrying out sporadic minelaying. For the naval fliers, anti-submarine missions were also elevated to high priority following the Royal Navy submarine successes against Germany's invasion and supply fleets and the withdrawal of U-boats from Norway.

From the end of March 1940 *F.d.Luft Ost* had been assigned strenuous ASW patrols within the Kattegat and Skagerrak, as well as the close cover of transport ships in preparation for *Weserübung*, restrictions on attacking sighted submarines having been lifted after *Wesertag*. In the conquered Danish town of Aalborg, *F.d.Luft Ost Generalmajor* Hermann Bruch had established his headquarters by 12 April, and the first seaplanes of *Küstenfliegergruppe* 906 alighted on Limfjord, west of the town, beginning the establishment of the new base *Seefliegerhorst* Aalborg. There were already numerous Danish mooring buoys available in the channel between the base area and Egholm Island, as well as a 300m pier and concrete slipway perfect for the maintenance of seaplanes. Not long thereafter, Bruch was moved from *F.d.Luft Ost* and appointed *F.d.Luft West*. He replaced Coeler on 25 April, the latter's attentions now fully required by command of 9.*Fliegerdivision*. *Oberstleutnant* Hermann Edert was promoted from command of *Küstenfliegergruppe* 606 and named the new *F.d.Luft Ost* in Aalborg. Small two-seat Ar 196 floatplanes of 5./BFl.Gr. 196 were also transferred to the command of Stab/ Kü.Fl.Gr. 906 on 13 April, to bolster the number of available aircraft as *Küstenflieger* serviceability rates wilted under the constant strain on men and machines imposed by anti-submarine patrols, mounted even during the hours of darkness by those crews training for night flying. Among the

Rear gunner/wireless operator aboard a Dornier Do 17 bomber, the first wheeled aircraft operated by the *Küstenflieger*, in this case *Küstenfliegergruppe* 606.

reported sightings and attacks listed within *F.d.Luft Ost*'s KTB is one on 29 April, in which an Ar 196 attacked a submarine north-north-west of Skagen Island. From a height of 230m, two 50kg bombs were dropped as the target submerged, and were seen to strike the hull immediately forward of the conning tower. However, the explosion was so violent that the Arado was damaged and forced to make an emergency descent, the crew later being rescued by an He 115.[23]

On 16 April *Hptmn*. Wiegmink's *Bordfliegerstaffel* 1./BFl.Gr. 196 was ordered by *F.d.Luft* to provide a *Kette* of Arado floatplanes for the purpose of submarine hunting in the sea area stretching from the west coast of Denmark across the Skagerrak, and from the southern Norwegian coast to the island of List. Aircraft 'B', 'F' and 'M' were assigned beginning at 0715hrs that day, leadership of the small sub-unit being handed to *Oblt.z.S.* Jürgen Quaet-Faslem. He was to take his orders directly from *F.d.Luft West*, and began operations immediately, although disaster overtook them on their first mission when aircraft 'M' dropped out of the loose *Kette* formation while off the southern tip of Langeland and attempted an emergency alighting. The Arado rolled over for reasons that remain unclear, and Observer *Lt.z.S.* Siegfried Andrasch and *Uffz.* Heinz Rösken were both killed.

It was two Arados of 5./BFl.Gr. 196 attached to *Küstenfligergruppe* 906 that sighted the disabled minelaying submarine HMS *Seal* on 5 May, after Lt Cdr Rupert Philip Lonsdale, RN, had been forced to bring his boat to the surface with heavy damage caused by a mine explosion. HMS *Seal* had sailed from Immingham on the last day of April, and had laid its planned field of fifty mines south of the Swedish island of Vinga in the Kattegat to block the waters used by German supply convoys bound for Norway. Lonsdale had already narrowly avoided attack by an aircraft of *Küstenfligergruppe* 906 as well as German ASW trawlers. He had been forced to lay his minefield not in the primary location, but at the first alternate provided by his Admiralty orders in the event of heavy enemy activity. Within forty-five minutes their task was complete, and *Seal* crept away. Still aware of the proximity of German patrol craft, and in shallow

Kriegsmarine officers inspect gunfire damage inflicted on HMS *Seal* by the Arado aircraft which ultimately captured the submarine.

water that did not exceed 100ft and left little room for manoeuvre, *Seal* drifted with the current to avoid hydrophone detection. At 1830hrs the sound of wire scraping the outside hull was distinctly heard by the crew, followed twenty-five minutes later by a severe explosion aft, just as the men were about to eat their evening meal. In the heavily mined Kattegat they had apparently snagged a moored mine, probably German though potentially Danish, as they had also sown their own defensive fields before the German invasion.

Although all of the crew were unharmed, the boat shipped nearly 130 tons of water in the partially flooded aftermost mine compartment, and several attempts at surfacing the heavy submarine failed. Life-sustaining oxygen, compressed air for blowing tanks, battery power to turn the screws, and morale all ran low, and one final attempt to surface was made at 0110hrs on 5 May. Almost miraculously, the damaged boat rose to the surface, where Lonsdale immediately jettisoned code books and secret material as his crew smashed the ASDIC gear and radioed an urgent situation report to the Admiralty. The submarine's rudder was jammed, and attempts to steer towards Sweden using only the engines failed after the starboard diesel engine seized solid. Out of options, Lewis guns were manned on the bridge as HMS *Seal* wallowed hopelessly in the swell.

In Aalborg, the previous day's sighting of HMS *Seal* by the reconnaissance aircraft prompted the despatch of several aircraft from *Obstlt*. Lessing's *Küstenfliegergruppe* 906 in a prolonged hunt for the submarine. First to sight the stricken vessel were *Lt.z..S.* Günther Mehrens and his pilot, *Uffz*. Walter Böttcher, in the attached 5./BFl. Gr. 196 Arado 6W+IN. Below, Lonsdale harboured the forlorn hope that Mehrens would possibly mistake them for a disabled Swedish submarine, but the Arado opened fire with machine guns and made a bombing run, Lonsdale ordering his Lewis gunners to return fire. A second Arado, 6W+EN, commanded by *Lt.z.S.* Karl-Ernst Schmidt and flown by *Uffz*. Sackritz, soon arrived to join the fray, and on *Seal*'s conning tower Lonsdale himself manned one of the Lewis guns after German fire wounded Lt Cdr Terence Butler in the leg and an able seaman who was taken below for treatment. One of the Lewis guns jammed, and Schmidt's machine-gun fire perforated the submarine's port ballast tank, causing *Seal* to list badly. The arrival of *Lt.z.S.* Nikolaus Broili's larger He 115, 8L+CH of 1./Kü.Fl.Gr. 906, coincided with the second Lewis gun jamming, and Londsdale realised that, to have any chance of saving his crew, his vessel would have to be surrendered. A tablecloth was waved from the battered conning tower, and HMS *Seal* capitulated to the *Küstenflieger*.

Schmidt alighted nearby, and demanded that the captain swim over to be taken captive. Lonsdale handed command of HMS *Seal* to his navigation officer, Lt Trevor Beet, before being taken aboard the Arado and flown to Aarlborg. Mehrens later also descended and took aboard Coxswain Marcus Cousins. Aboard the Heinkel, Broili flashed Morse messages to the floating Arados, instructing the observer officer to board the submarine, but they were either unseen or ignored. Instead, the two seaplanes took off once more with their captives, leaving the Heinkel to stand off and monitor *Seal* until the arrival of the submarine-hunting converted trawler *UJ 128* to complete the capture of boat and crew, who were removed by an armed boarding party. HMS *Seal* was towed towards Germany, the *U-Jäger* being replaced by the salvage tug *Seeteufel* until the minelaying submarine was pushed against the sea wall at Friedrichshafen.[24]

On 12 April *Luftflotte* 5 was established in Hamburg under the command of *General* Erhard Milch (who was simultaneously named *Fliegerführer Nord*) to control all air operations in Norway and Denmark. Taking control from Geisler's X.*Fliegerkorps*, it and its composite units, including transport and maritime aircraft, were made directly subordinate in the command chain to Milch's new office. Geisler's staff had already begun moving to Oslo, creating signals and supply networks, as Milch's *Luftflotte* staff did not begin arriving in Norway until 24 April. Shortly after *Luftflotte* 5 had been firmly established, Milch handed command to *General* Hans-Jürgen Stumpff, former Chief of Luftwaffe General Staff and commander of *Luftflotte* 1.

At the end of April the *Küstenflieger* units were spread beneath a widening canopy of mixed Kriegsmarine and Luftwaffe commands, increasingly geographically dispersed as the battle for south and central Norway drew to a close, while the struggle for Narvik still balanced precariously between defeat and victory for the Wehrmacht

Maritime Units, 30 April 1940, and chain of command

Gen.d.Lw.b.Ob.d.M (*General der Flieger* Hans Ritter)
   F.d.Luft West (Jever, jointly subordinate to MG West) *Generalmajor* Hermann Bruch

Kü.Fl.Gr 106, *Obstlt.* Hermann Jorden (Nordeney)
(subordinate to 9.*Fliegerdivision* for minelaying missions)
- 3./Kü.Fl.Gr. 106 (Borkum), *Major* Hans-Joachim Kannengiesser, He 115
- 3./Kü.Fl.Gr. 506 (Nordeney), *Hptm.* Ernst-Wilhelm Bergemann, He 115
- 3./Kü.Fl.Gr. 906 (Nordeney) *Oblt.* Max Schöne, He 59 — converting to He 115.

Kü.Fl.Gr. 406, *Major* Karl Stockmann (Hörnum)
- 2./Kü.Fl.Gr. 406 (Hörnum), *Oblt.* Hans-Joachim Tantzen, Do 18
- 2./Kü.Fl.Gr. 906 (Hörnum), *Hptm.* Hans-Bruno von Laue, Do 18
- 3./Kü.Fl.Gr. 406 (Hörnum), *Hptm.* Gert Gustav Konstantin von Roth, Do 18
- 2./Kü.Fl.Gr. 106 (Rantum), *Hptm.* Franz Schriek, Do 18
- 1./Kü.Fl.Gr. 406 (Rantum), *Oblt.* Horst Kayser, Do 18

Staffel 1./BFl.Gr. 196 (Wilhelmshaven), *Hptm.* Gerrit Wiegmink, Ar 196

Kü.Fl.Gr. 806, *Oberstleutnant* Wolfgang von Wild (Uetersen)
- 2./Kü.Fl.Gr. 806 (Uetersen), *Hptm.* Friedrich Hahne, He 111J
- 3./Kü.Fl.Gr. 806 (Uetersen), *Hptm.* Richard Linke, He 111J

Kü.Fl.Gr. 506, *Major* Heinrich Minner (Trondheim)
(subordinate to X.*Fliegerkorps* for *Weserübung* operations)
- 1./Kü.Fl.Gr. 106 (Trondheim), *Hptm.* Friedrich-Franz Schroetter, He 115
- 1./Kü.Fl.Gr. 506 (Trondheim), *Oblt.* Eberhard Peukert, He 115
- 2./Kü.Fl.Gr. 506 (Trondheim), *Hptm.* Wolfgang von Zezschwitz, He 115

Transozeanstaffel (Travemünde), *Hptm.* Friedrich von Buddenbrock, Do 24, Do 26, Ju 52. (Subordinate to X.*Fliegerkorps* for *Weserübung* operations)

F.d.Luft Ost (jointly subordinate to *MG Ost*) *Obstlt.* Hermann Edert.
Kü.Fl.Gr. 606, *Obstlt.* Hermann Edert (Holtenau)
(subordinate to X.*Fliegerkorps* for *Weserübung* operations)
- 1./Kü.Fl.Gr. 606 (Holtenau), *Hptm.* Wolfgang Lenschow, Do 17
- 2./Kü.Fl.Gr. 606 (Holtenau), *Hptm.* Werner Lassmann, Do 17
- 3./Kü.Fl.Gr. 606 (Holtenau), *Hptm.* Heinrich Golcher, Do 17

Gruppe Busch, *Hptm.* Hermann Busch (Copenhagen/Aalborg)
   1./Kü.Fl.Gr. 706 (Copenhagen), *Oblt.* Wolfgang Beitzke, He 59
   2./Kü.Fl.Gr. 706 (Copenhagen) (temporary unit), He 59
   1./Kü.Fl.Gr. 806 (Copenhagen), *Hptm.* Hermann Busch, He 111J

Kü.Fl.Gr. 906, *Obstlt.* Hermann Lessing (Aalborg)
   1./Kü.Fl.Gr. 906 (Aalborg), *Major* Hermann Kaiser, He 59
   5/BFl.Gr. 196 (Aalborg) *Hptm.* Helmut Bertram, Ar 196

The somewhat makeshift re-formation of *Küstenfliegergruppe* 706 had begun during January 1940 at Kiel-Holtenau, with the sole operational *Staffel* being 1./Kü.Fl.Gr. 706, equipped with elderly He 59. Without a Staff unit, they were amalgamated into the *ad hoc 'Gruppe Busch'*, under the command of *Hptm.* Hermann Busch of 1./Kü.Fl.Gr. 806. On 20 April an additional single He 59, NE+TD, was released from service in the transport unit *Kampfgruppe zur besonderen Verwendung* 108 and attached to Busch's command, becoming the sole unit of a temporarily established 2./Kü.Fl.Gr. 706 and renumbered 6I+IK, soon rolled into 1.*Staffel*. The primary focus of *Gruppe Busch*, based between Aalborg and the small

Major Hermann Busch, former commander of 1./Kü.Fl.Gr. 506 before taking command of I/KG 26.

harbour at Thisted, was anti-submarine patrolling of the Skagerrak and Kattegat. However, its service was relatively brief; all of the He 59s were ordered to be transferred during mid-June 1940 to the *Seenotdienst* for conversion to air-sea rescue aircraft, while the *Staffel* retrained and re-equipped with Ar 196s and He 115s, after which the *Gruppe* would assume a more orthodox structure. Busch was promoted *Major*, and on 20 April transferred to KG 26, where he took command of I.*Gruppe*.

For the operational Luftwaffe, the strength of their dedicated maritime units at the end of April 1940 amounted to 9.*Fliegerdivision* and certain elements of X.*Fliegerkorps*:

9.*Fliegerdivision, General der Flieger* Joachim Coeler, (Jever)
    KG 4, *Obst.* Martin Fiebig (Fassberg), He 111P
        I./KG 4 (Copenhagen-Kastrup), *Obstlt.* Hans-Joachim Rath, He 111H-4
        II./KG 4 (Oslo), *Major* Dietrich Freiherr von Massenbach, He 111P
        III./KG 4 (Lüneberg), *Major* Erich Bloedorn, He 111P, Ju 88A-1
    I./KG 40 (Copenhagen/Kastrup), *Major* Edgar Petersen, Fw 200C-1
    KGr. 126 (Marx), *Hptm.* Gerd Stein, He 111H-4
    3.(F)/*Aufklärungsgruppe* 122, (Stavanger), Do 17, Bf 110

Luftflotte 5 (Oslo) *General* Hans-Jürgen Stumpff
    X.*Fliegerkorps*, *Generalleutnant* Hans Geisler
    KG 26 'Löwen' (Trondheim Vaernes), *Generalmajor* Robert Fuchs, He 111H
        I./KG 26 (Trondheim Vaernes), *Major* Hermann Busch, He 111H
        II./KG 26 (Trondheim Vaernes), *Major* Martin Vetter, He 111H
        III./KG 26 (Trondheim Vaernes), *Major* Viktor von Lossberg, He 111H
    KG 30 'Adler' (Westerland), *Obstlt.* Walter Loebel, Ju 88A
        I./KG 30 (Jever), *Hptm.* Fritz Doench, Ju 88 A
        II./KG 30 (Westerland), *Hptm.* Claus Hinkelbein, Ju 88 A
        III./KG 30 (Marx), *Hptm.* Gerhard Kollewe, Ju 88 A

Ultimately, the outcome of the struggle for Narvik was decided nearly 2,000 kilometres to the south-west. From 5 May, following the Allied evacuation of Namsos, additional air units that had been subordinated to X.*Fliegerkorps* were withdrawn to Germany alongside elements of KG 30, in preparation for the planned attack in the west. During the night of 9 May the codeword *Danzig* was issued by *OKW* in Berlin to all subordinate major commands, signifying the opening of Hitler's cherished assault on the Low Countries and France, beginning at 0535hrs the following morning. During the night, seven aircraft of 9.*Fliegerdivision* dropped mines off the Dutch and Belgian coasts: near den Helder, Ijmuiden, Hook of Holland, in the Scheldt, and off Flushing, Zeebrugge and Ostend. Further minelaying operations were also undertaken over successive nights, including the He 115s provided by *Küstenfliegergruppe* 106, by which time land forces had made significant headway in The Netherlands and Belgium. Meanwhile, both KG 4 and KG 30 attacked shipping off the Belgian and Dutch coasts, claiming notable success against destroyers engaged in Operation *Ordnance*, the evacuation of Dutch government staff and monarchy, and the small British force that had landed in the Hook of Holland on demolition missions.

A pilot of KG 30 reports to *Geschwader Kommodore Oberstleutnant* Loebel in a photograph staged for the benefit of a Propaganda Company photographer.

Twelve He 59s allocated to 3./KGr.z.b.V. 108 for *Unternehmen Weserübung* took part in the invasion of The Netherlands as part of '*Sonderstaffel* Schwilden'; a provisional seaplane unit formed for the purpose and placed under the command of *Hptm.* Horst Schwilden, *Staffelkapitän* of 3./KG 26. Schwilden had taken part in the Spanish Civil War as an *Oberleutnant* pilot with AS/88; he was no stranger to the operation of the large Heinkel floatplanes. The *Sonderstaffel*'s task was the securing of key bridges in Rotterdam on the morning of the invasion, crucial for the advance of German armour. It carried 120 men of 11./*Infanterie Regiment* 16, comprising platoons commanded by *Lts.* Gottbehöde and Fortmann, plus twenty-two engineers from the 2./ *Pionier Bataillon* 22. The assembled infantry and engineer company was commanded by *Oblt.* Hermann-Albert Schrader, and the twelve Heinkels approached the Willems Bridge over the River Maas during the early morning assault, splitting into two separate flights of six aircraft to envelop the target from both east and west. The aircraft alighted on the river virtually unopposed, and the troops were disembarked successfully in rubber dinghies. They secured the Willems Bridge amidst crowds of bewildered civilians, and a nearby railway span and the Leeuwen and Jan-Kuiten Bridges were also captured without loss. Four Heinkels were damaged while manoeuvring within the confined waterway and later completely wrecked while stationary on the river during a brief attack by Dutch gunboats. The remaining Heinkels suffered minor damage while being held in readiness to act as ambulance transports for wounded troops. Following the successful operation, the *Sonderstaffel* was disbanded.[25]

    The decision to withdraw Allied forces from Narvik was not made until 24 May, and until then the battle continued to rage. Fresh Luftwaffe plans were laid to base long-range Ju 88s in Trondheim, capable of reaching the Arctic battleground and of supporting troops struggling on the ground. The Junkers were to be commanded by *Major* Harlinghausen, freshly awarded the Knight's Cross on 4 May while still Chief of Staff to X.*Fliegerkorps*, and now back on operational flying while also holding the newly established office of *Fliegerführer Trondheim*. The intention also to use the highly effective but short-range Ju 87 dive-bombers remained dependent on the provision of an airfield between Trondheim and Narvik. Meanwhile, the Kriegsmarine also advocated aerial minelaying with the newly developed TMA mines (moored influence mines designed to be laid by U-boat torpedo tube) near the Stroemen Channel in Rombaken Fjord, to frustrate continued Royal Navy gunnery support provided by destroyers and cruisers. At the time of the proposed minelaying operation there were only eight TMAs in existence, and they would have to be transported by He 59s, which would have to touch down on the water to lay their mines. Staff at X.*Fliegerkorps* enthusiastically backed the idea, requesting that an additional nine mines be dropped in the narrow Stroeman Channel itself, though the dangerously constricted airspace made this suggestion impossible to accommodate.

On 22 May four He 59s of 1./Kü.Fl.Gr. 706 departed from Copenhagen, each carrying a single TMA mine. One aircraft, 6I+IH, was forced down near Godøy island, Giske, with engine damage, where it was scuttled and the crew rescued. The remaining three He 59s successfully laid their mines and had returned to Copenhagen by 24 May. Encouraged by this success, a further mission was mounted four days later which deposited five more mines at the narrow entrance to the Tjelsund.

The fighting in Norway involved myriad isolated skirmishes between Wehrmacht and Allied forces, also including aircraft of *Seenotflugkommando* 2, which highlights the difficult distinction between humanitarian and military service within which the *Seenot* aircraft operated. As a result of action on 15 May, *Oblt. der Reserve* Wilhelm Branger was taken prisoner as an enemy combatant by Norwegian troops. Earlier that day, *Lt.* Willi Meier's He 111H of III./KG 26 had been forced down with engine trouble near Alstahaug during an anti-shipping attack near Narvik, whereupon local Norwegian militia approached and demanded the crew's surrender. Following an initial German refusal, the militiamen opened fire on the stranded crew, wounding one and forcing the remainder to surrender. The wounded man was taken to hospital in Sandnessjøen, while the others were transported by fishing boat to a makeshift prisoner-of-war camp. Responding to earlier distress calls made by Meier before his forced landing, Branger's *Seenot* Heinkel He 59, D-AKUK, arrived some time later and alighted in the bay, whereupon Branger went ashore to discover the whereabouts of the missing bomber and crew. Branger was told by locals that the crew had been captured and moved, the wounded man and possibly other prisoners being held in the nearby town of Sandnessjøen.

The wreck of the He 111 was plainly visible, and, coming under rifle fire from Norwegian militia guards, Branger decided to lift off and proceed instead to Sandnessjøen to liberate the wounded crewman. Alighting at 1730hrs, Branger and an accompanying *Uffz.*, both now armed, went ashore again, walked to the small local hospital and demanded the release of any wounded Germans being held there. Although the chief physician initially refused to comply, he was subsequently ordered to do so in a telephone conversation with the Norwegian police commissioner at nearby Nesna. Meanwhile, as the luckless Branger was preoccupied with the protracted negotiations, the Norwegian naval trawler HMNoS *Honningsvåg* arrived in the bay, its captain having been ordered to seize the He 59 and capture its crew. Branger and his companion were taken prisoner by a landing party, but the two remaining *Unteroffiziers* aboard D-AKUK initially refused to surrender. A warning shot from the trawler settled the matter. Branger and his three crewmen were handed over to the Norwegian police. Although D-AKUK was taken in tow, it proved impossible to move, as it had firmly grounded in a low tide. After sustaining damage to its wings and pontoons during the attempts to pull it free, the aircraft was finally dragged out of Leirfjord and sunk three days later.

Seaplanes continued to transport men and equipment to German forces at Narvik, landing in Rombaksfjord to the east of the town itself. This, combined with Ju 52 parachute drops inland, maintained the fighting efficiency of Dietl's men. A reinforced infantry battalion making its way from Trondheim to link up with the troops in Narvik was also supplied by regular seaplane rendezvous. On the part of the operational Luftwaffe, the crews of the He 111 bombers were handicapped in their battle against Royal Navy forces because they possessed neither the training nor the specialised bomb sights needed for precision naval strikes, and the number of Ju 88s available for dive bombing and reconnaissance remained low as KG 30 steadily relocated to the Western Front. Overly optimistic Luftwaffe reports constantly cited the severe damaging or sinking of capital ships and even aircraft carriers, but without substance, so much so that Kriegsmarine officers stated on record their extreme scepticism at most success reports filed by the Luftwaffe General Staff. To compound their problems, Hurricane and Spitfire fighters were now based at aerodromes north of Narvik and began to take a heavy toll of the unescorted bombers. However, von Falkenhorst short-sightedly demanded that the Luftwaffe continue to concentrate its efforts at Narvik on ground support, rather than re-establishing the air superiority that would allow successful attacks against both the Royal Navy and Allied troops. Backed by the incoming commander of *Luftflotte* 5, Stumpff, this misdirection of available air power did little to lessen Dietls' misery, and despite a small number of reinforcements reaching the battle, German forces were expelled from Narvik on 28 May by fresh British forces that had been successfully landed by ship two miles to the east.

The position of Dietl's *Gebirgsjäger* was extremely precarious, and consideration was given to a forced march to nearby Sweden for internment as the staffs of X.*Fliegerkorps* and *Luftflotte* 5 wrangled over how best to use their available forces. Amid bitter arguments, the *Fliegerkorps*' Chief of Staff, *Genmaj*. Ulrich Kessler, resigned his command at one point in protest at what he considered the woeful and careless misdirection of his men that had resulted in unnecessarily heavy casualties. However, events on the Western Front had already played their part, and on 24 May the British finally resolved to evacuate their troops from Narvik. In truth, the splitting of Allied land forces between fighting for Trondheim and Narvik had already doomed the Allies to overall failure, British planning being muddled as to its actual strategic objective. Although Narvik and its access to Swedish iron ore mines was the prize, Trondheim was perhaps the key to controlling both north and south with its strategic position at the narrow waist of the country. Vacillating between the two objectives robbed both of success, and between 4 and 8 June the Allied troops in Norway were successfully evacuated by sea in Operation *Alphabet*.

Part of the British withdrawal was sighted by He 115 S4+EH of 1./Kü.Fl.Gr. 106 during a reconnaissance over the rugged coastline around Narvik. Following the initial sighting, a probe northward yielded confirmed contact with the battleship HMS *Valiant*. However, air support hastily summoned from HMS *Ark Royal* bounced the Heinkel, and it was shot down east of Bodö by Skuas of 800 Sqn FAA. Its pilot, *Fdw*. Franz Augustat, managed to shake off the pursuing Skuas, but his aircraft had been hit in the starboard engine, and gunner/wireless operator *Uffz*. Willi Schönfelder was wounded in the shoulder after firing only a single burst of return fire. Aircraft commander and observer *Lt.z.S*. Rembert van Delden bandaged the wounded gunner, and the Heinkel staggered back towards Trondheim. With his compass behaving erratically in the northern latitudes, van Delden used his sextant to plot a course, but after an hour they were forced to ditch in the sea with fuel exhausted. Although the aircraft's radio equipment had been damaged they were successful in transmitting distress calls before they alighted, whereupon the heavy swell ripped the starboard float clean off its struts. Nonetheless, the Heinkel remained afloat, enabling its crew to abandon it in their rubber dinghy after jettisoning anything of potential intelligence value. The three crewmen were in their dinghy only briefly before another of the *Staffel*'s He 115s, flown by *Oblt.* Peterjürgen 'Pitt' Midderhoff, an experienced air-sea rescue pilot, arrived on the scene as a result of their hurried radio transmissions. Despite the swell, Midderhoff alighted and recovered the stranded crew, although his aircraft's propeller blades were badly bent by impact with the choppy water as the Heinkel crashed through the peaks and troughs of wind-driven waves. Despite the damage, Midderhoff was able to take off again, using the swell to help catapult the aircraft upward and, after sinking the abandoned aircraft with gunfire, he successfully returned to Trondheim with the rescued crew.[26]

The day after Midderhoff's spectacular rescue of the downed Heinkel crew, 10 June, Norway officially surrendered, and the I./KG 40 Focke-Wulf Fw 200 flown by *Oblt.* Heinrich Schlosser sank the largest ship lost by the British during Operation *Alphabet*, the 13,241grt armed boarding vessel HMS *Vandyck*. Schlosser attacked the ship with bombs off Andenes, as it prepared to assist in the evacuation. Direct hits sent the former cruise liner under, killing one officer and five ratings. The remaining twenty-nine officers and 132 ratings took to their boats and rowed ashore, where German troops captured them.[27]

KG 26 *Kommodore Oberst* Robert Fuchs photographed aboard one of his bombers. His award of the Knight's Cross on 6 April 1940 for *Geschwader* leadership was the first such decoration granted to a member of the Luftwaffe's bomber arm. (NARA)

The *Küstenflieger* were heavily involved in supporting the invasion of Norway through reconnaissance and anti-submarine patrols, this He 115 of *Küstenfliegergruppe* 506 being photographed at Trondheim. (Australian War Memorial)

Although the Norwegian campaign was successful, German losses had been severe, particularly to surface ships of the Kriegsmarine. The crisis confronting Raeder and his staff in the face of such depletion had the knock-on effect of halting construction of the carrier *Graf Zeppelin* completely. Raeder ordered the worked curtailed. The guns were to be removed for use as coastal defence for Norway, as the carrier's fire-control system was still incomplete, elements having been supplied to the Soviet Union owing to contractual demands included within the 1939 non-aggression pact. On 6 July 1940 the *Graf Zeppelin* was towed to the Baltic port of Gotenhafen, beyond the likely range of British bombers, and it became a floating storage space for Kriegsmarine hardwood supplies. Construction of 'B' had already been stopped on 19 September 1939, the hull later being dismantled and its components used elsewhere.

Nevertheless, by the time Norway had surrendered the Allied Western Front had collapsed, Belgium and The Netherlands had surrendered, and the Dunkirk evacuation of the shattered remains of the British Expeditionary Force had been completed. Göring's operational Luftwaffe had been tasked with annihilating the cornered enemy trapped

HMT *Lancastria*, her hull crowded with survivors, sinking off Saint-Nazaire after being hit by bombers of KG 30. This disaster remains one of the world's worst in terms of its death toll, never properly ascertained, but estimated to have reached at least 3,050 people, possibly as high as 5,000.

against the Channel coast, but had comprehensively failed, and although British losses of men, equipment and ships were heavy, Britain was not yet defeated.

Aircraft of both KG 26 and KG 30 had taken part in the attacks against The Netherlands and France, and on 17 June Ju 88s of II./KG 30, which had moved to a forward base at Le Culot, Belgium, bombed shipping gathered at Saint-Nazaire as part of Operation *Aerial*, the British evacuation of ground forces nearest the French Atlantic ports. The bombers found the heavily-laden 16,243-ton liner *Lancastria*, requisitioned by the Admiralty for service as a troopship, anchored off the entrance to Saint-Nazaire's harbour. The liner's skipper, Capt Rudolph Sharp, a veteran seaman from Liverpool, was held in high regard both by company and crew, and had previously captained the liners *Lusitania*, *Mauritania* and *Olympic*. He had already taken his ship to Lorient, where he was found superfluous to evacuation requirements and redirected onward to Saint-Nazaire, arriving at 0400hrs on 17 June. HMT *Lancastria* was anchored in twelve fathoms, barely 22m, at Charpentier Roads, near the harbour's entrance, the ship's draught being too great to allow it to enter port. While the *Lancastria* swung lazily at anchor in the turbid water carrying silt from the mouth of the Loire River, Saint-

Nazaire was in a state of bedlam, as retreating Allied troops destroyed their heavy equipment and whatever installations might be valuable to the advancing Wehrmacht. British officers of the Royal Navy Volunteer Reserve (RNVR), acting as embarkation control, boarded *Lancastria* to assess the number of troops it could accommodate. Sharp was heard to reply '3,000 at a pinch'. By midday Sharp and his crew had embarked an exhausted 5,200 dishevelled soldiers and airmen, as well as many British civilians, some of whom had worked for the Fairey Aviation Company in Belgium and had retreated all the way across France. The British destroyers HMS *Highlander* and *Havelock* shuttled between shore and ship throughout the day, until attempts to keep track of the number of evacuees were abandoned completely. Finally, packed beyond capacity, *Lancastria* received clearance to sail for England, but remained at anchor, Sharp and his officers erroneously believing that U-boats posed the most prominent threat, and opting to await an armed escort.

As the Luftwaffe appeared over Saint-Nazaire, Sharp had the ship's boats swung out in the event of emergency, and at 1557hrs II./KG 30's Ju 88s attacked *Lancastria*. Sharp rushed to the bridge, reaching the wheelhouse as four high-explosive bombs bracketed his ship. Two passed through the deck planking. One detonated inside number two cargo hold, packed with at least 800 RAF men, and the other smashed through

Dornier Do 26 aircraft of the *Transozeanstaffel* were used to ferry men and equipment to the beleaguered garrison at Narvik, temporarily attached to the transport group '*Kampfgeschwader zur besonderen Verwendung* 108'.

number three hold, where it released gallons of heavy fuel oil into the water. A third bomb arced directly down a smokestack and exploded in the engine room, while the last missed by mere metres, its blast sufficient to hole the great liner below the waterline.

The *Lancastria* sank rapidly by the head, listing initially to port before a sudden intake of water rolled the hull over to starboard. Many were trapped inside after the main internal staircase collapsed, and, with KG 30 bombers continuing to strafe the anchorage, neighbouring vessels could not remain stationary long enough to be effectively useful as rescue ships. The ASDIC trawler HMT *Cambridgeshire* was the most successful, with over 1,000 survivors dragged aboard. Within fifteen minutes *Lancastria* had rolled back to port, the stern briefly rising above water before it finally went down.

The exact number of dead has never been established, but it is known that at least 3,050 people were killed, estimates variously rising to 4,500 or 5,000 dead. Even without this revised death toll, the horrifying statistic of people killed during the sinking gave the *Lancastria* the tragic title of the worst British merchant loss in history. Captain Sharp, who survived the ordeal, stated that there was no panic on board, even up to the final moment as the hull slid beneath the sea. In words taken from his report to the Department of Trade:

A Do 26 of the *Transozeanstaffel* in Hemnfjorden on 13 May 1940.

> The spirit of the men in the water was wonderful, they even managed to sing whilst waiting to be picked up. [But . . .] not everyone who had a lifebelt was saved . . . I should estimate that 2,000 were saved by lifebelts and another 500 in boats and rafts, so that 2,500 people were saved out of a total of about 5,500. I lost 70 of my crew of 330.

The loss of life was so shattering that Prime Minister Winston Churchill forbade the publishing of news of the disaster in the English press, clamping a 'D-notice' on it. He felt that the country's morale could not bear the burden of this terrible event. In his voluminous Second World War history he later wrote:

> When this news came to me in the quiet Cabinet Room during the afternoon I forbade its publication, saying: 'The newspapers have got quite enough disaster for today at least'. I had intended to release the news a few days later, but events crowded upon us so black and so quickly that I forgot to lift the ban, and it was some years before the knowledge of this horror became public.

Survivors were forbidden under King's Regulations to mention the disaster. Those killed were listed as 'missing in action', leading to the assumption by most bereaved relatives that they had probably died during the bloody retreat from northern France. However, the story of the sinking could not be contained and, after appearing in the *New York Times*, it finally broke in English newspapers on Friday 26 July 1940, albeit belatedly and quietly. The official report is still sealed until the year 2040 under the Official Secrets Act.[28]

By the end of the French campaign several maritime bomber pilots had been awarded the Knight's Cross for their cumulative service since Operation *Weserübung*. *Oberleutnant* Werner Baumbach of 5./KG 30 was so awarded on 8 May for his attack on the French Group Z off Namsos, *Oberst*. Martin Fiebig, *Geschwaderkommodore* of KG 4, received his on the same day. The following five all received theirs on 19 June: *Maj*. Fritz Doench, *Gruppenkommandeur* of I./KG 30; *Hptm*. Claus Hinkelbein, *Kommandeur* II./KG 30; *Oblt*. Franz Wieting, *Staffelkapitän* 6./KG 30, 'for noteworthy success against enemy warships and shipping in the North Sea'; *Fw*. Willi Schultz, 6./KG 30, 'for hits on Royal Navy surface units off Norway, including the cruiser HMS *Suffolk*'; and *Hptm*. Arved Crüger, awarded for his '*Staffel* leadership during *Weserübung*, the subsequent anti-shipping campaign against the United Kingdom and the invasion of France'.

The naval air arm played little part in the defeat of the Allies' western forces, instead continuing minelaying and the harassment of shipping, both military and merchant, in the North Sea. By the middle of June the improvised group commanded by *Major* Walter Schwarz, *Gruppe* Schwarz, comprising 3./Kü.Fl.Gr. 406 and 2./Kü.Fl.Gr. 906, both equipped with Do 18 flying boats, was based at Stavanger-Sola (See), ten kilometres south-west of the town on the shore of Hafs Fjord. Previously used by the Norwegian Naval Air Service, the base had an established infrastructure that the Luftwaffe improved further over their years of occupation. The Dornier Do 17s of 3./Kü.Fl.Gr. 606, based on the nearby airstrip, also formed part of the *Gruppe*. This forward base increased the range of reconnaissance missions into the North Atlantic approaches, though the ageing Do 18s showed limitations, both in combat and endurance. During June the seaplane tender *Hans Rolshoven* was based in Stavanger Harbour as support for *Gruppe* Schwarz, acting as the general communications hub for all naval aircraft operating along the south-west Norwegian coast by means of its powerful radio gear. *Gruppe* Schwarz was soon reinforced by the Ar 196s of 1./BFl.Gr. 196 and renamed *Küstenfliegergruppe* Stavanger on 14 June, after Schwarz had departed for Germany and was replaced by *Major* Karl Stockmann.

The Norwegian seaplane bases also provided support for shipborne aircraft during June, when the Kriegsmarine mounted Operation *Juno*, a sortie by the battleships *Gneisenau* and *Scharnhorst*, the heavy cruiser *Admiral Hipper* and four escorting destroyers. Their objective was the disruption of Royal Navy forces supporting Allied troops still engaged in the final weeks of fighting in Narvik. While *Juno* succeeded in sinking the carrier HMS *Glorious*, two destroyers, one minesweeper, one troopship and an oil tanker, *Scharnhorst* suffered heavy damage from a torpedo fired by the destroyer HMS *Acasta*. Badly holed and with forty-eight men killed, *Scharnhorst* was hounded by British aircraft as she headed first for Norway for emergency repairs, and then south towards Kiel's shipyards. The battleship's Ar 196s were flown in continuous combined reconnaissance and anti-submarine patrols, and all German U-boats were instructed to avoid the area through which the battleship would pass. During one such patrol, on 21 June, observer *Oblt.z..S.* Peter Schrewe and pilot *Uffz.* Gallinat had taken off from *Scharnhorst* in Ar 196 T3+BH at 0045hrs, alighting at both Trondheim and Bergen for refuelling and brief rest during their extended and exhausting patrol. At 1645hrs they sighted a diving submarine, and dropped two 50kg bombs, which were recorded as landing only 3m from the conning tower. The vessel's stern rose clear of the water as the boat dived, leaving a vague smudge of an oil slick behind. Estimated as a 1,000-ton submarine, the single deck gun was visible to Schrewe as it dived, and the boat was considered probably damaged by the attack. The Arado subsequently alighted at Stavanger-Sola, where the starboard float was found to be damaged, requiring brief repairs before the aircraft returned to *Scharnhorst*. In fact they had attacked *Kaptlt*. Otto Kretschmer's *U99*, which had strayed into the area proscribed for U-boats. It had suffered minor damage on what was its maiden patrol from Germany, bound for the Atlantic, and was forced to return to Wilhelmshaven for repairs.

Nonetheless, the small Arado floatplanes based in Norway proved their worth in anti-submarine patrols during July, when they were largely responsible for the surrender of another British submarine, HMS *Shark*. At around 2215hrs on 5 July, Ar 196 T3+LH, piloted by *Lt.z.S.* Gerhard Gottschalk, accompanied by wireless operator/gunner *Uffz.* Gerhard Manjok, sighted *Shark* running on the surface, recharging depleted batteries while on patrol thirty-five miles west of Feistein, south-west Norway. The midsummer nights were never completely dark at that latitude, and Gottschalk immediately attacked from astern with bombs and machine-gun fire.

> At 2210hrs I dived from 800 metres and released the first bomb from 400 metres . . . The bomb hit amidships, just behind the tower. The submarine vanished, but shortly after, the stern reappeared and I attacked again. The boat vanished before I was in a position to release the bomb, though. Again the stern appeared, and this time I dropped the bomb from 400 metres. It detonated on the starboard side of the tower, three metres off and somewhat aft. The submarine was lifted slightly out of the water, sank quickly and then came back up, stern down and with a severe list. It slowly righted itself, but the stern remained deep in the water. The fore end of the submarine was strafed by cannon and machine-gun fire. Eventually the submarine vanished, leaving a large oil patch.[29]

The *Shark* was badly damaged and sinking, stern first. Lieutenant Commander Peter Buckley attempted to control the descent using the port motor, the only one still functioning, but succeeded only in draining the already depleted batteries. With little choice, he ordered all the remaining compressed air to be used to blow main ballast, and arrested the descent at a depth of 91m. The submarine began to rise, out of control, and reached the surface at an ungainly angle, where it came under renewed attack. A second Arado had arrived to continue the battle, and the *Shark*'s crew manned guns and attempted to fight them off. Aircraft T3+GH, piloted by *Lt.* Eberhard Stelter with *Uffz.* Helmut Stamp in the rear seat, also dropped its bombs on the stranded submarine and continued circling and strafing, the aircraft being hit by Lewis-gun fire from *Shark*'s bridge.

Gottschalk's aircraft was hit in the starboard wing, causing slight damage and forcing a return to base, where he swiftly exchanged it for another machine and returned to the scene, replacing Stelter, who returned to Stavanger. A third Arado, piloted by *Oblt.z.S.* Junker, had reached the scene, along with two Bf 109s which made repeated strafing passes. In Stavanger, Do 18 flying boats were fuelled and armed so that they might add their weight to the battle.

Aboard *Shark*, the situation had become hopeless. The final ascent had spilled battery acid into the bilges, creating chlorine gas, while Petty Officer James Gibson was killed by German gunfire and several men had been wounded by the attacking aircraft, including Buckley, who had been hit in the head and legs.[30] Under constant fire and with the Dornier flying boats also arriving, led by *Major* Karl Stockmann (*Gruppenkommandeur Küstenfliegergruppe* 406) in M2+FK, Buckley decided to surrender.

Junker noticed the sudden cessation of return fire as the Messerschmitts continued their strafing runs, and also saw men aboard the submarine raising their hands and frantically signalling with lights. To forestall any further attacks he impulsively set his Arado down alongside HMS *Shark*, though the port float had been seriously holed by Lewis-gun fire and immediately took on water as he brought the aircraft to a halt immediately alongside. Junker and his gunner, *Oblt.z.S.* Gerhard Schreck, jumped aboard the submarine with pistols drawn, while behind them their aircraft drifted away and capsized. The two Germans surveyed the scene aboard the wrecked conning tower, exchanging some words with the injured Buckley, but were unwilling to go below decks and investigate the situation further. Junker successfully communicated with a Do 18, which landed and retrieved both German airmen as well as Buckley and Sub-Lt Robert Barnes, transporting them to Stavanger.

Behind them, the circling aircraft monitored HMS *Shark*, the British crew now gathered on deck and awaiting the arrival of four minesweepers, which attempted to take control of the stricken submarine and bring her into harbour. Boxed between *M1803* and *M1805* and underslung to keep her afloat, the submarine was taken in tow by *M1806*, but began to sink by the stern after the British crew had been removed. The Germans had failed to prevent a surreptitious scuttling of the boat, the departing British crewmen having left the main ballast tank vents slightly open and disabled all pumps. As the Germans were unable to control the sinking submarine, the tow line was hurriedly cut and HMS *Shark* went down twenty-five miles west-south-west of Egersund.

The likelihood of the submarine being successfully captured intact was, in fact, virtually nil, regardless of its scuttling. German *B-Dienst* radio interception had detected HMS *Southampton* and *Coventry* of the 18th Cruiser Squadron and four destroyers of the 4th Flotilla being despatched from eastern Scottish bases to reconnoitre the area off Skudesnes as a result of Buckley's distress calls. While aircraft of *Luftflotte* 5 prepared an interception strike, the minesweepers were ordered to scuttle *Shark* and return to port, rather than face certain destruction by superior enemy forces; a measure that proved unnecessary. Coastal Command also joined the search for *Shark*, but found nothing, while the approaching surface forces experienced frequent air attacks that damaged HMS *Fame* and forced the search to be abandoned.

While the small and nimble Ar 196s were proving valuable for short-range coastal missions, the limitations of the Heinkel He 111J had impeded operations by *Küstenfliegergruppe* 806, and the decision was taken to re-equip the *Gruppe* with the more reliable and versatile Junkers Ju 88. During June all three *Staffeln* were relocated to the large training airfield at Uetersen for conversion to the new type, a process completed by 10 July. By this stage the so-called *Kanalkampf*, the concerted Luftwaffe attacks on English Channel shipping, was beginning, as Göring attempted to lure Fighter Command forces into battle over the water in the overture of what became known as the Battle of Britain. The objective was aerial superiority over Britain, either to force Churchill's government to sue for peace or as a prelude to potential seaborne invasion, something for which the Wehrmacht was woefully unprepared. The operational Luftwaffe's maritime units, KG 26 and KG 30, had maintained a degree of activity harassing shipping within the North Sea, KG 26 also mining east-coast harbours, but emphasis was now placed on the bombing of

Luftwaffe pilots and Kriegsmarine observers of the *Küstenflieger* that had taken part in attacks on British shipping off Norway photographed on 2 June following a press conference for foreign correspondents at Goebbels propaganda Ministry in Berlin. Second from left is renowned Stuka pilot Martin Möbus, while at far left is *Leutnant zur See* Rolf Thomsen of *Küstenfliegergruppe* 106. He later found fame as the commander of *U1202*.

British industry and military centres, and eventually changed to night area-bombing as the Luftwaffe failed to break Fighter Command.[31]

On 15 August the maritime strike aircraft of Geisler's X.*Fliegerkorps*, still part of Stumpff's *Luftflotte* 5, were ordered to attack the British mainland from Norway across the North Sea, in concert with simultaneous bombing raids in the south by *Luftflotten* 2 and 3, based in France and Belgium. In a risky 'flanking' attack, sixty-five He 111s of KG 26 from Stavanger, escorted by thirty-five twin-engine Bf 110 heavy fighters, were to bomb airfields in the Newcastle area, while fifty unescorted Ju 88s of KG 30 from Aalborg attacked the No.4 Group Bomber Station at Driffield, Yorkshire. The Bf 110s of I./ZG 76 were provided with extra fuel drop tanks, and flew without rear gunners to minimise weight and extend their range. The Luftwaffe expected to find little or no opposition, but instead blundered into experienced Spitfire and Hurricane squadrons posted to rest and refit in the north of England. British Radio Direction Finding (RDF) had detected the incoming waves of German aircraft while they were still miles out to

TURNING NORTH AND WEST

sea, and the defending fighters were directed to intercept them. Though vastly outnumbered, the nimble fighters were more than a match the unwieldy Bf 110s and slow-moving Heinkels. As the Bf 110s went into their familiar defensive circles, the Heinkels scattered, some dropping bombs to little effect on the British mainland, but most jettisoning them to flee for Norway. In total, KG 26 lost eight Heinkels, ZG 76 seven Bf 110s and KG 30 seven Ju 88s destroyed, though the Ju 88s had better speed compared with the Heinkels and had managed to bomb their allocated target. Many others were heavily damaged, and the attack marked their first and last attempt to bomb mainland Britain from Norway. A decoy flight of He 115 floatplanes to the north failed to draw any of the defending fighters away from the attacking bombers, and not a single British fighter was lost, although twelve Whitleys were destroyed by Ju 88s bombing the No.4 Group Bomber Station at Driffield. The Ju 88s dropped 169 bombs of various calibres on the airfield, also damaging hangars and administrative buildings and killing seventeen RAF ground crew by fragmentation bombs and subsequent low-level strafing. However, the aircraft of X.*Fliegerkorps* played no further significant part in the Battle of Britain, being relegated to night area bombing from the airfield at Beauvais in France, or reverting to maritime harassment missions within the North Sea. Among those aircraft now relegated to the area bombing of Britain, a steady casualty rate continued to claim experienced maritime fliers misused on such traditional bombing missions. For example, *Obstlt.* Hans Geisse, *Kommodore* of KG 40, was shot down and killed over London on the night of 7/8 September 1940 in an He 111H-5, and the following night *Maj.* Johannes Hackbarth, pre-war Adjutant to *Generalfeldmarschall* Milch and now *Kommandeur* III./KG 30, was shot down by 602 Sqn Spitfires after another night bombing raid on London. Ditching his Ju 88 in the sea off the Sussex coast, Hackbarth was rescued and became a prisoner of war. Severely wounded, he had his leg amputated below the knee. He was repatriated on 28 November 1943 and relegated to staff duties.

From 15 September He 111s had even begun dropping LMA and LMB naval parachute mines on land targets, fused to explode either by contact or by a clockwork timer. British Army bomb disposal experts were advised against attempting to defuse any unexploded mines found, instead calling on naval personnel from HMS *Vernon*, the Royal Navy Mine Warfare Establishment. On 21 September 1940 Lt Cdr Richard Ryan RN and CPO Reginald Ellingworth were killed while attempting to defuse one such mine in Dagenham, East London, as it hung by its parachute on a warehouse in North Oval Road. Both were posthumously awarded the George Cross for bravery.³² In night attacks on London during December, KG 26 was also using the heavy SC2500 'Max' bomb, the largest conventional bomb used by the Luftwaffe, which was carried externally on a specially modified bomb rack. A post-war Allied intelligence report on German explosive ordnance records the huge bomb's appearance:

> Sky blue overall. SC 2500 is stencilled on the body in letters 3 inches high. Two yellow stripes are painted on the body between the tail fins. A few anti-shipping bombs have been found with the following stencilled on the body: *Beim Abwurf auf Land nicht im Tiefangriff und nur o.V.* (not to be released over land in low-level attack and always without a time-delay fuse). This type is thought to be filled with Trialen 105.³³

Leutnant Werner Baumbach receives the Knight's Cross on 8 May 1940 while a pilot with 5./KG 30. Baumbach went on to become a leading expert in maritime operations, eventually becoming *Gruppenkommandeur* of I./KG 30 before withdrawn from active service to help develop new bomber designs.

While the operational Luftwaffe's maritime forces were involved, the seaplanes of the *Küstenflieger* played no significant role in the fighting for aerial supremacy over Britain. Instead they continued making opportunistic attacks on whatever shipping could be found within the North Sea and English Channel. However, the required concentration of available aircraft against mainland Britain also allowed the Luftwaffe to erode the strength of the naval air arm once again. At the beginning of July Göring suggested that the duties of aerial reconnaissance be once again redistributed, proposing that the operational Luftwaffe handle all reconnaissance duties west of Britain, in the Orkney/Shetland area, within a strip thirty miles wide along the British east coast and in the Channel area south of 53°N, a line bisecting Den Helder and Cromer. The aircraft controlled by the Kriegsmarine would only carry out aerial reconnaissance of the North Sea, German coastal approaches and sea lanes to Norway, also undertaking anti-submarine operations within these areas. Therefore, to reinforce Luftwaffe strength and match its increased responsibility, Göring laid claim to the *Küstenfliegergruppe* 806 and its new Ju 88s, as well as the He 115s of 3./Kü.Fl.Gr. 106 and 3./Kü.Fl. Gr. 906 for 'reinforcement of the offensive forces'. All Kriegsmarine personnel already assigned to these groups were to be left in place for the time being. His proposal was forwarded to Raeder:

> Under my command, *Luftflotte* 2 and 3 are carrying out the air offensive against the British Isles from the Belgian-Dutch and the French coast. They are equipped with all means for reconnaissance and thereby assure surveillance of the coastal area occupied by us, as well as of the Channel. I request your agreement to this arrangement so that I can immediately issue all necessary orders. Göring

Göring had already provoked the ire of the Kriegsmarine during June, when he sent what was described as a 'rude telegram' (unfortunately no longer extant) to Raeder, regarding the Kriegsmarine's part of Operation *Weserübung*. Raeder immediately complained in conference with Hitler, who ordered Göring to apologise personally, and Göring complied. The fresh attempts to subvert naval authority over *Küstenflieger* units merely antagonised an already tenuous relationship. While internally raging at his opposite number in the Luftwaffe, Raeder tactfully agreed with Göring's view that all air forces needed to be marshalled for the impending battle against Great Britain. This was largely due to diminishing North Sea convoy targets for offensive *Küstenflieger* operations, and the fact that air support for Germany's major surface forces was being rendered superfluous as they refitted and repaired following *Weserübung*. Yet Raeder also noted that the 'surrender of naval air force formations to Commander-in-Chief, Luftwaffe, however, will have to depend on the tasks at present also falling to the Kriegsmarine.'[34] For, like the operational Luftwaffe, the naval air force had also been forced to reorganise and redeploy following the fall of France and the development of bases along the Atlantic seaboard.

During August 1940 the post of *Führer der Seeluftstreitkräfte West* (*F.d.Luft West*) was abolished and replaced by the position simply known as *Führer der Seeluftstreitkräfte* (*F.d.Luft*), which remained the domain of *Generalmajor* Bruch. The office of *F.d.Luft Ost* was also to be no more, replaced instead by '*Fliegerführer Ost*' which was, in turn, incorporated directly within *Marinegruppenkommando Ost* (*MGK Ost*) in all operational matters. While Hermann Edert departed the post of *F.d.Luft Ost* to take command of the Ju 87s of *Sturzkampfgeschwader* 3, *Obstlt*. Axel von Blessingh, commander of *Küstenfliegergruppe* 906 since July, took the chair as the newly appointed *Fliegerführer Ost*, based in Aalborg with 1./Kü.Fl. Gr. 906 (He 115s) and 1./Kü.Fl.Gr. 706 (He 59s) as his available forces.

The extension of the *Küstenflieger*'s operational area to the Norwegian regions of Tromsø and Kirkenes also demanded the allocation of additional forces. Raeder estimated that at least three *Küstenfliegergruppen* and two shipborne squadrons (the latter for submarine chase and escort duties) were required for this area alone. Meanwhile, the desired increase in co-operation between aircraft and U-boats in France would also demand at least one *Küstenfliegergruppe* and the surviving long-range reconnaissance Do 26s of the *Transozeanstaffel*. Therefore, Raeder replied to the *RLM* that, while surrender of *Küstenfliegergruppe* 806 to Commander-in-Chief, Luftwaffe, would be in order, it would be impossible to hand over any elements of *Gruppen* 106 or 906, as these would be needed for new tasks arising in the French sector. The surrender of *Küstenfliegergruppe* 806 was agreed on the conditions that:

> 1. The arrangement is prompted by the need for joint action from joint operational areas and is based on the fact that there is no operational battle Fleet at present available and consequently no necessity for a close tactical tie-up between air formations and surface forces.

2. *Gruppe* 806 is only ceded temporarily.

3. *Gruppe* 806 will continue to be staffed with naval observers.

4. The Luftwaffe undertakes, if so requested by Naval Staff, to use this group for naval air warfare for which it is especially qualified.

5. Combat tasks in the central North Sea will be taken over by the adjacent *Luftflotten*.

However, this diplomatic approach by Raeder quickly stumbled after a visit by Luftwaffe Chief of Staff Hans Jeschonnek to his Kriegsmarine counterpart *Admiral* Otto Schniewind on 10 July, after which Schniewind had noted in the *SKL* War Diary:

The statements made by Chief, Luftwaffe General Staff, reveal that the Luftwaffe aims at the surrender of all naval air forces by the Navy.

Nevertheless, on that day *Küstenfliegergruppe* 806 was transferred to the control of *Luftflotte* 3 and redesignated *Kampfgruppe* 806, part of IV.*Fliegerkorps* based in Caen-Carpiquet. Inevitably, it was never to return to full naval control, though it did continue maritime operations in British waters and later, during 1942, became a part of bomber group KG 54, which had previously lacked a third *Gruppe* in its order of battle. In fact, Göring had already also put into play the movement of 3./Kü.Fl.Gr. 106 and 3./Kü.Fl.Gr. 906 to Luftwaffe control prior to Raeder's response, the naval chief demanding their immediate return to Kriegsmarine command, and Göring responding with platitudes that merely delayed resolution of the issue.

In Brittany, Brest had begun to become established as one of the preeminent Kriegsmarine bases for U-boats and surface security forces, as well as providing repair facilities for future deployment of major warships, and *Generaladmiral* Saalwächter at *MGK West* requested the immediate transfer of maritime air forces to the region. As early as 18 June, four days before the French surrender, the *SKL* had formulated a directive noted within its War Diary for the aerial support of future U-boat operations from French bases.

> The Army's imminent capture of the French Atlantic coast and the resultant possibility of exploiting the naval and air bases there will entail the great advantage for U-boat warfare in the Atlantic that operations can be supported by air reconnaissance.
>
> For this purpose, utilisation of the bases on the French Atlantic coast by U-boats and coastal patrol formations is necessary. For air operations it is intended to establish a special *Fliegerführer* under *F.d.Luft West* and to assign him about one group of He 115s (later Ju 88s) and available *Transozean* aircraft. It will not be possible at present to assign more forces for this task.
>
> The Luftwaffe General attached to Commander-in-Chief, Kriegsmarine, has been instructed to make the appropriate preparations for the necessary transfers.
>
> A settlement of basic questions regarding joint or simultaneous operations by air forces and U-boats will be arrived at between *Befehlshaber der U-boote* [*B.d.U.*] and *Führer der Luft. (West)*. The establishment of a U-boat operational headquarters on the French Atlantic coast appears to be necessary for local cooperation in the operational area between the *Fliegerführer* to be established there and the operational control of the U-boats (for handing over results of reconnaissance, etc.). *B.d.U.* will investigate the matter and submit proposals.[35]

Following the occupation of the Atlantic ports, the head of the U-boat service, *Konteradmiral* Karl Dönitz, ordered the establishment of new U-boat bases at the existing naval and commercial harbours of Brest, Lorient, Saint-Nazaire, La Pallice and Bordeaux. During the afternoon of 26 July Dönitz held a conference with Bruch as *F.d.Luft West*, regarding the reconnaissance requirements of his U-boats and what aircraft were actually available to fulfil these requirements.

> At present there are only four Do 18s [2./Kü.Fl.Gr. 106] for reconnaissance from Brest. The range of these aircraft and their small striking power as compared with enemy aircraft makes it possible for them to make reconnaissance flights only as far as about square BE 3000 (approximately 150 West) and in a south-west direction. However, the area North of this is not to be covered, owing to the proximity of enemy air bases, so as to avoid unnecessary losses. This reconnaissance will be flown from tomorrow.
>
> From 29 July there will be Do 17s [Kü.Fl.Gr. 606], three Do 26s [*Transozeanstaffel*] and later a few He 115s [2./Kü.Fl.Gr. 906] available.

These types of aircraft can be used off the North Channel, where the most shipping is to be found at present. Unfortunately, the only U-boat available now for operation against this traffic, e.g. the convoy HX58, is *U34*.

For this purpose, the Do 17s of Kü.Fl.Gr. 606, under its new commander *Obstlt.* Joachim Hahn, were moved to the captured airfield at Brest-Lanvéoc. However, rather than becoming available for *B.d.U.* reconnaissance, the Dornier bombers became embroiled in bombing raids against British aerodromes and cities over the following weeks, under the control of IV.*Fliegerkorps* for all land-target operations. Luftwaffe plans to convert the *Gruppe* to He 111 bombers were fiercely resisted by Hahn, who considered the aircraft type unsuitable for the coastal operations for which his unit was originally designed. While the Dorniers were tasked with conventional bombing, Hahn at least insisted that a single aircraft be kept at readiness at all times for maritime work.

During September the tug-of-war between the Kriegsmarine and Luftwaffe over control of Kü.Fl.Gr. 606 reached absolute boiling point. Between 24 and 29 August Hahn's *Gruppe* had taken part in raids on the British mainland, and in response *SKL* and *MGK West* issued orders that all attacks against strongly defended mainland targets be immediately stopped in order to retain the unit's readiness for impending maritime operations. The aircraft were instead reassigned to reconnaissance of the southern Irish Sea and St George's Channel. However, on 6 September the Luftwaffe liaison officer at *MGK West* (*Generalstabs-Offizier d.Lw. in Stab/Marinegruppenkommanddo West*), *Oberst.* Hans Metzner, telephoned *SKL* and relayed urgent demands from Göring that Kü.Fl.Gr. 606 take part in Operation Loge, the bombing of London that began on 7 September and would last for seventy-six days; now known more commonly as 'The Blitz'. The Kriegsmarine, of course, refused.

There then followed an increasing cycle of fractious wrangling over dominion of Hahn's *Küstenfliegergruppe*. *Oberst.* Walter Gaul, a former *Reichsmarine* officer who had transferred to the Luftwaffe in 1934 and was the Luftwaffe Liaison Officer attached to Raeder's staff (*Chef Verbindungsstelle d.Ob.d.L. beim Ob.d.M.*), was informed by *Major* Torsten Christ, Luftwaffe General Staff Operations Officer, that Göring had unequivocally ordered Kü.Fl.Gr. 606 to take part in the assault on London, and requested the necessary agreement from Raeder to 'avoid unpleasant friction'. Gaul replied that Raeder's original orders were to be adhered to, and that Göring was outside of his authority giving commands to a unit tactically subordinate to the Kriegsmarine. Christ countered that as Hahn was a Luftwaffe officer his duty bound him to obey the orders of his superior officer. The discussion broke down completely, both sides being intractable in their opposing standpoints, though Christ somewhat menacingly assured Gaul that Kü.Fl.Gr. 606 would indeed take part in Operation *Loge*.

Finally, on 7 September, *OKW* ruled that Hahn's unit was to obey the wishes of the Luftwaffe Staff, Gaul being given a somewhat rewritten history by officers of *Luftflotte* 3 of how the original confusion and disagreement had begun:

> The Kriegsmarine had transferred *Küstenfliegergruppe* 606 to Brest. *MGK West* had given it hardly any assignments in connection with naval operations, so that the *Gruppe* commander (Hahn) had approached the Luftwaffe and asked about the possibility of taking part in attacks on England. *Luftflotte* 3 had then taken over this commitment in agreement with *MGK West*. After a time, *SKL* had forbidden the operations. This order was not complied with. On Thursday or Friday, *Generalfeldmarschall* Sperrle had reported to the *Reichsmarshall* along these lines and also added that it was obvious from the operational reports of Kü.Fl.Gr. 606 that the latter was not at all overloaded with work. He had therefore asked permission to include this *Gruppe* in his *Luftflotte* for Operation *Loge* ... the *Reichsmarschall* agreed with the view held by *Generalfeldmarschall* Sperrle and gave permission to include *Gruppe* 606 in the operation.[36]

With the endorsment by Alfred Jodl as *OKW* Chief of the Operations Staff, there was no more room for Kriegsmarine opposition. Hitler also confirmed that Hahn's *Gruppe* would take part in the raids, beginning on 8 September. Although they participated in the bombing of Britain from that point onward, the first truly noteworthy attack carried out by Hahn's Dorniers was during the early morning of 1 October, when four Do 17s led by Hahn took off from Brest to attack the RAF airfield at Carew Cheriton in Pembrokeshire. Skimming the surface of the English Channel to avoid radar detection, they arrived over the airfield and bombed from an altitude of only 30m. In total, the Do 17s dropped forty 50kg and 240 incendiary bombs before strafing the airfield, after which Hahn led his bombers back to Brest unscathed. They left behind them significant damage, one hanger and a number of buildings being totally destroyed, along with two Ansons. One man, AC2 John Greenhalgh, was killed, and another four ground crew were injured. *Oberstleutnant* Joachim Hahn continued to mount small and effective operations against the British mainland, and on 21 October he was awarded the Knight's Cross for 'meritorious operations against England', the first to be given to a member of the *Küstenflieger*.[37] During the night of 14/15 November Hahn's *Kampfgruppe* also took part in the infamous bombing of Coventry, during which, in the course of 469 separate sorties, the Luftwaffe dropped 394 tons of high explosive, 56 tons of incendiaries and 127 parachute LMB mines.

In return, between the last day of August 1940 and the end of the year, *Küstenfliegergruppe* 606 lost eighteen aircraft, the majority shot down on missions mounted against Liverpool. From these aircraft, only the crew of 7T+LH emerged relatively unscathed and able to fight again after making an emergency landing near Sizun on 21 September, following battle damage inflicted by British fighters. *Leutnant zur See* Jürgen von Krause and two of his crew from 7T+EH were captured on 11 October after being shot down by fighters near Anglesey following a raid on Liverpool, though his pilot, *Fw.* Josef Vetterl, was killed. Likewise, the entire crew of *Lt.z.S.* Hinrich Würdemann's 7T+AH survived being shot down and were taken prisoner on 20 October, following another raid on Liverpool. All of the remaining aircrew of those Dorniers brought down were either killed or posted as missing in action; their bodies never recovered.

Meanwhile, within the operational Luftwaffe, Coeler's 9.*Fliegerdivision* had been subordinated to *Luftflotte* 2 and transferred to the newly captured Dutch Soesterberg Airfield. Coeler still controlled minelaying missions, including the use of the He 115s of 3./Kü.Fl.Gr. 106 and 3./Kü.Fl.Gr. 906, and also had a small number of Fw 200C Condors attached from the complement of I./KG 40. The long-distance Condors were tasked with twelve minelaying missions between 15 and 27 July, resulting in the loss of two of these already-scarce machines. On the night of 20 July *Staffelkapitän Hptm.* Roman Steszyn was shot down by anti-aircraft fire while heading for the Firth of Forth, when he passed too close to Hartlepool's defences. Two of the crew were captured, while four, including Steszyn, were killed, his body later being washed ashore in The Netherlands. Four nights later, *Hptm.* Volkmar Zenker, *Staffelkapitän* of 2./KG 40, was lost during a mission to lay four LMA mines in Belfast

Advertisement in the pages of *Signal* magazine for the Arado Ar 196; 'The eyes of the Kriegsmarine, protector of the coast and successful hunter of enemy submarines.'

Harbour. The Condor successfully reached the dropping point near Black Head in the early morning darkness. Only three of the mines were successfully dropped, and Zenker opened his throttles to make a slowly climbing turn and attempt to drop the last remaining mine. This second pass was observed by gunners at the Greypoint artillery position, the Condor this time approaching only metres above the sea surface, following a descent made with engines at near idle to reduce noise. The last mine was successfully dropped, but as Zenker applied throttle to climb away once more, both port engines failed owing to an air blockage in their fuel lines caused by his gliding descent. With the aircraft suddenly banking to port and no room to manoeuvre, Zenker feathered both starboard propellers and ditched the Condor. He and only two others, *Uffz.* Heinz Hocker and *Gefr.* Lothar Hohmann, successfully escaped the rapidly sinking aircraft, but *Fw.* Willi Andreas and *Uffz.* Rudolf Wagner went to the bottom. Heinz Hocker gave the following account of the loss of his aircraft:

> Because of the impact the aircraft was full of water very soon. In the cockpit I saw my comrades Wagner and Andreas in the water, looking for an exit. I swam to the other exit in the back of the fuselage, called my comrade Hohmann and told him to get ready with the dinghy. I pushed open the main door and Zenker swam up to us. We left the aircraft. In pitch-dark night I called together my swimming comrades. I only had a distress signal in a tin and the dinghy which had not yet been inflated. For a very long time we called the missing comrades, but in my opinion they went down with the Condor.
>
> Swimming in the heavy swell, I had to inflate the dinghy, which took me eight hours, as the compressed-air bottle had not been connected to it after

its last servicing. Zenker and Hohmann climbed into the dinghy first. In the morning we noticed a steamship on the horizon which was heading for us. I realised that Zenker had exhausted himself, and so I took command. In case of capture we should state that we were a reconnaissance flight. Then I searched through Zenker's pockets and threw overboard anything which could prove to be suspicious. The ship which came towards us was manned by English soldiers.

The crew stood on deck with their rifles loaded, the officer had a pistol. I shot two red flare signals and threw overboard the pistol and ammunition box before putting my hands up. After being taken on board and searched, the sailors supplied us with rum. I was thankful about that, as I could not take any more.[38]

The three survivors had been rescued by the ASW trawler HMT *Paynter*, and were taken to the Olderfleet Hotel, which served as headquarters of the Naval Officer in charge at Larne. Under interrogation, in an effort to keep the Condor minelaying operations secret, Zenker and his men repeatedly claimed to have been the crew of an He 111 engaged in a reconnaissance flight.

The delicate Condor had shown itself patently unsuited to the rigours of minelaying, and the task was extremely unpopular with KG 40 Condor

An He 60 on the ice. Some floatplanes were equipped with special ice runners allowing operation from frozen surfaces during the Norwegian campaign.

crews, a personal appeal from Petersen to Hans Jeschonnek soon resulting in the Condors being ordered to discontinue minelaying missions. They were reconfigured for their intended role of long-range Atlantic reconnaissance from the airfields at Brest and Bordeaux-Mérignac. From there they scored their first minor success with the damaging of the Norwegian freighter *Svein Jarl* on 18 August, a straggler from Convoy OA199. Two men were injured in the attack west of Bloody Foreland, but the ship reaching Londonderry and was repaired. One week later another Condor sank the 3,821-ton SS *Goathland*, sailing from Pepel, Sierra Leone, to Belfast with a cargo of iron ore. Finding the ship 630 kilometres west of Land's End, the Condor from Brest made three bombing runs which finally sent the merchant ship under, all thirty-six crew successfully abandoning ship in lifeboats and later being rescued, despite the Condor's gunners strafing on each pass.

Although it was no longer using the Condors, 9.*Fliegerdivision* continued its minelaying missions, deploying small numbers of a new acoustic mine from 28 August for which the British initially had no countermeasure. Its secrets were revealed in October, when an unexploded example was retrieved by the British and successfully disarmed. Between 14 September and 30 October Coeler's unit dropped nearly 1,000 mines of different types in British waters, though exhaustive Royal Navy minesweeping helped prevent the closure of ports.

Trials with torpedo-launching He 111Hs were also under way by the middle of 1940, using aircraft of KGr. 126, which had been based in Marx until July 1940, when it was moved to Nantes. The experienced original *Kampfgruppe* commander, *Hptm.* Gerd Stein, had been lost in action after his He 111H-4 failed to return from a minelaying sortie off Boulogne. He was briefly succeeded by former naval officer and *Staffelkapitän* of 1./Kü.Fl.Gr. 706 *Major* Karl-Heinrich Schulz, but he too was soon out of action, after being injured in an aeroplane crash on 2 July, *Major* Holm Schellmann taking his place. Like his predecessors, Schellmann had a naval background, having entered the *Reichsmarine* in 1925 before transferring to the Luftwaffe eight years later.

On 22 July four He 111s of KGr. 126 arrived at Lanvéoc-Poulmic Airfield, which they shared with the recently transferred Dorniers of *Küstenfliegergruppe* 606. While other aircraft of KGr. 126 dropped their 1,000th aerial mine in British waters four nights later, a feat recognised in the *SKL* War Diary, in which they praised the unit's 'indefatigable and courageous activity under most difficult weather conditions and against strong defence', the four aircraft at Lanvéoc-Poulmic were scheduled to begin conducting combat trials of newly developed torpedo-launching gear for the He 111H-4; the external PVC bomb rack modified to carry two torpedoes. An initial planned operation was scrubbed owing to poor weather, and the four did not fly operationally until 28 July. However it was no success, according to the report they filed with KG 40 Staff in Oldenburg, under whose temporary operational control they had passed. While three of the Heinkels returned to their original airfield in Niedersachsen (i.e. Marx in Lower Saxony), the aircraft commanded by *Oblt.z.S.* Helmut Lorenz remained in Lanvéoc-Poulmic. A scattering of planned missions were scrubbed one after another until the middle of August when, in company with a second new He 111 arrival from Marx (commanded by *Oblt.* Josef Saumweber, formerly of 3./Kü.Fl.Gr. 706), Lorenz mounted a torpedo mission in the southern entrance to St George's Channel. Two torpedoes were dropped, one passing ahead and one astern of a targeted merchant ship despite being launched at close range and with only 1 degree separating the two torpedoes' set gyroscope angles.

The increasingly active Lanvéoc-Poulmic Aerodrome was attacked by Blenheim bombers on 11 August and again two nights later, killing two men and seriously injuring another five, though relatively minor damage was inflicted upon what was still a fairly rudimentary airfield infrastructure. The raids also failed to halt Lorenz's planned flights. Another mission was launched in the evening of the second Bomber Command raid, dropping two torpedoes which again missed ahead and astern of the targeted vessel. On 16 August an attempted attack on a small trawler west-south-west of The Smalls (wildly overestimated to be a ship of '5,000 tons', as opposed to its actual 294 tons) missed once again, at least one torpedo breaking surface several times before settling on to its course. Lorenz felt that he had conclusively proved that the launch gear was not yet functioning as intended. Kriegsmarine torpedo engineers had arrived at Lanvéoc-Poulmic, and further adjustments were made to the aircraft's release gear before its next daylight flight, on 19 August. Lorenz was down to his last four torpedoes, and 9.*Fliegerdivision* had twenty more shipped to the Kriegsmarine torpedo storage facility at nearby Brest, along with parachute mines and the associated tools required for their maintenance. Before these arrived, the last of the available torpedoes were fired in consecutive missions, all of which failed; three out of four being classified as gyro failures, as they circled after launch, and the fourth disappearing completely.

The relatively undeveloped infrastructure of the increasingly cramped airfield at Lanvéoc-Poulmic, as well as bouts of illness suffered by Lorenz, delayed further torpedo operations, and the two KGr. 126 Heinkels were moved to the more-developed Nantes Airfield instead. Not until 8 November was Lorenz active again with his torpedo operations, leading three He 111H-4s of 1./KGr. 126 to Brest-Guipavas in preparation for a mission the following day against convoy traffic in the Irish Sea. Like Saumweber, the last aircraft commander, *Oblt.* Friedrich Müller was also a former naval officer and a highly-experienced aircraft commander, and the Heinkels lifted off towards the Irish Sea in poor weather conditions, with low cloud and limited visibility. Their journey had not proceeded far from the French coast before a Blenheim Mk.IVF of 236 Sqn, Coastal Command, intercepted them at 1416hrs. Pilot Officer Dugald Lumsden was on independent patrol over the Western Approaches when he sighted the trio of Heinkels and immediately attacked. Lorenz's wireless operator, *Fw.* Peter Hermsen, was killed almost immediately when a bullet from the Blenheim hit him in the forehead. As the Heinkels separated and aborted their mission, pilot *Fw.* Walther von Livonius threw Lorenz's aircraft into evasive manoeuvres, but bullets ripped into the port engine and shattered cockpit instruments. Flight engineer *Flieger* Otto Skusa was badly wounded in the leg and, though the Blenheim made no more firing passes, the Heinkel went down into the Bay of Biscay. After the shuddering impact with the sea, the forward half of the Heinkel momentarily submerged before rising back to the surface and allowing the three survivors to escape. Their life raft had been riddled with bullets, and they were soon in the numbing cold of the Biscay water, kept afloat by their kapok lifejackets. After drifting for more than an hour, Otto Skusa was unable to remain afloat, lapsed into unconsciousness through blood loss, and slipped beneath the surface. Finally, their crash having been reported by Kriegsmarine artillerymen on the distant Ile d'Ouessant, a Breguet 521 Bizerte seaplane KD+BC of *Seenotflugkommando* 1, piloted by *Lt.* Paul Metges, recovered the two remaining survivors. The He 111 still had some way to go before it became a fully operational torpedo bomber.

During July, as the battle for air supremacy over Britain was poised to begin in earnest, Kriegsmarine commands stretching along the Dutch, Belgian and French coasts were ordered to co-operate closely with *Luftflotte* 2 and 3, who were to bear the brunt of forthcoming operations, and elements of the *Küstenflieger* (2./Kü.Fl.Gr. 906) were temporarily assigned to air-sea rescue duties to augment the available aircraft of the *Seenotdienst*. The air-sea rescue service played an important role in the recovery of downed crewmen of both protagonists from the war's earliest days. With increasing levels of combat over the North Sea and English Channel, the He 59s, painted white, and with large Red Cross markings and no defensive armament, flew an ever-increasing tempo of missions to retrieve airmen stranded at sea, not without considerable risk to themselves. During the early morning of 1 July He 115 M2+CL of 3./Kü.Fl.Gr. 106, under the command of *Lt.z..S.* Gottfried Schröder, crashed off Whitby through engine failure during a minelaying mission. At first light an He 59 of *Seenotflugkommando* 3, bearing the civilian registration D-ASAM, departed from Schellingwoude in The Netherlands. It was flown by *Uffz.* Ernst Otto Nielsen (untrained in night flying and therefore forced to await first light before departure) and commanded by *L.t* Hans Joachim Fehske. After Fehske had guided the aircraft to the Heinkel's last reported position by dead reckoning, he instructed Nielsen to approach the British coast in order to attain a firm navigational fix, flying between the coastline and a southbound convoy as they did so. Three Spitfires of 72 Sqn were scrambled to intercept, Flt Lt Edward Graham circling the brightly painted aircraft with brilliant Red Cross markings and the equally bold red-banded swastika of a civilian aircraft on its tail. He was initially undecided, and it took several minutes and the presence of the convoy nearby to convince Graham that the odd-looking Heinkel was hostile. In three separate strafing runs the Spitfires shot it down, noting no defensive fire and no evasive action taken, though Fg Off Edgar Wilcox also recalled seeing the 'enemy aircraft jettison some small objects which I thought were small bombs'. One of the Heinkel's engines had been quickly disabled and its radio equipment was smashed, and medical orderly *Uffz.* Struckmann was shot twice through the legs. After an emergency descent the aircraft began to sink tail-first as all four crew took to their dinghy, to be rescued by HMS *Black Swan* shortly thereafter. The He 115 crew that had been the object of their search-and-rescue mission were also eventually rescued after twenty-eight hours at sea and taken to Grimsby Harbour. Fehske and his crew loudly protested the shooting down of a non-combatant aircraft, though British investigators who examined the wreckage later claimed to find cameras aboard, suitable for use in reconnaissance work.

Eight days later a second plainly-marked *Seenotdienst* aircraft was brought down. The He 59B-2 of *Seenotflugkommando* 1, registered

D-ASUO, took off from Boulogne and flew via Calais to Ramsgate to look for any of six Messerschmitt Bf 110s shot down into the Channel during a convoy attack earlier in the day. The Heinkel, which approached to within sight of the convoy that was still transiting the Channel, had a covering *Staffel* of Bf 109 fighters, which was sufficient to convince the leader of a group of 54 Sqn Spitfires flying convoy cover that it was hostile. New Zealander Flt Lt 'Al' Deere led his Spitfires into an attack on the German fighters, a melée soon developing in which Deere collided with a Bf 109 flown by *Obfw.* Johann Illner, both aeroplanes limping away to crash-land safely. Two Spitfires were shot down with both pilots killed, while Fg Off John Allen attacked the He 59 and hit it with a single burst from his machine guns. As soon as the unarmed aircraft was damaged, pilot *Uffz.* Helmut Bartmann alighted on the sea within sight of the Kent coastline, where its floats became bogged down after running into a thick glutinous sandbank of the Goodwin Sands in the ebbing tide. Before long the Heinkel was taken in tow by the Walmer Lifeboat and beached near the lifeboat station, where its crew was taken prisoner. All four crew members were found to be registered with the International Red Cross, and apparently seized the opportunity to explain the purposes of the *Seenotsdienst* organisation and attempt to prevent future attacks on what was a humanitarian mission. However, a search of the aircraft's interior yielded the pilot's log book, in which Bartmann had recorded convoy positions and directions, justifying British conclusions that the aircraft could not be considered non-combatant. Interestingly, papers belonging to *Seenot* aircraft D-AGUI were also found that described the rescue of RAF Sqn Ldr Kenneth Christopher Doran on 30 April after his Blenheim IV of 110 Sqn was shot down during a bombing raid on Stavanger Aerodrome, Norway.

> 30/4./40. Verbal orders 1950hrs, search for Englishmen shot down about 10km west of Stavanger. Weather perfect. Visibility 50km, wind 130° 25km. Start 1952hrs. At 2015hrs oil spots in Grid Ref.3125. Sighted a man drifting in rubber dinghy, beside him a man swimming. We landed beside them 2200hrs. Sea strength 2. The dinghy drifted between the floats and was made fast. Both Englishmen hauled into the machine. The first, who was in the dinghy was slightly wounded on his chin, protested that he did not need first aid. We made him fast to the 'Tragbahn'. The second was already drowned. Artificial respiration in the machine had no effect. Owing to the rolling of the machine and the heavy load, the stern ladder broke.

Took off for return flight at 2055hrs and landed at Stavanger 2110hrs. It turned out later that the rescued Englishman was a *Staffelführer*, with the rank of major, the other who had been unable to get into the dinghy was his observer [Pt Off F.M.N. Searle].

Note: The companion ladder must be strengthened; that would make it easier to get people on board. Light rubber overalls reaching up to the chest are wanted – at least two per aircraft, as the crew get wet when carrying out rescues and often have a long return flight afterwards.[39]

A third He 59, D-AGIO, shot down on 11 July in the vicinity of a convoy south of the Devon coast, finally settled the issue as far as the British were concerned, and despite vehement German protests that the *Seenotdienst* aircraft were protected by articles of the Geneva Convention, on 14 July the British issued Air Ministry Bulletin 1254 in which they declared:

> Enemy aircraft bearing civil markings and marked with the red cross have recently flown over British ships at sea and in the vicinity of the British coast, and they are being employed for purposes which His Majesty's Government cannot regard as being consistent with the privileges generally accorded to the Red Cross. His Majesty's Government desire to accord to ambulance aircraft reasonable facilities for the transportation of the sick and wounded, in accordance with the Red Cross Convention, and aircraft engaged in the direct evacuation of the sick and wounded will be respected, provided that they comply with the relevant provisions of the Convention.
>
> His Majesty's Government are unable, however, to grant immunity to such aircraft flying over areas in which operations are in progress on land or at sea, or approaching British or Allied territory, or territory in British occupation, or British or Allied ships. Ambulance aircraft which do not comply with the above requirements will do so at their own risk and peril.

By specifically withdrawing any tacit or implied permission for the *Seenotdienst* to operate over the North Sea or English Channel combat zones, any perceived protection provided by the 1929 Geneva Convention was technically removed, as it required agreement 'between all the Parties to the conflict'. On Dowding's orders the British subsequently declared that, as of 20 July, *Seenotdienst* aircraft would be shot down without warning.

On that day, as it forecast, He 59 D-AKAR of *Seenotflugkommando 4* was intercepted and shot down by Hurricanes of 238 Sqn flying as convoy escort south of the Needles, near the Isle of Wight. The Heinkel was seen to make an emergency descent approximately three miles from the French coast, though it was never found. The body of pilot *Fw.* Herbert Dengel was later washed ashore on the beach at Mers-le-Bains. The remaining three crewmen were listed as missing in action.

During July the *Seenotdienst* was officially incorporated into the Luftwaffe as *Luftwaffeninspektion* 16 (Air Force Inspectorate 16), under the direction of *Generalleutnant* Hans-Georg von Seidel, the Luftwaffe's Quartermaster General. On 29 July *RLM* ordered all *Seenotdienst* aircraft be armed and painted as normal front-line aircraft. The civil registrations were dropped, the aircraft being given standard *Stammkennzeichen* (the military four-letter codes) instead. By November

Bordflieger Arado Ar 196s carried aboard capital ships proved their worth many times over, though that of the *Scharnhorst* also mistakenly bombed Otto Kretschmer's *U99* on 21 June 1940. (James Payne)

they had become fully militarised, being redesignated *Seenotstaffeln* rather than *Seenotflugkommandos*. Before completion of the camouflaging of all *Seenotdiesnt* aircraft, British aircraft began receiving return machine-gun fire from the white-painted Heinkels still carrying Red Cross markings, and more than one merchant ship also reported being strafed by *Seenotdienst* aircraft.[40]

Additionally, the British government, and Winston Churchill in particular, were aware that by allowing the rescue of trained aviators who had been shot down at sea they were returning them to action, whereas the fact that downed German aircrew generally landed on British soil, or at least descended in the no-man's-land of the English Channel, denied valuable manpower to the Luftwaffe. They therefore issued a fresh policy on 26 August regarding all German rescue vessels, which also encompassed the *Seenotdienst* air-sea-rescue boats.

> Sixty-four small vessels marked with the Red Cross and notified by Germans as detailed for rescuing airmen will not be recognised by H.M. Government as entitled to Red Cross protection, and after midnight 30/31 August will be liable to be captured and sunk. Till that midnight these vessels should be dealt with under Article 4 of the Tenth Hague Convention.

Following the fall of The Netherlands the *Seenotdienst* had benefited from the capture of thirteen incomplete Dornier Do 24K-2s in various stages of construction at the Papendrecht aircraft assembly plant on the northern bank of the Merwede River. Components for eleven more were also on site, as well as stored engines, all originally destined for the Dutch Naval Flying Service. Rather than being transferred to the *Küstenflieger*, the Do 24s were impressed into service with the *Seenotdienst* after inspection by *Flugkapitän* Karl Born, commander of *Seenotflugkommando* 1. The He 59 had proved suitable for the task, though it was unable to function well beyond a sea state of 3. The Do 18s of 3./Kü.Fl.Gr. 406 had also been appropriated for the task, and were moved to the Dutch base at Schellingwoude near Amsterdam and subordinated to *Luftflotte* 2 for their search-and-rescue missions. By October the additional Do 18s of 2./Kü.Fl.Gr. 106 were similarly being used by the *Seenotdienst* from the harbour at Cherbourg, while also flying reconnaissance missions over the Cornish coast. Although the Do 18 operated efficiently in the search-and-rescue role, its cabin was relatively cramped and unsuitable for the treatment of wounded men. Production of the Do 18 ended in August 1940, the final two entering service that month. The captured Dutch trimotor Do 24s, on the other hand, were perfect. For *Seenotdienst* purposes they operated with a crew of six, comprising pilot, observer/navigator (and aircraft commander), wireless operator, two flight engineers who doubled as gunners, and the tail gunner, who doubled as a paramedic. Two hatches were built into the aircraft's port side for recovering men from the sea, and eight bunks were provided amidships. Able to function in anything up to sea state 6, the Do 24 was flawless in its role as a rescue aeroplane, and by November 1941 limited numbers began to be produced in Germany.

In France, by the beginning of August, all of *Küstenfliegergruppe* 606 (Dornier Do 17), the *Transozeanstaffel* (Dornier Do 26) and the Do 18s of 2./Kü.Fl.Gr. 106 had transferred to the Brest area. Consideration was given to tasking the aircraft with attacks on merchant shipping off the northeastern Spanish coast, though the proposal was soon abandoned and the maritime aircraft began reconnaissance operations over the Bay of Biscay.

Commander of the U-boat service Karl Dönitz (second from left) had exacting requirements for aerial reconnaissance to assist U-boat operations. Eventually he would replace Raeder (in leather coat) as head of the Kriegsmarine.

The land-based Do 17s were based at Lanvéoc-Poulmic, across the Rade de Brest from the city itself on the north shore of the Presqu 'île de Crozon, and flying boats at the nearby station that had been first developed by the French Navy. Sited on the western shore of the Anse de Poulmic, the seaplane anchorage was protected from westerly winds but vulnerable to storms and high easterly winds. It had a single concrete slipway, and a quay stretching along the waterfront to the east of hangars that the seaplanes shared with the aircraft of Lanvéoc-Poulmic. As Lorenz and his torpedo bombers had noted, early conditions at the Lanvéoc-Poulmic airfield appear to have been less than ideal, particularly when more than just the Dorniers of Kü.Fl. Gr. 606 were allocated space at the base. Both Stab/KG 40 and the rest of KGr. 126, as well as Kü.Fl.Gr. 106, were scheduled to transfer to the small airfield for impending operations over the North Channel; a total of forty-two officers and 188 men with twenty-eight Heinkel He 111s combined. *Oberleutnant zur See* Fräsdorff of the advance party tasked with preparing the base for the incoming units immediately

Focke Wulf Fw 200 Condor aircraft of KG 40 became involved in long-distance minelaying missions during July 1940, a task which was unpopular with crews and for which the Condor was poorly suited, two being lost within twelve nights of operations.

signalled KG 40 at Oldenburg and KGr. 126 at Wittmundhafen with a list of complaints regarding Lanvéoc-Poulmic. His main grievances included overcrowding of both billets and runway; a poorly equipped headquarters building; inadequate fuel tankage, water supply and signals equipment; and the location of the spares depot, which was 160km distant. He lamented insufficient ammunition storage, not to mention a lack of available ammunition beyond one or two bombing and mining missions. Upgrading began as a matter of urgency, although on the evening of 23 August KG 40's new Deputy *Kommodore*, First World War naval aviator *Oberst*. Ernst-August Roth, signalled the advanced detachment at Lanveoc-Poulmic that both his KG 40 *Geschwaderstab* and KGr. 126 would instead be going to the airfield at Nantes, which was already in better repair and at a more advanced state. Roth later moved his Staff *Geschwader* to Brest-Guipavas, known as 'Brest-Nord' to the Germans, situated eight and a half kilometres north-east of the port city, before eventually returning to the Condor's home base at Bordeaux-Mérignac.

The wreckage of *Uffz*. Heinz Löffler's He 115 on the aft deck of SS *Highlander* following a failed attack on Convoy FN239 on 1 August 1940.

In the North Sea, the only unit ready for torpedo action was He 115-equipped 3./Kü.Fl.Gr. 506 based at Stavanger, and they launched fresh attacks throughout the month. From mid-August 1./Ku.Fl.Gr. 106, based at Norderney, became ready for torpedo operations, and another five aircraft of 1./Kü.Fl.Gr. 506, adapted to carry torpedoes, were ready by September. On the first day of August He 115Cs of 3./Kü.Fl.Gr. 506 attacked Convoy FN239 off the Scottish east coast. At least three torpedoes were fired, all of which missed. Frustrated by this failure, pilot *Uffz*. Heinz Löffler circled the target ship, the 1,216-ton coastal steamer SS *Highlander*, before attempting a strafing run. As his Heinkel approached from the port quarter it was hit by a bomb fired by the ship's Holman Projector, a makeshift defensive mortar that had been rushed into production to provide some form of anti-aircraft defence. This weapon fired grenades using compressed air, and one exploded immediately ahead of the oncoming Heinkel as Lewis guns also opened fire in its direction. It is possible that Löffler was wounded, as the aircraft was seen to sheer off dramatically, and its tail caught the port midships lifeboat davit as the aircraft crashed, the left wing breaking off and falling on the ship's poop deck while the rest of the aircraft carried on, sweeping away stern cranes and flattening the Holman Projector before falling in flames into the sea. Lewis gunner Able Seaman George Anderson recalled:

> We saw nothing of the airmen. But we could hear them screaming inside the plane as it toppled over.[41]

A second He 115C, piloted by *Fw.* Siegfried Gast, also made a strafing run and was brought down by the combined fire of *Highlander*'s Lewis gunners and anti-aircraft fire from the escorting sloop HMS *Weston*, crashing into the sea. No survivors from either aircraft were found, and two merchant seamen were injured on the SS *Highlander*. Anderson later discovered a bullet graze on his lip and a dent from another machine-gun bullet in his helmet, while a crewmate discovered bullet holes through both lapels of his jacket.[42] The merchant ship later steamed into the Tyne still carrying the remains of Löffler's aircraft on its poop deck.

The number of torpedo combat missions gradually increased, though supply of the temperamental LT F5a torpedo became a problem during September, stocks sinking to as low as thirty-eight. Werner Baumbach later wrote of the torpedo manufacture issue:

Its production was faced with great difficulties owing to the high consumption of metals involved. The LT F5, for instance, required 112½lb of chromium, 250lb of aluminium, 172lb of lead, 121lb tin and 825lb of copper. It was shortage of these raw materials, and not of manpower, machine tools or factory space, which impeded production.[43]

There were, however, at least some overdue successes for the *Küstenflieger* when Kü.Fl.Gr. 506 attacked Convoy OA203 on 23 August in the Moray Firth. The 5,053-ton SS *Llanishen* and 6,680-ton SS *Makalla* were both sunk by torpedoes, while the 10,119-ton SS *Beacon Grange* was also heavily damaged during the attack, though it was successfully towed into harbour by the tug *Buccaneer*. Three days later an attack by four He 115s of Kü.Fl.Gr. 506 against Convoy HX65 off Kinnaird Head resulted in the successful sinking of the 11,445-ton New Zealand cargo ship RMS *Remuera* by torpedo. The Heinkels struck immediately following a dive-bombing raid by eight KG 30 Ju 88s which sank the 5,030-ton SS *Cape York*. The Junkers' bombs burst on the ship's guard rails starboard of Number 2 hold, splitting the plates and decking and setting the stored lumber cargo on fire, though that same lumber kept the crippled ship afloat until the following day, when she capsized and sank. Thirty-one survivors were landed at Peterhead.

Ten minutes after the *Cape York* was hit, *Remuera* was strafed by a Ju 88 and narrowly missed by bombs before the ship's Chief Officer saw a torpedo track 30 degrees off the port bow and headed straight for his ship. It impacted below the waterline between the two rear holds (Numbers 4 and 5), flooding both. Within fifty minutes *Remuera* had sunk stern first, briefly resting on the bottom with its bow in the air before submerging completely, taking 4,801 tons of refrigerated cargo and 1,646 tons of general cargo to the bottom. All ninety-three crew and one gunner successfully abandoned ship and were rescued.

Sporadic torpedo operations continued with little confirmed success despite some overly optimistic after-action reports, before disaster overtook 3./Kü.Fl.Gr. 506 on the night of 15 September, when two of the *Staffel*'s aircraft mounted a torpedo operation against shipping in the Firth of Forth. The pilot of He 115 S4+GL, *Oblt.* Clement Lucas, had been briefed to attack an oil tanker expected to be part of Convoy FN79, approaching Methil anchorage from Southend under destroyer escort. Lucas's observer and aircraft commander was *Staffelkapitän Hptm.* Ernst-Wilhelm Bergmann. As well as wireless operator *Fw.*

Successful sinking of a British freighter photographed and reported in a German propaganda publication.

Ernst Kalinowski, the *Staffelkapitän* of 1./Kü.Fl.Gr. 506, *Hptm*. Hans Kriependorf, was also aboard as a passenger to gain first-hand experience of torpedo operations. Kriependorf had received pre-military pilot training with *DVS* Warnemünde before enlisting in the Kriegsmarine in April 1930 and transfer to the Luftwaffe during 1936, where he qualified as an observer and was subsequently posted to *Küstenfliegergruppe* 706.

The first aircraft attacked to little effect, the British Admiralty War Diary stating that a torpedo was fired at the convoy, 'possibly at [HMS] *Vivien*', which exploded ashore, missing its potential target by a wide margin. Lucas, however, sighted his target and circled for a period in the darkness before launching his own attack once he considered the situation most advantageous. But his low-level approach left him silhouetted against the moon as he made a textbook torpedo drop, which then carried his aircraft on a straight course for thirty seconds after launch, lest the aircraft's slipstream affect the torpedo's running. The

He 115 passed straight through the convoy and was squarely hit by anti-aircraft crossfire which disabled both engines and brought the floatplane down near HMS *Vortigen*.

The German crew ditched documents and maps before attempting to scuttle the damaged Heinkel with explosives and abandoning the aircraft. Unfortunately their attempts were in vain, as the Heinkel capsized but stubbornly refused to sink before two fishing boats rescued the crew from their dinghy and took the aircraft in tow toward Eyemouth, where it was beached.

Though the loss of the aircraft and two senior officers was a disaster for Kü.Fl.Gr. 506, which suspended torpedo operations for five days, Lucas at least claimed a hit amidships on his target. He had, however, not sunk an oil tanker, but the 1,264-ton Danish SS *Halland*, commandeered from the Dansk Franske shipping line by the Ministry of War Transport in 1939, and going down with seventeen men killed. Five were rescued by HMT *Hildena*, transferred to the Dutch steamer *Sparta* and later landed at Methil.

Bergmann was replaced by former Kriegsmarine officer *Hptm.* Franz Dyrchs, who led four aircraft of 3./Kü.Fl.Gr. 506 from Stavanger on 20 October to intercept the twenty-six ships of Convoy OA232, reported off the Scottish east coast. The convoy was intercepted off Girdleness, and after shadowing until darkness the aircraft attacked and claimed three ships sunk, totalling approximately 20,000 tons. *Oberleutnant zur See* Karl Barth successfully torpedoed what he estimated to be a '6,000-ton steamer', which he left in a 'sinking condition'. He had hit the 4,876-ton SS *Conakrian* midships on its starboard side, smoke and steam rising into the air as it slewed to a stop. Anti-aircraft fire stabbed into the night sky, and Dyrchs' Heinkel was hit and forced to make an emergency descent beyond the line of sight of the convoy and its escorts. Although it was damaged, makeshift repairs enabled the aircraft to take to the air once more, and Dyrchs returned successfully to Stavanger.[44]

Barth's success during the mission was widely celebrated, the daily Wehrmacht situation (and propaganda) report broadcast at noon (*Die Wehrmachtberichte*) mentioning Barth on Friday 8 November:

> With the recently reported sinking of a 6,000BRT steamer off the Scottish east coast, *Oblt.z..S.* Barth, commander of a seaplane, has sunk a total of 30,000BRT of enemy shipping.

Although Barth's skill as an observer and aircraft commander was not in doubt, he had not actually sunk the SS *Conakrian* during the attack on OA232. The steamer was indeed hit and her engines disabled, and twenty-nine crew were removed by the escorting destroyer HMS *Cleveland* while the ship lay anchored off Aberdeen with a skeleton crew left aboard, soon joined by convoy commodore, Cdr William Clyde Meek, RNR. During the following day it was towed into harbour for repair. Nonetheless, on 14 December 1940 Karl Barth received the second Knight's Cross to be awarded to a member of the *Küstenflieger* for his officially approved accumulated sinkings.[45]

On 3 October *Küstenfliegergruppe* 706 was directed by *Generaladmiral* Carls at *Marinegruppenkommando* Nord (*MGK Nord*) to establish regular reconnaissance flights over the Denmark Strait in support of the departure of the 'pocket battleship' *Admiral Scheer*, scheduled to leave Germany and break into the Atlantic on a solo raiding voyage during the last week of the month. An advance seaplane base was to be established on Jan Mayan Island by two converted trawler weather ships, *WBS4 Hinrich Freese* and *WBS3 Fritz Homann*, which would act as floating seaplane depots. The *Hinrich Freese* sailed from Trondheim on 19 October, carrying aircraft fuel and supplies and three Luftwaffe men led by *Oblt.* Franjo Gosodarić, a Croatian national serving in the Luftwaffe. The *Fritz Homann* followed six days later, by which time the first weather ship had already reached Maria Muschbukta on the western coast of Jan Mayen. While the *Fritz Homann* moored only briefly in the isolated bay before continuing to its weather reporting station in Quadrant AE 39, the *Hinrich Freese* awaited the coming of two He 115s of *Küstenfliegergruppe* 506, which arrived on 29 October. The first aircraft, S4+BK, was damaged upon alighting and sank into the frigid water shortly thereafter. With only a single aircraft remaining, *MGK Nord* cancelled the planned weather reconnaissance flights. The other He 115, S4+EL, was wrecked that night by a heavy North Atlantic storm while moored in the bay. With both aircrews aboard, the *Hinrich Freese* returned to Trondheim, arriving on 5 November. Despite the abortive attempt at aerial weather reporting, the *Admiral Scheer* sailed from Gotenhafen on 23 October 1940 and successfully broke through into the Atlantic Ocean. By the time of its return to Kiel on 1 April 1941, the 'pocket battleship' had sunk fourteen merchant ships and captured two more, as well as sinking the auxiliary cruiser *Jervis Bay*, escorting Convoy HX84 off Newfoundland.

The extensively glazed cockpit of an He 111. Torpedo-dropping trials undertaken during the middle of 1940 that resulted in the Heinkel becoming arguably the most effective torpedo-carrying aircraft of the Luftwaffe.

The combined bomb and torpedo operations by He 115s of 1./Kü.Fl. Gr. 706 experienced greater success during the first half of November 1940, as the *Staffel* concentrated its attentions on Britain's east coast convoy traffic, sinking five merchant ships and damaging two. Storms at the exposed anchorage at Aalborg had caused damage to an Ar 196 during September, forcing a pragmatic relocation of the base of operations to Thisted, a small seaplane station seventy-five kilometres west of Aalborg that was operational from August 1940 onwards. From there, the primary focus of *Küstenfliegergruppe* 706, despite its convoy attack successes, was the patrolling of the Skagerrak on both anti-submarine patrols and convoy escort of ships bound to and from Norway.

With the Battle of Britain decided, Norway now secure and the emphasis on maritime operations moving west and also, for the first time, into the Mediterranean following Italy's declaration of war against the

Allied powers during June, yet another reorganisation and reshuffling of the Luftwaffe and *Küstenflieger* was undertaken, partly at the instigation of the Führer himself.

During September Hitler had attempted to quell the fractious relationship that had developed between the Luftwaffe and Kriegsmarine chiefs and their respective staffs. In the first of what would be three directives, issued on 13 September 1940, Hitler recognised that, though all aerial forces needed to be consolidated under Göring's command for the concentrated attacks on Great Britain, the Kriegsmarine required its own reconnaissance forces under direct naval tactical command. However, with minimal naval operations possible following *Weserübung*, he reasoned that it was therefore logical to presume that such supporting aerial reconnaissance units would probably be underutilised, and therefore must alternate between Luftwaffe and Kriegsmarine command. Furthermore, Hitler reserved the right to decide such matters of allocation between the two service branches himself, as supreme military commander. He ordered *Küstenfliegergruppe* 606 (Do 17Z), 3./Kü.Fl. Gr. 406 (Do 18) and 2./Kü.Fl.Gr. 106 (Do 18) to be transferred to Göring's control, while *Küstenfliegergruppe* 506 (He 115) was to revert to the Kriegsmarine's governance as of 18 September. Two further Do 18 squadrons were scheduled to transfer to the Luftwaffe in the event of Operation *Sealion* going ahead, while another would be so assigned as soon as the cruiser *Admiral Hipper* had sailed and had been transferred to the operational umbrella of MGK West.

Naval air strength took a significant blow with these fresh decisions, but reorganisation was continued in order to rationalise and streamline the tangled web of command structure and logistical support. The aircraft controlled by *F.d.Luft* in conjunction with *MGK Nord* were also subordinate to *Befehlshaber der Sicherung der Ostsee* (*BSO*), formed from the staff of *Führer der Vorpostenboote Ost*, which had been stationed in Aalborg. Commanded by *Konteradmiral* Hans Stohwasser, the *BSO* office was responsible for security operations within the Baltic, including minesweeping, interdiction of contraband shipping and anti-submarine warfare, and the *Küstenflieger* aircraft assigned to the area unceasingly patrolled the entrance to the Skaggerak in search of enemy submarines.

During October Stab and 3./Kü.Fl.Gr. 106 was transferred to Barth in Mecklenberg for conversion to the Ju 88. In Cherbourg, 2./Kü.Fl. Gr. 106 and 3./Kü.Fl.Gr. 906 swapped their unit designations. The new 2./Kü.Fl.Gr. 106 also converted to the Ju 88 in Barth, while the redesignated 3./Kü.Fl.Gr. 906 continued its *Seenotsdienst* work with Do 18 flying boats. The sole remaining operational seaplane unit of *Küstenfliegergruppe* 106 was the He 115-equipped 1./Kü.Fl.Gr. 106, operationally controlled by *Küstenfliegergruppe* 406 in Brest but based at Hourtin, a captured French seaplane station fifty-five kilometres north-west of Bordeaux at the northern end of Lac de Carcans. There they shared the slipways with 1. *Seenotstaffel* and, from December, the *Sonderstaffel Transozean*.

Through September 2./Kü.Fl.Gr. 906, based in France, began conversion to the newly acquired Blohm und Voss BV 138 trimotor flying boat, and in Rantum towards the end of 1940 1./Kü.Fl.Gr. 406 also began the same conversion process. Having a distinctly short hull with a hydrodynamic step beneath flat sides, the aircraft became known as the 'flying clog' by its crews, though it was officially named the *Seedrache* (Sea Dragon). Although the BV 138 showed great promise, it was soon shown to be beset with problems. The A-1 variant needed strengthening of the hull, ailerons, and floats to improve its robustness, and the air intakes for the centrally mounted engine also proved to be prone to clogging, reducing the power output. However, its strong defensive armament made it more than a match for equivalent Allied aircraft likely to be encountered on long-distance reconnaissance. Further modifications would eventually render the aircraft a valuable addition to coastal operations.

By September the airborne torpedo had still not been fully accepted as a viable operational weapon by *SKL*, despite slowly mounting success in its use by the He 115. Between the beginning of April 1940 and the end of the year, *F.d.Luft* recorded 111 torpedoes having been fired and twenty-seven achieving a hit; a 24.30 per cent success rate that was claimed to have sunk or damaged 158,000 tons of shipping. On 19 November *F.d.Luft* reported that, during the previous seven weeks alone, forty-eight torpedo attacks had been mounted, of which fifteen were reportedly successful. *Generalmajor* Bruch subsequently asked for Dornier reconnaissance aircraft to assist the torpedo-carrying *Küstenflieger* units in target location, for the He 115 *Staffeln* on Norderney to be increased to three, and for his *F.d.Luft* office being granted control of a Heinkel He 111 *Staffel* of torpedo bombers. Predictably, the Luftwaffe demurred.

A weapon-stock return dated 28 October 1940 put the number of torpedoes cleared for operational use by the Luftwaffe at sixty-eight, and those of the Kriegsmarine at only eighteen, with eighty-three more yet to be inspected and approved for action. Even this meagre stock held by Raeder's maritime aircraft was soon to diminish, as during November Göring restricted all airborne torpedo operations, earmarking every available torpedo for the opening of Mediterranean operations and attacks on naval units in Gibraltar and Alexandria. The Heinkel He 111 had finally been considered successfully adapted for torpedo use, Helmut Lorenz having sunk the 1,166GRT French steamer *Medoc*, which had been commandeered in a British harbour and transferred to Polish command, sailing with an Anglo-Polish crew. In the evening of 26 November *Medoc* left Devonport carrying a cargo of ammunition, in company with the armed trawler HMT *Lombard* and under low cloud and riding a heavy swell. At approximately 1800hrs one of the ship's lookouts sighted Lorenz's Heinkel approaching from the port side. He believed it to be friendly, but sounded the alarm bell as a precaution. Lorenz's first pass, strafing the ship's decks, was answered by belated fire from a Hotchkiss machine gun as the Heinkel crossed the steamer's bow. Lorenz circled and made a textbook approach, dropping a single torpedo within four minutes of the Heinkel having first been sighted.

Oberleutnant Helmut Lorenz, a former Kriegsmarine officer who led the Heinkel torpedo trials mounted by *Kampfgruppe* 126.

The torpedo was plainly visible from aboard the ship before it impacted on the port side, blowing a huge hole in the boiler room. Soon enveloped in smoke and escaping steam, *Medoc* sank rapidly, and stored depth charges exploding on its way down wounded men who were struggling in the water and damaged the escorting HMT *Lombard* as she closed to rescue survivors. Of a complement of eighty-seven officers and men, thirty-nine were killed. Lorenz had validated the He 111 as a torpedo bomber, destined for Mediterranean operations within the New Year.

The size of the *Seeluftstreitkräfte* had eroded significantly since the Norwegian campaign as the operational Luftwaffe assumed greater responsibility for all maritime operations and continued to subsume *Küstenflieger* units, converting many to land-based aircraft. By January 1941 the lack of seaplane *Staffeln* would prompt Jeschonnek to close the three dedicated schools for maritime personnel: *Flugzeugführerschule* (*See*) 1, Warnemünde (which had grown out of the pre-war *DVS* school); *Flugzeugführerschule* (*See*) 2, Pütnitz bei Ribnitz; and *Flugzeugführerschule* (*See*) 3, Stettin.

Using newly established French U-boat bases, the battle of the Atlantic was already reaching a fever pitch that would not relent for two more years as Dönitz's wolfpacks attempted what the U-boats of the previous war had been unable to do; starve Great Britain of military and civilian supplies and force an Allied surrender. The Luftwaffe had comprehensively failed to bomb Britain into submission after the struggle against the RAF in the summer of 1940, and now Dönitz would request a higher level of co-operation between the Kriegsmarine and Luftwaffe than had previously been attained. Aerial reconnaissance, he believed, could be the lynchpin by which U-boat victory could be achieved and the balance of the entire war be tipped irrevocably in Germany's favour.

Seeluftstreitkräfte *and operational Luftwaffe maritime units and chain of command:*

1 December 1940

Gen.d.Lw.b.Ob.d.M (*General der Flieger* Hans Ritter)
    F.d.Luft, *Generalmajor* Hermann Bruch (jointly subordinate to *MG Nord* and *Befehlshaber der Sicherung der Ostsee; BSO*)
        Staffel 1./BFl.Gr. 196 (Schellingwoude), *Hptm.* Fritz Grohé, Ar 196

Kü.Fl.Gr. 506, *Major* Heinrich Minner (Nordeney)
  1./Kü.Fl.Gr. 506 (Nordeney), *Oblt.* Eberhard Peukert, He 115
  2./Kü.Fl.Gr. 506 (Nordeney), *Hptm.* Wolfgang von Zetschwitz, He 115
Kü.Fl.Gr. 706, *Obstlt.* Hermann Lessing
  (half) *1.*/Kü.Fl.Gr. 406 (Rantum), BV 138
  (half) 1./Kü.Fl.Gr. 406 (Trondheim), Do 18
  2./Kü.Fl.Gr. 406 (Trondheim), Do 18
  3./Kü.Fl.Gr. 506 (Trondheim), Do 18
  1./Kü.Fl.Gr. 906 (Stavanger), Do 18
Flieger Führer Ost, *Obstlt.* Axel von Blessingh (Aalborg, Kü.Fl.Gr. 906) (jointly subordinate to *MG Nord* and *BSO*)
  1./Kü.Fl.Gr. 706 (Aalborg) He 59/He 115/Ar 196
  3. Bordgflieger. Erg. *Staffel* (Aalborg), He 114/Ar 196
Kü.Fl.Gr. 406 (Brest) (jointly subordinate to *MGK West* and *F.d.L*)
  1./Kü.Fl.Gr. 106 (Hourtin), He 115
  5/BFl.Gr. 196 (Cherbourg), Ar 196
  2./Kü.Fl.Gr. 906 (Brest), BV 138
  Transozeanstaffel (Brest-Hourtin), *Hptm.* Friedrich von Buddenbrock, Do 26

Luftflotte 3, *Generalalfeldmarschall* Hugo Sperrle
  IV.*Fliegerkorps* (Dinard) *Generalleutnant* Kurt Pflugbeil
    Kü.Fl.Gr. 606 (Brest)*
      1./Kü.Fl.Gr. 606 (Brest), Do 17Z
      2./Kü.Fl.Gr. 606 (Brest), Do 17Z
      3./Kü.Fl.Gr. 606 (Brest), Do 17Z
    KGr. 806 (Nantes)
      1./Kü.Fl.Gr. 806
      2./Kü.Fl.Gr. 806
      3./Kü.Fl.Gr. 806
    3./Kü.Fl.Gr. 906 (Cherbourg)* (previously 1./Kü.Fl.Gr. 106) *Seenotdienst* Do 18

Luftflotte 2, *Generalfeldmarshall* Albert Kesselring
  IX.*Fliegerkorps* (Soesterberg) *Gen.* Joachim Coeler
    3./Kü.Fl.Gr. 406 (Schellingwoude) *Seenot* Do 18*
    (jointly subordinate to *Seenotgruppe* Schellingwoude)
    Kü.Fl.Gr. 106 (Barth)* *Obstlt.* Hermann Jorden

2./Kü.Fl.Gr. 106 (Barth) (previously 3./Kü.Fl.Gr. 906), Ju 88
   3./Kü.Fl.Gr. 106 (Barth), Ju 88
KG 4, *Obstlt.* Hans-Joachim Rath (Fassberg), He 111P
   I./KG 4 (Copenhagen-Kastrup), *Obstlt.* Hans-Joachim Rath, He 111H-4
   II./KG 4 (Oslo), *Major* Dietrich Freiherr von Massenbach, He 111P
   III./KG 4 (Lüneberg), *Major* Erich Bloedorn, He 111P, Ju 88A-1
KG 40 (Bordeaux-Mérignac), *Major* Edgar Petersen
   Stab/KG 40 (Bordeaux-Mérignac), He 111H
   I./KG 40 (Bordeaux-Mérignac), *Major* Edgar Petersen, Fw 200C-1, He 111H
KGr. 126 (Nantes), *Hptm.* Holm Schellmann, He 111H-4
(redesignated I./KG 28 during December 1940)
   Stab./KGr. 126, He 111H
   1./KGr. 126, He 111H
   2./KGr. 126, He 111H
   3./KGr. 126, He 111H

Luftflotte 5, *Generaloberst* Hans-Jürgen Stumpff
   X.*Fliegerkorps*, *General der Flieger* Hans Geisler
      KG 26 'Löwen' (Beauvais) *Generalleutnant* Alexander Holle, He 111H
         I./KG 26 (Beauvais), *Obstlt.* Hermann Busch, He 111H
         II./KG 26 (Amiens), *Major* Eckhard Christian, He 111H
         III./KG 26 (Poix-Nord), *Major* Günther Wolfien, He 111H
         Erg.*Staffel*/KG 26 (Lübeck-Blankensee), He 111H, Ju 88A
      KG 30 'Adler' (Eindhoven), *Obstlt.* Erich Bloedorn, Ju 88A
         I./KG 30 (Gilze Rijen), *Hptm.* Heinrich Lau, Ju 88A
         II./KG 30 (Gilze Rijen), *Hptm.* Eberhard Roeger, Ju 88A
         III./KG 30 (Amsterdam-Schiphol), *Major* Schumann, Ju 88A
         IV./KG 30 (Ludwigslust), *Hptm.* Heinrich Paepke, Ju 88A

(*Remained dependent on *Gen.d.Lw.b.Ob.d.M* for replenishment of supplies and personnel)

6

The End of the Beginning

The Atlantic Battleground

During the autumn of 1940 the *SKL* had requested that air bases be established at Lorient and Saint-Nazaire, to support U-boats deployed on the French Atlantic coast. Demonstrating the acidity that relations between the Kriegsmarine and Luftwaffe had reached, the Luftwaffe General Staff replied that inspections had yielded 'no facilities there suitable for the construction of air bases', adding that there was no guarantee that any more suitable places would be found within the vicinity. Nonetheless, operational Luftwaffe and naval air units were moved to the Atlantic coastal region during the latter half of 1940.

Dönitz had been expecting Luftwaffe co-operation since his U-boats first began sailing from the French Atlantic ports, hoping for aerial reconnaissance to augment the already effective information gathering of *B-Dienst*, the Kriegsmarine's radio intelligence service. On 14 August 1940 he had noted in the *B.d.U.* KTB that KG 40 was to fly reconnaissance in the U-boats' area of operations off the North Channel from that date onward, but that little had come of it. The Luftwaffe continually claimed a lack of available aircraft, and only single flights were occasionally made, and they provided reconnaissance reports of dubious value. By November Dönitz was appealing strenuously to both *MGK West* and *Nord* for reconnaissance aircraft to patrol regularly both north-west of Scotland and to the west of Ireland, and on 16 November he obtained agreement from *Generaladmiral* Saalwächter at *MGK West*. However, the immediate reconnaissance of the North Channel area was only partly carried out, because Do 26 P5+EH, which had been despatched by the *Transozeanstaffel*, crashed immediately after launching. Based in Brest and supported by the catapult ship *Friesenland*, the Dornier suffered engine failure after being catapulted from the ship, and plunged into the water, killing all six crewmen.[1] Furthermore, nearly all of the BV 138s of *Küstenfliegergruppe* 406, based in Brest, were grounded for an expected two months owing to technical faults that had come to light since their active deployment. Without their assistance, in heavy weather during the first two days of December, U-boats closed on Convoy HX90 and managed to sink eleven of its forty-one ships. Although this was a significant success (though over-claimed as eighteen ships sunk by the commanders involved in the confused melée), the U-boats soon lost contact, frustrated by escorts, bad weather and the limited range of vision permitted by a U-boat's low conning tower. In his War Diary entry for that day, Dönitz lamented the lack of supporting aerial reconnaissance:

> The major thing was to establish contact. This couldn't be done:
>   a) by the boats themselves . . . or,
>   b) by aircraft of which unfortunately only a very few were available:
> One Fw 200 from KG 40 Bordeaux, two BV 138s from Brest, *Gruppe* 406. They did not make contact.
> The situation therefore remained obscure during the day. This operation shows up the gaps which inevitably result from warfare with so few U-boats . . . But it is equally clear that these gaps can be very effectively filled, as far as making contact goes, by using aircraft. Even a few isolated reports would be of greatest value. But there are only two BV 138s from *Küstenfliegergruppe* 406 available for this task and one Fw 200 from KG 40, which is used for this purpose by arrangement with the *Gruppe*. Success is correspondingly small: they did not make contact.[2]

It was a theme that had been regularly voiced both by Dönitz and his naval superiors since before the war. Even the reverse use of U-boats to guide aircraft to targets had failed, as evidenced by *Kaptlt*. Wolfgang Lüth's attempt to have the 10,350-ton New Zealand Shipping Company merchant MV *Orari* finished off by Luftwaffe attack. Lüth had hit the motor vessel in the stern with one of his last two torpedoes, fired south-west of Ireland at 2046hrs on 13 December as he made his way back to Lorient after over a month at sea. As it was impossible to use the U-boat's deck gun owing to bad weather, the damaged freighter was free from further interference, and wallowed onwards at reduced speed. Lüth followed for six hours while transmitting beacon signal and weather reports for a planned KG 40 Condor mission during the early morning. With no other U-boats in the area, Dönitz was enthusiastic about the opportunity to consolidate co-operation with the Luftwaffe with a success to which a U-boat had made a major contribution, and to test the practicability of calling up aircraft by means of U-boat reports. Although

In an image captured by a military photographer using a long-distance lens, an He 59 of the *Seenotdienst* rescues the downed crew of a Bf 110. By the time this photograph was taken the rescue service's previous neutral colour scheme had been replaced with military camouflage and markings.

KG 40 undertook to despatch an aircraft, its take-off was delayed until 1100hrs, which meant that the aircraft would be unable to reach the target before 1400hrs. Meanwhile, Lüth reported that *U43* was forced to break away and continue its return passage owing to a dangerously low level of lubricating oil. The plan was stillborn, and *Orari*'s crew managed to cover the torpedo hole with tarpaulins and reach the Clyde, where they began repairs that returned the ship to service in March 1941. Dönitz was disappointed and frustrated:

> I very much regret this failure of my plan, especially as every individual success attracts the attention of the authorities which would be concerned in the organisation of a large-scale co-operation and proves its practicability better than theoretical exposition can. Co-operation is necessary.[3]

Once again, Dönitz summarised the aerial reconnaissance requirements of his U-boat service within the *B.d.U.* War Diary, and submitted a copy as a memorandum to Raeder's office in Berlin.

The war has shown that the tactics of operating several U-boats together against a convoy are correct and lead to great success. In all cases, however, the first contact with the convoy was a matter of chance. The convoy approached a U-boat. In other cases, when this did not come off, the boats were at sea for days to no purpose. Time was wasted in the operations area. Full use of the U-boats against the enemy is not being made because of the lack of any form of reconnaissance.

B.d.U. is aware that Naval War Staff has been advocating the necessary reconnaissance with the Luftwaffe Ops. Staff for a long time. *B.d.U.*'s views on co-operation with the Luftwaffe are as follows:

a) The U-boat is of little value for reconnaissance. Its radius of vision is too small. It is too slow to be able to cover a large sea area in a short space of time, and we have insufficient numbers to attempt to do so. To use them for this purpose also wastes their fighting power. The U-boat can achieve much more if it does not have to hang around for weeks waiting for its prey to turn up, but, by means of previous reconnaissance, can be directed to the area where the enemy actually is. Every service arm has its own means of reconnaissance — except the U-boats.

b) By the use of long-range reconnaissance, the Luftwaffe can provide us with clear and definite information as to the whereabouts of the enemy, and can thus provide operational control with data on which to base the disposition of the U-boats.

c) The Luftwaffe can also support immediate U-boat operations by flying exhaustive reconnaissance of the area in which the boats are disposed, by reporting the valuable targets immediately and thus ensuring that enemy units within range are actually attacked, and that no enemy formations pass through the area occupied by U-boats without their even detecting them because of their small visual range.

d) But potential co-operation between aircraft and U-boats does not end simply with reconnaissance. The aircraft should shadow by day until the boats reach the enemy, bringing up the boats by using beacon signals; if contact is lost, it can be regained by aircraft after first light of the next day, etc. It is therefore a question of the closest tactical co-operation for a single co-ordinated operation.

e) The performance of these missions will in no way restrict or hamper normal air attacks against merchant shipping. In fact, it can only be an advantage to the U-boats if these aircraft attack and sink and damage ships, worry, divert and scatter the enemy. The areas in which the U-boats are stationed offer good prospects of success for aircraft attacks, because the U-boats occupy the busiest shipping areas. Aircraft attack need not be limited even if the U-boats are in the immediate vicinity. The only thing which the aircraft must not do is to attack submarines. Experience has shown that the danger of mistaking enemy submarines for our own U-boats is too great to permit the aircraft to attack, even if it is certain that it is dealing with an enemy submarine.

f) The best thing would be to discuss this form of co-operation directly with the Luftwaffe units concerned and try it out in practice. But in order to foster genuinely effective co-operation it is necessary: 1) to have sufficient forces; 2) to have a clear ruling as to command and control.

Once a convoy has been sighted, the subsequent co-operation — such as shadowing by an aircraft making beacon signals — must be controlled by the man who is directing the convoy operation, though this will not encroach upon the tactical leadership of the Luftwaffe Officer commanding the air unit engaged. This means that *B.d.U.* must decide where reconnaissance is to be flown and how many aircraft are to be used in each case, and have the available means at his disposal if a unified and rational method of co-operation is to be achieved. Close co-operation has so far been carried out with the following units:

a) *Küstenfliegergruppe* 406 Brest, which is tactically subordinate to *MGK West*. Their long-range BV 138 aircraft are, however, grounded for about two months because of technical defects.

b) KG 40 Bordeaux. No official contact. A degree of co-operation achieved by personal agreements. Type Fw 200. At present, generally only about one aircraft out by day.

c) *Luftflotte* 5 flies reconnaissance of a certain area from time to time by special request. So far only carried out once. Recently requested again but refused because of lack of available aircraft.[4]

Pilot and observer aboard a Dornier Do 17, both wearing standard-issue Luftwaffe steel helmets.

Mindful of Dönitz's recommendations, and somewhat chastened by Hitler's previous directive that heavily favoured Luftwaffe control of naval air operations, Raeder had fresh memoranda prepared for another meeting with the Führer, scheduled for 27 December 1940, as the tempo of operational flying was reduced by poor weather. Within its text, Raeder pushed for a small list of imperatives: the return of *Küstenfliegergruppe* 606 to Kriegsmarine tactical control, responsibility for aerial torpedo operations to rest with the Kriegsmarine, the intensification of Atlantic aerial reconnaissance in support of U-boat operations, and permission to use naval air units in strikes against enemy warships. To support his application on behalf of the U-boat service, Raeder despatched Dönitz to a meeting with *General* Jodl to present his observations in person. The meeting was both constructive and convivial. Dönitz asked for a daily reconnaissance sweep by twelve Fw 200s, and Jodl, in turn, raised the matter directly with Hitler.

Although most of the Kriegsmarine requests were treated with consideration by the Führer, perhaps indicating the loss of prestige that Göring had suffered within the halls of *OKW* as a result of the Luftwaffe's failure to destroy the BEF at Dunkirk and the RAF over

Britain, few concessions were granted. On 6 January 1941 a directive was issued by the Führer that ordered I./KG 40 (Fw 200) to be assigned to the Kriegsmarine to operate directly under *B.d.U.* control; something that had already been promised by the Luftwaffe since August 1940 but never delivered upon. Göring was instructed to bring the squadron to a strength of twelve Condors, maintaining that number 'if necessary by assigned additional aeroplanes of type He 111'. Hitler also, however, confirmed the transfer of the Ju 88s of *Küstenfliegerruppe* 806 to Luftwaffe control and attachment to *Luftflotte* 3.

While Hitler's directive demonstrated that the importance of aerial reconnaissance to Dönitz's U-boat service had been acknowledged and accommodated, little else was given to Raeder and the Kriegsmarine. Nonetheless, Hitler's decision signified a leap forward for the U-boats, albeit one that still required technical hurdles to be overcome before truly bearing fruit. The rate of Condor serviceability was extremely low, as the civil aircraft's airframe was not up to the rigours of operational military service over the Atlantic. However, while Dönitz was justifiably pleased, Göring was far less so, as it transpired that Hitler's decision had been made while the Luftwaffe chief enjoyed one of his many holidays in Paris. Not having been consulted, Göring was furious at what he saw as an attempt to subvert part of his domain once again to Kriegsmarine control. The Luftwaffe chief immediately summoned Dönitz from the Paris *B.d.U.* office to his own headquarters train, lying in a siding at La Boissière le Déluge, between Paris and Dieppe. This was the first meeting of the two men, and Göring attempted alternately to persuade and threaten Dönitz to return KG 40 to Luftwaffe control.

> Over coffee he heaped upon the Admiral remarks that Dönitz described in his report as 'distinctly unfriendly.' 'You can be sure of one thing,' Göring snapped, 'As long as I live, or until I resign, your *Grossadmiral* Raeder will never get a fleet air arm.' Pointing out that he, Göring, was 'the second man in the state,' he threatened that even if Dönitz should somehow get his hands on KG 40 he would not be likely to find replacements for its long-range aeroplanes. 'I need Fw 200s too,' he shouted, 'and it'll serve you right!'[5]

They parted as what Dönitz later described as 'bad friends'. The matter remained unchanged, and I./KG 40 was retained by U-boat headquarters, though obviously the Kriegsmarine and Luftwaffe's intractable dispute over operational control continued. The former protocols of spring 1939 were completely abandoned by Göring due to what he had termed the 'urgencies of war'.

Although the Fw 200 was a stopgap measure, it had already begun to prove its worth within the Atlantic battleground. By the end of 1940 KG 40 had been credited with sinking 800,000GRT of enemy shipping, though this estimate was far higher than the reality. Nevertheless, it was a notable start to Atlantic missions, and had cost the loss of only two aircraft thus far. The first had been on 20 August, when *Oblt.* Kurt-Heinrich Mollenhauer's Fw 200C-2, F8+KH of I./KG 40, crashed into Faha Ridge, Mount Brandon, County Kerry, Eire, during a meteorological mission made in dense fog. Most of the crew suffered broken limbs, but recovered and later became the first internees in Camp Curragh, County Cork. The second loss was the Fw 200 flown by *Oblt.* Theophil Schuldt, *Staffelführer* of 2./KG 40, which crashed off the Irish coast for unknown reasons during another meteorological mission. The pilot's body and that of meteorologist *Regierrungsrat* Dr Johannes Sturm were washed ashore some time later.

Bernard Jope of KG 40. A veteran of the Spanish Civil War he was awarded the Knight's Cross on 30 December 1940 following the destruction of SS *Empress of Britain*.

The most successful single attack had taken place on 26 October, when *Oblt.* Bernhard Jope attacked the 42,348-ton liner SS *Empress of Britain* seventy miles north-west of Donegal Bay. The liner was returning from transporting troops to Suez via Cape Town, carrying 224 military personnel and civilians plus a crew of 419 men. Jope sighted the ship and immediately dived out of the cloud cover on a strafing and bombing run, dropping six bombs, two of which hit (the ship's master reported five). The first bomb exploded in the main lounge, which immediately caught fire and sent dense clouds of black smoke spreading throughout the ship's enclosed areas. Although the liner's speed was increased and exaggerated zig-zagging undertaken, a second bomb struck as Lewis gunners returned fire, hitting the Condor several times before the attack was over. The fire aboard *Empress of Britain* rapidly spread, overwhelming all efforts by the crew to contain the blaze. Captain Charles Havard Sapworth gave the order to abandon ship at 0950hrs, only thirty minutes after the first attack. Most of the crew and passengers were picked up by the destroyers HMS *Echo* and ORP *Burza*, and the anti-submarine trawler HMS *Cape Arcona*, which also recovered an apparently substantial quantity of gold bullion being transported from South Africa. A skeleton crew remained aboard to fight the blaze that raged throughout the day and night, the ship floating on an even keel but gutted by the inferno, with its hull plates visibly glowing red. The only hope of salvage now seemed to be if the flames died out of their own accord. However, it was not to be. The stricken ship was sighted by *Kaptlt.* Han Jenisch in *U32* and finished off by torpedoes, though the nearby destroyers remained unaware of the U-boat's presence and believed the explosions to have been caused by the fire reaching the fuel oil bunkers.[6] Almost miraculously, considering the machine-gunning by Jope's Condor and intensity of the ensuing blaze, only twenty-five crew members and twenty passengers were lost.

Jope, a veteran of bomber missions during the Spanish Civil War as a member of K 88, returned successfully to Bordeaux-Mérignac and was feted for the achievement of seriously damaging the second largest ship operated by Britain, and the largest ship to be sunk by U-boat in the war. Mentioned in the *Wehrmachtberichte* of 29 October, he was awarded the Knight's Cross on 30 December 1940.

With little by way of aerial opposition within the Atlantic, by the end of 1940 the Condors of KG 40 harvested a deadly toll of enemy shipping sunk or damaged. Indeed, between August and February 1941 the unit claimed over 343,000 tons of ships sunk. Even allowing for wishful thinking and the resultant over-claiming, it was a remarkable success. During December all available KG 40 aircraft were used to fly reconnaissance for the approach of the cruiser *Admiral Hipper*, returning from an Atlantic raiding voyage to Brest Harbour for routine maintenance, and this forestalled any co-operative U-boat reconnaissance for several days. However, after *Hipper*'s departure from Brest on 9 February 1941, five Fw 200s of I./KG 40 attacked Convoy HG53 in co-operation with the U-boat *U37*, which had already struck, sinking two ships, and was providing position reports for both the Luftwaffe and the *Admiral Hipper*, which was in the vicinity of the Azores at that time. Led by *Hptm*. Fritz Fliegel, the Condors bombed and sank the 2,490-ton SS *Britannic*, carrying 3,300 tons of iron ore from Almeira, the 1,759-ton SS *Jura* with 2,800 tons of pyrites, the 967-ton Norwegian freighter *Tejo*, carrying wine, and the 2,471-ton *Dagmar I*, on a voyage from Malaga for the Clyde with 1,100 tons of oranges and oxide. Between them, the destroyed merchant ships lost twenty-seven men. The steamer *Varna*

The wreckage of *Oblt*. Erich Adam's KG 40 Condor F8+DK which crash landed in Portugal before being blown up by its crew who were briefly interned before repatriation to Germany.

was also heavily damaged. Its entire crew was rescued, although the ship did not finally sink until 16 February. In return, Fw 200 F8+DK, flown by *Oblt.* Erich Adam, was hit by anti-aircraft fire and damaged, breaking away to crash-land in Moura, Portugal. The crew sabotaged the abandoned aircraft and were briefly interned while trying to escape in civilian clothes in the Safara area. Transported to Moura, they were placed in the Grande Hotel before repatriation to Germany. Attempts to bring the *Admiral Hipper* into action against HG53 failed, though the cruiser sank a straggler on 11 February. Instead, *Hipper* abandoned the chase and attacked Convoy SL64, sinking seven of its nineteen ships. For the first time a capital ship, U-boat and aircraft had successfully co-operated against an enemy convoy, demonstrating the potential of joint Kriegsmarine-Luftwaffe operations.

Thus-far unidentified Luftwaffe *Leutnant* who served as pilot during weapon testing for the Heinkel He 115. His personal photo album provides a unique glimpse into the behind the scenes development of the Luftwaffe maritime force, including his role as pilot of an He 115 in the film '*Kampfgeschwader Lutzöw*'. (James Payne)

However, although KG 40 was garnering obvious success against merchant shipping, Dönitz was unsatisfied with the level of co-operation between the aircraft and his U-boats. The method by which sighting information was relayed to individual U-boats was extremely ponderous, as the aircraft could not communicate directly by radio with the U-boats themselves owing to a lack of equipment and trained personnel, and differing radio procedures. The reporting aircraft would shadow while transmitting long-wave homing signals via a trailing aerial, these being picked up by U-boats and retransmitted by short signal to *B.d.U.*, who plotted the various beacon signals and attempted to eliminate navigational errors before retransmitting a corrected position to the U-boats at sea. This procedure took valuable time, the aircraft frequently having then shifted location or departed owing to a lack of fuel if operating at extreme range. Additionally, location of convoy traffic itself was difficult for the Luftwaffe crews. In a typical mission to the sea area west of Ireland, a

Filming of the Heinkel He 115 scenes for the film *'Kampfgeschwader Lützow'* 100 kilometres west of Warsaw in August 1940. The aircraft used was an He 115 B1/C, probably BH+AM that was being used for torpedo trials at Travemünde and was later lost in a bad landing on 28 December 1942 while serving with *Küstenfliegergruppe* 906.

Condor possessed enough fuel to stay on station for approximately three hours before forced to return. During this time crewmen would be sweeping the sea with binoculars, the aircraft tending to fly at about 500m altitude, which allowed a search radius of around twenty kilometres in bright clear weather; frequently not the case in the Atlantic.[7]

Also, apart from the lack of available dedicated reconnaissance aircraft, which were frequently diverted to special bombing missions, it appeared that the British were re-routeing their convoys further to the north, pushing the intercepting U-boats towards Iceland. Aircraft of KG 40 based at Bordeaux could only effectively cover the south-eastern corner of this most northerly U-boat disposition, even if the long-range Condors departed from France and flew a circular route to land in Stavanger or Aalborg for refuelling. Dönitz reasoned that KG 40 could therefore really only provide information on shipping traffic in the southern sector, at that time patrolled only by Italian boats of the newly created BETASOM command, and for whose fighting value Dönitz harboured little respect.

> Immediate co-operation with our own boats is not possible. This state of affairs is unsatisfactory. There are considerable difficulties involved in the transfer of the whole *Gruppe* to Stavanger and Aalborg, and the advantages to be gained by such a move are outweighed by the many disadvantages which would result. The matter must be discussed with the Commanding Officer of the *Gruppe* as soon as possible.[8]

At a discussion between Dönitz and *Major* Petersen of I./KG 40 on 13 February, in which Dönitz requested that some aircraft be permanently relocated to Norway, it was concluded that a transfer of I./KG 40 was impossible at that point in time and unlikely to be made before the spring, as bad weather frequently hampered the operational effectiveness of the Scandinavian airfields. Dönitz therefore requested, via Petersen, that the Luftwaffe develop facilities at both Stavanger and Rennes to enable such operations in the future, while individual aircraft would begin to use the circular route, refuelling in Norway before making a return flight the following day. The threat posed by these returning Fw 200s was very much recognised by the British Admiralty.

> Enemy air attacks are being carried out in bad weather on ships and ports on the East coast with comparative immunity owing to the inability of our

aircraft to take off to counter them. C-in-C Rosyth urges that the enemy bases on the coast of Norway should be bombed. A Blenheim is to patrol over Stavanger Aerodrome nightly from 23 February in order to endeavour to keep Fw 200 aircraft from taking off during dark hours.[9]

On 19 February Bernhard Jope's Fw 200 was on armed weather reconnaissance near the Hebrides, before landing in Stavanger, when his crew sighted Convoy OB287 eighty miles north-west of Cape Wrath. Jope attacked through rain showers and, ignoring a pair of towed barrage balloons, dropped three bombs on one ship, two of which missed astern and the third hit the quarterdeck, and three on another, one a direct hit on its boiler room, which exploded. However, through lack of fuel he was unable to linger and transmit beacon signals for the benefit of U-boats, and despatched his sighting report and co-ordinates before heading via Fair Island to Stavanger.

Behind him, Jope left the 5,642-ton SS *Gracia* sunk, all forty-eight crewmen being rescued, and the 5,559-ton Royal Fleet Auxiliary tanker SS *Housatonic* still afloat but with its back broken and settling into the sea. Eighty survivors, some injured, one of them critically, were taken aboard HMS *Periwinkle*, which soon lost contact with the drifting wreck in a snowstorm. Last reported afloat during the course of the following day, the tanker was not seen again.

Alerted by Jope's radioed report, Dönitz quickly moved available U-boats south of Iceland to intercept, while the Condors continued to attack.

> Convoy OB287 was attacked this morning for the third day in succession in the North West Approaches . . . SS [sic] *Scottish Standard*, *St Rosario* and *D.L. Harper* are reported to have been damaged in the attacks today and yesterday. All attacks were made on the flanks or stragglers by single aircraft appearing suddenly from clouds or snowstorms. The escort was quite unable to cover the entire convoy and [HMS] *Wanderer* reports that continual escort (air) during daylight is essential if similar cases are to be avoided. It had been suggested that ASV [air-to-surface-vessel radar] transmissions might assist enemy aircraft to find convoy, and these were stopped after the dawn attacks this morning with subsequent immunity.[10]

Both the SS *St Rosario* and SS *Rosenborg* had been damaged by bombs on 20 February, the *D.L. Harper* also being damaged and sustaining a leak in its bunker. The 6,999-ton motor tanker *Scottish Standard* had been hit by Jope on his return trip to France from Stavanger during the following day, and abandoned by its crew. Jope reported two ships hit, one damaged and the second, estimated at 3,000 tons, destroyed by a hit in the boiler room and subsequent explosion. Jope then circled the convoy and transmitted beacon signals for the benefit of approaching U-boats. In his after-action report he maintained 'it was possible to calculate the exact position of the convoy by dead reckoning'. However, at *B.d.U.* it was found that the Focke-Wulfs' combined navigational reports of the convoy's location were so vague that U-boats were unable to make contact, and the chase was finally abandoned by the evening of 21 February.[11]

Greater success was achieved following a sighting report of OB288 south-east of Lousy Bank, made by an Fw 200 returning from Stavanger. The position report enabled *U73* to make contact and guide other U-boats, which collectively sank nine ships. Between 25 and 27 February Günther Prien's *U47* made contact with OB290 in the North Channel, and in a reciprocal operation, guided both other U-boats and Fw 200s of I./KG 40 to the convoy, where the Condors sank eight ships. It was a distinct high point in operations by the Condors, but subsequent attempts over the following two weeks to bring U-boats into action against convoy traffic sighted by the Fw 200s failed. The frustration of the situation at *B.d.U.* can be seen in Dönitz's War Diary entries:

2 March: One of the two aircraft detailed for reconnaissance to the North returning to Stavanger, reported a convoy at 1030 in AM 2920 (inexact). The course was given as west, only after further enquiry. The position was improved by the report of a bombed steamer in AM 2991. This position was assumed to be correct.

3 March: Aerial reconnaissance saw nothing of the convoy. It is questionable which position the aircraft has in fact reached, with the uncertain fix. It is still possible that the area to the south of the reconnaissance lines is covered. It is also possible that the convoy carried out an evasive movement after the air attack on 2 March, probably followed by one to the north . . . The situation strengthens suspicion to a conviction, that the convoys react to air attacks by greatly altering course — a course which must have seemed obvious to the English, with the development of co-operation between aircraft and U-boat. In this connection, therefore, KG

40 is only to attack isolated vessels; convoys though are to be shadowed unobserved, if possible, and not attacked. A lamentable, but necessary restriction. It remains to be seen how such questions should be decided after the statement of the *Fliegerführer Atlantik* under C-in-C Luftwaffe. Whether an unobserved shadowing is altogether possible with the large Condor aircraft also remains to be seen.

4 March: The Condor returning from Stavanger reported a convoy putting out in AM 2554, course 3000 at 0900. The composition is the same as that of the convoy of 2 March. It is possible that this is the same convoy, which, owing to the especially unfavourable weather conditions, has been lying practically hove to. The convoy cannot now be reached before darkness . . .

5 March: The reconnaissance lines did not bring any success up to the hours of darkness. Up to now, all attempts to operate on aircraft reports have remained without success (except in the case *U73* and *U96* on 22 February). The reasons are as follows:

a) Insufficient reliability of aircraft positions. A deviation of 70 nautical miles on 20 February must be attributed to the D/F ing of *U96*. In addition, it may be suspected that on this, and the days following, the aircraft positions were incorrect, the radio interception reports correct.

b) With the former method, the aircraft reports only gave one position, and the course given might only be that steered at the time.

c) For the most part, the U-boats detailed for operations could not intercept the target until the next day. During this long interval the first report will have decreased in reliability. Also, the uncertainty resulting from this cannot be compensated for, even by the operation of a wide U-boat rake.

Another method of co-operation must therefore be found in order to obtain a more exact position and course of the target from the reports of several U-boats in succession. Until this has been tried out there will be no more U-boat operations undertaken on aircraft reports. In spite of this, aircraft reconnaissance is important in the area not covered by U-boats.

Ordered for KG 40's operations:

a) Routine flights daily, with at least two aircraft if possible, reconnaissance west and north-west of Ireland.

b) Take off at intervals of one to two hours on the same flying route.

c) Convoys are the target. These are to be reported as quickly as possible (for the time being giving just course and speed). Contact is to be maintained as long as fuel supply allows.

d) The second, and all following aircraft, fly to the convoy reported by the previous aircraft and make their own complete reconnaissance report according to paragraph c). The report of the first aircraft can be checked by that of the second. Each aircraft must therefore report according to his own navigation, regardless of the report sent by his predecessor.

e) Convoys may be attacked until further notice.

Lunch break for the He 115 pilot during the filming of '*Kampfgeschwader Lützow*'. The one-piece summer flight suit (*Flieger-kombi für Sommer*) manufactured in a heavy brown/white flecked cotton and a long diagonal zip fastener from waist to shoulder was standard issue to Luftwaffe crew. (James Payne)

By March 1941 the aircraft of I./KG 40 had reverted to Luftwaffe control once more. After intense lobbying of *OKW* by the highest echelons of the Luftwaffe, Hitler issued a new order on 28 February, in which the Luftwaffe was given domain over the lion's share of naval aviation, stating baldly that there were no plans for the establishment of a separate naval air arm. Although reconnaissance over the North Sea in areas north of 52°, the Skagerrak and exits of the Baltic Sea, and ASW flights between Denmark and Cherbourg remained the preserve of the naval air service, Norwegian coastal reconnaissance and over the North Sea in areas including Shetland, the Orkney and Faroe Islands were to be handled by the Luftwaffe, by a newly created position designated *Fliegerführer Nord (Norwegen)* (Commander Air North, Norway, subordinate to *Luftflotte* 5). The *Kommodore* of KG 26, *Oberst* Alexander Holle, was appointed to this post in Stavanger, his men of Stab/KG 26 also forming the *Fliegerführer* staff and leaving KG 26 without a Staff flight. Hermann Bruch was in turn moved from *F.d.Luft* and appointed *Kommandierender General der Deutschen Luftwaffe in Nordnorwegen* on 21 April, headquartered in Bardufoss, Norway, acting as *Fliegerführer Nordnorwegen*. In Bruch's place as *F.d.Luft* came *Obstlt.* Friedrich Schily, pre-war *Kommandeur* of *Küstenfliegergruppe* 506.

The English Channel south of 52°N was also made the domain of the Luftwaffe, except for the protection and reconnaissance for convoy traffic. More importantly for Dönitz's U-boats, control of Atlantic reconnaissance and aerial cover for convoy traffic was transferred firmly to the Luftwaffe once more. However, Göring was ordered by *OKW* to establish a new post of *Fliegerführer Atlantik* (Commander Air, Atlantic, subordinate to *Luftflotte* 3), who would control reconnaissance missions for *B.d.U.*, meteorological flights, support for Kriegsmarine surface forces within the Atlantic and such offensive operations against maritime targets as were agreed between the Luftwaffe and Kriegsmarine. Hitler also ordered establishment of the post of *Fliegerführer Ostsee* (Commander Air Baltic) in preparation for the Führer's cherished Operation *Barbarossa* and the invasion of the Soviet Union. This new office would provide reconnaissance services for the Kriegsmarine within the Baltic Sea, particularly for *BdK* (*Befehlshaber der Kreuzer, Vizeadmiral* Hubert Schmundt), *FdM Nord* (*Führer der Minensuchboote Nord, Kapitän zur See* Kurt Böhmer) and *FdT* (*Führer der Torpedoboote, Konteradmiral* Hans Bütow based in Helsinki, Finland).

In France, the veteran former naval officer *Obstlt.* Martin Harling-hausen was appointed *Fliegerführer Atlantik*, with his headquarters in

Released in 1941, *'Kampfgeschwader Lützow'* followed a fictitious bomber squadron in its attack on Poland and subsequent operations against British shipping within the English Channel. The power of cinema propaganda was well harnessed by Joseph Goebbels, serving to both boost civilian morale and attract recruits.

the grand requisitioned Château de Kerlivio at Brandérion, fourteen kilometres west of Lorient. While the removal of most of the naval air units back to Luftwaffe command was far from ideal for the Kriegsmarine, at least in Harlinghausen they had an efficient and experienced ex-naval officer with whom to deal. Dönitz later described him as 'a man of exceptional energy and boldness', and the two men endeavoured to create a good working relationship.[12] Harlinghausen also articulated to Dönitz the independent operational doctrine with which his command would operate, his two central tasks being the reconnaissance reports locating convoys which could be attacked by U-boats, predominantly the domain of the long-range Fw 200, and attacks by shorter-range aircraft on enemy shipping nearer British coastal waters.

Nonetheless, Raeder gave vent to his extreme disappointment at the reversal of Hitler's previous decision, and the fact that none of his recommendations had been accommodated at all. Yet, despite a clearly worded memorandum, his last attempt at avoiding the 'serious limitations and dangers which will result from this for naval operations' was in vain, and the Luftwaffe reorganisation was undertaken during March. Correspondingly, Raeder saw the writing on the wall for his service, and during 1941 stepped up the channelling of *Küstenfliegergruppen* naval officers into the U-boat service. By the end of March 1941 most *Küstenfliegergruppen* had been detached from naval command, and the hierarchy of maritime aerial units changed dramatically once more.

Küstenflieger Command
Gen.d.Lw.b.Ob.d.M. (*General der Flieger* Hans Ritter)
   F.d.Luft (*Obstlt.* Friedrich Schily)
      Kü.Fl.Gr. 506 (Nordeney)
         1./Kü.Fl.Gr. 506 (Perleberg), Ju 88
         3./Kü.Fl.Gr. 406 (Hörnum), Do 18
         3./Kü.Fl.Gr. 906 (Nordeney), Do 18
         2./Kü.Fl.Gr. 906 (Hörnum), BV 138
         1./Kü.Fl.Gr. 406 (List), BV 138
      1./BFl.Gr. 196 (Wilhelmshaven), Ar 196
   Fliegerführer Ost (Aalborg), *Obstlt.* Axel von Blessingh
      Kü.Fl.Gr. 906 (Aalborg)
         1./Kü.Fl.Gr. 706 (Thistedt), He 59, He 115, Ar 196
         4.B.Flg.Erg.St. (Thistedt), Ar 196, He 114

Operational Luftwaffe Command Maritime Units
Luftflotte 2, *Generalfeldmarschall* Albert Kesselring
   IX.*Fliegerkorps*
      Kü.Fl.Gr. 106 (Schiphol)
         2./Kü.Fl.Gr. 106 (Barth), Ju 88
         3./Kü.Fl.Gr. 106 (Schiphol), Ju 88
Luftflotte 3, *Generalfeldmarschall* Hugo Sperrle
   Fliegerführer Atlantik (in co-operation with *B.d.U.* and *MGK West*)
      I./KG 1 (Amiens-Glisy), He 111
      Stab/KG 40 (Rennes), Ju 88 A
      I./KG 40 (Bordeaux-Mérignac), Fw 200
         3./KG 40 (Bordeaux-Mérignac), Fw 200
         4./KG 40 (Bordeaux-Mérignac), He 111
         5./KG 40 (Bordeaux-Mérignac), Do 217
      III./KG 40 (Brest-Lanveoc) *Maj.* Walther Herbold, He 111

3.(F)/123 (*Aufklärungsgruppe* 123), Ju 88, Bf 110
Kü.Fl.Gr. 606 (Do 17Z-2)
   1./Kü.Fl.Gr. 606
   2./Kü.Fl.Gr. 606
   3./Kü.Fl.Gr. 606
Kü.Fl.Gr. 406 (Brest)
   1./Kü.Fl.Gr. 106 (Hourtin), He 115
   5./BFl.Gr. 196 (Cherbourg), Ar 196
   2./Kü.Fl.Gr. 506 (Brest), He 115
   1./Kü.Fl.Gr. 906 (Brest), He 115

Luftflotte 5, *Generaloberst* Hans-Jürgen Stumpff
   Fliegerführer Nord (in co-operation with *MGK Nord*) *Generalleutnant* Alexander Holle
   Kü.Fl.Gr. 706 (Stavanger)
      2./Kü.Fl.Gr. 406 (Trondheim), Do 18
      3./Kü.Fl.Gr. 506 (Stavanger), He 115
   1.(F)/120 (*Aufklärungsgruppe* 120), Ju 88
   1.(F)/124 (*Aufklärungsgruppe* 124), Ju 88

X.*Fliegerkorps*, *General der Flieger* Hans Geisler
   1./(F) 121 (Catania), *Hptm.* Arnold Klinkicht, Ju 88D-1
   2./(F) 123 (Catania), *Oblt.* Gerhard Sembritzki, Ju 88D-1
   2./KG 4 (Comiso), *Oblt.* Hermann Kühl, He 111H
   5./KG 4 (Catania), *Hptm.* Heinrich Stallbaum, He 111H
   KG 26 '*Löwen*' (Stavanger-Sola) *Oberst.* Alexander Holle, He 111H
      I./KG 26 (Stavanger-Sola and Aalborg), *Obstlt.* Hermann Busch, He 111H
      II./KG 26 (Comiso), *Hptm.* Robert Kowalewski, He 111H
      III./KG 26 (Le Bourget), *Maj.* Viktor von Lossberg, He 111H
      IV./KG 26 (Lübeck-Blankensee), *Maj.* Franz Zieman, He 111H, Ju 88 A
   KG 30 'Adler' (Eindhoven), *Obstlt.* Erich Bloedorn, Ju 88A
      I./KG 30 (Eindhoven), *Hptm.* Heinrich Lau, Ju 88A
      II./KG 30 (Gilze Rijen), *Hptm.* Eberhard Roeger, Ju 88A
      III./KG 30 (Gerbini), *Hptm.* Arved Crüger, Ju 88A
      IV./KG 30 (Ludwigslust), *Maj.* Martin Schuman, Ju 88A
   LG 1 (Catania), *Oberst.* Friedrich Karl Knust, Ju 88A-4
      I./LG 1 (Krumovo), *Hptm.* Dipl.Ing. Karl Vehmeyer, Ju 88A-4

II./LG 1 (Catania), *Maj.* Gerhard Kollewe, Ju 88A-4
III./LG 1 (Catania), *Hptm.* Bernhard Nietsch, Ju 88A-4
IV./LG 1 (Tronsheim-Vaernes/Bardufoss), *Hptm.* Erwin Röder, Ju 87B

The most dramatic development, besides nearly all maritime air units being removed from naval control, was the movement of advance elements of Geisler's X.*Fliegerkorps* to the Mediterranean, *Luftflotte* 5 assuming direct control of operations in the area vacated by the *Fliegerkorps'* departure. The units listed above are Geisler's maritime strike units; X.*Fliegerkorps* also included fifty-three Bf 109 and fifty-five Bf 110 fighters, one hundred and sixty-four Ju 87 Stukas and seventy-six Ju 52 transport aircraft. The Luftwaffe Mediterranean initiative was in support of Italy's failing war in North Africa. After months of border skirmishes, on 13 September 1940 four divisions of the Italian Tenth Army based in Cyrenaica, Eastern Libya, had advanced into the British protectorate of the Kingdom of Egypt in Operazione *E*. The advance initially covered one hundred kilometres in four days, halting at Maktila, near Sidi Barrani. Five fortified encampments were constructed by the Italians as they awaited reinforcements,

A Dornier Do 18 shot down by British aircraft which filmed its sinking. The lightly armed Dornier proved highly vulnerable to enemy aircraft.

demonstrating a remarkable lack of offensive momentum. On the night of 7 December a vastly outnumbered British and Commonwealth force, well supported by the RAF and RN, launched Operation *Compass*, originally envisioned as a five-day limited operation to push the Italians back to the Libyan border, but culminating in the battle of Beda Fomm, which ended on 7 February with the virtual destruction of the Tenth Army.[13] The British, led by Gen. Richard O'Connor, had advanced to the shores of the Gulf of Sirte, and stood poised to end the threat of Axis forces in Libya entirely had O'Connor been permitted by his superiors to continue onward and take Tripoli. It was at that moment that Churchill made a monumental blunder and ordered the advance stopped, the captured territory to be held by minimal forces and the bulk of troops redeployed to Greece.

Hitler, on the other hand, ordered a small German land force despatched to Libya, commanded by *Generalleutnant* Erwin Rommel, his formation named the *Deutsches Afrika Korps*. Geisler's incoming *Fliegerkorps* was on hand to provide support, and his responsibilities had been spelt out in Führer Directive 22, issued on 11 January 1941:

> X.*Fliegerkorps* will continue to operate from Sicily. Its chief task will be to attack British naval forces and British sea communications between the western and eastern Mediterranean.
>
> In addition, by use of intermediate airfields in Tripolitania, conditions will be achieved for immediate support of the Graziani Army Group [Tenth Army] by means of attack on British port facilities and bases on the coast of western Egypt and in Cyrenaica.
>
> The Italian Government will be requested to declare the area between Sicily and the North African coast a closed area, in order to facilitate the task of X.*Fliegerkorps* and to avoid incidents with neutral shipping.

Geisler's expanded instructions made X.*Fliegerkorps* responsible for the initial engagement of Royal Navy fleet units, especially those at Alexandria, attacks on enemy shipping in the Suez Canal (including minelaying) and within the Straits of Sicily, while also preparing for possible deployment against targets in the Ionian and Aegean Seas. Geisler established his headquarters in the San Domenico Palace Hotel at Taormina, a seaside resort town at the foot of Monte Tauro, within sight of the brooding Mount Etna, and was ready for operations by 10 January. During the following day, X.*Fliegerkorps* had their mission parameters expanded to include attacks on British supply dumps and ports where incoming materials were being offloaded in Cyrenaica and western Egypt. Aircraft were to stage these attacks through forward airfields in Tripolitania in support of scattered Italian ground forces dug in to halt the British advance to Tripoli, which was the planned disembarkation port for Rommel's troops. During February Geisler's mission was expanded once more to include flying escort for German troop and supply convoys from the Italian mainland to North African ports. At a time when the Luftwaffe was already being stretched in western Europe, and the shadow of war with the Soviet Union loomed, it had already become involved in the dreaded 'war on two fronts'.

During January 1941 the airfield at Catania became the principle Luftwaffe base and main terminus for flights to and from North Africa. Among the first X.*Fliegerkorps* aircraft to arrive were Ju 87s of StG 3, Bf 110s of ZG 26 and bombers of LG 1, KG 4 and KG 26. The Heinkels of *Major* Helmut Betram's II./KG 26 spearheaded the deployment of that unit, based initially in Catania before moving to the airfield at Comiso, seventy-seven miles to the south-west and soon to be one of the major staging points for attacks on Malta. Harlinghausen accompanied the KG 26 aircraft to Sicily, and was thus absent from the French office of *Fliegerführer Atlantik*, while among the new arrivals were *Oblt*. Josef Saumweber, Helmut Lorenz and Friedrich Müller of 1./KGr.126, who had helped pioneer the use of torpedoes by He 111s while based at Lanveoc-Poulmic. They and their crews, along with two others led by Georg Linge and Rudolf Schmidt, were transferred *en masse* to 6./KG 26 to become the first cadre of *Geschwader* torpedo pilots. A torpedo workshop was established at Comiso by technicians attached to 4.*Flughafenbetriebskompanie*, II./KG 26, equipped with the few airborne torpedoes stockpiled after Göring had petulantly demanded that the six held by *Fliegerführer Atlantik* and the five with *F.d.Luft* in Stavanger be given up and flown by Ju 52 to Comiso.

Raeder forcefully argued that the loss of torpedoes for *Küstenflieger* aircraft rendered naval warfare against Great Britain unsustainable, and in conference with Hitler demanded the release of torpedoes to the *Küstenfliegergruppen* that were trained in their use, alongside the establishment of He 111 torpedo squadrons to be placed under *F.d.Luft* command. Striking while the iron was hot, he also pleaded for improved modern reconnaissance aircraft types for assisting U-boat warfare and the increased use of aerial mines off the western English ports, especially in the Firth of Clyde. Hitler merely asked Jodl, as head of *OKW*, to investigate these requirements, pointedly stating that 'matters of prestige' remained outside his decision-making powers. However, on 26 November Göring maintained his order to put a block on the use of aerial torpedoes, instead to be amassed for operations against the British Mediterranean fleet and the ports of Gibraltar and Alexandria, though these two ports were subsequently deemed too shallow for torpedo attack. He also ordered the establishment of his own air torpedo group, raising further objections from Raeder, who once again asked for the torpedo embargo to be lifted, maintaining that Germany could not release its pressure on British coastal convoy traffic in the interest of maintaining the naval blockade. He remained adamant that aerial torpedoes could only be successfully used by specially trained personnel who were, in his view, men from the Kriegsmarine. His objections were, however, overruled.

On 10 January, before the X.*Fliegerkorps* torpedo aircraft were cleared for service, other units made their Mediterranean combat debut.

The Blohm & Voss BV 138 was initially beset with design flaws but soon proved a reliable and rugged aircraft, this particular one belonging to *Küstenfliegergruppe* 706.

Convoy traffic bound for Malta from both Gibraltar and Alexandria had converged on the island in the British Operation *Excess*, both convoys arriving successfully after fighting through unsuccessful Italian air and naval attacks that cost two Savoia-Marchetti SM.79 torpedo aircraft. From the formidable Royal Navy escort forces, only the destroyer HMS *Gallant* of Force A suffered major damage, when her forward magazine was detonated after striking a mine near Pantellaria, the ship being towed stern-first to Malta with sixty-five crewmen killed and fifteen injured.

However, later that same day X.*Fliegerkorps* mounted its first successful attack on the ships of Force A, which comprised the battleships HMS *Warspite* and *Valiant*, the destroyers HMS *Nubian*, *Mohawk* (towing *Gallant* to Malta), *Dainty*, *Greyhound*, *Griffin* and *Jervis*, and the carrier HMS *Illustrious*. Fleet Air Arm Fairey Fulmars from *Illustrious* shot down a shadowing Italian aircraft, and two torpedoes later launched at low level by SM.79s were dodged by HMS *Valiant*. However, the Fulmars, which had descended to wave-top level to engage the Italian bombers, were surprised by the arrival of eighteen KG 26 He 111s and forty-three Ju 87s escorted by ten Bf 110s. HMS *Illustrious* continued launching Fulmar and Swordfish despite being the focus of the German attack, the British crew watching Ju 87s diving from an altitude of 12,000ft. The pilots delayed the release of their bombs to the last moment, bringing their aircraft lower than the height of *Illustrious*' funnel as they pulled their Stukas out of the dive. HMS *Warspite* was lightly damaged by a bomb, and *Illustrious* was struck by five direct hits and one that failed to explode, as well as a near miss that disabled the rudder. The bombing continued throughout the day, the Luftwaffe being joined by Italian Ju 87s. *Lehrgeschwader* 1 despatched three Ju 88s against the damaged carrier, but they were intercepted and driven off by Hurricanes from Malta, jettisoned their bombs and turned tail to run. *Illustrious* finally reached the relative safety of Malta at 2130hrs, with 126 dead and 91 wounded aboard.

> Shortly after noon today air attacks commenced on the Battle Fleet, which was covering the westbound convoy into Malta. Dive bombers, high-level bombers and torpedo aircraft were employed. Five of the bombers were Ju 87 with German markings; these attacked with great determination and skill, suggesting German personnel. This was the first really large-scale air attack to which the Fleet had been subjected. *Illustrious* was hit with six bombs and proceeded to Malta with severe damage and casualties,

THE END OF THE BEGINNING

Two photographs that show the devastating attack on HMS *Illustrious* in January 1941 as the Luftwaffe moved into the Mediterranean.

steering by engine. Sixteen of her aircraft were destroyed, but the remainder landed at Malta. Fulmars shot down six Ju 87s and two S.79s and damaged others.[14]

The German debut had yielded success, but at some cost. In addition, Wellington bombers attacked Catania Airfield on the night of 11 January. Six Heinkels of II./KG.26 were destroyed or damaged, plus two Ju 88s of III./LG 1. Further attacks by the Ju 88s against *Illustrious* as she lay stationary in Malta's Grand Harbour failed to inflict further damage, but five German aircraft were lost following the attack on 16 January. One collided with an Italian aircraft and was completely destroyed, two

A Junkers Ju 88 photographed from the ground during the attack on HMS *Illustrious* in Malta's Grand Harbour, 16 January 1941. (Leighton John Edward)

others were written off after serious damage from defending Fulmar fighters and anti-aircraft fire caused them to crash-land back at Catania, one reached the Sicilian coast and crashed near Pozallo after suffering heavy flak damage, and the fifth was shot down by a Fulmar; pilot *Oblt.* Kurt Pichler, observer *Fw.* Willi Strauchfuss, radio operator *Fw.* Heinz Kopecz and gunner *Fw.* Hermann Busch were all subsequently posted as missing in action.

Meanwhile, *Maj.* Helmut Bertram, former *Staffelkapitän* 5./BFl.Gr. 196 and now *Gruppenkommandeur* II./KG 26, took part in the first KG 26 raid mounted against the Suez Canal. The new German arrivals hastily assembled an attack against reported convoy traffic, as an early attempt to sink ships within the Canal could, according to Geisler, not only potentially block the vital Allied transit route, but also demonstrate the capabilities of the Luftwaffe both to the enemy and to their Italian ally.

The *Regia Aeronautica* granted the Luftwaffe use of the airfield at Benina, near Benghazi, as a forward staging post for operations within the eastern Mediterranean and against North African land targets. However, they instantly perceived that little co-operation was forthcoming from their newly arrived allies, a tangible air of assumed superiority accompanying the Luftwaffe into their new battlefield. Two Ju 88s of the reconnaissance *Staffel* 1.(F)/Aufkl.Gr. 122 landed at Benina at dawn on 15 January, their arrival unannounced to the Italian authorities and counteracting a standing Italian order for daylight operations only from the airfield. The Junkers had been tasked with a reconnaissance sweep of the Suez Canal to locate the convoy for Heinkel bombers that would follow shortly. Nine aircraft from KG 26 flew to Benina the following day, led by Bertram and with Harlinghausen as observer aboard the Heinkel commanded by *Hptm*. Robert Kowalewski, an ex-*Reichsmarine* officer and long-term friend of Harlinghausen.[15]

The Luftwaffe *Seetankschiff Clara*, one of a small number of tankers launched to supply Luftwaffe maritime bases with fuel rather than compete with the needs of the Kriegsmarine. *Clara* was constructed under orders from the *RLM* during 1938 and entered service in 1941 in the Baltic and North Sea.

The two Ju 88s took off at first light to begin their search. In the first, 7A+FH, pilot *Obfw.* Hermann Peters attempted to take to the air in strong wind, overshot the runway and collided with a parked Italian SM.79 Sparviero bomber. Both aircraft were destroyed, and all four German crew died in the resultant blaze.[16] The second Ju 88 fared better, but reported no trace of the convoy before diverting to land on the Italian controlled island of Rhodes to refuel. A third Ju 88 despatched on 17 January also failed to make contact.

Instead, Harlinghausen ordered one of the Heinkels in Benina to be emptied of bombs, and the aircraft subsequently arrived over Alexandria in good weather and reported shipping in the Canal, approaching Suez from the south. The remaining eight Heinkels departed between 1800 and 1830hrs, expecting to return by 0400hrs the following morning. However, the raid was a disaster. Only a single Heinkel returned, commanded by *Lt.* Werner Kaupisch, who had suffered engine trouble and jettisoned his bombs east of Alexandria. Strong winds caused delays to the other returning aircraft sufficient to cause fuel starvation. While Italian authorities ordered extra airfield lights to be switched on to aid navigation as sand storms began forming over the desert in Marmarica, radio communication was received that two of the seven remaining Heinkels had missed Benina in the abysmal visibility and been forced to ditch. Of the other Heinkels, one crew baled out and the remainder were forced to land. Italian ground forces formed rescue parties to search for survivors.

Harlinghausen had divided the force in two to sweep the waterway's eastern bank in opposite directions near the reported convoy position. The northbound Heinkels, led by his aircraft, sighting nothing. After reaching Port Said and reversing course they finally detected merchant ships hove-to offshore, though a hurried attack failed and the Heinkel crews faced a daunting return journey at their aircrafts' maximum range. In violent winds and a blinding sandstorm, Kowalewski was forced to belly-land his fuel-starved bomber in the desert, successfully bringing it to a halt among the endless wind-scoured sand dunes. Harlinghausen, Kowalewski and their crew set fire to the aircraft before beginning the 280-kilometre walk to Benghazi. The blackened remains of the aircraft were sighted by searching Italians after daybreak, but no trace of Harlinghausen or the Heinkel crew was seen. After four days, *Lt.* Werner Kaupisch, who had joined the hunt in the sole surviving Heinkel, finally found them and landed on the flat sand to pick up the exhausted men and return them to Benina.

Of the other Heinkels that had made emergency landings, three crews were taken prisoner by British and Australian troops, among them *Maj.* Bertram, who, as commander of the aircraft flown by *Lt.* Hans Folter, had put down out of fuel to the west of Tobruk. The four-men crew had been captured twenty miles east of Fort Maddalena after a gruelling march in the desert. Bertram was soon replaced in command of II./KG 26 by Kowalewski.[17]

The German disaster caused some small measure of satisfaction among the Italian officers of V *Squadra Aerea* (5th Air Fleet), who regarded the Germans as having been difficult and unwilling to accept local knowledge from the regionally experienced Italian airmen. The Luftwaffe operation had been hastily put together and poorly planned and executed. Designed to show German efficiency in action, it had instead betrayed the Luftwaffe pilots as ignorant of desert flying conditions and guilty of overconfidence. The conditions in which the German crews found themselves were completely alien, even for veterans of the fighting in western Europe. On hot days, the temperature inside the glazed cockpits of Luftwaffe bombers could reach 70° Celsius, and, navigating amidst the barren wastes of a desert landscape, the Luftwaffe men had been guilty of recklessness. General Francesco Pricolo, Chief of Staff of the *Regia Aeronautica*, suggested in a letter to X.*Fliegerkorps* that:

> The incidents that have occurred on this flight are predictable due to the worsening weather conditions, and resulted in painful human losses and material damage, which perhaps could have been prevented if greater contact was made with the local air force commands. They could have provided valuable advice derived from long experience acquired in the particularly difficult desert environment. I wish to communicate the above fact to this Liaison Office, in order to obtain the collaboration between the air forces of the Reich and Italy that is required for every aspect in an ever-closer manner with the greatest mutual interest.

Away from the Mediterranean, the *Küstenflieger* on the Atlantic coast had also suffered losses due to a mixture of enemy action and accidents. On 23 January an He 115B-2 of 1./Kü.Fl.Gr. 906 crashed in poor visibility south of Brest, and two days later, over the Bay of Biscay, He 115 M2+KH, under the command of *Lt.z.S.* Hans-Dieter Fürl, failed to return from its mission, no trace of the aircraft or crew being found. Although its fate remains unknown, three Blenheim VIs of 236 Sqn,

Coastal Command, led by Flt Lt Malcolm Robert McArthur, were flying an anti-Condor patrol when they encountered and engaged an He 115, though no 'kill' was claimed.

While patrols by the shorter-range aircraft continued relentlessly, Dönitz remained vexed by the lack of successful co-operation between the long-distance aircraft of KG 40 and his U-boats. Aside from the difficulties of untested aircrew over the sea, *B.d.U.* was also engaged in a tug-of-war over the few available KG 40 units with *MGK West*, wanting them for scouting for fleet, *Sperrbrecher* and minesweeping operations. Despite this, the relative success of independent attacks by Fw 200s against merchant ships had clearly registered with the Allies. Churchill's fear of British strangulation at the hands of U-boats and aircraft was foremost in his thinking during the first half of 1941.

> We must take the offensive against the U-boat and the Focke-Wulf wherever we can and whenever we can. The U-boat at sea must be hunted, the U-boat in the building yard or in dock must be bombed. The Focke-Wulf, and other bombers employed against our shipping, must be attacked in the air and in their nests.[18]

Instructions were issued to Bomber Command on 9 March 1941 to concentrate their main operational effort against targets posing a threat to British merchant shipping. While most of this energy was directed against industrial plants manufacturing U-boat components, construction yards and U-boat harbours themselves, the aircraft of KG 40 were also targetted.

During March 1941 only three merchant ships were sunk by I./KG 40, which, although having twenty-one Condors on strength, could muster an average of only six or seven serviceable machines during the course of the month. The *Gruppe* had, however, expanded to four *Staffeln*, three operational and one training, while a further two *Gruppen* were being formed. In January 4./KG 40, equipped with He 111s and commanded by *Hptm.* Paul Fischer, became operational, and the following May two further *Staffeln* were established, flying the Do 217. Fischer's Heinkels were replaced by Do 217s during June, and the three Dornier *Staffeln* were brought together as II./KG 40 under the command of *Hptm.* Wendt Freiherr von Schlippenbach. During March III./KG 40, commanded by *Maj.* Walter Herbold, was created, flying He 111H-3s owing to the lack of available Condors, but in training at

The battleship *Gneisenau* photographed in the North Sea alongside a low-flying He 111. Kriegsmarine-Luftwaffe cooperation seldom reached a level enabling effective inter-service operations.

Lüneberg until July, whereupon it transferred to *Fliegerführer Atlantik* based in Cognac.

As part of Bomber Command's initiative, a bombing raid on Bordeaux-Mérignac by twenty-four Wellingtons on the night of 12 April destroyed two Condors, a pair of He 111s and a Do 215, and badly damaged hangars and airfield buildings. That same night Stavanger-Sola Airfield was also bombed, one Wellington being brought down by ground fire and crashing into the roof of a bakery, where it exploded. This destruction of grounded aircraft was followed by the first Condor confirmed as shot down by an enemy fighter when, on 16 April, Flt Lt Bill Riley's Bristol Beaufighter of 252 Sqn Coastal Command attacked *Oblt.* Hermann Richters's Fw 200C-3, F8+AH, and sent it plunging into the sea in flames off the Irish coast, killing the entire crew. On the following day *Oblt.* Paul Kalus' 1./KG 40 Condor, F8+FH, was posted missing, and the body of an airman was washed ashore in the Shetlands over a month later. Yet another Condor was lost when *Oblt.* Ernst Müller of 3./KG 40 and his crew ditched off Schull Island, County Cork, and were interned. The final casualties of the month were suffered on 29 April, when *Oblt.* Roland Schelcher of 1./KG 40 was also shot down off the Shetlands by flak from Royal Navy ships, causing the loss of the entire crew. On the balance sheet that no longer favoured the Germans, KG 40 sank eight merchant ships during April.

Increased reconnaissance flights in support of *B.d.U.*, comprising three Fw 200 Condors and three He 111s (4./KG 40) in the air simultaneously, the former from Bordeaux and the latter from Stavanger and Gardemoen Airfield near Oslo, were scheduled to begin from 25 April, but 'technical difficulties' delayed their instigation. U-boats had been specifically moved to the area to be covered by the aircraft from Stavanger, but without eyes in the sky they struggled to find the enemy. Furthermore, when the delayed flights began, two days later than originally scheduled, the two Fw 200s spearheading the mission were damaged on their outward passage while attacking a merchant ship, forcing them to break off the action and return to base. They had not followed their briefing instructions to avoid actual combat. The Heinkels completed a journey of over 3,000 kilometres from their Norwegian airfields to land at Vannes, carrying only two 250kg bombs, a route that would be followed repeatedly until July 1941.

However, aerial reconnaissance by I./KG 40 had distinctly failed as far as *B.d.U.* was concerned. The tenor of his war diary entry for 28 April displayed his opinion of the usefulness of *Fliegerführer Atlantik*:

> *U123* made contact at 0106 with an inward-bound convoy in AL 2326 ... Radio message to *U123*: attack permitted, continue to shadow ...
>
> Air reconnaissance was requested for the area in which the convoy had been reported. The aircraft sighted various groups of destroyers and a convoy in AE 8932. It consisted of five ships, strongly escorted, and was inward bound. *U143* was informed accordingly. The reconnaissance aircraft did not on the other hand succeed in picking up *U123*'s convoy, which proves how inadequate a reconnaissance with <u>few</u> aircraft is even against a <u>reported</u> target.

Kapitän zur See Hans-Jurgen Reinecke, Staff Operations Officer in *SKL* between 1938 and 1941, later charged that a major difficulty in co-operation between U-boats and aircraft was the Luftwaffe's unwillingness to attack a convoy's escort and thereby leave the merchants to be torpedoed by U-boats. Göring's desire for 'headlines' led him to send his aircraft in to wage a tonnage war, attacking merchants and frequently scattering a convoy while U-boats were depth-charged by unchecked escort ships and unable to keep pace with the departing merchants. If they had indeed attacked in concert, bombers could have dealt with the escort while the U-boats concentrated on the slower merchants, potentially harvesting a far greater toll than that achieved, even against the hard-hit Arctic convoys.

On the other side of the coin, *Fliegerführer Atlantik* had also experienced frustration, as on at least one occasion an aircraft transmitted detailed and accurate bearings of convoy traffic while shadowing, only to learn later that *B.d.U.* had no U-boats within the area at all, a fact of which neither Harlinghausen nor his staff had been made aware

In the meantime, aircraft of the *Küstenflieger* and maritime units of the operational Luftwaffe continued to wage war against British shipping within the North Sea. The winter of 1940-41 had been considerably milder than the previous one, and the icy period in which seaplanes could not function had been relatively short. The increased number of *Küstenflieger* units that had converted to land-based aircraft also rendered them operational within the parameters of normal weather considerations. However, Luftwaffe demands in attacking land-based objectives led to the more frequent use of such maritime units over British soil. Both 2./Kü.Fl.Gr. 106 and 3./Kü.Fl.Gr. 106 were used in raids on Britain under the command of 9.*Fliegerdivision*, and suffered casualties in trained naval aviators. *Staffelkapitän Hptm.* Walter Holte of 3./Kü.Fl.Gr. 106 and his crew were killed on 21 February when their Ju 88A-5 crashed near Noordwijkerhou in The Netherlands during a planned raid on London, and on 14 March another of the *Staffel*'s Ju 88A-5s was lost during a bombing raid on Glasgow. *Oberleutnant* Hildebrand Voigtländere-Tetzner's aircraft was intercepted by Spitfires of 72 Sqn, and its starboard engine erupted in flames when Flt Lt Desmond Sheen attacked in bright moonlight.

> As I opened fire I could see my tracer bullets bursting in the Junkers like fireworks . . . when I turned in for my next attack I saw that one of the Hun's engines was beginning to burn, but just to make quite sure of him I pumped in a lot more bullets, then I had to dive like mad to avoid ramming him.

The Junkers spun into the sea off the Northumberland coast in flames. None of the occupants survived.

Other *Küstenflieger* crews brought down were luckier. On 17 February Do 17Z-3 7T+JL of 3./Kü.Fl.Gr. 606 was shot down near Windsor by

American-born Sqn Ldr James 'Jimmy' Hayward of 219 Sqn. His unit was operating the first Beaufighter nightfighters when he attacked the Dornier as it returned from bombing London; *Lt.z.S.* Rolf Dieskau and his crew survived the attack and were captured. *Oberstleutnant* Joachim Hahn's *Küstenfliegergruppe* 606 began to convert to the Ju 88 during early 1941, and was flying the new aircraft operationally by March. Following this conversion, the inevitable shift to full Luftwaffe control that Göring had pursued since July 1940 was completed in May 1941, when *Küstenfliegergruppe* 606 was officially redesignated *Kampfgruppe* 606, with an operational strength of sixteen Ju 88s.

With enemy fighter aircraft posing a growing threat to *Küstenflieger* daylight operations, more missions were planned for the hours of darkness. These, however, not only lowered operational efficiency on all but area-bombing raids, but also did not necessarily make the task any less dangerous. On the night of 18/19 May Hahn's Ju 88s took part in a raid against convoy traffic reported north-west of Ireland, and lost

An He 115 being loaded with a practice F5 torpedo, its dummy warhead denoted by the striped paintwork. The bomb bay doors obvious in this photograph allowed internal stowage of the torpedo.

four aircraft. *Hauptmann* Rolf Beitzke, *Staffelkapitän* of 2./KGr. 606, was shot down by flak near Falmouth and crashed into the sea, only the body of gunner *Fw.* Richard Pape later being washed ashore. *Oberleutnant* Günther Hitschfeld's aircraft, 7T+AH, crashed into the top of a hill near Yelverton in Devon, tearing off both propellers and the lower gondola before the shattered Ju 88 careered to a halt in the bottom of a valley. Although the cause of the crash remains unclear, the aircraft's tailplane had received at least one hit from an 0.303 bullet. Hitschfeld and all three of his crew were killed, their bodies being recovered from the wreckage and interred in Sheepstor Churchyard. *Oberleutnant* Helmut Eiermann's Junkers crash-landed at Lannion upon its return, having suffered extensive damage. Eiermann had already survived being shot down during *Weserübung*, when his Do 17 was hit by flak from a Norwegian MTB on 17 April 1940 and he had forced-landed north-east of Arendal. This time he was not so fortunate. Both he and gunner *Gefr.* Max Schwarzer were killed in the crash, and the two survivors were both injured. The final loss to *Kampfgruppe* 606 was *Lt.z.S.* Werner Neudeck of 2./KGr. 606, whose Ju 88 crashed six kilometres west of Thierry Harcourt after its fuel supply was exhausted. Neudeck was killed and the remaining crew injured, wireless operator *Uffz.* Heinrich Jänchen later dying of his wounds. A final Ju 88, flown by *Oblt.* Peter Schnoor of 3./KGr. 606, belly-landed at Lannion, but the aircraft was later repaired and returned to action. In return, Convoy HG61 reported being bombed by German aircraft north-west of Ireland at 0016hrs on 19 May, but suffered no damage.

Far to the east during that same day, the battleship *Bismarck* slipped her moorings at Gotenhafen and headed for the Danish Straits, shepherded by Luftwaffe aircraft including Ju 88s of I. and II./KG 30. Shortly thereafter, the battleship was joined by the heavy cruiser *Prinz Eugen*. Aboard *Kapitän zur See* Ernst Lindemann's *Bismarck* was *Flottenchef* (Fleet Commander) *Admiral* Günther Lütjens and his staff of over sixty men. The two heavy ships were beginning Operation *Rheinübung*, an Atlantic sortie to pillage the Allied merchant convoy routes. Once beyond the range of Luftwaffe cover they were shadowed by the Royal Navy before they fought the Battle of the Denmark Strait on 24 May, in which HMS *Hood* was sunk, leaving only three survivors. However, *Bismarck* had already taken damage during the brief action which forced her to break away from her planned course and head towards France, where the *Scharnhorst* and *Gneisenau* were already undergoing repairs in Brest Harbour following their own successful raiding voyage. Instead, *Bismarck*

The Fw 200 Condors of KG 40 became a mainstay of U-boat support work, though not without significant inter-service difficulties.

headed for the larger dockyard at Saint-Nazaire. Two large concrete mooring blocks had been built for *Bismarck*'s use in Brest's outer harbour, but Saint-Nazaire was the only shipyard capable of accommodating the battleship. *Luftlotte* 3 was informed of *Bismarck*'s movement by *MGK West* at 1600hrs on 24 May, *Generalfeldmarschall* Hugo Sperrle hurriedly reinforcing *Fliegerführer Atlantik* within two days with extra bomber *Gruppen*: I./KG 28 in Nantes and the pathfinder force KGr. 100 at Vannes (both He 111), and I./KG 77 (Ju 88), II./KG 54 (He 111) and III./KG 1 (He 111) all based at Lannion. While the *Prinz Eugen* peeled off to continue the planned raiding voyage, *Bismarck* was harried by British forces, their pursuit aided by oil leaking from the battleship's ruptured hull. While Dönitz formed two U-boat patrol lines to set up a potential ambush of the pursuing Home Fleet ships, Göring issued orders on 25 May for *Fliegerführer Atlantik* to provide the fullest possible support for the incoming *Bismarck*, and Harlinghausen ordered all aircraft under his command to be brought to immediate readiness. However, though the aircraft numbers available to him were impressive, eventually totalling 218 committed to cover *Bismarck*, the vast majority of the hastily added units had no experience of maritime warfare and navigation, let alone in the squally weather conditions sweeping across the North Atlantic as a low-pressure front from the north-west bought violent storms.

Condor reconnaissance by a single aircraft of I./KG 40 on 26 May detected HMS *Rodney* and four destroyers travelling in formation, but sighted no other ships, as the Focke-Wulf was at the absolute limit of its range and only briefly on station. Bereft of air cover at such distance from friendly shores, *Bismarck* was attacked that same evening by Swordfish of HMS *Ark Royal*, which attacked with torpedoes between strong rain squalls and disabled the battleship's steering.

While *Bismarck* was heading toward destruction, Harlinghausen had allocated three Fw 200s, seven Ju 88 reconnaissance aircraft, forty-two Ju 88 bombers, twenty-nine He 111s and fifteen He 115s to the task of supporting the approaching ship. The Condors, eight Ju 88s and ten He 115s took off on their armed reconnaissance flight in the darkness at 0307hrs, the Fw 200s sighting heavy British forces steaming from Gibraltar to cut off the disabled *Bismarck*'s retreat. As the aircraft transmitted beacon signals for distant U-boats, B.d.U. was notified of their position. Eight Ju 88s of KGr. 606 took off in the early morning, and five of them were able to detect direction-finding signals that were being steadily transmitted by *Bismarck* until 0845hrs. An hour later they arrived at the scene of *Bismarck*'s last stand, as she was engaged by two heavy ships and two lighter units. The Ju 88s delivered a hasty and unsuccessful spoiling attack on a pursuing cruiser, frustrated by 'Gladiator aircraft', probably confusing *Ark Royal*'s Swordfish for the biplane fighter. Unable to outrun or outmanoeuvre its pursuers, *Bismarck* was finally cornered and sank at 1101hrs, disabled by gunfire and scuttled by the German crew as they abandoned ship.[19]

During the final battle the Admiralty recorded HMS *Cossack* and *Norfolk* coming under attack by 'land-based aircraft' from 1000hrs, though the bombers achieved nothing. Within the hour *Bismarck* had been sunk. Of the crew of 2,221 men, only 114 survived. Eighty-five were rescued by HMS *Dorsetshire* and twenty-five by HMS *Maori*, until lookouts aboard *Dorsetshire* reported sighting a possible periscope and the two British ships broke off their rescue mission and returned to the main body of Force H. Three other men were later found by *U74*, which arrived at the scene of the battle but had been unable to assist *Bismarck* in high seas that prevented torpedo use. A German *Vorpostenboot* later rescued a further two. The *Bismarck* had carried four Ar 196 aircraft of *Bordfliegerkommando* 1./BFl.Gr. 196 and their associated crews and technical personnel, numbering four Kriegsmarine observer officers, four NCO pilots and ten technical personnel.[20] Of these, only 26-year-old technician *Mechanikerobergefreiter* Ernst Kadow survived, rescued by HMS *Dorsetshire*. One of the Arados had been made ready to catapult in the last-ditch defence of the *Bismarck*, but a torpedo hit below the catapult station had disabled the pressurised air system and the aircraft could not be launched. With the ship moving at speed and waves up to ten metres high it was impossible to lower any aircraft into the water, and the prepared Arado was later pushed overboard into the sea.

Luftwaffe attempts to intercept and attack Force H as it withdrew were unsuccessful, many of the German crews being unfamiliar with nautical navigation and completely failing to locate their targets, while occasional bomb runs mounted by single aircraft missed their mark. A further plan to despatch a concerted attack by 150 bombers at dusk was abandoned, as contact with the Royal Navy force had been lost. It was briefly regained by an He 115 of *Küstenfliegergruppe* 406, which reported the ships' course 'no longer determinable' in fading light, at the aircraft's range limit and sailing beneath low cloud through drifting squalls. The following day an Fw 200 regained contact at 0750hrs and

The emblem adopted by KG 40's long-distance bombers.

sixty-three aircraft mounted staggered attacks on the retreating British. The Commander-in-Chief of the Home Fleet requested urgent fighter escort, and Hurricanes, Hudsons and Blenheims were rapidly scrambled to assist.[21] None had arrived before HMS *Norfolk* came under attack at 0915hrs and was damaged by splinters from near-misses. HMS *Ripley*, *Tartar* and *Mashona* were also attacked, evading through a combination of full speed and rapid course changes, although the *Mashona* was hit at 0924hrs by a Heinkel of I./KG 28, the bomb penetrating the port hull abreast of the fore-funnel and exploding in No.1 Boiler Room. Badly holed, the ship listed heavily, and all unnecessary gear was thrown overboard to save her. However, after forty-five minutes the ingress of water could not be stopped, and *Mashona*'s list increased in the Atlantic swell. The order was given to abandon the destroyer and, during a temporary lull in the air attacks, HMS *Tartar* picked up survivors before the battered ship was finished off with gunfire from the freshly arrived HMS *Sherwood* and HMCS *St Clair*, finally capsizing and sinking. Sid Dobing was aboard the 'Tribal'-class HMS *Mashona* when the Luftwaffe attacked.

> We were very low on fuel. And we were in company with one other destroyer, HMS *Tartar*, when the German Air Force located us. They had left their bases and were looking for the British fleets, and found two lonely destroyers, carried out some heavy attacks and eventually we were straddled by bombs and we lost 47 men, and we were ordered to abandon ship. We were picked by HMS *Tartar* after a period of time. She was still under attack, and then the Germans had to go back to base and get some more planes and bombs, and during that lull we were picked up and then we came under heavy attack again, but eventually made our way by the *Tartar* to Greenwich on the Clyde, and from there we were sent on survivors' leave, and then back to another ship.[22]

Interestingly, Luftwaffe reports show that while I./KG 28 and KGr.100 both lost an aircraft each during take-off, none were lost to enemy action while in battle with Force H, although a Hudson of 233 Sqn claimed an He 111 destroyed and HMS *Tartar* reported another shot down.

> At about 1000 *Tartar* was engaging one He 111 on the port beam at about 3,000 yards' range when one round probably from the 4-inch mountings was seen to hit. Pieces could be seen falling away from the machine and a

trail of smoke was noticed. This machine flew on for about half a minute, when it was seen to dive towards the sea, the smoke increasing. On striking the water a large cloud of smoke appeared and one wing could be seen sticking up. None of the crew baled out. This aircraft was originally reported as having been shot down at 1025, but subsequent investigation shows that the time was nearer 1000.²³

While *Prinz Eugen* successfully avoided interception, she too was compelled to sail for Brest, as her raiding mission became unfeasible when engine trouble developed north-west of the Canary Islands. Furthermore, the eight supply ships that had been sent into the Atlantic in advance of *Bismarck* and *Prinz Eugen* sailing, to provide fuel and supplies in prearranged positions, were hunted, and all except *Spichern* were destroyed. *Spichern*'s captain, *Kapitän* Köhlsbach, was the sole commander among the supply ships to exercise wireless discipline, whereas the remainder transmitted prolonged radio communications, easily tracked by British direction finding. Aboard *Prinz Eugen*, *Kapitän zur See* Helmuth Brinkmann had been dismayed by the carelessness of the supply ships' captains, concluding that after refuelling from *Spichern* on 26 May it was too dangerous to remain in the area with faulty machinery.

The loss of *Bismarck* was the death knell for Kriegsmarine major surface operations, Hitler forbidding further Atlantic sorties and the remaining capital ships never again threatening convoys in that area. Luftwaffe attempts to render assistance had been thwarted by a lethal combination of bad weather and hastily gathered forces of which the majority had limited — if any — experience of operations against naval forces.

While the *Bismarck* drama played out, both the *Küstenflieger* and KG 40 continued their unconnected operations within the North Sea and Western Approaches. On the day that *Bismarck* perished, Convoy WS8B, carrying troop reinforcements to the Indian Ocean, and from whose escort HMS *Maori* had been detached to join Force H, was attacked off the Irish coast at 0825hrs by a single Condor, which approached at right angles to the convoy's direction of travel. The Condor flew over the entire convoy at a height of only 200 feet and dropped two bombs near the 11,330-ton troopship MV *Abosso*, the rear ship of the port-wing column. 'Although aircraft was heavily engaged during approach, attack was well pressed home, but since no other bombs were seen to fall it is thought

'Long-range bomber over the Atlantic' written by Carl G.P. Henze, Volume 88 of the weekly German Youth War Library series extolling the virtues of the Wehrmacht and Waffen SS, instigated by Reich Youth Leader Baldur von Schirach and written with the full approval of all service High Commands.

possible the aircraft may have been damaged.'[24] The Condor departed, flying ahead of the convoy, while the *Abosso* dropped temporarily out of station with minor engine-room damage. This was soon repaired, and the ship was back in position by midday.

Only three ships were sunk by I./KG 40 during May, as opposed to seven during April, with a single Condor shot down. The loss was keenly felt by KG 40, however, as the Focke-Wulf was piloted by *Oblt*. Hans Buchholz, an ex-*Reichsmarine* officer who had been credited with sinking ten merchants totalling 61,000 GRT of enemy shipping, and damaging a further eight ships estimated at 48,000GRT during his tenure with KG 40. Buchholz had been awarded the Knight's Cross on 24 March 1941 for 'courageous attacks on heavily defended convoys in the North Atlantic'. His aircraft, F8+DH, was hit by a single defensive 12-pounder round fired by gunners aboard SS *Umgeni* off Northern Ireland. The shell detonated on the Condor's nose, and it ditched in flames only 500 yards from the merchant ship. Two crewmen were wounded and drowned before they could be rescued, but five were taken aboard as prisoners. Wireless operator *Obfw.* Paul Schmidt and Buchholz were the two men killed, the loss of the highly-decorated veteran being a blow to both KG 40 and the German propaganda machine.[25]

Condor operations within the Atlantic had already unexpectedly peaked, and the strength of forces available to *Fliegerführer Atlantik* had been dramatically reduced in support of expanding Mediterranean operations as the Wehrmacht entered the war in the Balkans, attacking Yugoslavia and Greece before the greatest gamble of Hitler's military; the invasion of the Soviet Union.

7

Blue Water, Grey Steel

The Mediterranean and Eastern Fronts

GENERAL DER FLIEGER Hans Geisler's X.*Fliegerkorps* continued its raids against Malta, the unsinkable British aircraft carrier from which Axis supply convoys from Italy to Malta were vulnerable to attack. By 12 January X.*Fliegerkorps*' Sicilian presence comprised eighty Ju 88A-4 bombers of LG 1 and twelve Ju 88D-5 reconnaissance aircraft at Catania, eighty Ju 87R-1 dive-bombers of StG 1 and StG 2 at Trapani, twenty-seven He 111H-6 torpedo bombers of KG 26 at Comiso and thirty-four Bf 110C-4 fighters of ZG 26 at Palermo. The damaged HMS *Illustrious* in Valletta's Grand Harbour remained a priority target, and though the German Ju 87 and Ju 88 dive-bombers made repeated attempts to sink the carrier, they failed. The heavy bombing inflicted further damage on her and surrounding targets, but the toll taken by defending RAF fighters and anti-aircraft guns was severe, over forty aircraft being shot down between 16 and 19 January 1941. HMS *Illustrious* survived and was eventually able to slip out of harbour and make her way through the Suez Canal to the US Navy repair yard at Norfolk, Virginia. The cruiser HMS *Southampton*, however, had been sunk on 11 January; heavily damaged by Ju 87s south-cast of Malta, she was scuttled by a torpedo from HMS *Gloucester*, which had also taken several hits.

Geisler maintained pressure on the island with all the forces available to him, his bombers and dive-bombers soon coming under the enhanced protection provided by newly arrived Bf 109 fighters. Armed reconnaissance missions were flown along the coasts of Cyrenaica, where, on 19 February, 6./KG 26 suffered its first loss within the Mediterranean when one of the original torpedo bomber pilots, *Oblt.* Josef Saumweber, flying He 111H-5 1H+MP, was shot down and captured, two of his crew being killed. The mission marked the first use of Luftwaffe torpedo aircraft within the Mediterranean; an unsuccessful attack by sixteen Ju 88s and a torpedo-armed Heinkel *Kette* on Convoy

AC1. The four merchant ships had departed Alexandria, bound for Tobruk and Benghazi, and Saumweber was shot down by heavy anti-aircraft fire from the escorting corvette HMS *Peony* and taken prisoner.

Air-sea rescue for crews forced to ditch in the Mediterranean was the domain of 6.*Seenotstaffel*, which moved to Syracuse during February, equipped with nine He 59s and Do 24Ns. The rescue aircraft were soon also operating from the Italian seaplane bases at Marsala and Cagliari, and three He 59s were based in Tripoli by April 1941. On 25 February the Ju 88s of 7./KG 30 arrived at Gerbini under the command of *Staffelkapitän Oblt*. Hans-Joachim 'Hajo' Herrmann, who had been awarded the Knight's Cross on 13 October 1940, during his time as *Staffelkapitän* of 7./KG 4. The remainder of III./KG 30 followed within the following week, led by *Maj*. Arved Crüger, who had become *Kommandeur* during November 1940. 'Hajo' Hermann later wrote of Crüger in his autobiography:

> Arved Crüger, my *Kommandeur*, was tall and good-looking, which was why he had been chosen as an aide-de-camp to Emmy Göring [Hermann Göring's second wife] in Kampen, on the Island of Sylt. We used to joke about him handing her beach robe to her, passing her cooling drinks, until finally it became too much for him and he went to the front . . . [in November 1940]. My *Kommodore*, *Major* Bloedorn, became *Kommodore* of KG 30 and was replaced by . . . Crüger, an excellent pilot, a considerate leader and, above all, a kind man, of whom I was very fond. His leadership was relaxed and informal, but because of the example he set it was positive and conducive of loyalty also.¹

By the time of Crüger's arrival, Herrmann's *Staffel* was already in action, subordinated to *Oberst*. Friedrich-Karl Knust and Stab./LG 1. The newly arrived Ju 88s took part in the heaviest raid on Malta thus far, on 26 February, when every available Luftwaffe bomber hammered the besieged island. The Royal Navy had already been forced to withdraw fleet units from Malta to Alexandria during January, and by the end of March the RAF was no longer able to mount offensive anti-shipping operations from Malta and all bomber units were either withdrawn or destroyed on the ground. It appeared that X.*Fliegerkorps* had achieved the first of its objectives and asserted domination over the central Mediterranean. Rommel's gathering forces in Libya could now receive full resupply with little Allied interference.

Major Arved Crüger, commander of III./KG 30 as it relocated to the Mediterranean.

Despite a disastrous start, missions to the Suez Canal had successfully begun, and aerial minelaying caused periodic closures and resultant delays in Allied shipping of reinforcements and supplies to the Middle East from around the Cape of Good Hope. On 8 May *Oblt.* Eberhard Stüwe's Heinkel He 111H-5, 1H+BC, was shot down during a raid on Suez, but he and his crew were successfully rescued by the *Seenotdienst* and returned to action after ditching at sea. The central Mediterranean convoy route was now regarded by the British as too hazardous until such time as regional RAF and Fleet Air Arm units could be bolstered, and the situation was not helped by having to await the arrival of the carrier HMS *Formidable* as replacement for the damaged *Illustrious*. Thus, the Luftwaffe had temporarily tilted the naval balance of power within the Mediterranean. The effect was also felt ashore, despite that Allied defeat of the Italian 10th Army and V *Squadra Aerea* (5th Air Fleet).

Rather than obey the military maxim of exploiting success, and allowing Allied troops to push on to Tripoli and dispose of Mussolini's North African empire before Rommel could become established ashore, Churchill had forcefully argued for a diversion of maximum strength to Greece, to which the Greek government agreed on 24 February.

Royal Navy monitor HMS *Terror*, sunk after damage inflicted by Ju 88s of KG 30 and LG 1 on 23 February 1941, robbing British forces ashore of its bombardment capability that had aided the advances of 'Operation *Compass*'.

The Allies had yet to encounter the forward elements of the *Deutsche Afrika Korps*, and at that moment denuded their air, naval and ground forces in North Africa by beginning a complex transfer to the eastern Mediterranean and Aegean Sea. Churchill believed that Cyrenaica could be held with minimal forces as a buffer between the Axis and Kingdom of Egypt. Events were to prove him wrong.

The harbours at Tobruk and Benghazi, recently captured by the British, came under intense bombardment and mining by X.*Fliegerkorps*, rendering them virtually useless as maritime transport or supply points. The attacking aircraft frequently refuelled at the well-established Italian Castel-Benito airfield south of Tripoli before their return flights to their Sicilian airfields, while others were beginning to use the Italian-occupied island of Rhodes as a replenishing point. This brought British truck convoys, airfields and troops concentrations into range, and they too came under increasing aerial bombardment. Rommel reached Tripoli on 12 February, ahead of his first combat elements, pushing them immediately into action once they were ashore, supported by elements of X.*Fliegerkorps* controlled by the newly established *Fliegerführer Afrika*, the office held by *Generalmajor* Stefan Fröhlich, former *Kommodore* of KG 76.[2] Although his immediate forces comprised Ju 87 dive-bombers and Bf 110 heavy fighters, he was able to call on the support of the Ju 88s and He 111s when required.

The torpedo-carrying aircraft of KG 26 mounted further operations during February, while Benghazi was frequently raided by the Ju 88s of KG 30 and LG 1, the latter damaging the monitor HMS *Terror* so badly on 23 February that she later sank while under tow. The 7,300-ton Royal Navy ship had been crucial to the success of Operation *Compass*, her heavy guns shelling Italian positions during the lightning British advance. *Oberleutnant* Theodor Hagen, flying L1+GS, claimed to have hit it with two bombs, but in fact both had narrowly missed. Even so, the resulting pressure wave through incompressible water was still enough to fracture the hull, and *Terror* foundered the following morning. Following the loss of *Terror*, all Allied ships were withdrawn from Benghazi owing to its inadequate anti-aircraft and fighter protection, reducing front-line supply of British forces solely to overland convoys that straggled to the distant Egyptian border. That same evening the destroyer HMS *Dainty* was bombed and sunk after leaving Tobruk Harbour during an attack by thirteen Ju 88s of III./LG 1, a single 450kg bomb passing though the captain's cabin and detonating in the fuel tank. The ensuing blaze spread to stored ammunition, which exploded, killing sixteen crewmen and wounding eighteen before the ship went down. The Luftwaffe had swiftly neutralised the naval support and maritime resupply that had been crucial to the success of the British advance.

In addition, KG 26 flew armed reconnaissance missions to the western Mediterranean, where it is credited with sinking the 3,089-ton British steamer SS *Louis Charles Schiaffino*, a commandeered freighter formerly of French Algerian ownership. It was hit and sunk by torpedo off the Algerian town of Collo on 25 February by aircraft of II./KG 26, finally signalling the first successful Luftwaffe torpedo operation within the Mediterranean. However, torpedo operations were limited by available stocks, the entire German inventory of aerial torpedoes in March 1941 numbering only thirty-seven. Even so, it was to the eastern Mediterranean that the weight of X.*Fliegerkorps* was now directed, though ordered to strictly observe the limits of neutral Greek territorial airspace.

From 4 March the bulk of Royal Navy Mediterranean forces were engaged in covering Operation *Lustre*, the movement of Allied troops from Egypt to the port of Piraeus, Greece, on the outskirts of Athens. Mussolini had begun an ill-advised attempted invasion of the Greek mainland through Albania on 28 October 1940. It was swiftly repulsed,

Italian troops being pushed back for months of stagnant winter warfare marked by unsuccessful offensives and counteroffensives. In the meantime, RAF squadrons were despatched to Greece in honour of a declaration of assistance that had been signed in 1939, should Greece be militarily threatened. British infantry also arrived on Crete, enabling local forces to be despatched to the Albanian Front. Churchill had long harboured an obsession with warfare in the Balkans that now spanned both world wars, and, rather than reinforce O'Connor in the desert and bring about an end to Axis power in North Africa, he argued forcefully for the transfer of the bulk of British Mediterranean strength to Greece, this being granted on 22 February 1941.

Hitler was aware of the threat to the Romanian Ploiești oilfields that the RAF now posed, and had already ordered the planning of an invasion of the northern coast of the Aegean Sea, expanded to all of Greece if deemed necessary; Operation *Marita*. A regular supply from Ploiești was crucial to Germany's oil reserves, and neighbouring Bulgaria had been pressured into joining the Tripartite Pact on 1 March, allowing the passage of Wehrmacht troops to the Greek border in preparation for *Marita*, scheduled to begin on 6 April. British regional policy aimed at persuading Turkey and Yugoslavia to join the Allied cause had failed. The Turks remained politically aloof, and Yugoslavia was already under pressure to join the Tripartite Pact, which it finally signed on 25 March. The stage was set for *Marita* until a group of Serbian nationalist officers overthrew the Yugoslavian government in Belgrade with a *coup d'etat* on 27 March, subsequently refusing to honour the signed Pact. At first shocked, and then increasingly angry, the Führer hurriedly issued Directive 2 for the Greek invasion plans to be expanded to include a simultaneous attack on Yugoslavia codenamed Operation *Strafe* (Punishment). Within the Directive, the role of the Luftwaffe was spelt out:

> The Luftwaffe will support with two *Gruppen* the operations of 12th Army and of the assault group now being formed in the Graz area, and will time the weight of its attack to coincide with the operations of the Army. The Hungarian ground organisation can be used for assembly and in action.
>
> The possibility of bringing X.*Fliegerkorps* into action from Italian bases will be considered. The protection of convoys to Africa must, however, continue to be ensured.

The invasion was still set for 6 April 1941, and major units of X.*Fliegerkorps* began to shift their attention to the eastern Mediterranean basin in attempts to find and destroy Royal Navy and Royal Australian Navy units and convoy traffic of Operation *Lustre*, which by 2 April had moved the British 1st Armoured Brigade, the 2nd New Zealand Division and the 6th Australian Division from Egypt to Greece. It was planned to bring the 7th Australian Division and Polish Independent Carpathian Rifle Brigade as well.

The resultant lull in Luftwaffe pressure on Malta, as Geisler handed responsibility for attacks against the island to the Italian air force, allowed the Royal Navy to create the 14th Destroyer Flotilla, which was based on the besieged island at the beginning of April to restore an offensive naval presence. Subsequent early successes against Axis convoys during that month justified the decision, despite the ships' vulnerability to Axis air bombardment which, though diminished, continued. The flotilla's greatest single achievement was the sinking of an entire German supply convoy of five steamers and escorting Italian destroyers off Kerkennah during the early morning of 16 April, for the loss of HMS *Mohawk* to torpedoes from the Italian destroyer *Tarigo*.

The Luftwaffe and *Regia Aeronautica* war now focused on the east, and on 16 March *Hptm.* Kowalewski, *Gruppenkommandeur* of II./KG 26, climbed aboard the torpedo-carrying He 111 flown by *Lt.* Karl-Heinz Bock of 6./KG 26. In company with a second Heinkel flown by *Lt.* Rudolf Schmidt, Kowalewski led an armed reconnaissance of the sea area west of Crete, sighting and attacking a Royal Navy group that included the battleships HMS *Barham* and *Valiant*. Amidst fierce anti-aircraft fire both aircraft dropped their torpedoes perfectly before they were forced to break away out of the range of the enemy guns, claiming two possible but unconfirmed hits on both battleships.

Reported to the Italian Navy, their acceptance of the likelihood that both heavy units had been disabled, and knowledge that HMS *Illustrious* had been removed from the Mediterranean (without knowing that HMS *Formidable* had replaced it) contributed to the Italian decision to sail the bulk of the formidable Italian fleet to attack *Lustre* convoy traffic. The 'AN' convoys headed northbound and 'AS' southbound, travelling in ballast. The Italian Operation *Gaudo* was put together following German pressure to mount offensive action against the British shipping between Greece and Egypt, the *Supermarina* agreeing on the proviso of air support from both the Luftwaffe and *Regia Aeronautica*. Using one the best-kept secrets of the war, the Allies were forewarned by Enigma decryption, and temporarily suspended *Lustre* convoying while sailing the British Mediterranean Fleet to engage the enemy. The subsequent battle of Cape Matapan, between 27 and 29 March, was disastrous for the *Supermarina*. It ended with the Italian battleship *Vittorio Veneto* damaged, three heavy cruisers and two destroyers sunk, and another destroyer heavily damaged before withdrawing. Over 2,300 Italian sailors were killed and 1,105 rescued as prisoners of war, while the Allied forces suffered four light cruisers damaged, two torpedo bombers shot down and three men killed.

A single reconnaissance Ju 88 was sighted as the British recovered survivors, and Admiral Cunningham ordered rescue work curtailed and the fleet withdrawn out of bomber range. A plain-language signal was sent to the Chief of the Italian Naval Staff, advising him of the remaining survivors, estimated to number at least 350, and the hospital ship *Gradisca* later arrived from Taranto and recovered 160 more shipwrecked men.

Sixteen Ju 88s of III./KG 30 and twelve of II./LG 1 attacked the retreating British, the first sign of the promised Luftwaffe air support, but to little effect. HMS *Formidable* was narrowly missed by bombs dropped in the face of concentrated anti-aircraft fire. At least one LG 1 Ju 88 was brought down by Fulmars of 803 Sqn, *Uffz.* Georg Kunz's L1+EP of 6./LG 1 crashing into the sea, but not before gunner *Gefr.* Josef Leitermann hit the Fulmar piloted by Sub-Lt A.C. Wallace with return fire, causing enough damage to force it too to ditch into the sea after a failed attempt to land on the carrier's deck. Both Wallace and Leading Airman F.P. Dooley were rescued by the destroyer HMS *Hasty*. Kunz, Leitermann, observer *Gefr.* Fritz Schmidt and wireless operator *Uffz.* Walter Fischer were likewise rescued, and taken prisoner. *Leutnant* Alfred Pletch of KG 30 was also brought down, his Ju 88 caught by a Fulmar fighter as it pulled out of its dive and ditching several kilometres from the scene. His location was fixed by 'Hajo' Herrmann as the *Staffelkapitän* flew his aircraft to Benghazi for refuelling, and the crew were later rescued from their dinghy by a *Seenotstaffel* aircraft.

Major Arved Crüger, leading III./KG 30, claimed three hits on HMS *Formidable*, which was reported during the following day's *Wehrmachtberichte*:

> Combat aircraft under the command of *Major* Crüger successfully attacked a strong English naval force in the afternoon hours of 29 March

in the sea area west of Crete. Despite fierce flak and fighter interception they obtained three direct hits on an aircraft carrier. During the air attack a British Hurricane fighter was shot down. All of our aircraft returned to their base.

In recognition of this perceived victory, Crüger was awarded honorary Italian pilot's wings during April for his service in support of Italian naval forces.

While Matapan had been an unmitigated disaster for the Italian navy, and the desultory retaliation by X.*Fliegerkorps* achieved nothing, the cumulative effect of constant Luftwaffe missions in the eastern Mediterranean was being felt within the British Admiralty, yielding several claims of merchant ships sunk.

> Scale of air attack in Mediterranean is increasing very rapidly. Yesterday AS22 was twice attacked once by as many as thirty Ju 88s. Would it be possible to spare the two heavily armed escort ships *Flamingo* and *Auckland* from Red Sea Force?³

Wartime postcard depicting a successful Do 18 reconnaissance mission.

Newsreel footage shows score markings on a Condor's tail plane being updated.

On 2 April *Hptm.* Joachim Helbig's eight Ju 88s of 4./LG 1 attacked convoy AS23 off Gavdo Island, damaging the Greek SS *Teti* and sinking the 5,324-ton British SS *Homefield* and 4,914-ton Greek *Coulouras Xenos*. Salvage parties boarded the two latter ships, but they were both hopelessly wrecked and subsequently scuttled by explosives and gunfire from HMS *Nubian* from the escort of fast convoy ANF24. This convoy was also attacked twice, the steamer SS *Devis* being damaged during the first dive-bombing attack by *Hptm.* Kollewe's II./LG 1, and on 3 April the 10,917-ton liner MV *Northern Prince*, carrying ammunition and several thousand tons of powder from Britain for Greek munitions factories, was sunk in the Antikithera Channel north-west of Crete. The ship had taken two direct hits amidships, and began to belch thick smoke as the crew scrambled to abandon ship, fearing the sympathetic detonation of the lethal cargo. Ten minutes later the requisitioned Atlantic liner exploded.

Despite this success, the losses to 'AN' convoys were relatively minor, and the planned transfer of men and material from Egypt was successfully completed, setting the stage for the impending battle for Yugoslavia and Greece. Heinkel bombers of II./KG 26 were moved to Foggia Airfield during April, while the Ju 88s of II. and III./LG 1 relocated temporarily from Catania to Grottaglie, fourteen kilometres east-north-east of Taranto, committed to the attack on Yugoslavia and the bombing of land targets. This left Crüger's III./KG 30 as the sole *Gruppe* on Sicily, and when Operation *Marita* opened on the night of 6/7 April, Crüger's initial target was the Greek harbour at Piraeus, the country's largest port, which had been used for the transfer of troops during Operation *Lustre* and was still filled with shipping.

Crüger's Ju 88s carried a mixed load of mines and bombs. 'Hajo' Herrmann later wrote that the assigned weapon load was two mines to each aircraft, but unofficially he took it upon himself to add two 250kg bombs to each of his 7.*Staffel* bomber's load. Crüger apparently found the unorthodox weapons load while making a last-minute inspection, and instructed them to be removed, wryly commenting to his subordinate: 'And try and look a bit happier next time!' Herrmann gave the order, but, after Crüger had departed, managed to ensure that it was not obeyed. Following take-off, bad weather forced some 8.*Staffel* aircraft to jettison their mines, as they suffered severe icing while attempting to fly above a Greek mountain range, the clogging ice making it imperative that the

Hans-Joachim 'Hajo' Herrmann of KG 30.

aircraft's weight was immediately reduced. Despite this, most aircraft of KG 30 successfully laid mines across the narrow harbour entrance, Herrmann electing to begin his *Staffel*'s minelaying run from landward, throttling back to a little above stalling speed and deploying dive brakes before dropping, violently nose-up, to only 300m altitude before the mines were released, whereupon full throttle brought the aircraft back under control and they headed away from the enclosed harbour mouth. Once the mines had been dropped, Herrmann's *Staffel* gained height and returned to drop their bombs, beginning the destruction of the port. Their effectiveness was far in excess of what the Luftwaffe had expected. Royal Australian Navy Able Seaman Patrick Bridges was aboard corvette HMS *Hyacinth* in Piraeus Harbour as the attack developed, and wrote of it in his diary:

> Sunday April 6, 1941: Mass air attack here tonight. Hit one ship full of TNT, which burnt for four hours then blew up. A sheet of the ship's side tore through our bridge and killed Lt [Ronald] Humphrey. Ship broke away from the jetty and we had to abandon it. We pulled it back and tied

Piraeus harbour after attack by KG 30. At right of this photograph is the burning SS *Clan Fraser*. The subsequent explosion of its stored TNT cargo sank many other vessels and rendered the harbour unusable by Allied forces for ten days. (Australian War Memorial)

up and then ran the gauntlet through blazing oil and burning ships and magnetic mines with only half a ship's company.

> Monday April 7, 1941: Piraeus is still burning furiously. Sky is black with oil smoke and ammunition and dynamite is still exploding. Both our skiffs are holed. Bridge and boat deck are either wrecked or burnt. Great lumps of steel and shrapnel all over the deck. Drifting wreckage all over harbour. One plane came over to see damage . . . Waiting for raiders now.[4]

The 7,529-ton SS *Clan Fraser* was carrying 350 tons of TNT, and a further 100 tons was aboard a lighter moored next to the cargo ship, when three of Herrmann's unauthorised bombs hit *Clan Fraser*; one forward, one amidships and one aft. Six crew members were killed and nine wounded as the survivors evacuated the ship. The battered freighter could not be towed from port owing to the danger posed by the new mines strewn across the harbour entrance. The ship burned for five hours, its hull glowing red from bulwarks to waterline, before finally exploding, devastating the entire port and shaking buildings and shattering windows fifteen miles inland in Athens. The sound of the blast was heard as far as 150 miles from Piraeus. Following the initial explosion, fires spread rapidly to other merchant ships, including a second steamer loaded with ammunition, the SS *City of Roubaix*, which also detonated in a massive fireball, turning the harbour into an uncontrollable inferno. In total, twelve large merchant ships and at least fifty smaller craft were destroyed. Harbour installations and seven of the twelve berths were so severely damaged that Piraeus was completely unusable for ten days, robbing the Allies of the regional port most suitable for large vessels. More than twenty merchant ships in bays adjacent to Piraeus were stranded, as they had been moored awaiting coal and water, and were rendered vulnerable to the air attacks that would soon follow. The Luftwaffe suffered no casualties, though Herrmann's Junkers was hit by anti-aircraft fire that damaged the port engine and forced an emergency diversion to Rhodes, rather than the longer return to Sicily.

While the majority of X.*Fliegerkorps* assets were subsequently engaged in supporting the land offensive in Greece and Yugoslavia, Piraeus and its environs, as well as the port city of Volos, were attacked again by bombers of LG 1, III./KG 30 and II./KG 26, sinking further ships. They included the 2,561-ton Greek hospital ship *Attiki*, which went down in the Doro Channel (the first of six hospital ships sunk by the

Luftwaffe during April), and the 8,271-ton MT *Marie Maersk* at Piraeus, the tanker later being raised and repaired by the *Regia Marina*.

Disaster soon overwhelmed the Allied Expeditionary Force that had been landed in Greece. Outnumbered and outmanoeuvred by the Wehrmacht, the Allies were pushed steadily back, while Yugoslavia had crumbled almost immediately, surrendering on 17 April. The previous day, the British had bowed to the inevitable and decided to abandon Greece, the seaborne evacuation being codenamed Operation *Demon*. At that moment in North Africa, Rommel had been on the offensive since 24 March, eventually pushing the inexperienced forces that had been left to hold Cyrenaica back to the Egyptian border, from where O'Connor had launched his brilliant attack a year earlier. The troops that were sorely missed in Libya after being moved to Greece now found themselves in another Dunkirk-style evacuation, made more difficult by Hermann's devastating success at Piraeus. Beaches and smaller ports were used as embarkation points, small naval vessels and local craft being used to shuttle waiting troops to merchant and naval ships lying stationary offshore. It proved to be a boon to the Luftwaffe, who subsequently attacked without respite, the maritime strike aircraft reinforced by Ju 88 bombers of KG 51 and Stukas of St.G. 1 and 2.[5]

Almost unbelievably, the British evacuation was remarkably successful; 50,732 men, including some Greek and Yugoslavian troops, were successfully lifted from the Greek mainland between 24 April and 1 May. However, four major troopships were sunk by German air attack: the 3,791-ton MV *Ulster Prince*, 16,322-ton SS *Pennland*, 11,406-ton SS *Slamat* and 8,085-ton SS *Costa Rica*, as well as the destroyers HMS *Diamond* and *Wryneck* and myriad smaller ships. Churchill's misdirected folly had cost British and Commonwealth forces 12,000 men killed, wounded or missing, and 209 aircraft, 8,000 trucks and all of the Expeditionary Force's armour and artillery were destroyed, along with mountains of stores and supplies. It had also cost the recently conquered portion of Libya, putting Allied forces once again with their backs to the Egyptian border. Nor was that the end of the calamity overtaking Allied Mediterranean forces.

With mainland Greece and the Aegean Islands now in Axis hands, Crete remained the single Allied possession before the shores of North Africa. The island was defended by only six RAF Hurricanes and seventeen other largely obsolete aircraft, including Gladiators and Fulmars, giving the Luftwaffe virtually complete dominance and enabling the launch of the largest airborne assault yet undertaken; Operation *Merkur* on 20 May. Commanding the Luftwaffe presence over Crete was *General der Flieger* Wolfram Freiherr von Richthofen's VIII.*Fliegerkorps*. Von Richthofen, cousin of the First World War flying aces Manfred and Lothar, had served as a pilot during that conflict, and after joining the new Luftwaffe in 1933 had been a direct subordinate to Ernst Udet in the *Technisches Amt* (Technical Development Section), with whom he did not get along. Arrogant to the point of bluntness, the conceited von Richthofen became one of the Luftwaffe's most gifted officers, serving in the Condor Legion, where his once avowed aversion to dive-bombers was thoroughly altered. He became one of the foremost exponents of close air co-operation with ground forces, though he frequently showed little interest in, if not disdain for, Luftwaffe maritime operations. Following his return to Germany during 1938 he had been *Geschwaderkommodore* of KG 257, later redesignated KG 26, at its home base of Lüneburg.

Oberst Knust's LG 1 was transferred to von Richthofen's VIII. *Fliegerkorps*, I and II *Gruppen* being deployed to the recently captured

The reality of maritime patrols for bomber crews of all nations; the observer aboard and He 111 scouring the horizon for elusive enemy shipping.

Eleusis Airfield near Athens, while III./LG 1 remained at Benina near Benghazi, from where it supported Rommel's troops during their advance. Knust also took control of the nine serviceable torpedo bombers of *Hptm.* Kowalewski's II./KG 26, though by the launch of *Merkur* he had been replaced as *Kommandeur* by *Obstlt.* Horst Beyling.

Von Richthofen's available strength return at the beginning of May listed:

StG 2: three *Gruppen* totalling seventy-one Ju 87s;
LG 1: two *Gruppen* totalling forty-two Ju 88s;
II./KG 26: of nine He 111s;
KG 2: three *Gruppen* totalling seventy-seven Do 17s;
JG 77: three *Gruppen* totalling sixty-one Bf 109s;
ZG 26: three *Gruppen* totalling fifty-six Bf 110s;
7./LG 2: of four Bf 110s;
4.(F)/Aufkl.Gr. 121: of five Ju 88s.

By 23 May these were reinforced by sixty-five more Ju 87 dive-bombers of StG 1 and StG 77. During the days preceding the opening of *Merkur* the heavy cruiser HMS *York*, which had been disabled by Italian explosive motorboats in Crete's Suda Bay, came under intense bombardment by VIII.*Fliegerkorps*. She was hit several times by dive-bombing Ju 88s of LG 1, and was later wrecked by demolition charges before the British evacuation.

The torpedo bombers of II./KG 26 launched a number of attempted attacks during the battle for Crete, using the last six operational torpedoes available to them, though none were successful. The sole aircraft torpedo sinkings were achieved by the SM.79s of the Italian 281st *Squadriglia*. Instead, the Heinkels were more successful with conventional bomb loads, adding their weight to attacks against the Royal Navy north-east of Crete. The Ju 88s of KG 30 were also heavily involved in the attack on shipping around the embattled island, joining LG 1 and the Dornier Do 17s of KG 2 on 22 May in relentless bombing of the Royal Navy Force C of four cruisers and three destroyers that was attacking a seaborne German reinforcement convoy south of the island of Milo, badly damaging HMS *Naiad* and *Carlisle*. To reinforce *Fallschirmjäger* forces on Crete, the Germans despatched convoys of small vessels carrying *Gebirgsjäger*, immensely vulnerable to enemy naval forces. As the sole escorting Italian torpedo boat *Sagittario* bravely mounted a torpedo attack while laying smoke, the Luftwaffe pounded the attacking Royal Navy ships, allowing most of the German convoy to retreat successfully. Force C itself was already running short of anti-aircraft ammunition, and under unrelenting attack was forced to break away to rendezvous with the formidable Force A, commanded by Rear Admiral H.B. Rawlings and centred on the battleships HMS *Warspite* and *Valiant*, as well as two cruisers and the attached Force D of three cruisers and four destroyers. The ships made contact in the Kythera Channel, where the Luftwaffe found them once more, HMS *Warspite* being hit by a bomb dropped by a Bf 109 of LG 2 while the destroyer HMS *Greyhound* was hit twice and sunk. HMS *Kandahar* and *Kingston* were despatched to its assistance, the cruisers *Gloucester* and *Fiji* providing anti-aircraft support despite running low on ammunition. The commander of *Fiji* later told Admiral Cunningham that the 'air over *Gloucester* was black with 'planes', and *Gloucester* was hit by several bombs at 1550hrs after exhausting her anti-aircraft ammunition and impotently firing star shells, the only ammunition remaining.[6] Badly damaged, she came to a stop with her superstructure shattered and flames spreading throughout the ship. Bombs continued to rain down, preventing HMS *Fiji* from stopping to pick up survivors, though she dropped life rafts over the side before she was forced to depart. Of the 807 men aboard at the time of HMS *Gloucester*'s sinking, only 85 survived to be captured by the Germans. The body of Capt H.A. Rowley was washed ashore at Mersa Matruh, Egypt, four weeks later. There was no attempt by the Royal Navy to return after nightfall to search for survivors.[7]

Meanwhile, two bombs hit the battleship HMS *Valiant* and another scored a near miss on *Fiji* as she returned from the scene of *Gloucester*'s demise, close enough to damage the bottom plates of the hull and bring it to a halt with a heavy list to port. *Leutnant* Gerhard 'Fähnlein' Brenner of 2./LG 1 was among the relay of Ju 88s shuttling between Athens and Kythira Straits to bomb the Royal Navy ships. His first three separate attacks yielded near misses, but his final sortie of the day centred on HMS *Fiji*, now fringed by a spreading oil slick around her stern. Brenner dived at a steep angle before releasing his bombs, and three impacted on the cruiser, which quickly rolled over and sank, killing 241 men, 523 survivors later being rescued under cover of darkness. It was a victorious day for the Luftwaffe, and *Hptm*. Kuno Hoffmann, *Gruppenkommandeur* of I./LG 1, was awarded the Knight's Cross on 14 June, *Oberst* Herbert Rieckhoff, *Geschwaderkommodore* of KG 2, and Gerhard Brenner receiving the same decoration on 5 July 1941.[8] On 22 May VIII.*Fliegerkorps* had flown thirty-eight sorties against Royal Navy groups, launched six torpedoes and claimed ninety-three hits by bombs from Ju 88 bombers, forty-one from Do 17s, one hundred and eleven from Ju 87s, eleven from Bf 110s and five from Bf 109s. That day, von Richthofen lost seven Ju 87s, two Ju 88s, three Bf 110s and one Bf 109, with four officers and twelve NCOs and men missing, four dead, six badly wounded and eight with light injuries.

Although the Royal Navy had prevented the planned seaborne reinforcement of the *Fallschirmjäger* on Crete by successfully intercepting two troop convoys under inadequate Italian escort, the battle for the island was lost within days, and another evacuation was ordered a week after the first Germans had landed. By this stage the Royal Navy had already taken a fearsome battering at Luftwaffe hands, and it showed no signs abating as the evacuation began on the night of 28/29 May. The island surrendered on the first day of June.

The toll on the Royal Navy during the Cretan battle had been severe, though had the Luftwaffe been willing to bomb by night it would have been greater. Admiral Cunningham had deployed four battleships, one aircraft carrier, eleven cruisers, a minelayer and thirty-two destroyers in the defence of Crete and its consequent evacuation. Of these, air attacks by German and Italian aircraft had severely damaged the two battleships HMS *Warspite* and *Barham* and the carrier HMS *Formidable*, which was hit by bombs and required twenty weeks of repair work. Three cruisers were sunk, HMS *Gloucester*, *Calcutta* and *Fiji*, and five others badly damaged, and six destroyers were lost, with a further seven requiring lengthy dockyard repairs. Approximately 16,500 men had been rescued from Crete, but the British and Commonwealth forces suffered 3,579 men killed and missing, 1,918 wounded and 12,254 captured in another calamitous defeat. Somewhat ironically, as the Cretan disaster was about to unfold, Churchill abruptly issued orders that Rommel must be stopped at all costs and that 'not only must Egypt be defended, but the Germans have to be beaten and thrown out of Cyrenaica', presumably by the very troops he had demanded be moved to Greece. The exhausted Admiral Cunningham later ruefully wrote to the First Sea Lord:

> There is no hiding the fact that in our battle with the German Air Force we have been badly battered. I always thought we might get a surprise if they really turned their attention to the fleet. No A/A fire will deal with the simultaneous attacks of ten to twenty aircraft.[9]

The Wehrmacht was triumphant within the Mediterranean. However, the clarity of hindsight tells us that a serious tactical blunder was made almost immediately, when the Reich Air Ministry ordered that the aircraft of Geisler's X.*Fliegerkorps* which had remained in Sicily be transferred to Greece to undertake operations against British forces within the Eastern Mediterranean. The aircraft of I. and II./LG 1 and II./KG 26 were soon joined by III./KG 30 and the two strategic reconnaissance *Staffeln*, 1.(F)/ Aufkl.Gr. 121 and 2.(F)/ Aufkl.Gr. 123. Flying from the Athens airfield, they were tasked with hunting Allied naval and merchant ships, attacking ports and coastal installations, mining harbours and waterways, and bombing military installations and RAF airfields within the Nile Delta region. Having exhausted their supply of torpedoes, the KG 26 Heinkels began using some of the marginally larger Italian F200 Whitehead-Fiume torpedoes, bought from the Italian forces and designated 'LT-F5W' by the Luftwaffe. These began arriving at Eleusis towards the end of May. The Italian torpedo was 45cm in diameter, weighed 905kg, carried a warhead of 200kg of explosives, had a range of 3,000m, a speed of 14 knots and could be launched by an aircraft travelling at 300km/h, the highest speed yet possible for German aerial torpedoes.

Geisler had successfully argued that the best method of supplying Axis forces in North Africa was via Greece and Crete. With the resultant diversion of Luftwaffe power, pressure on Malta was to be maintained by the *Regia Aeronautica*. Yet the latter had already failed to prevent a resurgence of the island as a viable military base from which to threaten Rommel's current lines of supply. Before long, convoys between Sicily and Tripoli were once again under regular British attack. Under orders from Berlin, Dönitz had unwillingly allocated U-boats to the Mediterrancan, beginning in September 1941, and although they claimed an initial toll of major Royal Navy ships, including the carrier HMS *Ark Royal* and the battleship HMS *Barham*, their success was short-lived. None of the boats would ever return to the Atlantic battle, which remained Dönitz's centre of operational gravity, a loss of experienced men and valuable U-boats at a time when they could still have made a difference in the Atlantic convoy war.

Far from these developments within the Mediterranean theatre, *Küstenflieger* continued to mount armed reconnaissance missions into the North Sea, predominantly carrying bombs, with occasional sorties by torpedo-armed He 115s when newly produced stocks of the weapon allowed. During the early part of 1941 2./Kü.Fl.Gr. 406 had converted from the antiquated Do 18 to the He 115, and 3./Kü.Fl.Gr. 406 was scheduled to convert to the BV 138 flying boat, though this would not be fully completed until the beginning of the following year. Both the first and second *Staffeln* returned to Norway, 1./Kü.Fl.Gr. 406 being based at Tromsø and 2./Kü.Fl.Gr. 406 at the established seaplane base at Trondheim, occasionally using Stavanger as an alternative location. These *Staffeln* were administratively controlled by *Küstenfliegergruppe* 706 at Stavanger. Constant patrolling of the Skagerrak and its approaches had been undertaken alongside offensive sweeps, and *MGK Nord* issued a communique to *OKM* on 24 April 1941 which included appreciation of the value of *Küstenflieger* forces:

> In general, it should be noted that, despite low force numbers, all demands for security and reconnaissance, and especially for mining missions, have been fulfilled in an exemplary fashion by *Kustenfliegergruppe* 706. The achievements of this unit are to be particularly appreciated in the reporting period as well as for the past winter months.[10]

Oberstleutnant Walter Weygoldt's *Küstenfligergruppe* 506 mounted occasional torpedo operations, though stocks of the weapon averaged five at any one time for the entire *Gruppe* as, although the embargo on their use elsewhere had been lifted, the majority continued to be shipped to the Mediterranean. With such a scarcity, Weygoldt pushed for the conversion of 3./Kü.Fl.Gr. 506 to Ju 88s as soon as possible, his He 115s showing severe handicaps in combat with enemy aircraft and suffering heavy losses. Schily had ordered that patrols near the British coast should be mounted only under heavy cloud cover or by night, though an increasing rhythm of effective nightfighter activity still posed a serious threat. During one such nocturnal mission, at 2312hrs on 2 June 1941, *Lt.z.S.* Friedrich Michael of 3./Kü.Fl.Gr. 506 scored a resounding success when he hit an aircraft carrier with two torpedoes in the approaches to the Humber, columns of water being thrown thirty metres into the air by the detonations. The location of the carrier, identified as either HMS *Indomitable* or *Hermes*, had been reported earlier that day, after she had been sighted by a Ju 88 of 1./Kü.Fl.Gr. 506 during an attack on shipping off the Yorkshire coast that sank the French SS *Beaumanoir* and its cargo of coal, and damaged the SS *Thorpebay*. At that moment *Küstenfliegergruppe* 506 had no torpedoes in stock, so *Obstlt.* Schily improvised a solution by despatching three crews to the torpedo testing ground at Grossenbrode, where they collected three He 111s carrying practice torpedoes. Once the weapons had been rearmed with live warheads, the aircraft were used to attack the sighted carrier before being returned to Grossenbrode. Buoyed by this success, Schily immediately communicated his congratulations to *Küstenfliegergruppe* 506.

> For the exemplary operational readiness shown today, due to the ongoing missions on the 2nd and 3rd of June, when 10,000 tons [of shipping] were destroyed with the weakest available forces, I commend *Gruppe* 506 and all military personnel and civilian employees involved.
>
> Special thanks go to *Staffel* 3./Kü.Fl.Gr. 506, which achieved the success of two torpedo hits under difficult conditions using a new aircraft model, and the likely damaging of an aircraft carrier. May the accomplishments of today be a spur to even greater success.
>
> The Commander-in-Chief of *Marinegruppe Nord*, *Generaladmiral* Carls, expressed his gratitude to both myself and my subordinate squadrons, and his special recognition for the achievements made yesterday.

The action was reported in the *Wehrmachtbericht* as two torpedo hits on a 'large British warship'. But Michael had actually torpedoed the 7,924-ton SS *Marmari*, a large freighter commandeered by the Admiralty in 1939 with two others and converted into decoy ships; in this case a plywood-panelled look-alike of HMS *Hermes*. Known for security reasons as '*Tender C*', *Marmari* had been part of Force W, designed to fool German aerial reconnaissance into chasing phantom capital ships. The decoy carrier was disabled while evading Heinkel torpedoes, the hull striking the wreck of the steam tanker SS *Ahamo*, sunk by mine during the previous April. The Kriegsmarine later despatched *Schnellboote S19*, *S20*, *S22* and *S24* to destroy what they believed to be an incapacitated carrier, and, despite defending fire from an accompanying minesweeper and the sloop HMS *Kittiwake*, *S22* and *S24* hit the ship with three torpedoes and sank what they reported as '6,000 tons, presumably a *Sperrbrecher*'.

By April, the build-up of Luftwaffe forces in the Mediterranean Theatre and the east for Balkan missions and in preparation for Operation *Barbarossa* necessitated refreshment of Luftwaffe Atlantic forces. To that end, 1./Kü.Fl.Gr. 106 relinquished its He 115s and departed from Brittany for Barth and conversion to Ju 88 bombers. It was the final component of *Küstenfligergruppe* 106 to undergo the change, and with all

The crew of an He 115 are brought ashore to their Belgian base. (Bundesarchiv)

three *Staffeln* now operating land-based aircraft the *Gruppe* commanded by *Hptm.* Wolfgang Schlenkhoff had its designation officially changed to *Kampfgruppe* 106 (KGr. 106), though the unit did not immediately pass completely outside Ritter's responsibility as *Gen.d.Lw.b.Ob.d.M.* until September. Once all sections had completed the change to Ju 88s, operations by KGr. 106 revolved around the night bombing of Britain. During one such raid on 28 June, Ju 88A-6 M2+CK failed to return, *Gruppenkommandeur Hptm.* Schlenkhoff and his three crewmen being posted as missing in action. *Major* Friedrich Schallmeyer took command of KGr. 106 until April 1942, when he was replaced by *Maj.* Ghert Roth, former commander of *Küstenfliegergruppe* 406 and intelligence officer at *Stab*/IX.*Fliegerkorps*. During September that year KGr.106 was finally redesignated II.*Gruppe* of the newly formed KG 6. Roth also killed in action when his Ju 88 was shot down on 8 September, during a night mission to Bougie, Algeria. The aircraft of *Kampfgeschwader* 6 were distributed both east and west, bombing British mainland targets and supporting Army Group North in bombing raids on targets within the northern Soviet Union. Only I./KG 6 transferred to the Mediterranean to continue anti-shipping strikes.

The Luftwaffe reorganised its western commands during March and April 1941 to assist in the blockading of Great Britain. Theoretically, their purpose was to provide anti-shipping units that could cover the entire coastline stretching from northern Norway to the Franco-Spanish border. This not only observed the strategic goals employed by the Wehrmacht against Britain, but also provided an imperative for the Luftwaffe to absorb further maritime units previously tactically controlled by the Kriegsmarine. On the northern fringe of this realignment of Luftwaffe commands, on 1 April, the post of *Fliegerführer Ostsee* was occupied by *Oberst* Wolfgang von Wild, *Kommandeur* of KGr. 806. Hermann Bruch subsequently moved from the position of *Führer der Seeluftstreitkräfte* on 21 April, to be appointed to the office of *Kommandierender Gen.d.Lw. Nord Norwegen* (acting as *Fliegerführer Nord Norwegen*) in Bardufoss, and von Wild stepped simultaneously into his vacated *F.d.Luft.* role, *Maj.* Hans Emig taking command of KGr. 806. Initially, von Wild's *Ostsee* command comprised only KGr. 806 and the Luftwaffe's own new maritime reconnaissance element, *Aufklärungsgruppe* 125 *(See)*, which had been established in Kiel-Holtenau. Two such units were formed during April 1941, with many men transferred to its ranks from existing *Küstenflieger* units:

Aufklärungsfliegergruppe 125 *(See)* (Kiel-Holtenau), *Obstlt.* Gerhard Kolbe.
   Stab/Aufkl.Gr. 125 (Kiel-Holtenau), He 60
   1./Aufkl.Gr. 125 (Kiel-Holtenau), He 60
   2./Aufkl.Gr. 125 (Thisted), He 114
   3./Aufkl.Gr. 125 (Holtenau), Ar 95A

Aufklärungsfliegergruppe 126 *(See)* (Travemünde), *Maj.* Hans-Bruno von Laue.
   Stab/Aufkl.Gr. 126 (Travemünde), He 60
   1./Aufkl.Gr. 126 (Travemünde), He 60
   2./Aufkl.Gr. 126 (Travemünde), He 60
   3./Aufkl.Gr. 126 (Travemünde), He 60

These reconnaissance units initially used the outdated aeroplanes that *Küstenfliegergruppen* were discarding, and still included a large proportion of Kriegsmarine personnel in their observer role. One such man was *Oblt.z.S.* Rolf Thomsen, posted to Aufkl.Gr. 125 at its inception. Thomsen's career is quite indicative of the path many Kriegsmarine officers followed into and out of the naval air service. Having joined the Kriegsmarine in 1936, he as posted as Watch Officer to the minesweeper *M89* in April 1938 before transferring to flying training at the *Fliegerwaffenschule*, Bug, Rügen. From the beginning of the war until September 1940 he served as an observer in 1./Kü.Fl.Gr. 106 before being made *1. Admiralstabsoffizier op. (Seeluftstreitkräfte)* on the *F.d.Luft* staff in Wilhelmshaven. In April 1941 he was appointed an aircraft commander and *1. Admiralstabsoffizier* for Aufkl.Gr. 125 for a year, during which he served within the Aegean and Black Sea (as Deputy Commander and *1. Admiralstabsoffizier*, Russia) before being transferred to Harlinghausen's torpedo department as a member of the *Staff/ Bevollmächtigen für die Lufttorpedowaffe*, while also serving as Adjutant for KG 26. Finally, in April 1943, he returned to the Kriegsmarine and began training for U-boat command. Thomsen later captained *U1202*, his U-boat being adorned with the crest of the '*Löwen Geschwader*', and he ended the war decorated with the Knight's Cross with Oak Leaves.

At the same time that the two *Aufklärungsgruppen* were formed, *Luftflotte* 5 established the post of *Fliegerführer Nord* in Stavanger from the Staff of KG 26, commanded by *Generalleutnant* Alexander Holle and responsible for anti-shipping operations, U-boat support and coastal reconnaissance north of latitude 58°N. By the time of Operation *Barbarossa*, Holle controlled the fighter aircraft of *Jagdfliegerführer Norwegen* as well as I./KG 26, II./KG 30 and IV.(Stuka)/LG 1. The sea area south of the dividing latitude remained the domain of *F.d.Luft*, whose assets were grouped around Jutland. During December 1941 Holle's office was subdivided into three separate commands: *Fliegerführer Nord (West)* under *Oberst* Hermann Busch, based in Trondheim and responsible for the southern Norwegian area up to 66° North latitude that ran through the islands of Nord-Herøy and Alsten; *Fliegerführer Lofoten*, under *Oberst* Ernst-August Roth, responsible for the area between 66° North and Altafjord; and *Fliegerführer Nord (Ost)* under *Oberst* Alexander Holle, based in Kirkenes and responsible for the Arctic area north of Altafjord to Finland.

Stripped to the bone, Raeder's naval air service was now a shadow of what it had once been, and continued to be further eclipsed in Göring's reshuffling. On the eve of Operation *Barbarossa*, *Oberst* von Wild, as *Führer der Seeluftstreitkräfte*, controlled only the four *Staffeln* of Kü.Fl.Gr. 506 based at Westerland, three of Kü.Fl.Gr. 906 at Aalborg, and the *Bordfliegerstaffel* 1./B.Fl.Gr. 196 in Wilhelmshaven. The remainder of the *Küstenfliegergruppen* were distributed between *Luftflotten* of the operational Luftwaffe. By the end of June 1941 the Luftwaffe possessed a total of nine torpedo *Staffeln*:

F.d.Luft:	1./Kü.Fl.Gr. 406, He 115, nine aircraft (four operational)
Fliegerführer Atlantik:	7./KG 40, He 111, eight aircraft (four operational)
	1./Kü.Fl.Gr. 906, He 115, nine aircraft (four operational)
	2./Kü.Fl.Gr. 506, He 115, nine aircraft (five operational)
Luftflotte 3:	II./KG 40 (three *Staffeln*), Do 217 (no operational aircraft)
IX.*Fliegerkorps*:	1./KG 28, He 111, eight aircraft (four operational)
X.*Fliegerkorps*:	6./KG 26, He 111, eight aircraft (none operational)

Within the Atlantic battleground KG 40 remained locked in missions alternating between U-boat reconnaissance and offensive shipping strikes. The Fw 200s continued long-distance reconnaissance, *B.d.U.* maintaining their primary role as that of shadowing aircraft, bombing attacks being considered a subsidiary task of opportunity. The smaller He 115 and Ju 88 units continued attacks on British coastal shipping and those targets found within the Irish Sea, while the twin-engine Bf 110s of 3./KGr. 123 mounted reconnaissance sorties over the English south-western coastal area.

The large Condors had begun to encounter heavily-armed Short Sunderland flying boats more frequently, and though they often fought inconclusive running battles, the steady drain of wounded men and damaged aircraft reduced operational levels and corresponding mission frequency. On 17 July *Oblt*. Rudolf Heindl's Condor successfully shot down a Whitley of 502 Sqn which was flying as anti-submarine escort for Convoy OB346. Heindl's wireless operator, *Oblt*. Hans Jordens, was killed in the exchange of fire, which marked the first confirmed aerial victory for a KG 40 Condor. However, the elation was tempered by the loss of Knight's Cross holder *Hptm*. Fritz Fliegel's Condor, F8+AB, the next day, shot down by anti-aircraft fire from merchant ships of the same convoy. Fliegel's wing was seen to shear clean away from the fuselage after the aircraft was hit, the entire Condor cartwheeling into the Atlantic with all crew lost; another indication of the relative fragility of the Condor's airframe. Fliegel had been commander of I./KG 40, and had received his Knight's Cross on 25 March for the credited

Part of a German newsreel film showing a Condor crewman preparing food during what were frequently gruelling Atlantic patrols.

Robert Kowalewski, a former *Reichsmarine* officer and highly successful bomber pilot. (Bundesarchiv)

sinking of seven ships and damaging of a further six. His was the most senior loss suffered by KG 40 thus far, his place as *Kommandeur* taken by *Hptm.* Edmund Daser, former *Staffelkapitän* of 1./KG 40. The inherent weakness of the Condor was improved somewhat in the upgraded Fw 200C-3, which was structurally strengthened and equipped with better Bramo 323R-2 radial engines. Derivatives of the new variant also had upgraded defensive weaponry and were fitted with a hemispherical dorsal turret, plus enhancements to the ventral gondola that allowed the fitting of a *Lotfe* 7D gyroscopically stabilised bombsight, based on the extremely effective American Norden bombsight. The Carl Zeiss *Lotfernrohr* 7 series of sights had been the Luftwaffe standard since the war's beginning, the 7C being the first to feature gyroscopic stabilisation.

Casualties had indeed been heavy in July. Five days after Fliegel's death, *Obfw.* Heinrich Bleichert's Condor of I./KG 40 was brought down by a 233 Sqn Hudson while attempting to attack Convoy OG69. The Hudson pilot, Fg Off Ron Down, recalled the successful engagement:

> Flying above the convoy, at about a hundred feet above the sea, was one of the big Focke-Wulf Condors. We were overhauling him fast. Whether he saw us or not I don't know, but at four hundred yards I opened up with about five bursts from my front guns, and I could see tracer bullets whipping past the nose of the Hudson in little streaks of light. But he missed us, and his pilot turned slightly to starboard and ran for it, parallel to the course of the convoy . . . Once he put his nose up a trifle, as though meditating a run for the clouds. He must have decided he couldn't make it and was safer where he was, right down on the sea . . . We drew closer and closer. The Condor began to look like the side of a house. At the end all I could see of it was part of the fuselage and two whacking big engines. My rear gunner was pumping bullets into him all the time. When we were separated by only forty feet I could see two of his engines beginning to glow.[11]

Bleichert successfully ditched in the sea, all the crew escaping to be captured apart from the on-board meteorologist, who had been shot through the heart by the Hudson's gunfire. The following day 1./KG 40 *Staffelkapitän Hptmn.* Konrad Verlohr was posted as missing in action after his aircraft was lost west of Ireland. In return, not a single ship was sunk during July.

ObFw. Heinrich Bleichert's Condor of I./KG 40 brought down by a 233 Squadron Hudson while attempting to attack Convoy OG69 on 23 July 1941.

Meanwhile, at Lüneburg during May 1941, II./KG 40 became the second bomber unit (after KG 2) to equip with the Do 217. The *Gruppe*'s 4.*Staffel* was originally intended to operate as a torpedo unit, but trials using two Do 217Es on loan from KG 2 as torpedo carriers were initially unsuccessful owing to persistent electrical problems. Some Do 217s had already been taken on the strength of the newly formed II./KG.40, based at Soesterburg in The Netherlands and Bordeaux, flying conventional anti-shipping bombing strikes from March 1941. The Do 217 had suffered episodic delays during its arduous development process, hamstrung by Luftwaffe command-level obsession with a dive-bombing capability which was only belatedly recognised as utterly impractical for an aircraft of this size, and dropped from the list of requirements by the *RLM* in mid-1941. Further trials and then tests resulted in the ability of

Another view of Bleichert's Condor, with OG69 visible in the background. All of the German crew except the onboard meteorologist were rescued.

An He 115 making landfall. (James Payne)

a Do 217E-2/R4 to deliver a single LT F5b torpedo held by a PVC 1006 carrying rack, but the variant was never used in action, the role being allocated instead to Ju 88s, which were much easier to modify.[12] Later attempts at modifying a Do 217K-07 to carry four LT F5b torpedoes on underwing racks were made during 1943, but ultimately deemed unsatisfactory and not pursued beyond initial trials.

During the summer of 1941 Petersen was ordered to form an independent 'Kommando' from I./KG 40 for transfer to the Mediterranean. There he was to fly anti-shipping strikes over the Gulf of Suez, the Suez Canal and into the Red Sea. Six Fw 200s and nine He 111s, the latter commanded by *Hptm.* Robert Kowalewski of III./KG 40, who had previously commanded the torpedo aircraft of II./KG 26, were despatched to Athens during August. Petersen, however, was not destined to remain at this new position for long, as he was posted during September to command the network of Luftwaffe testing sites (*Kommandeur Kommando der Erprobungsstellen der Luftwaffe*), while concurrently heading the research establishment at Rechlin focussed upon developing the Heinkel He 177 *Greif*, which was beset by design problems. In his stead as *Kommodore* KG 40 in Athens came *Obstlt.* Dr Georg Pasewaldt, previous commander of II./KG 40 and provisional *Kommodore* until the end of 1941.

'*Kommando Petersen*' flew missions over the Suez and Red Sea area for only a brief period during early September. After that, the Fw 200s returned to Bordeaux and the Heinkels to Soesterberg, from where they had originated. During their brief Mediterranean tenure they achieved no successes, but lost two aircraft. *Oberleutnant* Horst Neumann's Fw 200C, F8+GH, crashed into the sea near Cape Sounio after take-off on 5 September, killing all of its crew, and *Fw.* Werner Titz's He 111 was shot down by a South African Hurricane of 94 Sqn while engaged in a conventional bombing raid on Abu Sueir, Egypt, on 6 September, the whole crew being taken prisoner.[13] However, other units continued to raid the Red Sea approaches to the Suez Canal. The 5,718-ton American freighter SS *Steel Seafarer* was sunk by a Ju 88 of LG 1 on 5 September. The ship was travelling from New York to Suez, clearly marked as a neutral, with American flags painted on the hull sides, when the aircraft attacked in darkness at 2328hrs. The ship was steaming at 4 knots with navigation lights burning in clear weather, though strong winds had made the sea rough. A single bomb landed squarely, and Master John D. R. Halliday ordered the engines stopped and the crew to abandon ship. As they pulled away in three lifeboats, *Steel Seafarer* capsized and sank within fifteen minutes of being bombed. Neutral it may have been, but it carried 5,700 tons of munitions for British North African forces, one of many American-flag freighters carrying such cargo under lucrative charter terms from the British government.

The preparation for Operation *Barbarossa* saw *Luftflotten* 1, 2, 4 and 5 move east in small components to avoid security breaches during June. *Fliegerführer Atlantik* thus became the sole dedicated anti-shipping force remaining in the Western Theatre. IX.*Fliegerkorps* was employed on minelaying as well as night bombing of British land targets, while the aircraft of *Fliegerführer Nord* and *Lofoten* were largely confined to scouting within northern latitudes.

The Luftwaffe was an essential component of the ambitious attack in the east, nearly two-thirds of operational bomber *Kampfgruppen* — thirty-two in total — being deployed between the four committed *Luftflotten.* The main maritime component of this initial attack would be carried by elements of *Generaloberst* Alfred Keller's *Luftflotte* 1,

Significant casualties were suffered amongst trained maritime pilots and crew by their use in bombing mainland Britain as the tug of war over control of the Luftwaffe's maritime forces reached new intensity during 1941.

supporting Army Group North in its advance through the Baltic states towards Leningrad, and the Arctic elements of *Generaloberst* Hans-Jürgen Stumpff's *Luftflotte* 5 in Norway. Within this latter region maritime missions were co-ordinated by *Fliegerführer Kirkenes*, Nielsen having established his headquarters at the Kirkenes Airfield, initially as an independent detached unit, but soon subsumed to Stumpff's command. As well as supporting the ground offensive, Nielsen's tasks entailed the disruption of the straggling supply links between Leningrad and Soviet terminals on the Arctic Ocean: the harbours at Murmansk (particularly valuable as it was ice-free throughout the year), Kolskiy Bay and Arkhangelsk. The Kirov railway provided the primary link, and attacks against it and shipping within the Soviet ports were of high priority. In this unforgiving Arctic landscape Kirkenes Airfield and that at Banak, at the southern end of Porsanger Fjord and described by Hajo Herrmann as 'a God-forsaken Lapp village in a treeless, tundra-like area', were the only two airstrips suitable for his aircraft. Assigned to his command were ten Ju 88s of 5./KG 30 and He 115s and Do 18s of 1./

Kü.Fl.Gr. 406 at Banak, thirty-six Ju 87s of IV.(Stuka)/LG 1, ten Bf 109s of I./JG 77, six Bf 110s of Stab/ZG 76, and three Ju 88s of 1./Aufkl.Gr. 124 at Kirkenes, and a further seven reconnaissance Hs 126s and Do 17s of 1.(H)/Aufkl.Gr. 32 at Kemijärvi and Rovaniemi. Two He 111s and two Ju 88s of a weather reconnaissance section were also attached to his command, along with eleven Ju 52 transport aircraft for internal movement of men and equipment.

In the Baltic, *Fliegerführer Ostsee* was committed to the attack on the Soviet Union, guarding the northern flank of *Luftflotte* 1, all tasks carried out in close cooperation with Kriegsmarine Baltic commands, in particular *Vizadmiral* Hubert Schmundt as *Befehlshaber der Kreuzer* based in Helsinki, requiring up to date information regarding any major Soviet fleet movements. While larger bombers penetrated

Officers and crew of a shore-based Ar 196 *Staffel* celebrate completion of their 2,600th combat mission.

deeply within the eastern Baltic, the smaller aircraft of Aufkl.Gr. 125 flew repeated anti-submarine patrols and convoy escort for coastal supply routes used by German merchant ships. The totality of roles included searching for indications of offensive movement made by the Soviet Baltic Fleet, as well as minelaying, escort duties, bombing Soviet merchant and military shipping and supporting ground forces whenever possible. *Oberst* Wolfgang von Wild, whose headquarters were at Metgethen in the East Prussian Samland district, had directly under his control: Stab/Aufkl.Gr. 125, *Obstlt.* Gerhard Kolbe (He 60); 1./Aufkl.Gr. 125, *Hptm.* Friedrich Schallmayer (He 60); 2./Aufkl.Gr. 125, *Oblt.z..S.* Rolf Lemp (He 114); and 3./Aufkl.Gr. 125, *Oblt.* Kurt Lüdemann (Ar 95A). However, he also exercised tactical command over elements of the two Ju 88-equipped *Kampfgruppen* recently removed from the *Küstenflieger* service: KGr. 806, (*Maj.* Hans Emig) and 1. and 2. *Staffeln* of KGr. 106. Von Wild's other resources included *Hptm.* Karl Born's 9.*Seenotstaffel*, comprising a handful of He 59s, two pairs of Do 18s and Do24s, Junkers Ju 52 (M) '*Mausi*' minesweepers, and the air-traffic-control ship *Karl Meyer*, which was used as a navigational aid.

The '*Mausi*' had been developed in response to enemy magnetic minefields. A standard Junkers Ju 52 transport aircraft was fitted with an external duralumin Gauss loop of 14.6m diameter suspended

A Junkers Ju 52 '*Mausi*' minesweeping aircraft, photographed here on the Eastern Front. (Bundesarchiv)

beneath the fuselage, and a generator powered by a 270hp Mercedes engine in the forward fuselage, the aircraft being classed thereafter as a Ju 52/3m MS. A small number of similarly equipped BV 138C-1/MS floatplanes and obsolete Dornier Do 23 twin-engine bombers soon became operational, as the method proved effective in action though extremely dangerous. The aircraft flew low above the water surface, typically between ten and thirty metres, and the electric current was sufficient to explode the mines below, which could pose a danger to the aircraft. They generally operated in pairs, and two '*Mausi*' minesweepers were lost on 26 October in such a mine detonation near Harilaid Island, several crewmen being wounded.

While aircraft of *Luftflotte* 1 were tasked with devastating Soviet air units and achieving aerial supremacy over the northern sector, *Fliegerführer Ostsee* intended to attack the Soviet Baltic Fleet both at sea and in harbour with bombs and mines, tie up merchant shipping within the Baltic, and stop traffic through the White Sea-Baltic Sea Canal (the 'Stalin Canal'), primarily by destruction of the lock installations at Povenets on Lake Onega, which were the canal's highest locks above sea level and comprised seven timber gates named the 'Stairs of Povenets'. Destroying the canal's functionality could prevent the Soviet transfer of approximately forty-five submarines, fifteen destroyers and various minelayers from the Gulf of Finland to the Arctic Ocean, where the Kriegsmarine presence was thin at best. Familiarisation flights within the area were undertaken by *Fliegerführer Ostsee*, assisted by the Finnish Air Force and flying as far as Utti (Kouvola) in preparation for the *Barbarossa* attack.

On 22 June, the opening day of *Barbarossa*, most bomber groups were engaged in battering Soviet airfields, though *Major* Emig's KGr. 806 flew what was probably the longest single mission made by any Luftwaffe formation when it completed the 1,000-mile round trip from East Prussian airfields to the main base of the Soviet Baltic Fleet at Kronstadt, west of Leningrad, to lay twenty-seven LMB mines. Emig's aircraft achieved total surprise over the Soviet naval base. They were guided by a Finnish liaison officer carried aboard the lead aircraft, the monotony of the landscape and lack of navigational fixtures testing the Luftwaffe aircrafts' navigation.

The Ju 88s' final approach from the Ingermanland coast was made at low level, sweeping over Leningrad and reaching Kronstadt from the east. Consequently not a single anti-aircraft shot was fired, as the

The Ju 88s of *Major* Hans Emig's *Kampfgruppe* 806 mounted probably the longest single Luftwaffe mission at the opening of Operation *Barbarossa* with a 1,000-mile round trip to lay mines near Leningrad.

gunners misidentified the aircraft. Twenty-eight mines were successfully dropped before the Finn guided Emig's aircraft home via a prearranged air corridor over Finnish territory, landing at the liberated Utti Airfield where the aircraft were refuelled before returning to East Prussia. Despite the extraordinary effort, this initial attempt at obstructing Kronstadt sank only the small 499-ton Estonian ferry *Ruhno* in the Leningrad Sea Port Canal, killing three men.

The Kriegsmarine were also sowing extensive defensive minefields to pen the formidable Soviet naval strength in the eastern Baltic, and Emig's Ju 88s were thereafter committed to this minelaying drive over the following weeks. Emig's *Gruppe* began using Helsinki Aerodrome as a stop-off and refuelling point when engaged in missions to distant northern targets, and urgent work was undertaken by the Finns to extend the runway to 1,500m by demolishing five houses and cutting down surrounding forest.[14] Utti had initially proved unsuitable for the German bombers, and after the official entry of Finland into the war on the Axis side on 25 June, four KGr. 806 Ju 88s lifted off from Helsinki Aerodrome and headed for Kronstadt, where they tried unsuccessfully to bomb the Soviet cruiser *Kirov*, though Emig claimed the ship hit and damaged. Sporadic armed reconnaissance missions were also flown alongside the planned attack on the Stalin Canal launched from Helsinki by KGr. 806 on the night of 27 June.

With his Ju 88 armed with BM1000 '*Monika*' mines (essentially the LMB mine fitted with a tail unit that allowed dropping without a parachute, in the manner of a conventional bomb), *Maj.* Emig led the raid, which approached the target in three waves during the early morning hours at extremely low altitude to increase chances of success. Emig successfully dropped his mine, which destroyed the lock gate that he had targeted, but his aircraft was so low that it took the full force of the blast and crashed. Emig and his crew, Observer *Obfw.* Helmut Rudolf, Wireless Operator *Obfw.* Heinz Bodensiek, and gunner *Obfw.* Werner Hawlitschka, were all killed as the Ju 88 ploughed into the ground in flames near Lock Gate Number 3.[15] *Hauptmann* Erich Seedorf, *Staffelkapitän* of 1./KGr. 806, ordered the two following waves to bomb from an increased height of 100m, and no further losses were reported, though one other Junkers later made an emergency landing at Utti airfield. The Povenets lock installation was damaged by the attack, and by a second one made on 15 July, and boat traffic on the canal was interrupted until 6 August. As each destroyed gate was repaired, the Kriegsmarine requested fresh attacks to maintain the blockade of Soviet naval forces in the Gulf of Finland, and another bombing raid on 13 August kept the canal unserviceable for eleven more days, after which further air attacks on the canal were mounted on 28 August and 5 September. During one of the latter attacks, led by *Maj.* Wolfgang Bühring, *Kampfgruppe* 806 used SC1000 '*Hermann*' bombs with newly designed detonators specifically intended for low-level bombing, and succeeded in completely destroying a lock gate and severely damaging the lock basin itself. However, several Ju 88s were lost through premature detonation of the bombs, and their use was immediately curtailed by the Chief of Luftwaffe Supply and Procurement.[16] Finally, on 6 December 1941, in a -37 °C frost, Finnish troops captured Povenets and the southern end of the Stalin Canal. Retreating Soviet troops demolished locks and dams, and water from the watershed lakes began to pour into Lake Onega through Povenets village, which was almost destroyed. The Finnish troops were soon pushed back to the canal's western bank by fierce counterattacks, while the Soviets held the east, and they remained in these positions until June 1944.

Meanwhile, the former *Reichsmarine* aviator and *Kommandeur* of I./KG 54, *Hptm.* Richard Linke, took command of KGr. 806, which continued anti-shipping operations over the Baltic. On 18 July two Soviet destroyers attempted to attack a small German supply convoy heading for the Latvian port of Daugavgriva. Although the convoy escaped interception, the destroyers were caught within the Gulf of Riga by Linke's aircraft, hemmed in by the narrows east of Saaremaa island as they raced for the open Baltic. During the ensuing attack the 1,686-ton *Serdity* was so badly damaged that it was scuttled after the Soviet Navy had spent three days attempting to keep it afloat.

In the Arctic on the opening day of Operation *Barbarossa* the temperature barely reached 8°C, and cloud, rain, and lack of visibility severely hampered flying operations, and German ground forces did not open their assault toward Murmansk until the Finnish entry into the war. The delayed opening of this three-stage land attack, codenamed Operation *Silberfuchs*, removed any element of surprise, and although only 120 kilometres separated the German jumping-off point in Norway from the port of Murmansk, the advance soon stalled in the face of stubborn resistance and excruciatingly difficult terrain. Along the line of the Liza River, halfway between Petsamo and Murmansk, fighting devolved into trench warfare, resulting in little movement until 1944.

Fliegerführer Kirkenes was closely embedded with Wehrmacht ground troops within the Arctic circle, and frequently mounted operations in support of the stalled ground offensive, including the same type of attacks against Soviet airfields that had taken place throughout the front line in the early days of *Barbarossa*. Principle missions were only vaguely defined by instructions from *OKW*, but included interdiction of Soviet supply routes and protection of German convoy traffic, the only method by which Kirkenes could be resupplied. Numerically weaker than the Soviet air forces they faced, initial attacks on Soviet airfields, communication lines and power stations were very successful, despite *Barbarossa* already being three days old by the time the Northern Front was opened.

With no Kriegsmarine surface forces present until the following month, defence of the coastal region fell completely to Nielsen's air units, which helped to decimate a Soviet amphibious landing at Kutovaya, behind the German front line. Minelaying had begun following an initial reconnaissance flight in the early morning of 23 June, after which eight Ju 88s mined the Kola Bay and Polyarnoye, near Murmansk. More mines were laid immediately before Murmansk during the following day. Although little result was observed from these operations, Soviet minesweepers were kept busy ensuring the entrances to the Arctic harbours were swept. Even so, the Soviets made very little offensive movement in the Arctic Ocean throughout 1941.

On the same day that Murmansk had been mined, and before Finland officially entered the conflict, two He 115s of 1./Kü.Fl.Gr. 406 carried a Finnish sabotage group of sixteen men on a mission against the Stalin Canal, at that stage still untouched by the bombers of KGr. 806. Operation *Shiffaren* was carried out with the Finnish soldiers wearing German uniforms, the He 115s taking off from Lake Oulujärviat at 2200hrs on 22 June and then flying a low-level, convoluted route that bypassed Soviet airfields. Once they reached the fringes of the White Sea the two Heinkels turned south and arrived east of the canal, alighting on a lake, where they dropped the saboteurs in rubber boats. While the German aircraft returned under cover of Finnish fighter aircraft, the commando team reconnoitred the canal locks but found them too

Two He 115s of *Küstenfliegergruppe* 406 were used to ferry Finnish commandos that operated against the Murmansk railway in June and July 1941. (James Payne)

heavily guarded to attack, deciding that the task could be handled better by Emig's KGr. 806 instead. The Finns retreated, using their explosives against the Murmansk railway and eventually returning overland to friendly territory by 11 July, having lost two men in skirmishes with Red Army troops.

Within the Baltic, *Fliegerführer Ostsee* was heavily involved in supporting the ground attack on Tallinn, Estonia's seaport capital. The Red Navy destroyer *Karl Marx* was bombed in Loksa Bight on 6 August, and sank after attempts to keep the stricken ship afloat failed. By the end of August most bomber wings of *Luftflotte* 1 were being used against Soviet shipping evacuating Tallinn, as well as both military and merchant vessels within the Gulf of Finland and the Bay of Kronstadt, and on the Neva River and the Ladoga Canal. The mass Soviet naval evacuation of Tallinn enabled KGr. 806 to achieve its greatest successes, together with other *Luftflotte* 1 bomber units including nine He 111s of I./KG 4 and *Obstlt*. Johann Raithel's KG 77, which was gravitating towards anti-shipping strikes. Alongside *Hptm*. Linke's KGr. 806, I./KG 77 and III./KG 77, totalling fifty-nine aircraft, attacked and sank the 2,317-ton SS *Lucerne*, the 1,423-ton *Atis Kronvalds*, the 2,414-ton *Skundra* and the 2,250-ton ice breaker *Krisjanis Valdemars* as they attempted to leave Tallinn. The light cruiser *Kirov* was damaged, as was the 2,026-ton SS *Vironia*, a former Estonian ship that had been commandeered by the Red Navy for use as a staff vessel. The *Vironia* struck a mine from the formidable Juminda barrage intended to pen Soviet ships in the Gulf of Riga. Under severe bombing, the remaining Soviet evacuation fleet changed course and blundered straight into the minefields, where thirty-five ships, including four destroyers and three submarines, were sunk.

The Luftwaffe repeated their attack with additional aircraft from KG 1 and KG 4 the following day, and three more ships were sunk: the 1,270-ton naval navigational and hydrographic training ship *Lensoviet* and two troop transports, the 3,974-ton *Vtaraya Piatiletka* and the 2,190-ton *Kalpaks*. A further three were severely damaged and beached on the Finnish island of Suursaari, and a fourth that was also hit, and beached on Seiskari, offloaded 2,300 of the 5,000 troops she carried before limping onward to Kronstadt, where the captain, wounded in the bombing, was executed for cowardice.

Between the opening of *Barbarossa* on 22 June and the end of August, *Fliegerführer Ostsee* had flown 1,775 sorties. Of these, maritime forces had flown: 737 by Aufkl.Gr. 125; 610 by KGr. 806; 15 by Kü.Fl.Gr. 406; and 66 by 1./BFl.Gr. 196. An estimated 66,000 tons of merchant shipping had been sunk, and 17,000 tons so badly damaged as to be considered 'probables'. In return, von Wild had lost eleven Ju 88s, three Ar 95s, one Ar 196 and five Bf 109s.

During September *Fliegerführer Ostsee* was reinforced by the arrival in Riga of the fourteen Ju 88s of *Hptm*. Josef Sched's 1./KGr. 506, though a planned assault on Leningrad itself, the main target of Army Group North, had been cancelled by *OKW*. Instead, the city was to be placed under siege, effectively ending *Barbarossa* maritime operations within the Baltic. The penned Soviet Baltic Fleet would be pounded by conventional bombing and Stukas, including the now-famous attack by *Lt*. Hans-Ulrich Rudel on the morning of 22 September, when he scored a direct hit on the battleship *Marat* with an SC1000 bomb.

Following the fall of Tallinn, the conquest of the Ösel (Saaremaa) and Dagö (Hiiumaa) islands, which controlled naval transit to and from the Gulf of Riga, was begun. They were heavily fortified by their Soviet garrison of more than 20,000 men, and two distinct plans had been formulated; *Beowulf* I, to be launched from Latvia, and *Beowulf* II from the western coast of Estonia. The Luftwaffe established an *ad hoc* command for support of the operation, named 'Luftwaffe Command B', under *Generalmajor* Heinz-Hellmuth von Wühlisch, and beneath this umbrella were KGr. 806 and Aufkl.Gr. 125 of *Fliegerführer Ostsee*, as well as 2./Kü.Fl.Gr. 906, which was transferred to von Wild's command, joined by 3./Kü.Fl.Gr. 506 on 21 September.

Alongside *Fliegerführer Ostsee*, I. and II./KG 77 and elements of ZG 26 and JG 54 took part in the *Beowulf* II attack, launched on 8 September. Von Wild established his headquarters at Parnu with the Staff and 1.*Staffel* of Aufkl.Gr. 125, the last two *Staffeln* of the reconnaissance group moving to the small Finnish airfields in Haapsalu and Helsinki respectively. The larger Ju 88s of KGr. 806 and Kü.Fl.Gr. 906 and 506 remained based in the Latvian city of Riga. During the operation the Luftwaffe provided constant and valuable support to amphibious landings, acting as flying artillery, and on 16 September destroyed or disabled a fleet of some twenty ships in Triigi Bay that had been assembled to evacuate the Soviet defenders. By 17 September, with the bridgehead secure and the battle swung heavily in the Germans' favour, von Wühlisch relinquished command of the Luftwaffe's *Beowulf* forces to *Fliegerführer Ostsee*, and the *ad hoc* 'B' office was disbanded. That same day, *Hptm.* Richard Linke, commander of KGr. 806, was awarded the Knight's Cross.

Once *Beowulf* had been successfully concluded, *Hptm.* Gerhard Wojahn's 2./Kü.Fl.Gr. 906 was instructed to hand its Junkers Ju 88s over to the crews of *Hptm.* Ernst-Heinrich Thomsen's 2./Kü.Fl.Gr. 506, which had been based in Brest with elderly He 115 floatplanes in the Bay of Biscay. The two *Staffeln* were to exchange places by 6 October, 2./Kü.Fl.Gr. 906 returning to the Breton battlefront and 2./Kü.Fl.Gr. 506 moving to Westerland for conversion training. *Küstenfliegergruppe* 506 was now composed entirely of land-based aircraft, and on 19 October was redesignated KGr. 506. Its association with the Kriegsmarine effectively ended after Raeder agreed to a request made by Göring to relinquish command of the unit to *Luftflotte* 3.

Generaladmiral Rolf Carls, *MGK Nord*, immediately protested Raeder's decision to let go of KGr. 506, over which he had hoped to exercise tactical control during impending operations against supply convoys from Great Britain to Murmansk.

> If the Naval Staff stands by its surprising decision to relinquish command over *Gruppe* 506, then there remain under *F.d.Luft* only the five aircraft of *Staffel* 1./Kü.Fl.Gr. 706 and Arado aircraft of BordFlSt 1./BFl.Gr. 196. This would pronounce the death sentence for the naval air arm.[17]

Nonetheless, Raeder's decision held firm.

On 27 October *Fliegerführer Ostsee* was disbanded, KGr. 806 being transferred to *Luftflotte* 1 for deployment in southern Finland before an eventual move to the Mediterranean, where it would form the cadre of III./KG 54. The Ju 88s of *Hptm.* Josef Sched's 1./KGr. 506 returned to their original airfield at Westerland, in the centre of the island of Sylt, and *Hptm.* Franz Drychs' 3./Kü.Fl.Gr. 506 to the Danish Grove airfield near Karup until November. On the last day of that month all three *Staffeln* were transferred to Leeuwarden and placed under the command of IX.*Fliegerkorps* based in The Netherlands. As winter approached, the light floatplanes of Aufkl.Gr. 125 transferred to Pillau owing to increasingly difficult ice conditions in the eastern Baltic.

Wolfgang von Wild was promoted full *Oberst* and despatched to France, where he became acting *Fliegerführer Atlantik* at the end of October. His predecessor, Harlinghausen, had been wounded earlier that month when his He 111H-3 was hit by anti-aircraft fire during a combat mission over the Irish Sea. After nursing the aircraft back to France, Harlinghausen crash-landed near Vannes. He was rescued by French fishermen and hospitalised for three months.

At the southern end of the *Barbarossa* front, *Luftflotte* 4 had detailed IV.*Fliegerkorps* to support the Eleventh Army and attack the Soviet Navy and its bases on the Black Sea, in support of the vast ground offensive aimed at capturing the Crimean Peninsula. The major port at Odessa had held out against Romanian attack for over two months, supplied by regular night convoys from Sevastopol, as the Romanian Air Force Corps (*Corpul Aerian Roman*) was both underequipped and unprepared for anti-shipping missions. Luftwaffe bombers frequently raided Odessa and its approaches, Ju 88s of KG 51 sinking the 4,727-ton liner *Adzhariya* near the port on 23 July, killing four men, though the cargo that was being carried to supply the besieged garrison was largely salvaged.

In September *Luftflotte* 4 ordered *Oblt*. Horst Krupka's torpedo-trained 6./KG 26 to relocate its He 111H-6 aircraft from the Mediterranean to Buzău, Romania, and use a Romanian airfield that had been used for advanced flight training north of Bucharest, but comprised a grass runway unable to bear heavy aircraft after strong rainfall. Krupka was instructed to attack Soviet evacuation traffic from Odessa to Sevastopol and other Caucasus ports, as well as undertake night bombing of Soviet defensive positions around Odessa. Despite their transfer to *General der Flieger* Wolfram von Richthofen's VIII. *Fliegerkorps* roster, they remained officially on the strength of II./KG 26, still based in Greece as part of X.*Fliegerkorps*. Krupka was shot down on 8 October by anti-aircraft fire from Soviet ships near Odessa, but was rescued by an He 59 of 8.*Seenotstaffel*. However, he did not survive his second downing at the hands of ships' gunners, being posted missing in action with his crew on 15 May 1942 and posthumously awarded the German Cross in Gold.[18]

To augment Krupka's mission, a second *Staffel* of torpedo bombers was established at Buzău, also equipped with He 111H-6s. The veteran crews of *Hptm*. Wolfgang Lauer-Schmaltz's 1./KG 28 had previously been 1./KGr. 126, which had specialised in minelaying on the Western Front, and were therefore experienced *Seeflieger*. Detached from the main body of I./KG 28, the *Staffel* had subsequently undergone torpedo training and been made operational once again within the Black Sea.[19]

The first noted success for these torpedo aircraft was the sinking of the unfinished hull of the 2,150-ton MV *Pugachev*, which was attacked while under tow south-west of the Kuban Strait, laden with grain bound from Kerch to Novorossiysk. Six crewmen and seven Soviet soldiers were lifted off by an escorting patrol boat before the ship went down. The gradual evacuation of Odessa provided further occasional targets of opportunity. On 3 October the 11,868-ton MV *Dnepr*, a Spanish passenger liner that had been seized from Nationalist Spain in 1939 and mobilised as a hospital ship during August 1941, was sailing under escort from Novorossiysk to Sevastopol when three He 111s attacked at 1920hrs. Six torpedoes were launched from a range of 1,000m, and at least one hit and sank the liner within ten minutes. Forty people were killed, while the escorting minesweeper rescued another one hundred and sixty-three. Attempted torpedo attacks against the cruisers *Chervonaya Ukraina* and *Molotov* and major warships at Tuapse around the same period were, however, unsuccessful.

As German ground forces broke through the defences of the Crimea, *Stavka* ordered Odessa evacuated, and it finally fell to Romanian troops on 16 October. The Soviet evacuation by sea was extremely successful, IV.*Fliegerkorps* failing to inflict significant casualties on convoys generally travelling under cover of darkness. The final major lift was made on the night of 14/15 October, and a total of 350,000 soldiers and civilians were successfully evacuated to the Crimean Peninsula. At the tail end of the evacuation the Luftwaffe attacked a small convoy escorted by four torpedo boats for a reported seven hours in the Karkinitskiy Gulf. The mixed force of bombers and torpedo bombers launched repeated strikes, and one torpedo hit the 1,412-ton steamer SS *Bolshevik*, carrying only twenty soldiers and travelling in ballast. After being strafed, the ship was struck on its starboard hull by one of three torpedoes dropped. The blast destroyed the engine room and boilers and killed sixteen men, the remaining thirty-six survivors being rescued by the escorting torpedo boats.

Following the port city's fall, the Romanian Air Force Corps began reconnaissance and anti-shipping operations over the Black Sea with its 101st and 102nd Seaplane Squadrons, equipped with He 114C-1s and Italian CANT Seagulls. The Soviet Black Sea Fleet had handled the entire evacuation extremely well, and in the air the Soviet Air Force were particularly effective against the Wehrmacht land offensive against the Crimea until additional Luftwaffe fighter units were deployed to the region under the direction of experienced 'ace' Werner Mölders, who had been removed from operational flying and promoted *General der Jagdflieger*, i.e. head of the entire Luftwaffe fighter arm. In this capacity Mölders was in the Crimean area as part of a tour of inspection of Eastern Front fighter units. When the fighter presence in the sector was increased from one *Jagdgruppe* to three, *Oberst* Mölders himself directed operations from the ground by radio from the forward trenches. To assist Mölders's fighter onslaught, most bombers of IV.*Fliegerkorps* were largely concerned with the bombardment of Soviet airfields as air supremacy was gradually wrested from Soviet hands.

Between October and December 1941, 6./KG 26 alone claimed the sinking of 20,000 tons of Soviet shipping. The most severe loss suffered by the Soviets was sunk by torpedo bombers of KG 28 on 7 November. The 4,727-ton passenger ship MV *Armenia*, captained by Vladimir Plaushevsky, had been impressed into service as what the Soviets termed a 'sanitary transport', akin to a hospital ship but not officially classified as such, and still carrying four 45mm defensive guns. It was escorted by warships and enabled to carry weapons and reinforcements. Nonetheless, the ship was clearly displaying large red crosses painted on boards hung on either side and lying visible on deck. The *Armenia* had already made fifteen evacuation runs from Odessa to various ports, carrying a total of approximately 16,000 wounded men to safety. On 5 November the ship lay in Sevastopol Harbour, a target coming under increasing Luftwaffe pressure, and Plaushevsky was instructed to take aboard occupants of Sevastopol's main naval hospital. Loading began under chaotic conditions, lasting for two days before further directions were received, requiring the evacuation from Yalta of several other hospitals and their staffs as well as high-ranking Communist officials and their families. Already at capacity, *Armenia*, sailed from Sevastopol at 1700hrs with only two hours of daylight remaining, and proceeded east towards Yalta. Radioed orders sent the ships to Balaklava, where NKVD men loaded several heavy wooden boxes, since claimed to have contained gold and valuables from Crimean museums. The ship finally reaching Yalta at 0200hrs, where further wounded men, medical staff, Communist officials and NKVD officers and their families were taken aboard, no attempt being made to register them as they were crammed into any available space.

Plaushevsky was ordered to remain in port until an escort could be provided, though he was anxious to depart before sunrise brought the threat of Luftwaffe attack. Subsequent messages informed the captain that, with dawn approaching by the time loading had been completed, his ship should not sail before 1900hrs. However, as Yalta lacked any form of air defence, and Wehrmacht forces were only a day or so away from capturing the city, he disobeyed instructions and, rather than remain a stationary target in harbour, sailed at 0700hrs, bound for Tuapse. The *Armenia* was initially accompanied by only one patrol boat, but a second, as well as two Polikarpov I-153 fighters, joined the small escort as the overcrowded vessel made way. Officially, it carried 5,498 people aboard, though it is speculatively believed that as many as 2,000 extra unregistered wounded men were carried at the request of medical personnel, the decks being crowded with people who could find no shelter inside the fetid atmosphere of the congested hull.

The weather gradually deteriorated, and sporadic storms swept across the ship, although they were not strong enough to ground the Polikarpovs or enemy fliers. The ship was found forty kilometres south of Yalta by a solitary Heinkel He 111 of 1./KG 28, which approached at low altitude out of the thick storm clouds and dropped two torpedoes at a range of 600m. The escorting fighters failed to detect the bomber's approach, and gunners aboard the escorting patrol boats were unable to open fire due to increasingly heavy seas. The first torpedo missed, but the second impacted against the ship's bow, and she sank rapidly, disappearing within four minutes. Of the approximately 7,000 people carried, eight survived. Three were rescued by the escorting patrol boats, and five later came ashore on the distant Crimean coastline, among them a pregnant woman.[20]

On 1 December, the new post of *Fliegerführer Süd* was established in Saki from the now-defunct *Stab/Fliegerführer Ostsee*, *Oberst* Wolfgang von Wild being posted onward from his temporary command of *Fliegerführer Atlantik* to take charge of all Black Sea maritime Luftwaffe operations. He would remain in this role until 10 September 1942, when *General der Flieger* Konrad Zander replaced him, the post being redesignated *Seefliegerführer Schwarzes Meer* during the December following Zander's assumption of command. Von Wild's *Fliegerführer* headquarters was in the Romanian port of Constanza until it was moved to Bakhchysaray in the Crimea during July and then pushed forward to Kerch in September, as the Wehrmacht advance reached its zenith within the Black Sea campaign.

By the end of 1941 the Wehrmacht was exhausted by its advance into the gaping void of the Soviet Union. Swathes of territory had been conquered, but logistically *Barbarossa* assumed nightmare proportions.

The transport of men, supplies and fuel bound for the front line was extremely difficult because of the nature of the dust roads, which degenerated into glutinous mud in autumnal rains before the first winter freeze. This brought its own fresh problems to the mix, as temperatures reached zero and continued to plummet. Rail freight remained the logical alternative, but Russian tracks were of a different gauge to German, requiring conversion to accommodate German *Reichsbahn* rolling stock which would take months to become effective.

Away from the front lines, the back-room warfare between the Luftwaffe and Kriegsmarine had continued throughout 1941, and had expanded to encompass matters other than flying units. On 12 November *SKL* Quartermaster *Kapitän zur See* Hans Erich Voss reported that, with increasing Luftwaffe construction of seagoing vessels (*Flugbetriebsboote*, craft of various sizes used as crash and patrol boats), the Kriegsmarine faced competition for shipyard building space, as well as a loss of 'manpower with instinct for, and knowledge of, the sea' and trained naval personnel as the Luftwaffe recruited its own maritime personnel. Coupled with this fresh depredation, Raeder desired to retain qualified Kriegsmarine officers who had been attached to naval aviation units over which he now exercised little or no control. The rate of attrition among his U-boats had drained the manpower pool of skilled naval officers and, with only a fraction of the former *Küstenflieger* strength still in existence, on 13 November Raeder asked for the recall of between eighty and one hundred Kriegsmarine officers serving in flying units. Predictably, the Luftwaffe initially refused, maintaining that return to Kriegsmarine service was the decision of each individual officer after they had served within the ranks of the Luftwaffe.

Furthermore, with the removal of KGr. 506 from Kriegsmarine control, the very existence of *Oberst* Friedrich Schily's post of *Führer der Marineluftstreitkräfte* was called into question. *Generalleutnant* Hans Ritter held a conference with Raeder on the first day of December to raise the matter personally, stating baldly that:

> With the transfer of *Küstenfliegergruppe* 506, the *F.d.Luft*, with his staff of sixteen officers and about one hundred enlisted men, is in charge of only *Staffel* 1./Kü.Fl.Gr. 706 and *Bordfliegerstaffel* 1./B.Fl.Gr. 196. Of these two *Staffeln*, 1./Kü.Fl.Gr. 706 is for all practical purposes commanded by the Commanding Admiral, Defences East, while those aircraft of the *Bordfliegerstaffel* not aboard ship have orders to co-operate with naval units or coastal commanders for anti-submarine patrol. This results in a situation

whereby the whole *F.d.Luft* staff is inactive, waiting for the vague possibility that *Gruppe* 506 might temporarily return in connection with a specific naval operation. Reduction of the *F.d.Luft* staff appears unavoidable.[21]

Ritter recommended that a smaller replacement unit be created by Schily from a picked cadre of *F.d.Luft* staff, to be named *Fliegerführer Nordsee*, capable of enlargement should the naval air arm be rejuvenated at any point. However, though Raeder would not prevent Ritter from forwarding his proposal to Göring's staff, stating matter-of-factly that he would not view such a move as an 'unfriedly act', he refused to endorse the idea, unwilling to have 'lent his hand to the dissolution of *F.d.Luft*'. He ruefully remarked that, with few bargaining chips left in his hand, in all likelihood Göring would force him to agree to the proposed solution, as had happened after so many previous negotiations.

However, the Naval Staff did not wholeheartedly agree with Raeder, and Schily's staff began to be whittled away, initially by the removal of

SM 79 multipurpose bombers of the Italian Air Force, mainstay of their torpedo units.

his Ia (Operations Officer) and Ic (Intelligence Officer) at the hands of the Kriegsmarine. On 23 December *SKL* revised with Ritter the diminished geographical areas of responsibility for *F.d.Luft* in relation to *Luftflotten* 3 and 5, but the writing was already on the wall for Schily's office in its entirety. During January 1942 the Luftwaffe demanded that the *F.d.Luft* staff be downgraded to the equivalent of a *Gruppe* command. Raeder's resolve crumbled, and he made a personal appeal to Göring not to dissolve the *F.d.Luft* office, belatedly advocating adherence to Ritter's previous proposals. In a letter sent on 18 February he argued that:

> From the beginning the *F.d.Luft* has been the centre for the unified training of air units operating over the sea and in immediate co-operation with naval forces . . . Numerous units of your Luftwaffe have received most valuable officer personnel from this command. They were thereby enabled to carry out their missions over the sea in accord with the overall requirements of the war . . . If this staff should disappear, its valuable experience too will be lost.[22]

Raeder argued that the future appearance of the *Graf Zeppelin*, which was back on the table as a viable construction project after Hitler ordered completion of the carrier 'in the shortest possible time' on 13 March, would necessitate a small independent naval air arm. He maintained that Schily and his staff would be invaluable in maintaining the link between flying operations and naval staff, and the maintenance of its experience in all aspects of maritime operations. During meetings between Raeder and Hitler, the former pointed to the effectiveness of aircraft carriers in modern naval warfare having been amply demonstrated by the British crippling of the Italian fleet at Taranto in November 1940, the loss of the *Bismarck* to forces centred on a carrier, and the spectacular raid on Pearl Harbor mounted by the Imperial Japanese Navy's carrier fleet. Raeder, aware that he faced the complete demise of naval air power, was anxious to secure this last possibility for naval-controlled air protection for his heavy ships, informing the Führer that work could be completed within a year, and trials within an extra six months. Work was resumed on *Graf Zeppelin* in short order, with Hitler's full backing.

The *SKL* War Diary records, on 3 March 1942, that *Generaldmiral* Carls, a fierce advocate of an independent naval air arm, was also obviously unwilling to let the matter of Luftwaffe control over maritime operations drop, though he faced opposition even from within the Kriegsmarine Operations Staff:

> Concerning air forces; The Chief, Naval Staff, Operations Division, reports on the proposal from Group North of 17 January 1942 which concerns the creation of a naval air force. As the initial step, the proposal advocates the formation of a naval air force under the tactical authority of the Kriegsmarine, while the Ministry of Aviation would furnish the necessary aeroplanes, weapons (except for torpedoes) and personnel. The Commanding Admiral, Group North [Carls] considers the present time especially opportune for preliminary work, so that as soon as the Russian campaign is at an end and forces are released as a result we can promptly proceed with the proposed reorganisation.
>
> In the proposal from Group North the Naval Staff, Operations Division, fails to see a working basis desirable for organising what is later to become a naval air force. Such an air force must be based on a Navy possessing a large fleet, and its personnel must be homogeneous with that of the Navy. Neither prerequisite exists at this time, and neither of them can be created for the duration of the war. Therefore the Naval Staff considers it impossible to reopen the naval air force issue for the duration.
>
> Some time ago the Kriegsmarine reported to the Führer that it agrees to the temporary solution of the naval air force controversy but reserves the right to report again at some future date in order to acquaint him with the Kriegsmarine's basic views on the problem. The Chief, Naval Staff, desires that it be determined whether the moment for this report is now at hand in order to emphasize that the Kriegsmarine lays claim to a final solution in the form of its own air force.

Raeder pushed vigorously for a new *Fliegerführer* staff to be established for the Baltic and North Sea, made up of Schily and his immediate subordinates and responsible, at the very least, for KGr. 506 and B.Fl. Gr. 196, while still operating beneath the command of *Luftflotte* 3.

> I hope that you, Herr Reichsmarshall, will agree to one of these proposals, which will mean that the *F.d.Luft* Staff is kept intact in a different form. At the same time you will acquire in addition to administrative control, full tactical command over this staff, which has excelled in every respect. Raeder.

There is no evidence of any reply being received. Rather, on 7 April 1942, Luftwaffe Operations Staff ordered that the responsibilities of *Führer der Marineluftstreitkräfte* be transferred 'in every respect' to *Luftlotte 3*, which would now hold responsibility for its direction and allocated forces, while 1./Kü.Fl.Gr. 706 was transferred to *Luftflotte* 5. With this order, which was annotated as being made 'in general in accordance with the proposal made by the C-in-C Kriegsmarine to the C-in-C Luftwaffe', the independent naval air arm ceased to exist. From 28 May KGr. 506 was incorporated into the Luftwaffe's maritime strike *Geschwader* KG 26, eliminating the final force over which *F.d.Luft* exercised any kind of jurisdiction in the southern part of the North Sea, and leaving the office with no forces at its disposal.

8

Torpedos Los!

The Arctic and Malta Convoys and the Crimean Battle

ALTHOUGH THE TUG-OF-WAR BETWEEN the Kriegsmarine and Luftwaffe over maritime air units had all but finished, with Göring victorious as early as 1941, the conflict regarding torpedo development continued. While torpedo testing and design had rested with the Kriegsmarine there had been little forward movement beyond the original LT F5 design apart from the rudder alterations to allow its use by the He 115, the improved LT F5b (A1) becoming available from early 1941. Capable of a maximum speed of 40 knots, it became the standard Luftwaffe torpedo alongside the Italian LT F5W.

The lack of attention to development was not simply a matter of Kriegsmarine negligence. Despite ample demonstrations of the efficacy of the torpedo in the hands of Britain's Fleet Air Arm, the Luftwaffe had not taken an active interest in carrying out the required research work before 1941. Yet, when they finally did so, the Kriegsmarine strenuously resisted their efforts. Testing data already accrued by naval establishments was withheld from the Luftwaffe's Technical Division, and independent Luftwaffe co-operation with private armaments firms erupted in a petty and ridiculous bout of inter-service rivalry. As early as December 1940 Hitler had spoken to Jodl and Keitel regarding the problem, their conclusion being recorded within the *OKW* war diary:

> Any such disagreement between two parts of the Wehrmacht like this just put forward (concerning the use of aerial torpedoes – a dispute between *OKM* and *RLM*) again proves the need for a strong supreme command of the Wehrmacht. Such disputes demonstrate that differing views are held on many issues, which cannot be eliminated through discussions between the Wehrmacht parties involved . . . in this case the firing of torpedoes from aircraft did not evolve at all or even be finalised because the two parties could not agree whose task this was. Such a situation is irresponsible, for wartime decisions remain completely indifferent whether the Luftwaffe or

Kriegsmarine uses the aerial torpedoes; the only thing that matters is that the aerial torpedoes used by the Wehrmacht have the greatest chance of success.¹

The Kriegsmarine had flatly refused direct Luftwaffe requests for control of aerial torpedo testing until the end of 1941. Undeterred, the Luftwaffe finally established its own testing unit, the *Torpedoschule der Luftwaffe*, at the Grossenbrode plant on the Baltic coast, which had originally been built by the Hellmuth Walter KG company of Kiel during 1939 for testing torpedoes and steam-catapult launch systems. *Oberstleutnant* Karl Stockmann, the former *Kommandeur* of KGr. 406, was placed in command.

On 1 August 1941 the Italian Silurificio Whitehead di Fiume company received a German order for 2,000 torpedoes. As part of their trade deal the Luftwaffe was obligated to provide the factory with a complete set of machine tools and all raw materials, though logistical problems prevented this being completed before the Italian surrender in 1943, whereupon the company's factory was simply seized and relocated. Between 1942 and 1943 there was a further Luftwaffe request for development of a short torpedo of only 3.38m length for use by fighter aircraft, and, later, a wire-guided torpedo. However, these were still some years in the future when matters between the Luftwaffe and Kriegsmarine over the issue of torpedo development finally came to a head in December 1941. The subject was raised in conference within the *RLM* and finally brought before Göring, who requested that instructions be issued to Raeder 'from the highest authority' to begin negotiations over the transfer of aerial torpedo development to the Luftwaffe. Shortly thereafter, *OKW* issued a directive on the matter, discussed at *OKM*. The *SKL* War Diary recorded the result of the naval officers' meeting on 3 March.

> In compliance with the directive from the Armed Forces High Command, Operations Staff, of 9 January 1942, a detailed examination has brought about an agreement between the Commander-in-Chief, Kriegsmarine and the Commander-in-Chief, Luftwaffe on the feasibility of transferring the development and manufacture of aerial torpedoes to the Luftwaffe. On 3 March this agreement is submitted to the *OKW*, Operations Staff, in the form of a joint proposal from both branches of the service, recommending that the field of aerial torpedoes be transferred to the

authority of the Commander-in-Chief, Luftwaffe. The Commander-in-Chief, Kriegsmarine, adds the remark that, as far as releases of materiel and personnel are concerned, the Kriegsmarine has gone to the limit beyond which it can no longer be responsible for its present tasks. As soon as the Führer makes his decision the transfer can be effected without further delay.

On 11 April the Führer issued his verdict:

> The aerial torpedo weapon has proved its outstanding value to an increasing extent. It is advisable to do everything to perfect it for use by aircraft and to increase its production. I therefore order that the Kriegsmarine is to turn over to the Luftwaffe the development and production of aerial torpedoes. The transfer is to be effected based on the agreement reached between the two branches of the Wehrmacht on 3 March 1942.

Orders to this effect were issued by the Kriegsmarine's Ordnance Division, and the matter was handed completely over to Göring, who appointed a Special Commissioner to oversee Luftwaffe torpedo development, supply, training and operations. The man in mind was Martin Harlinghausen, who had finally been discharged from hospital in January 1942. An obvious choice, he was subsequently appointed Commissioner for the Aerial Torpedo Service (*Bevollmächtigter für die Lufttorpedowaffe/RLM*), and was finally able to forge ahead with improving the organisation and development of the Luftwaffe's torpedo bombers. Later, on 27 June 1942, his title would be changed from 'Office of Aerial Torpedo Inspector' to 'Office of Deputy for Aerial Torpedoes', under the direct command of Hermann Göring as Luftwaffe C-in-C. He retained the same rank and authority as a division commander, while also holding command of the aerial torpedo wing, KG 26, to which he had been posted on 6 January.

Harlinghausen also pushed for an official diplomatic request to Japan that they share their aerial torpedo technology, the Imperial Japanese Navy having had great success with the Type 91, particularly in shallow water, such as at Pearl Harbor. As part of the agreed exchange of technology between the Axis partners, the Imperial Japanese Navy despatched full blueprint plans for the Type 91 to Germany aboard the submarine *I30*, which arrived in Lorient on 5 August 1942 as part of the *Yanagi* missions. The torpedo type was designated LT 850 when in German service, but

An He 115 secured to the nearby shore by ropes and anchor. (James Payne)

although seventy were built, none were used operationally. Shallow water had been the main reason for the cancellation of planned torpedo attacks on the British Mediterranean Fleets in Gibraltar and Alexandria, drawn up during the autumn of 1941. The release height of thirty metres was deemed likely to result in torpedoes impacting the harbour floor, and the idea was abandoned. The Japanese torpedo possessed two unique characteristics that had enabled such shallow-water missions. The first was a rather elementary enhancement of wooden aerodynamic stabilisers attached to the tail fins to stabilise the torpedo in flight and ensure an angle of water entry that prevented it from going too deep. The wooden fins were designed to break away from the torpedo body upon hitting the water surface. The second feature was an anti-rolling controller and acceleration control system that prevented the torpedo rolling while in mid-air and enhanced the effect of the on-board gyroscope, allowing a launch height of twenty metres, a water depth of twenty metres and launch speed of 180 knots.

Harlinghausen instigated an ambitious plan to convert existing Luftwaffe units to a specialised torpedo bomber force comprising approximately 230 aircraft. The onset of winter and storms and ice within the Baltic showed the deficiencies of Grossenbrode as a year-round torpedo testing and training establishment, and a second centre was opened in the existing Italian torpedo training centre at Grosseto, on Tuscany's west coast, during November. The Luftwaffe contingent of this Italian centre comprised *Kampfschulgeschwader* 2, formed during October in Grossenbrode from the staff of the *Torpedoschule der*

Excellent close-up of the glazed nose of the same He 115. (James Payne)

Luftwaffe and still under Stockmann's command as *Kommodore*. His first Training Chief was the veteran *Maj.* Werner Klümper, assisted by *Oblts.* Toball, Lorenz and Fritz Müller. Situated only ten kilometres from the Tuscan coastline facing Corsica, Grosseto had been the site for Italian bomber training since 1935, the aerodrome having originally been built during the First World War for aircraft testing. From the outbreak of war the *Regia Aeronautica* had developed there a specialised torpedo training unit, and many Luftwaffe pilots had passed through its doors since 1939 as trainee guests of the *Regia Aeronautica*. Using the target ship *Citta di Genova*, tactics and technique were finely tuned, and Grosseto was destined remain the Luftwaffe's principle torpedo bomber school until June 1943, when an intense bombing raid by the United States Army Air Force (USAAF) on 20 May, and steadily increasing Allied air activity over the region, forced a move to the Latvian airfield at Spilve, north of Riga.

In addition, the testing site *Erprobungsstellung Süd*, intended for the testing of air torpedoes and underwater weapons, had been established in Foggia, Italy, during the second half of 1941. However, because of unfavourable conditions, work was generally carried out instead at Grosseto. At the end of February 1942 *Erprobungsstellung Süd* transferred to Cazaux, in France, south-west of Bordeaux, which became operational in May and was commanded by *Hptm.* Heinz 'Henno' Schlockermann. The ballistic properties of various types of bombs and containers were measured during test flights, as well as target equipment and bombing. Allied air raids in March and September 1944 severely damaged the centre's facilities and several aircraft, and on 10 October 1944 *Erprobungsstellung Süd* was officially dissolved.

By September 1942 Harlinghausen had organised a logistical support network that could provide for torpedo operations in every theatre of action, with company-sized groups of torpedo technicians located in Saki (Crimea), Catania (Sicily, with a small subsidiary support unit on Crete), Grosseto, Sorreisa and Bardufoss (Northern Norway), and Banak (with a small subsidiary unit in Petsamo) and Rennes (France).

During a three-week course at Grosseto, Luftwaffe crews were trained in the use of the aerial torpedo carried by the Heinkel He 111H and the newly developed Ju 88A-4/Torp. aircraft, the two types found best suited to such operations. The first Ju 88A-4 had been trialled and tested in Travemünde and found suitable for the task, and a crew from 3./KGr. 126 became the first to convert successfully to the type in Germany, after handing over their outdated He 115 at the beginning of 1942. The Ju 88A-4/Torp. had two PVC torpedo racks fitted in place of the underwing bomb racks, each capable of carrying a single 1,686lb LT F5b torpedo. An eventual dedicated torpedo-carrying production variant of this aircraft was the Ju 88A-17, which had the ventral gondola removed, a torpedo-aiming mechanism accommodated in a housing on the starboard side of the nose, and the crew reduced to three.

One of the two original Luftwaffe maritime units, I./KG 26 began conversion to torpedo bombers and had completed this by June 1942, whereupon its forty-two He 111s were moved to the airfields of Banak and Bardufoss in northern Norway. The unit was soon placed under the command of highly-experienced pilot *Maj.* Werner Klümper, who had been their chief instructor in Grosseto. *Hauptmann* Heinrich Möller was given command of III./KG.26, the next unit to convert, which changed from the He 111 to the faster Ju 88A-4/Torp. before being posted to Banak. From there the combined strength of KG 26's torpedo units would be used against the Anglo-American 'PQ' convoys to the Soviet Union, which were beginning to gather pace.

Within the Mediterranean, only the *Staffel* 6./KG 26 had previously converted to the torpedo bomber He 111H-4./6 (Torp.) during February 1941, but by April 1942 the remainder of *Maj.* Horst Beyling's II.*Gruppe* had followed suit. The Luftwaffe's brief supremacy over the Mediterranean following initial successes of Greece, Crete and the Malta bombardment had already eroded. Following the diversion of forces from the central to eastern Mediterranean and the new requirements on the Russian Front, control of the Sicilian narrows had been lost, and Rommel's supplies suffered accordingly as, despite its best efforts, the *Regia Aeronautica* was unable to subdue Malta or counter Allied air forces that were building in power now that the United States had entered the war on the Allied side.

During October 1941 the Royal Navy had been able to create Force K in Malta from the light cruisers HMS *Aurora* and *Penelope* and the destroyers HMS *Lance* and *Lively*, to operate against Italian supply convoys heading for North Africa. Their most stunning success came during the night of 8/9 November, against the convoy *Duisburg*, comprising two German and five Italian merchant vessels carrying 389 vehicles, 35,026 tons of munitions, 17,558 tons of fuel (including Luftwaffe aviation fuel) and associated troops and personnel. Information regarding the convoy, which was escorted by an Italian close destroyer escort and a distant cruiser and destroyer group, was betrayed by ULTRA, the ships being detected by radar (which Italian military vessels lacked) south-west of Calabria. All of the merchant ships and the destroyer *Fulmine* were sunk for no loss to the British. Three He 111s of II./KG 26 flew from Crete in an attempt to intercept Force K, but failed to locate it.

By mid-November 1941 only eighteen torpedoes were available for the aircraft of 6./KG 26 in Greece, and while two *Staffeln* that had been posted to Romania, 4./KG 26 and 5./KG 26, returned to Kalamaki, near Athens, the torpedo bombers of 6./KG 26 were moved in exchange to Saki in the Crimea during the following month.² There, they operated against Soviet shipping in Sevastopol and the Caucasian harbours. Until conversion to torpedo aircraft was undertaken at Grosseto, the Luftwaffe maritime strikes within the Mediterranean were limited to bombs. With these the Mediterranean aircraft of II./KG 26 pushed their activity into the Red Sea to attack ships at anchor and awaiting transit of the Suez Canal, temporarily blocked by the wreck of the 5,856-ton British tanker *Tynefield*, which had struck a German mine on 5 October. *Abwehr* intelligence had detected a build-up of enemy troops in Egypt, and anticipated the presence of troopships, notably the RMS *Queen Mary* carrying Australian forces to the Middle East. The Heinkels were despatched on armed reconnaissance missions, and during the early morning darkness of 6 October two aircraft of 5./KG 26 found moored merchant ships and attacked, sinking the 4,898-ton SS *Thistlegorm* at anchor at Sha'ab Ali, in the Strait of Jubal south of the Sinai Peninsula (in what the British designated 'Safe Anchorage F'). The merchant ship was the largest of those present, and both Heinkels broke away to head for base, low on fuel after failing to find any troopships. *Thistlegorm* was carrying ammunition and equipment as well as two steam locomotives and medical supplies, and the stored ammunition detonated and sent the ship down in minutes. Nine men were killed, and the survivors were rescued by HMS *Carlisle*. One of the two attacking aircraft, *Lt*. Heinrich Mengel's He 111H-5, 1H+JN, was subsequently hit by anti-aircraft fire and crashed. Mengel and at least one other crewman, *Uffz*. Johannes Haubold, were taken prisoner and later held at the Murchison PoW camp in Australia.³

Two days later, bombers of 4./KG 26 attacked 'Safe Anchorage H' at Zafarana, in the Gulf of Suez, and sank the 3,963-ton SS *Rosalie Moller*, carrying 4,680 tonnes of coal from Durham. Once again an aircraft was lost, this time *Fw.* Albert Schindler's Heinkel, shot down by anti-aircraft fire and its crew captured.

Despite Rommel's early North African success, the tide of battle had swung relentlessly back and forth throughout 1941. The Libyan ports available to receive supplies were small, limiting the number of ships that could offload at any given time, and convoys were frequently being intercepted by resurgent Royal Navy forces at Malta. The further Rommel advanced east towards victory, the longer his straggling overland supply lines became, and the greater the requirement for fuel. In December, as the invasion of the Soviet Union stalled before Moscow, *Generalfeldmarschall* Kesselring's *Luftflotte* 2 staff and *Generaloberst* Bruno Loerzer's II.*Fliegerkorps* were moved from the central Russian front to Italy and Sicily to reinforce the Mediterranean battle. Kesselring established his headquarters in the Villa Falconieri, overlooking Frascati near Rome, and was designated *Oberbefehlshaber Süd*, responsible for operations by II. and X.*Fliegerkorps* as well as *Fliegerführer Afrika*. The new *Kommodore* of KG 26, *Oberst* Ernst August Roth, was also the first officer to hold the post of *Fliegerführer Sizilien*, a relatively brief position within the Luftwaffe hierarchy, designed to bridge the gap between Kesselring's advance arrival and that of his entire *Luftflotte* staff from the Russian Front.[4]

December also saw further restructuring of Luftwaffe maritime units as a part of a general shuffling of units. *Oberst* Ernst-August Roth's Heinkel He 111H-equipped KG 28, which had been based in the Soviet Union, was disbanded and its constituent parts redesignated.[5] On 15 December I./KG 28, which was based at Seschtschinskaja Airfield, ninety kilometres north-west of Bryansk, was renamed III./KG 26, the existing III./KG 26 being renamed II./KG 100. Meanwhile, 1./KG 28, which had been moved during November to Kalamaki in Greece, became 7./KG 26. Within six months this would change once again, 7./KG 26 becoming 4./KG 26, and the most recent incarnation of III./KG 26, which had undergone torpedo training in Grossetto, being renamed I./KG 1, while another new III./KG 26 was formed by the intake and redsignation of KGr. 506 in April 1942, now equipped with Ju 88A-4/ Torp. bombers after two months at Grosseto, and beginning torpedo operations from Rennes under the control of *Fliegerführer Atlantik*. The former *Staffelkapitän* of 2./KGr 506, *Hptm.* Ernst-Heinrich Thomsen, became the new *Gruppenkommandeur*, and led six aircraft of his *Gruppe* into action on its first torpedo mission from Rennes during the night of

TORPEDOS LOS!

A Ju 88 of *Kampfgruppe* 506 loaded with torpedoes, showing the plywood extensions fitted to the rudder to prevent rolling upon entering the water.

3 August, attacking the small Convoy PW196 south-west of the Scilly Isles at 2300hrs. The merchant ships were already being harassed by German S-boats when the bombers attacked. Although the Luftwaffe crews claimed the sinking of six ships totalling 20,000GRT, and were credited by *OKW* with three, only the 5,800GRT tanker *El Ciervo* was hit by an air-launched torpedo, flooding the engine room and stokehold. The Fourth Engineer was posted as missing, presumed killed. The *El Ciervo* was able to limp into Plymouth Harbour, where the unexploded torpedo was found still lodged in the ship's stern. Not until the late summer of 1942 would III./KG 26 be transferred to Banak, Norway, for action against the PQ convoy route.[6]

Mediterranean torpedo operations began afresh in November 1941. Four Heinkels took off from Heraklion to search for reported convoy traffic east of Marsa Matruh. One aircraft turned back with mechanical problems and the remaining three became separated, two finding nothing as darkness fell, but the third sighted five destroyers heading east at high speed. Two LT F5W torpedoes were launched after an approach under heavy anti-aircraft fire, one missing completely and later sighted beached on the shoreline, and the other disappearing completely. While returning to Crete the Heinkel crew spotted a single large freighter under destroyer escort, but were unable to attack, now bereft of torpedoes and vulnerable to escort anti-aircraft fire during a purely strafing run that would have had limited effect on the ship's structural integrity.

Further torpedo patrols were made over the following weeks, seeking both military and merchant targets, but they achieved nothing, being frustrated by periodically rough seas, escorting Fulmar fighters or an inability to locate target ships. Not until 2 December did an He 111 from Heraklion report a definite hit on a merchant ship and another a possible on a destroyer, both of them erroneous, as no confirmed aerial torpedo hits from the aircraft of II./KG 26 or 1./KG 28 within the Mediterranean were registered by the Allies during November and December 1941. Dive-bombing Ju 88s of II./LG 1 claimed hits on steamers, but were also incorrect. Mistakenly credited to the Luftwaffe was a successful attack by an Italian S.79 torpedo bomber of 279ª *Squadriglia Aerosiluranti*, flown by Capt Giulio Marini, on 1 December. Three British destroyers had been stationed north of Derna to intercept Italian destroyers running supplies

A bomb-carrying Ju 88 in flight over the North African coastline.

from Navarin to the small Libyan port, and it was these that were attacked by a trio of S.79s. HMS *Jackal* was hit and damaged by a single torpedo. The British armed boarding ship SS *Chakdina*, part of Convoy TA1 from embattled Tobruk to Alexandria, was also attacked by Italian S.79s on 5 December and sunk while carrying around 380 wounded Allied soldiers away from the overcrowded Tobruk aid stations, as well as 100 German and Italian prisoners of war and 120 crewmen. Approximately 400 men drowned as the steamer went down.[7] Meanwhile, Blenheim bombers from Malta and the ships of Force K, reinforced by two cruisers and two destroyers of Force B, continued to savage Italian supply convoys in the face of ineffective German and Italian interference.

Italian forces in North Africa, and Rommel's *Afrika Korps*, were desperately short of supplies, and on 13 December two Italian light cruisers, the *Alberto da Giusanno* and *Alberico da Barbiano*, had been sunk while carrying emergency materials and aviation fuel (in containers on the open stern deck) to Tripoli. Believed to be protected by their speed, the two ships were betrayed by broken naval codes and intercepted in what has become known as the Battle of Cape Bon. A new initiative, Convoy M41 comprising eight ships, was then launched by the Italians, but it turned into catastrophe when the submarine HMS *Upright* sank two and another pair collided later the same day. The distant covering naval force was found by the Royal Navy, and the submarine HMS *Urge* torpedoed the battleship *Vittorio Veneto*, which was damaged and forced to return to port. The remainder of M41 also turned about, and a second convoy, redesignated M42, was prepared. This comprised four cargo ships under close escort by seven destroyers and a torpedo boat, plus a close-cover force of a battleship, three light cruisers and three destroyers. A strong distant cover force of two battleships, two heavy cruisers and eleven destroyers completed this extreme show of Regia Marina strength. Aircraft of X.*Fliegerkorps* were also brought to readiness in support, and when a Ju 88 of II./LG 1 undertaking reconnaissance near the convoy's track reported approaching Royal Navy forces, twelve He 111s of II./KG 26 took off from Heraklion to intercept. Although they successfully located the enemy, poor weather spoiled all attempted attacks. The Royal Navy ships of Force K claimed a torpedo bomber shot down. Further torpedo-carrying Heinkels failed to find the British ships again, and although they were attacked by dive-bombing Junkers Ju 88s at various points throughout the day they did not suffer significant damage.

Italian aerial reconnaissance simultaneously reported a British convoy headed for Malta, and it was attacked by German torpedo aircraft from Sicily, probably drawn from those under training at Grosseto. These reported a hit on an escorting 'cruiser', but in fact it was the disguised tanker *Breconshire*, which was missed by the intended torpedo shot. In the end, after unsuccessful Luftwaffe attacks and inconclusive naval clashes, both the Axis and Allied convoys safely reached their destinations, Rommel's hard-pressed North African forces finally receiving at least a small portion of their critical supply. In fact, it was during an attempted interception of the M42 ships as they returned to Italy that Force K suffered grievous damage after blundering into an extensive Italian minefield off Tripoli which sank HMS *Neptune* and damaged HMS *Kandahar* so severely that she was later scuttled. The cruisers HMS *Aurora* and *Penelope* were also badly damaged, and Force K was virtually eliminated in a single stroke as a threat to Axis shipping. Shortly thereafter, the battleships HMS *Valiant* and *Queen Elizabeth* were disabled in Alexandria Harbour by Italian special forces, and the balance of naval power unexpectedly shifted to the Axis within the central Mediterranean for the months that followed.

During December 1941 I./KG 54 was also transferred to the Mediterranean theatre. The *Geschwader*'s II./KG 54 underwent conversion to the Ju 88A-4 at Landsberg, but returned to the Eastern Front until November 1942. Under the command of *Obstlt*. Walter Marienfeld's KG 54 Staff, KGr. 806 and KGr. 606 also arrived to bolster *Luftflotte* 2's Mediterranean maritime strike forces, as a renewed offensive against Malta, and the supply traffic that kept the island alive, was about to begin.

On the Western Front, Sperrle's *Luftflotte* 3 possessed an average of 153 aircraft in total between July and September 1941, though the number that were serviceable averaged only 63 for the same period. During the last quarter, numbers began to rise, with an average of 217 on strength and 113 ready for operations. In the second half of 1941 Sperrle's forces mounted 2,438 sorties directed against targets at sea, 1,524 against land targets, and 1,687 marine minelaying missions, for the loss of 128 aircraft.

Fliegerführer Atlantik had spread its He 111 units to The Netherlands, where they engaged British east coast convoy traffic, periodically joined by Ju 88s flying from Breton air bases. Harassing operations against British shipping within the English Channel, Bristol Channel and Irish

Sea continued, using Ju 88s, He 111s and He 115s, the last occasionally equipped with torpedoes. However, as merchant ships were given greater anti-aircraft firepower and fighter protection grew stronger, losses among the slow He 111 units became severe, so much so that III./KG 40 was soon withdrawn from combat to rebuild and begin re-equipping with Fw 200 Condors. Although a switch to night attacks reduced the number of casualties to *Fliegerführer Atlantik*, it also rendered the attacks less effective, and at no point were British coastal shipping routes closed to traffic. During the last six months of 1941 *Fliegerfuhrer Atlantik*'s aircraft mounted 963 daylight and 1,475 night-time anti-shipping sorties. While some Heinkels from III./KG.40 had been seconded to Coeler's IX.*Fliegerkorps*, II./KG 2 had begun to equip with Dornier Do 217E bombers (KG 2 becoming the only *Kampfgeschwader* to convert completely to the Do 217). Attached to the Staff of KG 30, it operated from Evreux, Normandy, on anti-shipping and minelaying missions. However, a lack of bomber units in the west, and increasingly strident calls for a resumed bombing campaign of mainland Britain in retaliation for the rising scale of RAF raids on Germany, caused most of these maritime

A disabled He 60, its floats apparently holed and taking on water.

units to become increasingly used for night area bombing. *Luftflotte* 3 protested vigorously to the *RLM* about this misdirection of specialised forces, but was completely ignored. The new III./KG 26, established in April 1942 from *Kampfgruppe* 506, was posted from Rennes to northern Norway for action against the PQ convoy route, under the command of the former *Staffelkapitän* of 7./KG 26, *Hptm.* Klaus Nocken after Thomsen was hospitalised for nearly the entire summer following a serious accident.

The Condors of KG 40 were also fast losing their effectiveness at sea. With their operational area now generally centred upon the Gibraltar convoy route, the serviceability of the Fw 200s had become so poor that an average of only five or six aircraft were operational at any one time. Concurrently, the rate of attritional loss had not lessened. On 15 June three Fw 200s of I./KG 40 attacked Convoy HG65, and only one returned. *Oberleutnant* Eric Westermann's F8+KL was hit by anti-aircraft fire and crashed in flames near Amareleja, Portugal, four bombs having been jettisoned in an attempt to lighten the aircraft's load before impact as Westermann tried to reach the small town's dusty airfield. Manuel Ramalho, son of the town pastor, Domingos Ramalho, recalled the event:

> The aeroplane, a four-engine one, was broken in pieces. A bit of a wing here, over there a part of the cockpit with two charred corpses, machine-gun bullets, engine wreckage . . . The four dropped bombs were found half-buried in the ground after having fallen within a few hundred metres of the site of the aircraft wreck at Fornilhos, and the bodies of the six crew members were found in the two biggest pieces of wreckage. The presence of a locking device had fortunately prevented the bombs from exploding.[8]

The bodies of the German crew were transported to the morgue of the Hospital de Moura, identified from documents retrieved from their pockets, and given a dignified military funeral.

The second Condor brought down while attacking the same convoy was *Lt.* Otto Gose's aircraft, which was damaged by flak and made a forced-landing on a short airstrip at Navio in Spain. The Condor had taken severe damage, its flight engineer being killed and a fuel tank badly holed. A Ju 52/3m was flown immediately from Bordeaux-Mérignac with spare parts, fuel and a supporting ground crew. They repaired the aircraft, which was able to take off and return to France on 18 June, the

Mayor of Navia receiving an award from Madrid's German ambassador for his hospitable treatment of the stranded crew. Another Condor landed briefly in Spain on 5 July, when an aircraft of 3./KG 40 put down at Tablada, damage to its flaps having increased the fuel consumption and forced an emergency landing. Quickly refuelled, the aircraft was able to depart within hours and return to Bordeaux.

Although Condors had taken part in the sinking of fifty-six ships in the first seven months of 1941, during the rest of the year only four were either sunk or badly damaged. Low-level attacks were abandoned, and high-altitude bombing techniques used instead, and although the Lotfe 7D bombsight was an outstanding addition to the Fw 200, this change considerably reduced their effectiveness. Moreover, a new threat and potential deterrent to the Condors shadowing Allied merchant convoys was posed by the introduction of Fighter Catapult Ships (FCS) and Catapult Aircraft Merchant (CAM) ships, able to launch a single defensive fighter (but not to recover it). In fact only one Condor was actually brought down by a Hurricane from a CAM ship, when, on 1 November 1942, Fg Off Norman Taylor shot down *Oblt*. Arno Gross's F8+DS of 7./KG 40, killing all seven of the crew.

On the other hand, the introduction of the British escort carrier HMS *Audacity* (the captured and converted German merchant vessel SS *Hannover*) during September 1941 was a landmark in battling the German aircraft. Carrying eight Fleet Air Arm Grumman Martlets of 802 Sqn, *Audacity* took part in only four Gibraltar convoys between September and December 1941, but her aircraft shot down six Condors before she was torpedoed and sunk by *U751* on 21 December.

Fliegerführer Atlantik's official combat return for November 1941 listed eight ships sunk totalling 49,200GRT, seven by KGr. 606 and only a single 200GRT trawler by III./KG 40, and twelve damaged, totalling 50,032GRT, four by KGr. 606, five by KGr. 106 and three by III./KG 40. Furthermore, a Spitfire of 74 Sqn RAF, piloted by Pt Off A. Williams, was shot down in combat twenty miles west of St David's Head at 1810hrs on 26 November by a Ju 88 of KGr. 106, Williams being killed. In total, sixty-two Fw 200 sorties had been flown for *B.d.U.*, including eight 'special operations' in which *MGK West* co-operated. During the missions in support of the U-boats five convoys had been sighted and reported, beacons being transmitted for the benefit of Dönitz's boats. On behalf of *MGK West*, *Fliegerführer Atlantik* had mounted thirty-four Fw 200 sorties (ten in conjunction with tasks for *B.d.U.*), and fifty-eight

He 115 reconnaissance sorties against enemy naval forces or escorting German coastal traffic and incoming blockade runners from the Far East. Additionally, 103 ASW sorties were flown by Ar 196 floatplanes off the French Atlantic coast and seven Ju 88s, three He 115s and three Ar 196s were used in *Seenot* searches for downed aircrew. Forty-six Ju 88 and ten Bf 110 reconnaissance missions had been directed against British coastal convoy traffic to the east, south and west of the British Isles, and two Fw 200, sixty-four He 111, forty-one He 115, one hundred and sixteen Ju 88 and six Ar 196 combat missions were ordered by *Fliegerführer Atlantik* against targets at sea. An additional fifteen He 111 and thirteen Ju 88 missions had been tasked by *Luftflotte* 3 against land targets. Fifteen air battles had been recorded during the month of November. Four involved Fw 200s, six involved He 115s, five involved Ju 88s, one involved an He 111 and another involved a Bf 110. December 1941 yielded an even less successful combat experience for *Fliegerführer Atlantik*. A single ship was claimed as sunk by *Küstenfliegergruppe* 406 on the 19th, but the tanker *Lucellum* was only damaged five miles from Bardsey Island, although six crew and two gunners were killed during the attack. The Royal Fleet Auxiliary ship was towed into Holyhead and repaired.

On 17 December the only known operational mission by torpedo equipped Fw 200 Condors took place. At Martin Harlinghausen's bidding, six Fw 200s had undergone modification for use as torpedo carriers. Two torpedoes were carried, one under each outer wing, requiring modification of the flaps to accommodate the torpedo cylinder. Although the lightweight airframe was found to be capable of carrying the weapon, stability was greatly affected, as was the aircraft's general performance. A combat trial was made against British convoy traffic on the Gibraltar route, but the attack was swiftly abandoned after the first torpedoes launched passed wide of the mark. All six aircraft were subsequently relegated to transport duties, and use of the Condor as a torpedo carrier was never attempted again.

During December *Oberst* von Wild departed from the temporary position as *Fliegerführer Atlantik* that he had occupied during Harlinghausen's hospitalisation, being transferred to the Black Sea. In his place came *Generalleutnant* Ulrich Kessler, appointed on 5 January 1942 to a position he would hold until April 1944 and the dissolution of the post. His appointment was not a happy one, as the supportive emphasis that had previously been placed on developing the capabilities of *Fliegerführer Atlantik* was already diminishing in the face of improved

Kriegsmarine observer Rolf Thomsen in Luftwaffe uniform before his transfer to the U-boat service.

Allied strategy and tactics and increasing demands on a thinly-spread Luftwaffe. *Fliegerführer Atlantik* had become a second-tier position that lapsed into a virtual doldrums as operational exigencies drew Luftwaffe attention elsewhere. During January 1942 Kessler recorded only three attacks on merchant ships; two by *Küstenfliegergruppe* 406 which damaged two freighters, and a single 4,000GRT ship claimed as sunk by KGr. 106.

During the latter half of 1941 the Ju 88s of I. and II./KG 30 carried on the fight around the coastline of Great Britain, mounting armed reconnaissance missions against coastal naval units and convoy traffic, although they were increasingly diverted to attack conventional land targets. *Hauptmann* Eberhard Roeger, *Gruppenkommandeur* of II./KG 30, had been killed in action on 3 July while still based at Banak, shot down by a Soviet Polikarpov I-16 fighter of the 72nd Composite Aviation Regiment flown by Lt Vasiliy Volovikov. Roeger was replaced by Knight's Cross holder *Hptm*. Sigmund-Ulrich Freiherr von Gravenreuth, and the *Gruppe* continued flying strikes against Murmansk and Soviet coastal convoys, sinking the 1,660-ton destroyer *Stremilteny* in the Kola Inlet on 20 July before being transferred to Stavanger alongside I./KG 30 for North Sea operations until the end of September.

A Ju 88 of *Kampfgruppe* 806, formed from the transfer to Luftwaffe control of *Küstenfliegergruppe* 806. This aircraft, M7+CK, belongs to 2./KGr. 806.

The ex-*Küstenflieger Kampfgruppen* 106, 506 and 606 had all been present within the North Sea until they were posted elsewhere or amalgamated into different *Kampfgeschwader*, while the three seaplane *Staffeln* of *Küstenfliegergruppe* 906 were based once again in the west, stretched between France and Norway; 1./Kü.Fl.Gr. 906 at Brest-Hourtin, 2./Kü.Fl.Gr. 906 at Brest-Süd and 3./Kü.Fl.Gr. 906 at Tromsø. Like the whittling-away of KG 40, losses around the British Isles had been severe, more than sixty Junkers being destroyed during the last six months of 1941, particularly while engaged in conventional bombing raids. Improved RAF nightfighter units, anti-aircraft defences, searchlight belts and radar capabilities all added to the deck stacked against the German fliers. To make matters worse, the British had even begun to use the Luftwaffe's own navigation beacons against them.

To assist direction finding while bombing British targets, the Luftwaffe made use of radio beacons strategically positioned at various French locations. British scientists were able to receive the signals and then re-radiate them, amplified, using transmitters located in Britain. The beacons' original positions were therefore effectively falsified by the British transmitters, which were known as 'Masking Beacons' or 'Meacons'. It is believed that this caused three Ju 88s of KGr. 106 to fly into the ground in Yorkshire of the night of 9 July, after their crews were fooled into believing that they were over the North Sea. Not long after there came a more spectacular success, when a transmitter at Lympshan re-radiated the Brest beacon and caused *Uffz*. Wolfgang Hosic to land his Ju 88, 4D+DL of 3./KG 30, at Lulsgate Bottom on 24 July, during a bombing mission from Poulmic against Birkenhead. Low on fuel, the crew were convinced by the 'Meacon' that they were over France, and put down at 0620hrs, whereupon Hosic and his crew were taken prisoner. Their aircraft later underwent testing and evaluation bearing the British military serial EE205, and then joined the Enemy Aircraft Flight at the Central Fighter Establishment. A second Ju 88, M2+MK of *Kampfgruppe* 106, flown by *Uffz*. Erwin Herms, was also misdirected and landed at Chivenor in Devon on 26 November following an anti-shipping strike in the Irish Sea. Herms and his crew were likewise captured.

Germany had reached a fresh military crisis point at the end of 1941. Hitler had declared war on the USA, formalising a *de facto* state of hostilities that had existed since the previous year, particularly manifest in the Atlantic U-boat war. The Soviet Union had not been defeated but had rallied, aided by the incomparably severe Russian winter, throwing the Wehrmacht back from the suburbs of Moscow, and American and British aid was beginning to shuttle into Soviet Arctic ports, bolstering the Red Army's fight against the invaders. An initial *ad hoc* convoy, codenamed *Dervish* and consisting of six escorted merchant ships loaded with supplies that included fifteen crated Hurricane fighters, had arrived in Archangelsk on 31 August 1941, and the aircraft carrier HMS *Argus* had simultaneously delivered twenty-four RAF Hurricanes that were flown off the deck when within range and landed at Vaenga airfield near Murmansk. The paucity of Kriegsmarine forces and Luftwaffe strength in the far north allowed the convoy to go unnoticed.

The value of the Russian convoys was not purely military but political as well. In terms of total wartime tonnage received by the Soviet Union, approximately 23 per cent arrived via the Arctic convoys; 27 per cent via the United States through the Persian Gulf, a route active from mid-1942; and fully 50 per cent through the Pacific to Vladivostock, again from mid-1942. However, during 1941 the Arctic convoy route was the only workable method of assisting the Soviet Union, and the symbolism and military value of those convoys compelled the establishment of the 'PQ' convoys after the success of *Dervish*; convoys designated 'QP' and made up of the merchantmen returning to Great Britain in ballast. PQ1 departed Hvalfjord, Iceland, on 29 September, all eleven merchant ships arriving in Archangelsk on 11 October. The empty ships of *Dervish* constituted part of QP1, which headed back to Great Britain on 28 September, the remainder of the convoy being made up of empty Soviet merchants travelling to collect supplies. It was the beginning of what would become one of the most arduous convoy routes undertaken by the Allies during the Second World War, and the Royal Navy's Home Fleet was already overstretched when the order for Murmansk convoy escort was given. Protection for the PQ convoys was split into three groups. A Home Fleet escort handed the PQ ships over to close escort at Iceland, while heavy ships sailed as distant support. Nearer to Murmansk an eastern convoy escort would take over. By 20 December forty-seven ships had successfully reached Archangelsk in six convoys, only a single ship, the MV *Briarwood*, being forced to return to Iceland after suffering damage from ice as part of PQ3. To oppose them, the post of *Admiral Nordmeer* had been established in October 1941 as a part of *MGK Nord*, *Admiral* Hubert Schmundt occupying the position until August 1942. He was responsible for U-boat deployment and co-ordination of airborne reconnaissance within the Arctic Seas from his headquarters aboard the *Tanga* in Kirkenes.

On 5 March a reconnaissance aircraft spotted Allied Convoy PQ12 and, to join four U-boats already at sea, Hitler authorised the battleship *Tirpitz* and three destroyers to sail from their Norwegian billet and intercept. However, *Tirpitz* failed to find the convoy, which had been diverted on to an alternative course once the Admiralty had discovered that *Tirpitz* had put to sea. Instead, the Home Fleet was despatched to attack the battleship, which was sighted by a destroyer on 9 March and attacked by carrier-borne torpedo aircraft from HMS *Victorious*. *Tirpitz* successfully combed the tracks of the incoming torpedoes and escaped, while three KG 30 Ju 88s attempted to bomb the carrier in return, but narrowly missed with dive-bombing attacks. A single Soviet PQ12 straggler was sunk by the German destroyers and an escorting armed whaler capsized after severe icing of the superstructure before the bulk of the convoy arrived at Murmansk on 12 March. The following day *Obfw.* Hans Hermann's Ju 88A-5, 4D+IK of 2./KG 30, was shot down by the Soviet ASW whaler *Stefa* while attempting to attack the Soviet steamer *Sevaples*, both vessels having straggled from PQ12 owing to thick surface ice. Hermann and his crew, observer *Obfw.* Walter Mans, wireless operator *Uffz.* Werner Pfülle and gunner *Fw.* Heinrich Schlüter, were all killed, though whether by gunfire, the impact with the sea or freezing to death within minutes of being in the frigid Arctic water remains unclear.

The action against *Tirpitz* illustrated the weakness of German naval and air forces within the Arctic region. Strong enemy task forces were able to operate thus far without fear of effective air attack, and Hitler supported Raeder's view that greater Luftwaffe maritime forces were needed in the area, even at the expense of *Fliegerführer Atlantik*'s operational strength. The decision was made once more to accelerate construction of the carrier *Graf Zeppelin*, to allow formation of a task force comprising *Scharnhorst*, *Tirpitz*, *Graf Zeppelin*, two heavy cruisers and twelve to fourteen destroyers. However, the resumption of work on the stalled carrier project already faced fresh obstacles, including the fact that the previous Bf 109 carrier adaptation had been based on the now-obsolete Bf 109E. The fresh problems were discussed between Raeder and Hitler in conference on 16 April 1942.

> The total time necessary to complete the carrier does not depend on completing the hull and engines, but on changing the flight installations for the use of aircraft adapted from the Ju 87D and BF 109F. About two years are required to develop, construct, and test the catapults necessary for these aircraft. If it is possible to convert the existing catapults the time limit will be reduced by six months . . . The Führer points out that in general the Wehrmacht set their requirements too high.
>
> There are no torpedo aeroplanes. If a new type of special carrier aircraft is developed, mass production cannot be attained until 1946! The Naval Staff maintains that the results of our efforts so far do not justify continuing work on the carrier.[9]

Production of the Fieseler Fi 167 had been halted back in 1940, although development of a torpedo-carrying version of the Ju 87D had already begun during December 1941, envisioned for use within the Mediterranean against the Malta convoy route. Capable of carrying an F5W torpedo, one Ju 87D-1/Torp, coded BK+EF, had been transferred for trials to Travemünde on 16 December, though these were delayed for two weeks because of bad weather. Designated Ju 87 V25/Torp, the aircraft was a standard production Ju 87D-1 airframe, equipped with an underwing PVC 1006B torpedo rack. After a series of successful tests the Ju 87 was moved to Grosseto for be put further through its paces. However, when all further work on the *Graf Zeppelin* was once again cancelled, in February 1943, a provisional order for production models was also rendered invalid. Not one of the Ju 87Ds that had been converted for use as torpedo carriers was ever used in combat.

During March 1942 Raeder had requested that, in the absence of an operational aircraft carrier, Hitler order Göring to reinforce Norwegian Luftwaffe strength to cover fleet operations, and the Führer readily agreed. During October I./KG 30 had already returned to Banak, *Hptm.* 'Hajo' Herrmann's III./KG 30 being posted from the Mediterranean to the Arctic Circle in March, though 7./KG 30 was based at Trondheim, further to the south, and von Gravenreuth's II./KG 30 was moved during the following month. Within I./KG 26, based at Banak and Bardufoss, there were twelve crews available for torpedo operations with their He 111H-6 aircraft, as well as 1./Kü.Fl.Gr. 406 with eight He 115 torpedo seaplanes (of which only two were operational), and 1./Kü.Fl. Gr. 906 with six He 115s. Göring immediately ordered *Luftflotte* 5 and all its attached units to co-ordinate with Schmundt in operations against Murmansk convoy traffic. When a PQ convoy was expected, long-range reconnaissance by Condors of *Hptm.* Edmund Daser's I./KG 40, flying from Trondheim-Værnes (where they had been quickly re-based during March, despite this move having previously been denied to Dönitz), were to cover the sea area between Iceland, Jan Mayen Island, Bear Island and the North Cape. Whatever *Küstenflieger* aircraft were available would augment the reconnaissance operations at shorter range. All available maritime strike aircraft were withdrawn from active missions over the Finnish Front and based between Banak, Bardufoss and Kirkenes in preparation for convoy interception.

The Ju 88s of KG 30 were at first used for reconnaissance flights under the control of *Fliegerführer Lofoten*, *Oberst* Roth. Roth's command had no permanently assigned units, but instead received whatever was required for specific anti-shipping operations whenever the situation arose. On his own initiative, Herrmann once again ordered extra firepower to be installed in his *Gruppe*'s Ju 88s.

> A bomber diving and a ship under steam looked to each other like a moving dot in their respective sights. The difference was that on the ship's deck there were numerous heavy-calibre guns pointing at the bomber, while the bomber had only one feeble machine-gun pointing forward. It seemed to me to be advisable to augment the single machine-gun fitted as standard in the cockpit with two fixed guns that I could fire when I was at the controls of the aircraft. During steep or shallow diving attacks

I could fire at a rate of 1,800 rounds per minute from each gun, aiming at the upper decks and flak crews, who were usually unprotected, before releasing the bombs using the same sight. We equipped all our aircraft in this way, and whenever we attacked the convoys in either *Staffel* or *Gruppe* formation each crew was under orders to pick out its allotted steamer and engage it with a brief burst of continuous fire.[10]

On 20 March PQ13, consisting of nineteen merchant ships, set sail from Reykjavík, Iceland, with two destroyers, two trawlers and three Soviet armed whalers as close escort, commanded by the covering cruiser HMS *Trinidad*. A Heavy Cover Force of battleships, cruisers, aircraft carrier and destroyers guarded against any threat of the *Tirpitz* sailing once more. An erroneous report that the German battleship had put to sea had already forced PQ13's original planned departure from Iceland on 18 March to be aborted. The day after PQ13 sailed, returning convoy QP9 put out of Murmansk, escorted by the cruiser HMS *Nigeria*, the destroyer HMS *Offa* and two minesweepers. Gale-force winds and blinding snowstorms dispersed PQ13, and on the morning of 27 March three ships were sighted south of Bear Island by a BV 138 flying boat of 2./Kü.Fl.Gr. 406. Three U-boats of the '*Ziethen*' group were ordered to intercept, and *U209* was the first to engage, making a stern torpedo attack on the Polish steamer *Tobruk*, but missed. The weather moderated that afternoon, and Ju 88s of KG 30 began targeting stragglers separated during the storms. A pair of Junkers found the Panamanian registered 4,807-ton SS *Raceland*, whose Master, Norwegian Sverre Brekke, had decided to take the most direct route to Murmansk after losing the rest of PQ13, despite the passage taking the ship close to the Norwegian coast and Banak Airfield. After circling overhead, one of the Ju 88s dived and dropped two bombs which, though they missed the starboard side of the ship by twenty metres or so, created a shock wave sufficient to break loose part of a cargo of nitroglycerin, which exploded, blowing a hole in the forward starboard hull and stopping the engine. Defending machine-gun fire had failed to hit the Ju 88, and as *Raceland* sank slowly by the stern the surviving crew abandoned ship, the steamer disappearing into the icy water with the remainder of her cargo of explosives, tanks, trucks and aircraft.[11] A second straggler, the 7,007-ton British SS *Empire Ranger*, was also sunk by the Junkers, all forty-seven crewmen abandoning ship and being rescued by the German destroyer *Z25*, one of three from the 8.*Zerstörerflottille* that had joined the attack on PQ13.[12] Other KG 30 aircraft damaged the Panamanian SS *Ballot* and narrowly missed several other ships that were twisting frantically in evasive manoeuvring. The freighter *Ballot* lost steam following the attacks and fell away from a large body of ships that had gathered. Sixteen men prematurely abandoned ship and were picked up by the convoy vice-commodore's ship, *Induna*. Unfortunately, *Induna*'s attempt to corral five other vessels, including *Ballot*, into a group after the storms had abated caused her to become briefly stuck in ice, and she was found and sunk by *U376*. As weather conditions deteriorated once more, torpedo bombers of I./KG 26 attempted their first operations. but failed. Half of the flights were cancelled and the remainder found nothing in appalling visibility.

Despite the new bad weather front, the German destroyers had continued the attack. Lashed by strong winds and thick snowstorms, they sank the 4,687-ton SS *Bateau* before coming under attack by destroyer HMS *Fury* and cruiser HMS *Trinidad* in the early hours. *Z26* was badly damaged, and later sank following further attacks by the Royal Navy and the Russian destroyer *Sokrushitelny*. Ironically, HMS *Trinidad* was disabled by one of her own torpedoes after the weapon's gyroscope froze and sent it circling. As the German destroyers disengaged, so too did the British; *Trinidad* limped for the Kola Inlet, where it was patched up just sufficient to allow a return to Britain. From the sinking of *Z26* the remaining German destroyers rescued eighty-eight survivors, while *U378* found a further eight and headed for Kirkenes. By the time that the surviving ships of PQ13 began to arrive in Murmansk they had lost five to enemy action; two to aircraft, two to U-boats and one to a destroyer. However, their trials were not yet over, as two surviving ships, the SS *Empire Starlight* and SS *New Westminster City*, were sunk during a Luftwaffe attack on Murmansk Harbour on 3 April, the Polish merchant ship *Tobruk* being severely damaged.

The first attack on a PQ convoy had passed off successfully, but hardly spectacularly, for the Germans. However, they abjectly failed against its successor, PQ14, in April. After the convoy was detected by a patrolling BV 138, multiple bombing attacks were vectored towards it, but with no success, and five aircraft were shot down. A single ship was sunk by U-boat attack before the convoy reached Murmansk. Ironically, the inbound convoy was decimated not by the Luftwaffe or Kriegsmarine, but by the weather. During the night of 10 April PQ14 encountered heavy ice south of Jan Mayen, which once again dispersed the convoy body. Many merchant ships suffered ice damage and others failed to rejoin the main group, so much so that sixteen ships returned to Iceland, leaving only eight to continue to the Soviet Union.

The returning convoy QP10, which had departed on the same day that PQ14 left Reykyavik, suffered greater losses at German hands. Four ships were sunk, two by KG 30. A day after leaving Murmansk the SS *Empire Cowper* was bombed and sunk by II./KG 30, killing nine crewmen, and the freighter SS *Stone Street* was damaged and returning to port before a violent snowstorm forced the aircraft to break off the engagement. Before they departed, however, fierce defensive fire from the merchants and their escort shot down three Ju 88s and damaged others, including 4D+AC, flown by *Gruppenkommandeur Hptm.* Sigmund-Ulrich Freiherr von Gravenreuth, who was seriously wounded in the leg. After nursing his battered aircraft back to base, von Gravenreuth was hospitalised and his leg amputated below the right knee. Although he returned to active duty with II./KG 30 during October, fitted with a false leg, his leadership was ground-based.

Two days after the first attack, QP10 was found by a reconnaissance Fw 200 and attacked by twenty Ju 88s. An aircraft of III./KG 30 scored a direct hit on the stern of the SS *Harpalion*, blowing the rudder away and rendering the ship uncontrollable. Abandoned, she was later found and sunk by *U435* of the '*Robbenschlag*' group. Although the convoy was trailed by the Fw 200, which in turn was relieved by a BV 138, further attacks yielded no successes.

In Britain the Commander-in-Chief of the Home Fleet, Admiral Sir John Tovey, pleaded with the Admiralty to reduce the size of the PQ convoys, as the Luftwaffe and U-boats were now beginning to show a significant presence in the north of Norway. He urged the measure to be taken at least until the seasonal pack ice that forced ships nearer to occupied Norway had receded, but was ignored, as political pressure on supplying the Soviet Union was intense, rendering Royal Navy operational considerations a secondary concern. Convoy PQ15, comprising twenty-five heavily escorted merchant vessels, sailed in late April for Murmansk. Nine U-boats of the '*Strauchritter*' group gathered in a patrol line within the Barents Sea south of Bear Island, lying in wait for PQ15 or QP11, which had departed from Murmansk on 28 April. After one day at sea QP11 was sighted by a Ju 88 reconnaissance flight, which began shadowing, and a KG 40 Condor found PQ15 250 miles south-west of Bear Island during the following day.

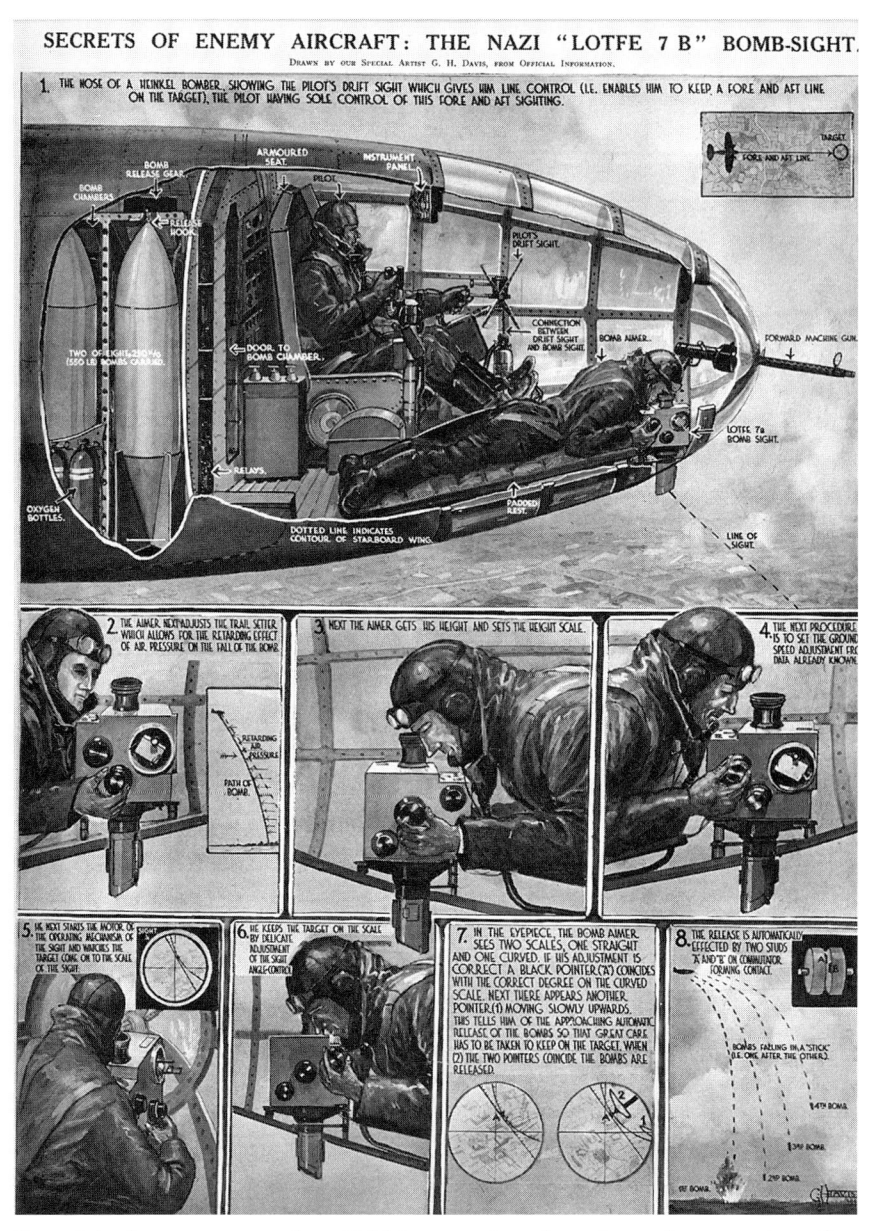

Surprisingly accurate wartime British magazine piece about the operation of the *Lotfernrohr* 7 bombsight.

Initially, German attention focused on the westbound convoy, and four KG 30 Ju 88s unsuccessfully attacked QP11 150 miles south-east of Bear Island at 0540 hours on the first day of May, suffering losses that included the *Staffelkapitän* of 9./KG 30, *Hptm.* Hans Hanke, who was reported as missing in action over the White Sea in his Ju 88A-4, 4D+XT. No aircraft attacks were successful against the returning convoy, though German U-boats and destroyers later sank the escorting cruiser HMS *Edinburgh* and a Soviet merchant ship, as well as damaging three other destroyers for the loss of the destroyer *Hermann Schoemann*. However, PQ15, the largest Murmansk convoy to date, suffered three steamers sunk by I./KG 26 torpedo bombers. The 3,807-ton SS *Cape Corso* exploded, killing fifty of her fifty-six crew; the 6,153-ton *Jutland* was heavily damaged and abandoned, with one passenger killed, the drifting wreck later being torpedoed by *U251*; and the 5,484-ton SS *Botavon*, torpedoed by acting *Gruppenkommandeur Oblt.* Bernd Eicke, was heavily damaged and later scuttled by the convoy escort, twenty-one crewmen being killed. Chief Petty Officer John Govey was aboard *Botavon* as a naval signaller:

> We couldn't hide our presence for very long before we were shadowed by the Blohm & Voss plane that circled round constantly from dawn to dusk, keeping a healthy distance from the guns of our escort. Then the fun began, air raid warning, and in they came, fifty plus, it seemed to go on for ever, as soon as the last one left another crowd could be seen on the horizon. Things quietened down as we began to go through some snow flurries and visibility was down.
>
> Still at full action stations (3 May 42) we could hear aircraft circling round, and after an hour and a half had got quite used to our air escort. Suddenly there was action; through a break in the snow came two Heinkel 111s and all hell let loose, they came in abeam of us and dropped torpedoes and flew over our bow from starboard to port. Meanwhile, as soon as I saw the torpedoes dropped I hoisted 'Emergency turn to Starboard'. By this time the air was full of flak and tracer bullets flying across the ship, I felt quite naked as the halliard I was holding fell limply in my hand, severed by the tracer bullets from the Russian *Krassin*. I immediately dropped on my face, but a glance in front of me made me realise that I had the shelter of canvas. I jumped up in time to see one Heinkel hit and plunge into the sea on our port bow, I looked to starboard and there were two tell-tale streaks of torpedoes coming towards us.

Slowly! Oh, so slowly we seemed to turn to comb the tracks, we had about 10 degrees to go. Then crash! the torpedo hit No.2 hold just forward of the bridge with a roar which was deafening, a huge wall of black shot up from the water and the ship shuddered with the explosion. We instantly heeled over to port, over we went, 30°, 40°. Christ! I thought we are going to turn over, 45° and then slowly back to an even keel. 'Away to the boats lads', yelled the Chief Officer.

Two of the attacking aircraft were shot down, and third crashed while returning to its Norwegian airfield. The damaged HMS *Trinidad* departed from Murmansk on 13 May after makeshift repairs had been completed, under escort by four destroyers, and was sighted during the following morning by an Fw 200 Condor. At 1852 hours two BV 138s relieved the shadowing Condor, and the first wave of a combined attack by Heinkel torpedo bombers and Junkers dive-bombers began at 2200hrs. Once again, Govey was part of the action, as he was returning to Great Britain aboard the escorting destroyer HMS *Matchless*:

[We] formed a screen on the *Trinidad* which flew the flag of Rear Admiral Bonham-Carter. We hadn't been under way very long before the fun began, and we were banging away at Junker 88s, it seemed for ages and ages. The skipper of *Matchless* was another cool sort, he had four signalmen covering the ship, spotting bombs in the air. As soon as a cluster looked as though they were coming in our direction we altered course. That's where I proved the theory, 'YOU DON'T HEAR THE ONE WHICH HITS YOU'. You see the bombs falling; when they are near, you lose sight of them, they hit the water, you hear the whine of their descent, followed by the noise of the explosion. It's a most peculiar feeling and not very good for the morale. At one time when we were bomb-dodging I spotted torpedo bombers dropping torpedoes a couple of miles away. I kept a good eye in that direction and duly reported 'TORPEDO TRACKS'. Leaving the torpedoes to look after themselves, the skipper calmly assessed the situation, turned to port and the menaces passed us on either side. Then disaster struck. At the end of a heavy bombing raid the *Trinidad* was hit with a bomb which penetrated to the recreation area, where a crowd of survivors were sheltering, and exploded with devastating effect. The explosion started the temporary patch leaking which had been put in at Murmansk, together with a fire which they were unable to contain, so the Admiral ordered the destroyers to take off the wounded and survivors.

> Each destroyer went alongside in turn and took their allotted numbers on board. Then we were ordered to sink her with torpedoes. We fired two fish into her and she sank, slowly and gracefully, bow first.[13]

Sixty-three British sailors were lost during the bombing of HMS *Trinidad*, including twenty survivors from HMS *Edinburgh* who were being taken home.

In the perpetual daylight of late May, the next incoming convoy, PQ16, was also found by one of eight KG 40 Condor reconnaissance aircraft despatched to search for traces of the inbound ships, with assistance from German Intelligence reports. *MGK Nord* had suggested that *Luftflotte* 5 hold bombers in readiness against British heavy naval forces likely to be acting as distant escort, but Stumpff replied that he was unable to hold *any* aircraft in reserve with such a paucity of available attack aircraft. The eight Condors operated in relays to maintain contact, sending D/F signals for U-boats and reinforced by BV 138s of 3./Kü.Fl.Gr. 406 once they were within the flying boats' range. For three days the shadowing was maintained, until 28 May, when Ju 88s of the reconnaissance *Staffel* 1./Aufkl.Gr. 124 took over as responsibility passed from *Fliegerführer Lofoten* to *Fliegerführer Nord (Ost)*. The two latter commands were co-ordinated to attack incoming supply convoys, as described by *Generalleutnant* Hermann Plocher:

> Newly arriving air units were stationed on a space-available basis at the airfields at Bodø, Bardufoss and Banak, and placed under the command of *Fliegerführer* Lofoten Islands, the command which directed the attack until the convoy reached a line extending from the North Cape to Spitzbergen. From that moment on, combat and reconnaissance responsibility passed to *Fliegerführer Nord (Ost)*, and the air units formerly assigned to *Fliegerführer* Lofoten Islands. Whenever possible, aircraft stationed at Bardufoss transferred to Kirkenes or Petsamo in order to take the fullest advantage of their operating range. Units operating from Banak remained there but were assigned to the new command (*Fliegerführer Nord (Ost)*), whose mission it was to keep the convoy under continuous attack for the remainder of the voyage and to follow up this attack with strikes on the terminal ports after the vessels arrived.[14]

During the intervening period, the incoming convoy was attacked by Ju 88s of KG 30, He 111 torpedo aircraft of I./KG 26 and the smaller

He 115s of 1./Kü.Fl.Gr. 406, which were seen to circle after releasing torpedoes, presumably to act as rescue craft for any aircrews brought down. Over the course of five days between 25 and 30 May, the aircraft sank six freighters and damaged two others (claiming ten sunk and five probables), though only one was hit by an aerial torpedo, the 5,170-ton freighter SS *Lowther Castle*, set on fire by the blast east-south-east of Bear Island. She finally exploded a day later. Several aircraft returned still carrying torpedoes, and two of the weapons were reported to have exploded immediately after release and on impact with the sea. An He 115 of 1./Kü.Fl.Gr. 906 also exploded shortly after take-off owing to another possible weapons malfunction, killing all three men aboard.[15] Poor communication between Kriegsmarine and Luftwaffe local commands had failed to bring about successful co-operation with the few U-boats available, so the effectiveness of the German attack was blunted.

Nevertheless, Allied Intelligence recorded that the Junkers pilots pressed home their attacks with great determination, particularly when thick clouds were scattered across the sky, providing cover for the approaching bombers while still allowing excellent visibility once they plunged downwards. Diving from cloud cover, they would release bombs at 1,000ft before pulling out of the 60° dive. On the other hand, when conditions were completely overcast, the Allies noted a perceptible slackening of effective Ju 88 dive-bombing. To Allied observers the torpedo attacks appeared far less determined, the Heinkels approaching at extremely low altitudes and releasing torpedoes at about ten feet from the sea surface, but at ranges and in such small numbers that enabled successful evasive action. The attackers lost several aircraft, including one He 111 shot down and another damaged by a 'Hurricat' launched by the CAM ship SS *Empire Lawrence* and piloted by Pt Off Hay. Following his successful sortie, Hay's aeroplane was struck by shells from over-enthusiastic American anti-aircraft gunners and he was wounded, but he baled out and was picked up by the destroyer HMS *Volunteer*. The CAM ship *Empire Lawrence* was among the six merchant ships sunk, suffering five direct bomb hits that ignited her cargo of explosives, sending a huge pall of smoke into the sky before she went down, with twenty-five men killed.

By 30 May shorter-range Ju 87 Stukas of I./StG. 5 joined the attacking air units before PQ16 reached Murmansk and Soviet fighter protection. The Luftwaffe airstrips at Banak, Kirkenes and Petsamo were attacked by Soviet bombers, which destroyed several bombers on the ground, and

A Dornier Do 217 of 4./KG 40, F8+DM. The fuselage *Balkenkreuz* has had its white portion largely painted over, probably for the benefit of night operations.

damaged barracks and hangars. Defending fighters were brought down by escorting Soviet fighters.

The remaining ships of PQ16 were attacked once more the day before arriving at the Kola Inlet. No more vessels were, sunk but several German and defending Soviet aircraft were shot down. Eight ships continued to Arkhangelsk, where the SS *Steel Worker* was sunk by Ju 88 dive bombing using incendiary bombs, and the Soviet submarine *ShCh-404* was damaged. Murmansk was becoming so heavily bombed and mined that, by July, Arkhangelsk had become the port to which incoming ships were directed.

At the end of the fighting over PQ16, German reconnaissance aircraft woefully misjudged the effectiveness of the attack, *Luftflotte* 5 claiming to have destroyed twelve identified steamers (totalling 86,000GRT) and an additional freighter of undetermined tonnage, as well as leaving five others (52,000GRT) in a 'sinking condition'. A single destroyer, twenty-two steamers (122,500GRT) and one of undetermined size were claimed to have been damaged, and two others (10,000GRT) 'probably damaged'.

The War Diary kept by *SKL* annotated the report with the comment that it was likely to 'include a few duplications, due to repeated hits on the same ships'. However, they also recorded that:

> Irrespective of whether the figures reported by *Luftflotte* 5 are correct in every detail, it can be stated that an outstanding success has been achieved in the fight against the PQ convoy traffic. The direct and indirect effects will probably be considerable and will also greatly relieve the Norwegian situation. The enemy has learned unmistakably what risks he takes by bringing strong expeditionary forces into the range of Luftwaffe.[16]

The returning QP12 had, however, escaped almost unmolested, although shadowed by a BV 138 and attacked by two Ju 88A-4s of KG 30. Aircraft 4D+IT was shot down by RAFVR Fg Off John Kendall in his 'Hurricat', which had catapulted from the CAM ship SS *Empire Horn*. The entire Junkers crew, pilot *Fw.* Martin Irrgang, observer *Obgerfreiter* Hans Bache, wireless operator *Ogfr.* Hans Müller and gunner *Gfr.* Heinrich Jungelaus, were later reported missing in action and never found. Kendall had been launched to attack the shadowing BV 138, but immediately lost contact with his fighter direction officer aboard *Empire Horn* and could not locate the flying boat. He chanced upon Irrgang's Ju 88, chasing the attacking bomber over the convoy and scoring multiple hits, the German pilot jettisoning bombs to lighten its load as smoke poured from both engines. As the bomber crashed into the sea, Kendall, low on fuel, decided to bale out rather than chance a risky ditching. He climbed to gain height near the destroyer HMS *Badsworth*, disappearing into clouds before the men below heard his engine cut out. The 'Hurricat' plummeted into the sea, and Kendall emerged close behind, his parachute canopy opening only fifty feet above the waves. The young pilot hit the water with such force that he was severely injured, and moments after being picked up he died aboard the British destroyer. Twenty-one-year-old Kendall had volunteered for duty within the Merchant Ship Fighter Unit in 1941, and was the first to shoot down an enemy aircraft and the only such pilot to be killed following a combat launch. He was later Mentioned in Despatches.

Though not yet catastrophic, the Allied losses from PQ16 had been heavy, particularly at the hands of the Luftwaffe, as opposed to a relatively meagre sinking rate achieved by Dönitz's U-boats. A brief respite followed the PQ16 and QP12 convoys, as Royal Navy strength was temporarily diverted to the Mediterranean in support of the *Harpoon* convoy to Malta, and the Luftwaffe bombers were moved back eastwards to the Finnish Front for attacks on ground targets. The torpedo aircraft of KG 26, unable to be so employed, were left to await the resumption of Allied Arctic convoys. Not until the middle of June would sufficient Royal Navy escort forces be assembled to allow the transit of PQ17, and this time they faced the renewed threat of the *Tirpitz*, as the Kriegsmarine had committed to employ heavy surface units against the next inbound convoy. By that stage the Luftwaffe within northern latitudes had also been strongly reinforced, and now mustered one hundred and three Ju 88 bombers, forty-two He 111 torpedo bombers, fifteen He 115 torpedo bombers and thirty Ju 87 dive-bombers, as well as eight Fw 200, twenty-two Ju 88 and forty-four BV 138 reconnaissance aircraft.

The lull had also been exploited by the Luftwaffe in refining already established tactics. Although, in the main, torpedo drops had failed against PQ16, the opportunity had demonstrated once more that skilfully interwoven torpedo and dive-bombing strikes could confuse enemy gunners and disperse their available firepower. Furthermore, the poor showing by torpedo bombers brought further formation-flying training as they employed Harlinghausen's proven technique known as the 'Golden Comb'. Using this method, torpedo bombers would approach out of the twilight sky in great numbers, spread line abreast, against ships silhouetted against a lighter horizon. All bombers would launch simultaneously, vastly improving their chances of hits.

While such preparations were under way in Norway, within the Baltic ten Norwegian ships attempted to break out of the Swedish port of Gothenburg, where they been sheltering since the German occupation of their homeland. The interned merchant ships had been the subject of months of bitter international diplomatic wrangles between neutral, Allied and Axis powers. Ownership was claimed by the Norwegian Shipping and Trade Mission (Nortraship), established in London during April 1940 to administer all Norwegian merchant vessels outside German-controlled areas, but also by the collaborationist Norwegian government headed by Vidkun Quisling. Known as the 'Kvarstad Ships', they had originally comprised forty-two valuable vessels, but some had already reached Britain, while others had returned to occupied Norway. During March, in an operation codenamed *Performance* by the British, ten were to attempt to break the German blockade and head for Britain. Beginning on 31 March, the ships sailed, but only two reached their destination. Four were scuttled after coming under fire from Kriegsmarine ships, two returned to Gothenburg and another two were sunk. One of the ten, the tanker *B.P. Newton*, which had already been shelled by *Vorpostenboote*, was repeatedly attacked on 1 April by Ju 88s of KGr. 506. Despite the defending Lewis-gun fire, two bombs fell only thirty metres from the ship's hull, and the detonations were so powerful that the tanker was physically lifted out of the water. Her captain believed that serious injury must have been inflicted, and the Luftwaffe crew claimed her as probably sunk or severely damaged at the very least. In fact, despite a hurried SOS reporting that manoeuvrability had been lost, after relatively minor repairs the *B.P. Newton* was under way again, and reached Methil the following afternoon. A single Ju 88A-4 of KGr. 506, S4+BL, was brought down over the Skaggerak during the interception of the Kvarstad ships, its four crewmen being posted as missing in action. The other successful escapee was the tanker *Lind*, which avoided two Heinkel torpedo attacks and reached Methil on 4 April.

Of the remainder, the 5,300-ton tanker *Storsten* was overflown by a Ju 88 during the afternoon of 1 April, and moments later was shaken by the blast of a mine against the hull. Although the Norwegian crew believed that the weapon was dropped by the Junkers, *SKL* recorded that 'at 1830hrs an aircraft sighted the sinking tanker *Storsten* inside the mined area of quadrant AN 5671'. This makes it highly unlikely that the Junkers had indeed dropped the lethal mine. Previously the *Storsten* had been sighted and machine-gunned by another Ju 88, and had returned fire with Lewis guns before vanishing into a fog bank. An attempted SOS transmission was abruptly broken off by the Junkers passing low overhead trailing a hook and line, which ripped the antennae completely off the ship.

Five additional aircraft were ordered into action against the Kvarstad ships, and at 1230hrs lookouts aboard the MT *Rigmor* spotted an aircraft which they were at first unable to identify as friend or foe. A strafing run by the attacking Junkers settled the matter, two bombs being dropped wide of the mark to port. Another pair of bombers began circling, alternately making strafing and bombing runs until a direct hit to starboard badly holed the hull and two near-misses astern caused further damage. The ship was listing heavily, her propeller shaft had been broken, and the bridge and radio room had been badly shot up by strafing attacks which had wounded the captain, William Gilling, and disabled the ship's single Lewis gun. As the crew frantically flashed an SOS light signal to approaching British destroyers, the tanker was attacked by two He 115 torpedo seaplanes of Stavanger's 1./Kü.Fl.Gr. 906. One hit the disabled ship, which still refused to sink. Attacking fire was then stopped, as the crew were seen to be abandoning ship. British destroyers finally arrived, but were unable to take the crippled tanker in tow as the Luftwaffe aircraft resumed their strafing attacks. Finally, at 1700hrs, the battered and floundering *Rigmor* was shelled and sunk by HMS *Faulknor*.

The battle against the Kvarstad ships was one of the last in which *F.d.Luft* played any significant independent role, controlling the activities of KGr. 506. During April 1942 the position of *F.d.Luft* was finally removed from connection with the Kriegsmarine, and *Oberst* Friedrich Schily was subordinated to *Luftflotte* 3, subsequently taking part in the planning of bombing operations over Britain by three bomber *Gruppen*. In a personal letter to Schily, dated 17 April, Raeder summarised his regret at the course of events which had led to that point.

> My original intention, to make your unit a strong instrument of naval warfare by steadily increasing its numbers and making use of technical advances, could not be realised. By order of the Commander-in-Chief, Air, issued in accordance with my proposal, you are detached from your tactical relations to the Navy and are transferred to the command of *Luftflotte* 3. This does not bring to a final close the efforts of the Navy to develop its own air arm. The Führer will make a decision about this matter at a later date . . . [17]

Although Schily's *F.d.Luft* office would not be officially abolished until 7 September 1942, when all of his allocated aircraft were completely absorbed into the structure of IX.*Fliegerkorps*, the post of commander of maritime air forces had finally, to all in intents and purposes, been made redundant.

During the first six months of 1942 Malta once again came under Luftwaffe attack, as bomber strength in Sicily was strongly reinforced during the beginning of the year. The opening of the renewed offensive was relatively modest, and it did not reach peak strength until March and April, 325 bomber sorties being mounted on 20 April alone. The decision had been made to invade the fortress island using airborne and sea landing forces (Operation *Herkules*), and targeting was shifted to the elimination of ground defence installations. Malta was bombed into a shambles and, once again, ran critically short of supplies, while Rommel's own logistical arteries across the Mediterranean flowed freely once again, the sole hindrance being the Italian logistical limitations regarding the organisation of seaborne transportation. It is widely considered that the resumption of unfettered seaborne supply allowed a successful resumption of the *Afrika Korps*' offensive operations. However, it was the very fact that Rommel's forces had been pushed far back into Libya, thereby possessing dramatically shortened supply lines, that allowed him to renew offensive action. Eventually, a lack of supply would defeat Rommel, but *not* because it could not pass a Royal Navy Mediterranean barrier. It was because it could not be trucked hundreds of miles to the advancing front line along vulnerable roads that straggled from small undermanned and cramped ports unable to cope with the demands placed upon them.

A British attempt during February to run a small convoy of three escorted freighters (MW9A) from Alexandria to Valletta had ended in complete failure owing to effective Luftwaffe attack. The 7,255-ton SS *Clan Campbell* was damaged and forced to shelter in Tobruk Harbour, the 7,262-ton SS *Clan Chattan* was hit and damaged so badly that she caught fire and was later scuttled, and the 7,801-ton SS *Rowallan Castle* was disabled by near misses. The *Rowallan Castle* was evacuated and taken in tow by the destroyer HMS *Lively*, but the decision was made to scuttle her when the escorting destroyers were warned that Italian battleship *Caio Duilio* had sailed from Taranto.

By the end of March 1942 only X.*Fliegerkorps* remained in the eastern Mediterranean, with the Ju 88s and Bf 110 reconnaissance aircraft of 2./Aufkl.Gr. 123 in Tatoi, north of Athens, I./LG 1 at Heraklion, Crete, 4./KG 26 at Kalamaki on Zakynthos Island, and both 2./Aufkl. Gr. 125 and *Aufklärungsfliegergruppe* 126 *(See)*, between the ports Skaramanga, west of Athens, and Kavalla in the Eastern Macedonian region controlled by Bulgaria. The 14 February combat returns of the *Aufklärungsfliegergruppen*, commanded from Athens by *Obstlt*. Hermann Kaiser, show that the reconnaissance units had now become a mixed bag of available aircraft after initial formation with the Heinkel He 60, including captured Dutch Fokker T.VIII. From a total of forty one, only twenty-one were available for active use:

2./Aufkl.Gr. 125, nine Ar 196 (eight operational);
Stab./Aufkl.Gr. 126, one BV 138 (non-operational);
1./Aufkl.Gr. 126, thirteen mixed He 60 and Fokker T.VIII (seven operational);
2./Aufkl.Gr. 126, ten mixed He 60 and Ar 196 (seven operational);
3./Aufkl.Gr. 126, eight mixed He 60 and Fokker T.VIII (one operational).

Meanwhile, in Sicily, II.*Fliegerkorps* mustered II./LG 1, KGr. 606, Stab/KG 54 and KGr. 806 in Catania, I./KG 54 in Gerbini and Stab, two *Staffeln* of II. and III./KG 77 in Comiso, as well as the Bf 109 fighters of JG 53 based at Comiso. During March *Maj.* Arven Crüger had been appointed *Kommodore* of KG 77, his unit already being heavily engaged in the bombing of Malta and morphing into a dedicated maritime strike wing. Only days after his appointment, a new attempt to supply Malta by Convoy MW10 began, as four fast freighters under the command of Convoy Commodore Capt C.A.G. Hutchinson aboard the auxiliary MV *Breconshire* departed from Alexandria on 20 March. The cargo represented salvation for Malta: a repaired SS *Clan Campbell* loaded with aviation fuel stored in four-gallon cans, ammunition and general stores; the 6,798-ton Norwegian SS *Talabot* carrying kerosene, aviation spirit and ammunition; the 5,415-ton SS *Pampas* loaded with army stores and foodstuffs; and the 9,776-ton *Breconshire* laden with fuel and stores. The merchants were heavily escorted by three light cruisers, HMS *Cleopatra*, *Dido* and *Euryalus*, the converted anti-aircraft cruiser HMS *Carlisle* and the destroyers HMS *Jervis*, *Hasty*, *Havock*, *Hero*, *Kingston*, *Kipling*, *Kelvin*, *Sikh*, *Zulu*, *Lance* and *Lively*, under the overall command of Rear Admiral Philip Vian. Seven destroyers had been sent to join the convoy from Tobruk, but HMS *Heythrop* was torpedoed by *U652*. She was taken in tow by HMS *Eridge*, but sank soon afterwards.

The convoy was immediately sighted by the Italian submarine *Platino*, and later shadowed briefly by six Ju 52 transport aircraft en route to Crete from North Africa, which reported the composition, speed, location and course of MW10. Reinforced the following day by the light cruiser HMS *Penelope*, with the destroyer HMS *Legion* from Malta, MW10 came under attack by Italian S.79 torpedo bombers, but their pilots appeared unwilling to press home their attacks, and dropped torpedoes at long range with consequent failure. Luftwaffe aircraft followed, with no initial success before news that an Italian surface force comprising a battleship, cruisers and destroyers had sailed to intercept. What followed is now known as the Second Battle of Sirte. A pair of British destroyers were disabled, and damage was inflicted on several other ships for little in return until the Italians broke away with the approach of darkness, which would have seriously disadvantaged the Italian ships as they were not equipped with radar.

Despite taking punishment, the Royal Navy had managed to shield the merchants from Italian attack, ordered them to scatter behind thick defensive smokescreens, and relied on developing storm weather conditions to cover their final leg to Malta. Yet despite this achievement the convoy was running significantly late, and engine trouble aboard the *Clan Campbell* caused the ship to slow down even more. With such delays, the merchants would still be at sea by dawn the following day, and vulnerable to the full force of Luftwaffe attack.

The following morning, as escort ships corralled the scattered freighters, they were sighted despite bad weather and low-hanging clouds by the crew of an Italian Cant seaplane, which pinpointed the convoy's location for the aircraft of II.*Fliegerkorps*. Within minutes Ju 88s appeared, and despite Spitfire and Hurricane fighter protection from Malta the SS *Clan Campbell* suffered several direct hits in low-level bombing attacks that killed the ship's Master, James Foster Vooght, and nine of his crew, and forced the remainder to abandon ship. In the rolling heavy sea the steamer soon foundered, and she went down twenty miles from the Maltese coast. An initial attack by Ju 88s of II./LG 1 on the SS *Breconshire* was repulsed by anti-aircraft fire from the escorting HMS *Carlisle* and destroyers, until three Bf 109 fighter-bombers of 10./JG 53, flying from Gela, hit the tanker with one 250kg bomb each. The first hit level with Number 1 hold, which was packed with ammunition, the second struck aft, and the third hit close to the port deck rail. With the ship holed below the waterline, the engine room quickly flooded, and *Breconshire* lost steerage and power. Less than ten minutes later a single Ju 88 flew through intense defensive fire to drop three near-misses on the port beam. A second low-level attack narrowly missed to starboard, and the ship wallowed out of control towards the defensive Zonker Point minefield. Despite constant attack with bombs and strafing machine-gun fire, the crew jury-rigged some steering while desperately attempting to stem the internal rising water level. Efforts to take the ship in tow when only nine miles from Valletta's Grand Harbour failed because the freighter's deep draught caused it to roll cruelly in heavy swell. During the early afternoon *Maj.* Arved Crüger led a flight of Ju 88s from Stab/

Cooperation between the Luftwaffe and *Regia Aeronautica* was frequently excellent at lower command level. This intriguing photograph shows our unidentified Heinkel test pilot (standing in the front row in civilian clothes) and a Luftwaffe *Flieger Hauptingenieur*, both flanking the Italian colonel. The other men include Italian torpedo bomber pilots, the remainder of the Luftwaffe He 115 crew in civilian clothes and even a German civilian pilot (glasses, back row centre). (James Payne)

KG 77 in a renewed attack. The weather had deteriorated, with near-gale-force winds from the south-east, and anti-aircraft support for the crippled ship had been increased by the addition of the cruisers HMS *Carlisle* and *Penelope*, and the destroyers HMS *Beaufort*, *Southwold*, *Hurworth* and *Dulveston*. Despite these handicaps, Crüger's flight pressed home their attack, managing a scattering of near misses and losing two aircraft during strafing runs, one of them Ju 88A-4 3Z+AA, flown by Crüger. He and his crew, observer *Obfw.* Erich Atzler, wireless operator *Obfw.* Ernst Raithel and gunner *Obfw.* Walter Wagner, were killed as the Junkers plunged headlong into the turbulent sea. Later, following news of the popular commander's death, *Obstlt.* Hermann Schlüter, former acting commander of KGr. 606, was moved to the vacant post of *Kommodore* of KG 77.

Over the days that followed the Luftwaffe continued to pound the stricken *Breconshire* and both remaining freighters which had reached

Another intriguing photograph belong to the German Heinkel pilot showing the Italian colonel from the previous image standing before an He 115 in Italy for torpedo trials and tests of ranging equipment. (James Payne)

Valletta with only minor damage. HMS *Legion* was severely damaged by a near miss on 23 March and beached, later being towed to Valletta, where she was bombed again and sunk when stored ammunition exploded. The following day HMS *Southwold* was sunk by a mine near the *Breconshire*, which was finally successfully taken under tow by the British naval tug HMT *Ancient* and anchored at Marsaxlokk on 25 March. The following day it was bombed once more and caught fire, eventually sinking in flames on 27 March. Both surviving freighters in Valletta had also been set on fire by relentless bombing. The *Talabot* was scuttled for fear that her ammunition cargo would explode, and all but two of *Pampas*'s holds were flooded. Only 4,492 tons of the 26,800 tons of supplies carried by MW10 had been successfully taken ashore.

Although the Luftwaffe had paid dearly for its success, the decimation of MW10 and the shambles to which Malta had been reduced, as well as the virtual annihilation of RAF forces on the island, convinced the Admiralty to evacuate all moveable surface vessels and submarines once more to Alexandria. The island bastion was yet again untenable primarily because of the Luftwaffe, and further convoys were suspended until aircraft carriers from Gibraltar could fly off further fighter aircraft to Malta as defence against the German onslaught.

During April, German and Italian army staffs had agreed on the shape of Operation *Herkules*, which was to be led by airborne assault and reinforced by sea. While Rommel prepared the second part of his 1942 offensive, which had already pushed forward to the Gazala Line west of Tobruk, Hitler and Mussolini decided to halt Rommel's advance after the recapture of Tobruk, whereupon *Herkules* would begin. However, Rommel's subsequent attack (*Unternehmen Venezia*), which battered its way east and had taken Tobruk by 21 June, showed no signs of abating, the *Afrika Korps* determined to pursue what they believed was a beaten enemy. Mindful of the losses suffered in the invasion of Crete, and with the Axis star obviously in the ascendant once more in North Africa, *Herkules* was cancelled. Instead, the logistical weight was thrown behind Rommel's plan to take the Suez Canal in a ground invasion of Egypt (*Unternehmen Aida*). By 25 June the victorious *Afrika Korps*' tank strength had been reduced to sixty, while the Italian XX Corps possessed only fourteen 'runners'. Within five days advancing forces had reached El Alamein, and they attempted to attack immediately and shock the Eighth Army out of their defensive positions with pure offensive momentum. The attempt failed, and both sides stagnated in complete exhaustion. Once again Rommel faced a supply line that meandered from Tripoli, 2,300 kilometres to the west, while the British poured men and material through the Red Sea directly into Egypt in preparation for their own counteroffensive, due for October.

By the middle of May, Luftwaffe pressure on Malta had slackened perceptibly once more, as units were either returned to the Eastern Front to support the advance into the Caucasus (*Fall Blau*), or transferred to *Fliegerführer Afrika* (only *Staffel* 12./LG 1) for direct support of Rommel's ground forces. Despite severe losses at the hands of II.*Fliegerkorps*, RAF fighter strength had gradually trickled back to Malta, and the last maximum-effort Luftwaffe attack against the island was made on 28 April. Shortly thereafter Stab, II. and III./KG 77 were moved to France, I. and II./LG 1 to Greece and the eastern Mediterranean theatre, followed by parts of I./KG 54. Remaining in Sicily under II.*Fliegerkorps* control were only KGr. 606, KGr. 860, Stab/KG 54 and the remaining parts of I./KG 54. Losses to those still engaged against Malta remained heavy, KGr. 806 losing two of its *Staffelkapitäne* in action, one to naval anti-aircraft fire and the other to Malta's defending Spitfires.

On 10 May the destroyers HMS *Lively*, *Jervis*, *Jackal* and *Kipling* sailed from Alexandria to intercept Axis convoy traffic bound for Benghazi. They were found by German reconnaissance aircraft the following day, and *Gruppenkommandeur Maj.* Joachim 'Jochen' Helbig led his I./LG 1 against the four destroyers, which had been instructed to return if engaged by enemy aircraft, as only limited Allied air cover from a single Bristol Beaufort was available. Surprised by the Junkers, *Lively* was hit during the first attack, which destroyed the bridge, holed the hull and killed the captain. A second strafing pass resulted in the destroyer being abandoned, and she sank 100 miles north-east of Tobruk with the loss of seventy-seven of her crew. Nine aircraft of II./LG 1 mounted a second ineffectual attack while Helbig refuelled and rearmed

The wreck of an RAF Beaufighter shot down on the North African coast photographed by a war correspondent accompanying Ju 88s on a Mediterranean shipping strike.

An He 111 of KG 26 showing the method of carrying two torpedoes (in this case minus detonators) on their PVC racks.

at Heraklion before returning to the action. His own bombs then hit HMS *Kipling*, while other aircraft of his *Gruppe* damaged HMS *Jackal* so badly that she was scuttled. *Kipling* finally sank the following day, and only HMS *Jervis* returned to Alexandria.

As Rommel advanced through Libya, Malta neared collapse, supplies for both the military and civilians having dwindled almost to nothing. In a desperate attempt to forestall the inevitable, two convoys were despatched; one from Gibraltar in the west and the other from Alexandria to the east, to split the besieging Axis forces and break through. From Gibraltar, Operation *Harpoon* comprised five freighters (Convoy WS19Z) and an American tanker carrying 39,000 tons of cargo and oil. They were escorted by the anti-aircraft cruiser HMS *Cairo*, the fast minelayer HMS *Welshman*, nine destroyers and four minesweepers, with distant cover provided by the battleship HMS *Malaya*, two aircraft carriers, two cruisers and eight destroyers. In the east, Operation *Vigorous* sailed from Alexandria with eleven freighters (Convoy MW11), escorted by 'decoy battleship' HMS *Centurion*, twelve destroyers, four corvettes and two minesweepers. Distant cover comprised eight cruisers and fourteen destroyers.

Almost upon departing Egypt on 12 June, *Vigorous* came under air attack, at first by Libyan-based Ju 87 Stukas and then, during the evening, by fifteen Ju 88s of KG 54 from Crete. The freighter SS *City of Calcutta* was damaged by a near-miss, took on a list and was ordered to divert to Tobruk.

During the following day, as part of the Allies' Operation *Albumen* to disrupt the Luftwaffe's maritime bombers, an SAS team consisting of Capt George Jellicoe, Lt Petrakis of the Royal Hellenic Army and four Free French commandos, Capt Georges Bergé, Sgt Jacques Mouhot, Cpl Jack Sibard and soldier Pierre Léostic, attacked Heraklion Airfield after being landed by the Greek submarine *Triton*. While the RAF mounted a diversionary raid, the SAS team destroyed one Ju 88A-4 and damaged seven others of I. and II./LG 1 with Lewis bombs. All six saboteurs managed to escape after their successful incursion, but they were betrayed by a Cretan peasant and 17-year-old Léostic was killed in a fierce firefight. The remaining Frenchmen were captured and later

Cover photograph of *Der Adler* magazine trumpeting Ju 88 anti-shipping operations within the Mediterranean.

interred at Oflag XC in Lübeck. Only Jellicoe and Petrakis escaped Crete and reached Egypt.

Despite this accomplishment, the air attacks continued, and by 14 June, only twelve kilometres from Tobruk, the 6,811-ton Dutch MV *Aagtekerk* was hit on the bridge by three bombs, setting the ship ablaze. With three men dead and steering destroyed, *Aagtekerk* turned lazy circles until the engine was stopped by a pair of volunteers in gas masks who braved the below-decks smoke and flame, the ship eventually running aground. The British 6,104-ton SS *Bhutan* was also bombed by aircraft of LG 1, and went down with six men killed, while the attackers lost three Ju 88 bombers. All available Kriegsmarine and Italian forces in the eastern Mediterranean were vectored on to the convoy, and shadowing aircraft homed S-boats of the 3. S-flotilla to the scene. During early evening the Luftwaffe unwittingly came to the aid of the Royal Navy, dropping brilliant flares designed to help pilots attack, but illuminating both the convoy and the waiting S-boats. Hurried radio requests transmitted to the S-boat headquarters at Derna for the cessation of flare use were not passed through quickly enough, and the advantage of surprise was lost. As each new Luftwaffe attack illuminated the sea ahead of *Vigorous*, the S-boats came under direct attack themselves from oncoming destroyers. Flotilla commander *Kaptlt.* Friedrich Kemnade desperately contacted the Kriegsmarine Liaison Officer to the *Regia Marina*, *Konteradmiral* Eberhard Weichold, with the message: 'Please no more bombing attacks, torpedo attacks impossible due to flares.' Against such odds their sole successes were the torpedoing of the cruiser HMS *Newcastle*, holed and forced to retreat to Alexandria, and the sinking of the destroyer HMS *Hasty*.

The Italian fleet had sailed to intercept, and, with *Vigorous* still under continuous aerial attack, fuel and ammunition supplies within the surviving ships were so low that it was judged they would be unable to reach Malta and stood no chance of defending against major Italian surface units. The convoy therefore turned back for Alexandria. Ironically, after the successful appeals of Weichold to Kesselring on behalf of 3. S-flotilla to end Luftwaffe flares, the returning S-boats were then shrouded in darkness and unable to find the main convoy again.

Meanwhile, *Harpoon* closed on Malta from the west. The procession had already been severely battered by Italian warships and air attack, initially by the *Regia Aeronautica*. Next came long-range reconnaissance Ju 88Ds of I./Aufkl.Gr. 122 from Libya, two of which were shot down

An Ar 196 being recovered from the sea. The seahorse insignia of *Bordfliegerkommando* 1./196 lay on a light blue shield. (James Payne)

by defending aircraft. On the evening of 14 June nine Ju 88s of KGr. 606 dive-bombed the carrier HMS *Argus* and narrowly missed, two being shot down by Sea Hurricanes. The following day I./KG 54 attacked, sinking the American 5,600-ton MV *Chant* with three direct hits, and disabling the 9,308-ton tanker *Kentucky* with a near miss. A second attack damaged the 5,601-ton British merchant *Bardwan*, and both she and *Kentucky* were sent to the bottom later that day by aircraft of KGr. 606. Of the two merchant ships that survived to reach Malta, the largest freighter in the convoy, the 10,400-ton SS *Orari*, detonated a mine near the harbour entrance and, though she managed to limp to a berth, lost much cargo outside the breakwater through the breach in the damaged hull. Malta, already on starvation rations, had its life prolonged for eight weeks.

The Luftwaffe began to exploit its maritime attack units fully, and their achievements reached a crescendo in 1942 with the struggles against PQ17 and PQ18 in the Arctic and *Pedestal* in the Mediterranean, these three battles marking the height to which Luftwaffe maritime operations aspired. After an enforced hiatus, the PQ convoys were recommenced in June 1942. The German summer offensive had opened on the southern

Russian steppe, initially appearing to repeat the stunning successes of *Barbarossa*'s early weeks. With Soviet forces in full retreat, Stalin's strident demands for supply by the Western Allies overruled any Royal Navy concerns regarding the Murmansk run. Admiral of the Fleet John Cronyn Tovey, responsible for the safe passage of the Arctic convoys, had raised Winston Churchill's ire by suggesting that the PQ convoys should be suspended until Luftwaffe airfields in northern Norway could be neutralised. 'If they must continue for political reasons,' he warned, 'very serious and heavy losses must be expected.'[18] Political pressure prevailed nevertheless, and PQ17 was assembled with thirty-five escorted merchants. British intelligence had warned of the likelihood of German heavy ships intercepting PQ17 as, following the dismal failure of U-boats against PQ16, the *Tirpitz*, *Admiral Scheer*, *Lützow* and *Admiral Hipper* had been gathered in Norwegian ports with sufficient fuel stocks accumulated to allow them and their destroyer escort to sail into action. The Kriegsmarine had planned Operation *Rösselsprung*, and while the Luftwaffe bombed, U-boats would shadow merchant ships of the next PQ convoy and report their position for the benefit of the surface fleet, provided it could be confirmed that there was no British aircraft carrier with the convoy escort.

The convoy sailed from Britain, first for Iceland and then onward to Murmansk, departing Hvalfjord on 27 June. At that point the close escort comprised six destroyers, four corvettes, three minesweepers, four trawlers, two anti-aircraft ships and the two British submarines *P614* and *P615*. The Soviets fielded five submarines — *D3*, *K21*, *K22*, *Shch402* and *Shch403* — to help cover both the incoming convoy and the outgoing QP13.

At a time when command unity was of paramount importance, preparations to battle PQ17 exposed the ongoing antagonism between the Luftwaffe and Kriegsmarine Staffs regarding maritime operations. On 8 June *SKL* informed Luftwaffe Operations Staff that an improved fuel oil situation would allow intensified surface action against Murmansk convoys, but that this would require increased levels of air reconnaissance.

> The Naval Staff knows increased reconnaissance will inevitably result in a withdrawal of bomber aircraft, the action of which brought such gratifying results against Convoy PQ16. It feels, however, that such a step is in the common interest and that the increased prospect of success on the part of the naval forces will compensate for the withdrawal of said aircraft.[19]

Furthermore, the Kriegsmarine requested that, alongside reconnaissance, the Luftwaffe be only permitted to attack enemy aircraft carriers and merchant ships, while the German surface units engaged the convoy body, thereby lessening the possibility of friendly-fire accidents. A detailed list of requirements was forwarded to the Luftwaffe, with requests that 'pertinent Luftwaffe commanders be instructed to meet all requests by *MGK Nord* and the Admiral, Arctic Ocean, which are within reasonable limits as far as the Luftwaffe is concerned'. In response, Luftwaffe Operations Staff instructed *Lufiflotte* 5 to comply as far as possible with naval requests for reconnaissance, but added that 'additional reconnaissance forces cannot be furnished. Under no circumstances are bombers to be used for reconnaissance tasks only.'[20] Instead, the Luftwaffe pointed to the successful air operations against PQ16, a repeat of which required the already weak *Lufiflotte* 5 bomber force to remain focussed on combat missions alone.

> The Chief, Naval Staff, agrees to the Operations Division's proposal that, should it become necessary, the attitude of the Luftwaffe Operations Staff be mentioned to the Führer, since it might easily decide the success of this operation. The directive of the Operations Staff to *Lufiflotte* 5 makes it clear that they believe that all that is needed for attacking convoys to Murmansk are bombers. This one-sided point of view cannot go unchallenged. Although the Luftwaffe's success against PQ16 was gratifying, a large portion of the latter, about twenty-five ships, did reach the port of destination. On the other hand, an operation such as *Rösselsprung* harbours the possibility of completely destroying an entire convoy if circumstances are at all favourable.[21]

Kapitän zur See Wilhelm Mössel at Luftwaffe Command submitted information on the planned Kriegsmarine *Rösselsprung* operation, and in return was promised reconnaissance forces of three *Staffeln* of Fw 200s, four *Staffeln* of BV 138s and reconnaissance *Kette* of three Ju 88s, each for use against the enemy's remote escorts or supporting groups.

On 1 July *U255* of the '*Eisteufel*' U-boat group sighted 'light naval forces' in quadrant AB 7166, and this was confirmed by *U408*, which had already begun trailing a pair of escorting destroyers through drifting patches of heavy fog. As two other U-boats began to shadow PQ17, *U456* vectored eight torpedo-carrying He 115s on to the convoy. The aircraft belonged to *Hptm.* Herbert Vater's 1./Kü.Fl.Gr. 406, temporarily based in Sörreisa, a seaplane station (*Seefliegerhorst*) at the head of Solbergfjord near Tromsø and the home of *Stab./*Kü.Fl.Gr. 706. During the attack, Vater's own aircraft, K6+HH, was shot down by anti-aircraft fire from HMS *Fury* and made an emergency descent near the convoy. As Vater and his two crewmen abandoned their sinking aircraft, HMS *Wilton* approached in an effort to capture them, but *Fw.* Karl 'Konny' Arabin alighted in his own Heinkel, under the command of *Oblt.z.S.* Karl-Hermann Burmeister, under the nose of the *Wilton* and near the life raft, and rescued the stranded men. Arabin struggled to take off amidst bursting anti-aircraft shells, but eventually succeeded and ran for Sörreisa.[22] The fierce flak kept all the seaplanes far enough from PQ17 to ensure that their attempted torpedo attacks failed, though with no further loss. A shadowing BV 138 of 1./Aufkl. Gr. 125 crashed while returning to harbour, hitting Kvalöya Island, Finmark. The pilot, *Ob.Gefr.* Walter Nebandahl, and flight engineer *Uffz.* Heinrich Krüger were killed, but the other two crew members recovered from their injuries.

Two days later a second BV 138 of the same unit went missing 300 kilometres north-east of Bear Island. All five men were posted as missing in action and never seen again.[23]

Further to the west, outbound QP13 was spotted by *U88*, but the decision was made to focus on the incoming laden merchants, and both Kriegsmarine and Luftwaffe forces were ordered not to engage QP13. The heavy units of *Rösselsprung* were activated, and *Tirpitz* and *Admiral Hipper* departed Trondheim, moving north to a closer jumping-off point should they be committed to action. Their movement was detected by Allied intelligence. The *Lützow* and three destroyers in Narvik had all run aground and were temporarily out of commission, but the two remaining capital ships joined *Admiral Scheer* and awaited orders to sail against PQ17.

On 4 July PQ17 suffered its first casualty at the hands of an He 115 of 1./Kü.Fl.Gr. 906 which had taken off from the seaplane station north of Banak, at Billefjord. Although seven aircraft departed, six failed to locate PQ17 in particularly foul weather, only *Staffelkapitän Hptm.* Eberhard Peukert dropping out of low cloud at approximately 0500hrs and launching his single torpedo. It hit the American Liberty Ship SS *Christopher Newport*. The 7,191-ton freighter was badly holed, with a rapidly flooding engine room, wrecked steering gear and three men dead. The survivors were lifted off and attempts to scuttle the ship failed, but at

0808hrs *Korvettenkapitän* Karl Brandenburg's *U457* found the drifting ship and sank her and her cargo of 8,200 tons of war material.

The Luftwaffe increased its attacks that day, their activities betrayed to the Admiralty by ULTRA decrypts, but failed to co-ordinate attacks in the way that operational doctrine demanded. At 1930hrs Ju 88s of KG 30 attacked PQ17 but failed to hit, the bombs released during their dive-bombing attacks falling wide of the frantically manoeuvring ships. Fully an hour later, twenty-five He 111s of I./KG 26, led by recently promoted and acting *Gruppenkommandeur Hptm.* Bernd Eicke (*Obstlt.* Hermann Busch having been appointed *Fliegerführer Nord* (*West*) at Stavanger), prepared to execute a low-level pincer attack from multiple directions simultaneously. Had the dive-bombing and torpedo attacks been combined, British defensive fire and evasive manoeuvring would have been effectively divided, but, as it was, both assaults suffered casualties to concentrated flak from escort ships and machine-gun fire from the merchants themselves. *Leutnant* Konrad Hennemann focused his torpedo run against the 4,871-ton British SS *Navarino*, which he hit with a single torpedo and sank, though his Heinkel was shattered by defending fire and disintegrated before crashing into the sea. All four crew were killed, and Hennemann was posthumously awarded the Knight's Cross on 3 September. His accumulated claimed tonnage of shipping sunk totalled 35,000 tons, and he was also mistakenly credited with sinking an American cruiser in his attack on PQ17.

A second Heinkel, flown by *Lt*. Georg Kaumayr, was also hit while lining up for a torpedo shot at a large freighter, unexpectedly dazzling sunlight blinding the pilot and crew to the proximity of the American destroyer USS *Wainwright*, which had come from the cruiser screen to refuel from the oiler *Aldersdale* in the convoy. On its way to the rendezvous the *Wainwright* assisted in repulsing two torpedo-aircraft raids, the first thwarted by long-range fire that kept the six attacking aircraft at sufficient distance to make their torpedo drops wholly inaccurate. The second resulted in the shooting down of Kaumayr's Heinkel. He had been accompanying Hennemann on his attack run, and the heavy anti-aircraft fire tore into his aircraft as it approached at high speed only twenty metres from the water surface. The Heinkel's radio gear was destroyed as a single torpedo was dropped, and the port engine suddenly misfired and began leaking hydraulic oil. Small-calibre hits smashed the Heinkel's instrument panel and, as Kaumayr banked away, 20mm cannon fire hit the oil tank. The remaining torpedo was jettisoned as flames began to consume the central fuselage, forcing an emergency descent. All four men abandoned the sinking aircraft and were subsequently rescued by the destroyer HMS *Ledbury*. Oberleutnant Heinz Jente of 2./KG 26 was also shot down east of Bear Island, his port engine being hit by flak before he could release torpedoes. Losing height despite jettisoning all weapons, Jente was forced to ditch in the icy water. The entire crew escaped from the sinking He 111H-6 and awaited the expected *Seenotdienst* rescue in response to radioed distress calls made before they hit the sea. However, rescue did not come until thirty-six hours later, when a Norwegian fishing boat passed their life raft by chance. Jente was awarded the German Cross in Gold on 21 August, the Knight's Cross on 29 October 1943, and in February 1944 became *Staffelkapitän* of 2./KG 26.

The USS *Wainwright* was instrumental in protecting PQ17 during her short tenure with the convoy. After the initial attack, a two-hour lull allowed *Wainwright* to resume refuelling, but large groups of Heinkels were sighted milling about on the southern horizon at 1820hrs, and USS *Wainwright* turned to port to clear the convoy as the attackers divided into two groups; one approaching from the starboard quarter and the other on the starboard bow. *Wainwright* took the group off her quarter under fire at extreme range, about 10,000 yards distant, and maintained heavy fire until it was considered dangerous for the convoy itself whereupon fire was shifted to the more dangerous bow attack. The flak proved so effective that only one aircraft managed to launch torpedoes between *Wainwright* and the convoy, the remainder prudently dropping their torpedoes approximately 1,500 yards from the destroyer, meaning a torpedo run to the convoy itself in excess of 4,000 yards. They were easily evaded. However, off the starboard quarter, two ships were hit. The first was the Soviet tanker *Azerbaidjan* carrying linseed oil. Catching fire, elements of the crew panicked and began abandoning ship while female gunners continued to fire at the enemy. Upon the realisation that their ship was not sinking despite the heavy fires caused by the explosions, the lifeboats were ordered by megaphone to return to help extinguish the flames, the ship falling out of station but later reaching Archangelsk on 24 July, albeit after losing her valuable cargo.

Meanwhile, *Gruppenkommandeur* Eicke had successfully torpedoed the Liberty Ship SS *William Hooper*, carrying 8,486 tons of military stores, despite rapid fire from the bow-mounted 75mm and stern 100mm cannon, and attempts by US Marine Midshipman Howard E. Carraway to detonate the incoming torpedo with fire from his Lewis gun. Three men were killed in the explosion, and the 7,177-ton ship was abandoned and subsequently sunk by gunfire from *Kaptlt*. Hilmar Siemon's *U334*. *Kapitänleutnant* Reinhard Reche, captain of *U255*, which had begun to attack PQ17, remembered the initial air attacks:

> At 1900hrs Ju 88 bombers roared overhead. We heard their bombs exploding and watched as one of the aircraft was hit and burned up in the sky. Then, from behind, came a swarm of He 111 torpedo bombers appearing flying close to the surface of the water, and roared past to the north. We reported the weather conditions around the convoy for the aircraft. It seemed that the large ships were no longer attached to the convoy.[24]

Despite the loss of some merchant ships, morale within PQ17 was high, as most torpedo attacks had been defeated, and the convoy was geographically at the closest point of its route to Banak airfield. While the Kriegsmarine refused to order the heavy ships of *Rösselsprung* into action until the whereabouts of enemy carriers could be ascertained, U-boats were thrown against PQ17. In Altafjord, *Vizeadmiral* Otto Schniewind aboard *Tirpitz*, and in overall command of the capital ships, seethed at his inability to put to sea and join battle. The deadline for sailing orders was 1300hrs on 5 July, otherwise the target convoy would be too close to the enemy coast. Finally, two hours late, Schniewind was given orders to sail, and *Tirpitz*, *Admiral Hipper*, *Admiral Scheer*, seven destroyers and two torpedo boats slipped out to sea. They were sighted near Ingot Island by the Soviet submarine *K21*, which fired a spread of four torpedoes at *Tirpitz* before going deep to avoid retaliation. Hearing two explosions, *Kapitan 2 ranga* N.A. Lunin believed he had hit the battleship, later reporting his attack and subsequent depth-charging by radio. The event had, however, gone unnoticed. Whatever depth charges had been launched were perhaps only cautionary discharges from destroyers detecting possible faint sonar traces. Further *Tirpitz* sightings were reported by British Consolidated Catalina aircraft and submarines, their messages intercepted by *B-Dienst* and causing undue consternation in *OKM*. After they had spent only six hours at sea, Raeder ordered the ships to be recalled, lest they become the target of carrier strikes. However, by that stage the destruction of PQ17 was already well under way.

On the British side, the news that *Tirpitz* had sailed caused virtual panic within the Admiralty, and at 2111hrs on 4 July the following message was transmitted to PQ17's escort:

> Most immediate. Cruiser force withdraw westward at high speed.

The messages escalated rapidly. At 2123hrs:

> Immediate. Owing to threat from surface ships, convoy is to disperse and proceed to Russian ports.

And at 2136hrs:

> Most immediate. My 2123./4. Convoy is to scatter.

It was a disaster in the making. Despite the absence of heavy surface units, the Kriegsmarine and Luftwaffe were now able to attack the dispersed merchant shipping that was now unescorted and leaderless. Despite the convoy having successfully driven off repeated air attacks with relatively minor loss, they were now ordered to break apart and lose the benefit of escorted group strength that was at the heart of the convoying principle.

The day after the scatter order had been given, the Luftwaffe returned. Six He 115s of 1./Kü.Fl.Gr. 906 attempted to attack during the morning, but were thwarted by bad weather and forced to return to Billfjord. Nonetheless, the scattered merchantmen were decimated by KG 26 and KG 30 along with gathering U-boats. *Kapitänleutnant* Hilmar Siemon's *U334* was also hit by Luftwaffe attack, a KG 30 Ju 88 dropping two bombs that damaged the steering gear. Siemon was escorted to Neidenfjord by *U456*, but not before sinking the 7,195-ton British steamer *Earlston*, which had already been disabled by the KG 30 aircraft during the same attack. While the battle raged, on 5 July, *SKL*, who believed that the convoy had been scattered as a result of the heavy air attack on 4 July, recorded:

> After evaluating success reports from raids by twenty-three He 111s at about 2000hrs on 4 July, *Luftflotte* 5 reports sinking four ships with a total tonnage of 24,000GRT and damaging five ships totalling 37,000 GRT so seriously that further sinkings are to be expected. Furthermore, six ships totalling 29,000GRT have been slightly damaged. The enemy defence is said to have been so strong that, unfortunately, our attacking forces suffered heavy losses. The action of 5 July, which was staged with the bulk of our forces late in the afternoon, yielded the following results: sixty-nine Ju 88s of KG 30 sank eight steamers totalling 51,000GRT, probably sank two steamers with a total of 14,000 GRT, and damaged six

steamers totalling 34,000GRT. There is no final report in as yet on the operation of the torpedo aeroplanes. According to the report of *Luftflotte 5*, our bombers found it difficult to get at the widely-scattered convoy. An organised defence was no longer possible. The actual figures of tonnage sunk are probably much higher than those given. Thirty-four prisoners were brought in by the He 115s which were in the action.

It had been an utter disaster for PQ17, and aboard escorting Royal Navy ships there were mixed emotions of anger, despair and depression as they departed from the convoy because of their phantom enemy; *Tirpitz* was back in a Norwegian Fjord, swinging at anchor.

The overclaiming of twenty-eight ships sunk by 7 July caused an overconfident *Fliegerführer Nord (Ost)* to pronounce the convoy annihilated, and the KG 30 bombers were redirected against naval and aviation installations in the Murmansk region. Elements of PQ17 straggled onward, however, and on 8 July Fw 200C-4 F8+EH of 1./KG 40 was shot down in the Barents Sea by the American merchant ship SS *Bellingham*, killing pilot and *Staffelkapitän Oblt.* Albert Gramkow and his seven crew. The following day several remaining PQ17 stragglers were sighted by U-boat. Five merchants had managed to reach Novaya Zemlya, where they joined eight escort vessels and the small *ad hoc* convoy attempting to reach Murmansk *en masse*. Hurriedly, KG 30 returned to its maritime missions alongside KG 26, and the 5,060-ton American steamer SS *Hoosier* was sunk by II./KG 26, while the Panamanian-registered *El Capitan* was disabled by near-misses scored by KG 30 that caused the ship to take on water and begin to sink slowly by the stern. The abandoned ship was finished off by *U251*. Then the Soviet freighter *Vishera* was sunk on 10 July. Further bomb hits were scored on the Soviet destroyers *Sokrushitel'nyy* and *Gremyashchiy*.

The attacks did not go unpunished. A single KG 30 Junkers, 4D+AH of 1./KG 30, flown by *Staffelkapitän Hptm.* Eberhard Schröder, was shot down by Soviet fighters and all crew lost. That same day, Ju 88 A-4 4D+QA of the training *Staffel* Erpr.St./KG 30 was also shot down, this time by Soviet flak over Iokanga on the Barents Sea coast. It crashed into the sea, all four crew being listed as missing in action. 'Hajo' Herrmann later recorded his impressions of the attack on PQ17:

> We raced down in formation, diving steeply through the cloud layer, emerging like devils, our machine-guns firing wildly. We descended lower

and lower, dropped our bombs and pulled up high into the sun, swiftly leaving the smooth white sheet of cloud below us . . . Anything we crippled but didn't sink would be finished off by the U-boats . . . Individual steamers battered their way through the drift ice. We found them.

As I flew back from the combat area one of my pilots called me up: the crew of a steamer had taken to their boats before he had carried out his attack. He had dropped his bombs, and the crew were rowing back to their ship to board it again and sail further on. He asked me whether or not he should fire on the men with his machine guns. I was at a loss. I tried to picture the situation. What would I do? I couldn't make up my mind. I told the pilot to take a note of the steamer's course, fly back to base and calculate the position of the incident by dead reckoning.

I telephoned *Kommodore* Bloedorn. He spoke to the Chief of the *Luftflotte*, who then spoke to me. I told him that in my opinion this was not a case of an emergency at sea. The crew had made a tactical evasion and should not be treated any differently from the crew of a scout car who have run away and taken cover from an attack from the air. Such soldiers would be looked upon as combatants, not as wounded or shipwrecked mariners. The *Generaloberst* was inclined to agree, but said that he would leave the decision to the Führer's headquarters.

I received the decision from Headquarters about two hours later: the men were to be treated as survivors of a shipwreck. If we had missed with our bombs, that was our incompetence.[25]

Finally, the ordeal of PQ17 was at an end. Only eleven of the thirty-four ships that had departed from Iceland reached the Soviet Union. Twenty-four had been sunk; sixteen by U-boats and the remainder by the Luftwaffe, killing 153 merchant seamen and disposing of some 430 tanks, 210 aircraft, 3,350 lorries and jeeps and 100,000 tons of materials bound for the Russian battlefields. In return only five Luftwaffe aircraft had been lost.

> Thus was achieved one of the most outstanding successes to be scored at one blow against enemy supply lines, through the most exemplary co-operation between the Luftwaffe and U-boats. A convoy carrying a full cargo of war materiel from America, some of which had been under way many months, was almost completely annihilated in spite of very strong escort, just as it was approaching its destination. Thus a severe blow has been dealt to Russia's armament and a serious breach made in enemy

shipping tonnage. The strategic, physical, and moral effect of this blow is similar to that of a lost battle. Aided by circumstances, the Luftwaffe and the U-boats, in five days of purposeful and unerring action, achieved what was to have been accomplished by the attack of the fleet forces on PQ17 in operation *Rösselsprung*.[26]

In fact, the damage caused to the Allies by the loss of PQ17 reached far beyond burning ships and dead bodies drifting on the frozen waters of the Arctic. Soviet authorities accused the Royal Navy of cowardice, and Allied commanders of lying about the extent of their losses and refusing to believe that so many ships could be lost in a single engagement. In the USA the well-known Anglophobe Admiral Ernest J. King, Chief of Naval Operations, was enraged at the loss of American shipping (fourteen of the merchants sunk), and refused to co-operate with the Royal Navy any further within the region, moving his forces instead to the Pacific to face the Japanese. To add insult to injury, the ships of QP13 that had evaded attack had suffered four merchant ships sunk and two damaged after the convoy was guided mistakenly into a British minefield off Iceland. Despite howls of Soviet protest, further PQ convoys were suspended, as British strength was required elsewhere for Operation *Pedestal* within the Mediterranean. Following the catastrophe of PQ17, the Royal Navy was determined that PQ18 would not sail until much greater escort strength could be provided, and the convoy would not depart for Russia until September.

Within the Mediterranean, significant portions of the Royal Navy's Home Fleet were detached to strengthen the escort for the WS21S convoy of fourteen merchantmen bound for Malta. Once more the island teetered on the point of collapse, and the all-out effort to push supplies through was escorted by a total of four aircraft carriers, two battleships, seven light cruisers and thirty-two destroyers in an operation codenamed *Pedestal*. The day after passing Gibraltar on 10 August the carrier HMS *Eagle* was sunk by *U73*. On a simultaneous operation, Operation *Bellows*, the carrier HMS *Furious* flew off its complement of thirty-eight Spitfires bound for Malta on schedule before turning back to Gibraltar under escort by eight destroyers. All but one of the fighters arrived safely. That evening the storm broke, and the Luftwaffe began its attack on the *Pedestal* ships.

German intelligence had detected a noticeable reduction in RAF activity over Malta and Egypt, and interpreted this to indicate a

Torpedo control mechanism housed beneath the nose armament aboard an He 111.

husbanding of resources to cover a forthcoming major resupply operation for Malta. Expecting diversionary attacks on *Panzerarmee Afrika*, and after reconnaissance aircraft detected 'lively submarine activity' within the western Mediterranean, the Luftwaffe began to redeploy aircraft from Greece to Sicily, while concurrently raising the combat readiness of units worn down through the bombardment of Malta. Joint torpedo and bombing exercises were planned with units of the *Regia Aeronautica*, but were forestalled by agents' reports of the passage of *Pedestal* through the Strait of Gibraltar. Kesselring harboured fears that Crete could also be threatened by Allied Eastern Mediterranean forces as a diversionary tactic, and ordered increased readiness of the Luftwaffe units in both Sicily and Crete. On 5 August he directed the redeployment of some Cretan aircraft to Sardinia and Sicily, though supply difficulty in Sardinia prevented the basing of long-range bomber forces on the island. Kesselring ordered II.*Fliegerkorps* to accommodate reinforcements from X.*Fliegerkorps* temporarily for imminent operations, and *Fliegerführer*

Afrika was forced to shift his operational focus from front-line ground support to escorting convoys bound for Tobruk. Luftwaffe Ju 88 bomber forces on Sicily (Stab, II. and III./KG 77, KGr. 606, KGr. 806 and I./KG 54) were bolstered by twenty Ju 88s from Cretan-based I. and II./LG 1 after they had completed their Aegean convoy-escort missions. Torpedo bombers from Grosseto were also quickly despatched to Catania, though there remains a certain amount of confusion over which aircraft they were. The He 111Hs attached to *Oblt.* Hugo Bock's training *Staffel* 1./ *Kampfschulgeschwader* 2 were certainly involved, although it appears that within the strength of this unit were aircraft of Stab and 6./KG 26, the latter still at that point engaged in operations from Saki, Crimea. It is possible that these aircraft had been detached for torpedo training, rendering them deployed under a *de facto* 'double unit designation'. Furthermore, an ULTRA decrypt of German radio communications on 8 August reads:

> 1040/11./8/42. EMERGENCY. A torpedo *staffel* of ten Ju 88 to transfer today from Grosseto to Catania. Secondly, twenty-five torpedoes to be flown from Kalamaki to Catania as early as possible today, all other air transport tasks from Greek area to be postponed if necessary.[27]

A lack of fuel in Crete may well have prevented the transfer being carried out immediately, but that still raises the question of whether ten Ju 88s were transferred from Grosseto or ten He 111Hs; three of *Stab* I./KG 26 and seven of 6./KG 26. Indeed, KG 26 had become quite dispersed by this stage of the war. Assuming that at least some element of 6./KG 26 remained in the Crimea alongside 4. and 5. *Staffeln, Staffeln* 1. and 3. were in Bardufoss and 2. *Staffel* at Banak, Norway, while III./KG 26 was in Rennes, France, now equipped with Ju 88A-4s.

Ultimately, between the Italian 287th, 146th, 170th, 144th and 197th Squadrons spread between Sicily and Sardinia, the *Regia Aeronautica* mustered 328 aircraft (90 torpedo bombers, 62 bombers, 25 dive-bombers and 151 fighters), while II.*Fliegerkorps* had been brought up to a strength of 456 aircraft, comprising 328 dive-bombers, 32 bombers and 96 fighters. Combined with major Italian surface units, Italian and German U-boats, S-boats and MTBs, the forces facing *Pedestal* were daunting, albeit known to the Allies through ULTRA decryption of Axis signals traffic.

The first air attack, mounted by thirty dive-bombing Ju 88s of LG 1 and KGr. 806 attacking simultaneously with six KG 26 He 111 torpedo bombers, was launched at twilight on 11 August. The Luftwaffe managed to evade fighters flown off the aircraft carriers, but was unsettled by heavy anti-aircraft fire that forced the torpedo aircraft to launch from a considerable distance and miss. Likewise, the Ju 88s experienced no success, though they mistakenly believed a cruiser and the carrier HMS *Victorious* had been hit and damaged. *Oberleutnant* Gerhard Stamp of 1./LG 1 later wrote:

> I well recall how none of us were very pleased about things when we had to move from our well-established quarters on Crete and transfer over to Sicily in readiness for the *Pedestal* battle. Any temporary move of this nature to Sicily involved a great deal of discomfort and upset, because our technical requirements, our personal needs and our servicing was all in the hands of strange ground crew who did not know our squadron, our machines or us. It was not their fault, they were already committed to servicing their own squadrons — we were extra work to them.
>
> On the attack, our pilot approached the target ship from her port side. He wanted to make sure that at least one bomb would be a direct hit.
>
> 'Ready for diving!' — the pilot would enter his dive within seconds. It was a textbook attack, as now I saw the big ship down there coming closer to the red mark ahead of my feet. This mark showed us when we were in the 60° angle for the dive. The pilot closed the radiator flaps of the engines. I saw the propeller indicator being moved back to the half-past-eight position, and now the air brakes came out, and our Ju 88 was shaking like a chained stallion.
>
> All of a sudden everything was literally flying in our cockpit. My heavy leather navigator's portfolio was moving around in suspension as the Ju 88's nose went down. I hung in my belts — all I had to do was keep my eyes on the altimeter. At 1,500 metres altitude I had to knock my pilot's knee, shouting 'Fifteen!' At 1,200 metres, a second knock — 'Twelve hundred!' At 1,000 metres a final clout on his knee, 'Thousand!' We now had our maximum diving speed of 600km/h and we would lose another 400 metres while flattening out automatically — so the bombs had to be dropped right now. The pilot pushed the red button on the left horn of his steering controls. One could physically feel the loosening of a total of 1,000 kilos of bomb weight, as the Ju 88's automatic pull-out returned the aircraft to level.
>
> Six Gs were pressing us into our seats and made our heads bow as if an invisible heavyweight had sat on our necks. My stomach, which had

almost come out of my throat when we started diving, was now somewhere else. My chin was torn downward and so was my tongue. The pilot did all he had to to bring us back to normal flying.[28]

One KGr. 806 Ju 88 was brought down by anti-aircraft fire, while LG 1 lost six aircraft, a seventh being shot down in error by Italian fighters near Sardinia. The following day there were fresh air attacks and more losses for the Luftwaffe, at least four aircraft being destroyed by Sea Hurricanes and Fulmars from the British carriers, as well as two claimed by Royal Navy gunners. To compound the German misery, *Oblt.* Axel Helmut Gerlich's Ju 88A-4, L1+ON, and *Lt.* Hans Hanneman's L1+HP were both mistakenly shot down by Italian flak over Sardinia. Hannemen and his crew were all killed, as was Gerlich, though the rest of his crew survived despite suffering wounds.

In return, aircraft of KG 54 and KG 77, in conjunction with Italian bombers, shook both HMS *Rodney* and *Nelson* with near misses and damaged the freighter MV *Deucalion*. Bombs from a Ju 88 straddled the ship, and one pierced the deck but failing to explode. However, a near miss caused enough damage to reduce its speed, with Number 1 hold half-flooded and Number 2 completely flooded. The freighter was ordered to leave the convoy and head for the North African coastal route to Malta, escorted by the destroyer HMS *Bramham*.

Amidst the wave of attacking aircraft, ten Italian S.84 torpedo bombers of 38 Group's 32 Stormo employed the 'Motobomba FFF Torpedo' in the largest use of the new weapon thus far. A 50cm-diameter electric torpedo, the 'Motobomba' was dropped from a height of up to 100 metres by parachute, which broke loose on impact with the water, the weapon's 3.5hp engine igniting to steer it in concentric spirals of between 500 and 4,000 metres until it found a target. Weighing 350kg and carrying a 120kg warhead, the torpedo had a top speed of 40 knots, though this dropped after a period in the water, and could continue running for nearly an hour. The weapon had been planned for initial use against Gibraltar during July, but the attack was aborted, its first successful employment coming a month later. Although its use against *Pedestal* failed to achieve a hit, the 'Motobomba' caused alarm aboard the Allied ships and helped to break up the convoy south of Cape Spartivento, Sardinia, diminishing the effectiveness of massed anti-aircraft fire. The Luftwaffe would later adapt the torpedo, designated LT 350, for its own use, though it was not used in action until 19 March 1943, in an attack on Tripoli.[29]

Throughout the day on 12 August *Pedestal* came under severe pressure from Italian aircraft and naval forces, which left only one aircraft carrier, HMS *Victorious*, with a functioning flight deck, the strategy to target the carriers first and eliminate aircraft protection almost succeeding. At 2038hrs, twenty-five minutes after sunset, thirty Ju 88s co-ordinated an attack with six He 111 torpedo bombers focused on the merchantmen. Escorted by six Bf 109s, the attackers hit the 12,800-ton SS *Brisbane Star* with a torpedo that blew a hole in its side and caused it to come to a complete stop, though it was later able to make way and reached Malta with most of its cargo intact. The 12,688GRT refrigerated cargo liner SS *Empire Hope* had its engines put out of action by eighteen near misses, then two direct hits on Number 4 hold caused part of the cargo of kerosene, coal and ammunition to explode, the stern catching fire. The crew abandoned ship and were rescued by HMS *Penn*. Although the blazing wreck was later torpedoed by the Italian submarine *Bronzo*, it still stubbornly refused to disappear until the wrecked remains were deemed a hazard to shipping and sunk by HMS *Bramham* off Galeta Island.

Only ten minutes later the 7,347-ton SS *Clan Ferguson* was hit and began to burn, its cargo of 2,000 tons of aviation fuel and and 1,500 tons of explosives later exploding and sinking the ship. The *Clan Ferguson*'s crew included eight navy and twelve army gunners and numbered 101 men in total. Twelve were killed as the remainder abandoned ship, along with thirteen passengers. Sixty-four men took to rafts, the remainder escaping in a single lifeboat which later drifted ashore in Vichy Tunisia, where they were interned. Of the men aboard the rafts, thirty-two were rescued by a German flying boat which alighted alongside during the following day, seven more by an Italian Red Cross aircraft, and the remainder were finally washed ashore on the Tunisian coast.

The damaged *Deucalion* was located creeping along the North African coastline and attacked once again. Torpedoed by an He 111 near the Tunisian island of La Galite, she caught fire and was abandoned before sinking in flames. The 12,843-ton MV *Waimarama* was among the final *Pedestal* casualties at the hands of the Luftwaffe. It was sunk off Cape Bon by Ju 88s of 3./KGr. 806 led by *Staffelkapitän Oblt*. Wolfgang Schulte. Direct hits by four bombs on this, the largest of the *Pedestal* ships, ignited aviation fuel stored on deck in flimsy cans, which exploded and sent the ship down in less than five minutes.

U-boat attacks whittled the convoy down further, while the Italian cruiser division sailed to intercept and 3.S-flotilla launched its own attacks from Porto Empedocle beginning in the early hours of 13 August. Italian MAS boats joined the fray and, although various sources quote different results, by the end of the night German S-boats had sunk four merchant ships and damaged a fifth. Later that day He 111s sank the badly damaged 12,436-ton MV *Wairangi*, but further attacks on 14 August failed to sink any more ships.

The Allied casualty list for Operation *Pedestal* was frightening. Only five of the merchant ships reached Valletta's Grand Harbour, and hundreds of lives were lost while battering the convoy through. Nineteen German aircraft were lost, along with forty-two Italian, including those destroyed on the ground and shot down by 'friendly fire' accidents. Royal Navy gunners and Fleet Air Arm fighters claimed seventy-four aircraft shot down, but destroyed forty-two; twenty-six from the *Regia Aeronautica* and sixteen Luftwaffe aircraft. The Fleet Air Arm lost thirteen aircraft on operations and sixteen additional Sea Hurricanes when HMS *Eagle* was sunk, while the RAF lost a Bristol Beaufighter, five Spitfires and a Sunderland. The Italian cruiser division failed to engage the enemy, an undoubted tactical blunder on Mussolini's part, for ultimately, although the convoy was a debacle comparable with such disasters as PQ17 in the Arctic, it resupplied Malta to such a degree that the island no longer faced starvation. Fighter cover above Malta was rejuvenated with the arrival of aviation fuel and machine parts and, ultimately, Malta revived as a functional military base. During August 1942 Axis convoys supplying the *Afrika Korps* came under attack once again. Thirty-five per cent of ships despatched were destroyed that month, and the figure rose in September. As Rommel appeared poised to strike a decisive blow in Egypt, his supply lines were threatened once again.

Panzerarmee Afrika launched its last great drive on 30 August. The attack, Operation *Brandung*, was an attempt to turn the Allied defensive line, but with the Allies forewarned by ULTRA, it was comprehensively defeated at the battle of Alam Halfa, and Rommel was back at his starting positions within six days. The stage was set for the Allied counterattack at El Alamein, which began on 23 October and initiated *Panzerarmee Afrika*'s long and permanent retreat.

Meanwhile, a temporary lull in Luftwaffe operations had allowed reorganisation of the Sicilian-based bombers. *Hauptmann* Rolf Siedschlag's KGr. 606 was finally incorporated into KG 77 as the new I.*Gruppe*, while *Maj.* Richard Linke's KGr. 806 became III.*Gruppe* of KG 54, their naval aviation origins but a distant memory. There then followed a renewed blitz on Malta, though with diminished effect and mounting Axis casualties. It began on 11 October and lasted only a week, the Luftwaffe suffering heavy losses in the face of a revived defence. More than thirty Ju 88s were destroyed, either through enemy action or subsequent crash landings. Among the casualties suffered on the final day of the offensive was II./KG 77 *Gruppenkommandeur Maj.* Heinrich Paepke, killed when his aircraft, 3Z+AC, collided head-on with a defending Spitfire off Valletta's south-eastern coast. That same day II./LG 1 *Gruppenkommandeur Maj.* Gerhard Kollewe was shot down by Spitfires of 126 and 249 Sqns off Valletta. Although Kollewe and his crew successfully baled out, only wireless operator *Obfw.* Martin Assum and gunner *Fw.* Paul Ballof were recovered alive from the sea, claiming that they had been strafed while in the water by a British fighter. The bodies of Kollewe and his observer, *Fw.* Bernhard Mähler, were later recovered and buried in Cagliari. Kollewe had been awarded the Oak Leaves to his Knight's Cross as commander of II./LG 1 on 12 August, his unit being credited with sinking 148,000 tons of shipping and two destroyers, and he having flown more than 250 missions.

While to the north and south the Luftwaffe's maritime strike forces had reached the summit of their achievements during 1942, within the Black

German Luftwaffe test crew aboard an unarmed He 115 near Foggia, Italy, 1942. (James Payne)

Sea the attritional battle against Soviet naval forces remained protracted and difficult. Although the Soviet Black Sea Fleet was quantitatively superior in every way to regional Axis naval forces, its continued use in support of army operations limited its effectiveness. Heavy units designed to contest naval control of the Black Sea were instead almost exclusively used in fire-support and convoy-escort roles, opposed by the smaller vessels of the Romanian and German navies present within the theatre. Luftwaffe operations were the domain of *Generaloberst* Alexander Löhr's *Luftflotte* 4, and attacks on the Soviet ships when engaged in bombardment missions lessened their fire support's effectiveness, Soviet commanders being trained to fire on the move in defence of air attack. By far the most lethal Luftwaffe asset in use against the Soviet Black Sea Fleet and its merchant convoys was the Ju 87 Stuka, which was hurled into action against targets of opportunity, frequently included shipping.

The eastern winter of 1941-42 was severe, and Luftwaffe operational levels fell dramatically, even within the warmer climes of the Southern reaches of the Russian Front. At the end of November 1941 the command staff of V.*Fliegerkorps*, a component of *Luftflotte* 4, had begun relocating from Rostov to Brussels. The intention was to convert it to a dedicated minelaying corps, until its commander, *General der Flieger* Robert Ritter von Greim, received direct orders from Göring to establish an emergency Luftwaffe tactical operations staff to counter a growing Soviet threat against the eastern Crimea, where Red Army troops had made some haphazard, though successful, landings despite Luftwaffe minelaying around Kerch. On 26 December Soviet troops stormed ashore on the northern coast of the Kerch Peninsula, establishing five bridgeheads up to one battalion in strength each. While huge resources were still engaged in battering Sevastopol into submission, the Germans were momentarily thrown off balance by the Soviet ability to land troops in force, supported by naval artillery.

Greim's hastily organised *Sonderstab Krim*, situated in Sarabuz Russkiy, north-west of Simferopol, was tasked with four chief responsibilities in support of *General der Flieger* Kurt Pflugbeil's hard-pressed IV.*Fliegerkorps*. These were the maintenance of reconnaissance over the Black Sea and coastal areas of the Crimean Peninsula; interdiction of Soviet maritime supply and troop movements, as well as those using the 'ice road' over the frozen Kerch Strait; strikes on troop concentrations in the Parpach position and rear areas; and fighter attacks against front-line Soviet airfields. Alongside fighter and dive-bomber units, Greim controlled the bombers of III./KG 27, III./KG 51 and I./ KG 100, though the situation was complicated in terms of equipment and training standards. There was no established supply system by which to equip the units gathered under Greim's command, and the few small forward Crimean airfields available to the Luftwaffe were unsuitable for major bomber operations. The supply situation was never resolved. *Major* Erich Thiel's III./KG 27 had its He 111s repurposed to enable anti-shipping missions after previously supporting the Wehrmacht's land advance, but the unit possessed neither bombs nor detonators suitable for anti-shipping strikes. A similar problem plagued III./KG 51, part of the only *Kampfgeschwader* equipped with Ju 88s in the Russian southern theatre. Furthermore, *Maj.* Ernst Freiherr von Bibra's III./ KG 51 was shuttled between the hastily prepared airstrip at Saki and its previous location at Nikolayev to help counter a Soviet ground offensive. Finally, *Maj.* Helmut Küster's I./KG 100, a specialised minelaying unit, possessed no aircrew trained in anti-shipping operations. Von Wild's

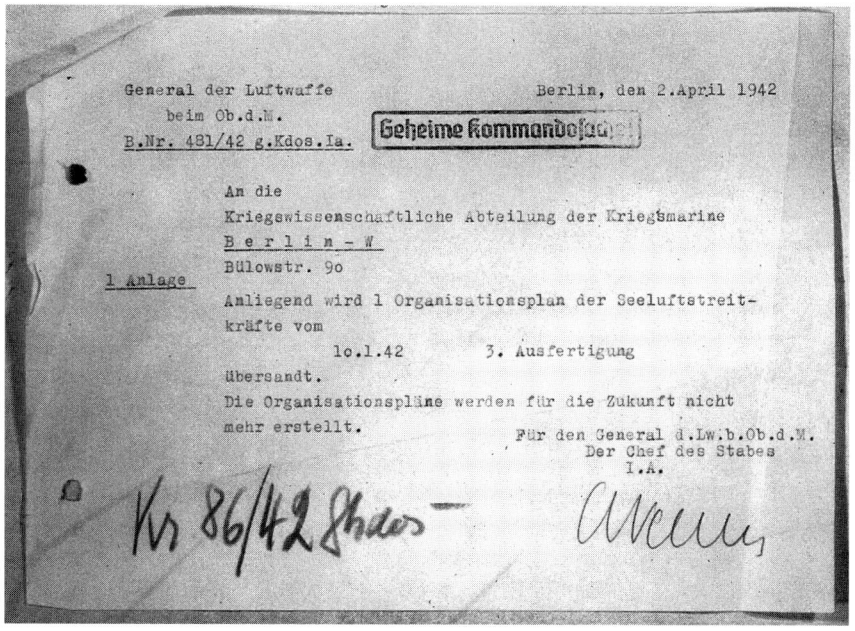

Communique reflecting the virtual dissolution of the *Luftstreitkräfte*; with no units on strength any longer 'organisational plans [which had been published monthly] will no longer be created'.

small *Fliegerführer Süd* command was also subordinated to Greim's *Sonderstab*, possessing as it did the necessary trained reconnaissance and 6./KG 26 torpedo aircraft.

However, although the aircraft and crews available to Greim may have lacked equipment or the specific training required for their tasks, they were far from ineffective. During January *Major* Helmut Küster's I./KG 100 began flying operations against shipping and troop concentrations from Focsani, Romania, before moving to the forward base in Saki, initially planned as a jumping-off point for anti-shipping strikes. From there they continued to mount repeated bombing raids despite frequent air attacks on the airfield. The *Staffelkapitän* of 8./KG 100, *Hptm.* Hansgeorg Bätcher, distinguished himself on 20 February by sinking a freighter headed for Sevastopol, estimated at 2,000GRT. Following demands from *Luftflotte* 4 that all supply ships be destroyed, on 6 February Bätcher attacked a sighted 7,500GRT tanker near Kerch Harbour, but encountered dense anti-aircraft fire. Circling out of visual range, he throttled back the engines to just above stalling speed to make as silent an approach as possible, and attacked once more, releasing his SC500 bombs manually, without bombardier control. A single bomb struck amidships, severely damaging the tanker, which Bätcher returned to finish off on 20 February, her cargo of fuel still trapped inside the stricken hull and sent to the bottom.

Perhaps unsurprisingly, the existence of *Sonderstab Krim* was brief and fraught with problems, and it was disbanded by Göring on 11 February after being further hamstrung by an inefficient supply network, inadequate communications staff and a lack of preparation that highlighted the hastily assembled emergency nature of the Staff. Nonetheless, the *Sonderstab* claimed the destruction of 25,000 tons of enemy shipping, seventy-six enemy aircraft, and 335 vehicles and fourteen artillery batteries, as well as the trains and troop concentrations attacked during its brief existence. Greim moved onwards to the support of Army Group Centre facing Moscow, forming *Luftwaffenkommando* Ost after being reunited with the remainder of his staff. At midnight on 18 February *Oberst* von Wild's *Fliegerführer Süd* assumed command over all Luftwaffe air units in the Crimea, and torpedo bombers of 4. and 5./KG 26 flew in to Saki from Greece to join 6.*Staffel* during that month, reinforcing the available torpedo force. The first success of the reunited II./KG.26 came on the night of 1/2 March, when the 2,434-ton SS *Fabritzius* was torpedoed and severely damaged, being claimed as a '6,000-

ton transport'. The stricken ship was grounded on the bleak shore near Bol'shoy Utrish, where it was further battered by gale-force winds and lay abandoned. On 23 March the 2,690GRT steamship *Vasilii Chapaev* departed from Poti under destroyer escort, carrying approximately 250 troops for Sevastopol. Forty miles from the Kherson lighthouse she was hit by a II./KG 26 torpedo and sank, with twenty-six crew members and eighty-six soldiers killed. The toll in Soviet shipping harvested by KG 26 over the following weeks was slow and steady, frequently involving heavy loss of life among Soviet troops being shuttled by any means into the inferno of Sevastopol.

Co-operation between von Wild's staff and Admiral Black Sea (*Admiral Schwarzes Meer; Vizeadmiral* Friedrich-Wilhelm Fleischer until May 1942) was fast and efficient. However, it still bore the hallmarks of uneasy Kriegsmarine and Luftwaffe relations, and was considerably more difficult when liaising with the command of *Lufiflotte* 4 as, once again, a relatively convoluted path was established for Kriegsmarine operational requests for maritime aircraft.

On 2 February 1942 *Lufiflotte* 4 requested a naval liaison officer to be attached 'in order to guarantee close co-operation between the *Lufiflotte*, [*Marine*]*Gruppe Süd* and *Admiral Schwarzes Meer*'.³⁰ S-boats, U-boats and minesweepers were about to become active within the Black Sea after being transferred laboriously from Germany by road, canal and waterway. *Marinegruppenkommando Süd* (*MGK Süd*) requested the posting of a fleet officer, the post temporarily filled by *K.K.* von Bothmer, Chief of Staff to *Seekommandant Ukraine* and a highly experienced man with proven logistical skills. By May *Konteradmiral* Robert Eyssen replaced him as the appointed liaison, Luftwaffe *Maj.* Werner Securius being among the officers alongside whom he worked. Following initial requests for aircraft to be made available for maritime reconnaissance, Fleischer's staff received a firm rebuke from the Luftwaffe, who made it clear that Eyssen alone, as liaison officer, was responsible for such appeals. Direct requests to Lutflotte 4 or *Fliegerführer Süd*, Fleischer was informed, were only to be made 'in urgent cases'.³¹ In return, following this reprimand, it was tartly remarked in the Admiral Black Sea War Diary that 'naval operations must not be disclosed by careless use of the telephone by the Luftwaffe'.

Fortunately, von Wild not only fully appreciated naval requirements, but also possessed a temperament patently suitable to his role, and he established a convivial rapport with his naval counterparts. Von Wild, whose staff reported a strength of eighteen officers and 200 men on 18

March 1942, continued torpedo operations against Soviet convoy traffic around Sevastopol throughout March, but with limited success. Although a spirit of willing co-operation existed between von Wild, Fleischer and their respective staffs, the number of aircraft available to *Fliegerführer Süd* for maritime operations fluctuated wildly, being dependant upon the situation at other points of the southern Russian Front, although floatplanes and flying boats of *Aufklärungsgruppe* 125 (*See*) remained on strength permanently from November 1941. The lack of extra maritime reconnaissance aircraft available directly to the Kriegsmarine was reflected in a telephone message from *Maj.* Securius on 3 April, in which he reported that four Cant Z.501 Gabbiano floatplanes, one Dornier Do 24 and two Heinkel He 114s were likely to become operational during the following day. Additionally, six Blenheims could be added, *if* the Romanian Air Force made them available from their Craiova Airfield.

Furthermore, on 12 March, Luftwaffe Operations Staff issued *Luftflotte* 4 with instructions that the centres of gravity for Black Sea anti-shipping operations were to be the ports of Sevastopol, Kerch, and Kamysh-Burun and their approaching sea lanes; Sevastopol being the point of maximum effort. Anti-shipping missions in the wider expanse of

A dummy torpedo is loaded aboard a Junkers Ju 87D during unsuccessful trials to convert the aircraft into a torpedo bomber.

The wreck of the 2,434-ton SS *Fabritzius*, torpedoed by KG26, ashore near Bol'shoy Utrish alongside the remains of a downed German aircraft.

the Black Sea were to be stopped, and aerial reconnaissance was only to be carried out in areas where bombers or torpedo bombers could reliably intercept sighted targets. Long-range reconnaissance was to be the very lowest rung of the Luftwaffe's operational ladder.

Löhr's *Luftflotte* 4, and by extension much of *Fliegerführer Süd*'s strength, was acting as flying artillery for land operations, and *Fliegerführer Süd* mounted anti-shipping operations that, though individually quite successful, *General* Hermann Plocher later described in his post-war study of the Luftwaffe in Russia as having the effect of mere 'nuisance raids', given the size of the Soviet Black Sea Fleet and its mercantile equivalent. Although this may somewhat understate the effectiveness of such anti-shipping strikes, which were 'felt very strongly' according to a 1943 Red Army General Staff study on the 1942 Crimean campaign, the offensive strength available to von Wild for dedicated maritime operations would never allow decisive operations. Nonetheless, between 19 February, when von Wild took over all Crimean air operations, and 9 August 1942 *Fliegerführer Süd* had flown 3,481 missions, claiming sixty-eight merchant ships sunk totalling an estimated 131,500GRT, as well as twenty-two military vessels. They also claimed damage inflicted on a further forty-three merchants, fifteen military vessels — including two heavy cruisers and a light cruiser — and a floating dry-dock in Sevastopol Harbour. Additionally, as well as ground operations against trains, wheeled transport columns, artillery emplacements and Soviet defensive positions, in fifty-six special nightly missions 351 aircraft had dropped 270 mines in the Kerch Strait, eighty-nine in Sevastopol Harbour and 279 in the Volga River near Stalingrad (predominantly laid by KG 100), as the Luftwaffe operated in support of the Sixth Army's drive towards the city.[32]

Von Wild's command had been stripped bare during May, when Wolfram von Richthofen had transferred to Simferopol at the head of VIII.*Fliegerkorps*. The tempestuous Luftwaffe commander was to operate independent of *Luftflotte* 4's command structure, answerable only to Göring, something that rankled deeply with Alexander Löhr and his staff. In command of all offensive Crimean Luftwaffe operations, von Richthofen immediately removed several of the all-purpose *Staffeln* that had been attached to *Fliegerführer Süd*. The effect of this was keenly felt by Admiral Black Sea:

> 1 May: Naval Liaison Officer to *Fliegerführer Süd* reported that from today the air forces in the Crimea were subordinated to VIII.*Fliegerkorps*. Only two bomber *Gruppen* were left to *Fliegerführer Süd* for attacks on ships and sea reconnaissance. This measure is only valid during the intended Kerch offensive, when sea reconnaissance must be restricted to the area off Sevastopol and the Crimea as far as Kerch Peninsula, the Sea of Azov and the north-east coast as far as Novorossisk. In view of the convoy assignments to be carried out, this reduction in air reconnaissance over the Black Sea is very regrettable, as aircraft taking off from Bulgarian and Romanian bases can fly only as far as 32° East. Moreover, only a few aircraft are available for that task, so that reconnaissance will by no means give a complete picture. For the time being, enemy movements and intentions must be deduced from the reports of Main Naval Direction-Finding Station, Constantza.

Von Richthofen's military star was in the ascendant. He had earned the full trust and support of Adolf Hitler, thanks to his unswerving obedience to instructions (including Hitler's infamous 'no retreat order' at the gates of Moscow in the winter of 1941) and his effectiveness as a military leader. His methods were direct, brutal and highly successful. To him was passed the task of reducing Sevastopol in support of *Feldmarschall*

Three of the crew of a BV 138 operating from Norway: pilot, observer, wireless operator.

Erich von Manstein's Eleventh Army and safeguarding the Crimean Peninsula from Soviet counterattack. What had once been a peripheral strategic objective was now assuming greater proportions than previously expected.

Von Richthofen immediately threw himself into his new task, and also promptly recorded his harsh observations of the *Fliegerführer Süd*'s state of readiness. On 27 May he recorded:

> Nothing has been done in the last months and, despite orders to *Fliegerführer Süd*, still nothing has been done in the last weeks.

To compound matters, on the following day von Wild despatched Heinkel torpedo bombers to attack a sighted Soviet cruiser and destroyers carrying troops bound for Sevastopol, but failed to obtain any results. The Red Army reinforcements successfully offloaded into the besieged port city, and von Richthofen was furious:

> *Fliegerführer Süd* attempted [to sink it] with the II./KG 26, the old group from Lüneburg. Absolutely pathetic. They fired off 29 torpedoes without any success!!

Despite von Richthofen's harsh opinion, von Wild had established an excellent understanding with his naval opposites, including the establishment of a small naval-air command centre in Saki, set up under the joint leadership of von Wild, *Kaptlt.* Heinz Birnbacher, commander of the newly arrived 1.S-boat flotilla, and *Capitano di Fregata* Francesco Mimbelli, commander of the Italian 4th *Flottiglia* MAS, which had also recently arrived in the Black Sea. Relationships remained locally good between the services, *MGK Süd* remarking that 'co-operation between naval and air forces in the operational zone exists, and without friction'. However, von Richthofen clearly underestimated the level to which the Luftwaffe, Kriegsmarine and *Regia Marina* could successfully interact, and issued orders on 10 June that were swiftly passed on by *Konteradmiral* Eyssen to Admiral Black Sea:

> As it is impossible always to be informed if and when submarines and light forces of the German and Italian navies are in Crimean waters, Commanding General, VIII.*Fliegerkorps* has given orders prohibiting his aircraft from making any attacks whatsoever on any submarines or light forces — including Russian vessels in the entire Black Sea.

Vizeadmiral Hans-Heinrich Wurmbach, who had taken over as Admiral Black Sea during May, was vexated by the heavy-handed Luftwaffe instructions.

> There is no valid reason why these air attacks on submarines and light forces should be prohibited in the whole Black Sea area, as at present the German and Italian S-boats and submarines are only operating in the Crimean area.

Eyssen was asked to request the prohibitive instructions be applied only to the Crimean area (north of 43° 30' N and west of 35° 40' E), and that Aufkl.Gr. 125, operating from Constanta, be allowed to continue their regular anti-submarine operations even within this area, as they worked closely alongside the regional Naval Special Duties Detachment and were constantly provided detailed information about all Axis naval movements. Almost surprisingly, given von Richthofen's bullish nature, within two days his request had been granted.

Elements of *Oberst* Gerhard Kolbe's Aufkl.Gr. 125 had been moved to the Black Sea in November 1941, Stab/A.F.Gr. 125 being based in Constanta (equipped with He 114s, Ar 196s and BV 138s), and the BV 138s of 3./Aufkl.Gr. 125 being based at Varna.[33] The floatplanes and flying boats operated rotating shifts of reconnaissance flights, and on 5

June BV 138 7R+DL crashed with engine failure. A rubber dinghy was sighted two days after the aircraft was listed as overdue, and *Schnellboote S72* and *S102* made their inaugural Black Sea sorties in an attempt to rescue the crew after an urgent request from Kolbe, as bad weather prevented an aerial search.

Fliegerführer Süd was heavily involved in adding every possible aircraft to the bombing of Sevastopol, particularly after von Richthofen was promoted and placed in command of *Luftflotte* 4 on 28 June. Austrian Alexander Löhr was moved to the Balkans, where he became commander of the Wehrmacht's Twelfth Army. Ultimately, von Richthofen would not be present to oversee the final assault on the battered port city, as Hitler's drive towards the Caucasian oil producing centres, *Fall Blau*, was about to begin, and VIII.*Fliegerkorps* headquarters had already relocated to Kharkov in preparation, von Wild once again being given command of all Crimean flying operations. Between 2 June and 3 July *Fliegerführer Süd* concentrated his attacks on oil storage, water and electricity works, artillery defences and enemy flak positions and airfields, ahead of the advancing Axis infantry, and also attacked shipping within the besieged harbour. During this period 23,751 sorties were flown, and in addition to inflicting considerable and extensive damage on ground installations and infrastructure, four destroyers, one submarine, three MTBs, six coastal ships and four freighters totalling 10,00GRT were claimed as sunk, for the loss of thirty-one Luftwaffe aircraft. Sevastopol finally fell on 4 July, as the final Soviet defensive land barrier was breached. Although sporadic fighting from isolated pockets of Red Army troops continued over the days that followed, the port city was finally in German hands.

The Black Sea remained a contested battleground, and on 1 August 1942 *Fliegerführer Süd* controlled III./LG 1 (thirty-two Ju 88s), II./KG 26 (20 He 111H-6 torpedo bombers, ten of 6./KG 26 having moved to Grossetto), Stab. and 2./Aufkl.Gr. 125 and, briefly, *Oblt.* Hans-Ulrich Rudel's training *Ergänzungsgruppe*/StG. 2 (twenty Ju 87s). On the night of 2 August the most concentrated attack by Luftwaffe torpedo aircraft within the Black Sea took place, when between six and ten aircraft of II./KG 26 attacked the Soviet cruiser *Molotov*, which was bombarding Axis forces in the Bay of Feodosia. Only a single Heinkel carried bombs, the remainder being armed with torpedoes, but skilful evasive manoeuvring foiled every torpedo launch. An aircraft of 4./KG 26 was hit by anti-aircraft fire and crashed in flames, the wreckage continuing to burn for three minutes after hitting the water. The cruiser was shaken by the blast

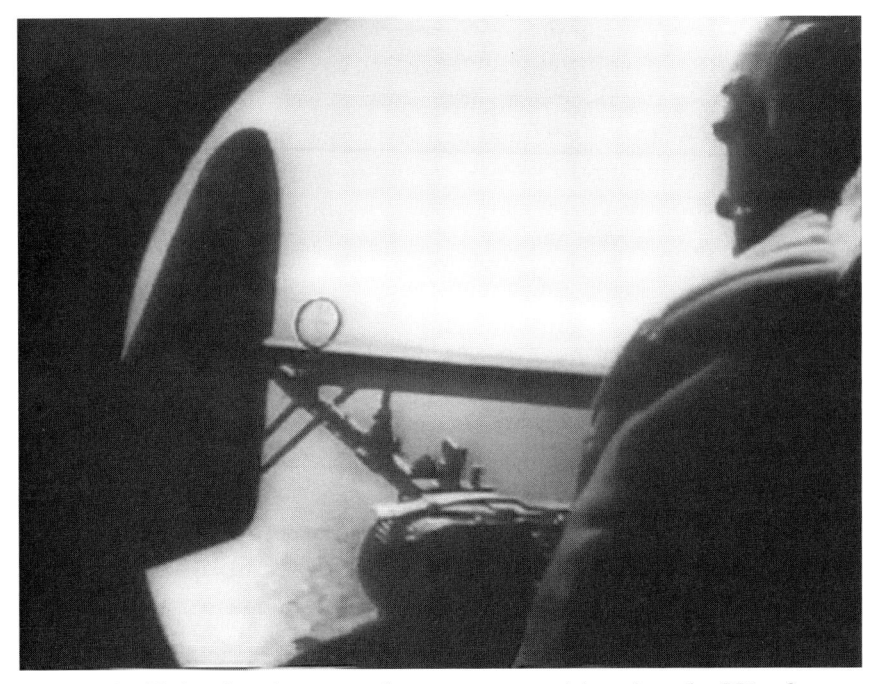

Newsreel still showing the exposed rear gunner position aboard a BV 138.

of a torpedo at 0127hrs, this frequently being attributed to the attacking Heinkels, not least of all by the after-action report compiled by the ship's captain. However, no such claim was raised by the German aircrews, and it appears that a separate attack by Italian MAS torpedo boats was responsible for the hit that blew off approximately twenty metres of the ship's stern. *Sottotenente di Vascello* Legnani's MAS 568 had been alerted to the presence of the cruiser by other boats of the same flotilla, and hit its port side with a pair of torpedoes before making off into the darkness, sporadically dropping depth charges as Legnani erroneously believed that he was being pursued by destroyers engaged in covering the *Molotov*.

This foiled attack marked the last major torpedo action within the Black Sea, although the front line would remain contested until 1944. Small Axis naval units skirmished continually with the Soviet Black Sea Fleet, its major ships withdrawing east as the Wehrmacht overran the western ports. However, despite *Fliegerführer Süd*'s relative success and the firmly established inter-service co-operation with the Kriegsmarine, the post was abolished during August 1942, around the same time that von Wild was hospitalised by illness. He did not return to active service until November, as *Lufttransportführer* I (*Südost*), Athens. On 15 October the new post of *Fliegerführer Krim* was established in Kerch, given responsibility for air operations in support of *Fall Blau*, and headed by the returned *General der Flieger* Konrad Zander.

As Luftwaffe operations stretched over the Casucasus, an unusual *ad hoc* unit was formed during the second part of 1942. *Oberleutnant* Hans Klimmer was apponted *Staffelkapitän* of *Küstenfliegerstaffel Krim*, created from twenty-four crews in training using the Focke-Wulf Fw 58 *Weihe*. Based at Bagerovo air base on the Kerch Peninsula, this small unit helped fill the ranks of a severely overtaxed Luftwaffe, patrolling the Crimean coastline, mounting armed-reconnaissance and ASW missions over the Black Sea, and providing aerial escort for transport convoys from Odessa to the Crimea. Over time the unit would morph away from nautical missions, being tasked from October onwards with nocturnal bombing of Soviet troop concentrations near Tuapse.

On the Arctic front, on 2 September 1942, the delayed convoy PQ18 sailed from Loch Ewe, bound for Archangelsk. The thirty-seven heavily-laden merchant ships, three minesweepers transferring to Russia, and one rescue ship were to be joined by eight more freighters from Reykjavik for the final leg. They were escorted by an unprecedented level of Royal Navy strength, including a close escort of destroyers, anti-aircraft ships, submarines, corvettes and minesweepers, a carrier force centred on HMS *Avenger* (albeit equipped with near-obsolete Sea Hurricanes), a 'Fighter Destroyer Force' of sixteen destroyers and the light cruiser HMS *Scylla*, and a distant cover force of battleships, cruisers and destroyers. Also, by September 1942, RAF Coastal Command had finally managed to establish a working base in northern Russia, equipped with Hampden torpedo bombers, photo-reconnaissance Spitfires and Catalina reconnaissance flying boats. Excellent intelligence sources included the successful tapping of the northern Wehrmacht teleprinter line that trailed through Sweden to Berlin, and ULTRA decryption painted a full picture of what faced PQ18, including the disposition of major surface units, the incapacitated state of *Tirpitz* due to mechanical problems and the location of waiting U-boats.

On the Luftwaffe side, the pause had allowed a rebuilding of forces with which to attack PQ18. *B-Dienst* conveyed the presence of HMS *Avenger*, and Göring ordered the aircraft carrier sunk as a priority target before assaulting the convoy proper. Arrayed against the incoming convoy were sixty Ju 88s of KG 30 at Banak, forty-six He 111H-6s and twenty-seven Ju 88 torpedo bombers of I. and III./KG 26 at Banak and Bardufoss (including the aircraft that had comprised KGr. 506), and fifteen He 115s of 1./Kü.Fl.Gr. 406. For reconnaissance, BV 138s of 1./Kü.Fl.Gr. 906 were available, as well as a handful of KG 40 Fw 200s and Ju 88s. Junkers Ju 87 Stukas of I./StG. 5 and Bf 109s of LG 5 also stood ready for closer-range attacks and to provide a defending fighter umbrella for the bombers.

On 8 September a BV 138 located the carrier group, earmarked for destruction by specific orders from the Luftwaffe command, but battle proper was not joined until 13 September. Failing to find the carrier, an initial attack in fine cloudless weather led by *Maj.* Eric Bloedorn at the head of twenty KG 30 Ju 88s attempted to disperse PQ18. They achieved no hits in their high-altitude bombing attacks, but neither did they suffer casualties, despite *Avenger* scrambling Sea Hurricanes at the first radar sighting of the incoming threat. However, the second strike, mounted by a combined force of seventeen Ju 88s of I./KG 30, dive-bombing simultaneously with the massed torpedo-bomber ranks of twenty-six He 111s of Klümper's I./KG 26 and seventeen Ju 88s of III./KG 26, led by *Hptm.* Nocken, achieved spectacular success in a three-wave attack. The Sea Hurricanes had run low on fuel and returned to the carrier, so the German bombers faced no aerial opposition, but they still had to run the gauntlet of massed firepower from every vessel, the Allied defences having been fully alerted by radar contact. Approaching at extreme low level in a textbook example of the 'Golden-Comb' wingtip-to-wingtip formation, the torpedo-bomber crews braved intense flak to drop torpedoes before overflying the convoy. In total, between He 111s and Ju 88s, eight merchants totalling 39,880 tons were hit in a space of mere minutes, either sinking immediately or being scuttled later by escort ships. Casualties were heavy, as many ships were struck by multiple torpedoes. Aboard HMS *Scylla*, Surgeon Lt Cdr J. L. S. Coulter witnessed the attack.

> They approached the convoy in line ahead from the starboard horizon. When level with the convoy they all turned towards it and attacked in line abreast. Each aircraft flew low over the water, and as the torpedoes were launched, each flew down the whole length of the convoy, firing its armament. There is no doubt that the attack was carried out with magnificent courage and precision, in the face of tremendous gunfire from the whole convoy and its

escort. The tanker [*sic*] in the next line abreast of us was hit early on by a torpedo which finished its run-in just above the tanker's funnel. At that second the whole tanker and aircraft were enveloped in a crimson wall of flame . . . When I looked down at the sea again, apart from a small occasional flicker of flame on the water, there was no sign of either the tanker or the aircraft, and I realised that they had both blown up.[34]

Four He 111s of I./KG 26 were hit by anti-aircraft fire and forced to ditch. *Leutnant* Johann Ruby's crew and one other were rescued by a Do 24 of 5.*Seenotstaffel*, and *Lt.* Arnold Harnau's crew was picked up by *U589*, only to be killed later when the U-boat was sunk with all hands the following day while trying to mount its own attack on PQ18. The fourth He 111, piloted by *Uffz.* Hermann Hiller (commanded by *Oblt.* Alfred Thöm), was seen to ditch, but no trace of the crew was ever found. *Feldwebel* Rudolf Hager's Ju 88A-4, 1T+KS of 8./KG 26, was shot down by naval gunfire. Two other Ju 88s were hit and damaged, crashing while attempting to land at Banak.

A BV 138 of *Aufklärungsgruppe* 125 (*See*) in Constanta, prepared with depth charges for an anti-submarine mission over the Black Sea. The tender (*Flugbetriebsboot*) at left, *Fl. C 3102*, was locally commandeered for Luftwaffe service.

At 1615hrs the convoy came under attack by nine He 115s of 1./ Kü.Fl.Gr. 406, though insufficient cloud cover, heavy anti-aircraft fire and relaunched Sea Hurricanes prevented a close approach and all torpedoes went wide. A single Hurricane was shot down that day, possibly while attempting to attack a shadowing BV 138 reconnaissance aircraft, killing Lt Cdr Edward W.T. Taylour, chief of *Avenger*'s 802 Sqn Sea Hurricanes. Hours later, at 2035hrs, twelve He 115s of 1./Kü.Fl.Gr. 906 also attempted a torpedo attack, but were similarly unsuccessful. Aircraft 8L+FH was brought down by flak, *Lt.z.S.* Heinz-Walter Schmuck and his two crew, wireless operator *Uffz.* Erich Kipka and pilot *Ob.Gefr.* Hans-Walter Keilert, being posted as missing in action. A final high-altitude bombing attack by I./KG 30 inflicted no damage, and two Ju 88s of 3./KG 30 collided while landing at Petsamo, one being written-off and the other severely damaged.

The following day saw fresh attacks as PQ18 sailed onwards beneath clear blue skies. However, according to German historian Cajus Bekker, Göring's personal hubris severely handicapped the Luftwaffe attack before it had begun.

> Göring was still smarting from the failure of the first Ju 88s to sink the aircraft carrier *Ark Royal* in the early weeks of the war, and the fact that she had recently been sunk in the Mediterranean by U-boat had rubbed salt into the wound. Moreover, he looked with envy at the success of Japanese naval aircraft against American aircraft carriers in the Pacific, and decided it was high time the Luftwaffe did something similar. Consequently, KG 26 was now ordered to concentrate every available plane exclusively against the aircraft carrier *Avenger*. Thus, they were sent to their doom.[35]

Hauptmann Nocken's III./KG.26 made the first attack, directed to focus solely on the carrier at the expense of all other targets. Having learned from the previous day, the Sea Hurricanes were only scrambled once the attacking bombers were visually detected, and approximately ten were ready for the torpedo-carrying Ju 88s as they approached. Nocken's crews desperately searched for *Avenger* and, once they had sighted her, were compelled to fly the length of the convoy to attain attacking position. Three were shot down, and two others were hit and forced to jettison torpedoes while breaking for home. Pilot *Fw.* Alfred Seidel and his gunner, *Uffz.* Walter Zachowski, were killed when their aircraft crashed while attempting to land at Banak. Observer *Lt.* Helmut

Natalis and wireless operator *Gefr.* Wilhelm Schuh were pulled from the wreckage dazed and wounded but alive. The other damaged Junkers landed successfully with two wounded men aboard. The few torpedoes that were successfully launched missed HMS *Avenger* completely.

At 1250hrs PQ18 was attacked by dive-bombers of I./KG 30, which once again attempted to hit the carrier. All of the bombs fell wide, and an aircraft of the staff *Kette* was hit by flak, the gunner, *Uffz.* Rudolf Haderlein, being killed. Twenty-two He 111s of I./KG 26 mounted yet another torpedo attack against HMS *Avenger* at 1410hrs. The original plan had been to co-ordinate their assault with dive-bombing by *Maj.* Werner Baumbach's III./KG.30, but the Ju 88s were late and the torpedo attack went in unsupported and facing the full weight of enemy fire. Although the 5,737-ton American freighter SS *Mary Luckenbach*, carrying a cargo of 1,000 tons of TNT, was successfully torpedoed, seven Heinkels were lost with their crews, and two others were damaged and crash-landed at Bardufoss. Horace Bell, Chief Radio Operator aboard the British rescue ship SS *Copeland*, saw the American ship torpedoed.

Wolfram von Richthofen. Harsh, overbearing yet brutally effective, his arrival as commander of *Fliegerkorps* VIII during the Crimean campaign caused considerable problems for the maritime operations of *Fliegerführer Süd*.

The leading plane came in to about 300 yards . . . before dropping his torpedoes and then swept on . . . As he passed, the gunner raked him fore and aft and bright tongues of flame flickered from his starboard engine. He dipped, recovered, dipped again and seemed just about to crash, when his torpedoes reached their mark and the ship simply vanished into thin air. As for the plane, it broke up into small pieces. In the stupefying moments of silence and inactivity that followed, we watched as an enormous column of smoke billowed upwards, slow, thick, black and ugly – no flames this time, just smoke, up and up until it reached the clouds. Gradually, from the overhanging top, there drifted down dust, like a shower of rain, and that was all.[36]

Only 200 yards from the exploding freighter, the American ship SS *Nathaniel Green* had a large amount of wreckage blown aboard, and bulkhead doors were damaged by the concussion of the blast. Initially, the crew believed that they, too, had been torpedoed, and headed for lifeboats in order to abandon ship before realising that their freighter remained seaworthy. Nonetheless, eleven men had been injured by the explosion, and HMS *Onslaught* evacuated five of the most severe cases. The 5,433-ton SS *Wacosta*, carrying 8,804 tons of war supplies and tanks, and sailing immediately astern of the *Mary Luckenbach*, was more severely damaged. Steam valves and oil lines were ruptured by the explosive force, and the engines disabled. While the ship was stationary, an He 111 dropped another torpedo that hit *Wacosta* near Number 2 hatch, blowing a hole in the starboard hull and ripping the deck apart. The ship began sinking by the head, and the entire complement abandoned ship, being rescued by HMS *Scylla* and the minesweeper HMS *Harrier*.

A further abortive attack by eighteen Ju 88 torpedo bombers of III./KG 26 followed at 1437hrs, several aircraft being shot down with no success achieved. Heinkel He 115s of 1./Kü.Fl.Gr. 406 and 1./Kü.Fl.Gr. 906 added their own weight to the attacks on 14 September, but again scored no hits in the face of fighter opposition and ferocious flak. While Kü.Fl.Gr. 906 lost three aircraft, a single aircraft of Kü.Fl.Gr. 406 was damaged and forced down while attempting to alight on the sea and rescue the crew of a downed Ju 88 of 9./KG 26. Nearby, *U405* retrieved the Heinkel crew and then pulled one of the Ju 88's survivors from the sea, also attempting to rescue men that lookouts had sighted seemingly tied to a dinghy. A worsening sea state prevented the U-boat from reaching the small inflatable, so one of the U-boat crewmen dived into the frigid water and affixed a line to the dinghy, which was then pulled in towards the U-boat. One occupant was found to be dead, and two others were severely wounded. Both subsequently died aboard *U405*, and their bodies were buried at sea.

Luftwaffe attacks continued over the following days, but with little success, including the accidental, and inaccurate, bombing of *U403* by He 111s on the afternoon of 15 September. The aircraft then went on to attack PQ18. Heavy anti-aircraft fire again claimed its toll, the bomber crews now apparently unwilling to make low-level or dive-bombing attacks, instead waiting above cloud cover to carry out level bombing from altitude. Not until nine torpedo aircraft of I./KG 26 attacked the convoy from astern on 18 September did the Luftwaffe claim a final victim, when 5,378-ton steamer SS *Kentucky* was torpedoed thirty-five miles west-south-west of Cape Kanin. The freighter avoided one torpedo, but the second hit forward of the bridge on the starboard side. The hatch of Number 2 hold was blown into the ship's superstructure, and fire broke out below decks as *Kentucky* slowly sank, its demise hastened by two bombs from a KG 30 Ju 88. All of the ship's complement was rescued by a British minesweeper.

Somewhat fanciful pre-war propaganda image showing the Focke Wulf Fw 58 *Weihe* as used by the ad-hoc *Küstenfliegerstaffel Krim*.

Ten ships of PQ18 had been sunk by Luftwaffe attack, and three others by U-boat. Paranoid about failure and damage to its capital ships, the Kriegsmarine had not been given permission to sortie its cruisers to add weight to the attack, leaving it instead to the U-boats and Luftwaffe. German claims were extremely optimistic, leading to disbelieving criticism from *SKL* on 23 September.

> A check of all data in the Naval Staff's possession discloses that a maximum of twenty-three merchant vessels out of the forty-five which assumedly made up convoy PQ18 did not reach their destinations, whereas the *OKW* communique dated 20 September announced the sinking of thirty-eight merchant vessels, *viz.*, the virtual annihilation of the convoy. In view of this gross discrepancy the Naval Staff requests the information in the possession of *OKW* and Luftwaffe Operations Staffs be passed onward.

The following day they received their clarification.

> Luftwaffe Operations Staff replied to the request of the Naval Staff concerning the reported success in the battle against convoy PQ18 as follows: 'The announcement that thirty-eight vessels of convoy PQ18 were sunk did not originate at Luftwaffe Operations Staff, which reported only twenty-three ships sunk (through *Robinson*). The *Kurfürst* intermediate command [Intelligence officers at the bunker complex that comprised Luftwaffe headquarters in Potsdam] added two probable sinkings to this number. The *OKW* added the eight vessels reported seriously damaged by the Luftwaffe to the number of vessels sunk. The Luftwaffe Operations Staff cannot be blamed for this. The matter is being investigated as carefully as indicated in the Navy's communication.'

Despite the fact that the first torpedo mission against PQ18 proved to be the Germans' single most successful such attack of the war, the battle for PQ18 marked the swansong of the Luftwaffe maritime strike force. Never again would such strength be mustered for a single battle. The price had been extreme: KG 26 had lost thirty-eight aircraft, with fifty-two crewmen missing in action, five killed and seven wounded, and KG 30 had lost six aircraft. In addition, the *Küstenflieger Staffeln* had lost five aircraft. Of the Luftwaffe's entire complement of trained torpedo bomber crews, 42 per cent had been lost in action against

Die Seeflieger der deutschen Luftwaffe magazine, published for maritime aircrew between 1941 and 1943.

PQ18. Göring's strict orders to attack HMS *Avenger* had caused unnecessary casualties and taken the impetus away from attacking valuable merchantmen which formed the very heart of the Soviet convoys. Furthermore, HMS *Avenger* emerged intact. Extremely effective defending anti-aircraft fire, the presence of Sea Hurricanes, periodically unfavourable weather conditions and imperfect co-ordination between dive- and torpedo-bombing attacks all contributed to the overall lack of success against PQ18 and the extreme number of Luftwaffe casualties.

Inertia once again overtook the Arctic Front operations. German intelligence gathered information about a potential PQ19 during October, but it never sailed. The Luftwaffe took the opportunity to attempt to rebuild the shattered units that had fought PQ18, though KG 30 was also assigned the task of bombing Murmansk and mounting missions in support of the Army once again. On 24 September *Luftflotte* 5 issued a communique to *MGK Nord*, in which it claimed that the 'extremely tight fuel situation' required the *Lufiflotte* to curtail or severely limit air transport services and reconnaissance and combat missions, except for those supporting the Army during decisive offensive or critical defensive operations. As far as naval operations were concerned, aerial reconnaissance would be limited to spot checks of general areas, or to locally concentrated coverage of areas known to be directly threatened by enemy activity. Raeder's headquarters staff were not amused.

> This most unpleasant new difficulty arising for the conduct of naval warfare is highly regrettable. In addition to the fact that, as reported by *MGK Nord* on a previous occasion, reconnaissance flights over the southern and central North Sea were discontinued a long time ago, the most elementary requirements of naval warfare for routine reconnaissance will also no longer be met from now on, either in the northern North Sea or in the Arctic Ocean. In view of the constant grave threat of enemy attacks on the northern Norwegian area, which is constantly emphasised by the Führer himself, the Luftwaffe is assuming a terrific responsibility in taking this step.[37]

Within days, the point had become moot. The bulk of the Luftwaffe's meagre maritime strength was rushed once again to the Mediterranean. While Rommel was in full retreat in the face of the Eighth Army advance from Egypt, on 4 November intelligence reports were received of another huge convoy massing in the Gibraltar region, believed at first to be a fresh attempt to supply Malta. The *Abwehr*'s intelligence machine had failed dramatically. The massive conglomeration of shipping was not bound for the island bastion at all, but instead swung south to approach the shores of Algeria and Morocco. The Allied invasion of Vichy North-West Africa, codenamed Operation *Torch*, was about to begin, as was the Luftwaffe's first attempt at countering a full-scale amphibious invasion.

Appendix

Main Aircraft of the Luftwaffe Maritime Forces 1935–1942

Reich Air Ministry Manufacturer Codes

When Göring's Air Ministry took charge of aviation in the Third Reich it introduced a standardised coding for aircraft types, as well as two-letter designations for all the major aircraft manufacturers. The aircraft concerned within this study all have prefixes that relate to the following manufacturers:

- Ar Arado
- Bf Bayerische Flugzeugwerke (replaced by Me in July 1938, though the the first operational aircraft to be so designated, the Me 210, did not enter service until 1941)
- BV Blohm & Voss (replacing Ha in September 1937)
- Do Dornier
- Fi Fieseler
- Fw Focke-Wulf
- Ha Hamburger Flugzeugbau (replaced by BV in September 1937)
- He Heinkel
- Ju Junkers
- Me Messerschmitt (officially replacing Bf in July 1938)

Arado Ar 95

A single-engine reconnaissance and patrol biplane designed and built in the late 1930s. No order was placed by the Kriegsmarine, but they were ordered by both the Chilean and Turkish air forces. Although the Chilean order was fulfilled, the Turkish machines were taken over by the Luftwaffe at the beginning of the war.

General characteristics
  Crew: Two
  Length: 11.10m
  Wingspan: 12.50m
  Height (seaplane): 5.20m
  Empty weight: 2,450kg
  Powerplant: One 656kW BMW 132De radial engine
Performance
  Maximum speed: 310km/h at 3,000m
  Cruising speed: 255km/h at 1,200m
  Range: 1,100km (594nm)
  Service ceiling: 7,300m
Armament
  One fixed, forward-firing 7.92mm MG 17 machine gun
  One moveable 7.92mm MG 15 machine gun in the rear cockpit
  Bomb load: One 800kg torpedo or 500kg bomb on underfuselage rack

Arado Ar 196

A highly successful low-wing shipboard reconnaissance seaplane. Introduced to replace the He 114 (which had in turn been rushed to replace the He 60), the Ar 196 was extremely popular with its crews. Robust, and handling exceptionally well on water and in the air, the Ar 196 could even hold its own in skirmishing combat, and after the demise of the surface fleet it continued to be used for coastal reconnaissance and ASW operations until well into 1944.

General characteristics
  Crew: Two (pilot and observer)
  Length: 10.96m
  Wingspan: 12.44m
  Height: 4.45m
  Powerplant: One BMW 132K 9-cylinder air-cooled radial piston engine
Performance
  Maximum speed: 311km/h
  Cruising speed: 267km/h
  Range: 1,080km (583nm)
  Service ceiling: 7,010m

Armament
  One fixed, forward-firing 7.92mm MG 17 machine gun
  Two wing-mounted 20mm MG FF cannon
  One moveable 7.92mm MG 15 machine gun in rear cockpit
  Bomb load: Two 50kg bombs

Blohm & Voss BV 138 **Seedrache** *(Sea Dragon)*

A tri-motor monoplane flying boat, the BV 138 had a twin-boom tail unit and short hull, which earned it the nickname '*Fliegender Holzschuh*' (flying clog) from its crews. It had three piston engines; a central engine mounted above the wing and driving a four-blade propeller, and two wing-mounted engines located at a lower level and driving three-blade propellers. A highly successful design, the BV 138 served throughout the Second World War, 297 being built between 1938 and 1943.

General characteristics
  Crew: Six (pilot, navigator, radio operator, nose gunner, rear gunner, upper rear gunner)
  Length: 19.85m
  Wingspan: 26.94m
  Height: 5.90m
  Empty weight: 11,770kg
  Powerplant: Three Junkers Jumo 205D opposed-piston diesel engines

Performance
  Maximum speed: 285km/h at 6,000m
  Cruising speed: 235km/h
  Range: 4,300km (2,321nm)
  Service ceiling: 5,000m

Armament
  Two 20mm MG 151 cannon in nose turret and rear upper fuselage
  One 13mm MG 131 machine gun in open position behind the central engine
  One to three 7.92mm MG 15 machine guns (optional)
  Bomb load: Up to six 50kg bombs or four 150kg depth charges under starboard wing root.

MAIN AIRCRAFT OF THE LUFTWAFFE MARITIME FORCES 1935–1942

Dornier Do J Wal *(Whale)*

A twin-engine flying boat with two piston engines mounted in tandem in a 'push-pull' configuration in a central nacelle on a parasol wing, one engine driving a tractor propeller, and other driving a pusher propeller. This configuration was used by experimental Fokker designs during the First World War, and Claudius Dornier firmly embraced the concept, though the advantages of a balanced aircraft and easier handling in the event of an engine failure were offset by disadvantages, including the rear propeller operating less efficiently in the disturbed air created by the tractor propeller. The *Wal* was used as a mailplane and by explorers such as Roald Amundsen before conversion to military use.

General military characteristics
　Crew: Two to four
　Length: 17.25m
　Wingspan: 22m
　Height: 5.62m
　Powerplant: Two BMW VI engines
Performance
　Maximum speed: 185km/h
　Cruising speed: 145km/h
　Range: 800km (432nm)
　Service ceiling: 3,500m
Armament:
　Up to three machine guns; one in the bow, the remainder amidships

Dornier Do 17

Although the Do 17 was secretly tested pre-war as a civilian airliner, it was soon realised that there was insufficient space within its fuselage for its six passengers. Nicknamed the 'Flying Pencil', the slender aircraft was developed as a bomber by the *RLM*. Popular with its crews, it was nonetheless vulnerable to determined enemy opposition.

General military characteristics
　Crew: Four
　Length: 15.79m

Wingspan: 18m
Height: 4.56m
Powerplant: Two Daimler-Benz DB 601A engines

Performance
Maximum speed: 425km/h
Cruising speed: 300km/h
Range: 660km (356nm)
Service ceiling: 8,150m

Armament:
Six 7.92mm MG 15 machine guns; one fixed in the nose, the remainder manually aimed in front windscreen, beam windows, and above and below, facing aft.
Bomb load: 1,000kg carried internally.

Dornier Do 18

An improved design based on the original *Wal*, retaining the high wing, metal hull and push-pull engines in tandem. The power was boosted by the use of Junkers Jumo 250 engines, and general aerodynamics and handling were improved. However, by the outbreak of war the Do 18 was virtually obsolete. Underpowered and vulnerable to enemy fire, it was still used in some quantity owing to the lack of a suitable replacement long-range reconnaissance aircraft for the *Küstenflieger*.

General characteristics
Crew: Four
Length: 19.23m
Wingspan: 23.70m
Height: 5.32m
Empty weight: 6,680kg
Powerplant: Two Junkers 205C-4 six-cylinder, vertically-opposed diesel engines

Performance
Maximum speed: 250km/h at sea level
Cruising speed: 190km/h (maximum endurance cruise)
Range: 3,500km (1,890nm)
Service ceiling: 4,350m

Armament
   Three 7.92mm MG 15 machine guns in bow and dorsal positions
   Bomb load: Two 50kg bombs under starboard wing

Fieseler Fi 167

A biplane torpedo bomber designed for use aboard the aircraft carriers of the Kriegsmarine, which were never completed. The Fi 167 had excellent aerodynamic qualities, including an extremely slow minimum speed for short take-offs and landings, and could carry a weapons load exceeding the original requirements. The Fi 167 was eventually deemed surplus to requirements, and only fourteen were built.

General characteristics
   Crew: Two (pilot and gunner)
   Length: 11.4m
   Wingspan: 13.5m
   Height: 4.8m
   Empty weight: 2,806kg
   Powerplant: One Daimler-Benz DB 601B inverted V-12 liquid-cooled piston engine driving a three-bladed variable-pitch propeller

Performance
   Maximum speed: 325km/h
   Cruising speed: 250km/h
   Range: 1,300km (702nm) or 1,500km (810nm) in reconnaissance role, with 300l drop tank
   Service ceiling: 8,200m

Armament
   One fixed forward-firing 7.92mm MG 17 machine gun with 500 rounds
   One 7.92mm MG-15 machine gun in rear cockpit on a moveable mounting, with 600 rounds
   Bomb load: One 1,000kg SC1000 bomb, or one 765kg LT F5b torpedo, or one 500 kg SC500 bomb plus four 50kg SC50 bombs

Focke-Wulf Fw 200 Condor

An all-metal, four-engine monoplane built originally as an airliner but adopted by the Luftwaffe for long-range maritime reconnaissance. Although comfortable and of long endurance in its designed role as a passenger aircraft, the Condor was not well suited to its military purposes. The airframe was particularly vulnerable to overloading when equipped with a full bomb load, hardpoints having been added to the wings for carrying bombs. The fuselage had been lengthened to create gun positions and a bomb bay, and some aircraft were destroyed while landing when the fuselage spine snapped. Its reputation among the Allies as the 'Scourge of the Atlantic' was formed during its earliest years of service, but by mid-1941 it had become increasingly vulnerable to Allied aircraft attacks.

General characteristics
  Crew: Five to seven
  Length: 23.45m
  Wingspan: 32.85m
  Height: 6.30m
  Empty weight: 17,005kg
  Powerplant: Four BMW/Bramo 323R-2 nine-cylinder, single-row air-cooled radial engines

Performance
  Maximum speed: 360km/h at 4,800m
  Cruising speed (maximum): 335km/h at 4,000m
  Range: 3,560km (1,923nm)
  Endurance: 14hrs
  Service ceiling: 6,000m

Armament
  One 7.92mm MG 15 machine gun in a Drehkranz D-30 forward dorsal turret
  One 13mm MG 131 machine gun in aft dorsal turret
  One 20mm MG 151 cannon in forward ventral gondola position
  One 7.92mm MG 15 machine gun in rear ventral gondola position
  Two 7.92mm MG 15 machine guns on moveable waist-gunner mountings
  Bomb load: Up to 1,000kg of ordnance internally, or up to 5,400kg externally on four PVC 1006 underwing racks

Heinkel He 42

Biplane seaplane built for covert military training schools (*Deutsche Verkehrsfliegerschule: DVS*) from 1929. The second production series, designated He 42E, was the largest, with 189 machines built.

General characteristics
　Crew: Two
　Length: 10.5m
　Wingspan: 14m top, 13m bottom
　Height: 4.5m
　Empty weight: 1,550kg
　Powerplant: One 221kW (296hp) Junkers L5G
Performance
　Maximum speed: 185km/h
　Cruising speed: 160km/h
　Range: 800km
　Service ceiling: 3,700m

Heinkel He 59

A large twin-engine biplane, the He 59 was constructed under the cover of being a maritime rescue aircraft, but in fact was a versatile reconnaissance bomber capable of operating from both land and water. The aircraft had long endurance, an ample bomb load, strong armament and dependable seaworthiness. The second of the two initial prototypes, the He 59b, which flew in September 1931, was the only prototype fitted with a wheel undercarriage. The first, the He 59a floatplane, made its maiden flight in January 1932. Subsequent versions were all fitted with floats, beginning with the He 59B-1, of which sixteen were built, one being taken to Lipetsk in Russia for testing in January 1932. The subsequently improved He 59B-2 was the first version to go into major production. The first sixteen were built by Walter Bachmann's aircraft production firm based in Ribnitz, which specialised in seaplanes. A glazed nose originally provided for the bombardier was replaced by an all-metal nose with a smaller glazed bomb-aimer's position.

General characteristics
  Crew: Four
  Length: 17.40m
  Wingspan: 23.70m
  Height: 7.10m
  Empty weight: 6,215kg
  Powerplant: Two BMW VI 6.0 ZU watercooled V-12 engines
Performance
  Maximum speed: 221km/h at sea level
  Cruising speed: 185km/h
  Range: 942km (509nm); maximum 1,750km (945nm)
  Service ceiling: 3,500m
Armament
  Three 7.92mm MG 15 machine guns in nose, dorsal and ventral positions
  Bomb load: Two 500kg or four 250kg or twenty 50kg bombs, or one 800kg torpedo

Heinkel He 60

The He 60 single-engine biplane reconnaissance aircraft was intended for launch by shipborne catapult. The first prototype flew in 1933, but the heavy airframe proved to be underpowered with the original 660hp BMW V 1 engine, which resulted in sluggish handling qualities. A second prototype with a 750hp version of the same engine showed no significant improvement, so the final production model, the He 60C, reverted to the original powerplant. Aircraft were delivered for training purposes during 1933, and in 1934 the He 60 began to equip front-line units, including the shipboard aircraft of *Bordfliegerstaffel* 1./BFl.Gr. 196. The He 60 was of similar mixed construction to the He 59.

General characteristics
  Crew: Two (pilot and observer)
  Length: 11.50m
  Wingspan: 13.50m
  Height: 5.30m
  Empty weight: 2,735kg
  Powerplant: One BMW VI 6.0 watercooled V 12 engine

Performance
 Maximum speed: 240km/h at sea level
 Cruising speed: 216km/h
 Range: 826km (446nm) at 2,000m; maximum 950km (513nm)
 Service ceiling: 5,000m
Armament
 One 7.92mm MG 15 machine gun on a moveable mounting for observer

Heinkel He 111

Early variants of the He 111, Germany's most prolific medium-bomber design, had a conventional stepped cockpit with a pair of windscreens for pilot and co-pilot. They first saw action during the Spanish Civil War. The low-level performance of the He 111J attracted the attention of the Kriegsmarine, who saw its potential as a multipurpose bomber capable of carrying, mines, torpedoes or bombs. When it entered service with *Küstenfliegergruppe* 806, however, its performance proved disappointing. Not until the He 111P did Heinkel adopt the extensively glazed nose section that has come to define this famous aircraft. The most widely produced model was the He 111H-1 through to H-10, and though the Battle of Britain revealed the type's weakness in defensive armament, the aircraft was reliable and tough, and could withstand considerable punishment before being shot down.

General characteristics (He 111H-6)
 Crew: Five (pilot, navigator/bombardier/nose gunner, ventral gunner, dorsal gunner/wireless operator, side gunner)
 Length: 16.4m
 Wingspan: 22.60m
 Height: 4.00m
 Powerplant: Two Jumo 211F-1 or 211F-2 liquid-cooled inverted V-12m engines
Performance
 Maximum speed: 440km/h
 Range: 2,300km (1,242nm) with maximum fuel
 Service ceiling: 6,500m

Armament
  Maximum, seven 7.92mm MG 15 or MG 81 machine guns (two in the nose, one in the dorsal position, two in the sides, and two in the ventral position
  One 13mm MG 131 machine gun (mounted in dorsal and/or ventral rear positions)
  Bomb load: 2,000kg within main internal bomb bay. Up to 3,600kg carried externally (which blocked use of the internal bomb bay). Torpedoes: Two LT F5b torpedoes on external PVC racks.

Heinkel He 114

An unusual reconnaissance aircraft designed to be carried aboard ship, replacing the older He 60. The greater-span upper wing was strut-braced to the fuselage like a parasol wing, while the lower wing panels, which were about three-quarters of the size, were anchored to the lower fuselage longerons. Y-form interplane struts connected the upper and lower wings.

The He 114 floatplane was not particularly successful, its performance aloft being roughly the same as that of its predecessor, and it was particularly sluggish afloat. It was soon replaced by the highly successful Arado Ar 196, though it remained in service with the Romanian, Spanish and Swedish air forces.

General characteristics
  Crew: Two (pilot and observer)
  Length: 11.65m
  Wingspan: Upper, 13.60m; lower 9.04m
  Height: 5.23m
  Empty weight: 2,315kg
  Powerplant: One BMW 132K 9-cylinder radial engine
Performance
  Maximum speed: 335km/h
  Range: 920km (497nm)
  Service ceiling: 4,900m
Armament
  One 7.92mm MG 15 machine gun on moveable mounting for observer.
  Bomb load: Two 50kg bombs

Heinkel He 115

Despite the first prototype failing to impress in 1937, Ernst Udet informing Ernst Heinkel that the aircraft would never fly with the Luftwaffe, improvements resulted in a genuine multipurpose torpedo bomber, minelayer and reconnaissance aircraft. During continued test flights in 1938 the He 115 actually set eight world speed records in its class. However, before long the type became increasingly vulnerable to enemy fighters, and was discontinued. Production of the He 115D and E officially halted on 18 January 1940, though small numbers were still built until 1944 with periodic reopening of the production line.

General characteristics
  Crew: Three
  Length: 17.30m
  Wingspan: 22.28m
  Height: 6.60m
  Empty weight: 6,690kg
  Powerplant: Two 865hp BMW 132K 9-cylinder radial engines
Performance
  Maximum speed: 327km/h
  Combat radius: 2,100km (1,134nm)
  Service ceiling: 5,200m
Armament
  One moveable 7.92mm MG 17 and single moveable 7.92mm MG 15 machine guns in nose and dorsal positions.
  Bomb load: Five 250kg bombs, or two such bombs and one 800kg torpedo within enclosed bomb bay. Up to 920kg of mines

Junkers Ju 88

Despite developmental problems, this twin-engine multipurpose *Schnellbomber* became one of the Luftwaffe's finest and most versatile aircraft. Originally it was believed that the Ju 88's speed would make it immune to enemy fighter interception, and although this was shown to be wrong, it was still a highly-regarded machine. The Ju 88 was produced in several versions, including bomber/dive-bomber, torpedo bomber and heavy/night fighter. The basic airframe remained the same throughout the production of over 16,000 Ju 88s of the various types used in every major German combat theatre.

General characteristics (Ju 88A-4)
 Crew: 4 (pilot, bombardier/front gunner, radio operator/rear gunner, navigator/ventral gunner)
 Length: 14.36m
 Wingspan: 20.08m
 Height: 5.07m
 Powerplant: Two Junkers Jumo 211J liquid-cooled inverted V-12 engines

Performance
 Maximum speed: 510km/h at 5,300m without external bomb racks
 Range: 2,430km (1,312nm) with maximum internal fuel
 Service ceiling: 9,000m at average weight, without bombs

Armament
 One 7.92mm MG 81J machine gun on moveable mounting in front windscreen, firing forwards, with 1,000 rounds. One 7.92mm MG 81J machine gun on moveable mounting in lower fuselage nose glazing, firing forwards, with 1,000 rounds. Two 7.92mm MG 81J machine guns on moveable mount in the rear of the cockpit canopy, firing aft, with 1,000 rounds each. One 7.92mm MG 81Z twin machine gun on moveable mount in the rear ventral Bola position, firing aft, with 1,000 rounds.
 Bomb load: Up to 1,400kg of ordnance internally in two bomb bays rated at 900kg and 500kg, or up to 3,000kg externally.

Ju 88A-4/Torp. variant capable of carrying two LT F5 torpedoes on external PVC racks.

Notes

Chapter 1

1. These lightweight aircraft were used primarily for coastal patrol and reconnaissance. Having a small bomb-load capacity, an FF 29 flown by *Leutnant* Alfred von Prondzynski was the first German aircraft to bomb England when, at 11am on 24 December 1914, a single bomb landed in the garden of the house belonging to Mr Thomas Terson in Leyburne Road, Dover. There were no serious injuries, though John Banks was blown out of a tree next door at St James' Rectory, where he was collecting holly, and suffered some bruising. Little damage was caused beyond a ten-foot crater in the lawn and smashed windows. On 10 November 1918, just before the war ended, von Prondzynski was hit in the face by shrapnel. The somewhat basic treatment available at the time involved the insertion of a metal alloy to replace parts of his broken jaw, and subsequent septicaemia killed him a few years later.
2. James S. Corum, *The Luftwaffe; Creating the Operational Air War*, p.45.
3. *Oblt.z.S.* Friedrich von Arnauld de la Perrière was captured in December 1915 after his FF 33 aircraft came down near Nieuport with engine trouble. A French ship took him prisoner and landed him at Dunkirk. *U12* was rammed and sunk on 10 March 1915.
4. Both Osterkamp and Christiansen became major figures within the Luftwaffe during the Second World War. Sachsenberg, however, decried the drift towards war evidenced by the re-establishment of the Luftwaffe, and was secretly tried *in abstentia* by the Nazis for defeatism. He worked in the design and production of hydrofoils and saw no further military service.
5. This latest defeat left many *Freikorps* men with a burning hatred of Ebert's Weimar Republic, which they believed had stabbed them in the back. It also left many longing to 'liberate' the lands of the East from Bolshevik domination, a theme that would resonate loudly with future right-wing politics in Germany.
6. *Peace Treaty of Versailles, Articles 159-213, Military, Naval and Air Clauses*, http://net.lib.byu.edu/~rdh7/wwi/versa/versa4.html

Chapter 2

1. Heinkel's contribution to the rearmament of the Luftwaffe can barely be overstated. He was later designated a *Wehrwirtschaftführer* (defence industry leader) by the Reich government for his commitment to rearmament.
2. Quote from *Leutnant* Winfried Schmidt, *Luftwaffe; A Pictorial History*, p.14.
3. 'Application of Article 198 of the Treaty of Versailles', Conference of Ambassadors, Paris, 31 August 1926.

    Thirty-six existing members of the military were listed as already being trained pilots, twenty-four of them members of the *Reichswehr*, and the following from the Navy: *Oblts.* Coeler, Ritter, Siburg, Bruch, Krueger, Geissler; *Lts.* Roth, Bischoff, Schroeder-Zollinger; *Fhr.* Jordan, Ferber and Edort.
4. 'The Lohmann Affair', Central Intelligence Agency. https://www.cia.gov/library/center-for-the-study-of-intelligence/kent-csi/vol4no2/html/v04i2a08p_0001.htm
5. David Isby, *The Luftwaffe and the War at Sea*, p.25.
6. Mewes was finally persuaded to leave Heinkel in 1933 when Blohm & Voss formed the Hamburger Flugzeugbau GmBH to build seaplanes and flying boats. Later he was chief designer for Fieseler and partly responsible for the Fieseler Fi 156 Storch. Mewes was also largely responsible for the design of the Fi 167 torpedo bomber planned for service on the *Graf Zeppelin* before the carrier's construction was suspended.
7. In German military nomenclature, 'F' denoted 45cm diameter (as opposed to 'G' for 53cm), and '5' gave the approximate length in metres, in the case of this weapon, exactly 55.5cm.
8. Erich Raeder, *Grand Admiral* (first published as *My Life*), p.233.
9. *Ibid*, p.234.
10. *Ibid*, p.246.
11. Figures from *The Rise and Fall of the German Air Force, 1933-1945*, British Air Ministry publication No.248, 1948.
12. Hardegen subsequently served in 1./Kü.Fl.Gr. 106 and 5./Bo.Fl.Gr. 196 before being posted to the position of Intelligence Officer and company commander at the *Seefliegerhorst* Kamp. Severely injured in an aeroplane crash, he spent several months hospitalised and was left with a shortened right leg and bleeding stomach that required a special diet to manage. He transferred in 1939 to the U-boat service, and though his injuries would normally have disqualified him from active duty, later captained the famous *U123* and received the Knight's Cross with Oak Leaves. He died on 9 June 2018.
13. Aircraft were moored in a small harbour at the northern end of the seaplane base at Kiel-Holtenau, able to taxi straight out from the two slipways and take off. A crane was adjacent to the larger of the two slipways and thirteen large open shelters were provided for aircraft dispersal.

14. Nuremberg, Germany: International Military Tribunal, 1945-09-20, Cornell University Law Library, Volume: 014, Subdivision 35/Goering, Section: 35.04 (Kessler interrogation, 20 Sept. 1945). Kessler had served with the *Seeflieger* during the First World War and was promoted *Kapitänleutnant* post-war, becoming a specialist in the development of observer's equipment for *Marineflieger* before transferring to the Luftwaffe in September 1933.
15. Possibly one of the more unusual ideas put forward by Göring to Ernst Udet, a former First World War flying ace and head of the Luftwaffe's technical development section, was for the establishment of a private 'Luftwaffe Navy' under the command of Ulrich Kessler, who would be designated 'Commander of Security Ships'. These were to be fast patrol boats of over 1,000 tons displacement, armed with flak weapons and torpedoes and capable of circumnavigating the British Isles, in Göring's words, 'faster than any warship'.
16. *Berichtigungen der Anlage* 2 zu A IIa 3530/35 GKdos. Vom 11 November 1935.
17. Walter Gaul, *Navy-Air Force Planning and Build-up of the Naval Air Forces; Their Disbandment, and the Transfer of Naval Air Commitments to the Operational Air Force*. Essays by German Officers and Officials on World War II, Wilmington: Scholarly Resources Inc., Delaware, p.8.
18. Wever was killed in a flying accident in 1936, his place being taken by Albert Kesselring. The latter's forceful personality saw him replaced by Stumpff during 1937, who was finally succeeded by *Generaloberst* Hans Jeschonnek, former commander of the Greifswald training unit.
19. The seaplane base at List experienced large North Sea tidal changes and rough waters, as well as pack ice, between December and March. There were two launching ramps for the seaplanes immediately north of the harbour, with a large girder-type crane adjacent to them. Five large hangars and one small one were available.

Chapter 3

1. Wilberg had been one of Germany's first military pilots, transferring from the infantry to the *Luftstreitkräfte* in 1913. Later he headed the *Reichswehr*'s air staff for eight years during the 1920s, and was initially considered for the post of Chief of Staff by Göring after the creation of the Luftwaffe. However, Wilberg's mother was Jewish, which nullified this opportunity, though Göring had him reclassified as 'Aryan' due to his obvious talents, and he joined the Luftwaffe in 1934. He subsequently played a major role in the drawing-up of Luftwaffe operational doctrine, becoming a major strategist of the Blitzkrieg style of warfare. He was killed in an air crash near Dresden on 20 November 1941, while en route to the funeral of Ernst Udet, who had committed suicide.

NOTES

    Coincidentally, the premier Luftwaffe air ace at that time, Werner Mölders, was also killed in an air crash two days later while heading to the same funeral.

2. Scheele was a former army pilot of the First Word War who had commanded a *Schutztruupe* air unit of two antiquated biplanes in German South West Africa. The small unit surrendered in July 1915, two months after Scheele had been injured in a crash. Time spent after the war in Argentina gave him a command of Spanish, and he had returned to Germany and joined the Luftwaffe. He was killed as a passenger in an air accident shortly before the outbreak of the Second World War.

3. Klümper had joined the *Reichsmarine* in April 1932 as an officer candidate, and was one of only forty survivors of the sinking of the training vessel *Niobe*. He transferred to the Luftwaffe in April 1935. He later commanded the torpedo-plane squadron KG 26, and became one of the Luftwaffe's leading experts in torpedo attacks.

4. On 15 November 1938 he was transferred to the Staff of *Führer der Seeluftstreitkräfte*. He was killed in a friendly fire incident on 5 September 1939, when Junkers Ju 52 WL-AGZG, in which he was travelling as a passenger from Kiel to Jever, was mistakenly shot down by anti-aircraft fire from the *Admiral Scheer* near Wilhelmshaven.

5. General Staff Bulletin, Cadiz Maritime Department, 9 June 1937. AS/88 p.30.

6. Hefele attended General Staff training after departing Spain in February 1938 and was subsequently appointed provisional commander of I./Tr.Gr. 186. Eventually he became commander of II./KG 26, and was captured on 3 April 1940 after his He 111 (1H+AC) was shot down by Spitfires of 41 Squadron.

7. Somewhat cynically, among the twenty-seven nations' signatories were Italy, Germany and the Soviet Union, all directly aiding the opposing sides.

8. A single Danish crewman had been injured in the bombing attack and subsequently died of his wounds after having been rescued by fishing boat and hospitalised.

9. *Evening News*, Sault Sainte Marie, Michigan, USA, June 22, 1938.

10. *The Morning Tribune*, Singapore, Friday 24 June 1938.

11. 'Ha' was the abbreviation of Hamburger Flugzeugbau, which in 1937 was renamed Blohm & Voss Schiffswerft, Abteilung Flugzeugbau.

12. Both Kleyenstüber and Brey retained connections with Spain. The former was enlisted into the *Abwehr* during 1941 and made head of its Spanish office on 1 July 1944 with the rank of *Oberstleutnant*. Brey, too, later worked for the *Abwehr* while serving as the Assistant German Air Attaché in Madrid from October 1944.

13. David Isby, *The Luftwaffe and War at Sea*, p.86.

14. Ibid, p.33.

15. Ibid, p.34.

NOTES

16 *Luftflotte* 4 was established on 18 March 1939 in Vienna, commanded by *Generaloberst* Alexander Löhr and responsible for south-east Germany, Austria and Czech territory.
17 Text from 'Section III: Organisation' of the joint declaration, quoted in David Isby in *The Luftwaffe and the War at Sea*, p.37.
18 *Umfang und Ausrustüng der Marinefliegerverbände*: T-1022, Roll 2033, PG-22046-NID.
19 The Messerschmitt Me 210 was designed as an upgrade of the Bf 110, with an internal bomb-bay, high-speed streamlining and a dive-bombing capability. In reality it was a compete design failure, taking sixteen prototypes and ninety-four pre-production machines before being put into production, which was soon halted, as the aircraft as the aircraft remained extremely unpopular with pilots, who reverted to the elderly Bf 110. Messerschmitt's chief test pilot stated that the Me 210 had the 'least desirable attributes an aeroplane could possess'.
20 Karl Dönitz, *Memoirs*, pp.134-135.
21 Air force planning etc pdf, p.23.
22 Helmut Mahlke, *Memoirs of a Stuka Pilot* (Kindle Locations 1260-1261). Frontline Books. Kindle Edition.

Chapter 4

1 The seaplane base at Kamp offered ample take-off and alighting room on both the Baltic and Kamper Lake (Kamper See), each with its own concrete slipway, although icy conditions were a potential hazard during the winter months.
2 The spacious Nest seaplane base allowed take-off and alighting on either the Baltic or Lake Jamunder, but dangerous ice conditions existed during winter months. A single concrete slipway was available on both sides, connected to hangars by tracks.
3 Moreau had been responsible for the co-ordination of the airlift of Franco's troops from North Africa to Spain, and subsequently commanded the Condor Legion's VB/88 (*Versuchsbomberstaffel* 88) of Ju 52 aircraft. He died, aged 28, on 4 April 1939 in Rechlin, in a crash while testing the new Ju 88.
4 Paul Just, *Vom Seeflieger zum Uboot-Fahrer*, p.13.
5 *Ibid*, p.13
6 Helmut Mahlke, *Memoirs of a Stuka Pilot* (Kindle Locations 1375-1377). Frontline Books. Kindle Edition.
7 Von Wild had served as a naval cadet during the First World War, being commissioned in the *Reichsmarine* in 1923 and taking part in fighting in the Baltic as part of the irregular forces and as a member of Erhardt's Naval Brigade in Upper Silesia and Berlin. In 1934 he had transferred to the Luftwaffe.
8 KTB der *Küstenfliegergruppe* 506, 5 September 1939.

NOTES

9 KTB der *Küstenfliegergruppe* 506, 6 September 1939.
10 SKL KTB 25 September 1939.
11 Helmut Mahlke, *Memoirs of a Stuka Pilot* (Kindle Locations 1525-1531). Frontline Books. Kindle Edition.
12 Just, *Vom Seeflieger zum Uboot-Fahrer*, pp.14-21. Just was later observer aboard an He 111J and Ju 88 as part of Kü.Fl.Gr. 806 after 1./306 became 3./806. He took part in the bombing of London and anti-shipping strikes before he was ordered on 1 January 1941 to report for transfer to the U-boat service. He later rose to command *U546*, which was sunk on 24 April 1945, twenty-six of the crew being killed and thirty-three being rescued by American destroyers, including *Kapitänleutnant* Just.
13 Edwards was initially incarcerated in Itzehoe before transfer to Spangenberg Castle, near Kassel, designated Oflag IXA/H. He was repatriated to the UK in 1944 owing to poor health, and later resuming a post-war flying career with the RNZAF. Edwards passed away in Christchurch, New Zealand, on 8 July 1994.
14 *Berichte des Kommandanten zur Notlandung der He 59 M2+SL am 26.9.1939*, KTB *Staffel* 3/Kü.Fl.Gr. 106, PG-80059-ND.
15 Kapitzky was later promoted *Oberleutnant zur See* in October 1940, and returned to the Kriegsmarine the following year. After training for U-boat service he was promoted *Kaptlt.* and given command of *U615*. On a mission to the Caribbean *U615* fought a week-long running battle with enemy aircraft which resulted in the vessel being sunk on 7 August 1943. A popular commander held in high esteem by his crew, Kapitzky was killed on the bridge while directing the defence of his boat north-west of Grenada. Hit by machine-gun fire, he bade farewell to his crew before dying. Three other crewmen were killed (one while outbound after the boat was strafed in Biscay), and forty-three were rescued by the USS *Walker*.
16 20 September 1939. Sgt F.A. Letchford, the observer in Fairey Battle K9243 of 88 Sqn, piloted by Fg Off Baker, claimed the first RAF victory of the war. He claimed a German Bf 109 during a patrol near Aachen. The claim was later confirmed by French troops. In fact there were no Luftwaffe losses.
17 SKL KTB 26 September 1939.
18 Francke became almost a household name, but, as news of the continued existence of HMS *Ark Royal* gradually became known, his position within the Luftwaffe became more difficult. Facing derision from some other pilots for his promotion and decoration for a fictitious sinking, he later returned to aircraft testing at Rechlin, becoming involved in the development of the He 177.
19 Naval Air Force Planning pdf, p.41.
20 PG-80323-NID.
21 SKL KTB 9 October 1939.
22 Jolly was posthumously awarded Medal of the Military Division of the Most Excellent Order of the British Empire.

NOTES

23. http://australiansinthebattleofbritain.blogspot.it/2012/10/australians-in-battle-of-britain-21.html
24. Jak Mallmann-Showell, *Führer Conferences on Naval Affairs*, p.53.
25. SKL KTB 8 December 1939.
26. SKL KTB 24 December 1939.
27. Helmut Mahlke, *Memoirs of a Stuka Pilot* (Kindle Locations 1068-1074). Frontline Books. Kindle Edition.

Chapter 5

1. SKL KTB 6 January 1940.
2. *Bordfliegerstaffel* 1./196 KTB, 9 March 1940, T1022 R-3360, PG-80297.
3. *Report on the Interrogation of Survivors from U-595 Sunk on November 14, 1942*, January 30 1943.
4. Stab/KGr.126 was formed from Stab III./KG 26, 1./KGr.126 from 7./KG 26, 2./KGr.126 from 8./KG 26 and 3./KGr.126 from 9./KG 26.
5. The 62-year-old Merchant Master was posthumously awarded the King's Commendation for Brave Conduct.
6. *Kalgoorlie Miner* (WA), Friday 12 January 1940.
7. SKL KTB 30 January 1940.
8. See Bill Norman, *Luftwaffe Losses over Northumberland and Durham: 1939-194'*, pp.27-34, for eyewitness accounts of the loss of two Heinkels and the rescue of Schnee's crew.
9. Exhaustive post-war analysis by a number of authors and historians has established that the probability of the *Max Schultz* detonating a British mine remains the highest, though it is possible that the destroyer also entered the German minefield as it strove to assist drifting survivors from the *Leberecht Maass*.
10. *Sunday Herald*, 12 March 1990, 'Orkney's first war victim'. http://www.heraldscotland.com/news/11935500.Orkney_apos_s_first_war_victim/
11. SKL KTB 16 March 1940.
12. *KTB Küstenfliegergruppe* 506, 9 April 1940. PG80099.
13. Eight such *ad hoc* transport units were established for *Weserübung*: *Kampfgruppen z.b.V. 101-107*, established by the Luftwaffe, and *Kampfgruppe z.b.V. 108* by the Kriegsmarine.
14. Peacock's aircraft was part of a 9 Sqn detachment based at Lossiemouth, Scotland, to support the Allied expedition to Norway. Peacock was awarded the DFC almost immediately, and his Navigator, Sgt Ronald Hargrave, was awarded the DFM shortly thereafter. Both were killed on 6 June 1940 after being shot down during a bombing raid on Duisberg Railway Freight Terminal; the remaining crew given time to bale out by Peacock's actions, and later captured.

NOTES

15 Kampfle was promoted to *Oberfeldwebel*, and in April 1941 transferred to the *Bordflieger* complement aboard the battleship *Bismarck*. He was killed in its sinking a little over two weeks later.
16 The specially created transport units attached to X.*Fliegerkorps* were administered by *Lufttransportführer*, *Obstlt* Carl August Freiherr von Gablenz, former technical director for Lufthansa before transfer to the Luftwaffe in 1935, and former commander of the Blind Flying School.
17 Ledet Roba, *Hydravions de la Luftwaffe*, LeLa Presse, 2010.
18 All crewmen from both aircraft were taken prisoner, although *Oblt*. Hans Hattenbach, the pilot of M2+FH, was shot by a Finnish Ensign volunteer on 6 June, when he approached the perimeter fence at Skorpa prisoner-of-war camp and failed to heed orders to stop. Hattenbach was buried with full military honours in the presence of thirty prisoners and a fourteen-strong Norwegian military honour guard. The remaining prisoners were freed by the Norwegian capitulation not long thereafter.
19 Hugo Bracken, Imperial War Museum Oral History, www.iwmcollections.org.uk/collections/item/object/80011093
20 HMS *Suffolk*'s Report of Proceedings, J.W. Durnford, Captain, 26 April 1940.
21 Geirr Haarr, *The Battle for Norway: April-June 1940*, p.15.
22 ADM 199/476 pp.169-175 inclusive. '*A Report on the Namsen Fjord actions, the embarking and disembarking of Troops at Namsos, the manning of a shore defence position and experience gained against aircraft.*' Lt Richard Been Stannard, RNR.
23 KTB *F.d.Luft* Ost, 16-30 April, 1940, pp.77, 86, 87.
24 HMS *Seal* was repaired and subsequently commissioned into the Kriegsmarine as *UB* during 1941. Despite hopes that the *Grampus*-class submarine would help the German war effort, it was of limited value and eventually decommissioned in 1943, later being sunk by an RAF bombing raid on Kiel as it lay abandoned in a corner of the harbour. Lonsdale was held as prisoner of war until the end of hostilities, whereupon he and Lt Beet both faced courts-martial for the surrender of the boat. Both were honourably acquitted of all charges.
25 Although Horst Schwilden's military record remains murky at present, it appears that he was killed as *Staka*. Of 3./KG 26 on 25 June 1940, when his He 111H-3 was shot down by a Spitfire of 603 Sqn south-east of Turnhouse, Scotland.
26 'Pitt' Midderhoff was subsequently killed in action south-west of Hourtin on 22 February 1941, when his aircraft capsized during another attempted rescue mission. Rembert van Delden was later captured as IWO aboard *U131*, sunk on 17 December 1941. Franz Augustat was killed in 1944. Willi Schönfelder survived the war to enter politics in Zeven as a member of the Social Democrats. The wreck of van Delden's Heinkel lay undisturbed in 220m of water until it was discovered by oil workers in 1985.

27   10th Engineer Sub-Lt Ron Walter Purdy was among the surviving crew. A previously active member of the Ilford branch of the British Union of Fascists, Purdy was later recruited to make radio broadcasts for the German Propaganda Ministry, before being arrested by the Germans in 1944 after an unexplained absence in Berlin. After a brief and contentious stay in Colditz, he was moved to the post of translator for the SS *Britische Freikorps* unit. Tried after the war for treason, he was sentenced to death, but the sentence was commuted to life imprisonment. He was released in 1954.
28   Subsequently, Sharp briefly captained the *Antonia*, before being transferred to command another Cunard vessel, the SS *Laconia*. This 19,695-ton ship was torpedoed by *U156* on 12 September 1942, its heavy loss of life becoming the second most costly British maritime loss of the war. Sharp did not survive this second sinking.
29   Geirr Haarr, *No Room for Mistakes: British and Allied Submarine Warfare 1939-1940*.
30   Stoker James Walsh also died later of his wounds, on 7 July.
31   Among the North Sea anti-shipping missions carried out by KG 26 was an unsuccessful one on 22 July, after which a single Heinkel jettisoned its unused bombs on a target of apparent importance; a large manor house surrounded by wire and Nissen huts. It was in fact Duff House at Banff, serving as PoW Camp 5. Eight men were killed: two British guards and six prisoners from the recently sunk U-boat *U26* (*MaschObGfr.* Hermann Ackerman, *MatrGfr.* Heinz Heymann, *MechGfr.* Conrad Marschall, *MatObGfr.* Günter Nordhausen, *MatrGfr.* Rudolf Popp and *MatrHptGfr.* Kurt Redieck).
32   Sub-Lieutenant Richard V. Moore, RNVR, was the third and only surviving volunteer from this trio from HMS *Vernon* travelling across London, Essex and Kent hunting the unexploded mines. He was also awarded the George Cross.
33   OP1666: *German Explosive Ordnance*, US Navy, 11 June 1946, p.14.
34   SKL KTB 3 July 1940.
35   SKL KTB 18 June 1940.
36   David Isby, *The Luftwaffe and War at Sea*, p.52.
37   Hahn was killed on 3 June 1942 as *Kommodore der Kampfgruppe* 606 on the Eastern Front.
38   http://ww2talk.com/index.php?threads/belfast-lough-condor.20367/
39   It was Doran who had led the first offensive strike mounted by British bombers of the war, when twenty-seven Blenheims of 110, 107 and 139 Sqns attacked Wilhemshaven on 4 September 1939. He remained a prisoner of war until 1945, and was killed in the Ermenonville air disaster, near Senlis, France, on 3 March 1974.
40   For example, on 17 September the Master of the SS *Fireglow* reported that two mornings previously he saw Convoy FS81 'machine gunned by an enemy aircraft painted white with a superimposed Red Cross' (Admiralty War Diary, 17/9/1940).

NOTES

41 Brian Cull, *Battle for the Channel: The First Month of the Battle of Britain, 10 July-10 August 1940*, p.230.
42 Anderson was later awarded the British Empire Medal, along with Fireman Berth Whyman. The Master, Capt William Gifford, received the OBE, and Able Seaman William Birnie, Stewardess Miss Cockburn and Steward Laurence Smith Halcrow all received commendations.
43 Werner Baumbach, *The Life and Death of the Luftwaffe*, p.102.
44 Dyrcks later wrote a 69-page memorandum on techniques to be used by torpedo-plane pilots, and in December 1941 was moved away from the front line to become an aerial torpedo specialist in the Reichs Air Ministry.
45 Karl Barth was transferred to the Luftwaffe on 1 February 1942 with the rank of Hauptmann. He was killed over the Mediterranean on 9 November, 1942, as *Staffelkapitän* of 6./*Kampfgeschwader* 26.

Chapter 6

1 Pilot *Leutnant der Reserve* Otto Emmerich, observer *Oblt.z.S.* Helmuth Groos, wireless operator *Stabsfeldwebel* Christian Graf, second wireless operator *Feldwebel der Reserve* Erich Gruber, flight engineer *Feldwebel der Reserve* Heinz Hingst and second flight engineer *Feldwebel der Reserve* Heinz Rautenberg. The bodies of all but Rautenberg and Graf were recovered and later buried at Ploudaniel-Lesneven.
2 B.d.U. KTB 2 December 1940.
3 Ibid.
4 Ibid.
5 David Irving, *Göring*, p.465.
6 Jenisch himself was sunk two days later by the destroyers HMS *Harvester* and HMS *Highlander*. The wreck of the liner has since been explored by divers searching for the reported bullion. They found no trace of gold, though they did enter the bullion room, finding it empty apart from a single skeleton whose identity remains unknown.
7 On-board radar was still some time in the future for the Condors. Experiments with the air-to-sea *Atlas* and *Neptun-S* systems produced disappointing results later in 1941, and it was not until 1943 that the first effective radar sets began to be carried.
8 B.d.U. KTB 11 February 1941.
9 Admiralty War Diary, 21 February 1941.
10 Ibid.
11 The *Scottish Standard* was later found by *Kapitänleutnant* Heinrich Lehmann-Willenbrock's *U96*, bow down in the water and with obvious bomb damage to its superstructure. After the tanker was sunk by two torpedoes, *U96* was detected by a nearby destroyer and slightly damaged by depth charges.
12 Karl Dönitz, *Memoirs*, p.137.

13 Italian losses amounted to more than 5,500 men killed, 10,000 wounded, 133,298 captured, and 420 tanks, 845 guns and 564 aircraft destroyed. The Allies had lost 500 men killed, 1,373 wounded, 55 missing and 26 aircraft destroyed.
14 Admiralty War Diary, 10 January 1941.
15 Kowalewski had already earned the Knight's Cross on 24 November 1940, while part of *Stabstaffel/X.Fliegerkorps*. His award was granted for the sinking of 83,680 GRT of enemy merchant shipping, the damaging of a British cruiser, the shooting down of both an enemy fighter and flying boat, and successfully returning his crew on only a single engine following a successful raid on the Moray Firth.
16 Observer, *Oblt*. Walter Gensch, wireless operator *Uffz*. Ferdinand Paul Holec, Gunner *Fw*. Hans Janzen.
17 On 1 November 1942 Bertram was promoted to *Oberstleutnant* while prisoner. Transported to an 'Officers Only' prisoner-of-war camp in Dhurringile, Australia, he was part of the most successful escape from that particular camp on 11 January 1945, when seventeen officers and three adjutants tunnelled from a large crockery room, under the perimeter fence and emerged beyond the wire. After breaking out, the escapees scattered, Bertram running with *Fregattenkapitän* Theodor Detmers, commander of the sunk raider *Kormoran* and senior officer of the camp. They were recaptured after a week at liberty. Detmers was sent for a punishment month at the Old Melbourne Gaol, but after returning suffered a stroke and was partly paralysed. Bertram assumed the role of camp leader until the war's end and repatriation.
18 *Official History*, Vol. 1, pp.165–6, or *Official History*, Vol. IV, p.133.
19 The Royal Navy had lost contact with *Bismarck* after it altered course for Brest, unaware of the ship's new destination. Somewhat ironically, it was the decryption of a Luftwaffe Enigma message that provided the British with the ship's new direction after *General* Hans Jeschonnek, Luftwaffe Chief of Staff, radioed Berlin for the latest information on the whereabouts of the *Bismarck* on behalf of one of his staff, whose son was serving as a *Fähnrich* aboard the ship.
20 The aircrews were: Ar 196A-2 T3+IH, pilot, *Uffz*. Ernst Lange, observer, *Lt*. Günter Lademann; Ar 196A-2 T3+AK, pilot, *Fw*. Oskar Andersen, observer, *Lt.z.S*. Rolf Hambruch; Ar 196A-4 T3+DL, pilot, *Fw*. Josef Kempfle, observer, *Oblt.z.S*. Siegfried Mühling; Ar 196A-3 T3+MK, pilot, *Fw*. Werner Seeliger, observer, *Lt.z.S*. Martin Lange.
21 The aircraft originated from: 14 from KGr. 100; 13 from I./KG 28; 6 from KGr. 606; 5 from KG 1; 10 from KG 77; 7 from Kü.Fl.Gr. 406; 8 from KG 54.
22 http://www.thememoryproject.com/stories/136:sidney-robert-dobing/
23 HMS *Tartar*'s Appendix II to Letter of Proceedings dated 31 May 1941.
24 Admiralty War Diary, 27 May 1941.

NOTES

25 The survivors were *Obfw.* Otto Kroke (second pilot), Obfw. Erich Kielke (mechanic), *Uffz.* Erhard Milde (second wireless operator), *Fw.* Kurt Brattke (gunner) and Friedrich Keller (metereologist).

Chapter 7

1. Hajo Hermann, *Eagle's Wing: The Autobiography of a Luftwaffe Pilot*, p.98.
2. Unhappily for Army and Luftwaffe co-operation, Rommel's apparent arrogance and frequently brusque way of dealing with other officers left a lasting antipathy between him and Fröhlich, who loathed the *Afrika Korps* commander to such an extent that he avoided personal dealings with him at all costs.
3. Admiralty War Diary, 27 March 1941.
4. Patrick Bridges, diary, 1941, in private hands, reproduced at https://anzacportal.dva.gov.au/multimedia/publications/greece-and-crete/chapter-4-piece-australia
5. KG 51 operated under the control of *Luftflotte* 4, handing over its serviceable machines to LG 1 at the end of the Balkan campaign and refitting and relocating to Poland in June 1941.
6. Ken Otter, *HMS Gloucester; The Untold Story*.
7. 7.*Seenotstaffel* had been formed from five He 59s that flew from Amsterdam to Salonika via refuelling stops in lakes and riverways to provide air-sea rescue facilities after the beginning of *Marita*. Operational by 22 April, and later moved to Phaleron Bay near Athens following the Greek surrender, the Heinkels were joined by three Do 24Ns transferred from Sicily. The basing of 7.*Seenotsaffel* in southern Greece paid huge dividends during the invasion of Crete, when it rescued 175 *Gebirgsjager* from a caique convoy intercepted and sunk by the Royal Navy on 22 May. A further eighty-four were picked up by local fishing boats requisitioned by the *Seenot* service, including sixty-five British sailors from HMS *Gloucester*.
8. Brenner was promoted *Oberleutnant* and was later shot down by Sgt George Tuckwell in a 272 Sqn Beaufighter on 14 June 1942, as the Ju 88s of LG 1 attacked the Malta convoy codenamed Operation *Vigorous*. The crew were seen to escape their ditched aircraft and take to their dinghy, but were never recovered.
9. Correlli Barnett, *Engage the Enemy More Closely*, p.364. Taken from the Roskill papers.
10. PG-80321-NID, *Luftwaffe and Naval Services Supplement to the list 'Compilation of Activities by Formations of S.O. Naval Air Forces, 1941.'*
11. *Coastal Command*, His Majesty's Stationery Office, p.108.
12. The F5b was an improved variant of the F5a, with an increased capacity air tank and higher-performance engine. Weighing 750kg instead of the previous 775kg, the warhead weight was increased by 25kg and the torpedo could travel 4,500m

at 30 knots, or 2,000m at 40 knots. However, the whisker-type detonator was often found ineffective if the torpedo struck at an acute angle, rendering the weapon unreliable once more.

13 The remainder of Neumann's crew were: *Obfw.* Martin Heidenreich, Co-pilot; *Obfw.* Willi Laufmann and *Uffz.* Johann Schneider, Radio Operators, *Fw.* Willi Schilf, Mechanic, and *Uffz.* Franz Rabensteiner, Gunner.
14 From August 3./Aufkl.Gr. 125 was based at Helsinki. It was replaced during September by 1./Aufkl.Gr. 125 and an accompanying detachment of 9.*Seenotstaffel*.
15 On 1 July Emig was posthumously promoted *Oberstleutnant*. He was awarded the Knight's Cross on 21 August 1941.
16 *Generalleutnant* Hermann Plocher, *The German Air Force Versus Russia*, p.175.
17 David Isby, *The Luftwaffe and War at Sea*, p.62.
18 Krupka was replaced by *Oblt.* Wilhelm Kleeman, who was also awarded the DKG, on 10 July, before being transferred to the *Fliegerwaffenschule* (*See*) and in turn replaced by *Hauptmann* Karl Barth in time for a brief reappearance of the *Staffel* in Sicily.
19 The various components of KG 28 can be difficult to trace, as it underwent a dizzying number of redesignations and transfers before finally being disbanded at the end of 1941; Stab/KG 28 becoming temporarily Stab/KG 26, I./KG 28 becoming III./KG 26, and Erg.*Staffel* becoming 11./KG 100.
20 News of the sinking, one of the worst maritime disasters in history, was supressed by the Soviet government for decades. Although treasure hunters have searched for the wreck of MV *Armenia*, its location has not yet been confirmed.
21 David Isby, *Luftwaffe and the War at Sea*, p.64.
22 Ibid., p.65.

Chapter 8

1 Vgl. Eintragung ins KTB; OKW, Volume. I, Pg. 214 f.
2 The three *Staffeln* of II./KG 26 would not be reunited until March 1942, at Saki, Crimea.
3 While incarcerated at Murchison, Haubold committed suicide. He had received a letter from his fiancée, breaking off their engagement, and hung himself at approximately 2100hrs on 10 August 1943. He was buried in Murchison cemetery.
4 Roth had previously commanded *Kustenfliegergruppe* 106 before the outbreak of war, and had been deputy *Kommodore* of KG 40 and *Kommodore* of KG 28. He was awarded the German Cross in Gold on 17 November 1941.
5 This marked the end of a *Geschwader* whose history is very complex, various subordinate components having undergone at least ten redesignations between the outbreak of war and end of 1941.

6   8./KG 26 was disbanded during July 1943 and re-formed from 1./Kü.Fl.Gr. 906.
7   Among the German prisoners aboard was *Generalmajor* Johann von Ravenstein, commander of the 21.Panzer Division, who was rescued after two hours in the water by the ASW whaler HMS *Thorgrim*.
8   http://asasdeferro.blogspot.it/2015/06/focke-wulf-fw-200-condor.html
9   *Führer Conferences on Naval Affairs*, pp.274-275.
10 Hajo Herrmann, *Eagle's Wings*, pp.138-139.
11 The nine survivors that made landfall were treated for injuries by Norwegian civilians before being taken to the German naval hospital in Tromsø.
12 Interestingly, one of the British merchant seamen, Able Seaman Alfred Minchin, later joined the Waffen SS as a member of the *Britisches Freikorps* in November 1943. Indeed, it was Minchin who suggested that the unit's name be changed from the original 'Legion of St George' to the 'British Free Corps'. He survived the war.
13 https://www.world-war.co.uk/trinidad_loss2.php3
14 *Generalleutnant* Hermann Plocher, *The German Air Force versus Russia, 1942*, p.37.
15 Pilot *Hptm.* Walter Staack, observer *Lt.z.S.* Peter Kruse and wireless operator *Fw.* Friedrich Ossenkopp.
16 SKL KTB 28 May 1942.
17 David Isby, *The Luftwaffe and ahe War at Sea*, p.67.
18 Quoted by Roskill, *The War at Sea, op. cit.*, p.130, Tovey Despatch, 2 August 1942.
19 SKL KTB 8 June 1942.
20 SKL KTB 9 June 1942.
21 Ibid.
22 Burmeister was awarded the Ehrenpokal on 10 August. He had already distinguished himself in September 1940 by flying from Tromsø to Kapp Linné in southern Spitzbergen to assist in determining the feasibility of establishing a weather station, flying on to the Soviet weather station at Barentsberg in Grønfjord, before returning to Tromsø. Arabin was later promoted *Leutnant* and, towards the war's end, posted to fighter aircraft, flying an Me 410 in 2./SAGr. 126. Vater was appointed *Staffelkapitän* 1./KG 26 in August 1942.
23 Observer *Lt.z.S.* Hugo Siegl, pilot *Uffz.* Walter Kahl, wireless operator Herbert Jacob, flight engineer *Ogfr.* Helmut Bernhardt and gunner *Uffz.* Helmut Zellner.
24 *Images of War, Eyewitness Accounts of World War 2*, Volume 15, p.415.
25 Hajo Herrmann, *Eagle's Wings*, pp.149-150.
26 SKL KTB 6 July 1942.
27 ULTRA, ref. 1282/T5, T8.
28 *Images of War*, Volume 13, p.356. Stamp was awarded the German Cross in Gold on 24 March 1943 and the Knight's Cross for successful attacks

NOTES

on enemy shipping on 30 March 1943. In August 1943 he transferred to fighters, and by the war's end was credited with 400 combat missions (300 in bombers), five air victories and sinking 35,000GRT of shipping, heavily damaging another 45,000GRT and three cruisers.

29   The LT 350 was cleared for use by the Ju 87, Ju 88, He 111 (H-5, H-6 and H-11), He 115, Do 217 and Fw 200.
30   Mar. *Gruppe* Süd op B. Nr. 627142 gKdos, in BAIMA RM 35 111./21: *Kriegstagebuch des Marinegruppenkommando Süd*, für die Zeit vom 1.-15. Februar 1942 (under entry for 2 February 1942) - Hayward thesis, p.69.
31   Admiral Black Sea KTB 5 March 1942.
32   Erfolgsübersicht des *Fliegerführer Süd* vom 19.2 - 9.8.1942, III/L14-1, Aul.5. Bibliothek fur Zeitgeschichte, Archiv.
33   1./Aufkl.Gr. 125 remained in Norway, its headquarters at Billefjord, while 2./Aufkl.Gr. 125 operated in the Aegean, based at Scaramanga/Athens, after spending the November and December at Akkermann, Ukraine.
34   Surgeon Captain J.L.S. Coulter, *The Royal Navy Medical Service. Volume 2. Operations*, HMSO, London, 1956, pp.45-46.
35   Cajus Bekker, *Luftwaffe War Diaries*, p.330.
36   https://wrecksite.eu/wreck.aspx?37345.
37   SKL KTB 24 September 1942.

Bibliography

Books

Coastal Command, His Majesty's Stationery Office, (Air Ministry) 1942.
The Rise and Fall of the German Air Force, The National Archives, 2001.
Bekker, Cajus, *The Luftwaffe War Diairies*, Doubleday and Company, 1968.
Barnett, Correlli, *Engage the Enemy More Closely*, Hodder and Stoughton, 1991.
Baumbach, Werner, *The Life and Death of the Luftwaffe*, Ballantine Books, 1967.
Brebbia, C.A. (editor), *Structural Studies, Repairs and Maintenance of Heritage Architecture X*, WIT Press/Computational Mechanics, 2007.
Busch, F.O., *Unter der alten Flagge, 1914-1918*, Reimar Hobbing Verlag, Berlin, 1935.
Carsten, Francis Ludwig, *The Reichswehr and Politics: 1918 to 1933*, University of California Press, 1974.
Corum, James S., *The Luftwaffe*, University Press of Kansas, 1997.
Cull, Brian, *Battle for the Channel: The First Month of the Battle of Britain, 10 July-10 August 1940*, Fonthill Media, 2017.
Dabrowski, H.P., *Heinkel He 115*, Schiffer Publishing, 1994.
Dancey, Peter, *Lufthansa to Luftwaffe – Hitler's Secret Air Force*, Lulu.com, 2010.
Dönitz, Karl, *Memoirs*, Weidenfeld & Nicolson, 1959.
Fontenoy, Paul E., *Aircraft Carriers: An Illustrated History of their Impact*, ABC-CLIO, 2006.
Forsyth, Robert, *Shadow over the Atlantic: The Luftwaffe and the U-boats: 1943–45*, Osprey Publishing, 2017.
Goss, Chris, *Bloody Biscay*, Crécy Publishing, 2013.
Griehl, Manfred, *Torpedo Fluzgzeuge der Luftwaffe 1939-1945*, Podzin-Pallas Verlag, 2000.
Haarr, Geirr H., *The Gathering Storm: The Naval War in Northern Europe, September 1939-April 1940*, Seaforth Publishing, 2012.
Hayward, Joel S.A., *Stopped at Stalingrad*, University Press of Kansas, 1998.
Heinkel, Ernst, *He 1000*, Hutchinson, London, 1956.
Herrmann, Hajo, *Eagle's Wings*, Guild Publishing, 1991.
Hooten, E.R., *The Luftwaffe, A Study in Air Power 1933-1945*, Classic Publications, 2010.

Hümmelchen, Gerhard, *Die Deutschen Seeflieger 1935-1945*, J.F. Lehmanns Verlag, 1976.
Irving, David, *Göring*, Parforce UK, 2002.
Isby, David, *The Luftwaffe and the War at Sea*, Chatham Publishing, 2005.
James, T.C.G., *Growth of Fighter Command, 1936-1940, Air Defence of Great Britain, Volume 1*, Routledge, 2002.
Jung, Dieter, Wenzel, Berndt and Abendroth, Arno, *Die Schiffe und Boote der Deutschen Seeflieger 1912-1976*, Motorbuch Verlag, 1995.
Just, Paul, *Vom Seeflieger zum Uboot-Fahrer*, Motorbuch Verlag, Stuttgart, 1979.
Kemp, Paul, *Convoy!*, Arms and Armour Press, 1993.
Kemp, Paul, *Friend or Foe: Friendly Fire at Sea, 1939-1945*, Pen and Sword, 1993.
Klaauw, B. van der, *The Fokker T.VIII*, Profile Publications No.176, Leatherhead, 1967.
König, Christian, *Erste am Feind: Bordflugzeug und Küstenaufklärer Heinkel He 60*, Helios Verlag, 2017.
Laureau, Patrick, *Condor: The Luftwaffe in Spain 1936-1939*, Hikoki Publications, 2001.
López, Rafael Permuy and O'Donnell, César, *Sea Planes of the Legion Condor*, Schiffer Publishing, 2009.
Mallmann Showell, Jak. P., *Führer Conferences on Naval Affairs*, Chatham Publishing, 1990.
Marriott, Leo, *Catapult Aircraft: Seaplanes that Flew from Ships Without Flight Decks*, Pen and Sword, 2007.
Murray, Williamson, *Strategy for Defeat, The Luftwaffe 1933-1945*, Quintet Publishing, 1986.
Neitzel, Sönke, *Der Einsatz der Deutschen Luftwaffe über dem Atlantik unde der Nordsee 1939-1945*, Bernard & Graefe Verlag, 1995.
Norman, Bill, *Luftwaffe Losses over Northumberland and Durham, 1939-1945*, Pen and Sword, 2002.
O'Hara, Vincent P. and Worth, Richard, *To Crown the Waves: The Great Navies of the First World War*, Naval Institute Press, 2013.
O'Hara, Vincent, Dickson, David W., and Worth, Richard, *On Seas Contested: The Seven Great Navies of the Second World War*, Naval Institute Press, 2014.
Otter, Ken, *HMS Gloucester, The Untold Story*, Pen and Sword, 2017.
Raeder, Erich, *Grand Admiral*, Da Capo Press, 2001.
Schmidt, Rudi, *Achtung – Torpedos Los!*, Bernard und Graefe Verlag, Koblenz, 1991.
Schuster, Richard J., *German Disarmament After World War I: The Diplomacy of International Arms Inspection 1920-1931*, Routledge, 2006.
Spang, Christian W. and Wippich, Rolf-Harald, *Japanese-German Relations, 1895-1945: War, Diplomacy and Public Opinion*, Routledge, 2006.
Stenman, Kari and de Jong, Peter, *Fokker D.XXI Aces of World War 2*, Osprey Publishing, 2013.
Suchenwirth, Prof. Richard (author), Fletcher, Harry R. *The Development of the German Air Force, 1919-1939* (Kindle Edition), Valmy Publishing, 2017.

Thiele, Harold, *Luftwaffe Aerial Torpedo Aircraft and Operations*, Hikoki Publications, 2004.
Thompson, Adam, *Küstenflieger*, Fonthill Media, 2014.
Treadwell, Terry C., *German and Austro-Hungarian Aircraft Manufacturers 1908-1918*, Amberley Publishing, 2010.
Vajda, Ferenc A. and Dancey, Peter, *German Aircraft Industry and Production, 1933-1945*, Airlife Publishing, 1998.
Zöller, Paul, *Die letzten Junkers-Flugzeuge I: Frühe Junkers-Entwicklungen von der Junkers J1 bis zur Junkers A50*, Books on Demand, 2017.

Articles, Magazines and Reports

Images of War, Eyewitness Accounts of World War 2, Marshall Cavendish, London, 1988.
Notes on inter-Allied aeronautical control commission for Germany 1920; FO 1032./42, National Archives.
The Lohmann Affair, CIA Historical Review Program, 22 September 1993.
Baxley, Major Brian T., *9 April 1940 German Invasion of Norway*, March 1997. Research paper presented to the Research Department, Air Command and Staff College, USA.
Elefteriu, Gabriel, *Air and Naval Power in the Black Sea, 1941-1944*, 26 June 2016. Essay written in March 2011 at the War Studies Department, King's College London (National Security Research Fellow at a Westminster policy think tank).
Gaul, Walter, *Navy-Air Force Planning and Build-up of the Naval Air Forces; Their Disbandment, and the Transfer of Naval Air Commitments to the Operational Air Force*. Essays by German Officers and Officials on World War II, Wilmington: Scholarly Resources Inc., Delaware.
Gould, Major Winston A. USAF, *Luftwaffe Maritime Operations in World War II: Thought, Organization and Technology*. Research Report, Maxwell Airbase, Alabama, 2005.
Hayward, Joel S.A. *Seeking the Philosopher's Stone, Luftwaffe Operations during Hitler's Drive to the South-East, 1942-1943*, dissertation, University of Canterbury, 1996.
Hamilton, Keith A., 'The Air in Entente Diplomacy: Great Britain and the International Aerial Navigation Conference of 1910', *The International History Review*, Vol. 3, No. 2 (April, 1981), pp.169-200.
Huix, Francisco González, 'La pérdida del vapor Delfín. Un naufragio con tres autores', *Revista General de Marina*, Spain, January-February 1998.
Koestner, Marc S., *The Luftwaffe's Support of Naval Operations during World War II, 1939-1941*, Canadian Forces College. CSC 30, Master Defence Studies.
Mattesini, Francesco, *Il Convoglio PQ18: 'Operazione EV'*.
Plocher, *Generalleutnant* Hermann, *The German Air Force Versus Russia*, USAF Historical Division Aerospace Studies Institute, 1958.

Rennie, Robert, *The Problem of Ernst Heinkel: Nationalism and State Power in Early Twentieth Century German Aviation*, Appalachian State University.

Stoll, Hans G. Lt Col, USAF, *Luftwaffe Doctrine and Air Superiority Through World War Two*. Research report submitted to the Faculty, Maxwell Air Force Base, Alabama, April 1994.

Tavoy, Tal (Ph.D.), '1930s German Doctrine: A Manifestation of Operational Art', *Military Review*, May-June 2015, pp.56-64.

Torroba, César O'Donnell 'Las pérdidas de buques mercantes republicanos causadas por hidroaviones de la Legión Cóndor durante laguerra civil Española (1936-1939)', *Revista de Historia Naval* N°43. 1993.

Web Resources

Axis History Forum —www.axishistory.com
Das Archiv der Deutschen Luftwaffe — www.luftarchiv.de
German Luftwaffe — www.germanluftwaffe.com
Lexicon der Wehrmacht — www.lexikon-der-wehrmacht.de
Luftwaffe der See — www.luftwaffe-zur-see.de
Military Campaigns — Major Battles and Operations — www.asisbiz.com/history.html
The Battle of Britain Historical Society — www.battleofbritain1940.net
The Luftwaffe 1933-1945 — www.ww2.dk
The Luftwaffe Blog — http://falkeeins.blogspot.it
Warbirds Resource Group — www.warbirdsresourcegroup.org

Index

Page numbers in *italics* refer to captions.

People

Barth, Karl, 236–7
Baumbach, Werner, 184, 205, *212*, 233–4, 415
Bloedorn, Erich, 194, 244, 265, 290, 395, 416
Bruch, Hermann, 42, 81, 88, 187, 191, 214, 216, 240, 242, 262, 311
Buddenbrock, Friedrich von, 123–4, *140*, 192
Busch, Hermann, 42, 82, 193–4, *193*, 244, 265, 312, 390
Christiansen, Friedrich, 10, 13–14
Coeler, Joachim, 22, 73, 81, 97–8, 99, 104, 130–1, 134, *136*, 137, 158, 187, 194, 219, 222, 243, 353
Crüger, Arved, 175, 205, 265, 290, *291*, 296–7, 299, 377, 378–9
Dönitz, Karl, 71, 216, *230*, 242, 245–7, 250, 251, 256–8, 259, 262, 263, 276, 282, 307, 355, 362, 372
Faber, Walther, 12, 13, 14–15, 21
Fuchs, Robert, 83, 166, 194, *200*
Geisler, Hans-Ferdinand, 21, 33, *35*, 42, 66, 73, 76–8, 83–4, 97–8, 112, 127, 147–8, 152, 165, 167, 171, 175–6, 180, 191, 194, 210, 244, 265–8, 272, 289, 295, 307
Göring, Hermann, *19*, 27, 28–34, 36, 40–1, 48, 58–62, *64*, 66, 68–72, 93, 108–9, 123, 127, 131, 134–5, 137, 158, 163, 201, 209, 213, 215, 217–18, 239, 241, 250–2, 262, 268–9, 278, 280, 283, 290, 312, 330, 336–7, 340, 341, 342, 362, 404, 406, 410, 415–16, 418, 424
Hahn, Joachim, 42, 217–19, 280
Harlinghausen, Martin, *51*, 52–5, 56–8, 83, 159, 167, 196, 262–3, 268, 273–4, 279, 282–3, 312, 330–1, 342–4, 345, 356, 373
Herrmann, Hans-Joachim 'Hajo', 290, 296, 299–301, *299*, 320, 367, 394–5
Jeschonnek, Hans, 34, 60, 92, 215, 222, 242
Kesselring, Albert, 40, 67, 68, 243, 264, 348, 385, 397
Kessler, Ulrich, 22, 35–6, 42, 199, 356–7
Klümper, Werner, 46–8, *46*, 345, 346, 416
Kowalewski, Robert, 265, 273, 274–5, 295, 304, *314*, 318
Loebel, Walter, 84, 147, 158, 194, *195*
Lorenz, Helmut, 223–4, 231, 241–2, *241*, 268, 345
Milch, Erhard, 20, 31, 34, 191, 211
Mössel, Wilhelm, 73, 92, 388
Petersen, Edgar, 84, 85, 173, 194, 222, 224, 257, 318–19
Pohle, Helmuth, 115–16, 119
Raeder, Erich, 22, *23*, 27, 29–30, 32, 33–4, 36–40, 58, 59–62, 63, *64*, 68, 71–2, 78, 93, 122–3, 127, 129, 134–5, 137, 138, 148, 159–60, 168–9, 183, 201, 213–15, 217–18, *230*, 241, 247, 250–1, 263–4, 268–9, 312, 330, 335–8, 341, 361–2, 375, 392, 424
Richthofen, Wolfram Freiherr von, *59*, 303–4, 306, 331, 410–13, *419*
Ritter, Hans, 21, 72–4, 81, 91, 124, 127, 191, 242, 264, 310, 335–7
Schily, Friedrich, 43, 262, 264, 308–9, 335–8, 375

INDEX

Sperrle, Hugo, 44, 67, 68, 218, 243, 264, 282, 352
Stockmann, Karl, 103, 123, 192, 206, 208, 341, 345
Storp, Hans, 45, 56, 115–17
Storp, Walter, 107, 115, *117*, 136
Stumpff, Hans-Jürgen, 191, 194, 198, 210, 244, 265, 320, 369

Thomsen, Rolf, 210, 311–12, 330, 357
Wild, Wolfgang von, 82, 89–90, 192, 311–12, 322, 329, 330, 334, 356, 405–13, 415
Wolff, Karl-Heinz, 45–6, 49, 56
Zander, Konrad, 23–4, 26, 33, 42–3, 67, 69, 73, 81
Zenker, Volkmar, 219–21

Luftwaffe units

Luftflotte
Luftflotte 1, 68, 92, 191, 319, 321, 323, 328, 330
Luftflotte 2, 58, 68, 73, 83, 93–4, 97, 102, 109, 134, 213, 219, 224, 229, 243, 264, 348, 352
Luftflotte 3, 68, 215, 218, 243, 251, 262, 264, 313, 330, 338, 352, 354, 356, 375
Luftflotte 4, 331, 404, 406–10, 413
Luftflotte 5, 191, 194, 198–9, 209, 210, 244, 249, 262, 265, 266, 312, 320, 339, 362, 369, 371–2, 388, 393–4, 424

Fliegerkorps
II.*Fliegerkorps*, 348, 377, 378, 381, 397, 398
IV.*Fliegerkorps*, 215, 217, 243, 331, 332, 333, 404
V.*Fliegerkorps*, 404
VIII.*Fliegerkorps*, 303–4, 305, 331, 410, 412, 413
IX.*Fliegerkorps*, 243, 264, 310, 313, 319, 330, 353, 375
X.*Fliegerkorps*, *51*, 83, 112–14, 120–1, 127–8, 132–3, 137, 144, 147, 148–9, 150, 152, 158–9, 162, 165, 167, 171, 176, 191, 192, 194–5, 196–7, 199, 210–11, 244, 265, 266–70, 275, 289–90, 292–7, 301, 307, 313, 331, 348, 351, 376, 397

Fliegerdivision
9.*Fliegerdivision*, 134, 136–7, *136*, 187, 192, 194, 195, 219, 222, 223, 279
10.*Fliegerdivision*, 83, 97, 104, 112

Geschwader
JG 53, 377, 378
JG 54, 329
JG 77, 304, 321
KG 1, 264, 282, 328, 348
KG 2, 304–5, 316, 353
KG 4, 134, 136, 182, 194, 195, 205, 244, 265, 268, 290, 328
KG 6, 310
KG 26, *46*, 83–4, 106, 107, 113, 115, 120–1, 124, 131, 134, 136, *138*, 143, 147–8, 151, 152–3, *155*, 156–9, 160–1, 166, 175, 180, 183, *193*, 194, 196, 197, *200*, 202, 209–12, 244, 262, 265, 268, 270–3, 275, 289, 293, 295, 298, 301, 303–4, 307, 312–13, 318, 331, 333, 339, 342, 346–50, 351, 354, 362, 364, 367, 369, 373, 376, *383*, 390–1, 393, 398–9, 406–7, 411, 413, 416–22
KG 27, 405
KG 28, 244, 282, 285, 313, 331, 333, 334, 348, 350
KG 30, *51*, 83, 106, 107, *112*, 113, 115–19, 119–20, 121, 131, 134, *135*, 136, 147–8, 152, 158, 160, 175, 179, 180, 184, 194, 195, 198, 202–2, *202*, 205, 209–11, *212*, 234, 244, 265, 281, 290–3, *291*, *292*, 296–7, *299*, *300*, 301, 304, 307, 312, 320, 353, 357, 359, 360, 362–5, 367, 369–70, 373, 390, 393–4, 416, 418–19, 421, 422, 424
KG 40, 131, 134, 173, 194, 200, 211, 219, 221, 222, 231–2, *231*, 244, 245–7, 249, 251–62, *253*, *254*, 264, 276–8, *282*, 283, *284*, 286, 287–8, 313–19, *316*, *317*, 353–5, 358, 362, 365, 369, *371*, 394, 416
KG 51, 84, 302, 331, 405
KG 54, 215, 282, 326, 330, 352, 377, 381–2, 384, 386, 398, 400, 402

459

INDEX

KG 76, 292
KG 77, 282, 328, 329, 377, 379, 381, 398, 400, 402, 403
KG 100, 166, 348, 405–6, 410
KG 157, 34, 49
KG 257, 303
KG.z.b.V. 107, 172–3
KG.z.b.V. 108, 172–3
LG 1, 113, 265–6, 268, 271, 289, 290, *292*, 293, 296, 298–9, 301, 303, 304, 305, 307, 312, 319, 321, 350, 351, 376, 377, 378, 381–2, 384, 385, 398–9, 400, 403, 413
LG 2, 304, 305
LG 5, 416
StG 1, 289, 304
StG 2, 289, 304, 413
StG 3, 268
StG 5, 370, 416
StG 77, 93, 304
Trägergeschwader 186, 80, 83, 87–8, 90
ZG 26, 268, 289, 304, 329
ZG 76, 180, 210–11, 321

Gruppen
Aufkl.Gr. 32, 321
Aufkl.Gr. 121, 304, 307
Aufkl.Gr. 122, 273, 385
Aufkl.Gr. 123, 307, 376
Aufkl.Gr. 124, 321, 369
Aufkl.Gr. 125, 311–12, 322, 329, 330, 376–7, 389, 412, 413
Aufkl.Gr. 126, 311, 377
BFl.Gr. 196, 43, 141–2, 146, 164, 187, 188–7, 190, 192, 193, 206, 242, 243, 264, 265, 272, 283, 329, 330
KGr. 100, 282, 285
KGr. 106, 310, 355, 357, 358
KGr. 123, 313
KGr. 126, 148, 194, 222, 224, 231–2, 244, 268, 331, 345
KGr. 406, 341
KGr. 506, 329, 330, 335, 338, 339, 348, 374, 375, 416
KGr. 606, 281, 283, 352, 355, 377, 379, 381, 386, 398, 402
KGr. 806, 243, 311, 322, 323–5, *324*, 326–30, 352, *358*, 377, 382, 398–400, 401, 402

Küstenfliegergruppen
Kü.Fl.Gr. 106, *32*, 42, 49, 82, 86, 99, 100, 105, 128–9, 134, 139, 171, 176, 177, 178, 180, 182, 183, 192, 199, 213, 215, 216, 219, 225, 229, 230, 231, 233, 239–40, 243–4, 264–5, 279, 279, 309, 312
Kü.Fl.Gr. 206, 50
Kü.Fl.Gr. 306, 82, 94, 96, 102, 104, 124–6
Kü.Fl.Gr. 406, 82, 102–3, 120–1, 124–5, 175, 182, 192, 206, 229, 239, 240, 243, 264–5, 307–8, 313, 321, 327, 329, 362, 363, 369–70, 388, 416, 418, 420
Kü.Fl.Gr. 506, 52, 82, 86, 89–90, 91, 100, 102–4, 111, 125–6, 129, 136, 171–2, 176, 178, 180, 183, 192, *193*, 233, 234–6, 243, 264–5, 308–9, 312, 313, 329, 330
Kü.Fl.Gr. 606, 82, 101, 112, 114, 120, 125–6, 192, 206, 216, 217, 231, 243, 265, 279
Kü.Fl.Gr. 706, 82, 89, 94, 113, 114, 125–6, 137, 193, 197, 214, 222, 223, 238, 243, 264–5, 330, 335, 339, 389
Kü.Fl.Gr. 806, 124–6, 139, 145, 166, 192–3, 243
Kü.Fl.Gr. 906, 125–6, 128, 130, 136, 138, 140, 145, 164, 172, 187, 190, 192–3, 206, 213, 214, 215, 216, 219, 224, 239–40, 243–4, 264–5, 275, 312, 313, 329–30, 358, 362, 370, 375, 389, 393, 416, 418, 420

Transozeanstaffel, 123–4, *140*, 176–7, 185–6, 192, *203*, *304*, 214, 216, 230, 243, 245

Fliegerführer Afrika, 292, 348, 381
Fliegerführer Atlantik, 260, 262–3, 264, 268, 277, 278, 279, 282, 288, 313, 319, 330, 334, 348, 352–3, 355–7
Fliegerführer Kirkenes, 320, 326
Fliegerführer Krim, 415
Fliegerführer Lofoten, 312, 319, 362, 369
Fliegerführer Nord, 191, 265, 312
Fliegerführer Nord (Norwegen), 262
Fliegerführer Nord (Ost), 312, 369, 394
Fliegerführer Nord (West), 312, 390
Fliegerführer Nordsee, 336
Fliegerführer Ost, 214, 264
Fliegerführer Ostsee, 262, 311, 321, 323, 328–30, 334
Fliegerführer Sizilien, 348
Fliegerführer Trondheim, 196

Ships (naval)

Acasta, HMS, 206
Admiral Hipper, 158, 174, 206, 239, 254–5, 387, 389, 392
Admiral Scheer, 57, 99, 141, 237, 387, 389, 392
Afridi, HMS, 185
Ancient, HMT, 380
Answald, SMH, 8
Arab, HMT, 184
Argus, HMS, 359, 386
Ark Royal, HMS, 104, 106–8, 113, 186, 199, 283, 307, 418
Audacity, HMS, 355
Aurora, HMS, 176, 346, 352
Avenger, HMS, 415–16, 418–19, 424
Badsworth, HMS, 372
Barham, HMS, 295, 306, 307
Beaufort, HMS, 379
Bedouin, HMS, 104
Bernhard von Tschirschky, 74, 75
Bittern, HMS, 185
Bismarck, 281–4, 285, 337
Black Swan, HMS, 225
Blyskawika, ORP, 137
Blücher, 37, 147
Bramham, HMS, 400, 401
Breconshire, HMS, 352, 377–80
Burza, ORP, 253
Cairo, HMS, 383
Cambridgeshire, HMT, 204
Cape Arcona, HMS, 253
Carlisle, HMS, 304, 347, 377–9
Centurion, HMS, 383
Cleopatra, HMS, 377
Cleveland, HMS, 237
Cossack, HMS, 283
Coventry, HMS, 209
Dainty, HMS, 270, 293
Deutschland, see *Lützow*
Diamond, HMS, 302
Dorsetshire, HMS, 283–4
Dulveston, HMS, 379
Eagle, HMS, 396
Echo, HMS, 253
Edinburgh, HMS, 113, 119, 367, 369
Eridge, HMS, 377

Eskimo, HMS, 104
Exeter, HMS, 142
Fame, HMS, 104, 209
Faulknor, HMS, 375
Fiji, HMS, 305–6
Formidable, HMS, 291, 295–7, 306
Friedrich Carl, SMS, 8
Furious, HMS, 37, 116, 396
Fury, HMS, 104, 364, 389
Galatea, HMS, 175
Gallant, HMS, 270
Gipsy, HMS, 128–9
Glasgow, HMS, 113, 175
Glorious, HMS, 37, 206
Gloucester, HMS, 289, 305, 306
Gneisenau, 37, 110–11, 113, 140–1, 206, *277*, 281
Graf Zeppelin, 62–6, *63*, *64*, *68*, 70, *72*, 79–80, 87–8, 94, *103*, 201, 337, 361
Greyhound, HMS, 270, 305
Griffin, HMS, 184, 270
Günther Plüschow, 74, 76, 86, 101
Gurkha, HMS, 175–6
Hans Rolshoven, 42, 74, 75, *89*, 100, 105, 130, 138, 206
Harrier, HMS, 152, 420
Hasty, HMS, 296, 377, 385
Hermes, HMS, 308, 309
Heythrop, HMS, 377
Highlander, HMS, 203
Hildena, HMT, 236
Hood, HMS, 107, 115–16, *117*, 160, 281
Hurworth, HMS, 379
Hyacinth, HMS, 300
Illustrious, HMS, 270–1, *271*, *272*, 289, 291, 295
Indomitable, HMS, 308
Intrepid, HMS, 156
Iron Duke, HMS, 119, 162
Ivanhoe, HMS, 156, 177
Jackal, HMS, 351, 382–3
Jaguar, HMS, 113
Jervis, HMS, 111, 113–14, 270, 377, 382–3
Jervis Bay, HMS, 237
Juno, HMS, 120–1, 306
Kandahar, HMS, 305, 352

INDEX

Karlsruhe, 174
Kipling, HMS, 180, 181, 377, 382–3
Kirschan, 74
Kittiwake, HMS, 309
Köln, 110, 141, 175
Königsberg, 175
Lancastria, HMT, 202–5, *202*
Lance, HMS, 346, 377
Ledbury, HMS, 391
Legion, HMS, 377, 380
Lively, HMS, 346, 376, 377, 382
Lombard, HMT, 241–2
Lützow, 100, 387, 389
Malaya, HMS, 383
Maori, HMS, 283, 286
Mashona, HMS, 104, 285
Matabele, HMS, 104
Matchless, HMS, 368
Mohawk, HMS, 119, 270, 295
Naiad, HMS, 304
Nelson, HMS, 104, 400
Neptune, HMS, 352
Newcastle, HMS, 385
Niger, HMS, 111
Nigeria, HMS, 363
Norfolk, HMS, 161, 283, 285
Nubian, HMS, 270, 298
Offa, HMS, 363
Onslaught, HMS, 420
Paynter, HMT, 221
Penelope, HMS, 346, 352, 379
Penn, HMS, 401
Peony, HMS, 290
Periwinkle, HMS, 258
Prinz Eugen, 37, 281–2, 286
Queen Mary, RMS, 347
Rauenfels, 176
Rawalpindi, HMS, 141
Remuera, RMS, 234
Ripley, HMS, 285
Rodney, HMS, 104, 105, 175, 283, 400
Roon, SMS, 9
Royal Oak, HMS, 119
Scharnhorst, 141, 146, 206–7, 228, *281*, 361
Scylla, HMS, 415–16, 420

Seal, HMS, 178, 189–91, *189*
Selkirk, HMS, 111
Shark, HMS, 207–9
Sherwood, HMS, 285
Sokrushitelny, 384
Somali, HMS, 104
Southampton, HMS, 113, 116–17, 119, 175, 209, 289
Southwold, HMS, 379
Spearfish, HMS, 104
Sphinx, HMS, 152
Stuttgart, SMS, *4*, 9–10
Suffolk, HMS, 178–82, 205
Tartar, HMS, 104, 285
Terror, HMS, *292*, 293
Tirpitz, *168*, 360–1, 363, 373, 387, 389, 392, 394, 415
Trident, HMS, 174
Trinidad, HMS, 363, 364, 368–9
Truant, HMS, 174
Upright, HMS, 351
Urge, HMS, 351
Valiant, HMS, 160, 199, 270, 295, 305, 352
Vandyck, HMS, 200
Vernon, HMS (shore establishment), 129, 211
Victorious, HMS, 360, 399, 401
Vivien, HMS, 235
Volunteer, HMS, 370
Vortigen, HMS, 235
Wainwright, USS, 236
Warspite, HMS, 177, 270, 305, 306
Welshman, HMS, 383
Weston, HMS, 233
Wilton, HMS, 389
Wolf, SMS, 8–9
York, HMS, 304
Z1 Leberecht Maass, 89, 152–9, *155*
Z3 Max Schultz, 152–7
Z4 Richard Beitzen, 152, 154–5
Z6 Theodor Riedel, 110, 152, 155
Z13 Erich Koellner, 152, 154–7
Z16 Friedrich Eckoldt, 110, 152–5
Z25, 363
Z26, 364

INDEX

U-boats

U12, 8
U13, 101
U32, 253
U34, 217
U37, 254
U43, 247
U47, 119, 259
U73, 259–60, 396
U74, 283
U88, 389
U96, 260
U99, 207, 228
U123, 278
U143, 278
U209, 363
U251, 367, 394

U255, 388, 392
U334, 392, 393
U376, 364
U378, 364
U403, 421
U405, 420–1
U408, 388
U435, 365
U456, 388, 393
U457, 390
U537, 146
U589, 417
U595, 146
U652, 377
U751, 355
U1202, 210, 312

Ships (merchant)

Motor Tankers
Marie Maersk, 302
Rigmor, 374–5

Motor Vessels
Aagtekerk, 385
Abosso, 286–7
Armenia, 333–4
Briarwood, 360
Chant, 386
Deucalion, 400, 401
Dnepr, 332
Northern Prince, 298
Orari, 246–7
Pugachev, 331
Ulster Prince, 302
Waimarama, 401
Wairangi, 402

Steamships
Ahamo, 309
Ballot, 364
Bateau, 364
Beacon Grange, 234
Beaumanoir, 308
Bellingham, 394

Bhutan, 385
Bolshevik, 332
Bremen, 25
Brisbane Star, 401
Britannic, 254
Cape Corso, 367
Cape York, 234
Chakdina, 351
Christopher Newport, 389
City of Calcutta, 384
City of Roubaix, 301
Clan Campbell, 376–8
Clan Chattan, 376
Clan Ferguson, 401
Clan Fraser, 300, 301
Conakrian, 236–7
Copeland, 419
Costa Rica, 302
Craigronald, 8
Delfin, 47–8
Devis, 298
Edith, 53
Empire Cowper, 365
Empire Hope, 401
Empire Horn, 372
Empire Lawrence, 370

463

INDEX

Empire Ranger, 363
Empire Starlight, 364
Empress of Britain, 252, 253
Fabritzius, 406, 409
Goathland, 222
Gowrie, 148
Gracia, 258
Halland, 236
Hannover, 355
Harpalion, 365
Highlander, 232, 233
Homefield, 298
Hookwood, 129
Hoosier, 394
Housatonic, 258
Ivan Kondrup, 148
Jean Weems, 50
Jura, 254
Kentucky, 421
Laris, 50
Llanishen, 234
Louis Charles Schiaffino, 293
Lowther Castle, 370
Lucerne, 328
Makalla, 234
Marmari, 309
Mary Luckenbach, 419, 420
Nathaniel Green, 420
Navarino, 390
New Westminster City, 364
Northwood, 148

Nuria Ramos, 48
Oakgrove, 148
Orari, 386
Oswestry, 8
Pampas, 377, 380
Pennland, 302
Raceland, 363
Reculver, 148
Rio de Janeiro, 173
Rosalie Moller, 347
Rosenborg, 258
Rowallan Castle, 376
Slamat, 302
St Rosario, 258
Steel Seafarer, 319
Steel Worker, 371
Stone Street, 365
Sunion, 55
Talabot, 377, 380
Teddy, 111
Tempo, 151
Teti, 298
Thistlegorm, 347
Thorpebay, 308
Thorpeness, 54–5
Umgeni, 287
Upminster, 148
Vironia, 328
Wacosta, 420
William Hooper, 391